The Open Gardens of Ireland

By Shirley Lanigan

The Butter Slip Press

NOTICE

VISITORS AND NEIGHBOURS ARE WELCOME TO SEE
THIS PLACE AND PLEASURE GROUNDS

RULES No1 .... No Flowers To Be Pulled
No2 .... Not To Walk On The Grass
No3 .... No Admission During Divine Service On
Sundays, Or for Boys Or Girls Without Their Parents
No Dogs Admitted
SEATS ARE PROVIDED FOR ALL TO
REST ON AND ENJOY THEMSELVES

First published 2017.
The Butter Slip Press,
12 Greenfields, Kilkenny, Ireland.
Tel: + 353 56 7752 180. + 353 86 3895 638.
e-mail: info@thebutterslippress.com
ISBN 978-0-9955825-0-7

© Copyright for text: Shirley Lanigan.
© Copyright for typesetting, layout, design: The Butter Slip Press.
Orders/Distribution: Robert Towers, 2 The Crescent, Monkstown, Co. Dublin, Ireland.
Tel: + 353 1 2806532.
e-mail: rtowers16@gmail.com

ACKNOWLEDGMENTS

There are so many people to thank. I will start with family: Michael, Mary Kate and Michael junior for peerless cheerleading. Maureen, Paddy, Mary and Billy, Zoe, Stephen and Zara, Dorothy and Michael senior, Niall and Toni, Grainne and Denis and specially to Dor who lent John to me. Shane and Clare, Aidan and Alicia, thanks for the encouragement.
Ray and Lorna McNally, Judith, Marina and Lorraine thanks for being kind. Owen and Sandra Ardill, thank you so much. Thanks always to Gobi Kearney for magnificent enthusiasm. Thank you Paul and Georgiana Keane and the fabulous Titus. Kay McEvilly, I am very grateful. Gerry Daly, you are always such a support and Frances MacDonald, you are generous with advice. Big thanks to Dorothy Jervis, Joan Evans, Michael Classon and all the Donegal Garden Trail crew. It is different up there. Margaret Gormley, Hugh Carrigan and Anne Teehan of the OPW - Thank you all.
Neil Porteus and Trevor Edwards, I am grateful for the advice on Ulster gardens. Carol Marks, thank you for the advice. Nora and Stuart Brownlow your generosity is much appreciated. Theresa Hayes, Stephen and Louise Austen, thank you all. Thanks to Daphne Shackleton for pointing me in the direction of more work. Edward Hayden, you are the best. Anne Marie Kavanagh, thanks for everything. Jonathan Williams, I am grateful for all your kindness. Blaise Smith and Orla Kelly, patiently advice givers both, thank you. To Karol Ryan for the help and oceans of calm. John Keane I am grateful. You do love a deadline.

For Michael, without whom there would be show and no road.

Contents

Galway

Angler's Return

*Toombeola, Roundstone, Connemara. Co. Galway. Tel: 095 31091.
e-mail: info@anglersreturn.com www.anglersreturn.com Contact: Lynn Hill. Open: Contact for annual details. Not wheelchair accessible. Special features: B&B. Herbal flower walks. Tiny campsite (Booking necessary). Directions: Take the R341 from Ballynahinch to Toombeola road. Signed to the right.*

Some readers may remember John Moriarty the poet-philosopher who, as well as writing, shared his thoughts with the nation on the radio in the 1990s as he battled terminal illness. In the middle of his struggle, he managed to inspire and uplift those who listened to his talks.

On arriving to see the garden at the Angler's Return, the first thing its owner, Lynn Hill, did was make it clear that much of the work that went into creating the garden was put in, not by her, but by John Moriarty. In the 1970s he moved into a neighbouring cottage. One day he arrived into her garden offering help and so began a relationship that helped to mould the shape and spirit of what is a simple garden with a special atmosphere.

Like the other Connemara gardens worth visiting, this feels as if it has been only slightly tamed. Being dominated by a wood, it has that blessed feeling of being completely natural although nature is rarely so tended. Under the trees, mossy grass has been encouraged to grow and it takes on the appearance of water flowing over protruding rocks in a stream. In the spring the ground is littered with bluebells and wild garlic.

Opening up paths within the woods was one of the first tasks undertaken by John and Lynn. They sank steps into the hills under the closely planted slim birches and over time these have become colonised by hart's-tongue ferns and wood sorrel. Making our way along, we passed a huge megalithic-looking boulder that stands bolt upright in the wood, called 'John's Stone'.

The old house and its garden were once part of the neighbouring Ballynahinch Estate. That history is echoed in 'Maharaja Ranji's Gate', an ornate little fancy that marks one entrance into the wood garden. At the turn of the century the Maharaja Ranjitsinhji, who used Ballynahinch as his summer home, had the gate made especially in England, sending two estate workers over from Connemara to personally escort it to its Galway home.

The vegetable garden takes up an opening in the trees, and while Lynn announced that 'this is not a flower garden', it was clear that this is not a hard and fast rule however, as there are splashes of old-fashioned cottage favourites like arums, poppies, lupins and roses growing between the vegetables. The century-old *Rhododendron luteum* which has such a great scent, is the star in this corner of the garden. The No Flower rule is breached again in a sunny gravel garden to the side of the house where you can enjoy your coffee surrounded by an abundance of cosmos, lupins, Michaelmas daisies and roses. It was this garden that first made me slow the car to investigate the place several years ago. I am glad I stopped.

Ardcarraig

*Oranswell, Bushypark, Co. Galway. Tel: 091 524336. e-mail: lornaoranswell@gmail.com
Contact: Lorna MacMahon. Open: Contact for details of annual Open Days, otherwise strictly by appointment. Special features: Plants for sale for charity. Directions: Situated off the N59 about 5 km out of Galway. Take the second left turn after Glenloe Abbey Hotel. The garden is 250m up the road on the left with a limestone entrance.*

Ardcarraig is one of those special gardens that has a lasting effect on people. I have spoken to visitors from overseas on several occasions, who, when they hear mention of the words 'gardens' and 'Ireland' will ask if I know 'the garden belonging to the woman in Galway.' Invariably, they are thinking of Lorna

MacMahon's garden.

Ardcarraig has been hugging the hilly land at the southern end of Lough Corrib since 1971 when Lorna and her husband Harry arrived to take over a scrubby one-acre site around their new home. They took out its humps and hollows and transformed them into one of the most innovative and beautiful private gardens on the island. Following the harsh contours of the land, the site is divided into separate garden rooms, each distinctive and linked by rising, falling and snaking paths.

As mentioned, the original garden surrounded the MacMahon home. Since then, there have been changes, chiefly in the arrival of Lorna's new home, a cool glass and steel structure which seems to have landed like a fabulous space ship among the plants without ruffling as much as a leaf. It gives a complete new appearance to the garden. The coupling of hard-edged contemporary architecture and trained jungle is a great success. The sight, out of the corner of an eye, of a metal span or an expanse of clear glass contrasts brilliantly with the rampant plant life. If Tarzan and Jane lived in the 21st century, this might be their jungle home.

The first of the different rooms is a dry gravel garden, made up of low-growing heathers, tall grasses and evergreen shrubs such as *Chamaecyparis filifera*, with foliage like dreadlocks. Lorna has a passion for dwarf conifers as well as a serious bone to pick with the nurseries that sell baby giants to unsuspecting novice gardeners under the impression that they are buying dwarf trees.

From here the garden quickly morphs into the hot stuff border, an exuberant flourish of kniphofia, plum-coloured opium poppies or *Papaver somniferum*, agapanthus, erigeron and South African plants that include watsonia and wine-coloured hemerocallis.

Running downhill from the building, there are umbrellas of scented rhododendrons draped with red sheets of *Tropaeolum speciosum*. Catch too, the powerful contrast between massive gunnera leaves and the fine foliage of *Acer japonicum* 'Aconitifolium'. This particular tree once lived elsewhere in the garden until Lorna decided that it would look better near the house. So she uprooted it with the help of an obliging man called Tommy and it is now known as Tommy's tree.

The path runs past a chamaecyparis battling a big *Rosa* 'Albertine', between layered shrubs. The trees gradually transform into a dark wooded canopy. Making its way through this, the trail emerges out into the pond garden. Here you get wild growth among giant hostas and astilbes, trilliums and erythroniums, as they fight for space with candelabra primulas in the damp ground. The primulas grow in what Lorna calls 'disease proportions'. All these plants combine to produce a lush abundance that is almost overwhelming. One remarkable small tree I spotted in an opening is the *Rubus lineatus*, which has such singular, ridged foliage.

In the dark wet world under the trees, the ferns take their chance to grow like weeds, while out in the sunny opening nearby, prehistoric looking restios and a weeping *Fitzroya cupressoides* glory in the sun. 'The whole idea is to go from light to shade and back out to the light again,' explained Lorna. At this point the trail reaches a little stream, another shaded spot and the moss garden. Moss is a natural phenomenon that looks so right that Lorna rightly wonders why so many people try to rid themselves of it, rather than encouraging it.

The stone lantern garden, inspired by Japanese gardens, is uninterrupted by flower colour and has a sense of purity about it. A small stone bridge links this with Harry's garden. Lorna made this in the late 1990s as a memorial to her late husband. The obliging landowner next door sold her an extra piece of rough land. She thinks he was intrigued at what might become of it. No doubt he is now impressed. In the place of gorse, bramble and rough grass there are plants gifted from family and friends, from golden acers and blue Himalayan poppies to francoa and a flowering stewartia. All this exoticism is held inside a boundary of native birch and hawthorn and a recently built and perfect looking outer stone wall.

It struck me when climbing up and down the formidable hills, on narrow little paths, that Lorna, an elegant, birdlike lady, manages to do all the carting and carrying of plants, tools and wheelbarrows around by herself. Anyone else would want a staff of at least four.

Ballynahinch Castle Hotel

Ballinafad, Recess, Co. Galway. Tel: 095 31006. e-mail info@ballynahinch-castle.com www.ballynahinchcastle.com Contact: Reception. Open: All year. Special features: Hotel. Restaurant. Teas. Guided walks around the grounds can be booked. No dogs. Directions: Travel on the N59 from Galway. After Recess village, take the R341 to the left, signposted Roundstone/Ballynahinch. The hotel is about 4.5 km along on the right.

Prince Ranjitsinhji, the Maharaja of Newanger, one of the most famous cricketers ever, made a trip to Ireland in 1924. He fell in love with and bought Ballynahinch Castle, and spent his summers there for the remaining ten years of his life, making friends and fans in large numbers. Earlier, Ballynahinch was home to Richard Martin, more commonly known as Humanity Dick, the famed 19th century MP and animal rights defender. Ballynahinch is as much of interest to historians as garden lovers. The grounds were laid out under the stewardship of the Maharaja in the 1920s. They are dominated by extensive woods and wooded walks.

The castle straddles a wide ledge mid-way down a steep hill that falls downhill towards the Owenmore River. Rising up from the ledge there is a lawn flanked by two sweeps of stone stairs. These are heralded by a smart statement planting of climbing white roses and white arum lilies. Seeing wild strawberries colonising the walls on either side of the stairs sets the tone for a visit here. The stones are also laced through with maidenhair fern or *Asplenium trichomanes*, a delicate-looking plant with black veins and bright green leaves. On the other side of the drive, the castle walls are almost smothered under the weight of scented jasmine and ivy.

Below the castle, there are several more stepped terraces and ledges over stone walls, draped over with roses and two fabulous wall-backed old Japanese acers, cotoneasters, white valerian, agapanthus and bergenia. The acers surely date to the early garden. This network of walls, flowerbeds and grass ledges is linked by steps, and the whole affair looks out over a wide bend in the river. Those of a nervous disposition might flinch a little at the sight of the drop from the castle and its terraces to the water below. It is magnificent and a bit terrifying. This is most certainly not a garden for unsupervised children. It is a place blessed in its surroundings.

The planting, simply and subtly decorates it, rather than trying to compete with such grandeur. The wooded walks go in all directions from the castle, some visible as they make their way out and along the river, crossing the water to the woods on the other side. The woods are scattered with some fine examples of pine and cedar, beech and oak, both statuesque and gnarled old specimens.

At going to press, a restoration of the walled garden was happily underway. It will be interesting to see the resulting new kitchen garden, in which they are reinstating paths, hedges and a water feature.

Brigit's Garden

Pollagh, Roscahill, Co. Galway. Tel: 091 550905. e-mail: info@brigitsgarden.ie www.brigitsgarden.ie Contact: Jenny Beale. Open: All year 10am-5.30pm. Special features: Wheelchair accessible. Coffee shop. Gift shop. Family events. School tours. Dogs on leads. Directions: Signposted in Roscahill village from the N59 Galway to Connemara road, 22 km from Galway.

Roscahill is a tiny village on the road from Galway to Connemara and it is that modest size that makes the community-run Brigit's Garden most remarkable. The venture was set up in 2000. They brought Chelsea Flower Show winner Mary Reynolds in to design the

gardens, themed around Irish folklore, its festivals, stories and myths. The results are as quirky, interesting, useable and eco-aware as one might expect from the talented designer. The whole project covers over 11 acres, and is divided into different areas devoted to among others, Saint Brigit. This is a place perfectly made for an idle wander between apple circles, newt-filled ponds and massive living grass sculptures depicting rotund earth goddesses. These are only a few of the items to expect in this entertaining place. I came across cubes made of thyme within an offbeat looking raised herb garden. Walking past a willow wall, you might wander into a poppy field, come upon an example of a managed mixed native hedge, a cowslip studded meadow, a crannog, or a wooden sculpture.

This might seem a bit dull but my favourite features were the boundary walks, under arched canopies of hawthorn, hazel and other native trees. These managed, yet slightly wild walks, are bounded by, among other things, ash trees left to grow around massive boulders and glacial boulder piles, like a collection of Henry Moore works in storage, waiting to be put on display.

The place is a living, nature textbook and is used as such to teach school groups about wildlife, horticulture and nature. Yet it can be enjoyed simply as a series of wild, flower gardens and woods. Anyone planning a garden in the countryside would do well to take a turn around this garden before imposing something alien on their surroundings.

Cashel House

Cashel, Connemara, Co. Galway. Contact: Kay and Lucy McEvilly. Tel: 095 31001. e-mail: sales@cashelhouse.ie www.cashelhouse.ie Special features: Hotel. Garden courses. Annual Planting of the Potatoes Day. See website for annual details. Restaurant. Guided tours can be arranged. Directions: South of the N59 between Oughterard and Clifden. Well signposted.

Driving from Oughterard to Cashel, passing Lough Corrib and a string of smaller lakes with the Maumturk Mountains for company and the ever-changing light, you might question the desire to hunt out a cultivated garden in the middle of such overwhelming natural beauty. But, like the sheep that are akin to landowners on the pock-marked roads, the garden at Cashel House holds its own very nicely within a wooded boundary, in the middle of the bog.

The house, seen from the drive, looks as though it has flowers and shrubs climbing in its windows and doors. The paths seem to have been all but lost behind plants, making the building appear to sit in the middle of a huge flower bed. This effect works from inside the building too: Sitting in the conservatory, masses of white lychnis, red 'ladybird' poppies and lilies stand at eye level, while a little bridged stream can be seen flowing past, unusually close to the house, as the windows appear under siege from climbing roses.

The flower borders sprawl out from the house toward large mixed shrub borders and beyond these, a rising encirclement of woods. I wondered about such abundant growth in the middle of desolate Connemara, when I remembered: Kay McEvilly, the lady of the garden, began her horticultural career at the age of four. She grew all the lupins and delphiniums here from seed. Kay knows her plants, special and not, and loves them equally as long as they perform. Passing a ribbon of *Alchemilla mollis* sneaking out onto the drive, Kay paused to admire its water-resistant leaves. 'I'll not stop good expansion,' she smiled and then paused to note a cuckoo singing nearby. 'We're on pure peat,' she told me, as we made our way past ranks of eucryphia – one with a huge *Clematis montana* climbing through it. The path ducks under a venerable looking bay arch leading into the vegetable garden, but at only about a decade old, this bay is proof of the enviable fertility here.

In the vegetable garden, the number of lesser-spotted crops is worth studying. The crops are hemmed in by *Euonymus japonicus* 'Microphyllus Variegatus' more simply known as box-leaf euonymus. It defines the lines of kohlrabi, lovage, red kale, Florence fennel and sorrel, all destined for the hotel kitchen. I admired a sweep of lavender and assumed it was being grown as a cut flower, but they grow lavender to make ice cream. These pretty crops are backed by equally pretty walls of *Rosa* 'Wedding Day' and *R.* 'Rambling Rector'. Kay put in an experimental fruit garden at the top of this area to demonstrate what can fit in so tiny a space. A 6 x 5 x 2 metre triangle is all she needs to grow pears, apples, gooseberries, cranberries and strawberries, with space to spare. 'My great discovery here was the supersonic rabbit deterrent. It's fabulous. Until I put it in, the rabbits ploughed through everything I sowed.'

Flanking the other side of the house is what looks like a dense wood. But stepping inside, it turns out to be an almost hollowed-out woodland stream garden full of camellias underplanted with hostas, ferns and primulas. All the wooden benches here were made from trees that came down in storms. Happily still standing despite so many batterings, is the tallest *Robinia pseudoacacia* on the island, a huge *Davidia involucrata* and an eight-trunked liriodendron. Much of the canopy towers way overhead. My breath was taken away by the 20-metre-tall parrotia.

We stepped out of the quiet shade and into the dazzle of a sunny area called Mary's Garden. In the summer, this is a highlight; a special flower garden created at the edge of the woods; an explosion of delphiniums, lupins, phlox and roses all twined together to make a garden that almost blinds the visitor with colour and flower as they emerge from the dark wood. It was made as a tribute to Kay's late sister Mary, another keen gardener and is the sort of mad flower garden that Mary once worked, alive with bees and wildlife as it was with flowers. As we sat in the middle of all these flowers and perfume, some American students walked by and thanked Kay who they referred to as; 'you guys, for the *awesome* garden.'

Coole Park

Gort, Co. Galway. Tel: 091 631804. e-mail info@coolepark.ie www.coolepark.ie
Special features: Partially wheelchair accessible. Tea rooms. Open: Grounds all year round. Free admission.
Directions: Follow signs from Gort.

Coole Park, famous from the WB Yeats poem, 'The Wild Swans at Coole', was home to Lady Augusta Gregory, who along with Yeats and Synge, was largely responsible for the revival of the Irish theatre at the turn of the 20th century. Today Coole is a pale ghost of what it once was, a park without a house. While there are some interesting nature walks and trails through the grounds, the place is of limited interest to gardeners. The walled garden has had some work carried out since my last visit: A long shrub border has been added to the top of the garden and there are a few good specimen trees including a fine *Abies nordmanniana* and the famous Autograph Tree, a copper beech carved with the names of George Bernard Shaw, Douglas Hyde, George Moore (AE), Synge, Sean O'Casey and the two famous Yeats brothers, W.B. and Jack. The park also boasts some fine tree-lined trails in the large surrounding woods. It is good place for a picnic and the day I visited there were several big groups enjoying Sunday feasts in the grass.

Do not leave Gort without paying a visit to Burke's hardware shop, decked out in a riot of tin bins and buckets, sweeping brushes and signs advertising silage tape, hurls and good mucky carrots. A little way down the street, Keane's Saloon Bar also does a mean line in farm and garden tools.

Cordarragh Farm Garden

Headford, Co. Galway. Tel: 093 35628. 087 4677790. e-mail: cordarraghhelen@outlook.com
Contact: Helen Veale. Open: For occasional Open Days. Contact early in year for annual dates. Special
features: Wheelchair accessible. Children welcome. No dogs due to working farm. Plants for sale. Directions:
On application.

Listening to gardeners talk about how they work their gardens is much more informative than a solo trot around. Simply looking, on the calm day I visited, I would not have known that Helen Veale's garden could be such a windy spot. As we trailed between an island bed made up of 'Bantry Bay' and 'Dublin

Bay' roses on one side, and the red-flowered spice bush or *Calycanthus occidentalis* and scented daphne on the other, I was interested to be told that gales apparently whip around this surprisingly exposed garden at a dreadful rate and Helen needs to use her wits to outfox them.

She has been working this farm garden for seven years, and in that short time she has brought it from 'concrete', as she put it, to a flourishing, young garden that will continue to mature and fill out in the years to come.

Helen started by enclosing the house within a series of garden rooms, starting with a rather dinky little blue garden that she not only planted up but built the walls for too. In the centre of this, the wind-proofing comes in the pleasing shape of a four-arched pergola and a summerhouse in the middle of the converging flower beds. 'You need something like this to get away from the wind,' she laughed as we stood underneath looking out through jasmine and schisandra curtains at deep purple and magenta 'Matucana' sweet peas, blue camassia, *Rosa* 'Reine de Violettes', perovskia, campanula and delphinium. Massed blues are gorgeous.

The farm which the garden is named after, is a mere hop over the low stone wall around the vegetable garden. This means that those vegetables are nicely placed for access to vital manure supplies. Look out for oddities such as the spiral trained gooseberries. This clever training method helps to avoid the picker getting scratched by thorns. Apart from accessible gooseberries, there are other fruit bushes, neat lines of salads and root vegetables, arranged for their look as well as for productivity.

In an extra wind defeating measure, Helen laid wooden paths in her big polytunnel, making it prettier and more pleasant to work in because she likes to spend as much time as possible in here, away from the gales. Next, we visited the patio garden by the house where we came across more climbers – wisteria, schisandra, *Akebia quinata*, and more rambling roses, - quite an exotic set of wall plants.

The drive is lined by young, developing cobnuts, filberts and hazels. It leads out to the last garden, which is based around a little roofless cottage that Helen transformed into a vine, peach and apricot house, which oversees the latest garden room, her flower orchard. This too is surrounded by a hip-high stone wall. I left admiring the little exhibition of old rusting tools discovered as she dug the garden.

Errisbeg House

Roundstone, Co. Galway. Tel: 095 35834. e-mail destacpoole@gmail.com www.roundstone.ie
Contact: Richard Duc de Stacpoole Open: By appointment. Special feature: B&B. Directions: Take the Ballyconneely road out of Roundstone. A few hundred metres beyond the Garda Station follow the sign to the right marked 'Stables and Errisbeg House'.

Richard Duc de Stacpoole was quick to tell me that he is not the gardener, but the caretaker. His job is to mind the garden his grandmother created. He presides over a place that is so wild and natural it could be a backdrop for a gothic novel. Its seas of grass, spiked with jutting rocks, are as beautiful as any composition the best designer might conjure up. The rustle of the surrounding trees fills the air and there are beehives humming with life. White flowering arum lilies or *Zantedeschia aethiopica* are among the few splashes of flower and colour here. There are also some entwined jasmine and shrub roses, as well as foxgloves sprouting from rocky crevices and free-standing specimens of rhododendron. Mostly this is greenery however, from gigantic gunnera leaves, dramatic *Osmunda regalis* ferns and, with one of the signatures of the western gardens, moss as thick as a Navan carpet. These all melt together to create pictures of beauty that sit comfortably into the wild surroundings. As I admired some of the huge boulders around which the lawns wash, I wondered how hard it must be to cut the grass here. Richard told me he manages nicely with a push-on mower and a strimmer.

A feature peculiar to the garden are the several sunken streams that run over and back across the space. Indeed there are streams everywhere. Gurgling water is a constant, as are wet, spongy greens. Wear your wellies. The Connemara landscape beyond the garden is always in the line of sight and I was told the waterfall that I could see tumbling down a very distant hill was making its way in the direction of this garden and the surrounding stream, which it sometimes floods.

This is a wild rugged maze of a garden, perhaps not for the smart edge-obsessed visitor, but a treat for anyone of a romantic bent.

Errislannan Manor

Ballyconneely Road, Clidfen, Connemara, Co. Galway. Tel: 095 21134. e-mail errislannanmanor@eircom.net www.errislannanmanor.com Contact: Stephanie Brooks. Open: By appointment. Not wheelchair accessible. No dogs. Special features: Riding school. Connemara pony breeding and sales. Directions: From Clifden, take the Ballyconneely Road. Drive over three bridges and then turn right uphill signed for the 'Errislannan Equestrian Centre.'

On my most recent visit, the estimable, Mrs Brooks had turned 90. When we previously met, a few years before, she had been simultaneously babysitting a new Labrador pup, feeding a pony and issuing orders to a girl giving riding lessons, yet she still found time to conduct me around the garden. This time I thought I should offer to walk alone. She agreed but told me to come back afterwards for tea and doughnuts.

Told that you will be visiting areas named the Dog Kennel Lawn, Dingley Dell, the Laundry and Horse's Grave, you will have some idea that this might be a country garden and you would be right. It is also a welcoming one, right from the entrance which is an arching avenue of ash trees, under-planted with mounds of rhododendrons and hydrangeas.

Off to the left of the drive is a body of water which, I thought initially was the sea but it turned out to be a small lake called Lough Nakilla. The house has an uninterrupted view over this gleaming body of water. The short avenue of field maples here, underplanted with daffodils, is of interest because up until 1950, daffodils were grown at Errislannan, packed in shoe boxes and brought to Clifden for the train to the Dublin flower market.

As I arrived, I spied an exercise ring a little way off where ponies were being schooled and beyond this, two ponies straight out of central casting galloped down a distant hill. The route to the garden leads through an iron gate, past a stand of tall yellow inulas that came home as seeds in a pocket from Tresco many years ago. The air of peace and tranquility in this garden is marked. I heard a cuckoo, which set the tone. They seem to be widespread in Connemara.

The path cuts between a short line of trimmed yews, past more hydrangeas including 'one untidy lady' as Mrs Brooks described a bulging *Hydrangea aspera*. The pink *Rosa* 'Albertine' close by is not much tidier. There are also beds of peonies, *Stachys byzantina*, monarda, red astilbe, veronica and *Rosa* 'Paul's Himalayan Scarlet.'

There is something special about gates in a garden and another gate lures you on from here into an area of small trees including red flowering hamamelis, a ginkgo and a lichen-encrusted *Cercis siliquastrum* or the Judas tree.

As a garden dating back to the 19th century, there are still remnants of that older, more regulated scheme to be seen: The walled garden is sloped and at the top, a line of cordylines stand like smart soldiers looking down over the garden. It is almost possible to imagine the ladies in white dresses and straw hats playing croquet on the lawn below these, such is the lingering memory of this almost vanished garden. The orchard is home to a mix of young and old trees and surrounded by a sheltering escallonia hedge. It has such an air of tranquility about it, with light layers of history strewn over the wild landscape.

Back in the 21st century, visitors can visit the bluebell wood in late spring. This wilder part of the garden is where the native trees are joined by embothrium, eucryphia and more hydrangeas.

Gleann Aoibheann

Beach Road, Clifden, Connemara, Co. Galway. Tel: 095 21148.
e-mail: breandanoscanaill@eircom.net Contact: Breandan O'Scanaill. Open: By appointment. Partially
wheelchair accessible. Supervised children welcome. Dogs on leads. Special features: House tours. Teas. Tours
of a selection of other Connemara gardens can be arranged. Directions. Driving on the Beach Road out of
Clifden, Gleann Aoibheann is the 6th house with gates facing the road.

The unusual old house at Gleann Aoibheann was built by the D'Arcy family, important landowners in Clifden, at the beginning of the 19th century. It has passed through several families over its 200 years, each of which added to the house and garden. Some of the older trees are thought to have been planted by the D'Arcys, but most of the garden work was undertaken at the beginning of the 20th century, with alternating periods of development and neglect ever since.

Breandan O'Scanaill is the current owner and it is going through another period of development, as a wildlife garden. As with so many good Connaught gardens, this two-and-a-half acre plot is impressive in the way it blends into the rough landscape around it. 'I nearly prefer wildlife to plants' Breandan told me. He works completely organically.

The Beach Road out of Clifden is a magical place, overlooking the sea, yet pulling into Gleann Aoibheann, the visitor doesn't feel they are being taken from one special landscape as much as being lured into another. The garden faces south and the steep hill behind it provides protection from prevailing winds, rendering it remarkably sheltered. Added to this, it is fortunate to enjoy fertile soil.

The hilly site is composed of sweeps of wildflower lawn interrupted by naturalistic groupings of shrubs and trees, ponds and, out on the edge, extensive woods. Breandan mows different paths through the grass depending on where the best stands of wild flowers happen to crop up each year. When we do walk on permanent paths, they are the beach-stone paths that were laid out in the 1920s. One of these rises up behind the house under a canopy of rhododendrons and a selection of different oaks including the willow leaf oak or *Quercus phellos*, a

Turkey oak, a red-flowering Indian chestnut and a sweet chestnut or *Castanea sativa*. It would be hard to stand out, but among this mass *Acer ginnala*, a tender and unusual tree, has fared remarkably well in the protected micro-climate. There are a good number of acers and hollies scattered through the garden. In the spring, the ground underneath all these is sheeted with bluebells.

Below the hill, we walked between explosions of herbaceous perennials and shrubs from yellow ligularia and purple loosestrife to white shasta daisies, pink *Hydrangea aspera* and camellias. Breandan points out a favourite here in the shape of a *Platanus orientalis* with serrated leaves and a special *Valeriana pyrenaica* that has been in the garden since the 1830s. Despite the number of exotic imports this is a garden with a native feel. The small wildflower meadow in front of the house with its early purple orchids is striking. Adding further to the wild feel is the huge carcass of a fallen tree, left to slowly decompose, providing homes for a whole world of plants from echiums and a kiwi to a big sprawling *Rosa* 'Wedding Day.'

We finished up our visit at the house, which is wrapped up in a century-old wisteria and fringed with all sorts of perennials.

The overall memory of this garden is the easy and stylish way Breandan mixes his ever-growing collection of unusual and good looking plants, so that they look as though they naturally arrived. To spend a few hours wandering up hill and down slope between these beauties is to time well spent.

Kylemore Abbey

Connemara, Co. Galway. Contact: Reception. Tel: 095 52001 e-mail: info@kylemoreabbey.com www.kylemoreabbey.com Open: Grounds: Daily all year 10am-5pm. Garden: Mid-Mar - Oct. See web for annual dates. Special features: Partially wheelchair accessible. Museum in Castle. Restaurant. Gift shops. Directions: On the Leenane to Clifden road (N59) 9 km from Leenane.

The romantic story of Mitchell Henry who bought the lands at Kylemore Abbey for his wife Margaret is the stuff of novels. In 1852, while honeymooning in Connemara, Margaret fell in love with the area and ten years later, Henry bought 9,000 acres and built her a castle. This achievement involved more than dewy-eyed romanticism and deep pockets. He imposed an impressive demesne on the rough land at the foot of the Twelve Pins, employing hundreds of workers to realise his vision. The story ended sadly however. Margaret only lived to enjoy her extravagant gift until 1875. On a trip to Egypt, she died of Nile fever. Henry later sold the property.

At the beginning of World War I, the Irish Benedictine nuns, who had been in Ypres since the Reformation, fled their war-torn base in Belgium. They moved to Ireland, where they bought Kylemore and opened a girls' school.

In the garden, a lack of manpower and money led inevitably to deterioration despite the efforts of successive gardeners. In 1996, however, the rot was stopped. Studying some of the famous Lawrence Collection photographs taken at the turn of the 20th century, and with money from the Great Gardens of Ireland Restoration Fund, the nuns set out to save the walled garden. Today it is possibly as handsome as when it was created.

The first of its sections is quite different from most traditional walled gardens. There are no tall herbaceous borders. Instead, this is an example of Victorian formal bedding where annuals are grown in massive numbers to create borders like floral carpets. Height is scarce and delivered by tall cordylines, phormiums, trachycarpus, tree ferns and in one area an unusual, large metal circular trellis with hanging baskets. This seasonal garden is interesting from an historical perspective.

Two of the original 20 greenhouses have been restored and house tender plants and cats snoozing on the electric propagation heat mats. The footprints of most of the others are all that remain along with intriguing looking bits of pipes and sumps and the remains of Victorian heating and watering systems.

Three features worth investigating are the restored gardener's house, a tool shed and the bothy. The gardener's house is a representation of the house the head gardener lived in, complete with its little flower garden. It is fully furnished, true to period and filled with the details of everyday life. The bothy was home to the garden boys who had to sleep close to the boilers they were charged to stoke 24 hours a day to keep the glasshouses constantly warm. As for the tool shed, horticultural anoraks will always enjoy a display of old and obscure implements.

The fruit and vegetable gardens have been fully restored and are among the best examples seen on the island. Healthy vegetables grown in handsome arrangements are always attractive and the sight of a nun with a trug full of carrots and onions serves to remind that this garden still feeds the residents of the Abbey along with being a huge tourist attraction. The adjacent water, woodland and fern gardens are also beautiful and the young orchard of native Irish apples will be worth watching as it develops. Walled and kitchen gardens are often a distance from the house. In the case of Kylemore, the garden is two kilometres away. The estate papers do not explain that distance, but one theory is that Henry positioned the garden so that Diamond Hill could be seen in its full glory from within its walls. Today a shuttle bus brings visitors on the long road leading to it. More energetic visitors can walk to it through the woods if they wish.

There are extensive woodland walks. Henry planted an oak wood, as well as plantations of lime and beech, Sitka spruce, alder, native wych elm (*Ulmus glabra*), and Monterey pine. The nuns continue planting to this day, concentrating on oak. Make a point of looking at the rough land around the garden as you leave. It is hard to see how so much could be wrested from so little. This is a constant theme in Connaught gardens.

Portumna Castle & Gardens

Portumna, Co. Galway. Contact: Reception or Tel: 0909 741658 e-mail: portumnacastle@opw.ie.
www.facebook.com/portumnacastle Open: Ap-Oct., 9.30am-6pm daily. Group tours can be arranged.
Supervised children welcome. Dogs on leads. Special features: Working kitchen garden. Semi-restored castle.
Guided tour as part of ticket price. Directions: Situated in the town surrounded by Portumna Castle Park.
Follow the signs from Abbey Street.

Richard Burke, 4th Earl of Clanricarde began to build Portumna Castle and its gardens in 1618 on an impressive site overlooking Lough Derg, on the border of Galway and Tipperary. The castle is one of the finest surviving examples of an Irish semi-fortified house of this period. The grounds are thought to have been laid out in the most modern style of the time as his wife had come from the court of Elizabeth I and was *au fait* with fashion.

The gardens are divided into two distinctive areas. The first is a recreation of a formal Jacobean garden laid out to the front of the castle. It is a smart, substantial array of perfectly proportioned paths and geometric beds of roses. The heavy scent of roses from raspberry ripple-coloured *Rosa mundi* and *Rosa* 'Chapeau de Napoleon' fills the air in summer. Well-raked gravel paths and lawns foil the rose beds neatly and the house lords it over the whole show. Standing on its steps, gives the best view of the design.

The second area is a walled kitchen garden, sited just over the wall and reached by way of a gate. To state that the difference in style between the two is dramatic would be something of an understatement.

This is like leaving a deportment class and entering into the middle of a riot. The explosion of flower, colour and sheer variety is a joy. Neglected for over 100 years, restoration on the kitchen garden began in 1996 under the care of a number of local organic enthusiasts. Archaeological research led to the discovery of ancient seed in the soil and the Irish Seed Savers Association helped with sourcing heritage seeds using that information. Meanwhile, many of the old paths including a turning circle for a pony and cart were uncovered and restored.

Today, following years of development the kitchen garden is a busy, pleasant place, full of vegetables, and fruit grown in little orchard areas, herbaceous borders, summerhouses and arbours draped in jasmine, roses and honeysuckle. The espaliered apple trees, entwined with an unknown red noisette rose stay in the memory.

Even on days when there are plenty of visitors around, the seclusion of each little part of the walled garden means that a visitor always feels as though they have the place to themselves. The woods around the castle have been smartened up and are also worth a walk.

Renvyle House

Renvyle Peninsula, Co. Galway. Tel: 095 43511. e-mail ronnie@renvyle.com Contact: Reception. Open: By appointment. Special features: Hotel. Directions: Take the Connemara Loop from Letterfrack to Tully Cross. Turn left in Tully in the direction of Renvyle.

Sometimes you are very happy you stopped to check out a garden and not necessarily because it is a perfect example of horticultural brilliance. Sometimes, the atmosphere of welcome and warmth is enough. The hotel at Renvyle, with its arts and crafts style building is unusual in Ireland. The hotel itself, busy as it was, when I stumbled in unannounced, felt welcoming and open. The gardens equally so. I came across chef Tim O'Sullivan in the herb garden picking this and that for the kitchen. He told me that he gets five cuts from a parsley plant before pulling it up – something to test at home. This herb and vegetable garden is surrounded by roses and flowering fuchsia, with a raised rosemary circle in the centre that is a bee magnet, so it is both productive, informal and pretty.

The drive up to the house gives glimpses of an orchard and a rose garden to one side but the waterside setting is what dominates the front of the house. A little lawn fringed with nepeta leads in under a stand of sheltering trees and from there, straight out to the water. There are lawns and mixed shrub beds, hydrangea walks and a bluebell wood through which you can walk. Someone loves building benches and walls using sea cobbles as there are a number of these scattered about the place. I was intrigued by the apple trees, mainly Irish cultivars, planted by dignitaries, and found all about the place in odd corners.

One of the walks leads through the woods, through drifts of Queen Anne's lace and daffodils, wild garlic and of course bluebells. This leads to the first orchard, planted up a few years ago with cider apples, which will in time produce Renvyle cider.

Wild flowers and a light touch are the words that sum up the garden. It not preened but it has heart and personality and, most welcome, it is run on organic principles.

Ross Castle

Roscahill, Co. Galway. Contact: George and E. Marshall McLaughlin. Tel: 091 550183. e-mail info@rosscastle.com www.rosscastle.com Open: All year. Special features: Tours of castle by appointment to groups. Refreshments by appointment. Functions can be organised. Accommodation in castle and courtyard. Directions: Driving through Roscahill toward Galway city, take the signposted left hand turn for Ross Castle and follow for a short distance.

Overlooking Lough Corrib, Ross Castle, like so many grand houses, enjoys views that almost render the need for a garden redundant. Until recently this old garden was indeed just that. Standing at the castle and looking over the parkland studded with trees, it has the venerable look of a place long cared for once. How looks can deceive: Mrs. McLaughlin explained that when they came to the house back in 1985 the park was invisible under decades of neglect and rampant growth.

Her husband's family, the Martins, left Roscahill and Ireland for America during the Great Famine. Returning in the 1980s, they would spend three months with a JCB just clearing field trees from the park. Then the castle had to be restored and the gardens retrieved from their slumber. A few decades of work later and the gardens and castle are once again handsome and fit for purpose.

After a drive under a canopy of tall ash, beech and oak, the avenue opens elegantly onto a sunny lawn and the lough. The roof of a little boat house peeps up from the water's edge and of course, on cue, two swans glided across the water.

The gardens proper are reached through an arch in a stone wall covered in a big red rambling rose. This is the rather magical entrance to the large walled garden. Huge yews that probably started as small topiary decorations, today dominate an ordered arrangement of grass paths between formal gravel paths, box beds and shrub plantings, all centred on a huge urn.

There are gates on opposing side walls that give views out on to the park in one direction, and into the kitchen garden, which is still being developed and restored, in the other. The path then leads on through a laurel hedge and into the greenhouse garden. This is a singularly pretty little area built around a long canal-like pond. The most spectacular apricot tree which takes up the greenhouse, was dripping fruit. Research found these to be delicious.

Around the greenhouse there is a puzzling and diverting maze of box-enclosed garden rooms, with big, golden flowered lysimachia and aquilegias and splashes of other cottage garden flowers around a sundial.

It is hard to envisage the state of the place back in 1985. Mrs. McLaughlin pointed out the cobbles that had to be unearthed in the courtyard. It too, was a jungle when she first saw it. Today the planting around the edges is easy and colourful, made largely of buddleia, roses, hostas and anemones in beds at the base of the stone walls. They left one huge field maple in the centre. This was just one of the wild trees growing in here when they arrived.

The original castle, built in 1539 by the 'Ferocious' O'Flaherty's was 'Georgianised' in the 18th century. Previous cow sheds were incorporated into the castle, which was in turn remodelled as a fashionable country house with courtyard. Apart from working on the grounds, the McLaughlins set out to restore the castle. Guided tours given by George can be arranged for groups. I recommend one, in particular to see the handsome vaulted brick basement. Proceeds from these tours go toward helping a girl's school in Kimlea in Africa.

Rosleague Manor

Letterfrack. Connemara, Co. Galway. Contact: Mark Foyle. Tel: 095 41101.
e-mail: info@rosleague.com www.rosleague.com Open: Mar-Oct by appointment. Special features: Hotel.
Events. See website. Directions: Situated south of Letterfrack on the N59. Signed.

Rosleague is yet another place surrounded by the rough majesty of Connemara. The gardens turn out to be an unexpectedly lush pleasure. The manor sits on top of a hill overlooking the sea. It is a house that seems to have the feel of an early 20th century tennis party. There is an air of comfort and leisure about both house and gardens. They are good looking but relaxed. Paths run out from the house between mixed beds of shrubs and herbaceous perennials that actually feel a bit like mazes. Hypericum and phlomis, hardy geranium, scented *Rhododendron luteum* and pruned up arboreal rhododendrons all melt together in big loose walls of happy clashing colour. As the saying goes; 'the colours would take the eye out of your head.'

They would, and you would not complain. This sort of exuberance is a pleasure. The paths tunnel through the scented cram, slowly making their way down to the sea. One veers off into a little mixed wood, rising, falling and winding between oak and ash on trunk-lined paths. In one place the path passed a temporarily fenced off area where three happy, scrub-clearance pigs lay about, snoring in a happy heap on top of each other. The ground in the shade here is littered with ferns and soft with moss and every so often you glimpse the sea. In late spring bluebells sheet the place. At one point, the wood opens out to an orchard and wildflower meadow with paths mown between the apple trees. The wood, meanwhile, eventually makes its way down to the sea and a view of the Twelve Pins in the distance.

A newly created garden to the side of the house took my interest on my most recent visit. This turned out to be a small vegetable garden set unusually, in a clearing in the middle of another wood. Take the goat path uphill and in under the trees and along past some sweeps of hydrangea. The wooded walks run under ridiculously tall, straight, beech, oak and larch and the tall canopy lets a sweet soft light in. The paths branch in several directions, some leading around the open vegetable garden and one leading into it. They do afternoon tea. Of course they do.

Woodville House Walled Garden

Kilchreest, Loughrea, Co. Galway. Tel: 087 9069 191. e-mail: info@woodvillewalledgarden.com www.woodvillewalledgarden.com Contact: Margarita Donohue. Open: Open seven days. Closed Nov-Jan. Supervised children welcome. No dogs. (Working farm). Not wheelchair accessible. Special features: Museum. Garden videos on rainy days. Tearoom. Gift shop. Plant sales. Seasonal events. Directions: From Loughrea on the N66 turn right in the village of Kilchreest. After 1.2 km, take the 1st turn left. Woodville Walled Garden is the 3rd entrance on the right.

As I arrived into the cobble-floored café and shop at Woodville Walled Garden, a visiting Chinese family, obviously having had a good time, tried to convince me that they worked there. I couldn't blame them. I wanted to to do the same when the time came for me to leave.

I had spent my visit almost staggering from one surprise to another. For a privately run walled garden, covering 1.5 acres, run by a small staff, the ambition of Woodville is remarkable. Walking along between one pair of deep mirroring, herbaceous borders, leads to another set of double borders. Come to a corner and there is yet another double border, running perpendicular, and then another one and these do not include the extensive wall borders. This is large-scale high maintenance stuff.

The smart use of repeat planting gives unity to each of these borders: In the mixed shrub and flower borders, *Viburnum* 'Mariesii is used successfully at intervals in this way. Elsewhere, crenelated box walls enclose another garden quarter. In the middle of all these flower borders there are attractive vegetable beds, while out on the walls, I spied lines of expertly trained fruit trees. I made my way through arches in hornbeam walls, almost expecting that to be that, only to find more - sometimes bowling green lawns, sometimes another flower border. This is a garden that keeps giving.

Parts of it date back to 1780 and when Margarita Donoghue, whose baby it is, began to work the garden, it was in need of restoration, so she enlisted the help of the talented designer, Daphne Shackleton. Together they began to to rein it in and the results are here today, an utter delight, run by a tiny team of great workers. Irish cultivars and heritage plants have been used throughout, so look out for these.

The old dovecote, built into the walls, is rather romantically home to a flock of white fantail doves whose job is to decorate the place. Meanwhile out in the mature woods to the side of the walled garden there are some pleasant woodland walks into which fairies seem to have arrived, in much the way that they have appeared in a good number of gardens around the country...

I finished up in the tearoom, with a slice of lemon cake and a fascinating trip around the museum to Woodville and Lady Gregory, who had links with the house. Look for the framed letter from a member of the family, back in the 19th century, looking to 'borrow friends for my nephew.'

Zetland Country House & Garden

Cashel Bay. Callow, Connemara, Co. Galway. Tel: 095 31111. e-mail info@zetland.com www.zetland.com. Special features: Hotel. Contact: Colm Redmond. Open: All year. Directions: Travelling on the N59 from Galway, turn left after Recess onto the R340. Turn right 4.5 km along the R340. The hotel is situated on the right about 1 km from the turn. Signed.

The gardens at Zetland House are yet again another take on the theme of trees, rocks, rhododendrons and views of the waters and wilds. Although the Victorian hotel once stood naked and bare to the elements, unprotected on a rough stony site beside Bertraghboy Bay, today, it is engulfed and protected by a substantial and mature shelter belt of trees. Within that shelter, a handsome array of mature, special shrubs and trees have been able to grow and thrive.

The sea is dominant however. Close to the house the main garden runs down to the bay. A seating terrace sits in the middle of some loose, mixed borders of colourful herbaceous perennials like mallow, lychnis, bergenia, roses and of course hydrangeas. Sitting here, the sea view is a blessed thing. A well weathered stone path and steps lead to the lawns below and to walks between the shrub borders through the wafting perfume of roses. The lawns are strewn with impressive rocky outcrops, some of which were harnessed as miniature ponds, surrounded by sprouts of fern and wild flowers. The feel is very much one of a relaxed slightly wild garden.

Views out to the sea and the landscape beyond are framed by curtains of rhododendron, myrtle, pines, field maples and Japanese acers, cordyline and horse chestnut. Lower storeys of flowering viburnums, hydrangea and fuchsia add colour and an extra puff of foliage to the billowing plantations. Is it manicured? No. The old fashioned welcome experienced indoors is similarly seen in the relaxed and attractive garden outside.

Take a look at the quirky collection of documents and photographs inside, including a picture entitled 'saving hay in Dublin Airport during the emergency'. These are part of owner Colm Redmond's collection. I first met Colm, a most enthusiastic man, as he emerged from the trees with a secateurs in one hand and a sheaf of bay leaves in the other, as he made his way to the kitchen.

Cashel House, Co. Galway

Leitrim

Lough Rynn Estate

Mohill, Co. Leitrim. Contact: The Manager. Tel: 071 9632 700. e-mail: enquiries@loughrynn.ie
www.loughrynn.ie. Open: All year. Call for seasonal times and dates. Groups by appointment. Directions:
5 km from Mohill on the road to Drumlish.

Lough Rynn was once one of the homes of William Sidney Clements, the third Earl of Leitrim, who, as one of the most notorious evicting landlords of the period, was famously ambushed and shot in 1878. On my first visit the house and grounds at Lough Rynn were deserted and ghostly.

Today, the house smells of life and polished wood. It is a busy, grand hotel surrounded by well worked gardens and grounds.

The stone baronial style manor is softened by planting of hydrangea and clipped box. Swept and sharply edged gravel walks lead out between expanses of lawn and statuary.

There are long woodland and lakeside walks, taking in an old boathouse, what looks like the remains of a lost rock garden and the remains of the 12th century Reynolds Castle.

I took a turn around with Piotr, gardener and all round enthusiast for the place. The walled garden, overlooking the Lough, is the highlight of the gardens. The style is unusual in that it is stepped into three levels, overlooking the water. In the first section, the walls are covered in the most perfectly trained closely set lines of cordoned and espaliered apples, pears and plums.

On the next level, yew walls create little rooms with roses over pergolas, on trellises and pinned to the walls.

The view of water from the bottom terrace is not easy to compete with, but mirroring shrub beds and lines of pleached beech that run the length of the garden, give a good account of themselves.

In one corner these is a sort of Rapunzel tower of a summer house with little iron balconies looking out over the water.

The Organic Centre

Rossinver, Co. Leitrim. Contact: Reception or Hans Weiland. Tel: 071 9854338.
e-mail: info@theorganiccentre.ie. www.theorganiccentre.ie. Open: Daily Mar-Nov. 10am-5pm. Partially
wheelchair accessible. Supervised children welcome. Please note, dogs on leads. Special features: Demonstration
gardens. Sunflower maze. Children's garden. Restaurant. Craft and garden shop. Plants and food for sale.
Courses. Community and school courses. B&B and hostel accommodation. Directions: Situated 3 km from
Rossinver on the R281 Kinlough Road between Manorhamilton and Bundoran.

The Organic Centre was established in 1996 to answer a growing demand for information on organic farming, land husbandry and gardening. Set on 19 acres of unspoilt north Leitrim limestone, the centre works in two ways. It offers a range of courses throughout the year aimed at professional gardeners, farmers cooks and interested amateurs. They offer everything from courses on how to make compost and become self-sufficient, to keeping hens, bees and encouraging wildlife. They cover willow sculpting, basket making and every conceivable sort of course on food growing, production and preservation one could hope to find.

There are examples of fruiting and edible hedges. The domestic and commercial vegetable plots are extremely useful to study.

Heritage gardens, planted up with seed obtained from the Irish Seed Savers and Henry Doubleday Research Association in the UK are as fascinating as they are vital in the protection of heritage vegetables.

The compost systems, green manure beds, apple orchards and propogating houses are all fascinating.

My most memoral feature this visit was Jill Scott's decorative polytunnel, where even in damp Ireland you can sit 'out' in a decorative garden safe from the wind and rain.

Mayo

Achill Secret Garden

Achill Island, Co. Mayo. Tel: 098 45103. 087 414 9895. www.achillsecretgarden.com
Contact: Willem and Doutsje van Goor. Open: By appointment. Special features: Accommodation, Apr-Oct.
Garden tour includes tea and home-made cake. Directions: Drive to Achill Island and take the L1405
south toward Bleanaskill. The garden is signposted.

You don't expect to find a garden that could be described as lush out on beautiful, but bleak Achill Island. Yet there has been such a garden out here for over 100 years. The house was once home to Alexander Williams, the watercolour artist, and Lady Noël and Sir Anthony Bevir, private secretary to Winston Churchill.

Today's gardeners, the van Goors arrived in 1997 and began working with the existing garden, to produce the place as it is seen today, a sheltered secluded, unusual garden on a wild, blasted island.

Doutsje told me how, in the natural scheme of things, it takes nearly a quarter of a century for a tree to reach a metre-and-a-half out here. The Secret Garden works because it is circled by a 40 metre shelter belt of trees through which the winds cannot cut. From time to time there are casualties however, when this happens they use the branches to make new fences throughout the garden. I studied these, unusual woven, organic fences that snake through the undergrowth. They add to the sense of romance and nature barely tamed in the place.

From just inside the gate it is apparent that there is something special about this place, an indefinable atmosphere. The drive seems to be a strange cobble-mixed-with-plaits design, which on a second look turns out to be made from lengths of old fishing rope. The seaside feel is further enhanced by the buoys and floats and other fishing paraphernalia hanging from trees, turned into little totems and pieces of art.

Willem is an artist and his work is distributed through the garden. It was to his overall design that

it was created while Doutsje's realm is in the vegetable garden down by the water. 'I do the functionality,' Doutsje said. 'Willem does the more intuitive work. He will walk around with a plant until he finds where it will be happiest,' she added.

The trail through the garden begins by way of a flat stone bridge spanning a stream into the woods, under a canopy of oak, larch, beech and lime. The trail continues on, leading out to an open, bright, grassy spot. This in turn leads back in through clipped box and *Lonicera nitida* hedging, into flowery corners where they pair wood natives with cultivated companions. The route is bounded by espaliered apples on one side and shrub roses on the other. Native ferns all but take over the paths at the height of the summer.

Willem and Doutsje have an understanding for the wild Irish garden that is to be admired. Using buckets of style and little money, the ideas to steal are everywhere, from the use of found objects, to sculptures sitting on blocks of wood painted grey, to imitate stone.

At one point the wood opens onto a Citrus Garden, a grouping of pots of kumquats and limes, that makes no sense and complete sense at the same time. In another corner, colourful drifts of agapanthus, lilies, hemerocallis monarda and dahlias are mixed with native ferns and exotic shrubs like Japanese kirengeshoma, under the partial shade of a tall paulownia. This is a garden that could drive the short-back-and-sides brigade to distraction and it is wonderful for that.

Ashford Castle

Cong, Co. Mayo. Tel: 094 9546 003. e-mail: reservations@ashfordcastle.com Contact: Reception.
Open: By appointment only. Wheelchair accessible. Supervised children. Special Features: Hotel. Golf.
School of falconry. Restaurant. Directions: In the village of Cong on the R436.

Ashford is a 19th century Gothic castellated manor house, set in extensive grounds by the north shore of

Lough Corrib, bordering Mayo and Galway. The long drive up to the castle is through a golf course and, as such, not as beautiful a drive as it could be, although the park trees are mature and handsome and there are two breathtaking *Cedrus libani* or Cedars of Lebanon on one of the stretches of green.

The grey limestone castle stands on a stretch of manicured lawn, edged with rhododendron. In recent years this lawn has been pulled into a more formal shape with the addition of borders defined by tight clipped box balls and seasonally appropriate white flowering annuals. The views from the castle are of this formal area and a backdrop of lake, trees and stone follies.

The Broad Walk, a wide straight path, leading away from the castle, has been improved considerably in recent years. The canopy has been pushed back so the walk is now much wider and brighter. The scrubby growth that had encroached on to the path is gone. The specimen trees, including fine oaks, pines, cedars, an extraordinary multi trunked *Thuja plicata* and a tulip tree, or *Liriodendron tulipifera,* can now be seen more clearly. Continual clearance of spindly growth from beneath the trees has improved the view through the larger woods too. Along its length, the path is divided into terraces by several sets of steps. Making your way down the avenue, the view takes in a sunken garden of square beds filled with annuals, box squares and yew pyramids.

Follies and mock castles crop up along the way too. One of these is the entrance to the walled garden,

an almost subterranean tunnel. The walled garden too has undergone major improvement. It was handsome before. It is now quite special. Emerging from one tunnel you find yourself entering another, this time one of hornbeam that stretches across the width of the garden. This is quite a welcome and the rest of the walled garden lives up to that welcome. There are beautiful double borders that look good from late spring right through to late autumn. The herb beds, formal and neat, are gorgeous and the vegetable beds look like mathematical creations. Pruned up silver pears, fine Japanese acers and flowering shrubs as well as an intriguing apple arch, provide something to look at all year round. Meanwhile the mature trees beyond the wall are a constant presence.

There are a number of walks scattered through the grounds, including a shrub-lined trail called Bea's Walk and a new lime tree avenue, nearly one km long.

A little formal area cut through with stone slab paths can be found in front of the thatched building near the golf clubhouse. Built around a Celtic cross on a grassed plinth, this is a confection of low yew walls, perennial borders of nepeta and stachys, rudbeckia and roses. It is fully wheelchair accessible.

Everything in Ashford is on the grandest of grand scales – Even the cottage garden. The upkeep is something to marvel. Martin Slattery, the man in charge of the gardens likes to do things properly. If you are a film fan make sure to see Squire Danaher's House from 'The Quiet Man.'

The Blue Bicycle Cafe

Main Street, Newport, Co. Mayo. Tel: 098 41145. e-mail: phillychambers@eircom.net www.bluebicycletearooms.com Contact: Phil Chambers. Open: Every day except Monday 10am-6pm. Seven days July and Aug. Special feature: Tearoom. Directions. In the centre of the town.

Tucked in behind an old Georgian townhouse and the Blue Bicycle Café, there is a quiet little town garden. Pots of flowering hydrangea and cordyline stand about on the gravelled area between benches and tables painted in deep peacock blue. In the summer this blue shade is well contrasted by the spreading tentacles of orange nasturtium, snaking along the gravel.

Follow a gate and set of steps set into the stone wall. They lead up to a little orchard and vegetable

garden bounded by fuchsia and self-sown maples, a peaceful, picturesque place in which to enjoy a cup of tea. The orange cake is recommended.

The garden is called the Princess Grace Garden after the iconic actress whose family came from Newport. The Princess does not have the garden to herself however: A plaque on the wall tells the story of the Danish Sea captain whose ship limped into Newport in 1792.

The Jackie Clarke Victorian Walled Garden

Jackie Clarke Collection Museum, Pearse St., Ballina, Co. Mayo. Tel: 096 73508. e-mail: clarkecollection@mayococo.ie Wheelchair accessible. Children welcome. No dogs. Contact: Reception. Open Tues-Sat., 10am-5pm. Special features: Museum. Archives. Events. Directions: In the centre of the town.

Jackie Clark was a businessman and collector who lived and worked in Ballina all his long life. He died in 2000 and his huge collection of over 100,000 Irish books, maps, posters, drawings, political pamphlets and newspapers, was donated by his wife to Mayo and the nation in 2005. Today the collection is housed in an old bank building in the middle of the Mayo town where it can be visited. A visit to the collection should not be without a trip around the walled garden attached to the museum.

Standing at the entrance my first thought was that this newly designed garden could be the very dream of a tidy gardener. If you like plants behaving very well, this is the place to visit. The wheelchair-accessible paths run the length of the space, between raised beds of big healthy herbs and vegetables, lines of clipped box that could have been cut with lasers and espaliered apple trees trained on wire fences.

Long flower beds planted up with sedum, allium, anthemis and nepeta, produce a billowing show in summer and there are picnic tables and benches set between the young trained ornamental natives and fruit trees.

One or two areas of long grass with wild flowers, clover and plantain, have been left to comport themselves and look loose and informal around a series of woven willow fences and arches. Every wall has its bird and bee box and the almost impossibly tidy compost system can be studied. It came as something of a surprise but it is a pleasure to report that this picture of perfection is gardened organically, showing that, at least on a domestic scale, there is no excuse.

The Clog Factory

The Quay, Westport. Co. Mayo. Contact: Evleen Mulloy. Open: As part of the Clew Bay Garden Trail. See website for annual details. Special features: Gaelige á labhairt. Air B+B. Directions: Take the R335 to Westport Quay. After the Quay Pub, turn left signed for The Greenway. Follow signs for the Clog Factory.

I fell for Evleen and her wild west garden from the moment we met. As we walked around between loose and informal mounds of roses and lupins, campanulas and peonies, she told me about the visitors who heave in and take to mowing the grass for her, so interested are they in the unusual Finnish push mower used to cut the grass here. I gave it a try to see what the fuss was about and discovered to my surprise that grass cutting can be fun. Evleen went on to give me demonstrations of the best tools for gardeners with tennis elbow and carpal tunnel troubles. She rounded off with the advice that the best tool in the shed is a tin of WD40.

There was a clog factory on this site until 1930, making wooden clogs for export to England. We looked at the flywheel from the old steam engine, today incorporated into a pond.

The garden is something of a family affair. The little white curved, stone wall garden was made by her daughter and a friend. This Mediterranean corner by the Atlantic, teams the gleaming whitewashed wall, gravel and bleached sleepers with campanulas, lavender and lime euphorbia.

Borders and beds knit into each other, linked by lawn and surrounded by natural, blending native hedges on the boundary. I like the widespread use of big perennials like four metre high hollyhocks and *Campanula* 'Lodden Anna'. We stopped in front of a stand of 'Stargazer' lilies when Evleen declared 'I lost track of subtlety there.'

The place is full of roses for which she blames Dermot O Neill's book. Evleen read it and fell for them in a big way. We walked between *Rosa* 'Ballerina', which flowers from May to October , *R.* 'Mme Alfred

Carrière' which is another obliging rose, easy and long lasting and stands of *Rosa* 'Graham Stuart Thomas' laced between deep blue delphiniums.

This is an open garden with a view of the Reek in the distance, which was quite a sight, with cloud coming down over the peak like a smoke ring.

The Cottage

Cross, Kilmeena, Westport, Co. Mayo. Tel: 098 25053. e-mail: daphguthrie@gmail.com
Contact: Graeme and Daphne Guthrie. Not wheelchair accessible. Open: As part of the Clew Bay Garden Trail. Contact for annual details. Otherwise by appointment. Directions. On application.

I first spotted Graeme and Daphne Guthrie's garden from the Westport Greenway when I came across a number of walkers and cyclists gathered on the path, looking up at a hilly garden that seemed to be laid on for their enjoyment. Back in 2000, when the Guthries came to live in this corner of County Mayo, that garden was nothing more than a field attached to a cottage. Graeme has been hard at work ever since and the results are on show, for all to see.

The steep garden starts at the house which is perched on the shoulder of a hill overlooking the Greenway, sweeping down the slope in a tumble of flowers and lawn, to a natural pond in a natural hollow. This is Mayo and it is stony. As Graeme worked the site he dug out stones, boulders and rocks and put them all to work, building low walls and embankments everywhere. These structures give shape to his design and hold in the flower and shrub borders full of phlox

and lupin, astilbe, geranium, cosmos and crocosmia. It is a busy, informal, colourful summer garden.

The pond at the bottom of the hill is a perfect case of making the best of a bad lot. The bottom of the hill was damp and soggy and otherwise useless, so Graeme made a virtue of this, digging out a pond that filled naturally and needs no lining. As a result it looks completely at home, surrounded with more unearthed boulders and planted up with lilies. In summer you will find cheerful orange nasturtiums trailing along the boulders. At the same time Graeme planted a range of native trees on the boundaries to help tie the garden into its surroundings as well as affording it some shelter.

Standing on the Greenway looking up at the garden and the surrounding sedgy, rough fields, it is not surprising that Graeme's garden stops traffic. Failte Ireland should give the man a medal.

Drimbawn Gardens

Tourmakeady, Co. Mayo. Tel: 087 7750 107. e-mail: franksteffans@eircom.net
Contact: Frank Steffens, head gardener. Open: As part of the Clew Bay Garden Trail. Partially wheelchair accessible. Contact for annual details. At other times by appointment. Directions: From O'Toole's pub in Tourmakeady follow the Lough Mask Drive. Cross the bridge and drive past the Church of Ireland ruin. The entrance is on the left.

Ninian Niven, the renowned garden designer created a garden for Catherine Plunkett in the mid-19th century on the banks of Lough Mask. Over time the garden went into decline until just over a decade ago when new owners Ronnie and Doris Wilson arrived and swept decades of neglect away. They cleared choking thickets of *Rhododendron ponticum*, restored and rebuilt the old garden and added their own touches to what they found. Drimbawn is once again a first

rate garden, a walk though which is like a feast for the senses.

The experience starts at the drive, where a massive effort, clearing rhododendron and laurel is ongoing, opening up what was a dark, lost space and leaving a replanted wood which can now settle in and develop. The little rills and stone-lined waterways designed by Niven have also been cleared and now run free, flanked by refreshed fern beds.

The walled garden, once lost under self-sown trees, was cleared and restored to a plan of Daphne Shackleton's. The combination of clean lines, beautiful stonework and what look like laser-cut, pleached hedges, contrast with the abundance of the herbaceous borders, vegetable beds, fruit and rose walls. The only thing to do was marvel. We walked past a greenhouse stocked with citrus fruits, along a sunny wall where some monster-sized *Echium canadensis* and *E. pininana* thrive unlike many parts of this island. Elsewhere we looked at auricula theatres and irises baking in their sunny beds under a line of 40 cordoned pear trees.

A surrounding of roses and sunflowers seems to be compulsory for all the vegetable beds. Artichokes share space with clematis, roses and peonies as the garden steps downhill towards a little pond and a view of Lough Mask. The way to the lough is through an elegant 'bulrush' gate and a wildflower meadow with

picturesque sheep.

The route runs along a restored ha-ha towards a developing arboretum. This is where the beehives are. Mown paths through the meadow continue on into the woods, past stone walls that local craftsmen made, and a beautifully placed sculpture by artist Bob Quinn. A hawk swept over us as we walked. The lawns become more manicured as they move towards the house. I like the quite modern garden up here, from the unusual curved hedges and stands of dramatic grasses, to the cool, restrained reflecting pool and chic thyme beds set into the slab stone terrace. The garden speaks as much of today as yesterday. The clever ideas are everywhere: The thyme smelled delicious and was alive with bees.

The Pleasure Garden is reached by way of a set of steps up to the woods, behind and above the house. Seas of bluebells and ferns and groves of rhododendron have been planted under the mature oak and beech that were here already. We met Peggy and Anne in the woods, two huge, fabulous pigs, doing their best to eat as many acorns as possible and allowing us to scratch behind their ears. From here we followed the stream downhill, where it met up with a series of other stone-lined streams, all worked by a pumping system that made a bog garden in the woods possible.

The orchard is a trial ground for 35 different apple trees and ten pear trees. Frank told me that 'if one is interested in apple diseases Cox's Orange is the tree to plant.' He can, on the other hand recommend 'Sheep's Snout' and 'Katy', 'an excellent red. Always healthy. I keep records and if an apple performs badly for five years, it's out,' he disclosed. The formal fuchsia hedge around the orchard is unusually tightly clipped.

The overwhelming pleasure to be had walking around a place as stylish and as well worked as Drimbawn is hard to describe. This is a garden that needs to be visited.

The Edible Landscape Project

Westport Town Greenway, Westport, Co. Mayo. Contact: Caithriona McCarthy or Paula Halpin Cannon. Tel: 086 6008 560, 087 2890 235. e-mail caithrionamcc@eircom.net ceresdesign@hotmail.com Open: As part of the Clew Bay Garden Trail. Directions: Various sites around the town. Signposted.

Anyone walking around the back roads of Westport cannot fail to notice that something interesting has been going on in and around a number of areas of open ground, along the famous Greenway walk, around the community centre and on bits of council land tucked here and there around the town. Orchards and vegetable plots, bee-keeping operations and young fruit gardens have been springing up in all corners.

Interesting old varieties of Irish apple are being planted along many of the public walks and there are horticultural classes, pruning workshops and classes on forest garden techniques being run on a regular basis. This project is in its infancy but hopefully it will develop. This is a project run largely by volunteers, the council, Leader groups, Transition Year groups from the local schools and the Men's Shed gents. Contact Caithriona or Paula for tours or information.

Enniscoe House

Castlehill, Near Crossmolina, Co. Mayo. Tel: 096 31112. e-mail: mail@enniscoe.com www.enniscoe.com Contact: Susan Kellett. Open: April-Oct., Mon-Fri., 10am-6pm. Sat., Sun., 2pm-6pm. Partially wheelchair accessible. Special features: North Mayo Family Heritage Centre. Tel: 096 31809 e-mail: mnhmanager@gmail.com Tea room. Museum. Directions: 3.5 km south of Crossmolina on the R315 to Pontoon and Castlebar.

Enniscoe was built in the early 18th century on the banks of Lough Conn with fine views of Nephin in the most beautiful part of wild Mayo. The garden as it is today has been growing and developing since a restoration project that started back in 1997.

The large walled garden is divided in two. Enter the first area, the ornamental garden, close to the house, through the visitor centre. The first sight is of long runs of healthy-looking box hedges, a happy picture in these days of box blight. Susan Kellett thinks and hopes that using only unaffected box from the garden will protect against blight. All the hedges were grown from cuttings taken from the ancient box plants that were here before the restoration. The resulting green walls provide a solidity and structure for both flower and shrub borders throughout the garden.

The sun-baked rock garden centres on an elegant wooden pavilion designed by Jeremy Williams. I love the rock garden, even as it runs a bit wild. It is not what the Victorians planned without doubt, but it is simply pretty. Mounds of stone combined with clove-scented dianthus, bellis, tiarella, ruby red sweet William and iberis, run the length of the wall, like colourful miniature mountain ranges.

They are all linked by carpets of creeping thyme, cerastium or snow-in-summer and lime green euphorbia, that flow over and between the rocks like lava. In summer the whole area is alive with bees and the compulsion to stop and study the teeming workers is irresistible. Generous amounts of red campion growing on and against the wall show that giving the wild flowers free rein can be a good policy. All that remains of a once extensive range of glasshouses are the base walls, the pipes and guts.

Several paths take off from here into the middle of the shrub borders which are full of aconites, roses and lupins between stands of viburnum, tree peonies and cherries. The ever-present box walls once again hem in the show.

The cordylines planted in the Victorian garden were nearly killed in the big winter of 2010 but some have re sprouted, 'coming back with grim determination,' as Susan puts it. They do not entirely delight her.

The divide between the two sections of walled garden is marked by a gothic stone arch. This is an archway in the wall, made from fossil stones and occasional bits of archaeology from a nearby

ruined abbey. A knowledgeable archaeologist could have a field day examining it. It was once used to house a damp, vertical fern garden. Beyond the walls, great oak, beech and other trees, tower above this show. We took the side gate, dripping *Clematis armandii* and *Rosa* 'Albéric Barbier' out and under these grand old trees, into a series of wooded walks.

The Tree Council of Ireland have planted 10,000 oak in a looped trail around the estate.

An organic vegetable garden takes up the second walled garden area, producing crops and providing the classroom for courses in growing. A series of old and new Irish apple trees can be found in here too.

Foxford Woollen Mills

Foxford, Co. Mayo. Tel: 094 9256 104. e-mail: info@foxfordwoolenmills.ie www.foxfordwoolenmills.com Contact: Joe Queenan. Open: Public space, open at all times. Special features: Woollen mill. Craft shop. Restaurant. Directions. Signed in Foxford village.

The Foxford Woollen Mills, formerly called Providence Woollen Mills were set up in 1892 by the Irish Sisters of Charity in an effort to bring decent employment to the poverty-stricken Mayo village. The mills have gone on to produce prize winning wool blankets famous the world over. Today, they still operate, making and selling from the shop. The community aspect of the Foxford mills is still seen in small horticultural ventures like the orchard of Irish bred apples chosen and planted by the Irish Seed Savers, in the mill carpark. They are there for the taking but I always seem to miss the perfect picking times.

In front of the shop, mills and workshop is an old greenhouse that houses a large, mature vine. Through the year, the staging beneath is laid out with pots of pelargoniums and herbs. Meanwhile upstairs through the restaurant, there is an almost secret roof garden where you can enjoy your tea and cake surrounded by planters of agapanthus and clematis.

Frogswell

Straide, Co. Mayo. Tel: 086 2106 166. e-mail frogswell@gmail.com www.frogswell.net Contact: Celia Graebner. Open: By appointment, Feb-Oct. Special features: Plants for sale. Directions: Travelling from Castlebar on the N5, turn left onto the N58. About 3 km along turn left at the first cross roads on the brow of the hill. Travel downhill and swing right at the level crossing. Take the second left and the garden is about 1/2 km along on the right.

Frogswell was started out in a wild part of Mayo in 1991 on virgin ground. This singular garden is built around a great number and variety of rare and unusual plants. Its style and shape are determined by those plants and their requirements and by the fact that Celia Graebner is an eco-friendly gardener, against the use of all chemicals and keenly interested in accommodating wildlife. It is a wild garden and not one for the tidy or fussy. I would liken it to a mad laboratory of plants rather than an ordered plot.

Celia believes that her plants should live in sustainable woodland and pond-side communities. They cannot be high maintenance because she grows a great mass of plants with limited time to give to individuals. The range is wide because her soil is both acid and alkaline, in pockets. The one constant is that the soil is deep.

The overall feeling is one of being in a jungle. On the ground there might be hostas, astrantias and any number of hardy geraniums. Overhead there could be a climbing aconitum or an unusual willow-leafed rose with a white flower. We slipped between rampant growth overhead while admiring erythroniums on the ground and made our way down to the hellebore nursery, where Celia trails a number of species and varieties. A little delicate *Geranium robertianum* 'Celtic

White' is only one of the 30 species and varieties that she grows.

This is an organic and sustainable research station as much as a garden. Do not expect neat flower beds and a classic approach. It is an example of wrestling gently with nature in order to study it. Wear wellies and bring a notebook.

Glensaul River Cottage

Tourmakeady, Co. Mayo. Tel: 094 9544 267. e-mail: alancourtney39@yahoo.com Contact: Alan Courtney. Open: By appointment. Not wheelchair accessible. Children welcome. Dogs on leads. Directions: On application.

The garden at Glensaul Cottage is half an acre of lush planting, water and rock, set between the Tourmakeady hills and Lough Mask. Alan Courtney designed and built his fine garden along the length of a fast flowing stream. Stone is another dominant feature, so it was hard to believe that the great slabs and boulders of limestone around which much of the garden is built, were all imported and then arranged so cleverly. In essence, the house stands in the middle of a massive man-made rockery and water garden.

The garden faces north, 'but it is sheltered' Alan explained, as we made our way between stands of scented fennel, lavender and hardy geraniums, under a rose arch and into the main area behind the house. The building, surrounded by its outdoor dining rooms and sitting areas, is itself like a living thing, almost invisible behind sheets of climbers, window boxes and planters.

When he began to work the site, Alan selectively removed some of the alder and willow that once dominated. He then proceeded to tuck his garden into the open space and between the surrounding trees. We looked at rhododendron and different species of fuchsia, tall plume poppies and tropaeolum clambering through big tiger lilies or *Lilium lancifolium*.

Growth here can be extraordinary: *Geranium palmatum* grows like a weed, as do the masses of *Primula florindae* that thrive in the damp soil along the waterside, beside exotic looking *Primula vialii* and grasses of all sorts. Alan studied botany in Britain before coming to Ireland. He has a love of plants and grows over 100 species of plant from seed every year, many of which he sources as a member of the Hardy Plant Society.

This is a wild garden with the added interest of homing so many unusual and rare plants, but it is more: On my travels, someone told me that this was the most beautiful garden that they had ever seen.

Mountain View

Bohea, Westport, Co. Mayo. Tel: 089 4545 623. e-mail: mountain2home@gmail.com Contact: Sally and Peter Churcher. Open: As part of the Clew Bay Garden Trail. Contact for annual details. No children under 12. No dogs. Directions: On application.

In 2004 the Churchers arrived in Mayo and bought a field on a hill facing Croagh Patrick. They had gardened in England but did not quite realise how hard it was going to be in the rough land of Mayo.

'We found ourselves just digging into rock,' Sally told me. But they are hard workers, consummate recyclers, composters and re-users. So, in their capable mend-and-make-do hands, the field has been transformed into a fine garden. It might be steep, but it is pretty. Goat track paths lead at angles between flower beds and natural rockeries. They planted fuchsia hedges to buffet and soften the gales that blast across the site. It works. Just look at the wind-shorn trees that feature in the surrounding landscape while the Churcher's plot is verdant and lush.

There is one very protected corner, to the side of the house and this is where Sally's cottage garden is to be found, entered by way of a clematis arch and surrounded by shrubs that fend off the wind. In here scabious, lupins, poppies and astrantia tumble together, favouring her outdoor sitting room with a changing show through the summer. It is hard to believe that the natural soil covering here is just a thin scraping.

Peter's vegetable beds are protected by box and escallonia. Looking at the healthy growth in here, the amount of work carried out on that meagre depth of soil to produce mangetout and cabbage can only be imagined. My favourite feature is the natural rockery, inspected from below as you walk along a scree path. The mix of euphorbia and fern, dianthus, foxglove and saxifraga is delightful. Finally, if you look up from the plants, Croagh Patrick greets you across the valley in all its glory.

Mount Falcon Kitchen Garden

Mount Falcon Hotel, Foxford Road, Ballina, Co. Mayo. Tel: 096 74472. e-mail: info@mountfalcon.com Contact: Alex Lavarde, Head gardener. garden@mountfalcon.com Open: As part of the Clew Bay Garden Trail and by appointment at other times. Special features: Wheelchair accessible. Children welcome with an adult. No dogs. Hotel. Tasting tours. Directions: Mount Falcon Estate is located 8 km from Ballina on the Foxford road, on the left. Signposted.

Arriving to visit the kitchen garden at Mount Falcon country house, I expected to be steered towards a walled garden. Instead, I was led back down the drive, and into the trees, beyond which there stood a most unusual Big House kitchen garden. It was in a large field and very much sans walls. With or without them, this kitchen garden is worth investigating.

Head gardener, Alex Lavarde has been running the garden since 2013. He feels that having started it from a grazed field, it suffers from none of the bank of diseases and pests an established walled garden can labour under. This is a productive garden, created to supply the hotel kitchen with as much produce as possible. He runs it on strict organic and sustainable grounds. There is a strong emphasis on the use of green manure, growing pollinating plants and encouraging a healthy ecosystem. Do not expect to see manicured edges and primped and preened borders. If some wild willowherb crops up on the edge of a bed it will be left there. Big runs of phacelia and nigella, marigolds and cornflowers provide colour between the neat rows of veg and fruit. The necessity of providing bees with both late and early flowers for pollen and nectar, is hugely important here.

We walked between hydrangea borders and *Rosa rugosa* hedges, grown to add height and colour to the project. They also grow willow walls, sculpted into arches and waves as an extremely pretty quick-fix fence. Alex plants sweet pea along the willow in summer.

Among the plants we ate as we walked, there were pods of purple mangetout and mashua, or *Tropaeolum tuberosum* which has attractive flowers and edible roots. We also looked at an unusual fruit called *Aronia melanocarpa*. From here it was into the tea garden and a heady walk between chocolate mint, and spearmint, chamomile, verbena and lemon balm.

An hour spent walking around this garden with Alex is worth a week's serious reading. He told me that he plants crocuses as early season bee benefactors. Willow catkins do the same work in March. Living in the west, he finds that runner rather than French beans fare better. They need less sun. He recommended growing red celery and, like leeks, harvesting it at the pencil-slim stage. Mexican tree spinach grown from seed is another intriguing crop found here, as are

'Longue de Florence' onions. He grows his asparagus through white clover which feeds the asparagus and keeps the weeds at bay.

I wanted to stay and live in the micro veg tunnel where tiny celery, lemon balm and pea shoots grow in trays. As we ate our way around and wandered through the bee-garden between the two tunnels, I learned that borage refills with nectar every two weeks. Finally I found out that Alex organises talks on the seven species of bats that live on the estate. As we left, we passed the latest feature here, a fruiting hedge of elder, wild cherry, spindle and apple.

Orchard Cottage

Muine, Carraholly, Westport, Co. Mayo. Tel: 087 6292 198. 087 6200 445. e-mail: ederiko@eircom.net Contact: Eriko Uehara and Ed Hopkinson. Open: As part of the Clew Bay Garden Trail. See website for annual dates. Otherwise by appointment. Groups under 20. Special features: Rare plants for sale. Entry charge to charity. Teas can be arranged separately. Not wheelchair accessible. Supervised children. Directions on application.

Driving up the lane leading to Orchard Cottage, I passed a gate under an arch of rambling roses and wished that this would turn out to be the garden for which I was looking. It did. I had already passed a herd of cattle swimming and mooing their way across the estuary a few metres down the road from the garden so the day had started with a bit of magic. That enchantment continued in the garden, with grass paths that cut through a scrum of flowers and ferns, old-fashioned roses and knots of clematis.

Ed started this garden about 20 years ago. Eriko began working it about five years later, bringing roses to the place and turning it into a sort of rose laboratory where she carries out her own trials, growing her plants without chemicals. The toughest varieties that she can recommend are: 'Ispahan', 'Alba maxima', 'Sir John Betjeman' and 'Tuscany Superb'. We walked under a large old apple, supporting a French moss rose, then made our way through arches of *Rosa* 'Rambling Rector' and *Clematis* 'Etoile Violette'. Both were grown from cuttings. Eriko also grows cut flowers in beds and among the mixes she was trying out when I visited, was a particularly dark nasturtium from the Sarah Raven seed catalogue. All sorts of dahlias, lychnis, snapdragons and sweet peas, scented stock and pot marigolds, elbow each other for space in the beds. In some places they are are joined by hardy Japanese vegetables while she grows tomatoes, edamame and soya beans in the polytunnel.

The whole enterprise is a fine example of a plot run on organic principles. The proximity of the sea and cattle swimming across the estuary came back to mind when Ed told me how, when the garden was flooded by seawater a few years ago, the salt water reduced the number of slugs they have had to deal with ever since.

Speckled Meadow

Bofara, Brackloon, Westport, Co. Mayo. Tel: 087 6298 716. e-mail: martymcelgunn@gmail.com Contact: Marty McElgunn. Open: As part of the Clew Bay Garden Trail. Contact for annual details. At other times by appointment. Directions: On application.

Bordered on one side by Brackloon Woods and the shoulder of Croagh Patrick, Speckled Meadow is a garden made for wildlife. The fields around Marty McElgunn's garden are appropriately 'speckled' with wild orchids and other native treasures. It was clear to Marty that he owed this extraordinarily beautiful landscape a debt of care so when he began to build his stone house in the rugged landscape a few kilometres inland from Westport, he stepped very lightly on the land 'and I started the garden first'.

The result is a creation of native hedges and informal borders of native and non-native flowering plants, with a strong emphasis on planting for the Irish honey bee. Species rather than named varieties dominate the colourful borders, so the look is delicate and pretty rather than showy.

On the day I arrived, a swarm of bees had left one of the hives in the garden and gathered on a wooden post like one heaving, humming creature. Marty explained to me how it would settle there over a period of about a day, sending out scouts to find a good place

in the vicinity to begin a new colony. It felt like a privilege to see this happen.

Leaving the bees, we walked on along grass and gravel paths, between edging made from the stones dug out of the fields, as well as willow and hazel hurdles and felled branches. We moved out of the sun and into the wood and stream garden, where found, and sometimes placed boulders, are as much of a feature as the plants around them. In the shade under the trees, a river of tall digitalis flowed downhill alongside the knobbled path. Hand-made bridges made from more felled branches led across the stream. It was heavenly, even if seriously requiring stout walking boots. Out in the sun, the meadow was full of wild flowers under an upper storey of Irish fruit trees.

The house is surrounded by a big area of gravel and found stone, spiked with self-sown wild flowers and ferns along with a few imports such as *Verbena bonariensis* and arums or *Zantedeschia aethiopica*, knautia and hardy geraniums. The beds are perched on stone ledges and the whole place feels as though it happened naturally, if only nature were so obliging. Marty has mastered that most difficult of tasks. He has worked with and imitated nature successfully.

Turlough Park Museum of Country Life

Turlough, Castlebar, Co. Mayo. Tel: 094 9031755. e-mail: tpark@museum.ie Contact: The manager. Open: Tues-Sat., 10am-5pm. Sun., 2pm-5pm. Wheelchair accessible. Children welcome. Special Features: Museum. Cafe. Shop. Directions: Take the N5 out of Castlebar for about 6 km. At Horkin's garden centre, take the left turn and the museum is a little way along on the left. Signposted.

I came across Turlough Park for the first time about 16 years ago. I pulled into the drive only to be chased away by earth movers and diggers busily working on some grand-scale landscaping venture. The results, now that they have matured are, to say the least, worth seeing.

The drive in, under mature park trees, runs past a little boating lake. This turned out to be the reason for the excavations back in 2000. The garden itself comes into view with a great flourish as you emerge through the trees from the car park. The first sight is of an immaculately tended Victorian flower garden. The house stands at the head of it, overlooking long runs of perfect, rolled and striped lawn with island beds full of bedding plants such as lobelia and pelargonium,

cut into the green at regular intervals. Expect all the usual in-your-face-colours associated with Victorian municipal-style borders.

The already mentioned greenhouse is stuffed to capacity with tender plants arranged on staging, from chillies of all sorts to birds of paradise or *Strelitzia reginae* and waxy hoyas, ruby *Rhodochiton atrosanguineus* and strange looking *Corokia virgata*. When we dream of owning the perfect greenhouse, it probably looks like this. I like that this house is usually open to visitors without having to seek special dispensation and advance booking.

Walking in the direction of the house and museum, one path ducks in under a trellised arch into a concealed garden room. This enclosure is home to a flamboyant flower garden with two mirroring borders full of herbaceous perennials. There are lupins, monarda, acanthus, phlox, salvias and delphiniums. One of the borders is backed by a beech hedge with towering park trees behind it. The other side holds an altogether more interesting sight, the vine house. This too can be visited, Inside, a massive, climbing *Pelargonium* 'Lord Bute' takes up an enormous amount of space. An almost fluorescent blue plumbago contrasts richly with the pelargonium's raspberry ripple flowers. Between them, they take up one side of the house. The other side houses a big fruiting peach.

The views over the lake below the garden take in a round tower in the distance and 40 acres of wooded trails. Separate to the garden, investigate the house building project, a display of different methods of constructing and finishing walls including historic renders, limes and plasters.

Westport College of Further Education

Newport Road, Westport, Co. Mayo. Contact: Cormac Langan. Tel 098 25241. e-mail: cormaclangan@westportcfe.ie Open: As part of the Clew Bay Garden Trail. Contact for annual details. Directions: From the town centre take the road for Hotel Westport at Holy Trinity Church and immediately take the next right into the college grounds. The garden is to the rear.

The student garden at the back of the college is compact and well worked. This is a practical laboratory as much as a garden, used by the students to carry out their practical work.

Windfalls Nursery

Castlebar, Co. Mayo. Tel: 094 9042 127. 094 9038 074. e-mail: andy.neary@hse.ie. Contact: Andy Neary. Open: Weekdays and as part of the Clew Bay Garden Trail. Telephone for seasonal times. Special features: Café on Thursday. Plants and cut flowers, home baking and crafts for sale. Directions: On the Humbert Way/Ring Road take the 2nd left after Corrib Oil.

Arriving unannounced to visit what I was told was a nursery with a garden attached, I came across three men relaxing outside a shed surrounded by buckets of flowers. Two were stripping foliage from some stems. Robin Cooper and Eamon Durkan are two of the 25 workers at Windfalls. The third gent leaned back and informed me that he was on his break. I could cheerfully have stayed to work here myself. This workshop is a charming and relaxed workplace.

The trainees and supervisors grow a good range of perennials and shrubs in beds and borders scattered around the grounds.

The gardens attached to the nursery include a little hobbit-like hill-and-dale garden made of shrubs and stoneworks, runs of mixed border full of cut flowers like delphiniums, cosmos, dahlias and grasses such as briza. These are also grown to attract bees and butterflies. One plant match that stood out was that

of veronica and *Orlaya grandiflora*.

The atmosphere of relaxed industry among the flowers makes for an enjoyable saunter, while the chance to buy both plants and flowers in such a surrounding is always pleasant. Before I left I had to return to take a second sniff at a rose called 'Princess Grace', growing in a poly tunnel beside a big peach. Gorgeous.

Woodlawn

New Road, Westport, Co. Mayo. Tel: 098 26023. e-mail: deirdre@hughes.ie Contact: Deirdre Hughes. Open: As part of the Clew Bay Garden Trail. Contact for annual dates. Special features: Plants for sale. Directions: On appointment.

Discovering Deirdre Hughes's large town garden in the middle of Westport was a real surprise. Deirdre is a propagator. She could propagate for Ireland. Division and seed, she does it all, and Woodlawn is filled with the results of her successes. As we walked around, she pointed out various 'mammy plants', the parents of so many of the herbaceous plants in the borders, in pots and under the trees. There were drifts of francoa, clumps of cowslips, kniphofia and campanula scattered throughout, each the progeny of one plant brought in many years ago. Gardens like this are always the most interesting.

The approach is up a short drive under sweet chestnut and spreading pink cherries that explode into double blossom late in spring. The shaded beds on either side of the drive are where Deirdre grows a rolling display of flowers. This starts with snowdrop, crocus, daffodil, chionodoxa and scilla. Later there are tulips and in the summer, campanulas, sedum, sweet William, cosmos and aquilegia. Her policy is

one of simply continuously adding new elements all the time. It works.

Deirdre has been gardening here since 1987 and in that time she has not just sown seeds and divided plants. She has moved earth to a depth of about two metres, changed the levels dramatically and transplanted trees. In the process she has created a huge rockery from boulders unearthed during the excavations. The rockery is like a natural outcrop, yet it is completely man-made, initially put in place to hold back a bank of earth. The tiny pockets of soil it accommodates were planted up with strawberries and these now cascade over the stone, between little alpines and self-seeding foxgloves. She grows the strawberries for ornamental purposes and so only the birds have access to the delicious fruit. I am not sure many of us could share Deirdre's ability to resist temptation.

Every corner is used as an opportunity to put together a composition of bulbs, flowering herbaceous plants and small shrubs. Climbers, roses, wisteria and clematis are put to work on every wall and there are massed ranks of pots gathered under every tree, filled with bulbs followed by annuals to ring the seasonal changes. As a plantaholic, Deirdre's need to constantly expand is an inevitability. A newly planted raised border at the back of the house is her latest project. It should suffice for the present but there is still a small field adjacent to the house at which she seemed to eye up with something of a glint.

Roscommon

Ardsoran

*Ardsoran, Lisserlough, Boyle, Co. Roscommon. Tel: 086 869 1141.
Contact: Saffron Thomas and Ian Stanley. Open: By appointment. May to Sept., and for specific open days. Not wheelchair accessible. Children welcome, but deep water so beware. Dogs on leads. Directions: On application.*

Set out in the middle of one of the more remote corners of Roscommon, Ardsoran is as much a horticultural research station as a garden. Artists, Saffron and Ian have, for the past 16 years, been slowly turning eight acres of wild soft, wet ground arranged in a small field system near Frenchpark, into a sculpture garden overlooked by a wooden cabin on a veranda.

Saffron grows all her plants from seed. She particularly likes dahlias, which, grown from seed, flower the next year with surprising results. The long borders full of her quirky dahlias, are visible from the veranda. Having studied them from on high, we walked down hill to see them more clearly, coming first to the hot bed. This is what Saffron calls her high performance bed. She likes it to look good from the house. Even in winter there should be something to see in this border. So seed heads and foliage are important.

We walked between tall stands of Mexican *Salvia confertiflora*, which has strange furry, orange flowers that reach up to two metres. It goes all summer, starting in May. Nearby, rich red hemerocallis or day lilies, set off the paulownia behind. Saffron loves a good old colour clash so we continued on past golden oregano, acid-yellow, jagged *Euphorbia similiramea*, golden geum and alpine strawberries all twined together in a happy cacophony.

In the middle of the bed we came on one of Ian's thrones, a grand chair made from elm. He also uses oak and ash. Further on, there was a monumental sized limestone piece, like a Valley of the Giants seed pod, that fell from the mother plant and rolled down the meadow. I loved the primitive looking stone foot with tiny pebbles for toes, upended in the woods. Meanwhile out in the sun, the bronze receptacle made from an old water tank, stands, majestic, in the wild grass.

We had already passed two small ponds as we marched down the hill but we now came to a larger one. There is no need to line the ponds here. They sit easily in the wet, heavy ground. Ian is responsible for the quaint plank bridges.

As well as being damp, the ground is also acid, making it perfect for growing blueberries. We tasted Saffron's favourite varieties, 'Berkley' and 'Blue Crop', both tasty berries. Saffron's dog likes them too.

The rough route we took through the garden is under a mix of native trees and tree peonies, cultivated dogwoods and Japanese acers. The contrast between wild and cultivated is a gentle one.

We finished up in the Jungle Tunnel among more tender plants such as loquats, a fabulous black clematis, amaranthus and a particularly sweet tomato called 'Sweet Aperitif'. Permaculture is the watchword in the garden. Meanwhile Ian uses every bit of wood harvested. Even the chippings are used to make wooden spoons. This is light touch gardening that will be of interest to organic growers and propagators.

Castlecoote House

*Castlecoote, Co. Roscommon. Tel: 0906 663794 e-mail: info@castlecootehouse.com
www.castlecootehouse.com. www.percyfrench.ie Contact: Kevin Finnerty. Open: Contact for annual details. Special features: Home of the annual Percy French Festival. Seasonal tea room. House and castle tours. Accommodation. Apple juice for sale. Directions: Driving from Roscommon on the R366 at the edge of the village of Castlecoote.*

When I arrived to see Castlecoote, I was told to expect some upheaval, as a new bridge was being built over the River Suck to reach the house. I asked if the old bridge had been washed away in a recent flood. The answer came back in a matter-of-act way: 'No it was blown up by Sarsfield in 1688.'

The man talking was Kevin Finnerty. Kevin has, since 1997, been restoring the shell of this fine Georgian House and three of the four towers from an older 16th century castle. Apart from resurrecting the house, which was a burnt-out shell when he arrived, Kevin has also been working on the grounds which are dominated by the River Suck. It flows in a 90 degree bend around the outer edge of the grounds. Those grounds are comprised of riverside walks through a bluebell, ash and ivy wood, a restored millrace and wildflower meadow.

To one side of the house is a venerable orchard made up of 48 varieties of old and new apples. The Irish Seed Savers found four varieties here that they thought were completely lost. All this is surrounded by the original moat. We looked at the way the parkland trees across that moat were planted, in staggered rows to reduce the west winds which would otherwise blast the orchard. One of the remaining towers of the old castle is found in the orchard too.

Castlecoote has a special atmosphere. As Kevin says: 'It's a very ancient place.' It is a very beautiful place.

Angela East's Garden

Boule. Co. Roscommon. Tel: 086 1649 656. Contact: Angela East. Open: For an annual summer charity day. Contact for details. Directions: On application.

It is incumbent on country gardeners to grow trees. Angela East believes that too. So when she and her husband decided to build a house in the country on the side of the Curlew Mountains, 19 years ago, they planted trees, before they ever put a block on top of another block. The programme began with an avenue of beech trees, both copper and green. Eventually they were joined by oak and maple.

The soil here is heavy, sticky and hard to work. It holds onto water and dries hard in droughty conditions, so Angela spends a great deal of time adding compost, the magic, cure-all ingredient to improve the ground. On the plus side there are pockets of acid soil and so rhododendrons do well here and Angela slots them in wherever she can.

The site takes in a number of rises and falls, and she used these to create a series of ponds that tip into each other, running downhill with little waterfalls as they go. These face the front of the house so Angela can enjoy the full impact of the sight and sound of moving water from the house. Although in the early year there is usually a population of tadpoles in residence so she cannot turn the pump on until they are grown and out of the water.

Around the house, there are mixed flower and shrub borders, and as one travels out, the planting simplifies into trees and some flowering shrubs. Seven Saint Bernard dogs live here so the need for substantial, simple planting is obvious.

Strokestown Park House

Strokestown, Co. Roscommon. Tel: 071 9633 013. e-mail: john.odriscoll@irishheritagetrust.ie Contact: John O'Driscoll. Open: Mar-Oct. Check website for seasonal times. Special features: Wheelchair accessible. Museum. Plants for sale. Restaurant. Croquet club. Family event days. Directions: Situated in the middle of the village of Strokestown on the N5.

The Pakenham family moved to Strokestown in the 1650s. Over the centuries, they built and added to the impressive Strokestown House, a process that culminated in the 19th century when they hit upon the idea that one of the tiniest villages in Ireland should have one of the widest boulevards in Europe: At just over 44 metres wide it would compete with the Champs Elysées.

Strokestown House is an intriguing place that conjures up images of feast and famine. The estate was at the heart of some of the most dreadful suffering experienced during the Great Famine of the 1840s. Today the outhouses and stable blocks, once known as 'equine cathedrals', provide the venue for the country's most comprehensive Famine museum. This is slightly ironic as the family's record during the Famine years was not unblemished: Major Denis Mahon, responsible for clearing tenants from his estates, was eventually assassinated in 1847.

Mrs. Olive Pakenham-Mahon was born to Strokestown in 1894 and continued to live there until her death in 1981. The property was sold to a local businessman as something approaching an untouched time capsule, filled with the furniture and miscellaneous bits and pieces of Big House life accumulated over centuries. It is a fine piece of social history. Today the place is run by the charity, Irish Heritage Trust and it is hoped that its future is secure.

Apart from taking over the aspic-encased house, a huge restoration project was started on the four-acre walled garden, which dates to the 1740s. In 1890 it was converted from a functional kitchen garden into a pleasure garden. By around 1940 however, lack of

manpower and money saw sheep and cattle grazing where immaculate flowerbeds and shrubberies once stood. The restoration work carried out in the 1980s has been consolidated and continues.

The walled garden is entered through an ornamental gate, made in 1914, with the words E.K. Harmon worked into the lacy ironwork. This was a gift to Olive from her *fiancé*, Edward Stafford King Harmon who would die in the trenches at Ypres, Belgium, shortly after their marriage. Its poignant presence sets the tone for a walk through the romantic old garden. The gate opens onto wide paths of gravel, lined with yews and one intriguingly placed liriodendron, backed by beech hedges and leading down to a formal lily pond which dates to the earlier days of the walled garden. Full-sized trees had to be removed from this pond during the restoration. Today, some of the water surface has been sacrificed to rushes as the pond homes several families of water hens and a sizeable population of newts.

The south facing herbaceous border is the biggest in Ireland and Britain, according to the Guinness Book of Records and is based on the original Victorian border. As an advertisement for organic gardening, the border couldn't be more spectacular. It includes big stands of heavily-scented, nodding crinum lilies and plume poppies or macleaya. In August, yellows and oranges come into their own and the bed puts on a great late summer and autumn show. Huge fennel plants, ligularia with acid yellow flowers on top of black stems, red-hot pokers or kniphofia, golden rod or solidago, fringed inula flowers and red geums shout at each other for attention. Work on this, as throughout the garden, is carried out by a small full time team and a growing number of volunteers, one of whom, an elderly gent, has known the garden since he was a small child.

The summerhouse in the centre of the walled garden was copied faithfully from an old photograph of Olive as a small girl, sitting inside the original with her nanny. Outside, the croquet lawn once again hosts a local croquet club. There is a further 'practice pitch' sited near the orchard. Tournaments and classes are regularly held through the summer.

The rose garden was recently replanted with different rugosa roses and old climbers, trained up obelisks and hanging in swags on ropes.

I love the hazel walk, which keeps a population of

red squirrels in autumn food. The ferns underneath are beautiful too.

The beech *allée* is made of two serpentine lengths of hedging. These include 26 niches or bays, each of which was designed to take a piece of sculpture. Today a project is underway with local schools to run an annual competition. The work of the winners will be displayed in the bays.

We made our way through a gateway in the wall, leading to the slip garden, a sort of assistant walled garden. This is where the collection of old apple trees, heritage vegetables and cut flowers are found. The glasshouses, one of which dates to 1780, are here also. After decades of ruin, today, big runs of agapanthus grow outside while inside there are vines and peaches and a quirky little collection of cacti, the story of which you should ask about. The fig growing in one house is thought to have been brought to the garden as a slip by the infamous Major Denis Mahon, from the the garden of Gethsemane in the Holy Land.

The workings of an old pineapple pit have also been unearthed and can be studied. The substantial vegetable garden rounds off the garden and I love the collection of old garden tools.

The final feature is an unusual Georgian teahouse, the first-floor tearoom of which is reached by an outside staircase. As the saying goes, the urge to begin building follies is God's way of telling us that we have too much money. So restoring follies must mean that every other job is now complete.

Finish off a trip with a turn along the looped woodland walk outside the walled garden.

The Old Rectory, Co. Sligo

Breeogue

Ransboro, Sligo. Tel: 086 1708 041. e-mail: ena.macloughlin@gmail.com. Contact: Ena McLoughlin. Open: Contact in spring for details of the annual open day. Partially wheelchair accessible. Special features: Pottery. Directions: From Sligo take the road toward Carrowmore. Ransboro is on the R292 in the directions of Standhill. Turn left at the sign for Ballisodare and 'Breeogue Pottery.'

'We bought the house and garden in 1963 and it had been left go to ruin. We've been working it ever since.' So explained Ena McLoughlin of the walled garden attached to her fine old house. What I like best about this garden is the gentle way that Ena carried out that work.

The walled garden is attached to the house. It had been an orchard and productive garden at one point but the only link to this incarnation were the remains of some paths and the footprint of a blown down greenhouse which Ena turned into a flower border.

The wall is curved and the paths and borders mirror that shape. The wide beds lining the walls morph from sun-loving phlox, oriental poppies and day lilies to shade tolerant ferns, Solomon's seal and hostas, as the aspect of the wall shifts from sun to shade.

'I bought one plant of that hosta twelve years ago,' Ena said, pointing to an impressively large hosta display. Although she does not know its name, it is quite a multiplier.

A 'Black Hamburg' grape vine that survived the loss of the greenhouse continues to grow happily although, as an outdoor plant there are no sweet grapes to eat any more. We stopped to look at it and a blackbird sitting in a nest, not yet fully camouflaged behind sparse spring foliage, stared us out and made us move along at a trot. The old pear next door will provide the bird with fruit conveniently close to home. later in the year.

The pergola and seating area in the middle of the bed has been planted up generously with 'Albertine,' 'New Dawn' and 'Arthur Bell' roses and the walk down the centre of the garden, is a double frill of lavender.

I think the sloped, cobbled courtyard is a beautifully preserved feature, complete with all its old farm buildings. These stone buildings are where the pottery is made. A large weeping willow and a golden ash grace the open square. I thought the steps leading up to a grain store, splashed with wild ferns were beautiful.

Behind the courtyard, the stone walled haggard was transformed 40 years ago, when it was planted up using beech, ash and Scots pine. The trees are impressively mature and the walls, set with a little stile, are perfect.

The house features in a book by Sean McTiernan called 'Under the Foot of Knocknaree.'

Cloghervagh

Near Lough Colgagh, Sligo. Tel: 087 2365 055. e-mail: martina.flynn22@gmail.com Contact: Martina Quinn. Open: For an open day annually. See the Secret Gardens of Sligo for details. Not fully wheelchair accessible. Special features: Refreshments and plant sales on open days. Directions: On application.

Cloghervagh is a garden set out on a hill overlooking the romantic Lough Colgagh, which has a strong connection with William Butler Yeats.

'That's 'The Lake Isle of Inisfree,' Martina told me as we stood in the middle of a cloud of hebe and golden conifers, all clipped to a height low enough to ensure a perfect view over the lake below, as well as the picturesque Sligo countryside.

Martina's is a pure flower garden, into which she fits as many blooms as she possibly can. So the place abounds with rose and clematis, iris and peony. It is all colour and scent and summer abundance. Even the little ponds are deeply surrounded with damp-loving candelabra primulas. She particularly loves *Primula bulleyana* that, as a happy plant, multiplies with enthusiasm here.

Sligo

The house appears to rise out of a rockery, surrounded by miniature junipers and thuja. The steps that lead up to it are edged by hardy geraniums, dianthus and different sedums.

We made our way down secret little paths, hidden behind the flower beds out on the boundary, ducking under and behind flowering shrubs, only to land out at another open viewing point which allowed us see both out of the garden down the valley to the lough, and back up into Martina's flower-busy creation.

One little feature has been built around a blacksmith's forge. This quaint little piece of country history makes a welcome, diverting sidetrack to the cheerful, busy garden.

Doorly Park

Sligo Town. Tel: 071 9114 506. e-mail: parks@sligoborough.ie. Contact: Lucy Brennan. Open: Constantly. Free. Direction: Drive south on Riverside from the centre of Sligo, Doorly Park is on the left.

This city park is full of the usual cycle and walking tracks, children's play areas and exercise machines, including an obstacle course. It also contains however, an excellent and unusual example of a public garden: In between all of the above, the council has planted raised herb beds to which people are welcome to come and help themselves. These are planted up on easily accessed ledges, alongside other borders, full of herbaceous perennials and grasses. There are also wire-trained fruit trees and lengths of trained wisteria, great swathes of spring bulbs as well as a young orchard, which in a few years will give people something else to pick. This is a fine civic gesture and one which seems to be well appreciated by the people of Sligo.

Easter Snow Cottage

Mullanyduff, Castlegal, Co. Sligo. Tel: 085 7601 333. e-mail: sligogardenflowers@gmail.com www.sligogardenflowers.ie Contact: Annette Coleman. Open: By appointment to groups. Not wheelchair accessible. Special Features: Flowers for sale. Directions: On application.

The road to Easter Snow runs through an expanse of sedge and damp ground, dotted with occasional turf piles, so I knew Annette Coleman was not exaggerating when she said she built her garden in a bog.

She arrived to live here a decade ago and got to work. Today her piece of bog is transformed; sheltered and protected within the belt of sycamore, chestnut and field maple that she planted in the early days. With that shelter in place and developing, Annette began the garden. She divided the two acre plot into individual rooms which would accommodate her flower and shrub borders. She harnessed the water and made a stream and wood garden, featuring native birch, many of which are self-sown. These grow over seas of self-sown foxgloves and other spring flowers and the sight of that wood in full flight is something to behold.

Out of the wood there are a whole range of formal and informal herb and flower gardens. The flowers are well arranged and look good, arranged as they are into 'rooms' but Annette had another agenda. Her creation was also to provide the raw materials for her cut-flower business. She raids the borders for flowers which she then turns into beautiful bouquets. There are dedicated picking beds but really the flowers Annette uses come from every corner. We walked along sniffing Harkness roses that smell like Turkish delight. She built a whole series of pergolas to hold some of the other favourites, from *Rosa* 'Madame Alfred Carriere' to 'Albertine,' 'New Dawn' and 'Compassion'.

I learned that 'airy-fairy cosmos' is a surprisingly robust cut-flower with a long vase life and there are so many dahlias here it is hard to decide which are best. At the moment, Annette favours *Dahlia* 'Cafe au Lait'

For all the cultivated plants, this is a pure country garden, shot through with areas of wildflower meadow and native hedges.

Lissadell

Ballinfull, Co. Sligo Contact: Reception. Tel: 071 9163 150. e-mail: info@lissadellhouse.com www.lissadellhouse.com. Open: Year round. See website for annual details. Special features: Museum. House tours. Exhibition gallery. Shop. Atmospheric tearoom and cafe in the old riding arena. Bicycle trails. Events. Directions: Drive 7 km north of Sligo on the N15. Go through the village of Carney and turn left at the sign for Lissadell.

The name Lissadell conjures up images of the historic, literary and political worlds of early 20th century Ireland, and of iconic figures like W.B. Yeats, Maud Gonne and Countess Markievicz.

Today, Edward Walsh and Constance Cassidy and their family own and run the famed house. They took on the massive project of restoring a dying estate in 2003, carried out an impressive project of restoration. They brought the place back to the heights of its glory but found themselves in conflict with Sligo County Council and were forced to close to the public as a result. Thankfully, they won the legal battle and Lissadell is once again in business, open to visitors, and we are thankful for that.

Lissadell's horticultural history is as compelling as its literary and historic pedigrees. Since the 1900s, it was home to a commercial seed potato, alpine and bulb growing business, a centre of horticultural excellence and home to Lady Gore-Booth's School of Needlework. The plant lists were famous and the methods of growing rare alpines were particularly admired, as they grew their stock outside in the rock garden, in specially built peat beds, rather than protected under glass. Their bulbs, particularly the daffodils were equally famous, winning prizes at shows in Ireland and England. Unfortunately, due to declining family fortunes, these enterprises dwindled away and the gardens went into serious decline from the mid-20th century. The almost derelict house and garden were bought by Edward and Constance. Working a brand of magic they should probably bottle, they have spent years bringing house and gardens back to life with the help of a small but busy team. In the garden there was also input from some of the country's best horticultural minds. The results have created a great garden visit and a place worthy of the horticultural heritage from which it stems.

Lissadell House is a strange, slightly forbidding, blocky house that feels like it must be overrun with ghosts. Overlooking the water and an expanse of wild flower lawn that melts into meadow, there are no concessions to fluff and flower around the house.

For flowers, visit the alpine yard. The path past the ha-ha trails through one of many expanses of wildflower meadow, on the way to the yard.

That yard is set out on a slope at the edge of the sea, looking across at Ben Bulben. It is terraced in places to accommodate the slope. At the top of the garden, a number of beds are held up on dry stone walls. These walls are themselves planted up with all sorts of vertical-growing plants, from dripping sedum to hummocks of saxifraga and miniature daphne.

On the beds overhead there are David Austin roses over lines of fluffed nepeta. The three-levelled stepped pond, made in the mid-18th century, is an unusual and pretty feature. Downhill from these, is the alpine yard proper, including a crevice garden. There are few examples of crevice gardens in Ireland. (See Drumnamallaght Road, Co. Antrim.)

A visit to see the Lissadell example should be a priority for anyone interested in the art of creating these complicated features. The Lissadell crevice beds are intricate and fascinating, perfect for up-close inspection. There are generous plantings of good-looking alpines like ramonda and oxalis and countless other small treasures ranged about. Meanwhile the clambering rock beds are a delightful concoction of towering *Echium pininana* and helianthemums, tiny dianthus, rock roses and bulbs. Early in the year there are examples of rare, miniature narcissi and erythroniums.

The mounds of stone used to create these features were in place but invisible, before the restoration started. They had to be dug out from under decades of debris and freed from under the huge trees that had self-seeded throughout the place. Old photos of the garden as it once looked, were used in the reconstruction and re-planting. They work this garden, as they do the estate, organically. It is particularly difficult to eradicate horsetail and I admired that even

Sligo

with this thug, they simply, constantly dig it, in an effort to wear it down.

The kitchen garden is surrounded by big yards and multiple greenhouse ranges. One of these has been restored and there are plans for the others. Meanwhile inside, two-and-a-half acres are divided by cross-paths and mature espaliered apple trees including 'Lissadell peach'. They grow a range of vegetables and the beds are laid out with military precision.

When the garden first opened, the star attraction here was the potato collection. During the years of closure due to the dispute with Sligo County Council over rights of way, the collection went into decline but it is once again being worked on and built up. I look forward to its being back at its full 180 variety strength.

Out in the wider estate, there have been many restoration projects carried out, from planting 14,000 oak and Scots pine, fuchsia and rhododendron, to conserving rare orchids and restoring the heritage daffodil collection. There are huge colonies of *Primula* 'Miller's Crimson' scattered through the various woods and in May the trails of wispy pink they sprinkle under the trees are unmissable, particularly through the Cathedral Walk. Stone walls are being restored and rebuilt everywhere and an old stone reservoir that fills from a stream on the land, has been re-activated. Kilometres of trails and tracks through the wood, lined by bluebell banks as well as fuchsia and *Rosa rugosa* hedges, are all the time being carved out.

Lastly they pulled the Victorian water ram back into service and it once again drives water around the estate. Do not miss the Victorian gardener's toilet, or the delicacy of the work on the cobble-floored barns. The constant clearing of *Rhododendron ponticum* scrub trees and laurel is another ongoing job and as if all this were not enough enterprise, out on a hilly area at the edge of the estate, Edward is busy building viewing mounds and open meadows where there were ugly conifer plantations. At this point nearly 50 of the 400 acres are in garden.

I finished up looking at the little folly that Eva Gore Booth used to retreat to, called St. Helena. This too is under restoration. The sheer industry of it all is a marvellous thing.

The Peace Garden

Mullaghmore, Co. Sligo. Open: All the time. Directions: In Mullaghmore, behind the church on the quay.

Overheard, two visitors in the Peace Garden:

'Do you live here?'

'No. I wish I did.'

Another question might be why one would need a garden in such an incredibly beautiful place. The answer is that there is always room for a garden, if it is a good garden. The Peace Garden, tucked in behind a wall on the edge of the quay is one such, created in a place touched by strife, and in need of healing.

It is a simple design, a walled garden with a square of grass surrounded by long wide borders, planted up on stone ledges, full of easy-to-mind, cheerful perennials and flowering shrubs. There is nothing not to love here: There are good plants, astrantia and cirsium, lupins and poppies, anthemis and cardoons. They share the space with wild bluebells and ordinary crocosmia, in a cheerful, colourful garden and a peaceful one too. Follow your curiosity through a little gate on the back wall to see the community vegetable garden and orchard with beehives and a compost system. There is beauty and peace here.

3, Two Mile Hill

Calry, Sligo, Co. Sligo. Tel: 087 2548 882. 087 7660 082.
e-mail: patriciafitzsimonsireland@hotmail.com Contact: Patricia Fitzsimons and Ben Flood. Open: By
appointment as part of the Secret Gardens of Sligo. Special features: Accommodation. Directions: Drive
towards the N16 from Sligo centre. Take the R286 towards Dromahair, then left to Calry. Drive for 1 1/2
km. The garden is on the left with green wooden gates (before Calry Church).

A garden that spills out onto the public thoroughfare, sharing its bounty with passers-by will always get my vote. Having driven through a tunnel of trees on a scenic road out of Sligo, a cleft chestnut fence came into view, fronted by arching ferns and crocosmia, leaving me no choice but to stop. Luckily it turned out to be my destination. The garden of Patricia Fitzsimons and Ben Flood.

The way into the garden is equally picturesque, through an iron gate, under the deepest shade of a huge multi-trunked, pruned-up laurel. The path underneath is made of gravel and sleepers. Boulders hold back fern and pink hydrangea borders. We walked under a dark tunnel of trees, all the while looking out onto a sunny circle of lawn with an intriguing piece of wirework sculpture. This is a stylish garden that holds itself to a limited palette of plants, with not many flowers, apart from a good number of hydrangeas and climbing clematis.

Patricia complained of the *Soleirolia soleirolii* or mind-your-own-business that has migrated to the lawn. Its allotted home was on the ground under a line of rocks and boulders and a run of fern-studded cotoneaster. The myob now forms the boundary between path and lawn and continues to spread much to Patricia's displeasure. In other places, perfectly trimmed box holds in masses of tall pink *Anemone japonica* and hellebores. The house meanwhile is well hidden behind sheets of wisteria, fuchsia and rhododendron.

An assured hand created the naturalistic lily pond behind and close to the house. It is shallow and graduated, edged with pebbles and gravel, and the little stream that leads into it is also pebble-lined, having trickled down a waterfall between more ferns and tall fox gloves. I could be fooled into believing that this all arose naturally.

The constant pull and tug between perfectly preened and loose and wild is a strong and appealing feature of this garden. To the rear, the wilder look is given free rein. Here, the wildflower meadow is simply broken up by mown paths, grass banks and grass walls and apple trees. Tall clipped hedges form a boundary that melts into the countryside and out on the boundary, is a little wood with a soft mulch path running through it. Restraint and exuberance, wild and smartly cultivated areas, as well as cleverly chosen plants make this a satisfying visit.

Ros Na Rún

Skreen, Co. Sligo. Tel: 087 4149 712. e-mail: ann.preston2@gmail.com. Contact: Ann Preston.
Open: By appointment to groups only. Wheelchair accessible. Children and dogs welcome. Special features:
Refreshmentscan be booked. Directions: On application.

'Everyone had a name for their garden except me,' said Ann Preston. The town land is called Ross and the Irish word for special is *rún* and so Ann's ten-year-old garden found itself named Ros na Rún. It is well named, with the Ox Mountains climbing steeply behind it and Ben Bulben visible from the house, the garden enjoys a special situation.

It is a flower fest from the front gate. As we walked, our route took us between bed after bed, stuffed with herbaceous perennials, flowering shrubs and climbers. Ann loves flowers and she grows almost everything in the garden from seed and cutting.

The lawn serves only as a route between the islands and along the boundary borders. The beds are in turn, tall and busy, open and revealing in some places, enfolding and secret in others. No matter what direction you look, there are flowers, from achillea and leycesteria, phlox, monarda and rose to arum and hollyhock, aconite and nicotiana under paulownia and acer. Images of Mildred Anne Butler's garden paintings come to mind.

Ann plays with colours and has come up with some sassy combinations. The pairing of pink mallow with soft lilac *Viola cornuta* or horned violets is a case in point. Silver blue erigeron beside the tall bobbles of raspberry coloured sanguisorba and michaelmas daisies is another. Even the ground under the apple trees has been stuffed and under-planted with astilbe and primula, phlox and lily. It would appear that

gaps are not to be countenanced and while the inner garden is completely busy, at all times the fields, wilder hedgerows and hills beyond, can also be seen. That adds immeasurably to the place. Ann planted the boundaries with a graduating mix of native hedgerow plants; blackthorn, ash, ivy and holly, threaded through with species and wild roses, honeysuckle and white hydrangeas. Pink annual poppies and monarda also insinuate themselves between these. The stone wall was built using the salvage from a ruined cottage on the land. As I left I saw yet another incidence of *Echium canadensis* growing in the wilds of Connaught.

The Old Rectory

Easkey, Co. Sligo. Tel: 096 49181. e-mail: lorelyforrester7@gmail.com. www.secretgardensofsligo.com Contact: Lorely and Robert Forrester. Open: For an annual charity day. See website in spring for date. Special features: Garden design. Directions: Signs in village on open days.

Hear the name 'old rectory garden' and what comes to mind? For me it is images from Jane Austen novels. Everything goes soft focus. The pace slows down. The flowers are scented and old-fashioned and I am in heaven. Happily it appears that this is also Lorely Forrester's idea too. She has been working the garden for many years, between garden design assignments elsewhere.

She explained that naturally, for a 230-year-old house, there was a garden here when she arrived. 'The earth was lovely and we had walls too, so we were lucky.' She repaid the compliment. We walked along along climber-backed flower borders, between healthy box walls and stands of all the favourite perennials: *Clematis macropetala* over aconites and *Geranium phaeum*, soapwort and galega, double pink roses of unknown nomenclature and origin.

Earlier in the season there are vivid blue camassias, dark red poppies and black tulips. She also loves aquilegias and peonies. In spring Lorely leaves the bluebells to clump in the grass, and simply mows around them. The resulting picture is soft, colourful and easy. The gravel is weed-free and she told me that she uses white vinegar to deal with any that sprout up between the pebbles.

We stopped to look at a five-trunked acer over a big froth of hydrangea, which itself stands over a

sea of London pride. This is a mad summer party of plants and there were roses everywhere. Many of these came from cuttings taken from old cottages along the coast road and so she doesn't know any of the names.

'I only know that they are good looking' she said. They certainly are, climbing over arches and up walls and trees with the mad energy that only rescue-roses seem to have.

Next door, the kitchen garden is a more ordered affair. But while the lines are straighter and the plants a bit more regimented, the flowers have crept into the formal corner too. From encircling ribbons of snowdrops early in the year, colonising the area around the frog pond, to the red *Rosa* 'Yeats' which was named by Lorely.

From here we took an arch into the orchard. A mix of old and new apple trees share the very Austenesque garden room. An apricot tree that managed to find its way into the mix, is doing fine although the fruits of course, never ripen. Hens, cats and two friendly lurchers accompanied us on our walk. I did not want to leave.

Slieve Daeane

Cleveragh Drive, Sligo. Co. Sligo. Tel: 087 6574 792. e-mail: anitakellyoconnor@gmail.com
Contact: Anita O'Connor. Open: By appointment to groups and for occasional charity days. e-mail for
details. Directions: On application.

'My parents laid it out in the the 1950s,' says Anita O'Connor of her garden, which satisfyingly, does feel like a substantial, suburban, 1950s offering. Set on the edge of the town, bordering the remains of an old estate, the garden started life by benefiting from the borrowed landscape of mature estate trees at the top of an open meadow beyond its boundaries.

Within the low hedges that divide the garden, there are all the features found in my 1949 edition of 'Practical Home Gardening' by Richard Sudell. We looked at rose garden, rockery, crazy paving, nice straight paths, fruit garden, vegetable plot and a certain, slightly higgledy-piggledy order.

In the rose garden, planted by her mother when the garden was in its infancy, the shrubs include *Rosa* 'Madame Butterfly' and *R.* 'Peace'. Her mother was also responsible for the big magnolia at the back of the plot. It was planted as an unhappy containerised plant, one of many inherited shrubs and trees around the three-quarter-acre garden. It is far from unhappy these days.

I loved the iconic little orchard, underplanted with spring bulbs that were dug up and saved from the old estate as it was being broken up. There are borders all around the house and a well-worked vegetable garden too.

The estate railings used throughout are a nice period feature. They have been draped with roses of unknown nomenclature, honeysuckle, wisteria and clematis, grown from cuttings. The rails are a beautiful linking feature. I like that much of the garden can be seen from most vantage points. Today this is something we try to avoid, but within this style of garden, it works.

Anita's enthusiasm for all things gardening shines out. After my visit, she conducted me down the road to the Cleveragh Park to inspect the work of Lucy Brennan, for Sligo County Council. Afterwards she brought me along to see the good looking public planting at Doorly Park.

The Yeats' Garden

The Model Arts Centre, The Mall, Sligo, Co. Sligo. Contact: Reception. Wheelchair accessible.
Special features: Arts centre. Gallery. Café. Events. Open: All year, dawn to dusk. Directions: On the Mall
opposite the Church.

Someone told me that they thought the Yeats' garden a bit scruffy. I think that is the point of it. As a homage to William Butler Yeats through an interpretation of his poem 'The Lake Isle of Inisfree,' this garden contains plants and features taken from the poem, right down to the bean rows and the hive for his famed honey bees.

There is also a small insinuation of a lake and the wild grasses, wild flowers and, if you wish to call them that - weeds. It is a gently put-together garden: Driftwood marks off informal clumps of specifically chosen plants like little gatherings of *Primula vulgaris* 'Lissadell', a reference to Yeats' links with the Gore Booth family and Lissadell House. Willow,

hornbeam and birch are the trees, and a suitably rustic wooden benches leans against an apple tree.

The island haven has been brought to life, complete with grassy mounds, stands of comfrey, hardy geraniums, bugle and nettles. The only part I am not in love with is the background painting of the lake isle. It possibly did not need to be quite so literal. Sited beside the unrelentingly stark but handsome Model Arts Centre building, this garden is an unexpected and rather attractive interlude.

As you leave the arts centre, look down to the left and to see a well worked modern vegetable garden attached to the gallery, laid out on terraces, hemmed in by silvered and weathered wooden palisades.

Carlow

Altamont Gardens

Tullow, Co. Carlow. Tel: 059 9159 444. e-mail: altamontgardens@opw.ie or
www.heritageireland.ie Contact: The Manager. Open: All year. See website for seasonal details.
Closed Christmas Day. Partially wheelchair accessible. Supervised children welcome. No dogs. Special features:
Free admission. Guided tours can be arranged. Events. Snowdrop Week. Picnic facilities. Tearoom. Toilets.
Coach parking. Directions: Leave M9 at Exit 5 for Rosslare. Continue along the N80 through Ballon and
N80/81 junction. Turn left at the next crossroads signed for Altamont Garden.

Altamont is a garden with an almost fanatical following. People adore the place and justifiably. Its history stretches back many centuries. Mediaeval monastic settlements, a nunnery and several families have been here and left their marks on this site by the River Slaney. The house seen today is a Georgian and Victorian creation, built over the foundations of an older castle. It is in the middle of a process of restoration by the State.

The garden, however is largely the creation of gardeners from the beginning of the 20th century, most notably Fielding Lecky Watson and his daughter, Corona North. The Watsons were Quakers who came to Carlow in the 1640s. Lecky Watson moved into Altamont in 1923 while his own home was being improved. He fell for the place and bought it. Corona, named after her father's favourite rhododendron, returned to Ireland to live, having served in World War II. In time she would become one of the most renowned Irish gardeners and plantswomen and when she died in the late 1990s, Altamont was given into State hands. Since then, the existing gardens have been well cared for by the OPW.

The house and garden are reached by a wide beech and sorbus avenue over a sea of daffodils. A huge *Rhododendron augustinii* named for the plant hunter Augustine Henry, stretches up the side of the building. From here the visit begins with a shaded spring wood garden, teaming hellebores and snowdrops under more beech and rhododendron. To the garden side of the house there is a little fish pool set into a slab-stone terrace, studded with iris and angel's fishing rod or dierama, self-seeded white sisyrinchium and violas.

The Broad Walk, a wide path going down to the lake, is straddled by a strange and memorable Mickey Mouse eared arch and walled in by stretches of 150-year-old clipped box. In spring, there are sheets

of snowdrops, snowflakes or leucojum, miniature irises and hellebores. The garden boasts an impressive collection of snowdrops. In summer it is a great, scented rose fest.

The path continues around the lily-covered lake, passing a magnificent specimen of white-flowering handkerchief tree or *Davidia involucrata*.

The Pump-House Walk leads past and under scented rhododendrons, and arrives at The Bund. This is a marl or clay wall, circling the lake and spiked with orange Welsh poppies (*Meconopsis cambrica*), creeping periwinkle or vinca and candelabra primulas. The raised wall holds in the lake but because it seeps in places, the ground around it is damp and therefore a perfect spot for primulas to do their thing.

The sight of this lake, surrounded by trees competing madly with with each other for attention is sublime. Thomas Pakenham (see Tullynally Castle, Co Westmeath) declared the *Pinus sylvestris* here to be the 'best specimen of Scots pine in the country'. The weeping silver birch and a Kilmacurragh cypress (*Chamaecyparis lawsoniana* 'Kilmacurragh') are also remarkably fine trees. During the Great Famine, 100 men worked for two years to dig out this lake by hand. A century later Mrs North and her husband Garry, would drain it and dig out a metre-and-a-half of silt and more than 60 fallen trees, before filling it again.

A path leads from the lake to the Ice Age Glen and arboretum, home to over 100 varieties of rhododendron and some venerable sessile oaks (*Quercus petraea*). As another reference to horticultural history, many of the rhododendrons came as seed from the plant-hunting expeditions of Frank Kingdon Ward in the Himalayas. In spring this area is golden with daffodils which in turn are followed by sheets of bluebells and ferns. At the bottom of the garden, the River Slaney cuts through the woods and the 100 Steps lead down to it. At the top of the hill a little temple sits in the field surrounded by sheep with a view of Blackstairs mountains. As in many other historic gardens around Ireland, the *Sequoiadendron giganteum* here was planted to commemorate the Duke of Wellington. In 1852 the collector William Lobb brought specimens to Europe from the forests of northern California. The Duke of Wellington had died the year before and it was felt that naming one of the tallest trees in the world Wellingtonia, in his honour, was appropriate.

Following the track from here leads to a white wisteria and rose covered bridge over the river and onto the Nuns' Walk. This walk is an almost over-mature avenue of beech trees under-planted with primroses, cyclamen, arums and ferns. It is heartening to see that those dying trees that needed to be taken out, have been replaced by young specimens.

Altamont Plants, The Walled Garden

Altamont Gardens, Tullow, Co. Carlow. Contact: Robert Miller. Tel: 087 9822 135. e-mail: sales@altamontplants.com www.carlowgardentrail.com Open: All year. Dec., closed Sundays. Special features: Nursery. Seasonal tearoom. Courses. Directions: In the grounds of Altamont Gardens.

The walled garden at Altamont is where you will find the Corona North Commemorative Border, created in 2000 to hold plants with a special link to the larger garden. It is not a traditional herbaceous border, but a mixed one, with something to interest the visitor from spring to the end of autumn. On one side the dominant colours are hot reds, plums, pinks and purples and the flowers include geums and roses, lupins and dahlias. On the other side you find cool blues, pinks, silvers and mauves. There is a lilac here which was bought from the nursery at Altamont many years ago. The tree grew too big for its intended home in Dublin and was returned to Altamont as a donation for the new border. There are special plants that found their way back to this garden from well known gardens and gardeners around the island and plants with stories are dotted throughout the borders.

Even the hard landscaping has a provenance - The granite steps dividing the borders were originally part of the quay walls along the Liffey in Dublin.

In contrast to the colour explosions found in those borders, the green garden is a cool, formal room made of box, robinia and lawn, gravel paths and smart uninterrupted straight lines. The nursery is attached, set within an attractive network of paths between beds bursting and busy with covetable plants. Two pretty stone pavilions stock both accessories and a tea room. Fairy lights strung along pergolas make the place pretty and functional for night time events.

The remaining area within the walls is given over to a vegetable garden and sloped lawns, defined and hemmed in by clipped box, all patrolled by slug eradicating fowl.

Arboretum Inspirational Gardens

Old Kilkenny Road, Leighlinbridge, Co. Carlow. Tel: 059 9721 558. e-mail: info@arboretum.ie www.arboretum.ie Open: Every day including bank holidays 9am-6pm. Sun., 11am-6pm. Thurs. 9am-8pm. Wheelchair accessible. Special features: Free admission. Garden centre. Restaurant. Events. Directions: Take exit 6 off the M9 to Leighlinbridge. The garden is 3km along, signposted off the road.

The award winning Arboretum is one of the best known garden centres in the country. Behind the big plant and accessories shop however is a garden well worth a stop over. It was set up to give visitors, particularly new gardeners, an idea of how various plants might be used at home. Set out on a hill, it is largely made of box enclosed plantings, from big puffs of lavender and architectural cardoons to sweeps of variegated hostas and stately looking *Zantedeschia aethiopica*. These single plant groupings are stylish.

It is an interesting garden. The names of plants are helpfully and practically marked on slate tags. This is where you can see just how big your *Euphorbia characias* will grow; a useful guide for the novice who otherwise might choose unwisely. The centrepiece is a maze that is just tall enough for small children to get lost in while parents can still watch from the terrace of the coffee shop, able to swoop in and fish them out if required. The staff are helpful, knowledgeable and willing to stop and talk about working the garden.

Borris House Gardens & Wood

Borris, Co. Carlow. Tel: 059 9771 884. e-mail: info@borrishouse.com. www.borrishouse.com
Open: May-Aug. See website for seasonal details. Partially wheelchair accessible. Special features: House
tours. Museum. Craft shop. Teas can be arranged. Events. Directions: In the centre of Borris opposite the
Step House Hotel.

Walk under the arched castle gate into Borris House on the main street of the village and the first thing to strike you is that someone here likes grass paths. There is a whole network wandering off in all directions, running into the woods, under and between small plantations of trees, towards the castle, and out to the park. These mown paths impose gentle definition to the place.

Invisible order comes courtesy of the ha-ha which divides the castle from from the sheep field and the outer park with its specimen trees. The castle stands on a wide gravel apron, looking out over all this and the mountains in the distance. A light dusting of roses grow up the walls and a fringe of fuchsia and vivid red dahlias, soften the look of the stone. There are loose, informal flower borders scattered about, with pieces of stone artefacts set between the flowers. The borders continue on out from the building, towards tree-lined avenues and little paddocks. But the main attraction is the lace garden and museum tucked in behind the castle.

With an idiosyncratic, lace-inspired gate leading into it, this small walled garden is a charm and quite modern in feel. I like the fact that the temptation to copy an older garden style was resisted, while still basing the design on the patterns of local Borris lace. The spare, open style, consists of different shaped borders divided and surrounded by wide irregular and angled pale gravel paths. The palette of colours in restricted to silver, white and green. The plants used include white lavender, cosmos, dahlias, hydrangea and chrysanthemums as well as white lupins and creamy hemerocallis. Overhead there are young eucryphias. The occasional splash of purple is deployed in the shape of fringed purple cardoon flowers. It is really a very pretty, modern garden, mixing loose, easy planting with a sharp lay out. Do not miss a quick trip into the laundry.

Finally, the garden outside the walls of the castle runs along the main road of the village in a colourful array of flowering shrubs under the boundary trees.

Clonegal Community Garden & Weaver's Cottage

Main Street, Clonegal, Co. Carlow. Tel: 086 2111 942. e-mail: clonegaltidyvillage@gmail.com www.clonegalkildavin.ie Contact: Mary Byrne, Tidy Village Association. Open: May-Sept. Special features: Free admission. Guided tours by appointment. Directions: Driving through the village the garden is just off the main street.

In general, when communities set about improving their environs for the Tidy Towns competition, they put a lot of energy into hanging baskets and trough planting, veering more in the direction of annuals rather than perennials. Clonegal does not work that way. Driving along its main and only street, the impression is that the village is one big private garden that has staged some sort of break out. It is as though gardening is the village pastime.

The village street is a great spree of mixed shrub and flower gardens that seem to have seeped out onto the roadside. The old granite and white washed shop fronts have been pounced on and decorated appropriately and enthusiastically and the impact is first rate. It helps that the village faces a picturesque stretch of the River Derry, but there are many who have spectacularly failed to take proper advantage of such treasures. I love Clonegal and would urge people to make the detour. A picnic by the river, a meal in its first rate restaurant or a drink in one of its bars would round off a visit to see the fruit and vegetable beds in the Community Garden.

Look in on the community vegetable plots and then take a tour through the little restored, 18th century Weaver's Cottage and the free museum. (Make a donation. All this endeavour costs.) The little garden behind the cottage is ranged on ledges above the house, with vegetables, flowers and fruit bushes.

Finally, do not miss Huntington Castle and its garden.

Delta Sensory Gardens

*Strawhall Estate, Carlow, Co. Carlow. Tel: 059 9143 527.
e-mail: info@deltacentre.org www.deltacentre.org Contact: Eileen Brophy. Open: All year, Mon-Fri., 9am-5.30pm. Sat-Sun. and public holidays, 11am-5.30pm. Jan., Feb. and Nov., closed weekends. Groups by appointment. Wheelchair accessible. Special features: Garden centre. Restaurant. Directions: Take Exit 4 off the M9. Look for Cannery Road, close to the Athy Road roundabout. The garden is signposted from here.*

There are times when the mere idea of something is enough to get you feeling good. The Delta Sensory Garden on the edge of Carlow town is one such place, a feast of gardening, set in the middle of the most unlikely surroundings of an industrial estate on the outskirts of the town. It is perfect that a utilitarian place of work should be graced by something so uplifting and enhancing. The gardens are attached to the Delta Garden Centre, a community enterprise. Each garden was created by a different designer. Some are contemporary. Some are more traditional but all were made as therapeutic places, devoted to entertaining the five senses. Trails lead between and link these and there are good design and plant ideas everywhere, from elegant living willow walls to examples of the indigenous, historic Carlow fence.

This was a unique Quaker innovation, a stone fence made of long slim lengths of local granite laid on low granite uprights.

Mary Reynolds's garden, inspired by Yeats' poem, 'The Stolen Child', is a wild corner; a mix of native trees, shrubs and water with a huge, green sculpture at its centre. It is a lightly tended place teeming with wildlife and even more than its neighbouring gardens, it gets wilder with each visit.

The roaring waterfall eventually lures you to the double ponds where the use of Virginia creeper as a draping ground cover plant strealing into the water, looks very good.

New developments are always underway and a recent addition is the Health and Wellbeing Garden, designed by Paul Martin, a cool confection of mirroring water, concrete arches and purple and white flowering agapanthus, artemisia, olive, iris, ferns and hydrangea. There is a giant games garden with

monster Jenga, chess, lawn darts and croquet, as well as quirky, stone tool sculptures. Meanwhile quiet areas can always be found tucked in little bowers, at the end of hazel walks, behind tall hedges, and in little sculpture gardens.

The rose garden was designed by Gordon Ledbetter, and has reputedly, the longest run of rambling roses on the island. It is made of standards, swags draped with climbers, ramblers and low growing carpet roses, all hemmed in by box walls. Pat Olwill tends these with care. An unusual wooden pyramid with a houseleek roof garden, dominates the centre of the garden. With permission, you may climb this to get a bird's eye view from the roof.

The heady scents of flowers and aromatic foliage are everywhere. Visitors are encouraged to touch spouting, splurting and dripping water features, rough and polished granite, limestone, wood, glass and metal sculptures. The temptation to run a hand over a surface is encouraged and, indeed, impossible to resist. For all the fine planting, it should be added that the garden is run by the most enthusiastic and friendly staff. They are to be congratulated.

Duckett's Grove Walled Garden & Pleasure Grounds

Keenstown, Co. Carlow. Tel: 059 9130 411. e-mail: info@carlowtourism.com www.duckettsgrove.ie Open: All year. Daylight hours. Wheelchair accessible. Supervised children. Dogs on leads. Special features: Free admission. Craft centre with tea room at weekends in summer. Directions: Take Exit 4 off the M9. Follow signs for Castledermot onto the R418. Continue for 6 km and turn right at the junction signed for Duckett's Grove.

Late summer is possibly the best time to visit Duckett's Grove. The large ghost of a house comes into view, in the middle of a field of wheat with nothing but estate railings to interrupt the view. The empty, bare gothic ruin is straight out of Hammer horror. Behind this is the walled garden. This was restored by Carlow County Council about a decade and a half ago. Just as the house has character to spare, the structure of the walled garden is perfect. A view of castellated roofs and towers presents itself on one side, while mature park trees are visible over the other walls. Within it, sections of granite overhangs, old greenhouse piping and corbels give clues to the comprehensive range

of glass houses that stood here in the estate's heyday. These days there are young fruit trees, box-enclosed rose and lavender beds and long walled-backed mixed borders. Iron benches provide focal points as well as resting points, and clipped box pyramids and walls add some height.

A shortage of funds and manpower however, mean that this is only a partially satisfying visit. The place has oodles of atmosphere and bone structure but it lacks in upkeep and ongoing input. I still love it. The big folly of an entrance is worth the detour.

Hardymount

*Hardymount, Tullow, Co. Carlow. Tel: 059 9151 769. 087 6316 415. www.carlowgardentrail.com
Contact: Sheila Reeves-Smyth. Open: Daily May-Aug., 2-6pm. Contact for appointment at other times.
Wheelchair accessible. Groups welcome. Special features: Guided tours. Refreshments by arrangement.
Coach parking on road. Supervised children welcome. Directions: Drive into Tullow from Dublin (N81).
Turn left at the bridge and right after the Statoil petrol station. Turn right at the crossroads. The garden is
600m along on the right, with a granite entrance. Signposted.*

Hardymount announces itself with a short drive past a wide spreading cherry and the second biggest Spanish chestnut (*Castanea sativa*) in the entire country. But the real reason to visit Hardymount lies in the walled garden, tucked behind the house.

'I grow what I like,' said Sheila Reeves-Smyth as she shooed away a pair of hens eager to follow us in through a gate in the wall. 'They cause all sorts of trouble among the flowers,' she continued. While hens are barred, Mrs. Reeves-Smyth welcomes visitors throughout the summer, and is as happy to show it in August as in May. This is not just a June garden.

Arriving at the gate you are met with the welcome sight of big expanses of lilac, perennial wallflowers or *Erysimum* 'Bowles' Mauve' purple aconites, downy, variegated mint, blue agapanthus pompoms, plum scabious and penstemon, and that is just the picture in one direction. In another, there are Californian tree poppies or *Romneya coulteri* with big fried-egg flowers, and acid yellow euphorbia, under blue and white dangling abutilon flowers. The abutilon appeared as seedlings after the demise of a parent tree in the bad winter of 2010. As we walked, on past a similarly stricken and recovered fig tree, and a perfumed *Cytisus battandieri,* Mrs. Reeves-Smyth puzzled over how a slight incline and a matter of a few feet in distance can determine whether or not a plant will survive a bad frost. We tip-toed between loose runs of nasturtium, scattered like floral explosions and reminiscent of Monet's garden at Giverny. Meanwhile, coming from the upper storey, the scent of old roses filled the air.

In early summer there are generous displays of peonies, none more loved by Mrs. Reeves-Smyth than the rich red single, *Paeonia peregrina* 'Otto Froebel'.

Old sundials and little stone cherubs from which hand digging forks dangle, provide engaging focal points and there are grand, knotty, espaliered apple trees with great personalities.

The surrounding granite walls are lined with unnamed, scented roses, lilies, hemerocallis, alliums and kniphofia, through which you can spy little quirks like the horseshoes, buried into the mortar and now used to support wires. We walked on, breathing in the scent of lavender, mint and sage, between asparagus and peas. A shovel stood in the ground among beetroot and potatoes, ready to dig out dinner.

The mature wisteria walk is under-planted with foxgloves and peach-coloured hollyhocks. The many shade of hollyhock here all came from one seed head given her years ago.

Obelisks, trellis, plantations of wine berries and the wisteria tunnel, all divide the space effectively, so each small division feels private and secluded.

Close to the house, the run of hostas grown on a shady wall is fabulous. 'Corona North told me to plant my hostas beside the pond. That way I can easily fill a bucket with water to administer to them.' Smart thinking.

I was reminded to admire the big osmanthus growing on the wall, and was told that it won a prize at the Tullow Show several years ago. 'It does rather shade out the kitchen but I'd rather have a dark kitchen than a blank wall!'

With this wisdom on board I·left, by the gate in the wall. The hens were still trying to sneak in.

Kilgraney House Herb Garden

Borris Road, Bagenalstown, Co Carlow. Tel: 059 9775 283. e-mail: info@kilgraneyhouse.com www.kilgraneyhouse.com Contact: Bryan Leech. Open: May-Sept., weekends and Bank Holidays, 2pm-5pm. Partially wheelchair accessible. Unsuitable for children. No dogs. Special features: Accommodation. Meals can be arranged. Art gallery. Herb oils from garden for sale. Car park not suitable for coaches. Directions: Drive from Bagenalstown to Borris on the R705. The garden is signposted.

I first discovered Kilgraney when I followed a tantalising brown sign down a side road off the main road. Kilgraney has continued to pleasantly surprise me over the past number of years. The house was built in 1820 and one might expect a certain style of Victorian garden around it. But Bryan Leech and Martin Marley had a more elastic vision of what would look good when took over the old house. They felt that the place could accommodate something more modern. They were right.

The garden is entered by veering off to the side of the house at the top of its tree lined avenue. This leads through a picket fence into a vegetable and fruit garden, with neat raised beds between crushed granite gravel paths. Potatoes, artichokes and beets line out in labelled rows. The only flowers here are the bright orange marigolds grown as companion plants to deter aphids. A huge trained cube of bay presides over the middle of the garden and a big ornamental vine stretches along the boundary stone wall.

From here follow a path out to an expanse of more bright, sun-glinting gravel surrounded by granite outhouses and a low stone wall. Those walls sprout thyme and origanum and while this is Carlow, on a bright day, it could be Provence. The striking stone sculpture by Niall Deacon dominates this sunny corner.

The garden changes continuously as it moves around the side of the house, to a courtyard overlooked by the back of the building and a range of outbuildings and cottages. This is the herb garden, home to a ruined bothy with a rogue elder growing through its broken roof and a large fig leaning against it. The beds are full of architectural angelica and fennel, as well as those likeable rogues; dark green mint and frothy lime lady's mantle. The square, raised beds were made from green oak which has weathered and silvered well. I had to admire the egg-shaped slate

pots, planted up with salvia. Nicholas Culpepper's famous herbal book, written back in 1653, was the inspiration and source for many of the medicinal and culinary herbs grown here.

The Cloister Garden was named as it is reminiscent of a monastic cloister, built around a little central slate pond. The upright, silvering oak posts, support golden hop and a vine. Sitting in the pews provided, take in another stylish feature; a four-cornered arch made from rusting steel spans, slowly being colonised by a twining jasmine, snaking its way up the struts. The foliage will eventually meet over the middle of the path. On warm days the scent of lavender, box, mint and oreganum fill the place. Boxed-in sage and rosemary beds compete with each other and on a sunny day the place is heady. At the bottom of this section of garden the pond is home to a small gaggle of Call ducks and other fancy fowl, quacking about and, presumably eating slugs. Standing here the view over the rolling patchwork of County Carlow fields and the huge skyscape is exceptional.

In the last few years, Bryan and Martin have developed a young fruit garden of apples, pears, plums and quinces. Nearby is another recent development, a Celtic circle garden made from huge boulders. I liked the wall bordering one of the walks in the wood, made from huge slices of tree trunk. There are also more traditional features such as flower borders and croquet lawns.

The older historic garden, can also still be seen in places, most particularly in the ghost of an ancient beech hedge that was left unclipped for so long that it turned into a series of gothic arches. The planting on the sunny house walls includes shell pink roses and frothy lavender.

It pays to follow brown signs.

Huntington Castle & Gardens

Clonegal, Co. Carlow. Tel: 053 9377 160. e-mail: info@huntingtoncastle.com www.huntingtoncastle.com Contact: Clare and Alexander Durdin Robertson. Open: May-Sept., 12-6pm daily. Partially wheelchair accessible. Children welcome. Special features: Castle tours, including the Temple of the Goddess Isis. Tearoom and gift shop open weekends May and Sept., and daily, June-Aug. Children's adventure area. Accommodation. Directions: Entrance is off the main street of Clonegal Village.

If Huntington Castle were to have a logo it might very well be the Chusan palm or *Trachycarpus fortunei*. Here in what is one of the coldest parts of the country in winter, these exotic looking beasts can be seen dotted about the garden, doing nicely. One, outside the castle walls seems hell bent on reaching the roof.

Having come along a drive between an avenue of limes dating back to the 1680s, arriving into the picturesque courtyard with its roaming hens, I walked about the garden with Alexander Durdon Robertson, five dogs and three small boys, most of whom had their wellingtons on the correct feet.

His family have lived here since the 1600s and along with his wife Clare, Alexander took on the enormous job of running, improving and presenting the castle and grounds to the public several years ago. Their boys might be small but already they help picking up sticks, which is good. This place eats up man hours. After tea and Victoria sponge, the tour proper began at the base of the castle, which appears to grow out of a knot of mahonia, roses, acer and those Chusan palms, along with a wisteria of such size and girth that it recently pulled down part of one wall. While the castle is of a great age, the gardens today largely date to the 19th century. They begin with formal terraced lawns and gravelled paths between lines of clipped Irish yews, stone urns and granite steps. Alexander has been pruning, tying in and taming the previously overgrown yews, bringing them back to a height of five metres. He showed me pictures of them in the 1880s when they were little round balls.

Leaving the formal terrace garden, one path ducks under the bordering wood, to the home to Huntington's most famous feature, the Yew Walk. If there were nothing else to see here, this would be worth the admission price alone, a fabulous occasion of romantic gloom. This line of yews is between five and seven hundred years old. The trees throw out stabilising branches that lean on the ground and keep them from falling. A cobbled path stretches invitingly beneath the brown arches and the light plays with the dark limbs, creating a magical atmosphere.

In the adjacent woods, the intrepid couple recently planted 20,000 spring bulbs, mainly snowdrops, bluebells and crocuses, among existing drifts of hostas and primulas. We walked through these, arriving at the lake and its small island over which another sky-scraping Chusan palm towers.

Over 3,000 tons of silt had to be dredged from the water which now sparkles clean and clear, surrounded by a laurel lawn, tall oak and beech planted in the early 1900s. The lake has populations of trout, newts and European freshwater eels.

Huntington was home to the first hydro-electric works in the country and the family hope, one day, to get the machinery back into working order as the old turbine house, down by the water, is still intact. Beside it, is one of several champion trees on the estate, an *Abies grandis*. Later, out in a clearing, we looked at two champion Siberian crab apples. Alexander's grandfather sent a lad to Kew to train and set up a direct line to bring in these as well as other interesting trees to Carlow. We passed an aged walnut that was blown over in the 1970s but failed to die, and resprouted. It still fruits today. There was also a mulberry struck by lightning, split in two, which also continues to fruit. The slightly unusual 1930s mass concrete greenhouse, homes a fig and a large vine which was taken as a cutting from the plant in the castle.

We walked out to the boundary to the new rose garden, planted to draw the eye along the garden to a view of Mount Leinster. Cross a little stream to get into this informally planted, formally devised garden. A wild rose walk is being developed to lead away from it back to the woods. Clare told me how Sheila Reeves-Smith of Hardymount has been generous with advice. 'She told us to put in crocuses down here and we put in 6,000. They're like little jewels.'

In response, Clare invented her own crocus planter that allows her plant one bulb and a quantity of sand per planting hole. She told me that it has 'an enormous success rate'.

Last task on the visit was to look at the apple orchard, a good September visit when the collection of native Kilkenny and Carlow apples can be inspected and tasted.

Leighlinbridge Garden Village

Contact: Mary Meany. Tel: 086 6027 751. www.carlowgardentrail.com Open: All hours. Directions: Leave the M9 at Exit 6 and follow signs for Leighlinbrigdge.

Leighlinbridge - pronounced *Locklanbridge* - is something of a class act. One might say, that as a village it was graced with a scenic, riverside setting: The River Barrow cuts through the village. There is also a grand old castle. But one might also add that not every similarly lucky village has made use of its good fortune. From the broad hedges that lead into the village from one direction, to the boundary walls bursting with pink, red and white valerian on another approach, the village earned its blessed place. Park the car and walk about to see the Four Seasons Garden with its statues, neat box walls and herbaceous planting, the window boxes and hanging baskets everywhere, and the river memorial garden with its array of monuments to the renowned dead of Carlow. It would be hard not to be absorbed by the eclectic

collection of monuments in the memorial garden by the riverside. Among these, there are tributes to the Carlovians killed in World War I, alongside Nurse Margaret Keogh of the South Dublin Union, killed as she tended a wounded man on Easter Monday 1916.

I thought I had seen all that Leighlinbridge had to offer when, by mistake, I came across the community garden. This is reached through an arched gate in a beech hedge that leads into the middle of a busy enterprise, with box enclosed vegetable beds full of climbing beans and lettuce. There are raised beds and polytunnels and plenty of flowers splashed about between the working and functional beds. Benches and tables laid on for the ease of the workers, under grand old apple trees, add the perfect finishing touch.

The Meadows

7, The Meadows, Myshall, County Carlow. Tel: 059 9157 530. e-mail: philippabaylissart@gmail.com www.philippabayliss.com. Contact: Philippa Bayliss. Open: May-Sept., 12pm- 5pm, daily except Thurs. Special features: Art gallery. Garden studio. Directions: Immediately outside the village of Myshall on the Kildavin road R724. Opposite the Garda station.

The countryside is littered with gardens that have one particular problem area that could defeat even a talented gardener. This is a rocky slope. I see an area like this regularly and fully understand the excuses for it being a bit less attractive than the rest of the garden; from soil erosion and flooding, to the difficulty of accessing the slope. From now on I will recommend that the owners of such problem spots visit Philippa Bayliss's garden. Philippa's whole garden is a steep, rocky site. Working it in a way that makes it look easy, she has transformed the place into one large rock garden. This is a tumble of small trees, flowering

shrubs, herbs, bamboos and grasses, herbaceous flowers and bulbs, that manages to look easy and artless. This garden is living manual on how to work an exposed, stony hill, in an unorthodox, stylish way.

For a start, apart from the gravel path that circles the house, the paths up through the garden seem known only to Philippa. She picks her way uphill and down like a mountain goat, between boulders and clumps of recumbent juniper and silvery blue *Festuca glauca*, explosions of agapanthus and watsonia. These paths are less defined, than hinted at, and they probably alter as growth fattens up and spreads out in summer. A programme of what she calls 'guardian planting' means that she tucks fragile plants in need of shelter in beside, and underneath toughies like phormium and hydrangea. Boulders are hauled in to create ledges on top of which other plants can find purchase. This was hard won yet it all looks as though it might just have happened. I have seen enough balding slopes to see this lush abundance for the achievement that it is.

I tracked after Philippa, up under *Aralia elata* and *A. spinosa*, between bonsai-trained dwarf conifers and fine Japanese acers, past well chosen pieces of sculpture and equally well placed rocks. The view from the bottom is one garden. From the top, where you stand above the roof of the house, it is a completely different garden. This is useful as Philippa is an artist and the Meadows is as much studio as garden. She has built a glass studio in the middle of the growth, surrounded by persicaria and *Sambucus niger*, martagon lilies and dahlias, galega and philadelphus. From here she can work all year round, studying and painting the garden in all its moods.

Rath Wood Maze of Ireland

Rath, Tullow, Co. Carlow. Tel: 059 9156 285. Contact: Reception. Open: Seven days. See website for details. Wheelchair accessible. Children welcome. Special features: Shop. Restaurant. Plant sales. Picnic facilities. Maze of Ireland (Admission charge.) Directions. Situated on the R725 from Tullow to Shillelagh.

A maze in the shape of Ireland, divided faithfully into the 32 counties - A daft idea and great fun too. Try to make your way through and out while simultaneously trying to remember the shape of the different counties and figuring out which of these you pass through as you wander through the maze is good fun. It is still quite young and developing. Promise yourself some cake if you get through it - and perhaps a plant from the nursery as a reward to bring home...

Altamont Gardens, Co. Carlow. Photo: Paul Cutler

Medina, Co. Dublin

Airfield Estate

Overend Way, Dundrum, Dublin 14. Tel: 01 9696 666. e-mail: info@airfield.ie. www.airfield.ie. Open: Mon-Sun 9:30am-5pm. Last admission 4pm. Wheelchair accessible. Supervised children. Guide dogs. Special features: Café. Garden shop. Museum. Events, Courses. Daily: 10am egg collection. 10:30am cows milked. 3:30pm animal feeding. House tours: Wed-Sun. 11:30am. 2:30pm. Directions: Travelling from Stillorgan on the Kilmacud Road Upper, Airfield is on the left and signposted.

Airfield started life as a small farm and cottage dwelling in the 1830s. In 1860 and again in 1913 it was extended by the Overend family to make a larger house and finer garden. The gardens went into decline in the 1950s and the suburbs encroached on the place, until eventually it became an island of neglected green in the city. In 1995 the Airfield Trust was set up with the aim of restoring it. Since then, the gardens have been overhauled, reconstructed and expanded greatly.

It all closed down for a major renovation a few years ago. I revisited it shortly after it reopened and several things struck me. It is now easy to find. The gardens have changed dramatically - A recipe for controversy. Some miss the old garden. It was loveable. I like this new incarnation too however.

I am not sure if I took the right route around: I entered by way of the restaurant passing through clean lines of hard landscaping and modern looking beds of cardoon, lavender and alliums. From there it was up steps between tall *Azara microphylla* and tree peonies, roses and walls of box, passing a little bothy and other garden buildings.

A lot of the planting is new but set between existing plants, and those new schemes of epimedium and asphodeline look good under mature abutilon and acacia. Whatever route you take, do not miss the Snake Gate and the walled garden in front of the house, where in summer you may find yourself drunk on the scent of the huge wisteria that covers the wall, trailing its sweet flowers down on the ground. In early summer the displays of tulips in here are first rate. This fast changing colour show is set between restrained developing yew walls. I love the flower-and-perfume-fest of the big herbaceous borders, pond, rose and herb gardens.

Tot's Garden was named for Laetitia Overend, one of the sisters who worked Airfield from the early 20th century. This is a romantic old wood, shaded and slightly wilder than the neighbouring areas. *Cedrus atlantica*, lime and maple stand over snaking paths, between insect hotels and big runs of hosta and fern, hellebore and pulmonaria. The pet's graveyard is in here, the final resting home of a whole population of Overend dogs, cats and newts. A collection of camellias make up a little Tea Garden where you will also find a rotating tree house.

Back out in the greater garden, the alterations are everywhere; from the contemporary concrete sleepers between stands of libertia, iris and fennel, leading to the greenhouse and cold frame yard, to the pond in front of the restaurant, with its cool, sharp lines. This marries surprisingly well with the bucolic sight of donkeys in a paddock next door. Close by, take the little walk uphill under a tunnel of native hawthorn, ivy and holly, to see the vegetable plots, the fancy fowl in their fancy houses, the goats and milking cows. These are all cheek-by-jowl with fenced-in espaliered apples, bee gardens, medicinal beds and a young vineyard.

The place is full of ideas worth stealing, from square metre beds and ornamental wooden fruit cages, to lines of crab apples grown over rustic hazel fences and a reed filtration system. The collection of historic breed potatoes grown here include the Lumper, bred in 1810 and so much a part of the story of the Great Famine.

This is a countryside visit set well within the city boundaries, and therefore, unique. Apart from everything else, thousands of native broadleaf trees have been, and continue to be planted in the woods, ensuring peace and quiet in parts of the garden. It was with something of a shock that I hit the noisy Kilmacud Road outside the gate.

Dublin

Arbour Hill Cemetery

(Including The United Nations Memorial Garden)
Arbour Hill, Co. Dublin. Contact: The manager. Tel: 01 8213 021.Open: Daily.
Contact for seasonal changes. Directions: Enter from Mount Temple Road.

I would not have expected a United Nations Memorial garden to have quite such a domestic atmosphere. It is all busy; a collection of bedding, painted benches, roses and flowering shrubs, hanging baskets and painted urns full of red pelargoniums. It is like someone's private garden, complete with picnic tables and gnomes. Not very militaristic.

Stepping through an arch in the wall I landed in the larger National Military Memorial Garden and an entirely different prospect. While it felt altogether more solemn and more like a memorial, this is a place more given to reconciliation and recognition than overblown military pomp. The different strands of the commemorative gardens take in the burial plot of the 1916 Rising leaders as well as the graves of British military personnel from the 19th century. The gardens are restrained and stately, incorporating fine mature acers, lines of yews, flowering cherries and laburnums. I got locked in, strangely appropriate, it does back onto the Arbour Hill prison.

Ardan

Windgate Road, Howth, Co. Dublin. Tel: 087 972 4271. e-mail: conall@europe.com
Contact: Conall O'Caoimh and Nuala Doherty. Open: By appointment to groups. Not wheelchair accessible.
Children welcome. No dogs. Directions: On application.

Nuala O' Doherty and Conall O'Caoimh were told that the site around their new house was a 'rough field'. 'That's not a field, that's a mountain,' was the verdict of Conall's father. The pair were however, keen. That was in 2002. Today it might still be burrowed into the upper reaches of Howth Hill, but this stylish, accomplished garden looks as though it might have always been here.

Self-taught gardeners, the pair got to grips with everything from botany to dry stone walling. The results include a walled kitchen garden, various little jungles, classic flower borders, woods and several water gardens.

Breaking the space into sheltered rooms was a necessity because the wind over Howth Hill can be formidable. Each room has its own style, from the yew-wrapped white flower garden, with white agapanthus, phlox, dahlias and clipped box, to the hot and cool herbaceous beds. One border is deep, full of lupins and delphiniums, roses and abutilon. The other backs onto the rocky hill and turns from border into a rock garden as it climbs the slope. It is possible to clamber up between low growing echeveria, dianthus and sedum, past a little stream that runs down the rock. The view up here, of the hot border below with all its rudbeckias, heleniums and roses, is a smasher.

We made our way past monster echiums and aralias, down an avenue of *Rosa rugosa,* under an arch of *Cornus kousa,* liriodendron, weeping beech and amelanchier. This leads surprisingly, into a native birch wood. These are close-planted trees with boulders, spring bulbs and ferns beneath.

The smart, clean-line pond garden with *Lobelia tupa,* arums and containerised equisetum is perfect.

We sat and studied good pittosporums and pruned-up phyllostachys bamboo, exotic *Tetrapanax rex* and airy *Verbena bonariensis* sitting under shelter of a bay hedge grown on top of one of Conall's walls.

I wondered about the crutch employed to hold one of the bigger trees upright and Nuala reminded me that the soil here is shallow, the wind strong and the going hard. Trees are regularly uprooted and blown away.

I thought I had seen everything, when we made our way into the vegetable garden to discover the copper-surrounded beds, designed to keep the lettuce and spinach slug-free!

Ardgillan Castle & Demesne

Balbriggan, Co. Dublin. Contact: Dominica McKevitt. Tel: 01 8492 212.
e-mail: ardgillancastle@fingal.ie Open: Daily from 9am. Closing times seasonal. See website for details.
Partially wheelchair accessible. No entrance fee to gardens. Supervised children. Dogs on leads. Special
features: Garden tours. Garden museum. Castle. Tea room. 'Paws' Dog café. Directions: Travelling north
on the M1, take the turn for Balrothery. The demesne is well signed.

Ardgillan greets you with a panoramic view of a long sweep of lawn, a gigantic cedar of Lebanon, herbaceous plantings, regiments of clipped yews and terraced rose and flower beds, the house and beyond that, the sea and to the north, the Mourne Mountains. While adults drink in all that, children will probably be found rolling down the hill.

The Reverend Robert Taylor built the house in 1738 and his descendants lived here until 1962. In the 1980s the house and 200 acres were taken over by Fingal County Council. Using the 1865 Ordnance Survey maps, the Council began to restore the formal gardens. The resulting garden is a varied and attractive affair, looked after by head gardener, Dominica McKevitt and her team.

Pictures of Ardgillan always include the Victorian greenhouse, the centrepiece of the walled garden. It was in the middle of restoration on my last visit but the rest of the gardens were more than diverting. The shelter afforded by the walls and surrounding mature woods make the climate in here especially clement. The inner free-standing fruit wall adds even more shelter. This unusual feature punctuates the two-acre site, whitewashed and niched in an example of Victorian ingenuity: Whitewash attracts maximum sunlight, and the niches improve air circulation behind the fruit trees.

Among the most attractive small trees in the walled garden there are several different azaras including the large leafed *A. serrata* set between good examples of loquat, *Drimys winteri* and *Dodonaea viscosa* 'Purpurea'.

Raised, sunny alpine and scree borders, beds dedicated to herbaceous plants and a dahlia garden are among the other features. In late summer, the combination of these dahlias with different species of fuchsia is a delight. There is also a well laid-out vegetable garden where they mix red-hot rocket, mizuna, and pumpkins. The herb garden never looked so well as it did on my last visit: I liked the use of deeply embedded slates to prevent the various mints from travelling.

Little gates divide and link the individual gardens, making them feel private and secluded. The maze-like Irish garden, houses a collection of native plants, plants gathered or found in Ireland, as well as some bred by Irish gardeners and found abroad by Irish collectors. It is a loose collection. The Irish fruit trees being trained along wires are popular. Knowing that a certain tree was bred in a certain county gives us the chance to pick a variety suited to our particular site and soil. It also goes some small way toward re-stocking our counties with trees of local interest.

The tiny greenhouses at each corner of the walled garden might be dilapidated but they are picturesque and hopefully they can be restored soon.

Dominica seems to live in a constant fight with the formal rose garden, battling to bring those that perform badly up to standard, beside their more amenable neighbours.

Add to the grounds, 8 km of paths that wind through the woods and park but three features should not to be missed - The Yew Walk, the Lady's Stairs and the Ice House. The stairs is a pedestrian footbridge which crosses the Balbriggan road and the Dublin to Belfast railway, supposedly to allow ladies cross to the sea to bathe. It is of course haunted by one of them. The Ice House was recently uncovered and lastly, for potentilla enthusiasts, the national collection is housed in a garden of its own close to the house. Dominica is in the middle of rejuvenating and properly cataloguing it.

I left her, as a man with a camera stopped her to ask about a flower he had photographed a few days previously, the location of which he could no longer remember. She was patience itself.

43 Beaumont Avenue

Dublin 14. e-mail: linda.murphy@teagasc.ie Contact: Linda Murphy. Open: By appointment to groups, June-Sept. Wheelchair accessible. Not suitable for children. No dogs. Special features: Teas can be arranged. Directions: On application.

Walking between well chosen and smartly tended shrub borders on lawn more akin to a carpet than plain old grass, making my way through gates in clipped hedging to further investigate a wooden greenhouse, it would come as no surprise to find out that Linda Murphy lectures on horticulture in the Botanic Gardens. This could double as an outdoor lecture room. I could also see it featuring in an Agatha Christie mystery, the perfect smart country garden attached to an equally smart lodge house. We sat in the conservatory under a well behaved, huge and heavily fruiting vine 'Muscat of Alexandria,' one of the oldest varieties of vines in existence.

The front garden is made up of a collection of Japanese acers over box walls and gravel. This is restrained and handsome, but practical too according to Linda:

'Acers are so easy. They echo the season. The growth is slow and they do the trick in an urban garden.'

The show proper is to the rear where an irregularly shaped site is divided and subdivided into little rooms. Most of these are formal, involving clipped hedging with different textured foliage, emerging and occasionally exploding up and out of the tidy hedges. This is the sort of smart exuberance that is hard to achieve.

The garden is largely based around shrubs and trees, trellises and green walls. The blooms come in the shape of roses, clematis, jasmine and stands of white hydrangea including *H.* 'Shakira' a great performer according to Linda.

'With shrubs and trees I know where I am – and how to maintain them.' Order is important here. Order and a crisp look. I loved it.

The Blackrock Hospice Garden

Our Lady's Hospice, Sweetman's Ave., Blackrock, Co. Dublin. Tel: 01 2064 034. e-mail: tconnell@olh.ie Contact: Tina Connell. Open: Each July for a few open days. Occasional coffee mornings and plant sales. See website for annual dates. Directions: Travelling up Carysfort Avenue from the N31, take the first left. Take next left and a little further on the Hospice is on the small roundabout.

Garden visitors will be well acquainted with Our Lady's Hospice Open Garden Trail, the scheme whereby generous gardeners all over South County Dublin and Wicklow join with the hospices in Blackrock and Harold's Cross by opening their gates to support the cause and raise money.

Tina Connell, of the Blackrock Hospice is the woman responsible for the much loved initiative. As well as helping others open their gardens for the Hospice, Tina has, of late, also been opening the

Blackrock hospice garden to visitors for a few days in July. She walked me around the large, busy flower border that sweeps in an exuberant curve outside the main ward windows at the back of the building.

This borders a long pond with a centrepiece fountain. It is modern, colourful and full of scents. There are also raised beds, worked by staff and patients. This is not all, there is more: Mary Reynolds' wild Chelsea Flower Show garden, famed in film, has found its way to live here and was in the middle of being tailored to the site when I visited. This is, as one might expect, all soft lines and rough stone, wild and native flowers, a romantic place and a garden in complete contrast to the rest of the grounds. Visit, contribute and support.

Burton Hall

Sandyford Industrial Estate, Sandyford, Co. Dublin. Tel: Reception: 01 2955 888. Ross Dawson: 086 3853 921. Open: 12.30pm–3pm. Summer months. By appointment only at any other times. Groups by appointment. Wheelchair accessible. Supervised children. Special features: Plants for sale occasionally. Teas may be arranged for groups. Courses. Directions: From the M50, drive to Beacon Court and turn right at the lights. Follow the road to the Luas junction. Continue and turn right at the next lights. Turn left at Woodies. Burton Hall is opposite the Jaguar dealership.

Burton Hall is a two-acre walled garden that somehow managed to avoid being flattened by its overbearing commercial surroundings, an extraordinary treat almost hidden in the middle of the offices and factories of the Sandyford Industrial Estate. (I always find it hard to locate the garden in the maze of roads between office blocks). Having suffered years of neglect, the garden was restored in the 1990s when work was carried out on both the ornamental and kitchen gardens within the walls, following plans drawn up in 1909. Today work continues under the supervision of Ross Dawson.

Burton Hall is plant-filled and a walk along the wide paths that cut between borders, is a walk between some great specimens. Among stands of more usual items like dierama, phlox, lilies, cephalaria, dianthus and tradescantia, it is good to see bold looking *Melanoselinum decipiens*, the giant black parsley and and *Iris* 'Martin Rix'. Alongside impressive beech and yew hedges, runs of restored bay hedging not affected by the two cold winters of 2009 and 2010, give a hint of the mild microclimate here.

The picture that stayed with me after my most recent visit was that of a long path bordered by wide runs of ground hugging *Acaena inermis* 'Purpurea' which is like a rose-coloured carpet. This in turn is backed by lavender and *Rosa* 'Perle d'Or' - Striking and scented, a three-for-one delight. 'It's not subtle,' Ross smiled.

Other memorable pictures are of the mini-forests of *Echium pininana*, *E. wildpretti* and *E. candicans,* running along the length of the south west-facing outer wall, in front of an equally impressive big *Rosa banksiae* 'Lutea'. Ross hopes that it and a white *Rosa banksiae* on the other side of the wall might meet at some point.

All around the walls, there are substantial shrub borders, with tree peonies, myrtles, bamboo and handsome *Strobilanthes atropurpurea*, with unusual pleated foliage. We looked at the *Salix contorta* in one corner, a plant with a history, grown from a cutting of a cutting from the Botanic Gardens in Glasnevin. Next door we admired the unusual *Stachyurus chinensis* which carries lime coloured flowers in spring.

There are vegetable beds and trained fruit trees as well as educational borders being used for horticultural classes. The wild wood meadow is Ross's current project, where he is planting understory, shade-loving plants and spring bulbs beneath a grove of cordyline, davidia and sophora. The tunnel of *Magnolia stellata* next door is a dream.

The St. John of God order runs the garden as a sheltered training project, where courses in gardening are given and teachers and students work the garden together.

Do not miss the 150 year old Monterey cypress with a girth of 10.3m and the strange 'Grasping birch' which grows from a huge dead stump.

Churchfield House

Rush, Co. Dublin. Tel: 086 8193 700. 01 8430 982. e-mail: peters.malcolm@gmail.com. Contact: Malcolm Peters and Anne Carrick. Open: By appointment only. No groups. Not wheelchair accessible. Directions: On application.

Non-gardeners might consider the sea view that this young coastal garden has to be a blessing, but with that view come howling gales. The garden had to be designed accordingly. Malcolm Peters and Anne Carrick have been working it, digging in, burrowing down and coming up with clever saline solutions for a dozen years now. To start with, they do love the sea view so the sheltering trees are deployed only where absolutely required. The species that work are phormium and cotoneaster, bay and Portuguese laurel. Within these, the looser mixed colourful borders of lavatera and cosmos, phlox and clipped box, penstemon, asters and lupins are given enough shelter to grow with gusto. Inside the shelter you might be forgiven for thinking that this garden is blessed on the matter of wind. We walked on smart lawns between long perennial borders and conifer beds, close to the house, and damp beds full of hosta, arums and primulas.

Well-made stone walls and fences, as sculptural as they are practical, are an integral feature in the structure. The wooden palisade with cotoneaster dripping down beside it into a little body of water is only one such stand-out sight and the dry river bed with pebbles, cistus and sea thrift is perfectly apt with the Irish sea within view.

Building up and cutting into the earth, there are a number of different areas, tucked like small sanctuaries containing pools and ponds, snug out of the cutting winds, surrounded by flowering lilac, ceanothus and silver *Salix rosmarinifolia*. Looking at the intricate rockeries and waterfalls it is clear that this gardening couple obviously love building as well as growing.

On a wind-free day, standing on the grassed plateau above several of the gardens, there is a fascinating view of the different borders and parts of various garden rooms. Hidden up here, within

a willow wall there is a wild garden that comes as a surprise, full of loose fennel and tansy, verbena and cow parsley, *Miscanthus floridus* and rudbeckia. In summer the scents here are tangy and herby.

Another route out leads down a set of steps to Monty's playground, where Monty, the dog, can swim in the rock pool surrounded by ferns and hostas. The L-shaped pool by the house with sleeper walls, gravel and stone paving is cool and good looking and I imagine off bounds to Monty. There is even an enclosed Japanese garden with bamboo and ferns built around a young *Prunus serrula*. Surprise on surprise, gardens within gardens, all worked with assurance and style. I look forward to seeing this garden again.

Deepwell

Rock Hill, Blackrock, Co. Dublin. Tel: 087 6125963. e-mail: deepwellgardens@gmail.com
Contact: Claire Nicholl. Open: As part of OLH Blackrock Open Garden Trail. See website for annual
details. At other times by appointment to groups. Directions: On application.

Deepwell is set in the middle of Blackrock, with tremendous views over Dublin Bay and across to Howth Head. It is a surprise to find such a sizeable formal garden in the middle of the town. The house was built in 1810, but was substantially changed and renovated in the 1840s. The gardens as they stand today are a recent creation, going back only to 1995. That planting was carried out by Helen Dillon but the house changed hands since then and its current gardener Claire Nicholl has spent the last two years dealing with some over enthusiastic growth, removing trees that began to shade the house, and bringing the garden back to heel.

Around the house with its swathes of scented *Trachelospermum jasminoides* and *Jasminum officinale* there is an intimate ledged garden, cut right into the hill, providing some fruit, in a few small apple trees. A little box and bay garden frames beds of mint and thyme, alpine strawberries and rosemary and the grape vine on the the house wall also fruits, without ripening. It feels like Monte Carlo rather than Dublin.

From here the garden falls down from the house in terraces, in runs of trailing rosemary and lavender. At the bottom of this drop, the parterre is defined and held in with a double backing of trellis and violet-flowered buddleia in a good mix of smart and loose. The meringue-white 'Margaret Merrill' and pink 'Nathalie Nypels' roses, like two prim ladies, sit well together. The rest of the planting is simple and made up of white Japanese anemone, bluey-silver perovskia, asters, agapanthus and catmint.

A cool, minimalist central pond and fountain, guard the small temple, which looks back over the garden and up toward the house, centring on the dramatic run of steps.

Where the garden borders the sea there are a number of small trees, including a *Robinia pseudoacacia* and corokia, fronted by sheets of lamb's ears or *Stachys byzantina*, sprawling comfortably onto the gravel. The planting became too wild down here and there was much pruning and even hacking back taking place as I last visited. The sea view is always there however and will distract while the new planting takes.

The big border by the tennis court is a busy mix of *Rosa* 'New Dawn' over great swathes of crinum lilies, hollyhocks and herbaceous clematis grown over tree stumps. Artichoke, echium and brilliant little Californian poppies all jumble together in happy chaos. We passed a beautifully pruned up pittosporum and *Prunus serrula* over a bed of hostas. The golden aggregate used in the paths matches the ochre coloured house. These pick up even the smallest drop of sun and light that reach the garden to get on a dull day.

Out to the side of the garden, the sun is in small supply under the grove of mature beech and birch trees. These are under-planted with honesty, cyclamen and spring bulbs, hellebores, euphorbia and lychnis, plants that do not mind shade. One huge beech has a big swing and a zip line from its branches. Temptation.

Drimnagh Castle

*The Long Mile Road, Drimnagh, Dublin 12. Tel: 01 4502 530.
e-mail: drimnaghcastle@eircom.net Contact: Reception. Open: All year. Mon-Fri 9am-4pm. Other times
by appointment. Partially wheelchair accessible. Supervised children. Guide dogs only. Special features:
Guided tours can be arranged. Norman castle with flooded moat. Events. Venue hire. Directions: travelling
on the Long Mile Road toward the city centre, Drimnagh Castle is on the left behind the Christian Brothers'
school and is well signed.*

Drimnagh Castle, situated incongruously on the traffic-clogged Long Mile Road, was, until 1954, one of the oldest continually inhabited castles in Ireland. It is a magnificent example of a feudal stronghold; the only castle in the country still surrounded by a flooded moat. These days the moat is filled with fish – a bit disappointing to children hoping for crocodiles.

The main garden is a formal 17th century style parterre, a neat confection of box walls enclosing herb beds over which clipped bay laurels float. Gravel paths cut through these and the whole place is enclosed in a whitewashed stone wall leading out from the castle courtyard. A hornbeam *allée* was being clipped by staff on my most recent visit. The garden is charming and provides the perfect atmospheric view from out of the leaded castle windows.

Before leaving, go through the gate in the stone wall at the edge of the parterre, and into a part of the grounds which, until a few years ago, was used as a dump. This is a new little vegetable garden that in a more workaday way, seeps atmosphere and history. It is laid out under the castle walls, bounded by stone outhouses and the moat, fed from a small stream called the Bluebell. If you imagined a lady walking about the parterre garden with a psalter in hand, you could certainly imagine a few hardy retainers slogging away at the garden work out here.

Life as a dump meant that this area had been altered very little and the small disturbance made by the organic vegetable beds, continues with that low intervention policy on this historic site. The steps down from the castle wall into the moat, have been colonised by an opportunistic yew. I saw beehives and birds and the lads working the veg beds told me about hawks and badgers that frequent the garden. They sell their 'Goose Green' honey at open days. We could have been in the deepest countryside in the far reaches of history.

Scattered around are some intriguing, free-standing dry stone walls, including a beehive hut modified to make a bread oven. There are stiles, curves and flourishes. These were built as part of a recent stone building workshops held here. Bring your notebook and camera. Ask to see the blacksmith's shed too…

Dubh Linn Garden

*Dublin Castle, Dublin 2. Contact: The Manager. Tel: 01 6458 800. e-mail: dublincastle@eircom.net.
Open: Mon-Fri. 10am-5pm. Directions: Behind Dublin Castle.*

Set in behind the impressive and intimidating range of buildings that make up Dublin Castle, behind the Garda Drugs Unit, the head office of the Revenue Commissioners, massive Norman round towers, multi-coloured painted Georgian buildings, gothic revival churches and the brick building that houses the Chester Beatty Library, the Dubh Linn garden comes as something of a surprise.

It is quite a simple design, made up of a large expanse of lawn, broken up by a Celtic knot design stone labyrinth set into the grass. A path circles this, dotted with oak benches providing seats in the sun for what looked like an unusually worried looking population – Perhaps customers of the Revenue or the Gardaí? One bench in the sunniest spot was taken up by an enormous long tabby cat basking himself and refusing to share the bench.

The main planting is found up on raised ledges

behind the benches around the wall. This is a loose mix of acanthus, senecio, *Jasminum officinale* and aralia. Behind these, the wall is draped in Virginia creeper or *Parthenocissus quinquefolia*.

The problem with this otherwise decent garden is that the beds were being dangerously overrun with weeds on the day of my visit. While I can understand how some gardens might become a bit weedy, the gardens attached to such well maintained, wealthy State buildings, should be smart.

Before leaving, take a look at the monument to the Gardai who died in the line of duty. The other memorial, is the altogether happier salute to the 7,000 athletes and 3,000 coaches who took part in the Special Olympics in Ireland in 2003 by sculptor John Behan.

The Duignan Garden

21 Library Road, Shankill, Co. Dublin. Tel: 01 2824 885. e-mail: carmel.duignan@gmail.com Contact: Carmel Duignan. Open: Occasional open days summer and autumn. See Facebook page for details. At other times by appointment to groups. Directions: At the Loughlinstown Roundabout on the M50, take lst left onto R837 signposted Shankill. First right and first left into Library Road.

I last visited Carmel Duignan's garden on an early October day. She was shaking her head: 'I should be putting it to bed but it won't go!' The garden was still at the top of its game. Carmel's garden is a remarkable place, a town garden that still manages to contain more unusual and rare plants grown beautifully than many larger gardens. It is something of a horticultural Tardis. A silver-tongued estate agent, would describe it as 'deceptively spacious.' They would then skip diplomatically past the fact that it is a garden worked relentlessly by a hardworking gardener, neglecting to inform the viewer that these are the sort of good looks that do not happen by themselves.

From the first instant, a tumble of notable things comes parading past the visitor. In the main back garden, the first sight is a jungle-like combination of schefflera knotted through a tall tree dahlia and *Salvia corrugata*, a plant from Ecuador that is, as its name suggests, corrugated. Carmel said that the dahlia never flowers in this climate. She grows it for the foliage.

From there the show just gathers momentum, with *Dahlia* 'Admiral Rawlinson', *Fuchsia boliviana*, *Tetrapanax papyrifer* 'Rex' and big trumpet-flowered brugmansia that lives outdoors all year round. There is nothing ordinary here.

Carmel has a talent and interest in propagation and experimentation and she takes full advantage of the sheltered aspect the garden enjoys, to raise plants not often seen in Irish gardens. Many of the agapanthus grown here were raised from seed and consequently include some rarities. Yet for all its experimentation,

this is no haphazard lab-garden with all the nuts and bolts on show. The arrangements are well thought-out combinations of colour and texture, height and shape.

The rectangular site slopes up gradually with a central lawn dividing deep mixed borders on either side. We stopped to look at a striking black, thorny *Kalopanax pictus*. Not as unusual but certainly as striking as the pale lilac *Geranium* 'Rozanne' that she uses along the front of both borders to tie different plant combinations together.

The colour mixes everywhere are strong and assured. So there will be a vivid yellow tansy with black ophiopogon grass, black dahlias with blood-red *Rosa* 'Bengal Crimson' and red cotinus. Carmel has what she calls an 'ecclesiastical love' of red and purple, seen in one corner with a *Clematis* 'Polish Spirit' climbing through red roses. Elsewhere the whites and greens of *Hydrangea* 'Annabelle' *H.* 'Limelight' and limy aralias create a cooler look.

Plants that have Irish connections are to be found throughout the garden. Among the choicest Irish items, she pointed out *Clematis* 'Glasnevin Dusk' with dark purple flowers, a fuchsia named after Christine Bamford who bred them in Wexford and a *Deutzia* 'Alpine Magician' named by the botanist and horticultural taxonomist or the National Botanic Gardens, Charles Nelson.

This visit seemed to throw up salvias everywhere, from the gorgeous synthetic blue *Salvia patens* 'Guanajuato' to scarlet *S.* 'Royal Bumble'

It is a garden that one could wander through and

enjoy without a shred of horticultural knowledge, simply admiring. But for those with a more serious interest, it is a treasure trove of fabulous sights owned by a guide who can satisfy the curious with insight and information. I left with a few seed heads of the remarkable looking *Stipa barbata*, which look like pieces of airy sculpture. Over Christmas they got more attention paid to them than any of the other Christmas decorations…

St. Enda's Park & Pearse Museum

Sarah Curran Road, Rathfarnham, Dublin 16. Contact: Reception. Tel: 01 4934 208. e-mail: brian.crowley@opw.ie www.pearsemuseum.ie Open: All year. See website for seasonal changes. No entrance fee. Wheelchair accessible. Dogs on leads in the grounds, but not within the walled garden. Special features: Pearse Museum. Tearoom. Nature trail. Study centre. Events. Directions: Travelling up Grange Road, turn right after the petrol station on the right, onto Sarah Curran Road. The park is signposted.

The grounds surrounding the Pearse Museum in Rathfarnham make a great suburban park. The playing fields are well used. Dog-walkers, groups of children playing and joggers busily exercising populate the place. St. Enda's is attractive. It feels safe and open. Within the park, and attached to the house that Patrick Pearse used for his innovative and famous boys' school in the early years of the 20th century, there is a fine walled garden.

This garden can be first seen first from a parapet that runs out in a semicircle from the side of the classically proportioned granite house. It is from here too that the full extent of the recent addition of a stark but handsome modern glass extension to the house, can be seen.

This view of the garden from a height makes a grand welcome. It gives you the chance to meet the tall monkey puzzle and sweet chestnuts eye-to-eye, before walking underneath. There are also lavender walks, sculptures by Liam O'Neill, an initial glimpse of a yew walk and sense of the order in which this garden is maintained.

The long, deep, informal bed baking in the sun against the newly extended building has been changed substantially, in keeping with its new backdrop. Today it is very modern, with loose arrangements of tall pale yellow *Cephalaria gigantea, Inula magnifica,* different cortaderias and *Verbena bonariensis,* all competing in the show-off stakes. At the back of the bed, and sometimes, interestingly, toward the front, these tall but see-through plants make the whole scheme appear light and gauzy.

A gate in the far wall beckons visitors out to a stone pergola that I remember hosted roses. It was awaiting new plants. The sunny courtyard beyond houses a yellow fremontodendron accented by yellow walls and a little pond.

Back in the walled garden, on a sunny day the paths lined by low lavender hedges could fool someone into thinking they are in a warmer country. I walked past a woman showing some friends her favourite shrubs in one corner, a michelia, a magnolia, some Japanese acers, a scented and striped *Rosa mundi* and philadelphus. Good taste. In the centre of the garden there is that yew walk, perfect lawns and a step-stone carved out presentation of Patrick Pearse's poem, 'The Wayfarer'. There was work being carried out on the other side of the iron gate in the bottom wall of the garden. The ground out towards the woods was being dug. Something to investigate at a later date.

Garden of Remembrance

Parnell Square East, Dublin 1. Tel: 01 6472 403. www.heritageireland.ie Contact: The Manager. Open: Ap-Sep 8.30am-6pm. Mar-Oct 9.20-4pm. Directions: Behind the Rotunda Hospital.

I have never warmed to the Garden of Remembrance. It might seem harsh but there is a clinical atmosphere, a preponderance of hard landscaping, long runs of concrete and stone. The Oisin Kelly monument is suitably moving and beautiful and the planting of roses and tulips, seasonally changing and well-kept, is well maintained. However, that long stretch of pond with its coloured tiles depicting swords and shields is somewhat harsh. I have known the place since I was a tiny child and could never love it.

Grangegorman Military Cemetery

Blackhorse Avenue, Dublin 7. Contact: OPW Tel: 01 8213 021. Open: All year 10am-4pm. Directions: At the Castleknock end of the Avenue set behind a stone wall and blue gates.

Grangegorman Military Cemetery is in an intriguing garden setting. The graves of Irish men who were part of the British military can be seen here in this picturesque corner beside the Phoenix Park. It opened in 1870s and the grand old oaks and Spanish chestnuts, sequoias, weeping purple beech, pole-straight pines and spreading yews, indicate its age. There are poignant graves to unknown airmen, to those in the pals brigades of the Dublin Fusiliers' from World War I, as well as a soldier killed on Easter Monday 1916. Take a tour Thursdays at 11am from March to October.

Harold's Cross Hospice Garden

Our Lady's Hospice, Harold's Cross Road, Dublin 6. Tel: (01) 4068 700. Contact: Eileen Nolan. Open: Annually in May for the Harold's Cross Festival. See website for dates. Wheelchair accessible. Supervised children. Dogs on leads. Special features: Plants for sale. Events. Directions: Travelling on Harold's Cross Road in the direction of the Canal, the Hospice is on the left, signed.

The Harold's Cross hospice was in the middle of a large expansion programme when I last visited it. They had built a new wing of single patient rooms, each of which gives onto its own garden, into which chairs or beds can be wheeled on good weather days. The gardeners, headed by Eileen Nolan, were getting down to the business of turning these courtyards into lush gardens.

The main feature here however is the rose display.

This is an old-fashioned flower and vegetable garden, with arbours and pergolas draped in honeysuckle and roses, summerhouses, snug in sheltered sun traps close to lines of fruit bushes and apple trees, placed to tempt patients with a little something nice, and a grand array of plants for sale lined up in equally tempting lines outside the greenhouse. The proceeds of plant sales go towards raising funds.

The rose garden is only part of the offering here however. There is an old lime tree walk and little corners of planting tucked everywhere, visible from inside the building and out. The summerhouse garden with its copper roof and *Rosa banksiae* pergola, which some people may remember from its display at Bloom a few years ago, is another charming addition to a beautiful array of gardens.

Irish National War Memorial Gardens

Islandbridge, Dublin 8. Tel: 01 6770 236. 01 6472 406. Contact: The manager Open: All year. Mon-Fri 8am-dusk. Sat-Sun 10am-dusk. No entrance fee. Wheelchair accessible. Dogs on leads. Special features: Two book rooms containing the names of 49,400 Irishmen who died in World War I. Visit by prior arrangement. Guided tours may be arranged. Directions: Enter from Con Colbert Road or take the bridge from Parkgate Street travelling south and turn right for the park, signposted.

The War Memorial Gardens is one of the lesser-known fine gardens in the country, though it is thought by many to be one of the most beautiful memorial gardens in Europe. Designed by the renowned architect Sir Edwin Lutyens (1869–1944. See Heywood, Co. Laois), it was built in the 1930s on an historic site called Long Meadows along the banks of the River Liffey.

The gardens, covering about 50 acres, suffered for years from a national tendency to ignore World War I, despite the deaths of thousands of Irishmen in that conflict. They were neither visited nor tended for many years. Today, however, the place is well maintained and, in recent years it has become more popular.

The memorial itself is divided into large garden rooms. The main feature is a raised lawn enclosed by granite piers and book rooms, where the names of all those who died are listed. There are pergolas, a pair of mirroring sunken rose gardens, formal ponds and good looking splayed flower borders. It is a very handsome garden, beautifully planted, in a fine site overlooking the river. Finish with a walk along the waterside watching the the rowers train.

Iveagh Gardens

Clonmel Street, Dublin 2. Tel: 01 4757 816. www.heritageireland.ie Contact: Margaret Gormley. Open: All year. See website for seasonal hours. No entrance fee. Partially wheelchair accessible. Children welcome. Dogs on leads. Special features: Events. Directions: Enter by Clonmel Street, off Harcourt Street, or through the grounds of the National Concert Hall, Earlsfort Terrace.

Until recently the Iveagh Gardens was one of Dublin's greatest secrets. Formerly the private garden of Iveagh House, it was donated to the State by Lord Iveagh in the 1930s. Screened on all sides by houses and tall office blocks, the garden is still a secluded, peaceful spot in the middle of a frantic city, providing an oasis amid the chaos and noise of the surrounding streets.

In 1865 Ninian Niven, working for Lord Iveagh, laid out a public garden for the International Exhibition of Arts and Manufacture. The design was based on the Italianate and French style of park design and included a cascade, fountains, a rosarium with scented old roses, and rustic grottos. The most novel feature of the place, however, was the archery ground, used for competitions among both ladies and gentlemen. This sunken green, along with most of the other features, still survives. The low box maze, just high enough to confound a toddler is also part of the original design and was based on the Tudor maze at Hampton Court in London.

The cascades are beautiful, surrounded by rock formations, tree ferns, a rustic, hobbly staircase and viewing point. The design of the gates leading into, and the railings up along the staircase are of an unusual and striking design and worth the visit alone.

For many years the Iveagh Gardens were neglected. Now however, it is in the hands of the OPW, and has been restored.

Because so much of the charm of the place was its slightly dilapidated, rather faded grandeur, the restoration work was done with a very light hand. Ghostly plinths stand bereft of their statues while parts of other statues lie on beds of ivy, peeping out from among the bushes. Hunt out the stumpery set in a shaded corner, an intriguing little feature, adding to the romantic feel in here.

Knockrose

The Scalp, Kilternan, Co. Dublin. Tel: 01 295 8371. 087 619 3455. e-mail: ttknockrose@eircom.net
Web: www.knockrose.com Contact: Tom and Patricia Farrell. Open: May-Sept. By appointment to groups.
Not suitable for children. Not wheelchair accessible. Special features: Art exhibitions. Classes. Venue hire.
Part of the Dublin Garden Group. Teas can be arranged. Plants for sale. Tours. Vintage car collection.
Directions: On application.

Patricia Farrell grew up at Knockrose, milking cows and helping with occasional jobs around the family farm on the cold, north side of the Scalp, a glacial hill on the border of Dublin and Wicklow. Today, along with her husband Tom, Patricia continues to work. These days that work is in the garden that her mother began here three-quarters of a century ago.

Knockrose is a true country garden, a mix of really ancient, old, and new, in an informal and organic spill and mix. It spreads out around the stone farmhouse and a collection of sheds and outhouses, complete with haggard and courtyard. It could all have come from Beatrix Potter and it has an atmosphere of peace and tranquility that is impossible to exaggerate.

The site has been occupied since before memory and those layers of history cannot but add to the experience of a climb up through the different garden rooms in the hilly garden, under the canopies of old *Magnolia soulangeana* and mature Japanese acers, past *Rhododendron williamsianum* with the most wonderful furry underside to its leaves.

'Who's going to look at the back of the leaves?' laughed Patricia as we walked on under a pergola covered in *Rosa* 'Sander's White, and by way of rough

granite paths, along a perfect bouncy lawn that was being pecked by magpies hunting for leatherjackets, much to Patricia's consternation. In one opening we slipped between an arrangement of stone mushrooms, past little copper plaques carved with Japanese haiku by artist Susan Cuffe. We made our way between hibiscus and special fuchsias, scented and unusual *Lonicera syringantha*, dahlias, *Rosa* 'Grootendorst' and pots of *Leucojum autumnale*, under old apple trees and spreading cherries. Airy pieces of art threaded through their branches, waved a bit in the breeze.

The layers of garden are visible everywhere: A standard wisteria has taken over and colonised the skeleton of an amelanchier that died and in one spot there seemed to be a death match raging between *Rosa* 'Rambling Rector' and *Garrya elliptica*. It might be chilly on the hill but the growth is exceptional.

We stood under a big knot of *Rosa* 'Stanwell perpetual' to draw in the Turkish delight scent. Close by there was a welcoming bench squashed between native ferns and more rarefied *Woodwardia fimbriata*. Everywhere there was a feel of a garden exploding with life and growth.

I could happily be left to live in the little walled vegetable garden, the sun trap wall, the massed crinum lilies and raised beds full of peas and climbing 'Cobra' beans. Look for the famine pot set into the granite paving. Patricia remembers using it to hold the whitewash she painted the outhouses with when she was young. Tom roped the old harrow in to support climbing roses in nothing short of a touch of genius.

Before I left I took a look at an old photograph of the sanatorium known as 'The Country Club for Wounded Soldiers' that was set up here during World War I. The men were brought up here by the Red Cross to recuperate in the clean air of the countryside. The men lying outside a wooden pavilion could not have found a more magical place in which to recover from their awful experiences.

Lamb's Cross Garden

3 Hillcrest Downs, Lambs Cross, Sandyford, Dublin 18. Tel: 087 7777 637. 01 2957 313. e-mail: patriciak@esatclear.ie Contact: Patricia Maguire. Open: To groups of two or more as part of the Dublin Garden Group. See website for annual details. Not wheelchair accessible. Not suitable for children. No dogs. Directions: On application.

My most recent visit to Lamb's Cross garden found Patricia Maguire concerned for the fate of her garden. A road widening scheme threatens a portion of it and she was, understandably, concerned. I do not know how the powers that be could look on such a creation and see fit to slice through it.

This is a truly secret garden, hidden away behind the Maguire's house. They have made a collection of garden vignettes that work individually and then hang together seamlessly. In a space covering perhaps a half-acre, Patricia has spent the past quarter of a century creating a series of formal lawns, flower borders, alpine and scree beds. Her informal ponds and streams, island beds and boundary borders are planted cheek-by-jowl. Not even the tiniest corner is left unplanted but the abundance is never less than under complete control.

Of the small trees and shrubs, many are trimmed and trained into ordered shapes. Look for the clever pruning-up of the remains of an old privet hedge, as well as the stack-of-draughts and lollipop-pruned conifers. There are scree beds, a greenhouse full of special things and a work area that is annoyingly perfect. Add to these, a number of planters full of miniature alpine landscapes. Could there be more? There could, in the shape of a wild wood ravine and stream garden, out at the boundary. They built a wooden platform to overlook the plantations of ferns and hostas, growing on the sloping bank down to the stream. I can only hope the road wideners reconsider.

Marlay Demesne & Regency Walled Gardens

Grange Road, Rathfarnham, Dublin 16. Tel: 01 4937 372. e-mail: parks@dlrcoco.ie. Open: All year. Check website for seasonal changes. No entrance fee. Partially wheelchair accessible. No dogs. Special features: Historic house. Craft shops. Coffee shop. Tennis courts. Golf course. Playing fields. Miniature railway. Events. Directions: Leave the M50 at Exit 13. Take the road signed to Rathfarnham which leads to Grange Road. Marley is accessed from the car park.

Set in the middle of great expanses of parkland, mature woods and walks, the Regency walled gardens at Marlay Park come as something of a surprise. The rest of the demesne, while it is a great green lung in the city, with lots of amenity value, is essentially a park. But tucked in behind a grove of ash, oak and yew, there is a quaint cottage like something from one of Grimm's Tales. Inside there is a tearoom, and thorough the trellis-surrounded back door, yes, the back door, is a garden to knock the breath out of the unsuspecting, and even the suspecting visitor. I never walk through that gate without a heart-skip.

This is a restored garden of great merit. Along the north wall of the first of the three garden sections, you come to a shaded grove shot through with winding pale gravel paths under and between shrubs and trees. Under the taller storeys there are solid clipped box balls, architectural acanthus, sprawling salvia and euphorbia. This area is, in essence, the wilderness to the neighbouring formal garden.

Out in the sun, benches painted in soft green *eau de Nil*, line up along precisely edged paths that slice between perfect lawns, studded with different sized and shaped flower borders.

The order and neatness of the lawns and gravel paths is in sharp contrast to the over-the-top explosions of colour, height and texture in the beds. Mixes of hollyhock, scabious, achillea, aconites, stachys and different varieties of hardy geranium seem almost shoehorned into the beds. These loose flowers were until a few years ago held in by crossed rustic stick hurdles about 40 cm long but these seem to have been dispensed with. This is a pity. They were stylish.

Large planters full of colourful flowers and tender banana plants mark the angles where lawn meets path.

A grotto or 'Wet Wall' on the north wall, between shaded beds of arums and ferns, drips water. It is slowly being colonised by hart's tongue fern, or *Asplenium scolopendrium.* Meanwhile on the sunny south-facing wall, the quaint summerhouse continues the Grimm's tales theme. This house is a mix of thatch and rustic poles, another popular feature in early 19th century gardening.

The second walled garden is where the vegetable and cut-flower garden is sited. Widely spaced goblet-trained fruit trees stand over neat circles of earth cut out of the lawn. In the vegetable beds, rows of chard contrast with oregano and parsley. I love the peacocks here but gardeners rightly find these birds, symbols of refinement, beauty and nobility, nothing more than a bit of a pest, happy to eat and damage the flowers and foliage as well as the slugs they should be eating.

The productive beds are just as good looking as the ornamental areas: The sculptural globe artichoke bed is beautiful and the pear and apple pergola walks are a source of fascination for anyone interested in how to train and shape fruit trees. For those who think gardens take too long to grow, these fruit arches were only planted in 2001 yet they are already impressively mature. Past chive walls, we hit the raspberry and potato patches, medlar and currant bushes, rows of loganberries, plums and pears.

Leaving this garden you notice the unusual garden sheds with curved walls. These were the bothies where the labourers slept. The way out is under an ancient, wisteria that spans the opening in the wall.

Much as this garden continues to be a very beautiful place, it seems clear that the number of workers being deployed has fallen since I last wrote about it. I sense something of a struggle to keep up what was an impressively high standard of care. Given the fact that Marlay Park has, unlike many other large gardens, become something of a successful commercial summer festival venue, a little more money spent of the care of its centrepiece garden seems not a huge request.

Medina

Thormanby Road, Howth, Co. Dublin. Contact: Karl Flynn. Tel: 01 8324 720. Fax: 01 8320 026. e-mail: k.flynn@teknika.ie. Open: Occasional charity days. Otherwise, to small groups by appointment. Partially wheelchair accessible. Supervised children. Guide dogs. Directions: At the Marine Hotel, Sutton Cross, turn right at the sign to Howth Summit. Drive for about 3 km until the summit appears at the top of the hill on the right. Medina is ten houses along from the summit, on the right. The name is on the gate.

Karl Flynn has taken pictures of his Howth garden every week since he began working it 30 years ago, recording the constant changes. He would need to. It is a substantially different garden today to the one I swooned over when I first saw it back in 2000. Listening to him talk, I think it will be different again in another year or so. He began working on the garden before he even moved into the house, slowly transforming it from a typical long stretch of grass with lines of predictable shrubs into the extraordinary exotic jungle it is today. The main garden is to the rear of the house, rising steeply up from the building toward Howth summit, where it is occasionally swallowed into the clouds.

There is not much depth of soil before reaching solid Howth stone. Karl regularly resorts to the pick-axe and maintains that the steps up through the garden 'made themselves' having lain in wait under a thin veneer of soil for his arrival. Looking at the massed exotics growing in lush abundance, it is hard to conjure up a picture of barren rock.

In the front garden, the first thing I remembered were cordylines. There are still cordylines here, fabulous multi-stemmed specimens, found between *Trachycarpus wagnerianus, T. fortunei* and a number of extraordinarily tall specimens of *Dicksonia antarctica* and the froth of a pale *Azara microphylla* 'Variegata'. As I admired them, Karl laughed and said they might be gone the next time I call. 'It's not low maintenance gardening', he continued. He is honest.

The house stands on a ledge above this, at the top of an astelia-flanked stairs. *Astelia nervosa* 'Westland', is his favourite, a resilient good-looker. The ledge looks out over elegant *Dicksonia fibrosa* and *Dryopteris wallichiana.*

Karl loves foliage plants and the garden is an impressive display of leaf colour and texture. Tree ferns could not look more at home than in the mist and cloud that regularly descend here.

The entrance to the back garden is by way of a sleeper arch that heightens anticipation, as a pale gravel path leads past a brugmansia that carried over 30 dangling flowers. It lives outside all year.

I spotted a spiral staircase. It leads up to a gravel and alpine roof garden over the boiler room. From here the view of the garden is one of *Cyathea cooperi* and mad echiums, the canopies of maturing acers, waterfalls and a pond. We climbed back down to visit the Japanese inspired area, a covetable concoction of water, gravel, boulders, stepping-stones, acers and rhododendrons, with a bamboo wall and a cedar house.

The few flowers that are here are subtle – from colonies of wild cowslips and the soft purple-blue of mint bush (*Prostanthera rotundilfolia*) and *Sollya heterophylla* with delicate bluebell flowers. 'It's not a colour garden. I don't use colour'. Karl said. Instead he plays with remarkable looking foliage plants from *Pseudopanax crassifolius* and exquisite *Rhododendron macabeanum,* 'studded' *Aralia chinensis*, spreading cherries and hoherias, eucalyptus and *Dicksonia sellowiana.* I loved the wisteria, fighting for space with a eucalyptus.

In a small garden the pruning and shaping are vital to creating walking room. Paths and secret ways cut through the plantations, allow all these glories to be seen to best effect. There is even space for a little lawn, with rocks peeping up through the grass.

If Karl loves something he will fight for it: Look for the huge ceanothus that fell over a few years ago. He hauled it back into position with ropes.

I left with a picture of the tree fern lying along the ground and still growing, with ferns growing from its trunk. Perfect.

Merrion Square

Dublin 2. Open: All year. Seasonal times change. Special features: Events. Summer markets.

The garden at Merrion Square, once the property of the houses on the square, is today one of Dublin's more popular open parks. It was always made up of sweeps of lawn bounded by mature trees but the gardens have undergone a restoration and upgrading in the past number of years. Mixed shrub and flower borders have been put in at various points as well as some new young plantations of trees. These accompany

an unusual historic exhibition of Dublin gas lights.

There is also an eclectic mix of statues, from one of Bernardo O'Higgins the Irish Liberator of Chile, to the rather strange multi-coloured statue of Oscar Wilde, to a throne in memory of the comedian Dermot Morgan, and a memorial to members of the Irish Defence Forces killed overseas. Look out for the tight-rope walkers practicing on Sunday afternoons.

Mornington

Saval Park Road, Dalkey. Co Dublin. Tel: 087 2256 365. e-mail: dalkeygarden@gmail.com.
Open: By appointment to groups Ap-Sept. Partially wheelchair accessible. Special features: Gardening
classes. Directions: At the T-junction in Killiney with Fitzpatrick's Hotel in front of you, turn turn left on
to Dalkey Avenue. Drive 300m to a roundabout. Take the first exit onto Saval Park Road. The garden is
on the left behind a long wavy hedge.

When a garden is close to the sea, it seems appropriate to read a direction that reads 'look for a long wavy hedge'. The hedge in front of Annemarie Bowring's garden in Dalkey is suitably reminiscent of the sea. Inside the gates, the garden around the climber-enveloped house, echoes its seaside status in several places, from dry beach pebble beds to raised ponds with flying fish sculptures in a 'sea' of *Stipa gigantea.* Annemarie's style of gardening has a witty, light touch.

The dry stream bed features, at different times in the year, foxgloves, agapanthus and zappy, magenta-coloured *Lychnis conoraria* with soft silvery leaves. Annemarie brought a dry river garden to Bloom in 2015. She is good at this.

The house faces north so it is unusual to see such healthy bulky stands of agapanthus around the steps to the door. Coupled with a particularly good purple form of fuchsia, these agapanthus flowers are not something you will need to be directed to see. Annmarie is extremely fond of them: She has divided and divided them, slotting them, to good effect into the long grass garden that bounds the drive.

This airy border weaves in and out, bounded by a wide pebble ribbon that 'finishes' it perfectly. It is all pinks, blues and silvers, delphiniums and lupins, libertia and sanguisorba, lychnis and sea kale or *Crambe maritima*, self-seeding *Stipa tenuissima* and tall *Calamagrostis acutiflora* 'Karl Foerster' grass. The result is height and movement from early summer right up to winter. Orange tulips in early summer inject electric pops into the summer bed.

There are, also seaside-themed vegetable beds complete with a beach hut style hen house. Gravel and sleepers combine well to define the style here and vegetables are sheltered between apples and thornless blackberries.

The shade is mostly light, delivered by *Prunus serrula,* good *Syringa vulgaris* 'Madame Lemoine' and the 'dirtiest tree ever' according to Annemarie, a eucalyptus which looks like it has a champion girth but with which she is not madly in love. I love the cherry, wrapped in a iron bench on the middle of the lawn.

Mount Venus Nursery

Walled Garden, Tibradden, Mutton Lane, Dublin 16. Tel: 01 4933 813. 086 3218789.
e-mail: mountvenusnursery@gmail.com www.mountvenusnursery.com Contact: Oliver and Liat Schurmann.
Open: See website for seasonal hours. Special features: Nursery. Mail order service. Garden design. Directions:
Take Exit 12 on the M50 and follow signs to Knocklyon road. Continue to Templeroan Road and turn
right. Drive to the roundabout and drive through onto Scholarstown Road. Turn right onto the R116 and
slightly left to Tibradden Road, driving straight to Mutton Lane.

The words of Cole Porter's 'You Do Something To Me' do not usually float across the mind walking around a plant nursery but Mount Venus is not a usual sort of plant nursery. Set within the weathered granite of an old walled garden, the nursery is a bit special. It might be a short hop from the manic M50, but it could not feel more remote.

Narrow paths pick their way between runs of bamboo and *Drimys winteri*, schefflera and *Cornus kousa*, unusual hydrangeas and fountains of ferns. The garden areas blend into the arrangements of plants for sale in an almost invisible way. Is it a plant in the ground or something for sale? Part of the garden or shop? The lines are a blurred and the result is an exotic series of horticultural vignettes.

Liat Schurmann's sculptures, tall elegant pillars, little sprites and figures lying between, sitting on top of and hiding behind the plants, emerge from the growth in charming, surprising ways. 'We are not so into hard landscaping,' Liat says with some understatement in this celebration of plants, plants, art and more plants.

Newbridge Demesne Traditional Farm And Museum

Hearse Road, Donabate, Co. Dublin. Tel: 01 8436 534. www.fingalcoco.ie. Contact: The Manager. Open: All year from 10am. Closing times vary. Partially wheelchair accessible. Dogs on leads. Special features: Exhibitions. Events. Tea rooms. Walks. House tours. Directions: Signed from the M1 travelling north of Swords.

Newbridge House is known for its rare breed animals and farming exhibits. From all sorts of pigs to fancy fowl, sheep, cattle and baby goats. There is livestock enough here to keep the most animal-mad family happily occupied.

The gardens are also well worth a visit, from the manicured parkland to the walled garden behind the neat Georgian house. The red brick walled garden has been undergoing restoration work for some time and arriving at the corner entrance, you can get fairly giddy at the extent and size of this well presented, well minded garden. There are several decent runs of herbaceous border, running perpendicular to each other in the middle of the garden as well as along the walls, with mixes of dahlia, nepeta, rudbeckia and agapanthus, rose arches, fountains and pergolas at the junctions.

There are long beds of soft fruit and wall-trained fruit trees and those with an interest in native Irish apples will like the orchards, both mature and juvenile. Take a walk between espaliered fruit trees through the centre of the garden, past some fiendish-looking farm implements

The two free-standing restored Victorian greenhouses are worth seeing before you leave to see the baby goats and pigs or the black swans on the pond in the park beyond the wall.

Oakdown Garden

16a Oakdown Road, Churchtown, Dublin 14. Tel: 086 0830 264. 01 2984 537. Contact: Jackie Horan. Open: One charity day in June for the OLH Hospice Trail. See website for annual date. Partially wheelchair accessible. Special features: Plant sales. Directions: On application.

I arrived on a wet day and met Jackie knitting dresses for Barbie dolls on their way to Africa as part of the Team Hope Christmas shoe-box appeal. The kitchen was lined with boxes getting ready to be posted off. Jackie divides her time between this work and her well-stuffed, pretty garden in Churchtown.

A garden migrating out to the footpath in front of a house is always a welcome sight. Pittosporum and sephora on the roadside are her gifts to passers-by. In truth the whole front garden is also open to them: Jackie prunes up and raises the canopy of the small trees and shrubs here, enabling her to fit in more plants and the passers-by to see more of everything. The beds are divided by squiggling little paths lined with granite boulders. It is a spree of white *Lychnis coronaria* under pruned-up *Pittosporum* 'Tom Thumb', pink perennial wallflowers and irises. There are alpines insinuated between every boulder, little sedum and dianthus, auriculas, ophiopogon and hepatica. *Cyclamen coum* grows in weed-like proportions and even *Primula denticulata* manages to do well despite the free-draining conditions. Among the stand out plants here is a metre-tall *Diascia personata*. Jackie smiled and said 'All I know is that it cost €2.'

The house provides a leaning post for the sort of huge pelargoniums that can only stay outside in coastal counties. Following the wall around the corner and through a gate, the way leads into a secreted-away little shade garden made up of ferns, hellebores and hydrangeas, thriving in the moist damp.

The main back garden is taken up with an informal rockery, surrounded by fruit trees, trained well along a wooden trellis, some fine cut-leaf acers and roses - all grown from cuttings.

Plants that remind her of friends and gardeners abound in the borders, including a stand of blue *Eryngium* 'Miss Willmott's' ghost, from Noelle Curran, who was a well known gardener in Dublin.

Jackie suffers from a disease that means that when she has a handful of cuttings she needs to plant them, a dangerous ailment when your garden is small. So they all get sold in aid of the Hospice and Team Hope. It is, as they say, all good.

Orchardstown Park Garden

10 Orchardstown Park. Rathfarnham, Dublin 14. Tel 087 204 4368. Contact: Mairead Harkin.
Open: Occasional Open Days for the OLH Hospice Trail. See website for annual dates. Not wheelchair accessible. Directions: See website.

The enthusiasm that emanates from the people who open their gardens for the Hospice is always noticeable. They put boundless energy into their fundraising days. Walking through Mairead Harkin's flower filled suburban garden, looking at this clematis and that holly, ducking under an arch covered with the pink Donegal rambling rose and admiring the still standing 50-year-old *Cytisus battandieri,* she told me about the artist friends who produces cards to sell on the day for the cause.

Mairead has been working her busy garden for many years and opening it for the Hospice for the past six. She is an informal gardener. When asked what the row of standard roses were, she replied that they were on sale years ago in the garden centre, minus labels, so she bought them at a bargain price. Who needs the names? It might be a small garden but she loves tall plants, including three metre tall perennials like *Cephalaria gigantea* beside *Cercis siliquastrum,* whose pink tiny flowers she adores. She also has a thing for dripping golden laburnum and white *Exochorda* x. *macrantha* 'The Bride'. In a tight space a lot is expected of an individual plant. These plants deliver.

The People's Park

George's Street, Dun Laoghaire, Co. Dublin. Open: All year. Wheelchair accessible. Dogs on leads. Special features: Restaurant. Directions. In the centre of the town.

The Victorian park in Dun Laoghaire has become one of the town's most attractive features since its recent restoration. Its heritage is called to mind in the beds of mad red pelargoniums and trachycarpus, but today it has the feel of a welcoming, modern meeting place as much as a garden. As I stopped to look at something, a gang of cool dudes walked past me, hunting for Pokemon: 'It should hatch in 6 seconds,' one of them knowledgeably informed his skateboard-carrying companions. I left them to the chase and followed a gate into a secluded gravel garden, full of tree ferns and bamboo, Japanese acers and clipped box. After the happy chaos outside, this is a quiet and peaceful place.

The big café stands on top of a ledge planted up with a riot of flowers, perfect for people and garden watching. That garden is made up of long mixed borders backed by actinidia or kiwi, little avenues of roses under gingko and beds of geraniums of all sorts. The place is all go, with spouting fountains and beds of cosmos. Every lamp post is festooned with exploding hanging baskets There are benches everywhere and children running riot.

You cannot but be cheered in the middle of such

a busy, well used park on any given summer day. Well done Dun Laoghaire Rathdown. I think the upkeep must be a nightmare.

I left having enjoyed a few minutes puzzling over the eclectic selection of commemorative trees and wishing that I could nose about the little red brick gate lodge.

Phoenix Park: Aras An Uachtarain

The Phoenix Park, Dublin 7. Tel: 01 8213 021. e-mail: phoenixparkvisitorcentre@opw.ie www.phoenixpark.ie. Contact: Reception. Open: Seasonal. See website for details. Tour bus collects and delivers visitors from Phoenix Park Visitor Centre. Wheelchair accessible. Supervised children. Guide dogs. Entrance free. Special Features: House tours.

I wanted to see the gardens of the Aras for many years and when I finally got to visit, they did not disappoint. From the lawn like a billiard table with its nail-clipped yews and an uninterrupted view of the Dublin Mountains, to the wildflower meadows planted by Mrs. Higgins and the Peace Bell Monument set up by Mrs Aleese, the numerous trees planted by the De Valeras and the daffodil collection introduced during Mrs. Robinson's tenure, the stables full of Garda horses and not forgetting President Higgins, who waved at me from a distance as he was going about his business and I made my way around –The Aras is, as the saying goes, 'doing the State some service'.

The historic gardens cover 130 acres and are the only OPW run gardens in the country with full organic status. This matters because it means that the President is able to impress every visiting Head of State or dignitary at official dinners with the highest quality home grown food, from the apple juice they drink to the vegetables and fruit on the dinner plates. They know it was all grown in the house gardens. That is special.

Close to the house, the emphasis is naturally on flowers. There is the formal area, with its seasonally changed beds of canna and salvia. This is like the compulsory question on the exam paper. It must be answered. The dairy garden, to the side of the house, is however, the most charming, alluring little place, with its pretty scented display of pink and white, old Irish roses, combined with lavender, all centred on a grand *Magnolia grandiflora*.

There are several walled gardens, some featuring great bulging, busy flower borders. I was impressed by the restored Victorian curvilinear greenhouse where the vines, planted outside, grow in through little openings in the base of the walls, to ripen inside the bright, warm house.

The dahlia collection takes up the centre of one garden, and huge numbers of these explosive plants are stuffed inside razor-sharp box and yew walls. The fact that they are colour-themed injects some order on these otherwise unruly plants. The outer walls home herbaceous borders, a punchy collection of hydrangeas and some fine old lead planters. I recently learned that lead planters subside under their own weight and need to be pulled back into shape. These planters, on government business as they are, showed no such slovenly tendencies. Apart from looking good, the borders provide the Aras with all its flowers.

The unusual concertina wall in the fruit garden is worth noting. This was another Victorian invention, a design that would soak up maximum light and warmth for the crops. Today, the fruits and vegetables with the important job of impressing visitors are grown in ordered rows along the walls and in the middle. They will be required in the kitchen but they must also look good in the meantime.

Outside the walled gardens we walked along the Queen's Walk, named after Queen Victoria. I picked up an acorn from one of the trees planted by the same lady. Many famous visitors have left their mark by planting a tree at various points around the gardens and the plaques are fascinating to pore over.

Before leaving, we made our way along the 230 metre long sensory border, where the plants are gathered into groups, coupled with pieces of art, to tickle the senses of touch, sight, sound, smell and taste. I noted that the gravel paths we walked on had been weeded with organic citronella.

As we left we were observed by a pair of Garda

horses, enjoying a sunny day off in the Park between bouts of doing the state some service.

Farmleigh

The Phoenix Park, Dublin 7. Tel: 01 815 5914. e-mail: farmleighinfo@opw.ie. www.farmleigh.ie Contact: Sharon Doyle. Open: All year. See website for seasonal details and for details of closures in case of government business. Wheelchair accessible. Supervised children. Guide Dogs. Special features: Café. Tours. Events. Directions: Drive up Chesterfield Avenue in the park towards Castleknock. The garden is signed to the left.

The Phoenix Park is a remarkable place. But no less remarkable are the individual gardens within the great city park. Farmleigh, in a hidden corner of the park was once the property of the Guinness family. It is now owned by the State and came as a stunning surprise to the public when it was first opened to visitors several years ago.

In the short time since it was unveiled, it has become one of the favourite national treasures, not only as a garden but as a venue for a whole range of garden activities, talks, demonstrations and expositions. But it needs no special activities to make it worth a trip. A walk around the grounds is all it takes to make one fall for the place.

Tended by a small number of seriously talented gardeners, Farmleigh is like a master class in Big House gardening. There is so much about the place that is impressive, particularly the tiny number of people who manage it.

The visit starts properly at the coach yard, a charming place in itself with a huge wisteria and appropriately overstuffed window boxes. But the American red ash *Fraxinus pennsylvanica* just outside the yard is the wow plant here. It is a fine tree at the best of times but breath-taking in autumn when it turns scarlet, and rears above the courtyard like a flaming cloud.

The way into the garden proper leads up through a fern walk, which in spring is home to a collection of hellebores, anemones, snowdrops, daffodils and crocuses.

The conservatory is next in line, full of lemon trees, cannas, and an abutilon that could well be the tallest in Ireland. *Dracaena reflexa*, is an unusual striped yucca-like plant that certainly calls for attention and we inspected a banana called *Ensete ventricosum*. Adelaide Monk grew this two-metre tall plant from a seed planted in 2009. The exotic good looks of these plants are matched only by the attention to every little detail of their care.

The path to the pond and boathouse runs between a walk of magnolias that feature fine specimens of *Magnolia*, 'Elizabeth', *M.* 'Leonard Messel,' *M.* 'Atlas' and *M.* 'Milky Way'.

The walled garden is of course the centrepiece of the garden. It boasts impressive flower and shrub borders, fine statuary set in among well designed walks and all sorts of interesting plants, from old unidentified tree peonies, and day lilies to tall cynara or artichoke. Lanning Roper, the American landscape architect, was responsible for the design. He had a great love of sculptural plants and his yew-backed borders here are perfection. I love the cut-flower borders full of lined-up verbena, aquilegia, sweet pea and thalictrum.

Meanwhile the tulip displays are worth seeing in early summer. Mad orange and shocking pink tulips planted through blue camassia are just one of the flashier combinations.

There are rose, wisteria and clematis pergolas, gorgeous magnolias including the great scented *M. kobus*, which is like the best possible version of *Magnolia stellata*.

Adelaide grows so many of the plants in here from seed, a particular love being agapanthus which, she says 'thrive on abuse.' Their only draw-back is that they just take a long time to grow and require a lot of patience. The greenhouse is a hub. In summer it is used for growing a number of different chillies and tomatoes and in winter, it is hauled into service to mind oleander seedlings, as well as over-wintering semi-tender plants sheltering from the weather. Hauling huge numbers of pots in and out of the greenhouse is only one of the jobs the small team does every year, twice a year.

Outside, vegetables and fruit trees share the space with flowers and the ever present deep tall yew hedges. There are two miles of yew hedges in this garden cared for by Noel Ford who is a perfectionist when it comes to hedging. One section or another is generally under rejuvenation which is an interesting sight in itself.

On the subject of hedging, the Dutch garden is a favourite. This is one of very few examples of a topiary garden on the island. The contrast between sharp spirals, cones and peacocks and sunken beds of fluffy nepeta and tulips is effective.

The grounds are extensive and take in lakeside and wooded walks and some truly fine specimen trees. The formal pond lawn is beautiful and the small decorative restored dairy should be hunted out.

Come for special events by all means but make time to visit it for its own sake too, and say hello to the horses and donkeys in the paddocks, at least some of which have represented Ireland in international showjumping competitions.

Walled Victorian Garden

Phoenix Park, Dublin 7. Tel: 01 8213 021. e-mail: phoenixparkvisitorcentre@opw.ie www.phoenixpark.ie. Contact: Reception. Open: All year. Wheelchair accessible. Dogs on leads. Special features: Restaurant. Growing demonstrations first Sat. every month 10.30am. Vegetables from the garden sold at weekends. Directions: In the Phoenix Park, close to the visitors centre near the Castleknock gates. Signposted.

The Phoenix Park is one of the greatest jewels the country possesses. It is one of the greatest city parks in the world and home to a huge number of individual features: polo grounds and hospitals, the Dublin zoo, several walled gardens, Victorian tea rooms, a castle, the official homes of both the President of the Republic and the United States ambassador to Ireland, the headquarters of the Garda Siochana, the official government hospitality venue of Farmleigh, the Ordnance Survey Office, herds of deer, play grounds, Viking burial sites, the Wellington monument, massive numbers of fine trees, individual parks and gardens. It comes as no surprise to find that it is also the workplace of over 2,200 people.

Standing in the middle of the huge park, just beside Ashtown castle, the oldest building here, is where the walled kitchen garden can be found. This is a good place to start. This restored Victorian ornamental fruit and vegetable garden is a gem. Enter it from the central main entrance to catch the best first view of the main event; the central walk between the double borders. These long beds are stuffed to capacity with changing perennials, from alstroemeria and agapanthus to achillea, aconitum and agastache, and these are only the As. They look good from spring right up to the beginning of winter. The two beds are corseted in at the front by box and backed by wire-trained fruit trees, which will eventually look like overgrown candelabras.

Behind the trained trees you will find vegetable beds that make perfect demonstrations beds, like living textbooks on kitchen gardening. Among these there are herb gardens, rotation beds, soft fruit bushes, lines of strawberries and well arranged lines of lettuce and leek. Meanwhile a dozen or so rhubarb forcers sit at the edge of a bed waiting for a job of work. From mid-summer on, the little sunflower field becomes more and more dramatic and brash, as the neighbouring pumpkin patch fills up with swelling monsters, destined for for Halloween festivities.

Good housekeeping and upkeep are the things that set a vegetable garden apart and this is an impeccably maintained garden, one that would send you home with a yen to get growing. It is worked by helpful and knowledgeable staff, happy to stop for a few minutes and answer questions. They also give regular demonstrations on growing through the summer season.

The long range of greenhouses and vine houses built by Jacob Owen in 1850 on the south-facing wall still awaits restoration. Hidden behind a hoarding, they will be a great addition to the garden eventually. Meanwhile, a small orchard of Irish cultivar apple trees has being planted outside the wall.

Also outside the walls there are some magnificent trees, cedars of Lebanon, giant Scots pines, holm oaks and blue cedars. The miniature maze of box beside the castle is fun for children and from here the choice of things to do and see in the park stretches out in front of you. You can even take a tour on a Segway these days.

Don't miss a visit to the People Park, down at the main entrance at Parkgate Street. This garden came about as part of a forward-thinking civic plan in the 1830s to create a 'Healthy People's Garden' complete with flower beds and drinking fountains of clean water for the populace to enjoy. The huge rockery here is in the middle of restoration. This has been re-sited three times in its long lifetime and today it is fronted by unusual ribbon beds, where eight rows of bedding are laid out precisely in strings of colour along the ground.

Close by, under the shelter of the trees the unusual modern 1950's shelter designed by Raymond McGrath, jars somewhat with the Victorian feel, but it is interesting nevertheless.

Lately a collection of rare hawthorns has been planted into the laurel lawn alongside 150 Princeton elms, planted in an unusual mound system. On my most recent visit, as we drove on past these, we spotted a huge gorilla sitting on top of a ten-metre pole inside the Zoo fence, surveying his world, the fantastic Phoenix Park.

The National Botanic Gardens

Glasnevin, Dublin 9. Tel: 01 8040 300. 01 8570 909. e-mail: botanicgardens@opw.ie www.botanicgardens.ie Contact: The Reception. Open: All year daily, except 25 Dec. Summer 9am-6pm. Winter 9am-4.30pm. Wheelchair accessible. No entrance fee. Car parking fee. Special features: Restaurant. Book shop and visitor centre. Courses. Lectures. Events. Guided tours: Mon-Sat 11.30am and 3pm (Admission charge.) Sun. 12pm and 2.30pm (Free). Directions: Situated on the north side of the city on Botanic Road.

The National Botanic Garden in Dublin is one of the loveliest botanic gardens in the world. It is beautiful at all times of year; functional, well loved by Dubliners and visitors alike; a place of recreation and serious botanical research and conservation; a green lung in the city; a haven for wildlife and a tourist attraction of the first order.

Founded in 1795, the Botanic Gardens constitutes Ireland's foremost botanical and horticultural institution. It played and continues to play a vital role in the conservation of rare, imported and unusual plants. Throughout its history, all the great gardens around the island have been involved in the division and sharing of plants with the Botanic Gardens, and it has been a great force for good in the world of Irish horticulture.

Education and research have played a part of the work of the Botanics since the 1700s, when six boys were taken on as apprentices, to be paid *if* their work was considered satisfactory. Today, it is still the classroom and laboratory for the horticulture students that will bring Irish gardening into the next century.

The plant collections are a delight, arranged in geographical and scientific groupings in a landscaped setting on the banks of the River Tolka. The layout incorporates rock gardens, alpine yards, rose gardens, order beds, herb and vegetable gardens, a pond, herbaceous and shrub borders, wall plants and an arboretum.

The four glasshouses include the Victoria house, built specially to house the giant Amazon water lilies beloved of generations of small children. Other houses contain succulents, palms, orchids, ferns and alpines. The curvilinear houses, built by Richard Turner in 1848 with additional work which he carried out with his son William 20 years later, are justly world famous. They have been magnificently restored. The Palm House, guarded by the 1870-planted Chusan palm (*Trachycarpus fortunei*) beside it, has also been restored. These elegant houses with their delicate cream paintwork, lacy iron veins and warm granite bases are the pride of the place. A specially developed shade of cream called 'Turner White' was used on the restored houses rather than the previous stark white. The reason for this is that the original paint had oxidised to a similar creamy colour soon after application.

There are so many sights to see at any and all times of the year throughout the garden. It might be a heavily-laden *Cornus kousa* white with flowers or bracts or the line of baby Wollemi pines that will one day be an impressive avenue or the temporary fun of a sunflower maze near the front gate, or the heat of the alpine house full of gravel-mulched pots of special plants. My own magnet is always the rockery. Its mix of gnarled little acers over alpines and small bulbs, low growing, spreading perennials and sub-shrubs always lures me in.

A recent addition to the gardens is the walled fruit and vegetable garden. This garden is run on strict organic principles. They grow over 200 different crops in here, using a range of different organic methods to both feed and protect the plants from pest and disease. It is a fascinating and educational display area.

One of the great features here is the willingness of the staff to stop and explain what they are doing. You will not leave without a tip on how to better grow your own vegetables at home. Look out for the square-foot beds, devoted to showing how many edible plants can be fitted into a postage-stamp sized border. The green manures are worth inspecting too.

There is always something worth seeing, from a temporary garden-related sculpture exhibition or the Viking house to the gardeners laying out a border of exotics for a summer display, almost using rulers to make sure the spacings between plants are perfect.

The Botanic Gardens have been a favourite haunt of Dubliners for centuries. A whole range of people use them, from painting groups studying and sketching the summer borders, to school classes being hauled along for nature walks, horticultural students studying the well-labelled plants and families out for a Sunday walk. If I lived in Dublin it would have to be next door to 'the Bots.'

Primrose Hill

Lucan, Co. Dublin. Tel: 01 6280 373. www.dublingardens.com Contact: Robin and Gay Hall. Open: Feb, one week 2pm-6pm. June-July, daily, 2-6pm. Not wheelchair accessible. Groups welcome, by appointment only.. Supervised children. Special features: House tours for groups. Plants for sale. Directions: In Lucan village, turn into Primrose Lane, opposite the AIB Bank. The garden is at the top of the lane. Buses must park in village as they will not fit up the drive.

On my most recent visit, Gay Hall, was getting ready to receive a group of visitors. The bus driver had announced that the bus would never make it up the drive.

'It's not supposed to make it up the drive. The people need to walk up the drive to see the place properly.' Quite so.

Primrose Hill is one of the favourite gardens among visitors. Attached to a Regency house attributed to the architect James Gandon, it is a plantsman's garden, created over the past 70 years by the Hall family. It has the look of a garden from another age; an old-fashioned, personal place, full of plants, flowers and scent and it starts at the drive.

The impressive, hardworking team of Robin Hall and his wife Gay, tend this stuffed-to-capacity garden. Robin's mother, Cicely, began work here in the 1950s when she took on the long-neglected site, turning it into a garden with a particular leaning towards

old-fashioned cultivars. The garden now has one of the largest collections of small flowering plants in the country, a famous and growing collection of snowdrops, which can be seen during the spring, alongside early narcissi, crocuses and aconites. It also holds a developing five-acre arboretum.

The beds in the walled garden are filled with red lobelia and magenta *Salvia grahamii*, yellow santolina, big papavers in a whole range of shades that do battle with each other in the early summer. Gutsy plant combinations stand out everywhere. *Rosa moyesii* sits in the centre of a border beside campanula and *Crocosmia* 'Lucifer.' Strong colours are more fun with which to work. Gold and pink, purple, yellow and plum mix in and out of each other, showing clearly that a gardener can get away with brazen colours if they approach them thoughtfully.

Plants live cheek-by-jowl in these beds and the weeds have only a small chance of moving in, given that their cultivated brethren have accounted for every bit of space.

Tiptoe over the little stone paths between dangling barriers of angel's fishing rods or dierama. This is a floral assault course, with *Anemone hupehensis* and *Digitalis lutea* self-seeding everywhere in the paving cracks, pushing and shoving for space with tall verbena, *Veratrum californicum* and steely-white eryngium. Masses of early foxglove spires are replaced by seas of phlox later in the summer so it always feels like a crush. You will have difficulty locating the paths at the height of the year.

The ground under Arctic beech and betula, tree peonies, mahonia and sweet-smelling philadelphus, is full of gardener's garters or *Phalaris arundinacea*, pale yellow sisyrinchium, lilies of all sorts and hellebores.

The sunny house wall is covered in an aged vine, intertwined with honeysuckle and together, the two gnarled trunks look like living scaffolding. Close by, in a shady spot, the fernery holds a sizeable collection of natives and exotics, and in front of it, the ground is carpeted with golden oregano, which gives off a wonderful smell when crushed underfoot.

My last visit saw Robin and Gay preparing to welcome a group of enthusiasts. Gay was arranging flowers in preparation. Those lilies were not picked from the garden. Garden flowers are too important to bring indoors.

Royal Hospital Kilmainham

Military Road, Kilmainham, Dublin 8. Tel: 01 6129 900. e-mail: info@imma.ie www.imma.ie Contact: Mary Condron. Open: All year See web for seasonal changes. No entrance fee. Partially wheelchair accessible. Dogs on leads. Special features. Museum of Modern Art. Bookshop. Restaurant. Guided tours can be arranged. Directions: Travelling along St. John's Road West by Heuston Station, turn left onto Military Road. The entrance is 200m along, on the right.

Built by James Butler, the second Duke of Ormond, in the 1690s, the Royal Hospital was modelled on Les Invalides, the retired soldier's hospital in Paris. Similarities between it and the Chelsea Pensioners Home in London are also striking. The Royal Hospital is considered to be Ireland's finest 17th century building. It is a fitting home to the Irish Museum of Modern Art (IMMA).

Lined along the north-facing front of the building, the restored garden stands below the hospital on a shelf of land looking out over the river Liffey and across to the Phoenix Park, which was also laid out as a deer park, by the Kilkenny Duke.

It is known as the Master's Garden and it is a magnificent place, worthy of a visit over and above any visit to the museum. In 1695 the governors of the hospital declared that 'a garden should lie all open to the north side of the Hospital for the greater grace of the house and for the recreation of the retired soldiers'.

Its five acres are formal in fashion, in keeping with the French-style building and, as was also the style, it can be seen and studied in full from the main reception rooms. The layout involves four large squares, each subdivided by horizontal avenues in a *patte d'oie* or goose-foot pattern. Hornbeam hedges along with pleached limes and lines of yew pyramids line the different avenues and they all converge on a central pond. Each path leads up to a focal point which will either be a piece of topiary or classical statuary. The planting is sparse and restrained, as much back-up colour to the hard landscaping as a focus in itself. Box hedges, lollipop-trained holly, statues and bright pale gravel, work together to create and ordered, imposing garden.

The straight lines of trees were given the name of Wilderness. Today the word conjures pictures of wild growth. In the 17th century it described a formal wood. The Master of the Hospital, at the time this feature was being laid out, was the Earl of Meath, who was in the process of carrying out similar work at Kilruddery in Bray.

At one time there would have been a section given over to vegetables grown by the soldiers. Today this is represented in a small sectioned-off herbaceous border, running down one side of the garden. Box-enclosed beds full of tulips, iris, nepeta and rudbeckia replace the cabbage and onions of old.

A wide formal stairway marked by lead urns,

leads down to the garden from the viewing terrace. A group of big chestnuts underplanted with seas of cyclamen, render this terrace a shady, sheltered place in the summer. The huge walls that drop down to the garden are draped and softened by expansive sheets of *Parthenocissus quinquefolia.*

In a garden such as this, upkeep is all. A flower border can go untended for a while and still look good. A garden of formal clipped greenery forgives nothing. It must be tended with clippiness and nail-scissors accuracy. Fortunately the garden enjoys this sort of attention.

Apart from the classical works in the Master's garden, there are some fine contemporary sculptures arranged about the upper gardens. On the way into the garden you will have passed large works by Tony Cragg and Barry Flanagan. A changing display of work is temporarily sited at the fountain in front of the restored tea house.

This tea house is an unusual stone and red-brick folly, the focal point in the garden. It is thought to have been built as a banqueting house. It also housed the gardener and his family in the early 20th century. The view from it, up through the garden is a perfect picture of the Hospital and its towering copper spire.

Outside the walls, the large hilly, wildflower meadow is cut twice yearly but otherwise left to nature. This area was the site of the old hospital graveyard. It leads up to the historic Bully's Acre, the oldest graveyard in Ireland.

Springhill Garden

17, Springhill Park, Killiney, Co. Dublin. Tel: 01 2853 184. Contact: Brian & Patty Maher.
Open: Open days for the OLH Hospice. See website for annual dates. Otherwise by appointment. Not wheelchair accessible. Directions: Off the Main Killiney Road.

Arriving home and looking at the notes taken in Patty Maher's garden I had to remind myself, faced with page after page of notes about different plants, that this was in fact, as it is described in the Hospice brochure, 'a small suburban garden'. The cram is impressive. We made our way between swathes of white hesperis and dierama, lychinis and stachys, scrums of astrantia, and epilobium, phlox and all sorts of hardy geraniums. Patty deploys 'Rozanne' widely and in the cracks between other things, forget-me-nots happily fill in any spare space.

I admired a kiwi or actinidia, and Patty told me that when Carl Dachus asked her what variety it was she was able to tell him 'Tesco'. She loves her roses and I swooned past stands of *Rosa* 'Many Happy Returns' and *R.* 'Gertrude Jekyll', *R. mutabilis* and 'Caroline Testout'. *Rosa* 'Frensham' might not have a scent 'but it flowers on Christmas Day' so she loves it. As Patty claimed, there is indeed no bare earth to be found here and the plants rule supreme.

It is also an attractive garden, filled with scent, busy with pruned-up pittosporums, pollarded *Cornus mas*, and *Sophora japonica*. Every opportunity possible is found to accommodate climbing clematis and roses. Patty gets good value for her acreage.

Interestingly, as an incredibly dry site, standing at the top of a two-metre drop, plants such as *Darmera peltata* and hydrangeas manages to do well here too. Great heaps of compost and mulch seem to have done the trick. Patty is an informative woman, full of tips on how to turn a tiny garden with dry soil into a tropical jungle. I spent an afternoon being charmed by both garden and owner.

Springmount

Rathmichael, Co. Dublin. Tel: 01 2822 032. Contact: Catherine O'Halloran. Open: May-July by appointment. Supervised children. Not wheelchair accessible. Directions: Travelling from Bray, drive up the Old Connaught Road, pass the Old Connaught Golf Club and continue a short distance. The garden is on the right-hand side, with a gate lodge to mark it.

The house at Springmount stands at the bottom of a wide straight drive. Like an interested crowd, all eager to see who is coming down the road, the trees and shrubs along that drive peep out from behind each other, trying to get a better view: Mature *Cornus capitata*, cut-leaf acer, eucryphia and crinodendron, tree heathers and dark cotinus. Underneath, lime coloured mop-head hydrangeas, fuchsias and crinum lilies crane their necks too. It makes for a fine welcome.

The house is covered in heavily-berrying orange cotoneaster, wisteria and jasmine and looks out through all this, onto a set of secret stone steps surrounded in honeysuckle, vinca and ivy, leading up to a secluded woody garden. Hebe and mahonia brighten the area under the canopy of pines.

Climbing up through a combination of one-third stone step, one-third box hedging and one-third mind-your-own business, the way leads in under an arch of *Clematis* 'Duchess of Edinburgh', through an enticing gate and into a big 'wow' of a garden. Spreading out in front is a vision of rolls of box hedge, like a line of police trying to hold back a riotous crowd of herbaceous flowers and shrubs. I noted roses, myrtle, *Clematis viticella* 'Alba Luxurians'

with greeny-white, frilled flowers. The greyish leaves of a backing hedge of cotoneaster foil them nicely. A rose arch over an iron bench provides a perfect corner place to sit and take it all in.

More cotoneaster hedging runs into yew, and another step up in the garden leads to a bench, royally guarded by urns on a little stage, and a sweep of steps snowed under by self-seeding nasturtium and aubrieta. A fountain and raised pond, surrounded by lush hosta and ferns, caught my eye in one quiet, cool spot.

At one point I walked through an arch in a beech hedge and landed in a box garden with a fountain and a summerhouse looking over to a trellis-enclosed little orchard. There are of course roses on the trellis and the apples and pears are old and full of character.

The sunny front of the house is covered in climbers, roses and jasmine being the main candidates. The building stands above, lording it over an informal rockery busy with azalea, penstemon, saxifraga, yet more roses and more fuchsia. Below all this action, the lawn leads to a long arched length of privet, framing a paddock and a view of the woods beyond.

Look out for the 'box' steps. Impractical. Beautiful. Everything a garden should be.

St. Stephen's Green

St. Stephen's Green, Dublin 2. Tel: 01 4757 816. www.heritageireland.ie. Contact: Margaret Gormley Open: All year. See website for seasonal hours. No entrance fee. Wheelchair accessible. Dogs on leads. Special features: Children's playground. Garden for the visually impaired. Concerts. Directions: Accessible from Grafton Street, Merrion Row, Earlsfort Terrace and Harcourt Street.

St. Stephen's Green is a much-loved public park, home to a thousand lunchtime sun-worshippers in summer and to duck-feeding children at all times of the year. The park dates back to the medieval period, when it was used as a common.

In 1663, Dublin Corporation decided to develop St Stephen's Green, building houses within the park and laying out a parade ground and walk as well as a

place of public entertainment, which famously housed a grand fireworks display in 1749. In 1815 the iron railings and the granite, chain-linked bollards outside the Green were erected. The Green was then locked to the public, a move which provoked general discontent. In 1877 Sir Arthur Guinness, Lord Ardilaun, rowed into the fray, declaring that he would pay for the Green's development as a public park. Work began: An artificial lake with a substantial waterfall and rockery was created. Formal flowerbeds and fountains were laid out and erected and a picturesque superintendent's lodge was built. Finally, in 1880, the transformed park was opened to the grateful public.

Only once was the Green involved in important historical events, when Countess Markievicz and the Irish Citizen Army occupied it during the 1916 Easter Rising. Afterwards the superintendent was praised by his superiors for continuing to feed the birds, at the risk of getting shot. Six waterfowl were killed and seven park benches were destroyed in the crossfire, but the superintendent survived.

The park looks much as it did in the time of Lord Ardilaun. At the centre are the formal flowerbeds and two elaborate fountains with beautiful ornamental bulrush spouts. The beds are used for colourful summer bedding; petunia, wallflower and tulips with phormiums as the more permanent fixture. The lake is the central feature of the garden, with its bridges, islands and rock work, all covered by mature shrubs.

The water in the lake is pumped from the Grand Canal.

Despite the sheltering barrier of trees and shrubs, which filter out much of the pollution, there is still enough environmental damage to prevent many specimens of plant from being grown in the Green. A significant number of the trees are London plane, *Platanus × acerifolia,* a species tolerant of pollution. Sycamore is also planted widely, along with evergreen holm oak. New plantings are being made all the time and groves of flowering trees and shrubs are dotted around the park.

A garden for the blind, with aromatic shrubs and herbs labelled in Braille, is a recent feature. There is a good children's playground, and the bandstand is used for performances throughout the summer. A sculpture trail including a bust of Countess Markievicz can be followed around the park with the help of an information panel at the Harcourt Street entrance. A series of information panels have been erected recently, telling the history and sundry stories about the park.

St. Anne's Park

Mount Prospect Avenue, Clontarf, Dublin 9. Tel: 01 8331 859. Open: All year until dusk. No entrance fee. Wheelchair accessible. Dogs on leads. Special features: Café. International Rose Trials in July. Lectures. Tours. Directions: Entrances on Mount Prospect Avenue and All Saints Road.

Covering 300 acres, almost half the size of the Phoenix Park, St. Anne's is a huge suburban park. Previously owned by the Guinness family, today it is cared for by the city and run by the Dublin City Council's Parks and Landscape service.

In the 1970s a man called Leslie Mitchell, of the Clontarf Horticultural Society, began the push to create a rose garden here on a grand scale. The resulting rose garden covers 14 acres and holds over 25,000 rose bushes in hybrid teas, floribundas, patio and ground-cover varieties, together with old garden cultivars. These days, the small number of workers available to care for the garden is not enough to maintain everything in order. I could gripe but I suppose the Council needs to divide its resources. A volunteer scheme perhaps?

Other interesting features at St. Anne's include a walled flower garden with a quaint clock tower. The last two times I visited however, both times during summer months, the gates were closed and I could not gain entry. The pond, rockery and and wood garden are wild and attractive. The sunken garden was being restored. I look forward to seeing it again. The trees are magnificent with yew and chestnut walks and a millennium arboretum among the very many sights.

The International Rose Trials held in July are a good opportunity to enjoy the flowers. Guided tours, talks, lectures and clinics on rose care are given at this time of year.

The Talbot Botanic Gardens Malahide Demesne

Dublin Road, Malahide, Co. Dublin. Tel: 01 8169 538. Garden Open: All year. Daily from 9.30am-5.30pm. Wheelchair accessible. Dogs on leads. Special features: Historic castle. Tea room. Craft shops. Tours of garden by appointment. Events. Directions: Driving from Fairview to Malahide, turn right at the sign for Malahide Castle. The entrance is on the left.

The castle at Malahide was lived in continuously by the Talbot family from the 1180s, when the lands were granted to Richard Talbot by the English Crown, until 1973 when the last of the family, Lord Milo de Talbot, died.

Despite the lengthy history of the demesne, the gardens, as seen today, are young, largely created by Lord Milo between 1947 and 1973. He was a learned and enthusiastic gardener who set out to create a garden full of tender and less common plants, many of them from Tasmania, New Zealand and Australia; all countries with which he had connections.

The variety of plants in Malahide is limited by the alkalinity of the soil, which is measured at 6.97 pH. This prevents the growing of acid-loving plants. In Malahide, visitors with alkaline soil in their own gardens for once need not be green-eyed at the numbers of plants on show that they cannot grow themselves. Genera well represented here include euphorbia, crocosmia, hebe, pittosporum, escallonia. It also homes the National Collections of olearia and clematis.

The gardens are divided into the pleasure grounds and the walled garden. The pleasure grounds, covering about 19 acres, are made up of varied rides and paths that meander between a bewildering number of species of trees and shrubs.

The walled garden is an exceptionally fine feature. It covers almost four acres and is divided into herbaceous and mixed beds, a spectacularly densely planted pond and the Australian garden. The collection of greenhouses, alpine and sunken houses scattered through the gardens, are for many visitors, the high points of the visit. The auricula house is like a sweet shop of delights. The Victorian greenhouse is an old one, donated to the garden by nuns in Blackrock in a grand example of re-cycling and reconstruction.

The list of superlative plants in this is a long one and the visitor falls from one to another. The rare trees include a fine *Cladrastis sinensis*. See it in June to admire the pea-like flowers. In autumn and spring its foliage is golden and dramatic. Its wood is also yellow, hence its common name - the yellow wood tree. It was a present to Lord Talbot from Hillier's nursery in England. The pittosporum hedge is another feature worth noting.

The Haggard is a small area within the walled garden and in here one of the great sights is the *Clematis nepalensis,* which carries hellebore-like yellow flowers on bare stems in December. *Rubus lineatus* is another lesser spotted shrub. The greenhouse was built by Lord Talbot in the 1960s and the planting has been held to that historic period. The organic regime worked here involves leaving the windows open from May to October, the employment of *Encarsia formosa* wasps, along with regular misting to stop red spider mite. One of the most notable things about Malahide is that they work almost completely without chemicals. Getting at the weeds and diseases early and often is the answer.

Incredible feats seem to be what this garden is about: Lord Talbot wrote 12,000 individual cards with the details of each specimen he collected and planted in his lifetime. These cards were detailed down to the price paid for each item. They have been gathered into a computer record to make an important academic resource.

Out in the pond garden the list of impressives increases more with the presence of a *Euonymus lucidus*. This is a tender shrub that lives outside here positioned against a sunny sheltered wall.

In the quaintly named chicken yard the rarities include a collection of Chilean plants like a *Berberidopsis cordifolia*, embothrium and an ancient-looking, gnarled leptospermum that overhangs the gravel path like an arch. The tower was thought to be a 14th century building. Recently they discovered that it was a 17th century pigeon house. Outside the wall look for the olearia collection and an *Escallonia revoluta* that experts from Kew say is the biggest in Europe.

Development and discovery are constant and

ongoing. The uncovering of eight fireplaces along the wall in the Alpine Garden gave rise to some interest. These were used to light fires to create smoke and deter frost from the tender plants in the little garden.

The newly created Cambridge house should not be missed, with its collection of treasures including a nearly extinct *Banksia serrata* which has a remarkable looking bark and fine scent. Although if it is perfume you want, arrive in September and die happy in the magnificent aroma of the well named *Luculia grandiflora* that also lives in here.

40 Templeroan Avenue

Knocklyon, Dublin 16, Co. Dublin. Contact: Caroline McMahon.
e-mail: carolinemcmahon100@yahoo.co.uk Open: One day in June for the sammcmahontrust.ie See the website for annual details and directions.

The overriding sense in Caroline McMahon's garden is one of order. She clearly takes no nonsense from her plants. I fell for the skill with which she inserts each plant and combination in her town garden, so that they all work to contribute to an overall pleasing picture, never allowed to run riot or dominate. She builds walls and structures with plants. Clipped and trained, deployed to carry out certain tasks, her shrubs and flowers work together to create a restful, handsome green retreat. There is flower and bloom here but not too much, Caroline's chief talent is in working with foliage, mixing textures and subtle shades, shapes, light and shade.

'They follow the rules,' she confided in me as I admired a particular composition of plants.

'I suppose I should probably say that I have a problem with topiary' she disclosed. If she does it is not in getting it right, but in limiting herself. The place is full of lollipops and columns, balls and pyramids, in ligustrum and yew, box and bay. They emerge from over soft mounds of hosta foliage and mounded Japanese acers. They peep from the side of the prettiest pale green painted shed which is an unusual squat shape, which makes the garden around it look bigger.

On the business of snipping, she informed me that *Cercis canadensis* is a small tree that 'you can snip as much as you like.'

You could perhaps sit under the *Robinia* 'twisty baby' by the back door, with its twinkling magic lights lighting up the branches, and think it all just happened, or walk under the arch of perfectly clipped variegated holly, over step-stones that seem to have squished into a gravel cushion, between perfectly shaped and clipped holly and box, euonymus and airy *Cornus controversa* 'Variegata'.

There are only dots of colour, from hydrangea and *Salvia* 'Hot Lips', to an occasional urn of red pelargonium, or a few wands of *Verbena bonariensis*. Colour is sprinkled around in sparing doses and the overall feeling in this smart garden is of greenery. Catherine admitted that she will occasionally clip the grass edge with a scissors. It shows. Perfection is the word that continued to bubble up as I walked around.

Add to this gorgeous creation, a crew of generous sisters who parachute in bearing delicious cakes for the annual busy charity day. The cakes, I am told are legendary.

Ticknock Garden

*Ticknock Hill, Co. Dublin. Tel: 01 2956 152. 086 8574 999. e-mail: info@previewco.com
Contact: Carmel Buttimer and James Grant. Open: Fri. 2-4.30 pm June-Aug. Partially wheelchair
accessible. Directions: e-mail for directions. GPS co ordinates: N53. 14.901 W6 15.17*

A garden 1,200 feet above sea level, Ticknock enjoys a remarkable position, just below the tree line and looking out over the whole of Dublin Bay. I cannot imagine how wonderful the glittery view of the bay must be at night. It is quite a sight during daylight hours. The garden is on the site of a Victorian gamekeeper's cottage.

Carmel and James came to live here in 1993 when the house was almost lost in the middle of a plantation of mature Sitka spruce. They were able to take out most of the trees, replacing them with broad leaf specimens in the outer acres of the large plot, but keeping the inner two acres of garden open and available for Carmel's new garden.

The price you pay for a view over the bay is that the garden faces north and gets very little sun from around Halloween onward. *Rhododendron ponticum* and gorse had to be removed and a deer-proof fence erected. Carmel began by building granite walls and ledges around the blank site and then she started to to garden.

Close to the house, we looked at the Japanese inspired pond, a natural feature with a fine red acer, *Kirengeshoma palmatum*, *Actaea spicata*, a range of azaleas and *Hydrangea villosa*. The ground around the gate seemed to be nothing but mud and instinct told her to plant it with candelabra primulas and arums. She also discovered that *Rhododendron arboreum* can live in damp too.

A whole series of paths lead between the different ledged terraces built into the steep hill. They allow you to see each garden from a different vantage point, above and below. Mixed beds of recumbent juniper berberis and *Cornus controversa* 'Variegata' paint a different picture from these vantage points. The whole series of wide and easy-to-negotiate paths come courtesy of her architect husband James. They lead past a range of flower and shrub beds, like islands in the rock-studded grass and guide us past maturing acer, liriodendron, hoheria and magnolia. The garden, at its altitude, is a late one: Philadelphus flowers not in early, but in late summer.

At the very bottom of the slope is where the tropical surprise sits, a little stone seating area beside a pond. This is the only wind-free spot in the whole place, filled with the scent of *Trachelospermum jasminoides* and the mad good looks of *Aralia spinosa*.

The views back and forth, up and down along the garden, are well thought out. It is a different garden at every turn. With its Ph and granite base, it is excellent for all acid-loving magnolias and camellias. Carmel has laid out rose, shrub and flower beds all around the house so that the views out, be they from bedroom or kitchen, are of acers, clouds of roses, hydrangeas and fluffs of hardy geranium.

Above the building, as it makes it way up the hill, she is currently working on a new garden, a wild place, where she is simply slipping shrubs into the rough boulder-strewn scrub. This is where her rhododendron, hydrangea and acer wood will grow. Watch this space

Tyrrelstown House

Powerstown Road, Tyrrelstown, Dublin 15. Tel: 01 8213 206. 086 2412 000.   *e-mail:info@* *tyrrelstownhouse.ie Contact: Olive or Mark Wilkinson. Open: Feb-Oct. By appointment to groups. Open days: 3rd Fri. and Sat., Feb-Sept. Special features: Daffodil Day. Venue hire. Plants, honey and eggs for sale. Teas can be arranged. Directions: Take Mulhuddart Exit 3 off the N3. Turn right at the lights and follow the R121 onto Cruiserath Road. At the roundabout (top of Damestown Ave.) take the third exit onto Powerstown Road. The house is on right after 2ⁿᵈ speed bump.*

There is a string of fine gardens dotted the length of the chaotic M50 and the tentacles that lead off it. So close and yet so far from the traffic and din, you will hear no racket louder than the birds, and there is nothing more jarring on the eye than a colour clash in a border. Mark and Olive Wilkinson's Tyrrelstown House is one such garden. Leave the hassled world outside and drive up an oak avenue, catching sight of specimen trees and white flower borders along the boundary lawns as you go.

The garden proper, begins to the side of the Georgian house under its huge blanket of *Parthenocissus tricuspidata*. A sweep of curved beech hedge and a little rose garden tucked into its shelter plays the part of appetiser. Over a mile of hedging stretches its way around this garden Mark told me, in the manner of a man concerned with its upkeep. We made our way in through a gate leading to a blue garden, all different shades of blue hydrangea, agapanthus, geranium, and wisteria. The rich acid soil is indicated by the number of thriving magnolias and camellias, embothriums and rhododendrons. King of the jungle here is however the grand old *Magnolia soulangeana*, with branches that drape and creep along the ground.

Curved gravel paths meander between these and runs of lawn, with more hydrangeas, hazy catmint or nepeta and peonies. In the spring, the ground is thick with bulbs, all zinging and colourful while the magnolias and acers are still in their wispy winter mode.

If Mark is the person who deals with trees, Olive is the flower expert and there are flowers in abundance, from the white beds out front and the herbaceous borders full of rudbeckia and asters, phlox and hardy geraniums, to big flowering shrubs, climbers and roses.

Generations of Wilkinsons have had fun working this garden, and what we had walked through at this point was just the first of two walled gardens. We continued into the second, older garden, where the walls are, in places, over 500 years old. In here, alongside more flower borders, they grow the vegetables, fruit trees and a handkerchief tree or *Davidia involucrata* that Mark has moved three times so far. His love of trees follows on from his father and we met a *Metasequoia glyptostroboides* that his father planted as part of a young and developing arboretum. Mark continues working on it. As old as the two walled gardens and various stone buildings around the house are, they are mere babies in comparison to the Norman keep that the garden is built on.

22 Weston Park

Churchtown, Dublin 1. Tel: 087 285 3834. e-mail: Contact: Olive Fitzpatrick Open: Under the OLH Garden Trail Scheme. See Hospice brochure for annual details and directions.

If you find yourself standing in the middle of a city garden with houses in front of you and houses behind you, and yet no houses can be seen, a deal of credit needs to be given to the maker. Kidnapped, blindfolded and set free into this garden I could have been in the tropics. Standing on the verandah behind Olive Fitzpatrick's house, looking out at the expansive umbrella of tree ferns and bamboos, fountains of huge *Hosta* 'Big Daddy' leaves, ricinus, *Tetrapanax rex* and a little Buddha on a plinth, I half expected to be offered tiffin, or spot a monkey scamper down a branch, rather than the blackbird that actually hopped past.

Olive's is a garden that I would happily move into and just stay. She has turned an approximate 150 metre long by 10 metres wide garden behind her suburban house into the most perfect version of a lush green garden I know.

Space is at a premium and so she clips up and hems in many of the shrubs. Carefully chosen trees from Sorbus 'Joseph Rock', *Pseudoacacia contorta* and fastigiate cypresses are deployed to block out any possible views of buildings in the vicinity. Arches hosting wisteria and roses are also used to obscure and block these views. She is entirely successful in creating a perfect secret city garden.'I spend my time looking for gaps and then I fill them,' she smiled. She fills them with suitable good-looking shrubs from *Garrya elliptica* and various cut-leaf acers, with hostas and *Dryopteris wallichiana*. Within the restrictions of space there are greenhouses and sheds, each of which lies camouflaged behind planting, only visible on approach. The football sized flowers on the agapanthus by the greenhouse, are first rate.

Like a sonnet, sometimes the best creativity springs from working within a tight set of rules and restrictions.

Kildare

Burtown House

Ballytore, Athy, Co. Kildare. Tel: 059 862 3148. e-mail: info@burtownhouse.ie www.burtownhouse.ie Contact: Lesley Fennell. Open: See website for changing annual details. Partially wheelchair accessible. Supervised children. Special Features: Snowdrop Week February. Gallery. Artist's studio. Shop. Restaurant. Farm walks. Plant sales. Directions: Travelling south on the M9, leave at Junction 3 and follow signs for Athy. Take the 2nd turn to the left, signposted 'Burtown House'.

The gardens at Burtown are more interesting than most. They consist of several separate garden areas around the Georgian house, each created by different members of the Fennell family. Lesley is however, the chief gardener and the person in charge of most of the gardens, including the large sunny borders around the house, the rock and woodland gardens, the formal hedging and topiary areas, the orchards, water gardens and rose walks.

The area around, and up against the house is pretty, with drifts of irises, peonies, thalictrum and alliums predominating. The wall planting includes a gigantic ancient wisteria and *Schisandra rubriflora* with scarlet flowers. Growing on the north-facing wall, this plant still reaches out about three metres and seems to thrive in the dry shade. It even survived the winter of 2010, enduring temperatures of minus 16. The lawns out from these beds are, in turn bounded by six mixed borders that hold some special plants including a tree peony named for Lesley's mother, *Paeonia* 'Wendy Walsh'.

The garden steps down from here in several ledges with a line of young limes that form an avenue out towards a natural swimming pond, a juvenile arboretum and wildflower meadow.

We took a wide gravelled walk between trimmed and trained young yews, away from the house, to a cross path under a pergola. The formality and tidiness of the yew walk balances the heaving floral bulk of the pergola, under the burden of *Rosa* 'Albertine' and clematis. Underneath there are informal splashes of *Hesperis matronalis*, tulips, miniature irises and double primroses. Beyond this is the orchard, full of venerable-looking apple trees in a daffodil and crocus meadow.

The next garden features a sunken, stone slab patio, full of self-seeding wild strawberries, hardy geraniums and *Alchemilla mollis*. The *Magnolia wilsonii* and some other light shrubs, form a grove to one side of this, adding height without enclosing the area too much. The family are related to the Shackletons so it is appropriate to find phlox from Beech Park, the famous Shackleton garden in Dublin.

Beyond the stone house is the oldest area in the garden - The big wood, set on an island with several bridges leading to it. It is a magical sort of place whose damp banks are full of trilliums, ferns, hostas and impressively tall *Cardiocrinum giganteum*. In spring there are plenty of hellebores too. Lesley added some pretty *Anemone nemorosa* 'Lucy's Wood' and an unnamed white double anemone. Erythroniums and epimediums do well under the tall beech trees, the homes of numerous bat, bird, and owl boxes.

The next garden is in the old stable yard. This is a sheltered high-walled square where James has been experimenting with a formal planting of pruned up and staked specimens of two-metre tall ligustrum, or privet, underplanted with lavender around a square of lawn. Its marked formality is in interesting relief to the looser feel of the garden outside the walls.

The walled kitchen garden close by is where the business of producing purple sprouting broccoli, leeks, beans, asparagus, currants and rhubarb for the restaurant goes on.

Moving from the kitchen garden back toward the house, the path takes in more flower gardens and an almost secret, semi-wooded area of acer, bamboo, shade-loving plants and a great spreading white-flowering cherry. With a flat head about ten-metres across; it casts a gentle shade over big spreads of snowdrops, aconites, bluebells and lily-of-the-valley.

Before I left, Lesley showed me a tree that has a special place here: It is an Oregon maple or *Acer macrophyllum*, a baby of the famous maple in the Front Square in Trinity College. Along with some other seedlings, her father found it on a rubbish tip in the college and transplanted it to an altogether finer life in a field below the house at Burtown, beside a beech and bluebell wood.

Castletown House

Celbridge, Co. Kildare. Tel: 01 628 8252. e-mail: info@castletown.ie or castletown@opw.ie
Open: All year. See website for annual opening times. Partially wheelchair accessible. Children welcome.
Dogs on leads. Special Features: Free admission to grounds. Headquarters of Irish Georgian Society. Café.
House tours. Events. Directions: From the M4 take Exit 6 signposted for Castletown. Stay in the left hand
lane and before the top of the slip road go into the third left lane. Gates are on the right.

Castletown House is one the finest houses in the country. Under the guardianship of the Georgian Society for decades, until a few years ago, it was not a widely visited garden venue. The grounds have, however been undergoing a major restoration in the past few years. It is a pleasure to see the revival of a once grand 18th century landscape park. There have been excavations, archaeological digs and reconstruction projects on garden features first laid out by 17-year-old Lady Louisa Conolly in the 1760s.

The serpentine pond once again, runs through the park finishing off in the gloomy and romantic wood beside the house. A series of cascades, waterfalls and dams were rebuilt along its length and a rustic stone bridge, that only a few years ago was little more than a cipher, is now restored, complete and handsome. Scruff and tatty growth have been removed from the park, uncovering forgotten vistas not seen in 100 years. These include a view of the lime avenue down to the picturesque schoolhouse on the edge of Celbridge village. It was almost completely obscured by self-sown trees until recently.

Paths through the grounds and along the Liffey were all unearthed, using clues from 18th century maps. Some of these paths allow views along the river that had also been lost long ago. One leads to an old bathing house. A little way along, an elegant Doric temple was being re-plastered when I visited and close by, a brick ice house was being repaired so that visitors will eventually be able to see how these landscape features-cum-estate facilities operated. The ha-ha, or sunken fence, once almost forgotten under self-seeded trees, has been brought back from the brink.

As I made my way through the grounds with the OPW architect, we bumped into Peter Kelly walking his dogs. Peter, now retired, comes from Castletown. He worked here as a young man and in recent years has become something of an unofficial advisor to the OPW. The architect quizzed him regarding the direction of an old drain and he was able to throw all sorts of light on its workings.

80 years passed in Castletown without any trees being planted. This is now being rectified. Beech and oak are being planted in numbers. As a result of all this the demesne is now a fascinating 'new' old garden.

Coolcarrigan House

Coolcarrigan, Coill Dubh, Naas, Co. Kildare. Contact: Robert Wilson-Wright. Tel: 045 863524.
e-mail: www@coolcarrigan.ie Open: As per website and at other times by appointment only. Supervised
children. Dogs on leads. Special features: Group lunches and tours by arrangement. Directions: Drive
from Clane to Prosperous and continue to the crossroads by the Dag Weld pub, from where Coolcarrigan
is signposted. Go through Coill Dubh. Pass the church. The garden is a short distance along on the left,
marked by black gates.

The Wilson-Wright family has been gardening at Coolcarrigan for six generations. Today, that history can be seen in the classic Victorian garden, the rockeries, lily pond, herbaceous borders, lawns, greenhouses and a collection of of shrubs and trees that runs to thousands.

The present owner, Robert Wilson-Wright, is the most recent member of the family to continue the tradition of gardening here. Minding an inheritance is important but Robert displays an infectious enthusiasm for the garden that stretches well beyond guardianship. In the last decade, he has added a further six acres and 250 species of trees to the growing venture. Pooled knowledge and work over such a long period gives this garden a special place in Irish horticulture as well as its own unique personality.

A visit begins with the more intimate area around the house. The chief attraction here is the border, a classic assembly of blue delphinium spires, bell-like campanulas, geums, dahlias, blue *Clematis integrifolia*, California tree poppies or *Romneya coulteri* and a host of other border flowers that are on the go from early summer to late autumn. It is flanked by a striking strawberry tree or *Arbutus unedo*, with tiny white flowers, edible strawberry fruit and a bark like a huge cinnamon stick.

Nearby the greenhouse is divided into separate, smaller houses. A memory of its being perfect on previous visits must have been mistaken because recently Robert took it apart, restored it and raised the roof height so that today, it is even more impressive than I remember. Along with the original grape vine, planted when the greenhouse was built in 1900, there are scented ginger lilies, peaches and a collection of passion flowers, which include the banana passion flower, *Passiflora antioquiensis*, a plant with deep pink flowers that frill out like tutus. Another specimen is the bizarre-looking *Passiflora quadrangularis* the flowers of which feature filaments like purple-and cream-striped jellyfish tentacles. There are also succulents and a pineapple guava or *Acca sellowiana* with edible, fairly tasty flowers.

The view out from the greenhouse takes in a naturalistic pond cut straight into the turf. The planting around the rim is sparse and for the most part restricted to grass. A few lilies decorate the water,

but generally, restraint has been shown and the water remains clear to reflect the sky and surrounding trees. In the damp lawns around it, wild orchids grow in almost weed-like numbers. There are several varieties here including pyramidal orchids (*Anacamptis pyramidalis*), common spotted orchids (*Dactylorhiza fuchsii*) and common twayblade or *Listera ovata*. Robert has implemented a light touch policy in the care of the extensive lawns and meadows and the effect on the wild flower population has been remarkable. He carries out just one cut in the summer. This is labour-saving and environmentally beneficial.

In the thicket beyond the pond we climbed in between shrubs to see a rare *Berberis valdiviana*, with unusual long yellow flowers and, close by another rarity, *Syringa pinnatifolia*. The plant expert Roy Lancaster fell in love with this when he visited the garden many years ago. Some time later, when re-introduced to the Wilson-Wrights, he remembered them as the owners of the shrub. It is that special.

While the main garden at Coolcarrigan is based on limestone, there is one area where the soil is acid, due to a pocket of bog. They planted it up with rhododendron and spring bulbs for an early year show. Many of these are planted around the two lakes that Robert created in recent years.

The arboretum, for which the garden is justly well known has benefited from a long time relationship with the British plantsman Sir Harold Hillier, whose knowledge contributed hugely to the significance of the Coolcarrigan collection. In recent years Robert has concentrated on a number of rarer oaks from South America. He is also working on thinning the larger old park trees to allow light spill down and the newly freed-up space in the lower levels. This is being planted with choice cotoneasters, magnolias, rare *Heptacodium miconioides*, *Nyssa sylvatica*, and varieties of sorbus. We revelled in the smell of the best smelling barley sugar tree or *Cercidiphyllum japonicum* I have ever come across and then I discovered that the tree was almost 50 metres away. In the walled garden Robert has developed a nuttery, with cobnuts and hazelnuts, Irish apple varieties, damsons and medlars.

Before leaving we went to inspect the new arboretum, where he has been creating paths through a large meadow and planting new trees. How it will look in 20 years he has no idea, but has this not always been the way with planting long term features like arboreta?

Burtown House

The Japanese Gardens & St. Fiachra's Garden

Brallistown Little, Tully, Co. Kildare. Tel: 045 521617/522963.
e-mail: dwardell@irishnationalstud.ie. www.irish-national-stud.ie Contact: David Wardell. Open: Feb-Dec. 23, daily 9am-5pm. Wheelchair accessible. Guide dogs only. Special features: Self-guided tours in ten languages. Guided tours. Café. Shop. Directions: On the edge of Kildare town, signposted clearly off the N7.

In 1906 Colonel William Hall Walker of Tully in Kildare, a man with a keen interest in Japanese gardens, brought a Japanese gardener, Tassa Eida, along with his family, to Ireland to create a Japanese garden on the Kildare plains. Tassa worked with 40 men for four years to develop the garden. The stories about his stay in Ireland are legion. He arrived as a man who neither drank nor backed horses and left, a poor man with a taste for both. But he also left a wonderful Japanese garden. In 2010 it celebrated its 100th birthday and some members of his family travelled from Japan to see the garden their ancestor built.

The miniature landscape is heavily laden with symbolism and meaning, based on the journey through life from birth to death. The symbolism is optional however and the place can be enjoyed simply as a garden full of handsome shrubs, trees, topiary and bonsai, waterside planting, paths and statuary. The garden is seen from a winding path that trails along, rising and falling, over and around rocky outcrops, past trees with carefully exposed root runs. By making choices about which path to take, you can visit different areas, each of which relates to a time in the life of man. A delicate teahouse, the site of occasional tea-making ceremonies, sits high on one outcrop overlooking the different gardens. It is surrounded by bonsai, some of which have been in the garden since 1906. The paths are rocky, moss covered and fern studded, sometimes picking their way up hills, sometimes partially submerged as stepping-stones through the hosta-lined stream. There is even a little raked gravel garden.

This is one of the busiest gardens in the country, attracting huge numbers of visitors each year. If you want to avoid the crowds, time your visit. Go on an out-of-season Monday or Tuesday. The garden does not depend on flowers or plants that should be seen in the summer, so a trip off-season will be just as rewarding, and perhaps even more enjoyable, particularly in early autumn when the acers begin to colour.

Attached to the Japanese Garden is the larger St. Fiachra's Garden. This is a wood dedicated to St. Fiachra, the Irish saint, known in France as the patron saint of gardening. This large, wild place has an artless and natural feel. The design is of simple walks through plantations of native oak, ash and willow. A lake, fed by natural springs, dominates the centre and the water has been trained over small waterfalls, with rock pools sited about the edges.

Simplicity is again the keyword for the planting by the lake. The woods are full of spring bulbs, wild garlic, aconites and wood anemone that have spread and naturalised under the light canopy. Fossilised trees stand like sculptures, giving the place an air of history and something ancient. Three beehive huts sit at one end of the lake, reminiscent of the monastic cells in which St. Fiachra and his monks might have lived. As this garden grows, it grows in charm.

While you are at the Japanese Gardens visit the Irish National Stud. Remarkably, people need to be told to be sensible. There is a sign at one of the fences reading 'DANGER! Horses bite and kick.'

Larchill Arcadian Gardens

Kilcock, Co. Kildare. Contact: Michael or Louisa de Las Casas. Tel: 01 6287 354. e-mail: delascas@indigo. www.larchill.ie Open: Summer Thur-Sun. Sept. Weekends only. Groups any time by appointment. Supervised children. Special features: Historic demesne. Rare-breed animals. Lecture hall. Poultry fairs. Directions: Take the Dunshaughlin Road from Kilcock and travel 5 km. Look for the signposts on the right.

Larchill is an unusual place, the only surviving example of an 18th century *ferme orné* or ornamental farm, on the island. This is a particular type of decorative landscape conceived as part of the Romantic movement. A garden like this is made up of walks and rides laid out around a park in which a series of follies and temples, grottos and mock castles are the focal points. There are framed views, monuments and ornamental plant schemes. Larchill was built between 1740 and 1780 by the Prentice family, a flax-growing Quaker family. It amounts to 60 acres of parkland, woods, canals and pleasure grounds. The lake alone covers eight acres.

Over time and periods of neglect, the *ferme* was almost obliterated until, in 1992, when the de Las Casas family took over the property and brought in garden historian Paddy Bowe who confirmed it to be a lost *ferme orné*. The lost lake was restored and various of the features were unearthed.

As a result, today we can enjoy a whole series of follies dotted around the park, situated in the woods, around the lake and in the park. These follies are strange and unusual, none more so than the fortification known as 'Gibraltar' set on an island in the lake, complete with battlements, turrets and gun ports. Apparently the family used to fight mock wars out here. The other folly is a classic circular temple. Did the Gibraltar folk fight with the Templars? Why the name Gibraltar? Was it due to the shape of the island, or as part of a literary conceit or cipher that displayed the owner's education and good taste? Such references were littered through gardens at this time. They were to tease and entertain visitors, testing classical knowledge and rewarding intellect.

Today the temples, gazebos and little structures are simply romantic. The Fox's Earth is bound in all sorts of wonderful stories about how someone, guilty about the number of foxes he had killed on the hunt, hoped that if he was reincarnated as a fox, he could escape in safety to live in the Fox's Earth. Are the stories with or without substance? Who cares for solid truth when there is colourful conjecture?

The bizarre animal pens and houses, including moated piggeries and little castles on top of which the resident goats stand, surveying the rest of the farm, are quaint. Hen-houses have gangways, walkways and look-out points, all castellated and self-regarding stuff for the pompous-looking fowl that reside there. It is posh and daft in equal measure. Meanwhile, the walled garden is charming and has benefited from a great deal of restoration work. Flower and shrub borders run around the boundaries and in the centre, there is a sunken box garden and pond with classical statuary. The flowers and herbs are arranged prettily. Fruit trees trained on wires divide the spaces between the smaller gardens, within the larger walled space and a fine rose walk.

At one end of the garden is an ornate dairy with stained-glass window. (See also Killruddery, Co. Wicklow). A herbaceous border runs the length of the walls, leading off from the dairy. At one corner the shell tower is unfortunately fragile but pretty in a faded sort of way. An intriguing set of steps leads up to the tower, which is at the present, off limits to visitors. I love its little revolving window.

The walled garden has a quirky and otherworldly feeling as befits a garden attached to something as whimsical as a *ferme orné*.

Lodge Park Walled Garden & Steam Museum

Straffan, Co. Kildare. Tel: 01 6288 412. e-mail: info@steam-museum.ie www.steam-museum.ie Open: May and Sept. Weekends. June-Aug. Fri-Sun and Bank Holidays, 2-6pm. Last entry 5.30pm. Wheelchair accessible. Supervised children. Horticultural and engineering students free entry. Special features: Steam museum and small shop. Steaming Kettle Teahouse Sun. and Mon. of Bank Holidays or by appointment. Directions: Straffan is signposted from the Kill flyover on the M7 at Junction 7, and from the Maynooth flyover on the N4 at Junction 7. It is approximately 8 km from both places. Follow 'Steam Museum' signs.

Before even entering the garden you have to be intrigued at the sight of a grumpy looking gargoyle in the wall, while high above, a weather vane swivels above a clock tower in the courtyard and at its summit a lovely fat pig, painted with the quartered family crest points out the wind direction. I thought of Trumpton and Chigley. Note too the small hole at the base of the wall through which the resident hens can trot in and out to get to their house, safe from the local hen-hating spaniel. You cannot but enter in happy expectation of a good visit. Open the heavy iron gate that leads inside. Duck in under tendrils of hanging *Vitis coignetiae*. Suddenly, in contrast to the handsome but stark exterior of the Palladian house overlooking paddocks and parkland, you are in a perfect old-fashioned walled garden.

The walled garden at Lodge Park dates to the 1770s but it was restored in the 1940s and again in the 1980s. It is a charming, relaxed flower garden.

A visit begins at the top of the long rectangular garden, along a path that runs its length, with various gardens leading away from the path to the centre of the garden as it makes way along.

The first picture is of a white garden full of lychnis and exochorda, frothy white potentilla, creamy agapanthus, sedum, lamb's ears, phlox, stock, anemone, white borage, rock roses and white variegated agave. This white extravaganza is built around an ornamental stone well-head. The greenhouse next to it is unusual. The outer wall is marked by a water-spouting lizard, spitting water into a rectangular lily pond. The path around the pond is edged with splashes of argyranthemums and an exquisite red passion flower (*Passiflora antioquiensis*). On a warm day with the sound of water, this corner feels quite exotic.

The path meanwhile, continues on, under an iron 'spider web' arch covered by *Rosa* 'Francois Juranville'

and on past a lean-to greenhouse on the south wall. This small house is an Aladdin's cave full of cuttings and baby plants from early spring. In the early months of the year, there is not an inch of space to be found between pots of plectranthus, little argyranthemum cuttings, alpine pelargoniums and salvias. They spend their first months in here with the huge bird of paradise or *Strelitzia reginae,* before being planted into containers to stand outside the steam museum for the summer. Outside this propagation house, on the red-brick south-facing wall there are trained greengages soaking up the heat.

The double, north-to-south borders are quite lovely. Backed by *Sambucus niger* 'Black Lace', they have been planted up with purple and blue iris, salvia, dahlia, eupatorium, forget-me-not and cornflower. Alliums, particularly *A.* 'Purple Sensation' add an

extra zing to the more solid colour blocks. *Verbena bonariensis* is allowed to seed about, giving the effect of a purple gauze over the borders. The black elders are pruned in spring to produce the best foliage. The font from St. Jude's Church nearby, stands in the middle of the wide grass dividing path.

Beyond it one can see a sharply clipped beech hedge with an opening that invites investigation. But the path, bordered by huge, clipped yews and its own beckoning gate in the distance keeps you on the main trail, down past a line of good looking shrubs including a magnolia, *Garrya elliptica* and abutilon, a tall trachycarpus and knotty corokia. In front of, and under these there are runs of alstroemeria and hesperis.

Then there is the *roseraie*, a sort of crown made of metal struts built to support *Rosa* 'Rambling Rector', *R.* 'Belvedere' and *R.* 'Alister Stella Grey'. Up close, it is like a sort of floral maze and it drenched with flowers from mid-June.

Eventually the path reaches the gateway and beyond the herbaceous border and tennis court over which it looks. In contrast to the darker double borders, this is all pinks and pale blues. There are campanulas and crambe, nepeta and early daffodils, all standing in front of a gigantic *Rosa* 'Felicite et Perpetue'.

This leads back into the main garden, around and through the *roseraie*, and from there into the north bed where the damp and shade-loving plants do best. There are lines of different hydrangeas from *Hydrangea aspera* 'Villosa' and *H. paniculata* sharing with *Schizophragma hydrangeoides* and Irish yew. Beneath these, hostas and hellebores smother the ground with their large leathery leaves. The perfect beech hedge, seen earlier is here again, visible from the other side and the opening in it draws the eye back out the sunny borders, past a line of both young and old apples, quinces and plums in the orchard.

Before leaving, take a tour around the steam museum and its intriguing tiny model of an old bath, copper cylinder and water heating mechanism!

Rathbawn Gardens

Kilteel, Co. Kildare. Tel: 0857109728. e-mail: rathbawngardens@gmail.com
www.facebook.com/RathbawnGardens. Contact: Ciaran Farrelly. Open: For occasional charity days. By
appointment to groups at other times. See Facebook page for annual details. Not wheelchair accessible.
Special features. Refreshments and plants for sale at open days. Directions: Signed from Kilteel on open
days.

New large gardens are a rarity and all the more exciting for that. Kathleen and Joseph Reynolds began gardening when they moved here, becoming more and more committed to the garden as the years went by and today they not only work it but have roped in a talented gardener Ciaran Farrelly to help. It is nothing if not a madly enthusiastic place.

I arrived to find Kathleen in the mucky siding of a little stream, planting primulas. The garden is laid out around the old house in the hills above Blessington. From the front of the building, it is all restraint, smart lawns, some mature trees and a number of flowering shrubs, including a particularly large specimen of chaenomeles or flowering quince. So much for restraint. The garden proper moves into full flow behind the house. Suddenly the picture is all abundance, peonies, swirls of box wrapped around rose beds and a general air of floral excitement.

The paths diverge, some in the direction of long formal ponds, some toward more secluded flower gardens in which the stars are exotic annuals like ricinus and salvias with puffs of cosmos. These are beds, where 'no rules apply'. Ciaran has a passion for growing salvias and dahlias from seed. This is seen in the bustling greenhouses, where thousands of plants are grown from seed for the great flower show that can be seen on the annual open day.

From the exotic border, the way leads under a long arched wisteria pergola out towards an informal pond and a sort of Japanese inspired garden made of boulders and waterfalls edged with mixed herbaceous plants and acers.

The garden features a steep hill, on top of which I spotted an intriguing building. It turned out to be the home of a grand old piece of machinery, that a century ago powered an assembly line. Even to someone who knows nothing about Victorian industrial history, this is a fascinating feature. The open wooden building in which it sits was made by a talented man called James Grace in the traditional way, using no nails.

The garden continues uphill, beyond a meadow and the machine house, towards another big pond, planted up with irises and home to several families of ducks and geese. The collection of young specimen trees on the slope, will in future take over from the line of almost over mature beech trees that runs down the side of the meadow today.

The route leads through an old iron gate, past stone buildings draped in climbers and into a wood garden, where the paths run between plantations of fern and vinca, hardy geranium and pulmonaria, hellebores, dead nettle and bulbs under native trees and rhododendrons. I was surprised to learn that this wood was only planted up in 2012. Nor is it finished yet. Through another old farm gate, the way leads out to a surprising formal double flower border. It took a few minutes to process the sudden sight of this. From early summer to the end of autumn this is an ever-changing mix of nepeta, tulips, alliums and cosmos, *Verbena bonariensis* and Californian poppies, between trained hornbeams and box walls. It all culminates on a view of the Hill of Allen beyond the garden.

As if all that was not enough, the Reynolds have set up a barn owl breeding programme. Kathleen was still working in the stream as I left to go home.

Kilfane Glen & Waterfall, Co. Kilkenny.

Kilkenny

Butler House Garden

Patrick Street, Kilkenny city. Tel: 056 7765 707. e-mail: res@butler.ie Contact: The Manager.
Open: Mon-Sun., 9am-5pm. No entrance fee. Wheelchair accessible. Supervised children. Dogs on leads.
Special features: Accommodation. Venue hire. Directions: Entrance is through the courtyard of the Kilkenny
Design Centre on the Parade in the centre of the city, directly opposite the castle.

This is a modest-sized town garden attached to Butler House, a Georgian dower house of Kilkenny Castle, which now operates as a guest house. The castle can be seen over the garden wall.

In 1999 a new design for the then slightly tired garden was drawn up by Arthur Shackleton. Work has since been completed and the result is a smart, formal garden that suits the old house. Shackleton's design is centred on a raised pond cut from Kilkenny limestone and surrounded by a circle of *Robinia pseudoacacia*. Radiating out from this, like spokes on a bicycle wheel, there are gravel paths, lined with box walls and yew cones, with wedges of lawn between.

The stone seats around the pond were once the base stones from Nelson's Pillar in Dublin. When the monument was blown up in 1966, the undamaged stones found their way out of storage and to Kilkenny, where they sat for many years, to be eventually turned into the seating arrangement around this pond.

There were lavender walks in the old garden, and so lavender been reinstated against the south-facing wall. The orchard has been jazzed up with spring bulbs and they allow the meadow grass under the trees is grow tall through the summer.

The new shrub borders along the outer walls are filled with flowering and easily cared for ceanothus, hypericum, mock orange, *Sambucus nigra* 'Guincho Purple', broom, buddleia and white shrub roses. A ledge above one of the old garden paths houses a peony border using plants rescued from the old planting scheme. This bed too, is enclosed in young box walls. The wooden summerhouse, at the bottom of the garden, looks back to the parthenocissus-clad house. Healthy white abutilon beside the wooden structure, shows that this is indeed a sheltered spot.

I love the *Rosa banksiae* 'Lutea' climbing the wall of the entrance to the National Craft Gallery crescent beyond the garden.

Clashacrow Garden

Clashacrow, Freshford, Co. Kilkenny. Tel: 087 2787 080. 087 9978 743.
e-mail: thelokef@gmail.com Contact: Fran and Peter Theloke. Open: By appointment to groups, May-
Sept. Not wheelchair accessible. Special features: Teas can be arranged. Accommodation. Directions: Driving
from Kilkenny to Freshford, turn left onto the L0005, 2 km before Freshford. Drive 1 km long the road
and the garden is on the right.

Along with a menagerie of fancy fowl, some goats, several dogs, and even a rabbit on a lead, the Thelokes run a country cottage garden of ridiculous charm. It would certainly be easy to imagine yourself sauntering about with a trug and a secateurs in hand, dead-heading the occasional spent bloom in the brimming-over flower borders that make up a good part of the garden. The rest involves shrub borders, willow walks, frog and newt ponds, a small vegetable garden and a wildflower meadow.

The house appears to have been dropped into the middle of a large border and is being overwhelmed by plants. On the sunny sides, there are all sorts of climbers, from honeysuckle to *Rosa* 'Madame Alfred Carriere' and wisteria, which has reached up so far that it hangs like curtains in front of the upper storey windows. Flowers wash right up against the house walls on the shaded side too, with a fern bed built to induce jealousy, stuffed with combination of ferns, variegated *Euphorbia* 'White Swan' and podophyllum or spotty dotty. The hens appear to be in charge here, marching in and out of these borders picking at slugs and earning their keep. Later on, walking through the meadow, between smudges of hardy geranium, we were joined by two white ducks waddling through the long grass.

When it comes to flowers, Fran has talent for combining colours, from the mix of bergenia with deep red leaves and red helenium, achillea, dahlia and scarlet crocosmia, gathered around large boulders. In another bed all the whites of hesperis, geranium and romneya gather together in an attractive mill.

Peter made the rustic pergolas and fences that hold up the various clematis and roses, behind borders of self-sown hollyhocks. We left here and walked up through the little orchard with its moon gate, made ingeniously from the metal ring of an ex-trampoline. This now has the more daunting job of supporting a 'Rambling Rector' rose.

As we walked, Fran fretted over a *Cornus kousa* that the goat had chomped, wondering if it might recover. There is nothing not to love here.

Coolcashin

Gathabaun, Freshford, Co. Kilkenny. Tel: 056 8832 443. 086 0616 133.
e-mail: reneecoolcashin@gmail.com Contact: Renee Fitzpatrick. Open: By appointment only. Not wheelchair accessible. Dogs on leads. Supervised children. Open to groups and for occasional charity days. Special features: Teas can be arranged. Flower arranging. Directions. Leave Gathabawn village by the Cullohill Road. Travel under 0.5 km. The garden is on the right.

Lucifer coming in the window is not something for which many of us would yearn. In the case of Renee Fitzpatrick's garden however, it is, as they say A Good Thing. Along with *Crocosmia* 'Lucifer' a great number of plants seem to be attempting to make their way into Renee's house, gathered around the windows, waiting for the chance. Meanwhile, for the past 35 years, she has spent as much time as possible outside, working the garden.

Renee is a flower arranger and so the place is filled, possibly even stuffed with flowers in a sheer mad colour party. Knowing that nearly all the perennials were grown from seed makes it even more impressive.

Standing at the house, looking downhill over the show and beyond it to the tapestry of Kilkenny fields, and on a good day, Mount Leinster in the distance, the garden looks like one large flower border. Echinops and lilies, delphiniums, roses, dahlias and hollyhocks,

lupins and geraniums, all flow and swirl in and out of each other, invisibly held up and perfect.

Only when you step down and into the middle of all this does the actual shape of the garden become apparent. What seemed to be one large border turns out to be two, divided by a snaking, path, the stones of which were dug from the field. Renee does things the hard way.

There is also a good lawn, maintained by Joe, Renee's husband, a scientific mower of lawns. He designed a green that requires no reversing of the mower and he brooks no interference with that efficient cutting regime. No tree or shrub is so special, that it can sit on the middle of the lawn, forcing him to mow around it. He believes that the mower's life should be straightforward.

An almost invisible ledge surrounds the house, separating it from the flower beds. Standing on this gives another view of the various borders. Among the more transient flowers, shrubs like pittosporum and box provide the show with permanence.

The garden is deceptive: Walking out through the flower borders, you eventually arrive at what looks like the boundary. This is actually an entrance to the wood garden, a necklace of oak, ash, davidia and beech, walnut, crinodendron, lime, liriodendron and variegated thuja. Underneath the trees, in spring there are drifts of bulbs.

Stepping back into the sun we reached a pond surrounded by gunnera, rodgersia, and primulas. It is here that Renee's bold red setter regularly takes to the water for a swim. She doesn't mind.

Croan House & Croan Cottages

Dunnamaggin, Co. Kilkenny. Tel: 087 2368 555. 056 7766 868. e-mail: info@croancottages.com. Contact: Francis Nesbitt. Open: By appointment to groups. Special features: Courses. Accommodation. Directions: Leave the M9 by Exit 10 onto the R699 towards Dunnamaggan and Callan. At the Y-junction turn right and then left onto the L5074, travelling 500m to the garden.

Croan House stands the top of a handsome, straight, wide lime avenue, planted in 1743. The next sight is the labyrinth, laid out on a grassed area beside the house. To be clear, a labyrinth is not a maze. There are many ways through a maze. There is only one way through a labyrinth, and there is one sure way to design one. Francis Nesbitt, its creator, told me how: 'You will need a long string, a stick and an accomplice. A nine-year-old daughter is ideal.' After much sum-doing, judicious mowing and growing wild flower plugs, the result is a labyrinth, spiked with blue, pink and black cornflowers, poppies, cowslips and nigella. Adding yellow rattle in the seed mix reduces the vigour of the meadow grass and encourages more wildflower growth.

It was some time after the Nesbitts moved here that they discovered a walled garden. It had been lost under self-sown trees and one of its walls had been knocked. Francis set to reinstating the wall, clearing the trees and restoring the place as a new kitchen garden. We shooed an array of fancy hens and peacocks out of the way as we made our way to see his new, old walled garden.

It is divided into rotation and permanent beds, with asparagus and kale, strawberry patches, black, white, red and blueberries. The soil is lime so the blueberries grow in containers. The greenhouse is a useful double height structure that fits a good sized fig and two heavily fruiting vines. Meanwhile, outside there are cherries, plums, pears and a young Irish apple orchard.

Francis operates Croan House and Cottages, as an organic small holding running courses on the different aspects of operating such a venture, from growing vegetables and fruit, to keeping bees and poultry, pigs, sheep and alpacas. He also runs cooking courses in tandem with the River Cottage farm in Britain.

Dangan Cottage

Thomastown, Co. Kilkenny. Tel 087 2500 380. Contact: Christopher Moore.
e-mail: cmoorespdec@gmail.com Open: By appointment to groups. May-Sept. Partially wheelchair accessible.
Supervised children. No dogs. Teas and lunches by appointment. Directions: on application.

'It's all about the place,' said Christopher Moore. When that place is a blessed spot on the banks of the River Nore, a five-acre miniature historic demesne built around a *cottage orné*, the site of a hermitage with a sunken moss house, an old mill, various waterways including an island and a miniature stone aqueduct, it must indeed be, all about the place. This place is a bit special and its garden, which Christopher is in the process of restoring, is also special.

It was built in the late 18th century by Mary Bushe, Henry Grattan's sister, as a dower house. She had previously lived at Kilfane, home to another *cottage orné*. Mrs. Bushe lived at Dangan probably from about 1786 until her death in 1816, spending her declining years creating this romantic little fantasy garden around her thatched house, according to the very latest taste.

In the intervening years, the thatch was removed and the rustic cottage was restyled several times, most recently in 1970, as a Regency lodge.

Today, Christopher is busy teasing the garden back to its original appearance, restoring the hermitage and strange underground moss house. He has rebuilt the lost bridge on the diverted river and is playing with the aqueduct.

He is also planting, adding to the existing spreads of cyclamen and spring bulbs, dividing and spreading carpets of anemones, aconites, snowdrops and bluebells. Informal box groves have being planted. These will be left grow and billow out in their natural form. When left to its own devices, box can be an excellent, informal winter presence in a garden. New young trees including cork oak and groves of yew, as well as herbaceous borders have all been planted. This is a garden on a mission.

I was taken by the ghostly, half-standing, half-living robinia supporting a fine *Rosa banksiae* and a host of ferns burrowed into its gnarly branches. Visible from here, the faux ruin that forms the entrance to the garden, hosts a white *Rosa banksiae* 'Alba plena' clambering up its walls.

The house provides a grand leaning post for some architectural looking espaliered pears, and *Echium candicans*, doing its best in cold Kilkenny. Clumps of *Iris lazica* flower all winter in this sun trap gravel bed and *Crinum powellii* does well too. The presence of a bench here must make it very hard to rouse oneself and see to the work. The combination of the surrounding flowers and scents, the view across the garden of the new *chinoiserie* bridge over the river, the chance of catching sight of an otter, or one of Christopher's tiny dogs chasing a duck, make the temptations to dawdle too numerous. Described in 1805 as 'the beautiful seat of Mrs. Bushe' Dangan Cottage is, over two centuries later, looking appropriately beautiful.

Kilfane Glen & Waterfall

Thomastown, Co. Kilkenny. Contact: Susan Mosse. Tel: 056 7727 105. e-mail: susan@irishgardens. com www.kilfane.com Open: July-Aug. Daily. 11am-6pm. Pre-booked groups of ten all year. Not wheelchair accessible. Supervised children. No dogs. Special features: Modern sculpture on trails. Teas: Wed., Fri. and Sun. during open season. Picnic area. Member of the Gardens of Ireland Trust. Directions: 3 km off the Dublin–Waterford Road (N9) driving from Thomastown.

Green gardens and woodland gardens, done well are probably easier to love than any other type but they are probably harder to make a success of than flouncier flower gardens. Restraint is required. Walking through

Kilfane Glen is like walking through the illustrations from a book of fairy tales.

The main body is a romantic garden which was originally laid out by the Power family in the 1790s on a 30-acre plot: There is the wood and deep in the middle of it is a glen, an artificial waterfall, *cottage orné* and a hermit's grotto. The waterfall tumbles into a stream which runs through the wood, crossed at several points by rustic bridges.

The original garden was lost over the centuries, swallowed by choking *Rhododendron ponticum* and laurel. But in the early 1990s, looking at an 1805 print that showed that there was a glen and waterfall with an ornamental cottage seemingly on their land, owners

Susan and Nicholas Mosse began to investigate. Their explorations in the rhodo-choked woods proved that the print was no work of imagination, but an historic document. Down in the glen, they found the footprint of the *cottage orné* which had been razed to the ground in the middle of the 19th century. They painstakingly rebuilt it, bringing in the late, designer, Sybil Connolly to design the interiors of the thatched cottage. The porch and outer walls were planted with a period planting of honeysuckle, jasmine and climbing roses.

Outside the cottage, and visible through the leaded windows, the workings of the artificial waterfall were found and the old machinery was cranked back into commission. After nearly two centuries, water was sent pouring out over the cliff.

Several new gardens were created to add to the historic one, including a blue orchard. At its centre, crab apples were planted in a circle and underplanted with grape hyacinths or muscari and bluebells. The orchard wall backs a bed filled with blue agapanthus, monkshood, delphinium and aubrieta. The gateway in the centre of this wall leads to the pond and an all-white moon garden, featuring angel's trumpets (*Brugmansia arborea*) and tall cimicifuga among the white and silver plants.

There are bamboo walks, a sort of hall of mirrors hidden in a laurel walk with a display of hostas in pots, and the vista, which is a view of Slievenamon through a clearing in the trees.

A contemporary sculpture trail includes work by two of the finest British sculptors, Bill Woodrow and David Nash. William Pye's copper water vessel is the centrepiece of the vista. It brims with water, reflecting the surrounding trees. Lynn Kirkham's living willow bench can be found here too. The maturing grove of Japanese acers is handsome and there is even that most fashionable of garden items, a stumpery, being developed in the woods.

In the end, the most appealing features in Kilfane are the many paths through the woods, going up and down hills, past gurgly streams, under dark tree tunnels, preferably in the rain.

Kilkenny Castle Park

The Parade, Kilkenny city, Co. Kilkenny. Tel: 056 7721 450. e-mail: kilkennycastle@opw.ie www.heritgeireland.ie Contact: Head Gardener. Open: All year. See web for seasonal details. No entrance fee. Wheelchair accessible. Supervised children. Dogs on leads. Special features: Castle tours. Tearoom, May-Sept. Free guided tours of the park 3pm on Sun., July and Aug. Art gallery. Bookshop. Playground (swings for children with disabilities). Events. Directions: Situated in the middle of the city.

This 35 acre park, set high over the banks of the River Nore, belongs to Kilkenny Castle, the former seat of the Butlers of Ormonde. The Butlers were one of the chief families in Ireland, arriving here with the Normans in 1169. They ruled much of the southeast up until the 19th century, contributing such luminaries as James, the first Duke of Ormond, to Irish history. The Butler family lived in Kilkenny until 1935 when they vacated the castle, selling it to the State in the 1960s for a nominal price of £60.

A castle has stood on this site since the 12th century. Only some of the details of the original gardens have survived, but descriptions of the first Duke's garden in the late 17th century still exist (see also Royal Hospital Kilmainham, Dublin). As an ally of Charles II, James was exiled in France, where he became interested in the French style of gardening. Returning with the Restoration of the monarchy in 1660, James restyled his Kilkenny residence, rather incongruously, as a French château with a garden to match. That arrangement included grottos and extravagant waterworks. These are long gone. Time marched on, tastes changed and today the gardens are largely the result of work carried out in the middle of the 19th century by the Irish garden designer Ninian

Niven. (See the Phoenix Park and the Iveagh Gardens, Dublin and Hilton Park, Co. Monaghan).

The grounds are divided into two distinct parts: a formal terraced garden to the north and parkland to the south. The terraced garden is made up of a sunken lawn planted with formal rose beds. Hybrid tea roses make up the bulk of the flowers, but there are also some older rugosa roses. These beds surround a substantial limestone fountain set within a cruciform network of paths. The garden looks up to the castle, which stands on a raised platform of stone balustrades covered in *Rosa* 'Dorothy Perkins'.

The much loved, well-tended, gently developed park is made up of rolling and sweeping lawns, broken by groves of park trees and large shrubs as well as specimens. At the bottom of the park, a small wooded area opens rather romantically onto a lily pond, grandly termed 'the boating lake' complete with a population of ducks and a pair of swans. The lake has been side planted with water loving plants. A wildflower garden is in development and, close by, there is a small ancestral burial ground for the Butlers and their dogs. Kilkenny loves its castle park and with good reason.

Kilrush House

Freshford. Co Kilkenny. Tel: 086 8240 028. e-mail: sallystgeorge@icloud.com. Contact: Richard and Sally St. George. Open: Feb.-April. By appointment to groups. Not wheelchair accessible. Not suitable for children. No dogs. Special features: House and historic ruins. Teas and lunches by appointment. Directions: On application.

Kilrush, or 'the church of the promontory', on the River Nuenna, has been in existence on this site since at least the 12th century and possibly earlier. The St. George family arrived in the 1400s, continuing the already in-train practice of building a new house here every 300 years or so. The most recent was a fine

Georgian house, designed by Daniel Roberston, who also carried out extensive work on nearby Kilkenny Castle. The 15th century tower house and a rare 13th century 'hall house', are also still here, ruined but fascinating to visit.

The St. Georges have been farming and gardening

here too, and the remains of older gardens can be spotted in the ancient limes along the avenue, in the remains of an old lime tree walk behind the tower house, in sunken lawns and mature shrubberies as well as some fine old park trees.

The current St. Georges, Sally and her husband Richard, are in the process of rejuvenating the gardens, with a particular bent on the spring wood gardens.

The results of their work are to be seen between February and April in an expanding show of early flowers, leading to and wrapping around the old house.

I think Sally must spend an inordinate amount of her time planting bulbs. Everywhere there are swathes of snowdrops and erythroniums, fritillaries and anemones. Invariably she is the one carrying out the division and the business of distribution.

I particularly love the runs of different daffodils including the finely scented and dainty variety, 'Tipper' planted on and around the strange mound to the front of the house. This mound is thought to have been the promontory on which the ancient wooden church was built.

Together Sally and Richard are also planting interesting and specimen trees, particularly limes, which she says, do well here. Planting for posterity. In the meantime, visit for the cheerful spring display and the fascinating history.

Lavistown House

Lavistown, Kilkenny, Co. Kilkenny. e-mail: info@lavistownhouse.ie www.lavistownhouse.ie
Contact: Des Doyle. Open: By appointment and for selected Open Days. Contact for details. Not wheelchair accessible. Supervised children (Water). No dogs. Special features: Courses. Teas can be arranged. Directions: Driving into Kilkenny on the Old Dublin Road, turn left at Duggan Steel. Travel for approximately 2 km and the garden is on the left, signposted.

The garden at Lavistown has had an interesting few years. Until the Valentine's Day storm in 2014, it was a rather tranquil place, comprised of peaceful wooded areas that put on a good spring show, with a venerable old walled kitchen garden and some colourful mixed borders. Then the storm struck. Trees fell in all directions, causing temporary chaos and a long term rethink.

The woodland garden that was, with its mature beech and oak which sheltered and cosseted the shade-loving trilliums, hellebores, pulmonarias and epimediums, was more or less swept away in one afternoon and in its stead there was a new, open, sunny, mess.

So the rethink commenced and the new plan around the old Georgian house began to be put into place. At going to press, the garden at Lavistown is still a work in progress but it is an interesting and tantalising one: There are open areas, being grassed, for the first time in over a century. A formal pond surrounded by yew sentinels was being instated. The open sunny flower and late summer borders had been joined by new sweeps of flower.

The stonework is impressive. New raised, ledged beds give a solidity to the otherwise fleeting borders all year round. They have also been creating little stone walls to mark new walks, as well as unearthing previously lost, walled walks. Once planted up, these are going to be wonderful. They are already full of character. Happily too there are still areas of spring wood for the aconites, anemones, hellebores and trilliums. Watch this space.

The Millennium Park

Freshford, Co. Kilkenny. Open: Constantly. Directions on the R693 out of the village.

In an inspired move, the people of Freshford created this young park 17 years ago on a site partially surrounded by the River Nuenna. Groves of trees, including a few each of beech, oak, ash and birch were planted, all of which are maturing well. The yew walk, trained over a series of metal arches, has recently become a reason to stop the car. The spans are almost hidden by yew. Walking through it brings you down to the old stone bridge and a shallow point in the river which can be reached by a semi-circular set of steps, rather like an old washing site. The river, with its little waterfalls is itself a picturesque sight.

Mount Juliet

Thomastown, Co. Kilkenny. Tel: 056 7773 000. e-mail hospitalitydesk@mountjuliet.ie www.mountjuliet.com Contact: Reception. Open: By appointment. Groups welcome. Partially wheelchair accessible. Supervised children. Special features: Tours. Hotel. Restaurant. Golf course. Riding school. Directions: Turn left at the top of the square in Thomastown and follow the signposts to Mount Juliet, about 4 km away.

Mount Juliet is a fine old estate and now one of the country's major golf courses and hotel complexes. The parkland has been largely remodelled to accommodate the golf course but it still boasts some wonderful trees, both within the extensive woods and as specimens. Within the demesne there is a double herbaceous border situated in the old walled garden. This border was designed by one of the few female garden designers of the early 20th century, Marguerite Solly Flood. A circular opening or gateway in the fig-clad dividing wall in the walled garden leads onto a broad grass path that divides the borders. Blues, pinks and creams melt together in a haze that is very easy on the eye. Tall delphinium, phlox, aster, hesperis, peony and a host of other plants weave in and out of each other in a show that is at its best in late May and June. There are additional deep mixed borders running around the outer walls, involving repeat planting of darker buddleia, cotinus, veronica and penstemon. On my most recent visit, the border was in need of a rejuvenation and I believe at going to press, work has been started on this task. The view out over the walls takes in some great mature cedars, beech and oak. Outside the walls, there is a rose garden with a small sunken pond.

There is also a rock and water garden close to the main house, and a woodland walk, underplanted in places with spring bulbs and ferns.

Ballylinch Stud, attached to Mount Juliet boasts an unusual sort of rose garden: The large number of stone outhouses scattered through the yard, along with every available length of wooden fence, have been pulled into service to host a number of rambling and climbing roses, some old and some new, in a grand cheerful display of flower through the summer. The varieties include 'Schoolgirl', 'Queen Elizabeth', 'Golden Showers' and 'Albertine'. Billy Townsend, who gardened here since 1959 when it was owned by Major Victor McCalmont, says he thinks some of the ramblers could be nearly a century old.

Rothe House Garden

Rothe House, Parliament Street, Kilkenny, Co. Kilkenny. Tel: 056 7722 893. e-mail: reception@rothehouse.com www.rothehouse.com Contact: Mary Pyke. Open: All year. April-Sept., 10.30am-5pm. Oct-March. Mon-Sun., 10.30am-4.30pm. Wheelchair accessible. Children welcome. Guide dogs only. Special features: Historic house. Museum. Archive. Book shop. Events. Plants for sale. Directions: On Parliament Street in the centre of the city.

In the late Middle Ages with the development of market towns, a population of merchants arose, setting up shop to sell their goods. A natural desire was to display the wealth they had built up and they did this through building impressive town houses above and behind the shops. Sometimes they built gardens.

Today in Ireland there are a mere handful of these Tudor merchant houses left. A few are in Kilkenny, the

Shee Alms House, Grace's Castle and Rothe House are the most complete examples. But there is only one known medieval town garden left on the island and it too is in Kilkenny, behind Rothe House on Parliament Street.

The history of the restoration of the gardens at Rothe House has been a long one. It took a few decades of push and pull, but the long lost 400-year-old garden first planted by merchant, John Rothe in the early 1600s on High Street, opened its gate a few years ago.

With the input of garden historians and archaeologists, the site has been laid out in a sensitive facsimile of a 17th century town garden. The long slim, sloped 'burgage plot', the same width as the house and shop it backs, runs out from the building to the old city walls. It is divided into orchards with freestanding and wall trained trees, herb and flower beds, clipped shrubs, a pergola and little areas of lawn. Look for the 13th century covered well in the middle of the garden. Period plants were sourced and the formal, geometric style is in keeping with the style of the mid-1600s. It was a garden created to impress and those fortunate enough to be shown around would be suitably taken by the latest fashionable plants and features they found in Mr Rothe's garden. There might even have been orders placed as a result of a visit.

It is a marvel to be able to study such a garden, given the centuries of neglect, decay and loss.

Pat Murphy's Garden

Johnstown. Co. Kilkenny. Open: Visible from the road. Directions: On the R435 out of Johnstown towards Galmoy. This is a drive-by garden that can be seen in its totality from the road.

There is something special about a length of hedge or a free standing shrub, pruned, preened and clipped into an unnatural shape, that appeals to the garden nerd in all of us. It is not such a popular practice in Ireland but that very rarity is what makes it easier to knock on a stranger's front door to ask about their work. Hopefully the artist in residence will look kindly on the nosy Parker. In this case the artist was one Pat Murphy, of Tullyvolty, Johnstown, County Kilkenny and he was most welcoming, although he did give a guffaw when I congratulated him. 'I'm not a gardener! I just like to keep the place clean,' he said.

I thought that there are many among us, calling ourselves gardeners who would be proud to keep our gardens this 'clean'. Mr. Murphy has been working his garden and impressing passers-by since 1951 when he took to growing hedges and evergreen shrubs. The hedges grew and the tidy-minded Mr. Murphy felt the need to 'trim the scraggy bits.' The results are charming, from berberis eggs, to holly and leylandii domes, tiered 60-year-old yew wedding cakes, beech cubes on stilts and lonicera hedges that look like squashed pillows, held in puffs behind post and rail fences, It is masterful. On a summer's day, just after everything has been trimmed, he stands back to look or climbs up on top of the house for his favourite view which is from the roof 'and it's perfect. Like a postcard', he said. It is indeed.

Shankill Castle & Gardens

Paulstown, Co. Kilkenny. Tel: 059 9726 145. 087 1377 982. e-mail: info@shankillcastle.com johngeoffrey@gmail.com Contact: The Cope family. Open: Every day July-Aug. and in February for snowdrops. Other times groups by appointment. Partially wheelchair accessible. Children welcome. Special features: Castle. Teas can be arranged. Artists' studio and gallery open by appointment. Events. Directions: Take Exit 7 off the M9 for Paulstown village.

Run by the fascinating Copes, a family of artists, farmers, archaeologists and historians, Shankill Castle was originally a Butler-built tower house, restyled and added to throughout its history. It is an eccentric place and well worth a visit.

I arrived most recently when the snowdrop display was in full swing and began my visit in the little churchyard, which would make the perfect backdrop to an old fashioned spooky film. Geoffrey Cope led me between lichen and moss covered grave stones, as well as seas of snowdrops and budding celandines that take over from the white snowdrops in March.

Among the flowers look for the grave of Mary Cody, who died, interestingly, on February 31st 1782. In between the stones, shrubs of box, yew and holly, hellebores extend the flowering season on the ground. Overhead a murder of noisy crows rowed in the tall beech and ash trees. The church ruin that gives the Castle its name - *sean caisle,* can be found here and the little lane leading from this to the rest of the garden is inexplicably called the Macduff Trench.

Drives and entrances to Shankill Castle provide the castle with much of its lore. One particular curse was rained down on the castle and in particular its drive, by an old priest who said that 'grass will grow on the avenue and the gates will never close.' As curses go this would not be among the most dreaded.

From the graveyard we made our way out to the laurel lawn. Spiked with tall ash and sycamore, this is an example of a rarely seen Victorian feature. It was around here that Geoffrey discovered a clump of rare white flowering celandines.

The stream wanders through the garden, flooding it occasionally and eventually arriving at the canal in front of the house, feeding it with fresh water.

There is also a walled garden that covers over four acres. Only part of it is being used to grow vegetables for the family but the remains of some old goblet-trained pears can be seen on the south facing brick wall and an apple arch walk down the middle is still attractive if seriously showing its age.

Outside the walls, a series of unearthed old paths run through more seas of snowdrops, one making its way along the outside of the walled garden, past a huge *Sequoiadendron giganteum*. 'There was another that was supposed to be the tallest on the island but it fell in the 1950s,' Geoffrey said as we walked past the baby giant and into the moated garden.

This is an unusual circular garden, surrounded by a tributary of the ever present stream. It is entered by way of a low, stone bridge and dominated by damson trees underplanted with hellebores, ferns, box and aquilegias. The rough marble boulder-edged paths were unearthed in recent years.

The chief feature in Shankill is the canal or pond. This was originally a formal, rectangular, stone lined canal, running in a straight line out from the house, in the style of the early 18th century. Evidence of this and the old garden can be seen on the 1832 Ordnance Survey map. The canal was redesigned in the 19th century, to look more 'natural'. Two wings, or serpentine curves were added. The sunken lawn in front of the house was also once part of the canal. Today it is home to unique and complicated polyhedral or multi-faceted sundial. Shankill is 28 minutes west of Greenwich in England, so add that number of minutes to get GMT.

Nearby is the Vista, another feature that harks back to the formal garden. This was probably part of a pair of angled walks running from the house and was designed to frame the sun as it set on the winter solstice. Close by, Geoffrey recently planted up a new yew walk leading from the castle. The garden marches on.

The Watergarden

Ladywell Street, Thomastown, Co. Kilkenny. Tel: 056 7724 690. e-mail: thewatergarden@camphill.ie Contact: The manager. Open: All year. Contact for seasonal changes. Admission free if using tearooms. Wheelchair accessible. Supervised children (River). Dogs on leads. Special features: Restaurant. Art gallery and craft shop. Nursery. Directions: In Thomastown, on the road to Bennetsbridge.

The Watergarden started life many years ago when a man began working on his own small, river-banked plot and quickly ran out of space for his growing plant collection. Bernard Walsh did what anyone would do, borrowing the unused ends of the neighbouring gardens, he continued to extend the plot along the river, incorporating and reclaiming the boggy bits from the line of village gardens, working these into one long creation, secreted away behind the village.

Over 20 years ago the garden was taken over by the Camphill Community. The community is a network of small groups set up to enable able-bodied and disabled people to live and work together. They run farm enterprises, crafts workshops and garden centres around the country. In the Watergarden, the Camphill workers have sprinkled an extra dusting of magic powder over what was already a charming garden. Along with making it wheelchair friendly they added in new walled vegetable garden, built bridges, summerhouses and arbours, rose walks and pond gardens.

There are benches and seats tucked into every corner and at every junction. The miniature watermill has been restored and the sluice gates and weirs have been repaired. At different points, the noise of the river runs from a gentle burble to a loud roar, but it is always present.

The planting is informal, divided into open flower gardens and shaded woodland and riverside walks. The old boundary walls have been planted with climbing and rambling roses and in the beds beneath there are hellebores, ferns, columbines, hostas and marginal plants like flag iris and lysimachia, all under the shade of weeping willow and contorted hazel.

All work here is carried out organically, making it even more attractive. The latest gardens are the two little hilly vegetable plots with terraces of vegetables held up on stone ledges, entered by way of an unusual ceramic-decorated gateway.

The community also runs a small nursery which stocks many of the plants featured in the garden. They sell these at reasonable prices. Good quality home-made lunches and teas are available from the tearoom, which has an outdoor eating area from where the garden can be observed and admired.

On my last visit, the rain had stopped play outside but the workers were still hard at it, making woolly Easter decorations for sale in the shop.

Woodstock

Inistioge, Co. Kilkenny. Contact: Claire Goodwin: 056 7794 033, 056 7758 797. John Delaney: 087 8549785. e-mail: john.delaney@kilkennycoco.ie www.woodstock.ie Open: All year. Oct-Mar., 9am-4.30pm. Ap-Sept., 9am-8pm. Groups welcome. Partially wheelchair accessible. Car parking charge. Supervised children. Dogs on leads. Special Features: Tours can be organised. Tearoom, April-Sept. Playground. Buggy shuttle to the walled garden in summer. Contact for details. Directions: Situated 2 km west of the village, up a steep hill.

We complain about county councils and how inefficient and expensive they are. This may be so but Kilkenny County Council can claim to have at least one great big feather in its cap. That feather is the garden at Woodstock, the seat of the Tighes between 1745 and 1922 when it was burnt down. The garden, described as one of the finest in the country had largely disintegrated when in 1997 the County Council and the Great Gardens of Ireland Restoration Programme took the place on. The outcome of this was to bring Woodstock back to something of its former glory.

A spectacular monkey puzzle avenue, made up of 31 pairs, thought to be the longest in Europe, was restored and new, young monkey puzzles (*Araucaria araucana*), were planted where older specimens fell. A second avenue of noble fir or *Abies nobilis*, almost half a kilometre long, running at an angle from the monkey puzzles, was disentangled from a great thicket of rhododendron, laurel and bramble. The first avenue had always been apparent. The noble fir avenue, on the other hand, had been completely obscured by the rhododendron. Returned to their glory, together they impart a sense of grandeur to an already grand place.

All over the pleasure grounds clearances have revealed gardens not seen properly for nearly a century: The yew walk and kitchen gardens, only barely discernible up to recently, were saved and restored. A box parterre was replanted outside the walled garden. This leads up to the rebuilt Turner greenhouse, which in summer is used as a tearoom.

The ornamental dairy is a strange-looking item that was submerged under centuries of soil build-up but can now be seen. Meanwhile, the substantial Victorian rockery has also been restored. Once again it is possible to walk through it, between moss-covered granite and marble boulders, past ponds, with newly planted *Trachycarpus fortunei* and *Rhododendron macabeanum* beginning to rise proud of the lower storey ferns and libertia. The rockery was created when 200,000 cubic metres of soil were removed from here to plant up the winter garden in front of the house. That winter garden is currently under grass but once it was an elaborate confection of fashionable bedding and at going to press work is being started to reinstate the beds.

The walled garden is operational again after so many years of neglect and you can once again walk on restored paths between expansive beds of vegetables, mixed shrub and herbaceous beds, wall-trained and espaliered pear trees.

The work has been, and is still carried out largely by John Delaney and his small band of gardeners. They garden through the growing season and when the garden jobs are in short supply in winter, they take on projects such as the building of new playgrounds and the reconstruction of lost features like the bamboo rustic bower, with the help of conservation experts. The bower is clad in sasa bamboo, which was grown and harvested in the garden.

They also restored an elegant iron rose pergola nearby. This is now planted up with *Rosa* 'Madame Alfred Carriere', *R.* 'Blush Noisette' and 'Rambling Rector.'

A red squirrel whipped up a tree as we walked past and John told me that there is a healthy population in the garden. The pine martens successfully hunt grey squirrels but they cannot catch the more nimble reds, who thrive here, eating monkey puzzle seeds.

Although the once-famed collection of trees has become sadly depleted over the years from storm damage and neglect, there are still massive wonders ranged about the grounds, including examples of *Sequoiadendron giganteum*, (Wellingtonia) *Thuja plicata* 'Zebrina' and *Cryptomeria japonica*. Planting is ongoing, in part to make up for the lost trees.

Long woodland walks wind their way through the estate, leading in one case to a Gothic teahouse perched in the trees, with a panoramic view over the valley and river below. It is easy to imagine yourself back in time, enjoying tea up here, with servants to ferry the picnic things up that *tarsome* hill.

Do not miss the recovered Turner gate. Having been lost many decades ago, it was donated back to the garden by a kind lady, Mrs. Carr, from Inistioge.

Clonohill Gardens, Co. Laois

Laois

Ballintubbert Gardens & House

Ballintubbert, Stradbally, Co. Laois. Tel: 087 312 7639. e-mail: myhost@ballintubbert.com Contact: Lorraine Fenelon. Open: Thurs. April-Sept., 10am-5pm. Very occasionally closed due to private events. See Facebook to check. Occasional Open Weekends. See Facebook. Not wheelchair accessible. Supervised children welcome. No dogs. Special features: Events. Refreshments and wood fired pizzas can be arranged. Plants for sale. Member of the Gardens of Ireland Trust. Directions: From Stradbally take N80 south, travel uphill through mountain gap for about 4 km. As the road falls, turn left at the Ballintubbert sign. Travel for 1.2 km along and garden is on left.

A Renault 4 decked out like a car-shaped mirror ball in the car park at Ballintubbert came as an unusual welcome and a bit of a surprise when I visited. Equally surprising, coming off a short drive under a mix of informally planted lime, betula and beech, was the sight of a long, formal canal. This stepped-down water feature runs directly out from the front of the Georgian house between two lime *allées* leading to a yew arbour and a viewing perch. Sitting on that perch, the view back along the water to the house, skirted by box walls and balls and framed by mature purple beech and sweet chestnut, is grand.

With an appetite suitably whetted, I set off to investigate further. An irresistible little gate in a wall beside the house led into a small courtyard and the home to a newly created fern garden. Little dryopteris and polystichum ferns have been tucked into niches in the stone walls where they will expand and mature. This will eventually develop into an atmospheric little nook. I continued on into the next antechamber, and

a long pergola under sheets of actinidia, clematis and vine. Walking under this, gaps and openings look out onto a vegetable garden. From here, a yew arch leads out, through a hornbeam circle and on, to the Lutyens garden. This area was modelled on the Lutyens design at Heywood, a few miles away near the village of Ballinakill.

Jennifer, the head gardener, led me around and we made our way between yew circles and rose beds, puffs of nepeta and *Alchemilla mollis*. Liscannor stone paths cut the right dash between the sprawling borders. Arches cut into the yew wall enticed us out to see the cloister created by the addition of another, outer circling hedge. Clever stuff.

Rose gardens and meadow gardens, a little temple, an orchard and an amphitheatre - we wandered from one area to another, between the different features scattered through the grounds.

Arriving at the back of the house, we came to a terrace, combining flower borders and mature apple trees set into the flag stones. From here we made our way into the sunniest corner, and the site of an informal flower garden designed for a previous house owner, by Jonathan Shackleton, of Fruitlawn garden, in Abbeyleix, also a few miles away.

I made my way through tall waving lemon coloured *Cephalaria giganteum*, *Rosa moyesii*, salvia and *Hydrangea sargentii*. Mature, spreading wisteria hid the enclosing walls. Tall stands of oak and other park trees outside the walls make this little flower corner feel completely secluded.

Jennifer works Ballintubbert in a biodynamic way, aiming to avoid the use of chemicals and to encourage wildlife. She is more than happy to talk about how effective various strategies are. This obviously makes a walk and talk a rewarding experience.

Castle Durrow

Durrow, Co. Laois. Tel: 057 8736 555 / 086 2692254. e-mail: info@castledurrow.com
www.castledurrow.com Contact: Peter and Shelly Stokes. Open: As part of the Laois Garden Trail. All
year, daylight hours. Partially wheelchair accessible. Supervised children. Dogs on leads. Special features:
Guided tours can be booked. Accommodation. Restaurant. Bar. Tearooms. Events. Member of the Gardens
of Ireland Trust. Directions. At the top of the square in Durrow.

The 300-year-old house set on the edge of Durrow village has been through many incarnations, from lordly seat to convent and local school, but it can have had few owners as dynamic as the current incumbents, Shelly and Peter Stokes, who have been running the grand old house as a hotel for nearly 20 years. In that time, Shelly has been enthusiastically tackling the garden.

On the day I visited, she was busy working on a new wooded rock garden, based around an old stone grotto. She was toying with the possibilities of what could be done with a hump and hollow of land on the edge of the garden. It was be part of an amphitheatre she was making, and the problem in hand was one of trying to work out where the actors could change and in what direction the audience should face. This is the sort of person who should be in charge of a Big House garden.

There are a whole series of features ranged about the grounds, from formal lawns and courtyard rose displays, to walled gardens full of ornamentals, orchards and wooded gardens, semi-wild walks along the river, and hilly grassed trails between bucolic meadows and parkland studded with mature trees.

Shelly took the sloped lawn running out from the house and terraced it, adding to the already existing old yews with roses, specimen trees and shrubs. The walled garden is next door and enjoys the same sloped orientation. The proximity to the house is interesting and the way Shelly has arranged it, divided into three long sections, has transformed it into a feature that can be seen from an elevated viewpoint before visiting. The central section is decorative, made of two long herbaceous borders, divided by grass paths. Beyond this is a herb parterre. Secreted behind a hedge, a sunken Italian garden complete with a decorative little canal is like a secret lovers' garden. The orchard is another romantic spot, a wildflower meadow run through by mown paths, old varieties of apple and a resident flock of ducks.

The formal courtyard garden is a picture, the garden equivalent of a perfume shop full of scented David Austen roses, enclosed in ruler-straight box-lined beds. This is a *tour de force* in high maintenance old-fashioned gardening.

My favourite part of the visit is however the walk that runs around the boundary, taking in an uncovered ha-ha, a newly planted-up spring wood and the hilly path that takes in the Erkina River, the Laois hills, the park trees and even a little folly. The fact that you can break off to have afternoon tea half-way around the visit only makes it more enticing.

Clonaslee Garden

Graiguefulla, Clonaslee, Co. Laois. Tel: 057 8648038. e-mail: annecostelloe@eircom.net
Contact: Nancy Costelloe. Open: As part of the Laois Garden Trail. Mar-Sept. By appointment only.
Partially wheelchair accessible. Supervised children. Dogs on leads. Special features: Teas can be arranged.
Directions: From Mountmellick travel on the R422. After Rosenallis go through a crossroads then take the
next right. Drive 1.8 km passing 'Rose Cottage' on the left. Turn right and the garden is a short way along
on the left.

Nancy and Jim Costello have been gardening at Clonaslee for many years. The garden covers possibly about two acres but neither Nancy nor Jim quite know the size. They are more concerned with keeping their perfect garden, perfect. The Costello's retired as farmers a number of years ago and since then they have all the time they want to work the place. It shows, from the sunny gravelled courtyard to the wood, pond, herbaceous and mixed borders, grass walks and collections of containers.

The show starts with gusto at the front gate, once the site of an old stone outhouse. Pulling down the derelict sheds, but leaving behind the sun-trapping, back walls, Nancy made a heat retaining garden where she grows different grasses, echinacea, ricinus, artichokes and the tallest crocosmia. This is a place that feels hot on the mildest of summer days. In stark contrast, a shaded wood garden can be reached by

way of a little stepping-stone bridge and an opening in the trees. The hosta-lined path leads to a pond fringes with primulas and ferns, including *Onoclea sensibilis* and *Dryopteris cristata*.

Back out in the open, two tall clipped yews mark the entry to the house, by way of a set of steps framed by trained box balls, lush variegated hostas and fluffy *Alchemilla mollis*. The building is guarded by huge pots of *Agave Americana* and fat cacti. The well constructed alpine bed by the house is one my favourite features. In among the warm coloured gravel and stone mounds there are tiny geraniums and erodiums, little clumps of yellow meconopsis and creeping thyme.

'It's all getting too tall,' is Nancy's complaint, and indeed the growth here has been notable, from a fine big *Cornus kousa* to a sky-bound blue cedar, the place is maturing beautifully allowing for the creation of tunnels through the maturing trees.

It might be a country garden but not one where the often observed rule of sticking to gentle pastels has any heed paid to it. Nancy matches yellow broom with orange speckled alstroemerias, tall fluffy red inulas, vivid red poppies and acid yellow gleditsia.

Arches and gateways, draped with roses, clematis, and other climbers lead from one area to another. Beech hedge *allées* lead towards enticing iron gates and on into further gardens. One route leads to the greenhouse garden, full of more colour and more flowers in every shade and size.

The productive garden is Jim's realm: We walked along tasting fruit from lines of red and black currants, and admired his kale and climbing beans.

The visit finished sitting under a wisteria and variegated euonymus arbour, tucked in between two house gables. It was snug and comfortable. Overhead, a little cat visiting for a few days from Dublin looked liked he might like to stay.

Clonohill Gardens

Clonohill House, Coolrain, Portlaoise, Co. Laois. Tel: 087 9962 864. 057 8735 091.
e-mail: clonohillgardens@gmail.com Contact: Enda Thompson-Phelan. Open: As part of the Laois Garden
Trail. May-Sept. By appointment only. Partially wheelchair accessible. No dogs. Special features: Teas can
be arranged. Bus parking. Member of the Gardens of Ireland Trust. Directions: From Dublin, take Exit
18 off the M7 in the direction of Mountrath (R445). Drive through the town towards Limerick. 1.5 km
after the town turn right signed Coolrain. Travel for about 5 km to a crossroads and a stop sign. Follow
the signs straight for Laois Angling Centre. At the T-junction turn left. The entrance to Clonohill Gardens
and Angling Centre is 100 m along on left.

Travel up a drive, lined on one side by young beech trees and foxgloves and on the other by a paddock of sheep and you're almost there. All is neat and tended. The smart money says the garden will be good and it is. The drive ducks in under a grove of tall trees and the first of Enda Thompson-Phelan's gardens, a little wood, appears. Enda has an eye for design and her treatment of this wood is assured. You walk along spongy, mulched paths lined with moss-covered boulders and tree trunks. The beds are full of shade-loving and in particular, spring flowering plants like hellebores, erythroniums and trilliums. There are ferns and hostas galore, ribbons and ribbons of them, flowing along the side of the path in the dappled shade like rivers of foliage. Enda loves them. I love the primitive stone sculptures and ornaments she sets about between the plants.

Eventually, the route leads out to a long sun-trap flower border, bright with zappy golds and acid yellows, a place for the sunglasses, backed by a long, stone barn. Even on a dull day the colours in this bed make it feel like summer. From Japanese acers and gleaming golden philadelphus, lysimachia, cistus and more bright variegated hostas, it gleams. From there, the path leads back into the shade, around the house which is deeply engulfed in all sorts of shrub and flower borders. Arches, heavy with climbers, direct you into yet another wood, but this time, more highly worked and ornamental than the first.

This area is full to brimming with flowers alongside the ferns. From within the wood, the sight of an open lawn washing up against this shaded flower wood, seduces the walker back into the open. You know you are being played with and it is a pleasure, being enticed this way and that with good design, well constructed vistas, cleverly aimed paths, and secrets unveiled as you round a corner. The walled garden is a very individual take on a feature we most of us think we know what to expect from. Enda's walled garden is a treat, a chocolate box full good things, well chosen and well tended.

She is a knowledgeable gardener who will happily talk plants, swop knowledge and send you home more informed and inspired than when you arrived.

Dove House Sensory Garden

Main Street, Abbeyleix, Co. Laois. Tel: 057 8731 325. e-mail: dovehouse@scjms.ie Open: All year. Mon-
Fri., 10am-4pm. Wheelchair accessible. Supervised children. No dogs. Special features: Braille signage.
Directions: Driving into Abbeyleix on the N8 from Portlaoise, the garden is through a set of blue gates on
the left, just after the Heritage Centre.

The Sensory Garden is set within the walled gardens of the Brigidine Convent in the middle of the picturesque village of Abbeyleix. In 1996 the Sisters of Charity gave the land to the town. This led to the gift being turned into a community garden and a series of sensory garden rooms. The aim is to appeal in particular to blind and visually impaired visitors. This involves braille-labelled beds, easily negotiated paths, and plants chosen for their leaf texture and scent as much as for flower colour.

The backbone of the garden is a circle of mature limes underplanted with bulbs. A path runs along and under the circle. There are smaller gardens set within and around the circle, from secret garden rooms, rose pergolas and lawns, one of which has a dolphin swimming through the grass toward a wildlife pond.

The garden has matured hugely over two decades and today there are plenty of hide and seek paths running between the High King's chairs built for children, and the little teahouse. If this looks familiar it is because it is based on the bandstand in St. Stephen's Green in Dublin. The sculpture garden adds another element with its wire-work foxes and paper *maché* bulls. The potager with a snug lime arbour teaches children about growing vegetables and the hornbeam maze is fattening up. I like the thatched summerhouse surrounded by scented roses. Sitting in here is a perfumed pleasure. Indeed there are seats scattered everywhere, beside raised beds of golden oregano and pineapple mint.

On an historic note, a rill or sunken, directed stream that once flowed through the town, can still be seen in the garden, where it wanders along by the paths and beds.

This is a sort of secret, sort of wild garden in the middle of the town, a peaceful place, running to keep up with itself on the matter of weeds but you cannot buy atmosphere.

Dunmore Country School

Swan Road, Durrow, Co. Laois. Tel: 087 1258 002. 057 8736 578.
e-mail: tanguy@dunmorecountryschool.ie www.dunmorecountryschool.ie. Contact: Tanguy de Toulgoët.
Open: As part of the Laois Garden Trail. Mar-Oct. By appointment only. Supervised children. Dogs on leads. Special features: Garden school. Classes through English or French. Classes on natural beekeeping (Warre hive). Garden tool sales. Teas can be arranged. Directions: Leave Durrow by the R434 and take the first turn right onto Swan Road and an immediate left. The garden is a few metres along the lane.

The prospect of a French country garden in deepest County Laois is an appealing one. Add in that you can visit and take a lesson in how to garden, through French, if you wish and the prospect of visiting becomes thoroughly fascinating.

To spend an hour in the company of Tanguy de Toulgeöt is akin to being marinated in a bath of garden knowledge. He is a man with a passion for growing edible and ornamental plants, in his own words, for 'nature and for taste.' He carries out his unique and experimental gardening on a most picturesque plot just outside Durrow.

It is not an old garden but it feels like it, from the house, snug in the middle of a scrum of pink roses, 'Pink Cloud, and 'Albertine' among them. Perennial *Phlox* 'Miss Lingard' and delphiniums, grow in profusion on stone ledges against the house and snaking, ascending gravel paths pick their way between expansive runs of nepeta and *Geranium* 'Rozanne'. To study how many plants can be fitted into a surprisingly small space is reason enough to visit Dunmore. Every corner has been used to accommodate impressive numbers of bulbs, perennials and annuals, usually with an additional fruit tree or rose bush overhead for good measure. Fallow areas are quickly seeded with phacelia, a green manure and bee magnet.

Tanguy's roses are everywhere, grown over peacock blue arches and obelisks. Their names read like romantic novels - gallica and 'Ville de Bruxelles', 'Petit du hollande', 'Jacques Cartier' which flowers from May to October, and 'Blush noisette'. Scented trails of mint, dill and verbena are woven between them.

Nearly everything in the garden can be used in the kitchen. Even the fences are productive, some of which are made of step-over, cordoned apples. The variety Tanguy favours is 'Pomme de moisson'. While it is hard work to prune it is worth the bother. The range of vegetables found between the flowers is both wide and eclectic, from perennial kale and cut-and-come broccoli to Babington's leek and a host of unusual salads.

This is a garden built on sustainable growing methods and the need to nurture the endangered bee population. Every plant here is grown for its use to bees and other pollinating insects. The garden combines both practicality and romance and for all its usefulness, it still feels like walking through a soft focus film. From the roadside entrance where the ditch sprouts white scented narcissi, *Anemone blanda* and geraniums, ox-eye daisies, cowslips and camassias, to the tall flowers and vegetables grown together, divided by rose arches and trained fruit trees, herbs and flowering shrubs, it is a most beautiful garden.

Even the surrounding hedges have been clipped like swags and festoons.

Visit early in the season to see the bones; well-made dry stone walls, iron arches, gravel paths bounded by slate and iron edging and the skeletons of trained fruit trees. As the season goes on, the flowers take over. The only paths that remain visible through the summer are the grass ones through the orchard. They skirt medlars, damsons, quinces and an Irish apple called 'Glory of the West', which is good for juicing. There are also several old unknowns that Tanguy grafted himself. He grows French apples for cider. The fruiting hedges full of black and red currants, mixed with *Rosa gallica* 'Versicolor', are raided for jellies and dried petals. 'Cut off the white base of the petals with a scissors' he advises for the best, sweetest petals. Bring an empty notebook. I have visited the garden several times and each time have come away with almost a notebook full of scribbles, written at a hundred miles an hour in an attempt to keep up with the torrent of information Tanguy dispenses.

Emo Court

Emo, Portlaoise, Co. Laois. Tel: 057 8626 573. 086 8107 916. e-mail: emocourt@opw.ie
www.opw.ie Open: All year, daylight hours. Wheelchair accessible. Supervised children. Dogs on leads.
Special features: Free admission but tours must be booked. Tea room. Gift shop. House tours, Easter-Sept.
Directions: From M7 take Exit 15 for Emo and follow the signs. At the roundabout take the 3rd exit. In the village turn right at the sign for Emo Court.

Emo Court was built in 1790 for the Earls of Portarlington and forms the second largest walled park in Europe after the Phoenix Park in Dublin. The gardens were first laid out in the 18th century, but development continued until the middle of the 19th. Emo's parkland and arboretum are a complete contrast to more flower-filled gardens. Their charm is in substantial features, like sweeps of lawn, views across the park to groves of trees, or over the huge man-made lake and woods. Among the most striking of these trees is a fabulous *Cupressus macrocarpa* or Monterey cypress, close to the house. It has over 20 trunks.

Since the demesne was taken into state care in the early 1990s, a great deal of work has been carried out on the gardens. Close by the house rolling manicured lawns are cross-banded by avenues of clipped and

trained yews. (The restored swagged railings near the house are worth noting.)

Running from the front of the house to what was once the main entrance to Emo, but is now a dead end, is the estate's most famous feature – The longest avenue of Wellingtonia (*Sequoiadendron giganteum*) in the country. At just over 160 years old, the trees are mere juveniles, and they will still be growing when Emo is on its umpteenth restoration.

An ornamental game larder stands by the garden entrance complete with ceiling hooks visible through the decorative windows, so that visitors could inspect and appreciate the bag from the estate's most recent shoot.

This area is called the Clucker, a wooded area where rhododendrons thrive in a pocket of acid soil. The path makes its way from here through another avenue of restored yews, eventually leading back out to the lawns and beyond them, to the Grapery, like the Clucker, a name of unknown origin. Here is where the special trees such as sequoias, weeping beech, *Picea smithiana* and *Pinus niger,* the black and Corsican pines are found. The path runs down to a pair of ornate golden gates which were possibly made by Richard Turner. (See National Botanic Gardens in Dublin and Woodstock in Kilkenny). The walled garden has an attractive bell tower and split-level gardener's cottage dating to the 17th century.

The centrepiece of the long restoration project was a complete overhaul of the 25-acre ornamental lake. 19 acres are under water and there are three islands. To bring this back to life, the whole lake was drained. Tons of silt and build-up, reeds and rushes were dragged out, and then it was refilled and once more transformed into a pristine body of water, complete with fishing stands and new walks. The temple by the sluice gates was used as a teahouse folly, built in the 1850s. Someone once said that you know you have too much money when you start building follies.

Fruitlawn Garden

Fruitlawn, Abbeyleix, Co. Laois. Tel: 057 8730146. e-mail: arthurshackleton9@gmail.com www.arthurshackleton.com Contact: Arthur Shackleton and Carol Booth. Open: As part of the Laois Garden Trail. May-Oct. By appointment to groups. See website for additional open day details. Wheelchair accessible. Children supervised. No dogs. Special features: Plant sales. Classes. Member of the Gardens of Ireland Trust. Directions: Take the Ballacolla road from Abbeyleix. After 4 km turn right to Shanahoe onto the L1653. Just under 1 km along, pass a large white house on the right. Fruitlawn is the next entrance between two stone buildings.

'A swarm of bees in May is worth a load of hay.
A swarm of bees in June is worth a silver spoon.
A swarm of bees on July isn't worth a fly.'
Arthur Shackleton and a friend were standing in his garden debating swallows and bees in the roof space over his house. It set the perfect tone for a visit to his old-fashioned country garden. Arthur is a renowned garden designer whose own base near Abbeyleix is a pleasure to visit in the summer months. It is like walking through an Impressionist painting, all colour, all light, all alive. He gardens in generous sweeps with wide borders divided by equally wide gravel paths. There is nothing pernickety here. This

is loose and relaxed, full of self-seeders like *Verbena bonariensis* and aquilegia, ladies mantle, forget-me-nots and violas, that grow into the paths, as well as into the borders.

There is structure too however. The main double border is defined by solid, plum pudding shaped box specimens, more 'splats' than balls, around which the perennials, flowering shrubs, bulbs and annuals sport. Many of the plants here come from the historic Shackleton walled garden, Beech Park, just outside Dublin, in Clonsilla. We looked at Beech Park camassias and double white trilliums. There are unusual and lesser-spotted plants everywhere. I like *Iris missouriensis* and a pretty *Bupleurum fruticosum* that came from the famed, late Better Farquhar of Tipperary. Drifts of tall phlox and *Campanula lactiflora,* roses and hardy geraniums form frothy clouds of colour that butt up against tree peonies. If, as a designer Arthur has a signature, it would probably be the tunnel, made in either hornbeam or beech and a tunnel is one of the first features to greet the visitor to Fruitlawn. This example is a fine long hornbeam version, perfectly squared off, cut with 'windows' to let in enough light so that the inside is as green as the lush outer branches.

Fruitlawn was originally the old walled garden and attendant yards attached to a big house close by. Arthur took the existing, dividing stone walls to host climbing plants, from *Rosa* 'Alister Stella Grey' and rather rarer *Schisandra rubriflora* and climbers like the pitcher flower climber, *Aristolochia macrophylla* which doesn't look as though it should live outside.

Do not miss the oak wood. It is only about the size of an average suburban lawn. Everyone tells Arthur that the trees are too close but he likes them, slim stretching straight up and elegant.

If informality is allowed in the flower borders and in the wild flower areas, in the kitchen garden order reigns supreme. The ground is given to neat rows of well behaved kale, asparagus and beans, trained fruit bushes and trees grown on wires.

This is a designer's garden that rather wonderfully, does not feel designed.

Gash Gardens

Castletown, Portlaoise, Co. Laois. Tel: 087 2737 883. 057 8732 247. e-mail: gashgardens@eircom.net. www.gashgardens.ie Contact: Mary Keenan and Ross Doyle. Open: May-Sept. Mon-Sat, 10am-5pm. Closed Sun. Otherwise by appointment to groups. Not suitable for small children. Special features: Teas can be arranged. Plant sales. Dogs on leads. Directions: Take Exit 18 off the M7 travelling through Mountrath to Castletown. Leave the village by the R545. The garden is signposted.

Mary Keenan is a plant expert of note. Along with her husband Ross Doyle, she has been developing the four-acre garden started by her father Noel many years ago. The task of teasing and changing a garden, ensuring its place into the future, adding to its existing features and creating new ones, working with the natural assets, and even the drawbacks of the site, is a complicated business. These changes are first seen in the front garden where Mary has created a cottage garden, full of old roses – She loves *Rosa* 'Chandos Beauty' as a fabulous pink scented double. I love where she placed a young *Acer griseum* perfectly to catch the sun through its papery, copper-coloured peeling bark.

The nursery is around the corner. Today it looks more like a series of raised beds than a nursery. There are more roses, here draped on swags, and sloped bank beds with *Silene fimbriata*, asters, geraniums and lupins. Colour themed beds include a pink and blue border starring sky-scraping, five-metre tall cardoons or *Cynara cardunculus*.

For anyone who has visited Gash before, the most memorable feature must be the Moon House. This is a little cave set in the base of a large rockery. You sit inside peeping out through a circular stone opening into a cascade of water coming from above. The roar of the crashing water is invigorating but the Moon House is only one, albeit most spectacular, of a number of water features at Gash. There are ponds, streams and rivulets crisscrossing the garden, travelling in all directions, dividing and linking different garden rooms, feeding the roots and dictating the sort of plants that do best here.

Mary likes rhododendrons and plants them in her limy soil by inserting them into acid mounds, a reminder that their feeding roots are only ever 20 cms from the surface. The collection of trees also includes *Metasequoia glyptostroboides* and liquidambar, flowering *Cornus mas* and *Cornus kousa*.

The style is flowing and informal, taking in an easy mix of natural-looking rockeries, planted up with sweeps of perennials and shrubs, seen to advantage from a raised viewing ledge. There are also dainty alpine beds, borders of herbaceous perennials, ponds and streams, mixed shrubs borders, laburnum walks and damp, shaded ferneries.

One of the stand-out planting schemes here is the circle of *Hydrangea* 'Annabelle' wrapped around an inner circle of *Hydrangea sargentiana*, grown for its strong foliage.

Her enthusiasms are scattered through the place, as in the collection of Solomon's seal relatives by one of the streams. These include evergreen *Disporopsis pernyi* and *Polygonatum verticillatum*. Overhead, a *Salix magnifica* with big leaves and dark stems, cuts a dash. Not for nothing is it called the magnificent willow.

Grasses are deployed in drifts throughout the place. *Stipa gigantea, Miscanthus sacchariflorus* and

bulrushes planted in numbers, create a strong visual statement as well as a background rustle in the slightest breeze.

The garden was extended out into the countryside with the planting of a mixed maple walk along the bank of the River Nore. This stretches for a quarter of a mile along the river and passes a stream that Mary and Ross have banked and added waterfalls to, making the walk even more attractive.

Mary continues to plant and expand: The latest features are two new natural-style ponds. She made one in an outlying paddock that constantly flooded and another in the centre of the garden where the ground is always wet. When it comes to water, the wisest route is to go with the flow rather than argue with nature.

Heywood Garden

Ballinakill, Co. Laois. Tel: 057 8733 563. e-mail: heywood@opw.ie www.opw.ie. Open: All year during daylight hours. Supervised children welcome. (Steep drops). Partially wheelchair accessible. Special features: No entrance fee. Guided tours by appointment. (Fee charged). Directions: 7 km from Abbeyleix, off the R432 to Ballinakill, in the grounds of Ballinakill Community School.

Edwin Lutyens was an architect whose work with the great plantswoman Gertrude Jekyll is well known to garden lovers. He created a small number of Irish gardens some with and some without the help of Jekyll. Along with the National War Memorial Garden in Islandbridge in Dublin, the formal garden at Heywood ranks as the best known of his Irish gardens. His garden at Heywood is a small but spectacular place, set in the middle of a greater demesne in the rolling Laois countryside and it is known and admired by garden visitors everywhere. Visiting it today, it seems incongruously attached to a modern secondary school. The reason for this is that Heywood House, the property to which it was attached was destroyed by fire in the 1950s. The formal garden that today appears slightly adrift of the world, was once overlooked by a large house.

Lutyens' garden was created on several levels of an embankment standing out from the now disappeared house. The main attraction of this formal garden is the sunken, circular, terrace with a central lily pond surrounded by spitting lead turtles and an oversized fountain shaped like a massive champagne glass, out of proportion to the pond. The turtles are reproduction, based on the only one not stolen before the garden was restored. It was saved by one time guardian of Heywood, Fr. Seamus Cummins, who stored it under his bed in a suitcase.

Jekyll designed the planting scheme and while her plans have been lost, a study of her garden at Hestercombe in England gave the gardeners at Heywood the direction they needed during the restoration. Her signature plants are herbaceous perennials such as calendula and nepeta, pink phlox and Japanese anemone, *Viola cornuta* 'Huntercombe Purple' and silver stachys, peonies, bergenia and *Rosa* 'Nathalie Nypels'. They run around the circular garden in two ledges.

Sit into the summerhouse built in grey, lichen-covered, split limestone and covered in jasmine. The sheltering outer walls, have been cut with circular windows, each of which frames a little vista, like landscape paintings on a drawing-room wall. The views include rolling parkland, distant church spires, the village nearby and cattle that came straight from central casting. The compositions are worthy of Constable and when the church bells in the distance ring, it is pure heaven. Lutyens is said to have declared that that no-one could touch the Irish stone masons for quality of work.

Leaving the formal circular garden, the path leads through an ornate wrought-iron gate to a short avenue of pleached limes and a pergola on a high ledge above and overlooking the lake, woods and wider pleasure grounds. The wall is cut with niches for pieces of sculpture. To the side of the path, lawns surrounded by more low stone walls and herbaceous borders also float above the fields below. Visitors with children should note that the low walls mask steep drops on the other side. The whole garden is on a raised ledge overlooking the parkland. Small children should not be left alone.

Linked to these two main areas is a maze of small garden rooms. Walking between the tiny enclosures you will come across hot borders full of geum, gold helianthemum, rudbeckia and kniphofia. There are also sundial rooms, little iris and hellebore gardens wrapped in yew hedging with stone bird baths and hide-and-seek hedges that create a sense of mystery.

But the Lutyens garden is only part of a bigger entity and within it, there are several small features that point to an older garden. These are the ionic pillars in the pergola. They came from the Old Parliament building in Dublin (today the Bank of Ireland, College Green). There is also a carved Coade stone shell-fountain in one of the little garden rooms and the plaque in the summerhouse, with lines from an Alexander Pope poem. These fragments date to the 1770s and are thought to have come from a folly once situated in the older garden out in the greater pleasure grounds.

In the 1990s the land came into the hands of the OPW. There followed an amount of detective work by the then Park Superintendent Patricia (Paddy) Friel. Using historic records, she researched the older garden and found a substantial romantic demesne that dated from the late 18th century, which had been almost forgotten. The years since have seen it unearthed and restored. The discovery has added hugely to an already fine garden.

This garden, Heywood's most recent discovery, down in the woods was created by Frederick Trench, a tenant of the original house. He was a fashionable, well travelled and educated man and his garden reflected the tastes of his time. It was made up of trails or rides past a series of features including a sham castle incorporating an arched window appropriated from Aghaboe Abbey, 20 kilometres away, in what could be termed an early form of vandalism. Gothic follies and a hermitage peep out from beyond woods and hills. There are orangeries, a bath house, plunge pool, an artificial lake with boat house, serpentine pools and streams. It is wonderful that this wild and romantic garden has been saved from oblivion. The two gardens together make up one of the most satisfying visits in the country.

Barmeath Castle, Co. Louth.

Louth

Barmeath Castle

Dunleer, Co. Louth. Tel: 041 6851 205. e-mail: annbellew@rocketmail.com. www.barmeath-castle.com www.boynevalleygardentrail.com Contact: Bru Bellew. Open: As part of the Boyne Valley Garden Trail. See website for details. Groups by appointment. Special features: Castle tours. Directions: On application.

Being told about one of the oldest archery grounds in Ireland, rustic stone bridges over serpentine lakes dating back to the 18th century and a walled garden 'almost back to its 1820's glory', makes a nosy visitor excited. These descriptions of Barmeath castle gardens were not exaggerated. First there is that view, a castle standing four square at the top of a grand drive. This fine building 'started off life rather modestly as a ten pound castle', Bru Bellew, the current incumbent, told me. In the 700 years or so since then, it has been improved several times, according to him, thanks to the propensity of its lords to marry heiresses.

Queen Maeve is thought to have camped on this hilly site before moving into the mountains where she captured the wild bull of Cooley. Later, in the 1200s the Bellews arrived with Hugh de Lacy. These bits of lore were doled out as we walked through a border of tree peonies that Bru's grandmother planted. From here we made our way into an oak wood with an understory of box, rhododendron, fern, myrtle and the occasional tree fern.

Leaving the woods, we made our way along paths edged by unusual low slate walls that hold back the rushes and willows on route to the Dam, an artificial river, and part of the overall garden design implemented by Thomas Wright when he came to Ireland in 1745. The whole garden, including this water feature had fallen into disrepair by the 1920s when Bru's grandparents took over the place. 'My grandmother was a keen gardener,' he explained as we walked past walls of pale pink fuchsia and more rhodos, with occasional views of rolling fields through openings in the greenery. A buzzard flew out over and past us as we moved back under a tunnel of willow, emerging out to the light and a view of Thomas Wright's fantastic bridge, a gothic confection of knobbled stone.

All along the water the wet ground suits an ever spreading run of candelabra primulas, and in the distance, the upper layers star some great explosions of rhododendron, planted in the 1890s.

We took a path through the beech wood to the walled garden, past a recently planted maze and along a walk between lines of hydrangea.

There was no record of it on the 1770 map and Bru thinks the walled garden was built in 1800. Until ten years ago it was a bit of a sorry neglected place, but the four-and-a-half acres have spent the last decade being hauled into shape. The results are impressive. Hornbeam hedging and a network of gravel paths divide the garden into regular plots of young orchards and vegetable beds while decorative borders run the length of the walls. One of these borders is an impressive 50 metres long. The walls meanwhile, are being systematically recapped by a talented builder, William McQuaid, who is also responsible for the octagonal brick summerhouse, a handsome little building surrounded by giant clumps of *Echium candicans*.

A rose walk made of a long series of iron arches, planted with pink roses over complimentary peonies, cuts through the middle of the garden.

We left by way of the archery ground, the oldest on the island, and made our way past lines of old Irish yews to the Victorian Dogs Graveyard and a laurel lawn, which they clip once a year.

All this restoration, it seems is thanks to a priest friend of Bru's who looked at the overgrown garden and said two words to him:

'Clear it'.

These were followed up by two more words several months later:

'Keep going'.

Wise words. Bru's feelings on the matter is that a garden either goes forward or backward. Barmeath is going forward, steadily.

Beaulieu

Drogheda, Co. Louth. Contact: Tel 041 9838 557. 086 6039 818. e-mail: info@beaulieuhouse.ie www.boynevalleygardentrail.com Open: As part of the Boyne Valley Garden Trail. See website for details. Other times by appointment. Partially wheelchair accessible. Supervised children. Dogs on leads. Special features: House tours. Teas can be arranged. Directions: The garden is on the right turn towards Baltray (R167) off the Drogheda to Termonfeckin Road (R166), 2 km from Termonfeckin.

Beaulieu House was built in 1628 on the banks of the Boyne and refurbished between 1710 and 1720. It bears the distinction of being the first non-fortified house of its kind on the island. The style of the redbrick house at the top of a short, wide, straight drive, is unusual for Ireland and looks as though it might have been borrowed from northern France or Holland. The bricks came from the Netherlands.

It has been gardened by eleven generations of the same family. In my visits there I have met three of those generations, starting with the late Mrs. Sidney Waddington, a tiny, but determined woman who worked it up to her mid-80s and battled to maintain the unusual old garden. Her daughter took over and carried on and today, Cara Konig, her granddaughter continues the work. It is looking beautiful.

The walled garden is set close by the house and is bordered by a mature wood. The Dutch artist Willem Van der Hagan, who painted several canvasses that can be seen in the house, as well as an allegorical work on the ceiling of the drawing room, was also reputed as a designer of walled gardens. If he designed it, this dates the garden to before 1732.

To get to the garden take a path, bordered by golden yew and fuchsia, which passes a small temple-like building and a faded and fragile old greenhouse with a small grotto and fernery. On stepping inside, you are greeted by a huge border on a wide ledge which looks down over the rest of the garden. Many of the plants are old cottage varieties that have been grown here for generations, adding to its charm. The flowers include white galtonia, variegated mallow, asters, phlox and rust-coloured phormium. Plants like exotic *Cautleya spicata*, which marries red stalks, red-veined leaves and vivid yellow flowers, and the Maltese cross (*Lychnis chalcedonica*) in a shade of red that scares off more timid gardeners, are just two among the bolder plants in the south-facing border. At eight metres deep, this bed holds an enormous number of plants in sometimes surprising combinations of leaf and flower: White agapanthus beside cream and green variegated sage, waves of anemone and the honey bush, *Melianthus major* are thoughtfully mixed. Big pink crinum lilies and kale or *Crambe cordifolia*, like sprays of gypsophila, make another memorable combination. The sundial is hours out of synch as it trundles along at its own pace, standing head-high over the flowers. Losing time here seems like the thing to do.

The path running the length of this dreamy old border leads down toward a summerhouse that looks like something in which the Crooked Man from the nursery rhyme might have lived. But before getting to it, you walk past a knot garden made of intricate walls of box surrounding splashy roses, purple heliotrope and antirrhinum. Two huge Irish yews, nearly 300-years old, hide a shady foxglove and hellebore garden to the side of this formal bed. Mrs. Waddington planted a eucryphia here in the 1950s, which she once declared 'almost too full of flowers.' It is. Its branches sag under the weight of blossoms.

Both border and knot garden sit on the raised ledge at the top of the garden. The level drops down to where the productive vegetable and fruit growing

areas are sited. The bank down to this area is covered in meadow grass, hardy cranesbill and other wildflowers. Down below, paths run under rose-covered arches and trellises covered with trained apple trees, into the vegetable and working kitchen garden. It is obvious that there is no large staff available to mind the Beaulieu gardens but despite manpower shortages and the resulting slight wild look, this is a garden with a truly magical atmosphere.

Collon House

Collon, Co. Louth. Tel: 087 235 5645. e-mail: collonhousereception@gmail.com www.collonhouse.com Contact: Michael McMahon and John Bentley-Dunn. www.boynevalleygardentrail. com Open: By appointment to groups only. Partially wheelchair accessible. Dogs on leads. Special features: Accommodation. House and garden tours. Lunches. Bus parking possible. Directions: Situated in the centre of Collon at the crossroads.

Although you can see tumbles of roses coming out over the walls and around the front gate, the gardens at Collon House are secreted away from view, revealing themselves only as you travel up the short drive under a laburnum arch, between rhododendrons, landing finally into an open gravelled area in front of the Georgian house.

A mixed border surrounds this area, full of the soft yellows of aconitum and cephalaria and a monster *Rosa* 'Rambling Rector' that managed to bring down a whole pergola which once ran the length of this border. The result of the chaos is that the remaining, free-standing pillars now accommodate good looking tangles of *Clematis jackmanii*, *Rosa* 'American pillar', honeysuckle, and a new secret garden tucked into the middle of the border.

This well arranged collection of shrubs and herbaceous plants is a far cry from the overflow garden full of evergreens that they found when Michael McMahon and John Bentley-Dunn arrived here in the 1970s. My visit was on a dreadful day, but the weather was unsuccessful in its attempt to make the garden less attractive. We sheltered from the spilling rain under the shelter of an Edwardian summerhouse, overlooking a square of textbook lawn, deep, mixed borders full of flowers and shrubs, held behind low box walls.

'When we started we decided to work with the 18th century house and create a garden in keeping with it. So what we have is a formal walled flower garden,' Michael told me. The design of five hemmed-in borders both looks well and is easier to work than one long border.

The line of potted box balls along the house wall are nail-clipper smart in a good contrast to the sprawling expanses of *Rosa* 'Bobbie James', 'Lady Hillingdon and 'Zephirine Drouhin' on the walls. I love the big cherry, clad in *Rosa* 'Bantry Bay' blocking off sight from the lower garden. Walking beyond it reveals a precisely cut and trained knot garden of box and a semicircular series of columns.

Everywhere around the garden there are pots, big ones full of roses, that 'do well if you really feed them' according to Michael. There are hydrangeas and lots of hostas, gathered together in their own shaded corner of the courtyard. I am not in the least surprised to find out that Michael's background is in design. The impressive style is only matched by impeccable upkeep.

Forest Edge

*5, Forest Edge, Stameen, Drogheda, Co. Louth. Tel: 087 4164 890. 041 9841 436.
e-mail: chobrienlynch@gmail.com See Facebook: Forest Edge Garden. www.boynevalleygardentrail.
com Contact: Christopher and Debbie O'Brien-Lynch. Open: May-Oct. By appointment. Groups up to
25 welcome. Not wheelchair accessible. No children. No dogs.*

There is no doubt which garden on this quiet road on the edge of Drogheda is *the open garden*. So many plants spill out onto the footpath, it announces itself from a distance. Forest Edge is a small garden attached to a semi-detached house but Christopher and Debbie O'Brien Lynch meet the conundrum of a lack of horizontal space with a vertical answer: This is a garden of layers, starting at the top with acers and pruned-up hollies, roses in the mid section and underneath hostas, ferns, self-seeding nigella and hardy geraniums. Plant-stuffed is the term.

Christopher explained to me that he built a set of terraces and steps on what had started as a slope 'for more surface area' and to fit more plants. He manages to pare and prune the upper layers, so that the sun gets down to the lower regions and the whole creation manages to appear see-through, busy as it is.

To the side of the house where the sun never reaches there is a little fern garden with *Dicksonia antarctica* and multiple pots of smaller specimens.

From here we moved to the middle garden, just behind the house and encountered a bewildering number of plants in pots and in the ground. This is high-maintenance stuff. Climbing, golden hop, *Rosa* 'Bonica' and *Clematis* 'Hotel de ville' obscure the walls. Walls of pruned-up bamboo draw the eye up as well as allowing the visitor to look through the plantation to the sight of yet more roses, or the summerhouse, into which a white wisteria has insinuated itself and grown huge in the process.

There are several ponds. The glint and sound of water are never far away in this jungle garden. One is surrounded by fossil-pocked stone and more pots of roses. Here and elsewhere, the pots are all in the same peacock blue.

One side of the garden is bounded by a mixed hedge, cut with windows so the neighbours have sight and enjoyment of each other's plots.

The garden is broken into several areas, of woodland, flower border and water, linked by paths that thread through and between the great mass of well minded plants. A carefully tempered jungle that should show that size need not be a barrier to adventurous gardening.

Killineer House & Garden

*Killineer, Drogheda, Co. Louth. Contact: Charles Carroll. Tel: 041 9838 563.
e-mail: charles.p.carroll@gmail.com www.killineerhouse.ie www.boynevalleygardentrail.com Open: As part
of the Boyne Valley Garden Trail. Contact for details. Groups at any time. Partially wheelchair accessible.
Special features: Historic house. Directions: Travelling north on the M1, take the first left to Drogheda/
Monasterboice after the suspension bridge. At the roundabout, take the Drogheda exit. Go through the
next roundabout, in the direction of Monasterboice. At the third, turn left for Monasterboice. The garden
is about 1 km along on the right, with a lodge and green gates.*

Killineer was built in the mid 1840s on a hill looking south over Drogheda, with 17 acres of garden attached. I would bet that it enjoys the distinction of having the most extensive laurel lawn on the island. This is an laurel grown as a hip-high 'lawn' through which tall oak, beech and ash trees, as well as more rarefied magnolia and *Cornus kousa* emerge and tower over.

On the other side of the drive is a man-made lake.

The house, looks from its perch, down over sloped and stepped lawns to the bottom of the hill. It takes in views of the lake, a little temple-like summerhouse and stands of specimen trees including a big *Thujopsis dolabrata* and *Chamaecyparis lawsoniana* 'Triumph of boskoop'. These have been pruned up so their lifted skirts allow one see to through them to views of the water and the greater grounds beyond. A good proportion of the garden at the bottom of the slope is light woodland, and in the woods, the damp ground is festooned with candelabra primulas. Charles Carroll has been busily encouraging their spread. He says this is an easy task because there are two underground streams here keeping the ground sufficiently moist.

In other areas, carpets of white lamium or dead-nettle spread out under the trees. Charles is not so pleased with that but it still looks good and its pale

foliage is spiked with ferns like dramatic *Dryopteris affinis 'Cristata'*.

Down here, one of the plants that must be seen, is the third biggest holly in the country. The strange knobbles on its trunk are indicators of age. Nearby, the spongy bark path runs under tunnels of rhododendron, among which there are red leafed *R. arborea* and *R. sinogrande*. There are newly planted baby acers, magnolias and rare rhododendrons everywhere.

Charles loves his trees and witness to this is the Caucasian wingnut or *Pterocarya fraxinifolia* which fell in a storm. With the help of a tractor, some friends, and plenty of rope, he managed to right the casualty and today it is heading skywards again.

The walled garden dates back to Regency times and alongside the big stone outhouses, this is a grand, if slightly sleepy part of the operation. Deep, mixed borders line the walls, and *Hoheria glabrata* and *Hydrangea villosa* mix it with fruiting figs and a greenhouse full to bursting with nectarines and apricots. Vegetable beds and wild flower squares take up the bulk of the one-and-a-quarter-acre space with extra wide paths dividing them.

The word substantial best describes these gardens, with their sweeps of lawn, well trimmed hedges, stands of trees and shrubs. The woods, shot through with streams, surround the more tended, cultivated areas and there is a sense of a subtly, gently reined-in garden.

Listoke Gardens

Ballymakenny Road, Drogheda, Co. Louth. Tel: 041 9832 265. (0)41 9844 742. 087 744 7057. e-mail: info@listoke.com www.boynevalleygardentrail.com Contact: Patricia Barrow. Open: As part of the Boyne Valley Garden Trail. Contact for annual details. Other times by appointment. Children welcome. Special features: Tea rooms. Plants shop in old wash house. Art gallery. Animals, pets and rescue animals.

I remember visiting Listoke a number of years ago. Patricia Barrow ran a well ordered garden reminiscent of a classic Edwardian country house. We floated along herbaceous borders, passing an old-fashioned lawn tennis court with a little pavilion. It stayed in my mind. Time has passed and while the purist might gripe about perfect edges, I think Patricia's garden is more interesting today, particularly as a garden to bring children. There is something especially

welcoming about the place. Between walking around the flower borders full of loose plantings of echinops and hemerocallis, to a backing of park trees beyond the walls, there is an easy feeling to this garden.

The path leads in under arched trees to an atmospheric wood garden with cornus and betula and rampant *Rosa* 'Rambling Rector' clambering over the neighbouring shrubs and trees in the mid-layer, and hellebores and bluebells underneath. There are actually big loose explosions of rambling roses everywhere in the garden. As we walked through the wood, she told me about how charming Gerard Depardieu had been when he came to shoot 'Asterix and Obelix' in among these trees.

Roses and lavender surround the tennis court to the extent that I had visions of players spending more time hunting among the flowers for the ball than playing.

Beside the court there is an old stone shed flanked by a similar sized yew, perfectly clipped to echo the shape of the shed, except that it occasionally sprouts a shoot of *Romneya coulteri*.

The garden is slightly ruffled. It feels like a place to enjoy getting lost in, a little like F. Hodgson Burnett's 'Secret Garden'. Along one walk we had to duck to get in under a dripping laburnum, catching a glimpse across a lawn, through an orchard. I came upon the recently restored greenhouse, back in its Edwardian glory and home to a collection of cacti. They turned out to not belong to Patricia. She is in fact, not overly fond of cacti. They belong to an elderly lady whose collection was in need of minding. It perfectly sums up Patricia Barrow. She restores her greenhouse and then lends its use to someone in need.

When we left it was to visit the menagerie, a collection of rare black ducks, fancy fowl, an abandoned baby barn owl staying with her as she tries to train it to independence and two house martins, from a destroyed nest. Patricia had been feeding them every 15 minutes - around the clock – throughout the previous ten days, using a tweezers. As I left a couple pulled up their car with a cardboard box containing an injured blackbird to see if Patricia might help…

Rokeby Hall

Grangebellew, Dunleer, Co. Louth. Tel: 086 864 4228. www.rokeby.ie www.boynevalleygardentrail.com. Contact: Jean Young. Open: As part of the Boyne Valley Garden Trail. Contact for annual details. Other times, groups by appointment. Special features: House tours. Teas may be arranged in advance. Bus parking. Directions: Take Exit 12 off the M1. In Dunleer turn onto the R170 to Clogherhead. 5 km on, turn right at the Grangebellew crossroads. Continue 1.5 km and the R170 becomes the L2275. Rokeby Hall gates are on the right.

The Georgian House at Rokeby has been through a long line of owners. Fascinatingly the current owner, the Young family, are once again doing what the owners of these grand old houses often did. They are building follies and temples, and in the case of Jean and her husband, an observatory on the lawn, reached by way of an equally new yew walk beside the house. Enthusiasms are a wonderful thing.

Their enthusiasms also ran to restoring the Turner conservatory that was built in 1850. Today the elegant building with its intricate iron work, is once again looking splendid painted in soft, 'Turner White'. The conservatory homes an exuberant mix of abutilon and brugmansia along with *Butia eriospatha*, more quaintly known as the wooly jelly palm and *Phoenix roebelinii*, the pygmy date palm.

It stands on a granite plinth overlooking box-lined flower borders in one direction, and a sweep of parkland in another, framed by curtains of beech, weeping cypress and oak, past young, ledged shrub and flower borders, juvenile rhododendrons and specimen trees, including a weeping evergreen oak, podocarpus and a multi-trunked thuja.

Out in the distance, beyond the orchard with its mown grass paths, a new temple or summerhouse, was being built when I visited. There is a great sense of activity and endeavour about the old house and grounds. I look forward to revisiting.

Tankardstown House, Co. Meath

Meath

Balrath House & Courtyard

Balrath, Navan, Co. Meath. Tel: 041 9825749. 087 9547883. e-mail: frances.balrathhouse@gmail.com www.balrathcourtyard.com Contact: Frances and Ray O'Brien. Open: As part of The Boyne Valley Garden Trail. See website for details. Wheelchair accessible. No dogs. Supervised children. Groups by appointment. Special features: Accommodation. Teas can be arranged. Landscape designer. Directions: Driving from Dublin to Slane on the N2 turn right at Balrath Cross onto the L1610. The garden is under 1 km along on the left.

The house at Balrath was built in 1760 with a walled garden that covers 1.5 acres overlooking the River Nanny. Frances and Ray O'Brien arrived to live here in 2003, taking over what was largely a vegetable garden. Ray is a landscape designer and so he transformed the space into an ornamental garden. 'We work it together' explained Frances.

'Ray is the designer. I'm the weeder and waterer!' As we spoke, Ray was busy working on a fern garden he has developed close to the house, a restful, white and green area, composed around a fine tree fern that has special memories. It has been living and growing here for a few years. Ray was surrounding this anchor with smaller new specimens of fern and white hydrangeas.

The overall garden is divided into a number of more intimate spaces, situated, between the grand old stone house and its associated courtyards and outhouses. There are several gardens, little rooms and private corners. The lines are all rounded and soft, with circular lawns enclosed within neatly clipped box hedges that also hold back exuberant mixed borders of irises and peonies, roses and towering echiums. Within the greater sheltering, soft shapes of the mature trees, they make optimal use of fastigiate slim conifers and clipped evergreens, which look extra sharp beside soft billows of campanula and acer. I like the injections of exoticism too, in the shape of *Trachycarpus fortunei*, which soldiers on here despite that fact that it can be a bit of a frost pocket.

The stone-lined pond is surrounded by irises and Solomon's seal. It is a sunny spot from where to sit and enjoy the sounds, the colours, scents - and the working bees and insects going about their business.

I love the ever present limestone walls, backing and sheltering the borders, and the snug little Four Seasons summerhouse. The perfect place to sit with a cup of tea and a good view of the action.

Boyne Garden Centre

Ardcalf, Slane, Co. Meath. Tel: 041 9824 350. e-mail: boynegardencentre@eircom.net www.boynegardencentre.ie. Contact: Aileen Muldoon Byrne. Open: Seven days. See website for details. Partially wheelchair accessible. Guide dogs only. Special features: Plants for sale. Teas can be arranged. Directions: On the N2 out of Slane turn left at the graveyard and follow the signs.

There are garden centres and there are garden centres. This one is a bit special. Set behind Aileen Muldoon Byrne's house and a garden full of flowers, the Boyne Garden Centre is a charmer.

'I grow all my plants to encourage pollinators,' Aileen told me. Hers is a nursery as much as a garden centre, where she brings along much of her her stock from seed, cutting and division and she has gold medals from Bloom and the Northern Ireland Garden shows to bear witness to that.

Aileen uses the house as the demonstration model of what can be done with the plants she sells on the colour and size matched benches in the nursery. One other point that I liked is that her plants, grown outside, are tough, and that too is a help to the gardener bringing them home. An inspiring place for the plant lover.

Bramley Cottage

*The Rath, Killsallaghan, Co. Meath. Tel: 087 6839 520. e-mail: jane@janemccorkell.com
www.janemccorkell.com. www.boynevalleygardentrail.com. Contact: Jane McCorkell. Open: As part of the
Boyne Valley Garden Trail. In June by appointment to groups. See website for annual details. Wheelchair
accessible. No dogs. Special features: Garden design. Directions: On application.*

A little over a decade and a half ago, garden designer Jane McCorkell arrived to live in this corner of Meath. She took on a worn out Georgian house and a blank slate where once there might have been a garden and began to experiment. This garden is as much her lab as anything. If something works for her she knows that she can recommend it to her clients. So as we walked we met all sorts of plants that she happily endorses from *Echinacea* 'Rubinstern' to reliable hornbeam for clipping and shaping.

The resulting garden is her own personal take on a traditional country garden. There is just the right amount of formality about it, with yew obelisks and box walls, hornbeam and rose arches that all hem things in and hold them up. But within those confines, the flowers are allowed to run riot and the result is a cheerful, pretty place.

Jane creates 'secret' lanes between box walls, hipped roses and cotinus. These might open onto a circular lawn or a little sitting corner surrounded by white Japanese anemones and roses.

Hunt out the, almost secret, outdoor garden room where you look through a window into a room full of *Echium pininana*, intent on escaping, with gleaming white hydrangea, bamboo and lime-coloured *Robinia pseudoacacia*. There is a definite feel of humour evident here.

Leave the house by way of a hawthorn walk that leads to a mixed border full of peony and rudbeckia, echinacea, elegant cephalaria and lilies, out to a woodland garden, all dappled light and soft greens. The well chosen small trees are everywhere, from weeping cherries and acers to liquidambars and betulas. Clipped box cubes set off the colourful splashes of phlox and veronicastrum, *Verbena bonariensis* and nepeta.

The large mixed borders, divided by a wide grass paths at the front of the house, are a delight all summer. Jane likes to use generous sweeps of each type of plant and the effect is one of abundance. There are sunken gardens and rose gardens full of David Austen favourites, mixed with upright yews and apple trees. I imagine a lot of Jane's clients simply point to her garden and say 'I'd like that'. So would I.

College Hill House & Gardens

Slane, Co. Meath. Tel: 041 9720 098. 087 1400 220. e-mail: college.hill.house@gmail.com. www.collegehillhouse.com. www.boynevalleygardentrail.com. Contact: Eileen O'Grady. Open: As part of the Boyne Valley Garden Trail. See website for annual dates. Dogs on leads welcome. Special features: Teas can be arranged. Directions: On application.

The house at the top of the hill in question was, until recently a parish priest's house. Eileen and Bruce O'Grady arrived here in 2000 with a horticultural gleam in their eyes. They began by pulling out lengths of mature and overbearing hedging, rebuilding retaining walls and turning grounds into a garden.

Bruce is a keen stone collector and his collection of cap stones, carved oddments and curiosities can be found scattered about, adding character and architectural solidity to this developing garden.

Arriving at the house you cannot but be impressed by the two big beech trees – one with an old fashioned swing. In spring the ground beneath is full of daffodils, bluebells and in autumn there are sprinkles of cyclamen. Beyond the trees is a raised area and a stone patio with a curved sweeping set of stone steps. Above it the O'Gradys painstakingly created an old-fashioned lawn tennis court with a view across to the Hill of Slane and Cree Wood.

The centrepiece of the front garden is a formal pond and fountain garden, bounded by an explosion of lavender that tips over the edge of its stone ledge.

It is still a bit too rare to see borders planted against house walls and the example here, stars some rarities like an annual delphinium among the peonies and phloxes, under big *Rosa* 'Rambling Rector' and *R.* 'Dublin Bay', both scrambling up the wall.

A distance out from the house, they excavated and built a stone- edged natural pond, featuring a carved arrow stone found onsite. Archaeological experts from Trinity College told them that it is older than the carved stones in nearby Newgrange. This venerable boulder brings with it a unique sense of the deep and long history of which this part of Meath is heir.

Kilgar House Garden

Kilcock, Co. Meath. Tel: 087 1344 950. e-mail: kilgargardens@gmail.com
Contact: Paula and Thomas Byrne. Open: For an annual open day and otherwise by appointment to groups.
See website for annual dates. Directions: On appointment.

Formality, personality and enthusiasm are not words found regularly sharing a space. Paula Byrne is someone whose garden combines all three with seeming ease. I use the word seeming because walking around between beds stuffed with roses and herbaceous perennials, tied in by solid box walls, edged with military-neat stone paths, backed by even neater beech and hornbeam hedges, it is still, for some unfathomable reason, possible to be fooled into believing that this all just happened.

Paula is a woman with the magic formula. She is only partially interested in what varieties of rose and peony she grows, cannot always recall the names of the tulips, but she has no hesitation remembering the name of the friend who helped build this gate or that greenhouse, this obelisk or that fence.

I love her garden in a way I do not always love formal gardens. It has her pleasant personality sprinkled everywhere. This is no surprise. She works it every single day. Rain only ever stops play momentarily, sending her into one of several little painted sheds to shelter until the shower passes and from what I could see, when inside the sheds she is busy arranging the tools, pots and whatnots so that they too look great. Jealousy trailed behind me on my walk.

Back out in the garden she loves her David Austen roses and plants them by the dozen, woven through with repeat plantings of blue haze nepeta and all sorts of hardy geraniums, crocosmia and anthemis, libertia and bulbs. The explosions of flower look even more explosive hemmed in by the box and beech, see-through trellis and step-over espaliered apples.

This is three acres divided into a number of garden rooms around the house. Glimpses of one can be caught when you are in another. Meanwhile, views of the Meath countryside can be caught through cream-coloured park fencing, elegant iron gates with even a little turnstile in one place.

Paula's sense of style is even carried into the vegetable garden where there are as many flowers as vegetables. The apple trees are underplanted with flowers and there are distracting cherry fields visible over the hedge. This garden would make a scruff want to pull up their socks.

The Francis Ledwidge Museum

Janeville, Slane, Co. Meath. Tel: 041 9824 544. e-mail: info@francisledwidge.com
www.francisledwidge.com Open: As part of the Boyne Valley Garden Trail. March-Oct. Every day, 10am-
5pm. Oct-March, 10am-3pm. Special features: Museum to the war poet. Bus parking. Directions: On the
N51 just outside Slane on the road to Drogheda.

In the summer months, driving into the village of Slane, you cannot miss a cheerful, busy little front garden on the side of the road attached to a small cottage. The Francis Ledwidge museum is housed in the cottage, this being the place in which the World War I poet was born and raised.

The garden is modest but pretty, with window boxes full of bedding, roses climbing the walls and little beds of herbaceous perennials. When you leave by the back door of the museum, into a little yard, go through an arch in the beech hedge, into the wood garden.

Ledwidge was called the Poet of the Blackbird and as if on cue, I found blackbirds singing up in the trees. This is a simple garden of rough grass spiked with daffodils in spring under the groves of oak, lime and sorbus. A path circles the place and there are several memorials to the poet. It is a quiet, peaceful spot that inspires one to drift and dream.

Loughcrew House & Gardens

Oldcastle, County Meath. Tel: 049 8541 356. e-mail: info@loughcrew.com www.loughcrew.com. www.boynevalleygardentrail.com Contact: Reception. Open: All year as part of the Boyne Valley Garden Trail. See website for details. Special features: Adventure centre. Coffee shop. Events. Directions: Leave Oldcastle going south on the R195. A little way along turn left onto the L2800. Garden is signposted and on the right.

In 1997 the Naper family took the bones of the old demesne that has been in their family since 1693 and restored it with the help of the Great Gardens Of Ireland Restoration Programme and garden designer Daphne Shackleton. The result is an eccentric collection of features, a sort of trip through a section of garden history in the hilly drumlin hills of north Meath.

St. Oliver Plunkett's family house and church are on the site. The Napers are related to the saint's family three times by marriage. Look out for the ground plan of the 17th century longhouse, laid out like a full sized architect's drawing near the entrance to the garden. The house was knocked in 1788 and replaced by a new house. There are also ornamental canals, a walled garden that has yet to be worked on,

a watermill, a viewing mound, an ancient yew avenue, formal gardens, an archery lawn, a variety of follies and a bridged lake with natural waterside planting. Rather like a big cabinet of curiosities. Loughcrew is filled with singular oddities, such as the small spring and waterfall, emerging from under the raised roots of a cedar tree.

For me, the grand-scale yew walk, made up of trees of indeterminate age, is worth the visit alone. To walk under these venerable old specimens is to experience a real sense of history. The viewing mound at one end of the yews was created to be climbed. From the top, one could survey the garden and surrounding countryside. It might not seem like a hugely impressive feature, but in pre-JCB days every shovel of soil and stone had to be hand-lifted and carted into place on the growing mound.

The long herbaceous border starts ordinarily enough, with standard herbaceous classics, like delphinium, aster and potentilla. But nothing in Loughcrew is ordinary, and it comes as little surprise that, halfway along, the border becomes a 'Grotesque's' border. Choice and colourful descriptions of the plants being grown include the unfortunately named *Vestia foetida*, described in the accompanying label as 'an unpleasant smelling shrub'. What is usually thought of as unprepossessing vinca is intriguingly described as 'beneficial for memory disorders, irritability and vertigo'. Pulmonaria, we are informed, is 'for all disorders of the lung, including fever and plague,' which is good to know. Finally, pulsatilla is 'a remedy for nervous exhaustion in women'. Phew.

The Stream Garden with its damp rich soil is busy with primulas, gunnera and ligularia. Beyond it the stone grotto is an eerie, romantic corner, a dark and fern-filled rockery. If I had to believe in fairies, I imagine they might live in here.

The Loughcrew cairns and passage tombs on the Hill of the Witch are close by, prominently signed and definitely worth a visit.

Oldbridge House & Battle Of The Boyne Site

Drogheda, Co. Meath. Tel: 041 9809 950. e-mail: battleoftheboyne@opw.ie www.boynevalleygardentrail.com Open: All year except for Christmas and New Year. Wheelchair accessible. Children welcome. Dogs on leads. Special features: Admission free to garden. House tours. Historic demonstrations. Restaurant. Events. Directions: Take Exit 9 on M1 and follow signs. Or follow signs from Donore village.

I arrived for my first visit, to what seemed like a festival of dogs being walked on leads one sunny Sunday. Assuming that there was a dog show, I was surprised to hear from one of the stewards directing cars and people, that this was just a typical Sunday. The dogs of County Meath are a fancy gang.

Making my way up the sloped lawns in front of the house toward the walled garden, between posh hounds and handbag dogs, I passed a rustic fence enclosure. A display of cavalry horsemanship was being given by a very entertaining and knowledgeable woman in period uniform. From her saddle she was in admirable, complete control of horse, crowd, and even stray children.

The walled garden is an interesting one. The large and vaguely triangular shaped garden, has been under restoration for some time and now is beginning to settle into itself. Standing at the entrance, the overall impression is one of great expanses of space. There are large areas of box-enclosed lawn, punctuated by lavender beds with clipped box cones to give height and punctuation. Along one wall, in contrast to those low growing, central features, there is a great length of herbaceous border, that in high summer, is an extravaganza of kniphofia, achillea, helenium, aconites and crocosmia. Beyond the backing walls, the view of park trees and rolling hills stretches off into the distance.

Restoration was still in hand and the beautifully built greenhouse was awaiting proper planting up. In front of the greenhouse and already settling in, is a young orchard.

The paths continues on, past restored dog kennels, leading eventually to the sunken garden. This is an unusual feature lined with octagonal walls in red brick. A circle of mature yews runs around the circumference, with grassy slopes running downhill into the centre.

Oldbridge is a pleasant family visit, as well as being of interest as a garden in development.

Ratoath Garden & Garden Centre

Raystown, Ashbourne, Co. Meath. Tel: 01 8256 678. e-mail: rathoathgardencentre@hotmail.com www.ratoathgardencentre.ie. Contact: John Lord. Open: All year. See website for details. Special features: Plant nursery. Teas can be arranged. Directions: On the R125 out of Ratoath.

Set behind the garden centre and nursery, there is a garden that could turn the most horticulturally averse visitor into a plant fan. John Lord is a man in the right job. He has a garden centre and adores plants. We walked through his American prairie garden full of veronicastrum, stipa, rudbeckia and aster, past informal wild pond gardens full of rushes, irises and lilies, under skyward-bound trees, between long meandering, mixed shrub and flower beds, falling from one great looking plant combination to another.

I fell for a cream coloured rose called 'Moonlight' and *Miscanthus* 'Cosmopolitan', a wonderfully tall grass with stark white stripes, planted over *Coreopsis* 'Zagreb', it is a real winner. Meanwhile *Hydrangea villosa* over stands of white pulmonaria and epimedium work well together.

The plants are arranged in big drifts that create memorable pictures. The word generous keeps coming to mind. The show kicks off quite late, in May, with tree peonies. But it then carries on late into the year and looks good right into winter.

'The rabbits would break your heart though,' John said as we walked around. Even rabbit-proof fencing is only partially effective. They find their way in and shear off the new growth of the best perennials. I asked what the secret to dealing with them was.

'If a plant gives me trouble. I get rid of it!'

Sonairte Eco Centre & Gardens

The Ninch, Laytown, Co. Meath. Tel: 041 9827 572. Facebook: info@sonairte.ie www.boynevalleygardentrail.com. Contact: Paddy Ryan (Gardener) Open: As part of the Boyne Valley Garden Trail. Contact for annual details. Child friendly. Dogs on leads Special features: Café. Bee museum. Shop. Directions: On the R150 out of Laytown.

I arrived at the Sonairte Eco Centre Garden to find a basket of windfall apples at the gate with a note inviting people to take one. As I left, I thought how very representative of the place this little offering had been. Sonarite is not about the most perfectly presented set of gardens. (They are not perfect). But there is gentle sense of work here that has its own attraction. It is a raggle taggle garden and I am sure the time and motion expert would want to put order on everything. But the plants are growing well and the old walled garden has an air of warm welcome that I cannot fault.

In order of appearance, I came across a museum to the Irish bee, a little book shop, a little eco shop selling jute string, organic plant food and organic seeds. In the café they served me a scone straight out of the oven – it was delicious. Then I made my way into the garden.

I walked between the apple trees from which those windfalls hailed. There were a good number of varieties. UCD recently carried out a survey to name some of the older varieties, and they were awaiting the results although gardener Paddy Ryan says he knows they definitely have 'Blood of the Boyne' and 'Lady Sudeley'.

Paddy loves this garden and told me that it has a good micro-climate, usually between 5 and 10 degrees higher than the surrounding countryside. It favours excellent growth, as it is on a south facing slope and is surrounded by brick walls which soak up and slowly release the heat.

Working on four year rotations, they were growing good courgettes and cucumbers, beets and spinach, flowers and peas.

Paddy is a fund of organic information and the place runs with a volunteer workforce. Swapping a few hours of your time for the sort of information you might pick up on growing productive plant seems like a fair exchange. Finally, before the Neat Police come after me, entry was free. These people are doing their best.

St. Mary's Abbey

Trim, Co. Meath. Tel: 087 2057 176. e-mail: phiggins@reganmcentee.ie. www.boynevalleygardentrail.com Contact: Peter Higgins. Open: As part of the Boyne Valley Garden Trail. By appointment. Special features: Historic house tours. Directions: On application.

When the direction to a garden tells you to 'start at the front gate of Trim Castle,' one of the most imposing castles in the country, and continues with instructions on climbing grassy hills and taking wooden bridges over the River Boyne, you know you are in for a treat. My directions also mentioned small ruins and round towers. Finally, I discovered that the garden I was looking for was located in the grounds of the ancient

building with gothic windows, at the top of the hill that I had in my sights since I left the castle. I felt like Anneka Rice on a treasure hunt.

The garden at St. Mary's Abbey is unique. It may not be the best tended gardens – it is not – but it is one of the most romantic. If you are fond of perfect borders and weedless perfection, perhaps look somewhere else, but if you fancy bumping into the ghost of some little 18th century waif or grey lady, this garden is for you. It oozes archaeology and history, with links to Jonathan Swift and The Duke of Wellington. I could be fooled into thinking I had landed in Barchester.

Laid out on three ledges overlooking the river and straight across at the castle, even the paths feel venerable. It is laid out on a sunny slope down to, and overlooking the water.

There are apple trees and a herbaceous border, a weirdly contorted *Trachycarpus fortunei* that takes two, ninety degree turns in its growth, some little greenhouses and a set of steps that lead straight down to the river. There is also a rampant and colourful rockery that leans up against the house with only the tops of two sub-terranean windows of some basement rooms visible over the stones and rosemary, aubrieta, pittosporum and clematis, perennial wallflowers and vinca.

There are also wall-trained figs and massed climbing potato vines. What there is mostly however is a peerless sense of history which, after a tour of the house, will hook the romantic novelist in you if not the strict horticulturalist.

Tankardstown House

Rathkenny, Slane, Co. Meath. Tel: 041 9824 621. e-mail: info@tankardstown.ie www.tankardstown.ie. www.boynevalleygardentrail.com Contact: Helen Byrne. Open: For one open day as part of the Boyne Valley Garden Trail. See website for details. Otherwise by appointment. Partially wheelchair accessible. Child friendly. Dogs on leads. Special features: Accommodation. Restaurant. Afternoon teas. Directions: Leaving Slane heading west on the N51, turn right onto the R163 and travel for 5 km to house.

The grounds of Tankardstown House are largely made up of parkland, a place of classic sweeps of lawn rolling between groves of mature trees beside the River Nanny. The classic design creates views and vistas from one picturesque area to another. Specimen broadleaf trees and conifers in the distance draw the eye and then direct it on and beyond to views of the Meath hills, fields and woods.

The walled garden, beside the big house, has been divided into two areas. The first is a pleasure ground with lawns and cross paths, mature yews and cedars and a few rose beds surrounded by espaliered pear trees. It is a pleasant place for a turnabout.

Next door is the more productive garden with angled beds busy with rhubarb, strawberries artichokes and kale. In here I spied more espaliered trees, including damsons trained on the walls. Clearly someone loves training fruit trees. In the polytunnel to one side of the garden, there is also a trained vine stretched along the upper support spans.

A practical working kitchen garden is always an interesting sight.

Birr Castle, Co. Offaly.

Offaly

Bellefield House

Birr Road, Shinrone, Co. Offaly. Tel: 086 6002 180. e-mail: angelajupe@gmail.com
Contact: Angela Jupe. Open: Feb: Wed-Sun. For snowdrops. Mid Mar-mid April: For heritage daffodils.
April-May: For tulips. May-July: For peonies, irises, roses. Other times by appointment to groups. Wheelchair
accessible. Small dogs on leads. Not suitable for small children. Member of Gardens of Ireland Trust. Special
features: Refreshments can be arranged. Plant sales. Events. Accommodation. Directions: 1km north of
Shinrone on the N492.

Angela Jupe is a force of nature, a garden expert and something of a serial garden restorer. Her latest garden, rescued from dereliction a few years ago, has been resurrected and is open for some time now, yet she never seems finished and is always developing new areas. The last time I visited, she was working on a walk around the perimeter taking in a little wood to one side of the house.

The house is at the top of a drive between fields of grazing horses, culminating on a little meadow studded with scarlet tulips in early summer - A stylish start.

Angela is in the middle of creating a new orchard to the side of the house but the garden proper begins through the courtyard behind the house in the old walled garden. When Angela arrived, to have called this a neglected mess, would have been kind. A walled wood might have been more appropriate. Scores of mature self-seeded trees and brambles meant that the only way the garden could be accessed was on all fours but Angela had moved here specifically because it had a walled garden. She held onto a small number of the trees to ensure that the new garden would start life with a certain level of maturity.

The space is divided into two levels. The first section, set out on the lower ledge is where she built her long greenhouse or sunroom. This bright house hosts a rampant passion flower, a grape vine and a collection of pelargoniums, among them a fabulous little *Pelargonium acetosum*. In front of this she created a dramatic water feature, involving a wall of water that tumbles from one raised pond down through a canal lined with damp-loving Japanese irises and into a circular pool.

Along the wall that runs parallel to this is a slightly raised mixed bed that is a particularly striking in late autumn, a bed full of salvias and seed-raised dahlias, perennial cornflowers and late gladioli. The colour palette is one of plum and purple, rich blue and watery lemon. I counted seven different species and varieties of salvia, among them *Salvia guaranitica* 'Amistad' and 'Black and Blue' *S.* 'Night Moth', *S.* 'Cavaliero celeste' and *S.* 'Red bumble'. The ground here suits them as they like lots of water but also good drainage. In with the salvias the dahlias include *Dahlia* 'Rip City', Angela's recommendation for the blackest of all the dahlias.

In the main area up on the higher ledge, there are long mixed borders running in all directions. These are largely colour co-ordinated. Down along one wall there is a 70-metre long mixed border full of purple lupins and plume poppies, rich pink campanula and blue nepeta. The stone wall behind the bed supports a range of roses and clematis. The bed turns a corner and continues on down the length of the next wall. Decoratively grown fruit bushes, feature strongly here. The space between the black, white and red currants has been used to grow strawberries. As the border turns another corner, the accent shifts to some of Angela's collection of peonies. These old garden favourites are one of her passions. She grows a number of species and hybrid peonies, many of them collected on her travels in France.

Down the middle of the garden is a pair of brilliant early summer iris beds overlooked by the *pièce de résistance*, a rather wonderful, Indian-inspired summerhouse, a towering confection made from salvaged items Angela accumulated over the years. Within it there are leaded windows salvaged from a convent, as well as a dramatic copper cupola she found in a salvage yard in England. Angela thinks it came from India. The interior has been decorated using mosaic tiles. It sings of fun and whimsy, suiting the flower-filled atmosphere in this seemingly effortlessly stylish garden.

Birr Castle Demesne

Rosse Row, Birr, Co. Offaly. Tel: 057 9120 336. e-mail: mail@birrcastle.com www.birrcastle.com Open: Daily. See website for seasonal hours. Groups welcome. Wheelchair accessible. Supervised children. Dogs on leads. Special features: Playground with huge wooden castle. Holiday cottages. Telescope demonstrations in summer. Carriage rides through grounds in summer. (Contact: Declan Cleere 087 6693237) Gift shop. Museum. Gallery. Tearoom. Tours can be booked. Member of Gardens of Ireland Trust. Directions: in the town of Birr, signposted.

The Parsons, Earls of Rosse, have been living in Birr since the 1620s. They are a singular family, earning reputations for themselves as scientists, astronomers, philanthropists, photographers and gardeners. Their most famous achievement was in the 19th century, with the building of 'Leviathan', the then largest telescope in the world. The family can also boast the invention of the steam turbine. In the past number of years Leviathan has been restored and exhibitions in the museum demonstrate the pioneering work the family carried out in all the areas mentioned above.

Meanwhile, the garden is made up of 150-acres spread between Offaly and Tipperary, filled with trees from all over the world, including, arguably the most impressive *Cornus kousa* in the country and a huge *Sequoiadendron giganteum* up which a red squirrel ran. In recent years they planted a whole grove of *Sequoiadendron giganteum* here, which as fossilised records show, once grew in this country. According to Lord Rosse planting these represents the return of our arboreal diaspora.

The Rosses subscribed to many of the great plant-hunting ventures of the 19th and early 20th centuries, including the Kingdon Ward, Wilson, Augustine Henry and George Forrest expeditions. Michael, the 6th Earl travelled to Tibet to collect plants, and after his marriage in 1937, he and his wife Anne collected in China. Many of the special trees that came about as a result of these expeditions grow in Birr today. Among these plants there is what could be the first *Metasequoia glyptostroboides* brought to this island.

Planting is constantly going on and the way to the walled garden is today lined by a young beech avenue that includes a large number of different species and varieties. Also outside the walled garden, there are lines of magnolias that should be investigated.

Filigreed iron gates lure visitors from the park inside those walls. The smallest hint of what may be seen is gleaned when one spots the restored greenhouse at the far end of a path.

This walled garden was redesigned in the 1930s by Anne to commemorate her marriage to Michael. She was an enthusiastic gardener, her family being the owners of Nymans, the famed English garden with which Birr is twinned. In here, the most famous plant is *Paeonia* 'Anne Rosse,' a yellow tree peony that came about as the result of a cross Michael made. In addition, the current Lord Rosse, Brendan, told me that both his grandparents have magnolias named after them.

Hornbeam *allées*, older than the 1936 garden, form a 'cloister' around the inside of the walls. Michael planted snowdrops under the hornbeams as a young man while home on leave during World War I. The cloisters have 'windows' cut into them, giving the visitor glimpses of the box parterres outside. Those parterres are planted in complicated patterns, incorporating big Rs for Rosse.

There is a rose garden here too, a romantic corner, full of old French roses, mainly cultivars from the 1820s to the 1890s. The list of names reads like creatures from a bodice ripping novel. So we have *Rosa* 'Duchesse de Montebello', *R. gallica* 'Versicolor' and *R.* 'Petite de Hollande' in flounces of pink, dusty mauve and plum.

The air of romance continues with the delphinium border, full of all sorts of delphiniums in blues, jewelled purples and pale lilacs, blended with catmint, tree peonies, thalictrum, inula and aconites, related to delphiniums but unlike their finer relations, not in need of staking. Beyond this sea of flowers, a Greek goddess standing in her bower is afforded some privacy by clematis and sweet pea cloak.

The century-old gnarled wisteria arches have such character. Then there are the iris and peony beds and the famed 200-year-old Tallest Box Hedges in the World according to the 'Guinness Book of Records'. Box has a remarkable scent: When you know that the smell is box, it smells good. But, like basil and Parmesan cheese, it is curiously reminiscent of cats when the source is unknown. Back in the miniature box garden, the multiple planting of *Syringa* 'Birr Sensation' is well named.

The way back out to the greater garden is by a path under a yew avenue. One route leads through the trees, to a Victorian fernery. Overhead, the dense canopy creates a dark, gothic atmosphere. The ferns and tree ferns look perfect in the damp green light, between moss-covered, glistening stones, beside ravines and bridged streams. The narrow goat-track path picks though these, travelling past the exposed roots of beech trees crawling down the bank. After heavy rain

when the stream is high, the roar of water over the falls is exhilarating.

Birr has many of the usual features expected in a great pleasure garden including, not a shell house, but a shell well, set down here in the woods.

The mixed borders leading up to the castle and tucked in under the outer walls of mock fortifications are flowing, herbaceous and informal. These are full of buddleia, echinops, white iris and inula. Do not miss the big, gnarled, pinned-up *Magnolia delavayi* behind the flowers.

Out in the open, in front of the castle is the Whirlpool Spiral. First planted in 1995, this spiral of 290 young lime trees or *Tilia cordata* travels in an ever-decreasing spiral, like a galaxy of stars closing in on a black hole. Out here too is the famous Carroll Oak. (The Carrolls predated the Rosses in the county.)

In under the castle walls, walk along the high and low walks, beside and above the river. Waterfall Point looks down the spring-flowering bank to the River Camcor below, and on towards a small suspension bridge that leads across to groves of cornus, acer, willow, cherry and pine on the opposite bank. This bridge was built in 1811, another legacy of the family's engineering endeavours. The view across to the garden beyond takes in an impressively large *Acer griseum* and *Parrotia persicaria* planted in 1936 and a rare *Carrierea calycina* 'the envy of Kew' apparently.

With Chinese family connections, the collection of plants from that massive country is being added to constantly, particularly in the open woods at the Tipperary end of the estate. In the next few decades these will be fascinating to watch.

Watch out for red tree labels. These denote a Trees of Distinction system set up to mark the special trees here. Among them must be the Fallen Giant, the Great Poplar, the tree that fell for Ireland, down by the bank of the river. Close by, is an unusual grove of *Decaisnea fargesii*, unusual Dr Seuss-like trees with shiny blue seed pods. Many of the special trees here have been planted in groves for extra effect.

There are many more walks and trails through the grounds than before, making it possible to always find a quiet corner – with its own special trees to study, including a 70-year-old common elm recently discovered among the exotics.

And to enjoy all those extra trails, today, you may spoil yourself with a carriage ride around the grounds.

Woodland Cottage Garden

Tullamore Road, Birr, Co. Offaly. Tel: 086 3051697. e-mail:nanoward@eircom.net
Contact: Anne Ward. Open: Garden visits by appointment. Dogs on leads. (Hens present). Special features:
Garden centre. Coffee shop. Member of the Gardens of Ireland Trust. Directions: Leave Birr on the Tullamore
road. Pass Lidl on the left. 100 m along the garden on right. Park outside gate.

Anne Wards' Woodland Cottage garden is just that, a cottage garden incorporating a little wood on the edge of the historic town of Birr.

The feel is informal and relaxed as a cottage garden should be. I like the way the house is tucked in between plants of every description. The building is clothed in climbers and fringed by mixed borders with a mix of roses, *Melianthus major* and masses of tulips. From here the garden heads off in all directions, by means of mown grass paths, between colour themed herbaceous borders, little rose gardens, raised alpine beds and shrub borders. It continues on out to a wood and Anne's young arboretum. She has been planting this in the shelter of three magnificent and aged beech trees. Under these, she created log-lined, mulch paths and planted up the ground with woodland favourites like erythronium and epimedium, hosta and fern, hellebore and the full range of spring bulbs.

The ground is peaty and moist and she has been trialling different trees in the conditions, from apples and different betulas to a baby sequoiadendron, a grove of hazel, oak, walnut and Spanish chestnut.

I love the easy, natural feel of this garden. It manages to combine good plants with an eye to nature and the needs of wildlife.

Tullynally Castle, Co. Westmeath.

Westmeath

Ballygillen Garden

Reynella, Delvin, Mullingar, Co. Westmeath. Tel: 087 1234 935. Contact: Evelyn and Alec Sherwin. e-mail: evelynsherwin2@gmail.com Open: June-Sept. By appointment only and for an annual open day. Contact for details. Special features: Plant sales. Directions. On the L1505 to Bracklyn from Delvin.

'I started 30 years ago and I've been working at it ever since,' Evelyn Sherwin says. She sure has. This is three acres of sheer high maintenance garden and woe betide the plant that misbehaves. Evelyn is a most enthusiastic gardener. She grows from seed and slip in a whole selection of green houses and potting sheds and the results end up in tidy, well-edged well-defined beds in her hilly, pretty corner of Westmeath.

There are island beds full of contrasting, clipped and shaped conifers that give year round structure to the place, while an equal number of flowering shrubs range about, adding seasonal splashes of colour and scent. There are beds of perennials and annuals everywhere too, full of the babies Evelyn raised in all her workshops. Elsewhere, busy rose beds stand in perfect order.

Between these, sweeps of impeccable lawn provide routes through which you can walk to inspect everything. Where the lawn finishes, perfectly kept gravel paths begin. There are stone benches to sit on but I do not think either Evelyn or Alec get much chance to use these. Evelyn told me that July and August are her favourite months. I visited in May and it was no slouch then either...

Belvedere House, Gardens & Park

Mullingar, Co Westmeath. Tel: 044 9349 060. e-mail: info@belvedere-house.ie www.belvedere-house.ie Open: All year from 9.30am. See seasonal closing on web. Partially wheelchair accessible. Children welcome. Dogs on leads. Special features: House. Visitor centre. Café. Gift shop. Play areas. Events. Directions: 7 km from Mullingar on the N52.

On hearing the history of Belvedere, you could be forgiven for thinking that you were being given the plot of a particularly gruesome Gothic novel. This is the deeply unpleasant story of the three Rochford brothers, their three homes, Belvedere, Tudenham and Gaulstown, and their appalling sibling rivalry. Their lives seem to have been one long run of dastardly carry-on, with stories of misfortunate wives locked up for decades, debauchery, duels, quarrelsome feuds and casual cruelties. One can imagine an intriguing sort of oppression hangs around Belvedere as a result of such a history of conflict. On my first visit, in the late 1980s, before its restoration, it certainly had the feel of a woebegone sort of place. Not so now.

The family history can still be seen today however, in the bricks and mortar of the Jealous Wall. This well named building is the largest Gothic folly on the island and a visible reminder of the Rochford feuds. It was erected as a mock ruin by Lord Belvedere to obliterate the sight of his brother's home, Tudenham, built next door to, and bigger than Belvedere.

In the 1990s, the dilapidated gardens and deserted house were taken over by Westmeath Co. Council. They underwent a programme of restoration and opened to the public in 1999. Today Belvedere is a source of pride in the county. It is a busy tourist attraction that hosts all sorts of events, concerts and fairs. The restored gardens are worth visiting, along with the Jealous Wall, in the lee of which sits a visitor centre, complete with a small display devoted to the much loved local man Joe Dolan.

At the front of the Georgian house there is a formal terrace stepping down from the building in a series of sloped spans of lawn, gravel ledges, heavy balustrades and statuary. It is all very self important-looking. Savage lions glower down from the steps. Trained yews add to the formality. This feature was added in Victorian times, a copy of the stone terrace at Haddon Hall in England. It overlooks Lough Ennell. Falling away from the side of the house, a wild-looking rock and wood garden tumbles downhill. It is all a suitably sombre backdrop for the Jealous Wall. On my most recent visit, the upkeep of the gravel left something to be desired along with the bare rockery and bramble-choked drop from the terrace.

The seven-acre walled garden was faring a lot better and looking very well. This too was built, not by the Rochford's, but by a later owner, Charles Marley, in the 19th century. The larger space is divided into five rooms, each with a different mood or feel. The Bell Gate leads into the garden and its chief feature; a double border backed by battlemented yews. The borders were designed to look good for much of the year. Spring bulbs give way to iris, catmint, thalictrum and phlox. Box corkscrews line out between the airier perennials adding punch. These beds run downhill towards a swag-decorated wall.

The Himalayan garden came about when one of the earlier owners participated in a plant hunting expedition, the bounty of which it boasts, from blood-red flowered *Rhododendron chamae thomsonii* to Himalayan blue poppies *Meconopsis grandis*. In the rose garden, look for the famous pink climbing *Rosa* 'Belvedere' named for the garden.

The greenhouses meanwhile, are filled with all sorts of exotics. The garden rounds off with the fruit, vegetable and herb garden. Some of the wall-trained and espaliered fruit trees here are particularly impressive. The small fountain pond is collared by masses of flowers and could compete for first prize as the finest sight in the garden, with the view downhill over the different rooms, expanses of lawn, specimen trees, a maze of walks and paths and small hidden summerhouses.

Tucked into the shadiest corner there is now a fairy garden complete with a stream, a bridge for an ugly troll and all sorts of fairy paraphernalia to keep little children amused.

In order to encourage bees and butterflies, the walk down the lake was planted with fuchsia, shrub roses, buddleia and eucryphia. Mature maple and ash mark the edge of the deeper woods. I loved the uncovered, reinstated and restored old cobbled paths in the woods.

Lough Ennell is as grand a body of water as such a house would require, with a wildflower meadow running down to the water's edge. There is also a network of paths through the 160 acres of park.

Tullynally Castle

Tullynally, Castlepollard, Co. Westmeath. Tel: 044 9661 856. e-mail: info@tullynallycastle.com www.tullynallycastle.com Contact: Valerie Pakenham. Open: Thurs. Fri. and Bank Holidays, April-Sept., 11am-5pm and for Heritage Week. See website for annual dates. Groups at other times by appointment. Supervised children. Dogs on leads. Special features: Season ticket available. Castle tours: Sunday 3pm April-Sept. At other times by appointment to groups. Play area. Discovery trail. Member of Gardens of Ireland Trust. Directions: Situated 1.5 km from Castlepollard on the Edgeworthstown Road, (R398)

For anyone with an interest in trees, Tullynally holds a special significance. It is the home of Thomas Pakenham, renowned author and tree expert. Travelling toward the castle, up the splendid oak avenue, past elegant skeletons of fallen trees re-sprouting with new shoots, serves to whet the appetite for this magnificent place. Tullynally was built in the 1600s by the Pakenham family. They still live here.

The castle is largely 19th-century Gothic in style, overlooking a park and garden that have been in almost constant development since the arrival of the family. There are records of plants being brought to Tullynally from plant hunting expeditions as far back as the 1700s and as you walk about, it is between plants that date to every era since then. For the future, it is exciting to see that the pioneering planting continues into the early 21st century in this horticultural treasure chest.

Tullynally Castle is the biggest castellated house in Ireland. The building is flanked by a yew hedge, which is also castellated. A giant wisteria climbs the house, softening the grey limestone, while splashes of agapanthus and orange Welsh poppies self-seed in the cracks in the flagged terrace.

The romantic landscape and garden beyond this, date from the 18th century. Among its most beautiful features is the Grotto, a curious stone bower perched on a bank at the top of a step-stone path. Peep inside to see the little carved wooden faces created by French sculptor and friend of the family, Antoine Pierson. The atmospheric little building overlooks an opened up area of lawn studded with specimen *Cornus controversa* 'Variegata,' mature Japanese acers, a *Magnolia campbellii* and a two century old *Acer campestre*.

Close by, Valerie Pakenham works the flower borders, playing with successional flowering perennials from early summer to autumn, in wall-backed borders. The summerhouse, that presides over the changing display, was built in the 1920s.

Here too is an unusual little sunken lily pond with a Victorian 'weeping pillar', completely mossed over and surrounded by lady's mantle, geraniums and ferns. Two Coade stone sphinxes guard the entrance to the flower garden. They were bought by Lord Longford in 1780, and are known as the Merry Maids.

The kitchen garden covers a huge, eight acres. It was built in the 18th century, when manpower was in no short supply. However, by 1840, when labour was still cheap, it was already being described as 'impossibly large for these times'. There were originally twelve greenhouses ranged along the long brick wall. Today there are only two left but the restoration work has been well done.

Valerie created the feature of the Indian bulls, copied from a temple on the sub-continent. They guard the Jeremy Williams pavilion in some style. The Irish yews here are thought to date to 1740.

Apples trained along the walls provide productive decoration. The avenue of blended, humped yew and box walls, knotted through with ivy and mahonia are known as the 'tapestry hedges'. They feature so many contrasting textures and shades of green and are one of the most charming examples of hedging I have seen.

Some of the huge area in the walled garden is today given over to a family of llamas that Valerie told me are good lawn mowers and easily minded, as well as having fetching good-looks.

In general, the routes through the garden are by way of mown paths cut through long grass spiked with *Narcissus recurva*, camassia, snake's head fritillaries and bluebells. One of these grass walks leads past Queen Victoria's small summer house and onto the 'bridge over the River Sham', named because it is not a river but a serpentine lake. Even the Sham's crocodile, standing on an island is bogus, and the ducks and black swans showed no interest in or fear of the wooden monster. The summerhouse too falls into the same category: Queen Victoria never visited the garden. This is a copy of one made for her elsewhere.

The path leads into the Tibetan Garden. This is on the site of an old American Garden planted by the second Countess of Longford in 1830 with acid-loving plants like camellia and azalea. Following a visit in 1834, the novelist and diarist Maria Edgeworth wrote of this feature: 'I never saw in England or Ireland such gardens...She has made the most beautiful American garden.'

The more recently planted Tibetan Garden is an exciting project, the product of a seed-collecting trip made by Thomas to Yunnan in China. There are new and interesting species of blue Himalayan poppies, yellow *Primula florindae* and tall *Primula poissonii,* whose lilac flowers bloom until November.

Tibetan birches and species tree hydrangeas spread out in the openings. We stopped to look at a 20-year-old elm with flowers like green double roses as we made our way through this jungle on a golf cart, trundling past four-metre tall *Cardiocrinum giganteum* grown among dogwoods, *Lilium auratum* and some recently discovered, species rhododendrons.

The Womb With A View should not be missed. This is a round, organic wooden pod on squat legs into which you can sit on either of two thrones. It too was made by Antoine, using fallen trees on the estate. It overlooks a mix of young specimen trees in an opening, sheltered by the surrounding tall beech and sycamore. In the distance you can see Lough Derravaragh and the hills.

The trail goes on past a pagoda decorated by Chinese plants including sorbus, white pine, betula and philadelphus. It also takes in what looks like a gingerbread house as it makes its way down to a viewing mound.

The development continues and the most recent additions include a new magnolia garden with 36 different species. 'For me it's magnolias with everything,' Thomas said, walking between *Magnolia* 'Wada's Memory,' *M. loebneri* 'Merrill,' *M. wilsonii* and *campbellii* and *M.* 'Peppermint stick'. We passed another of Antoine's wooden features, a red painted fence based on that seen on willow pattern plates.

Work continues: The upper lake was cleared of 150 tons of silt and further improved with the creation of a new waterfall. They also recently discovered a rock wall in the woods. Valerie explained that it came about

as a result of the spoil left over when the River Sham was dug out in the 1860s. A rockery was draped over the excavated soil to disguise it, turning leftovers into a feature. Until recently, it was lost under ivy. Today, the ferns are colonising it.

Valerie, as she explained, is in charge of maintenance and weeding as Thomas forges ahead, planting unusual and new plants. His most recent addition is a garden of plants in homage to the great Irish plant collector Augustine Henry, including two rarities, *Tetracentron sinense* and *Emmenopterys henryi.*

There are many remarkable trees here and among them are champions including a beech with a girth of 7 metres, and the 'Squire's Walking Stick', an unusually tall stick-straight oak. It was planted in the mid-1740s by the then Thomas Pakenham. Seek out the *Abies alba*, decapitated in the huge storm of 1839, in which 3000 people were killed. The tree re-sprouted with six new trunks.

These days, the current Thomas plants thousands of young oak and beech, from acorns and beechnuts harvested at Tullynally, but ask to see the Tesco walnut trees too, grown from a bag of walnuts bought in the supermarket a few years ago.

Kilmokea Country Manor, Co. Wexford.

Wexford

Ballinkeele Garden

Ballinkeele House, Ballymurn, Enniscorthy, Co. Wexford. Contact: Mary Maher.
Tel: 053 9138 105. 085 8308 147. e-mail: marymaher4@hotmail.com. Open: By appointment.
Special features: Accommodation. Directions. On appointment.

Speaking to Mary Maher as she climbed out of a border in the walled garden at Ballinkeele, it was clear that this is a hardworking gardener doing the work of many. Like so many large house gardens, where once there were teams of workers, today there is one and sometimes two people to keep the horticultural show on the road. Ballinkeele is a beautiful conundrum being taken care of by Mary.

She explained how she is reconfiguring the walled garden to make it a little easier to work. More shrubs and fewer herbaceous perennials is the best plan: Roses, clematis and flowering shrubs team with the nepeta, cosmos, dahlias and sedum and in summer it is pretty and colourful but not as hard to care for as an herbaceous border. The great expanses of red brick in the two walled gardens is impressive in itself. Vegetables and fruit trees take up a good amount of space, providing produce for the house. I like the restored summerhouse set into a long flower filled border, outside the walls.

Out in the greater grounds, there are well designed walks between mature rhododendron and fine old woods, spiked with flowering shrubs. The lake is gorgeous, surrounded by towering trees and mounds of flowering shrubs. There is a peaceful atmosphere in this long lived garden, with its rising and falling canopy of huge monkey puzzles and conifers, beech and oak interspersed with the occasional explosion of rhododendron.

The Bay Garden

Camolin, Co. Wexford. Y21 XH61. Contact: Frances and Iain MacDonald. Tel: 053 9383 349.
086 8436 624. e-mail:thebay@gmail.com www.thebaygarden.com Open: As part of the Wexford Garden
Trail. May and Sept., Sun. 2-5pm. Jun-Aug., Fri-Sun., 2pm-5pm. Partially wheelchair accessible. Guide
dogs. Groups welcome. Special features: Plants for sale. Garden talks and teas by arrangement. Garden
tours in Ireland and abroad arranged. Directions: Driving on the N11 travelling south, the garden is 1km
south of Camolin on the left.

Garden designers Frances and Iain MacDonald have spent the last quarter century working together here in Wexford, creating and playing with what is both their garden and shop window - and what a shop window.

When they first arrived they spent five years eradicating perennial weeds before ever beginning a garden. Five years spent killing weeds is a statement of intent. There are few of us who could put off the pleasure of planting up a garden for so long to make sure the place was weed-free. This place was built on 'patience and planning' and it shows.

Arriving at the front of the house you meet the cottage garden, surrounded by tall stone walls and the front of the MacDonald's double-fronted Georgian house. It could be straight out of a Jane Austen novel with shrub roses, white anemone, sweet-smelling tobacco plants (*Nicotiana sylvestris*) and lengths of chunky, clipped box. The upper parts of the house host a big wisteria, *Rosa* 'Cecile Brunner' and *R.* 'Mermaid.' The white-and-green foliage of *Euonymus* 'Silver Queen' does the same job at the lower levels. Bright gravel and stone paths divide the beds and draw light into this intimate little garden room. This is the sort of design that would look perfect in the small garden that fronts many period town houses.

Exit, however reluctantly, by a side gate into a large and open garden with big colour-matched beds set into an expanses of grass. In one island, pink geranium weaves between the sharp swordy leaves of a pink variegated phormium. Crinum lilies and pink-tinged goat's rue or *Galega officinalis* all melt together in strange combination that work fantastically. In another bed they have teamed reds, silvers and whites together successfully.

It is said that good bone structure will never fail a beauty, and the bone structure here comes in the shape of small trees such as cornus, azara, acer and lilac dotted through the beds.

The trail leads from this big open area, stepping down to a compact formal garden. This is a square divided by crossed paths into four smaller square beds, hemmed in by nepeta, and sharply colour divided. The first two beds are filled with white and shell-pink roses, white cosmos and anemone with delicate pink-and white-tinged *Gaura lindheimeri*. I love the plum coloured penstemon and roses matched with wine scabious. In the fourth bed, lemon-and-lime is the theme, with yellow roses, pale, butter-yellow *Anthemis tinctoria* 'E.C. Buxton' and lady's mantle or *Alchemilla mollis*.

The next treat is the red-hot border. Here there are exotic cannas, showgirl-red dahlias, crocosmia, tiger lilies, kniphofia and insanely orange rudbeckia all going together like a house on fire.

My favourite section is what Frances calls her 'funereal border', full of serious and sombre-looking plants. There is black grass, *Ophiopogon planiscapus* 'Nigrescens', *Scabiosa atropurpurea* 'Ace of Spades', *Physocarpus opulifolius* 'Diablo' and black aeonium. There is something voluptuous about black flowers from sweet William to irises, dahlias to cornflowers.

New additions arrive in the garden on a regular basis and a new area here called Jardin Sheila, is made up of a series of iron arches over which clematis, apples, roses and pears are being trained. It is an intriguing idea that I have yet only seen in its infancy. I think it will look great at the height of the summer. Next is the barn where a meandering trail winds between beds of different grasses speckled with flowers, like a firework display on the ground, informal and dynamic. Frances says that the only work ever needed here is one trip around with the strimmer in February. In exchange for that small effort she gets an ever-changing show for the rest of the year, particularly in July when the lychnis, geraniums, *Verbena bonariensis* and thistles are at their best. It looks great even in November when the first frosts hit the grasses. The planting here is so dense that the weeds may look elsewhere to find a footing. An arbour made of trained parrotia sits in the corner, taking the full blast of the sun.

The latest new garden houses a loggia overlooking a formal pond and two mirrored flower borders full of silver, blue and pink flowers. After the hoedown in the barn garden, the symmetry here is a surprise.

The wet garden was an expanse of wet flood-plain that they planted up using a boardwalk to cross the damp ground leading to a little summerhouse. Crossing it between crowds of astilbes, arums, ranunculus and rodgersia feels like traversing a little jungle. That jungle-atmosphere is enhanced further by the gigantic gunnera leaves that rise up behind the summerhouse at the other side of the boardwalk.

The growth here is phenomenal: Hunt out the huge *Pinus montezumae*, a giant at 30 years old, or the pretty *Cornus capitata*, and *Cornus satomi* in the Japanese area. A growing collection of trees is turning the sloped expanse into a semi-woodland garden. There is a good selection of betula, aralia, Spanish chestnut, beech, camellia, magnolia and conifers under-planted with bluebells and narcissi, primula and hellebore, epimedium and even dactylorhiza. It adds up to a glorious year-round display. 'When everything else is gone, the woods will be still here,' Frances said.

Fern-and container-gardens close to the house show that the MacDonalds never stop creating. Meanwhile the small vegetable garden to the side of the house carries no fewer than 55 different kinds of flowers and vegetables and takes up a space no bigger than the average postage stamp-sized new house garden. This shows just what can be achieved in a small space.

Lucy's Wood Garden

Colclough Walled Garden

Tintern Abbey, Saltmills, Hook Peninsula, Co. Wexford. Tel: 083 3064 159.
e-mail: colcloughwalledgarden@gmail.com. www.colcloughwalledgarden.com. Contact: Alan Ryan. Open:
As part of the Wexford Garden Trail. May-Sept., Mon-Sun., 10am-6pm. Oct-Ap., Mon-Sun., 10am-
4pm. Partially wheelchair accessible. Note that the garden is a 7 minute walk from the car park. Children
welcome. Dogs on leads. Special features: Teas can be arranged. Tours. Directions: Leave the R733 Ballyhack
to Wellingtonbridge Road, at the L4041 for Saltmills. The entrance is 1 km along.

I arrived at the car park for the first time, with no idea as to the shape of Colclough (pronounced Coke-Lee). I could see no walled garden, but a path into the woods, so I followed it, under the trees, past the remains of an intriguing cottage garden (Mr. Rose's cottage garden). On and on it went until finally, I hit an entrance in a wall and in through the gate, the garden. I was met by the admirable Alan Ryan, who whisked me off on a visit despite the fact that

he should have been closing up shop for the night.

The walled garden, which dates back to the early 1800s, was until recently, like so many places, lost to overgrowth. In 2010, 30 full sized Sitka spruce trees were taken out and a programme of restoration was embarked upon by Hook Tourism. Much of the work has been carried out by volunteers. The result is a wonder.

We walked through the garden, laid out as it was in 1830, between the two sections, east and west, one for ornamentals and one for vegetables, divided by an unusual internal wall. We crossed back and forward, over the little river that runs its length, using several of its five bridges. I was charmed.

The place is so well worked, using organic methods some of which Alan generously explained as we went. It is also beautifully presented, a real pleasure of a garden. Visit in September to taste the Irish apples from the orchard and any time in the summer to see the handsome arrangements of vegetables and flowers. They were in the final stretch of building a new greenhouse during my visit. I look forward to seeing it filled.

Coolaught Gardens

Clonroche, Enniscorthy, Co. Wexford. Contact: Caroline and Harry Deacon. Tel: 053 9244 137.
087 6446 882. e-mail: coolaughtgardens@eircom.net. Open: May-Sept 7 days. Other times by appointment.
Partially wheelchair accessible. No dogs. Special features: Plant nursery all year. Teas by arrangement.
Directions: On the N30, in the village of Clonroche turn at Greene's Supermarket. Drive 2.5 km to the
garden, signposted.

Coolaught is something many help-strapped gardeners might envy – a family affair. Harry, Caroline and their family work the place together. It is also something of a laboratory, where they experiment with as many plants as they can, so that when they sell a plant from their nursery, they can recommend it with confidence.

There are actually a whole array of gardens laid out around the old house and nursery. The most memorable in spring must be the crocus lawn to the front of the house. The sprinkling of thousands of *Crocus tommasinianus* that has been developing here for the past century, kicks off the year with panache. This small, square garden, the oldest corner of Coolaught, is surrounded by roses with names as romantic as their scents – *R.* 'Ferdinand Pichard' *Rosa de rescht*, and *R.* 'Blanc de Double de Coubert' over sheets of *Geranium* 'Hocus Pocus' and a fine big crinodendron.

Take a small gate from here into a laneway, that in turn leads to the first in a series of long borders running the length of the garden, turning corners and leading into woods, past flower-draped arbours and into small little sun rooms. The love of plants is obvious. There are over 80 varieties of clematis alone and if I began to count, there must be just as many different roses.

Open sunny spots, full of perennials give onto gravelly herb gardens, and from there, they duck under the shade of flowering shrubs and fruit trees. The barn garden is particularly good. This was built around an old stone barn, the home of a huge family of swallows. It is a purely romantic place, full of scent and colour through the summer. Swallows apparently operate like dynasties, with a family seat to which they return, generation after generation. They then leave for warmer climates when the Irish weather gets cold.

So the swallows seen in a building several hundred years old such as this one, could represent several hundred years and hundreds of generations of a single swallow dynasty.

Having heard Caroline mention it, I discovered that the Egyptian garden was a corner planted up with blue, red and gold, the colours she associates with Egypt, as well as a smattering of plants with Egyptian names. So *Agapanthus* 'Lily of the Nile' and *Hemerocallis* 'Nefertiti' are grown in combination with hedychiums, red rhododendrons and verbenas.

Since my last visit the acre-and-a-half arboretum at the outer edge of the garden has matured substantially. The number of trees reaching up to four and five metres is notable and the whole garden now only reveals itself as you walk around. Beech and rhododendron hedges cut off one area from another while reaching up, *Magnolia tripetala,* the umbrella magnolia, and *M. dentata,* rub in with golden larch, *Acer negundo* 'Kelly's Gold', different cornus, camellia, Wollemi pine and tree ferns. It is a sort of trip around the world of trees where, with the space for big specimens, the experiment continues.

Douentza

....

Knocknalour, Bunclody, Co. Wexford. Tel: 085 7613 768. e-mail: rachel.darlington65@gmail.com
Contact: Rachel Darlington. Open: Two annual Open Days and by appointment to groups at other times.
Not wheelchair accessible. Children welcome. No dogs. Special features: Teas and plants for sale. Rachel's
book for sale. Directions: Take the Bunclody road from Carnew. Turn left at the small Kilrush/Ferns sign.
Take the 2nd left. The garden is the 4th house on the right.

To call Rachel Darlington a garden obsessive is to understate it a little. She loves plants and she really loves unusual plants. Fond of growing from seed, her greenhouse is like a horticultural oven, while the garden is made up of the 'ones she prepared earlier'.

It is sited on a windy hill above Bunclody, on acid shale which is hard to work, but you would not know about all those drawbacks walking between the bulging, generous island beds that make up much of the garden. We made our way between colonies of carnivorous arisaemas grown from seed, sited under equally exotic looking *Tetrapanax Rex* and tree dahlias. Rachel uses large leafed, fast-growing perennials like these as often as permanent shrubs to foil and back the

flowers. Among her current enthusiasms, roscoeas and brugmansias, both of which are secreted and about the borders too, under the skirts of and between groves of roses, rhododendrons and a *Prunus serrula* with a peeling bark the colour of burnt marmalade

She plays expertly with colours, mixing dark acer and sambucus over red and black sweet William and pure black cornflowers. Pink *Rosa* 'Celeste' combined with purple *Continus coggygyra* was particularly pretty.

She likes to surprise too, by placing a succulent bed up on a reclaimed stone bank, filling it with aeoniums, echeverias and aloes, not plants that immediately remind one of the Wexford hills.

Style is important. Clever touches can be seen everywhere, from the box balls that melt into each other like buns on an oven tray, to the knitted scarves and 'leg warmers' on various of the trees – I suppose some of those exotics get cold here.

Meanwhile, the lawn that wraps up the many borders is itself a picture, tended by her husband Norman, when he is not tending sweet potatoes in the greenhouse between her cautleyas and succulents. This garden needs to work all year round, because in Rachel's words, it is looked at every day.

Make sure to see the Wexford Colours Bed. I can't think of a better use for hardy purple orchids.

The Hollwey Garden

Bunclody, Co. Wexford. Tel: 087 6700 138. e-mail: philiphollwey@gmail.com. Not wheelchair accessible. Contact: Philip Hollwey. Open: For annual charity day, other times by appointment to groups and individuals. Special Features: Garden design service. Directions: On appointment.

This garden is an excellent example of how to fit comfortably into the countryside. Philip Hollwey took the hilly north Wexford landscape around his one-acre strawberry field and pulled it in as backdrop and setting for a charming country garden.

The old cottage stands to the front of the sloped site, covered in 'Mme. Alfred Carriere' roses and fringed with irises and geraniums. The real show however, starts behind the house, with a series of little garden rooms within the larger acre-field. When I saw the little circular area, hedged in by hornbean,

created to house tall climbing beans and his nursery bed, I was smitten. Lucky beans. Lucky baby plants. Two, long sweeping, curving mixed borders enclose another garden room. High up the slope, there are further circular beech hedged rooms made to display pieces of sculpture, with nepeta-lined walks leading between. In the middle of it all is a wildflower meadow that could fairly star in a Cadbury's Flake ad. Wild flower meadows are not easy to create. There are more unsuccessful examples than enviable examples around. Phillip's is quite a sight, visually strong and yet at the same time an ethereal and airy place. It is just as we imagine the old-fashioned countryside to have been. From the meadow, a trail leads into a young wood, mainly comprised of native oak and betula, joined by rhododendrons and specimen trees, among them some developing Japanese acers. He made a path through the wood, bounded by ferns and grasses, leading to the top of the garden and a tree with a swing.

The most rewarding sight of the garden and countryside can be had from here as they both sweep downhill and away into the distance. The mirroring of the garden and the fieldscape beyond is worth the visit alone.

Glenavon Japanese Garden

Courtown Harbour, Gorey, Co. Wexford. Contact: Iris Checkett. Tel: 053 9425 331 085 2048 737. Facebook: glenavonjapanesegarden Open: As part of the Wexford Garden Trail: Aug., Fri. and Sun. 2pm-5pm. To groups by appointment. Not wheelchair accessible. Children welcome. Special features: Teas can be arranged. Directions: On application.

I arrived to visit Iris Checkett's garden, made my way up the drive past mature camellias, lawns and busy, mixed beds, assuming that we would retrace and inspect this area together. 'No no,' laughed Iris. 'This isn't the garden at all.'

This garden is about 40 years old. The garden Iris wanted to show me is much younger, tucked in behind the house, a surprise waiting to be discovered.

She led me to a large wooden, Japanese gate flanked by two big pots of lavender and indicated to it. Her late husband Reg, who loved her garden, designed the gate for her. We made our way through it and and into the garden proper.

This is her Japanese garden or as she called it, her Japanese style garden, a long slim space, broken into a number different areas, from stream and pond gardens to a teahouse or pavilion. We made our way down through the various features, between pots of clipped conifers and past pruned-up shrubs. There are so many sculptural pieces ranged about, from weird bog oak monsters to fine stone works, all placed to surprise and entertain.

I loved the stream that is not a stream, a clever piece of design that includes 'bedrock slabs' arranged to look as though they were uncovered by running water rather than put there by Iris. She understands how to arrange gravel, pebbles and boulders so that they look as though they were washed up by nature rather than placed by her.

The pavilion hovers above a grand iris and water garden, surrounded by gravel and bamboo. It both looks over its own body of water and the Irish Sea in the distance and it is Iris's evening cup of tea spot. We hung over the side of the railing to see the Koi below. Iris told me that the pond is a bit of a 'heron restaurant'. The pavilion also gives a good view of other features in the garden, from an unusual young avenue of *Liquidambar styracifolia* to groves of magnolia, camellia and pittosporums, which she plants everywhere, because, as she explained 'they grow for us.' The place is wonder.

John F. Kennedy Arboretum

New Ross, Co. Wexford. Tel: 051 388171. e-mail: jfkarboretum@opw.ie www.heritageireland.ie Open: May-Aug. Daily. 10am-8pm. April and Sept. Daily 10am-6.30pm. Oct-Mar. Daily. 10am-5pm. Wheelchair accessible. Supervised children. Dogs on leads. Special features: Exhibition centre. Seasonal tea room. Picnic area. Play area. Self-guiding trail. Miniature railway. Guided tours may be booked April-Sep. Directions: Travelling south on the R733 from New Ross, turn right 8.5 km south of New Ross at the sign for the arboretum.

The John F Kennedy Arboretum was set up in the late 1960s in memory of the Irish-American president, appropriately close to the old Kennedy homestead and it would seem a shame to visit one without a trip to the other too. The arboretum is huge, covering 250 acres, and is laid out in blocks and groves of trees joined by wide paths, runs of grass and lakes. Alongside the profusion of specimen trees, there are 200 forest plots. These scientific experiments were laid out to study how trees from different parts of the world grow as forests in Irish conditions.

Over 4,500 species and cultivars of tree and shrub from all temperate regions can be found here. The plants are arranged in a well-signed grid system. The arboretum is an educational facility with ongoing research into such problems as Dutch elm disease.

It is also a pleasant walk. The walks are divided into two main circuits, one of broad-leaved trees and one of conifers. Visit in late April to see the gigantic pink flowering *Magnolia campbellii* close to the entrance. The native wood walk with its bluebell and ferns, bridged streams and soft mulchy paths is a good place to start a visit.

Apart from the vast array of trees, there are displays of different hedging plants, varieties of shrubs, conifer beds, rockeries, lakeside and marginal plantings around the different water features. If you want to see a dozen different species and varieties of cotoneaster, this is the place to visit and the same applies to sorbus, ceanothus, spirea, berberis and a number of other plant families. Wild flower areas have been encouraged in a number of places.

The arboretum displays a wealth of trees and plants. It is worth taking a whole day to explore and appreciate it fully, taking in a walk to the viewing point. Up here, on top of the windy hill, the surrounding geography of Wexford, Waterford, Tipperary, Carlow, Wicklow and Kilkenny can be studied on a bright day as well as the view out to sea to the Saltee islands.

In recent years the arboretum has been taken in hand and a programme of improvement is underway. This is a great move and it will be wonderful to watch its progress.

Kinbark Nurseries & Garden

Carriglegan, Camolin, Co. Wexford. Tel: 053 9383 247. e-mail: noel@kinbark.ie. www.kinbark.ie Contact: Noel Kinsella. Open: As part of the Wexford Garden trail. Jan-Dec. Mon-Sat. See website for seasonal hours. Not wheelchair accessible. Children welcome. Dogs on leads. Special features: Nursery. Teas can be arranged. Directions: From Dublin on the N11 take the first turn right in Camolin, opposite the petrol station. Drive on and take the first turn left. At the next cross roads, turn left. Signed.

Noel Kinsella can only ever remember living in a garden and nursery. His father Charlie began gardening here on a bare field in the early 1980s and the garden has been growing ever since, so much so that the river that once formed the boundary now runs down the middle, bridged and central to the design.

There are several personalities present.

According to Noel, his mother, 'picks up bits and pieces from everywhere'. She has been at this for three decades so her influence on the plants is widespread. These days, it is Noel and his sister whose influence is being felt. The garden is a most interesting place, a maturing creation to which they continue to add. Every nursery should have such an inspirational 'shop window'.

Johnstown Castle

Murrinstown, Co. Wexford. Tel: 053 9184671/9171247. e-mail: info@irishagrimuseum.ie www.irishagrimuseum.ie Open: As part of the Wexford Garden Trail. All year, 9am-5pm. Partially wheelchair accessible. Children welcome. Dogs on leads. Special features: Agricultural museum and Famine exhibition. Tearoom open June - Sept. Peacocks in the courtyard. Directions: Coming from Dublin on the N11, or from Cork on the N25, take the Wexford–Rosslare bypass (N25) to the T-junction signposted for Johnstown Castle.

Impressive battlements at the entrance to Johnstown Castle announce to the visitor that this is something special. Moving up the drive, the big limestone castle comes into view, standing beside one of three ornamental lakes and flanked by some fine specimen trees including a good evergreen oak and an equally impressive blue cedar. The castle sits in the middle of about 50 acres of parkland, pleasure grounds and woods; an enjoyable place to walk. Legends of King John's visit to Ireland in the 1200s gave the castle its name (see also Curraghmore, County Waterford), but today's building dates back only to the 1850s, when the fabulously named Hamilton Knox Grogan Morgan built the castle on the site of Rathlanon Castle, the 15th-century home of the Esmonde clan. Johnstown is every child's idea of what a good castle should be – a confection of turrets, arrow slits and battlements. It was designed, along with the garden by Daniel Robertson, who also designed the Italian garden at Powerscourt (see County Wicklow).

The three ornamental lakes were designed to flow into each other, and cascades between the lakes were positioned so they could be seen to best advantage from the windows of the castle's main reception rooms. The old tower house can be seen along the same axis, fronted by the falling stream. This contrived view takes in the Robertson-designed Italian garden across the lake, where statuary and a balustraded walk stretch along the water. Lines of gunnera surround the lake along with a huge, splayed Japanese cedar (*Cryptomeria japonica*), which looks as though it is growing out of the water

The walled garden is entered through a gate towered over by a grand tall *Drimys winteri*. The sloped, sunny space was laid out in the 1850s, but was abandoned in the 1940s. However, in the 1950s, John Fanning, a well-known horticulturist, oversaw its reconstruction. This included the planting of the yew hedging and the two main central borders. These are traditional herbaceous borders, mirroring each other. The paths are cruciform, and one arm leads to a long run of greenhouses, built in the 1930s to replace the original, more impressive curvilinear houses. Unfortunately, the greenhouses are out of commission and out of bounds. The wall trained fruit trees, cordons and espaliered, are an echo of distant glories. As I get cross at the under-use of the walled garden I need to remember that Johnstown, once employed 200 workers, and now manages with only four gardeners.

Meanwhile, the walks throughout the grounds cut through tall avenues of beech, oak and other park trees. Among the more specialist plants there are runs of rhododendron, which are at their best in spring. I love this place and wish it well. In the meantime the agricultural museum is first rate and should not be missed. The display of Irish furniture is fascinating.

Kilmokea Country Manor

Great Island, Campile, Co. Wexford. Tel: 051 388109. 086 6641 946. e-mail: stay@kilmokea.com www.kilmokea.com Contact: Mark and Emma Hewlett. Open: Mar-Nov. 10am-5pm. Partially wheelchair accessible. Supervised children. Dogs on leads. Special features: Art and crafts for sale. Teas and light lunches. Hotel. Events. Guided tours by arrangement. Member of Gardens of Ireland Trust. Directions: From New Ross take the R733, signposted for 'Campile and the JFK Arboretum.' Pass the turn for the arboretum and continue for 1.5 km. Turn right at the signpost for 'Great Island ESB and Kilmokea Garden.' Drive 2.5 km and take the left fork to the entrance.

Kilmokea is in the unusual situation of being sited on an historic site that was once an island in Waterford Harbour. In the early 19th century, land reclamation joined the little pocket of frost-free land to the mainland. Soon after, a pretty Georgian house was built on the site. The garden looks venerable, laid out around the old house but it was in fact started in 1947 when the Price family created a formal garden within the kitchen garden walls. The enterprise was taken over by the enthusiastic Hewletts in the late 90s and they have minded and continued to develop the garden since then.

Kilmokea is a romantic place, full of surprises, good plants and design. Low walls, impressive tall semi-mazed hedges as well as elaborate topiary, deliver year-round structure. Many features in the well-divided garden would be perfect by themselves, for example, the iris garden – all straight lines with beautiful blue flowers over strappy leaves around big Chilstone urns. The precision of topiary bells, cones and mushrooms serves to make spreads of catmint, monarda and other loose herbaceous plants look even more flamboyant.

In one corner an Italianate loggia lords it over a formal lily pond with Chilean potato vine (*Solanum crispum*) and lobster claw (*Clianthus puniceus*) doing their best to smother it, making it an even more private and secluded corner to retreat to.

Self-seeding is enthusiastically encouraged. Desirable self-seeders, like echiums, for which the garden is well known, as well as love-in-a-mist or *Nigella damascena*, aquilegia and poppies, can be incorporated into most gardens by allowing them to germinate and then deciding which little plants to keep or dump.

Everyone loves the sight of opportunistic blooms emerging from seemingly impossible situations like the tops of walls. Occasionally a plant will park itself beside another surprisingly complementary plant, for which the gardener can, of course, take credit. The millions of seeds that an echium gives rise to should not scare novice gardeners. Like horticultural tadpoles, there may be countless seedlings but by the time the Irish weather has done its job, there will be no more than two or three plants alive, with luck.

The big kitchen garden reached by way of a cathedral of bamboo, is another one of the surprises. This is a busy, working but presentable vegetable garden, operated organically and built to wander through as much as to raid for food. Roses and herbs vie with beans and peas. Low, box walls enclose a sort of maze of beds, with as many roses as lines of lettuce, leek and potato and rose arches lead both into and out of this corner. Look for the little pet cemetery nearby…

Gates in walls feature widely in this garden. They lead to other gardens. I followed one and landed in a more secluded, more shaded area with ferns under camellias and rhododendrons and secret wooden summerhouses. This could be called the battle of the big leaves: Huge rodgersia, three-metre-tall gunnera, acanthus and bamboo make the garden feel positively tropical. I almost expected to see a coconut fall from the sky.

Taking another gate, I followed a trail across a road to yet another garden, this time a *real* secret garden – a wild wood and 'Horse Pond,' once used to bathe horses. Once past the pond, the level of the land falls down to a glade of tree ferns, candelabra primulas and trachycarpus; it is damp, sheltered and warm. Little feeding ponds drip into each other, overhung with ferns and *Euonymus planipes* with pretty red-quartered fruits. Walkways and bridges have been set into the trees. I was told that Emma built all of these. They give the feeling of walking on gangways through a giant greenhouse. There have been some additions to this garden, from the arrivals of fairies to a marooned pirate ship and a cowboy outpost, a Norman motte, and I was told that a Viking boat was expected. This place, with its network of trails and paths under gnarled old trees is the garden into which any child could move.

'David Price 1907-94 made this garden which he loved.' So reads a plaque in one corner of the garden. The same could be said about the Hewletts.

Kilmurry Nursery & Garden

Gorey, Co. Wexford. Tel: 053 9480 223. 086 8113 171. 086 8180 623.
e-mail: kilmurrynursery@eircom.net. www.kilmurrynursery.com. Contact: Paul and Orla Woods.
Open: As part of the Wexford Garden Trail. See website for seasonal opening hours. Partially wheelchair accessible. Special feature: Perennial nursery. Tearoom. Directions: Take exit 22 on the Gorey bypass. Travel on old road towards Gorey and take L5032 to Ballymoney. Go through crossroads. The garden is 4th on the left with a signpost at entrance.

Kilmurry Nurseries are among the best regarded perennial nurseries in the country. They grow and regularly win prizes at home and abroad. A visit to the garden that Paul Woods has been creating attached to the nursery for the last 16 years is to be recommended, as is a visit to the tearoom where his daughter's excellent cakes can be sampled.

This part of Wexford labours under Mackamore clay, a heavy, marl that is slow to drain, quick to waterlog and hard to work, so everything in the garden is a plant that can be grown in this tough medium, making it worth studying.

Start a tour at the edge of the nursery beside the tea room, with a fine pair of perennial borders enclosed by a tall hornbeam hedge at the back, and a neat, low box hedge at the front. These are old fashioned borders that start in spring with daffodils and camassias, followed by different varieties of monarda, which is almost a signature plant at Kilmurry. Hemerocallis, sanguisorba, lychnis and galega, *Romneya coulteri, Iris siberica* and phlox all feature. Late in the summer, a whole raft of asters come into their own.

The path disappears into the hedge, opening onto the house garden where the plants, very satisfyingly wash right up to the walls, so much so that in summer, it is hard to see the whole of the building, under *Rosa* 'Albertine' wisteria, *Magnolia grandiflora* and *Hydrangea petiolaris*. Narrow paths slink between head-height borders of shrubs, small trees, bamboo, grasses and flowers, including huge tall stands of *filipendula* 'Ventusa' - known as the Queen of the prairie.

This is where Paul's, 'famous actor trees', live. I met an *Acer capillipes* and some betulas that starred in 'Game of Thrones'. Other trees notable for their screen-star good looks are the unusual weeping *Cercidiphyllum japonicum* that has the elusive barley sugar scent. The one I really fell for was a 20-year-old *Magnolia campbelli*.

He placed tall, clipped yews in strategic spots, to close off and open up views across the garden. On the lower storey, the deep, moisture retentive soil is perfect for candelabra primulas, *Iris ensata* and lychnis.

The shade the trees cast as they mature allows Paul to grow semi-woodland plants like podophyllum and myosotidium alongside frilly black and pink hellebores.

In an opening in the trees we arrived at the sunken, evening sun sitting garden, full of the scents of lavender, David Austin roses, nepeta and agapanthus.

Paul spent the winter and spring of 2016 creating an impressive water feature, close by, using the wet clay and an existing stream. He diverted the water into three levels of pond and stream, and then built stone walls and waterfalls. No liner was needed. He was busy planting up the whole thing when I visited. I can only imagine the exotic jungle that is now developing.

The whole garden is a testament to the use of seaweed fertiliser. He says it hardens the plants up as well as feeding them. 'In the nursery, the first thing we do with our seedlings is give them a seaweed feed'. Advice worth following.

Lucy's Wood Garden

Barker's Road, Bunclody, Co. Wexford. Tel: 053 937 7256. Contact: Erika and Werner Marten. Open: May-Sept. by appointment. Groups welcome. Not wheelchair accessible. Directions: On the N80 driving from Carlow into Bunclody town turn right onto Barker's Road, opposite the road to Glanbia. Drive past a wood and the garden is 300m along on the left with a black gateway.

Arriving at the front gate that leads into a little courtyard in front of Erika and Werner Marten's garden, you have no idea of the size and scale of the operation that lies beyond the small enclosure. But having entered through a busy plant stuffed courtyard that feels continental the moment a whisper of sun appears, the place slowly unfolds, revealing itself to be a great big garden, filled with interesting planting schemes and the considerable enthusiasm of its energetic owner and gardener.

Erika embarked on this project in the early 1990s, taking a huge run of lawn and weaving a series of beds, big and small through it. She loves plants and the garden is her big laboratory, filled with cornus and tree peonies, acacias, acers magnolias and camellias. The paths and grassy routes through the island shrub

beds lead, in turn past fruit and vegetable gardens, Japanese beds of cut leafed acer, stone lanterns and tree peonies, raised beds, herbaceous borders, and benches from which to enjoy the views. The outer boundary is home to a number of camellias grown from cuttings. The upkeep is impeccable.

The vegetable beds run in a slope down towards the house, finishing off a rockery full of trilliums, erythroniums, ferns and hellebores. The house is barely visible behind a huge *Magnolia grandiflora* and an unknown pink camellia with the smallest fractal-like flowers.

We also looked at the little *Anemone* 'Lucy's Wood' named for this garden, which was previously worked by a talented gardener, Miss Evelyn Booth.

In the vegetable garden a washing line carried

nothing more than a whole line of gardening gloves.   The mark of a gardener!

Marlfield House & Garden

Courtown Road, Gorey, Co. Wexford. Tel: 053 9421 124. e-mail: info@marlfield house.ie
www.marlfieldhouse.com Open: March-Dec. By appointment with afternoon tea or lunch. Partially
wheelchair accessible. Directions: Leave the town by the road to Courtown. Signposted.

Since I last visited, the gardens at Marlfield have developed. Altogether there are ten acres around the house, including mature woods. The main features are the rose gardens and the long mixed borders seen from the restaurant behind the house. Sitting outside on a sunny day the show these put on can be enjoyed before rousing yourself to walk through the grounds.

To the other side of the old house the planting consists of mature magnolias, more roses and neat lines of box. A slope leads down to the woods from here and an enticing arch leads, intriguingly, into those woods, between shuttlecock ferns and spring bulbs under the big trees. Suitably mysterious. I got lost a few times. Following one fork on a path through the trees, brought me back out to the sun and the vegetable garden, between straight lines of herbs and hydrangeas, broad beans and tree peonies. Lines of old apples and young celery, carrots and courgettes make this a handsome, busy, well maintained vegetable garden.

Taking the rose pergola back towards the house led me past two funky looking wire work lounging hounds sprawled on the middle of the path.

Yew hedges with mature trees beyond distracted the eye off into distance for a moment, but first the long border in front of the hedge had to be studied. It was a picture, full of thalictrum and phlox, sedum and hemerocallis. Once again I was distracted by an arch in the hedge and followed it, out to the sequoia lawn and another long border, this time with more shrubs, like magnolia and cordyline, pittosporum and philadelphus, grown over easy runs of Japanese anemones.

I liked the single colour rose beds too. The scents among these on a warm day are heavenly. Do not miss the tulip displays in early summer.

Monksgrange Garden

Rathnure, Enniscorthy, Co. Wexford. Contact: Jeremy and Rosie Hill. Tel: 053 9255 071.
053 9255 145. e-mail: monksgrange@gmail.com. www.monksgrange.com Open: By appointment to groups.
Not wheelchair accessible. Special features: Teas can be arranged. Directions: On application.

Jeremy Hill is the tenth generation of his family to garden the grounds at Monksgrange. Up until about 1914 however, the family seems to to have spent more time playing with the building, adding wings and modifying the house than thinking about gardens. His grandparents took over the running of the place in that year and it is to their taste for the Arts and Crafts movement that the garden today owes its interesting current shape and style.

A long drive leads up through a wood, opening onto parkland studded with mature oak and on up through meadows to the winged, grey limestone house, standing on a gravelled apron up on a stone ledge.

The garden begins to the side of the house, with a set of steps leading up to a pleasure ground lawn past a fine mature *Podocarpus salignus* that is proof of what Jeremy calls their 'Cornish microclimate'. The sheltered situation along with acid soil, mean that a substantial number of special rhododendrons and borderline tender plants thrive here. Around the lawn we looked at a *Davidia involucrata*, *Rhododendron* 'Nancy Evans' and a tall if wind-battered liriodendron. The border running along the sun-trap stone wall mixes day lilies and epimediums, shrub roses and *Rosa* 'Lady Hillingdon'. This is a dry bed, yet there are lots of candelabra primulas here. A stone path runs up along the borders, rounding the corner where its style becomes pure Arts and Crafts, made of large square stone slabs softened by ferns and primroses. This area is below the main garden, and looks up to it. I liked the view up under the skirts of the big multi-stemmed *Cercidiphyllum japonicum* above us, and the smell of barley sugar it emitted. Jeremy's gardening grandparents chopped it right back in order to achieve the multi-stemmed look. Looking up from the path to the upward sloping garden, there are views through *Cedrus deodara* and some Irish yews, wide, splaying purple Japanese acers and a scented *Rhododendron luteum*.

Running down the slope is a stream, bordered by mossed stone slabs and colonised by ferns and skunk cabbage. The very air is romantic.

We walked under an arch, host to a rose and clematis that date back to his grandparents time. Jeremy told me that there old are records of the garden, its designs and plants, including glass plate photographs and a record of the planting that took place in 1920.

He has spent much time clearing the old rockery of leaf litter, uncovering the rock formations and planting them with mini rhododendron and podocarpus. Myrtles grow like weeds here and the cinnamon barks stand out from all corners. One particular specimen with eight trunks will stop any visitor in their tracks.

Do not miss the 1822 folly. This is a scaled down version of a ten pound mediaeval tower house, just big enough for a tiny flat. Could it be a five pound castle? Jeremy is in the middle of planting up a physic garden around it.

The trees and shrubs give the garden a feel of posterity, from champions like the *Drimys winteri* (bought as a sixpenny plant at a Red Cross sale in 1920) to chance happenings like the self-sown pink flowering rhododendron that appeared here a few years ago. He is very proud of it.

The end of May is when the garden is at its best, when the flowering shrubs, magnolias and rhododendrons, are in full flight. That said, it is lovely at all times of year.

Newtownbarry House, Gallery & Garden

Bunclody, Co. Wexford. Tel: 053 937 6383. 087 0569 805. e-mail: info@newtownbarryhouse.com www.newtownbarryhouse.com Open: As part of the Wexford Garden Trail. June-Aug. See website for details. Partially wheelchair accessible. Special features: House tours. Art exhibitions and classes. Teas can arranged. Member of Gardens of Ireland Trust. Directions: Leave Bunclody on the R746 Carnew Road. Cross bridge and entrance is on the left.

The Nortons opened their house and garden back in 2004 with the innovative idea of presenting the public with both a garden to visit and the chance to use it as an outdoor art class.

It is clearly an inspiring place. I travelled up a drive bordered by a stream with several weirs and waterfalls, up to a little lake, passing grand old park trees and specimen cedars, oaks and venerable lines of yew.

The gardens proper begin around the house. They are attractive but were not always so. The first of these, a sunken garden, was, until a few years ago, hidden beneath 50 self-sown trees. Clody Norton invited a man with a tractor in to clear a few of them, telling him that some day she planned to clear the garden. She went off about her business and arrived home to find that the whole area had been scraped bare. She knew something big had been embarked upon so she called in the renowned Iain and Frances MacDonald, and they created a rose garden design for the old tennis court on the upper level of the walled garden.

Today there are herbaceous perennials in the tram lines and roses where the service courts, net and baseline once were. The backing height is delivered using azara, mahonia and *Clematis armandii*.

Some time later Clody pointed to a place where she remembered there had been a set of steps, and so the sunken garden was rediscovered. In the years of neglect, the steps had been covered by leaf litter. Like archaeologists, following these down they found a lost garden, about two metres beneath the rest of the garden level. It was bounded by beautiful old stone walls.

Today the uncovered sunken garden features pink and white borders full of roses, wisteria, persicaria, rosemary and lavender. Clody thinks it predates her family's arrival at the house back in 1861. It could be 18th century and it is certainly on the 1840 Ordnance Survey maps. The grottos on either end date back to the 18th century.

It appears that the reason for making this unusual sunken garden, was not for some obscure design idea. It was created, according to family lore, because the building of the house required a lot of stone, so they mined it on the spot.

Whatever the history, the result is a happy one. Layers of planting up along the ledged walls make the atmosphere from down at the bottom of the garden, standing by the rectangular lily ponds, themselves surrounded by ligularia and iris, primula and hosta, like standing at the bottom of the hanging gardens of Wexford.

There is an atmosphere of pure romance through the place. Cardoons and agapanthus, scabious and geranium on the ground, jasmine and roses up the walls. It is perfect. Low box walls pull in the wilder herbaceous things. On top of the walls, the long ribbons of of scented lavender are divine. In the background there are huge stands of trees.

Leaving the sunken garden, the path ducks under a stone arched grotto. Emerging on the other side of this lands you in the wilder wood, where the trees, previously seen over the wall, can be properly viewed. The path runs through these, on under a *Carya ovata*, known as the shag bark hickory, a Champion tree of Ireland and Britain. The wood is suitably wild, with paths woven between beech, ash and oak, mad coloured Japanese acers, magnolias and, in the summer, philadelphus and hydrangeas.

'Dinky' Donoghue's wooden benches – beautiful seats made from the contorted old branches of fallen trees, were all made by Mr. Donoghue, a talented local man, whose skills of working wood are so aptly displayed in this perfect old country garden.

Susie's Orchard

Tomona, Kiltealy, Enniscorthy, Co. Wexford. Contact: Josephine Ann Fitzhenry. Tel: 053 9255 322. 087 2300 501. e-mail: josephineannfitzhenry@gmail.com Open: Open to groups by appointment. Partially wheelchair accessible. Special features: Teas can be arranged. Art classes. Directions: On application.

Josephine Fitzhenry's flower garden is a cheerful, busy and extremely well maintained place. From the front gate, the enthusiasm for colour, variety and display is obvious. The profusion of flowers is the first thing that hits you. There are rose borders and merry beds of aquilegia and phlox, delphinium, agapanthus, hemerocallis and aconites, hemmed in by estate fencing, clipped beech hedging and low walls of box.

Definition is given to the various gardens by arches occupied in the business of supporting a large number of roses and clematis, and pergolas used to host espaliered fruit trees. There are also tall hedges and gates everywhere.

The explosive growth in the borders is kept from becoming chaotic through the use of impeccably swept and maintained gravel paths, and neat lawns with perfect edging. I like the use of low clipped spheres of black *Pittosporum* 'Tom Thumb' as a boundary along one path. This is a place where order rules, but not at the expense of exuberance and a bit of fun.

Josephine runs art classes and there are some nicely placed stone works ranged about the garden. I also love the use she makes of neatly stacked logs by the shed as a garden feature in itself.

Keeping the outer beech hedges at a height that allows one see the surrounding hilly countryside from every point in the garden, is a good idea.

Tombrick Garden

Tombrick, Ballycarney, Enniscorthy, Co. Wexford. Tel: 053 9388 863. 087 2961 340.
Contact: Walter Kelly. Open: June-Sept., Fri-Sun. 2-6pm. Other times by appointment. Guide dogs only.
Partially wheelchair accessible. Special features: Plants for sale. Directions: Situated on the N80 between
Bunclody and Enniscorthy, 1.3 km north of the Ballycarney Inn, signposted.

Walter Kelly built the house at Tombrick in a small rectangular field on an extremely windy hill back in 1988. The following year he began to dig. Today, Tombrick gives visitors one of the most satisfying horticultural experiences to be found in a county full of great gardens. Walter is something of a magician. Walking through his mixed borders full of wonders, it is hard to see how this could ever have been 'the windiest site on a wind-swept hill'. It proves the wisdom of erecting a proper shelter belt.

The garden to the front of the house is made up of lawn surrounded by borders, not so dense that the sweep downhill to the River Barrow and the valley beyond cannot be seen. It is interesting to see such a grand healthy *Cornus controversa* 'Variegata' on such a gusty spot.

The real garden is however, to the side and rear of the house. It begins with a series of impressive ledged rockeries. From there it moves out into woodland walks, sunny pond gardens, orchards and long serpentine paths through mixed borders, filled with good and unusual plants, ridiculously healthy looking stands of Chatham island forget-me-nots, *Veratrum album* and disporum. Fuchsias are his passion and the range of different species and varieties scattered throughout the borders is excellent. His habit of planting them deeply brought all of his fuschias through the worst to the bad winters of 2010 and 2011.

The paths sweep up against massed, billowing ground cover plants, well pruned-up small trees including a smartly worked *Magnolia stellata* and invisibly supported tall herbaceous plants. The range and number of plants is stunning, as is the upkeep. He also manages to run a full farm and work this garden. I sometimes wonder if night work and a Davy lamp are involved.

Fancy fowl strut about the place, providing mobile entertainment and slug eradication. The fowl have their own pond which doubles as a water garden and home to collections of primulas, hostas and other damp-loving plants. A fat Suffolk ram observed us from his home in a paddock just visible through the trees, reminding us that we were on a farm.

Walter also uses stone well, mainly local granite in the shape of gate posts and standing stones, ledges and gravel paths.

The paths in particular give a sense of unity to the place, tying it together and trailing off in so many different directions, lighting up dark wooded areas and making sunny bright spots appear even brighter. They are more impressive because they are so well minded, swept clean and clear of leaves. This is a state of affairs that will leave lazy gardeners green with envy.

Wells House & Garden

Ballyedmond, Gorey, Co. Wexford. Tel: 053 9186 737. 087 9974 323. e-mail: info@wellshouse.ie www.wellshouse.ie Open: As part of the Wexford Garden Trail. All year. May-Sept. 10am-6pm. Oct-April 11am-4pm. Wheelchair accessible. Restaurant. Craft shop. House tours. See website for seasonal programme of events. Directions: Travelling south on the R741 from Ballycanew.

A wide and straight oak lined drive leads up to Well's House, a red brick house designed by Daniel Robertson, famed for his work on Powerscourt House in Wicklow as well as Johnstown Castle. The house, undergoing ongoing restoration, can be visited on guided tours. The gardens, meanwhile are only part of an overall complex of craft galleries, coffee shops, playgrounds, clay pigeon shooting grounds and other activities. This is an all-the-family place.

The gardens centre on the Victorian flower gardens, dating from 1832. Soon after Sabine and Uli Rosler took over the house and grounds in 2011, the son of previous owners presented them with the thrilling prospect of the original Robertson garden plans. They had no idea that these gardens ever existed, but nevertheless they launched into a restoration project to find them.

The old gardens, having been completely lost under weeds and rampant growth, were located and the footprints of the symmetrical borders and paths were retraced and reinstated, cut into smart lawn between even smarter golden gravel.

Now replanted under the advice of renowned plantswoman Daphne Shackleton, the terraces and formal beds in front of, and centred on the house, are happily back to life. Open a few years, and developing accordingly, the planting is soft and pretty, mixing peonies and nepeta, lavender, campanula and tulips, grasses and rudbeckias.

Mature magnolias, cedars, yews and rhododendrons and an unusual old *Crataegus* x. *lavallei* 'Carrièrei' frame the flower gardens and house and lead off toward a pond garden where even more formal bedding borders encircle a little pond. From there the way leads to a developing arboretum.

This new arboretum, until recently was choked by rampant laurel and *Rhododendron ponticum*. Today you will see young trees being added to the existing mature oak and beech. Unusually this is a people's arboretum in which people may buy a tree to plant. The garden is old but new, still developing and worth following.

Woodville House Gardens

New Ross, Co. Wexford. Tel: 051 422957. 087 9709 828. e-mail: woodville05@eircom.net www.woodvillegardens.ie. Contact: Gerald Roche. Open: As part of the Wexford Garden Trail. May-Aug. 10am-5pm. Other times by appointment. Partially wheelchair accessible. Special features: House tours. Teas can be arranged. Accommodation. Directions: Entrance at the junction of the N30 and R700 beside Mannions Pub 1 km from New Ross.

The Roche family have lived at Woodville since the 1870s. Recently I met Gerald, the fifth generation Roche dedicated to working the garden. Gerald came to love gardening as an adult but he did it with a vengeance. He has continued to both mind and develop the fine old place, including restoring, almost single-handedly, the elegant Victorian, Messenger greenhouse. As a result, the things Gerald does not know about curved window tiles are not worth knowing.

The slate-sided house stands on a height overlooking his constantly developing shrubberies and a sweep of lawn studded with trees, including a *Fitzroya cupressoides*, named for the captain of *The Beagle*, the ship that carried Charles Darwin to the Galapagos Islands. There are also walnuts, a *Crataegus orientalis,* which is thornless and bears orange fruit, as well as liquidambars and runs of rhododendron including scented *R. luteum.*

Once upon a time, the railway ran below the garden on its way to Enniscorthy. When it closed down, the resourceful Roches made use of a spring originating under the railway tunnel to fill a pond that they edged with angel's fishing rods and sisyrinchium. The pond is also a disguised swimming pool. Below it there is a wood and water garden, with various ponds that tip into each other. These can be seen from the vantage of a series of rope-railed steps down a bank of astilbe, bloodroot (*Sanguinaria canadensis*), ferns, including *Adiantum pedatum,* which has noticeably black stems. The flowers include trilliums, snowdrops and bluebells and all this happens under a tall canopy of ash, oak, holly, *Rhododendron macabeanum* and a camellia, run through by rampant clematis. The look might be natural and native but there are plants here from 37 countries, including *Veratrum album,* with accordion-pleated leaves. Deposits of glacial and acid sand allows the easy growing of acid loving plants in this part of the garden.

Stepping away, and heading up the hill again, the row of mature Monterey pines, *Pinus radiata,* reminded me of when the late Mr Roche told me that he leap-frogged them when he was 12 years old.

Woodville's walled garden is built beside the house. The general trend was for siting kitchen gardens, outbuildings and working parts of the estate away from the house, sometimes as far as a mile away. (See Kylemore Abbey, Co. Galway).

The stand-out features here are the Harry Potter-esque apple trees, old gnarled, one-time trained specimens with character to burn, including 'Bramley', 'Newton Wonder' and 'Allington Pippin', which apparently tastes of pineapple. But there are plenty of ornamentals here too, from indigofera and *Paeonia delavayi,*fascicularia, roses of all sorts and all the usual herbaceous perennials.

It takes enormous work to keep a walled garden to the standard and Gerald works it with gusto. We walked between long beds of lilies and dahlias, alongside substantial rows of peas, beans and asparagus.

The box hedges here are an important feature. There are double box walks, wavy hedges, hedges within hedges and some quirky topiary features.

At the end of one hedge a fox looks across the path longingly at a fat hen on the opposite hedge. She is the dinner he'll never enjoy. The book-ending pyramids are good too.

The walled garden is full to bursting – Lovely yellow *Rosa banksiae* 'Lutea' thrives under a north wall, along with fresh and healthy-looking Chatham Island lilies, *Myosotidium hortensia,* generally seen struggling and looking miserable in Irish gardens. Sow the seed fresh is Gerald's advice.

I was looking forward to seeing the greenhouse and it lived up to expectations. It was built in 1882, and having been fabulously restored by Gerald, it is now full of plumbago, clivia, scented brugmansia, unusual red nerines, vines, a century-old maidenhair fern gone wild and several abutilons.

Outside the gate, he has been adding to an existing wood, creating the Dairy Walk, and adding young walnuts, azara, euonymus and loquats. The garden is marching on.

Photo: Ger Lawlor.

National Botanic Gardens at Kilmacurragh. Photograph, Seamus O'Brien

Wicklow

Avoca Handweavers / Glencormac Estate Garden

Kilmacanogue, Co. Wicklow. Tel: 01 2867 466. Contact: Des Carton or Donald Pratt. Open: All year. Partially wheelchair accessible. Children welcome. No entrance fee. Dogs on leads. Special features: Restaurant. Garden shop. Nursery. Directions: Travel south along the N11. About 4 km after the turn for Bray, watch for the Avoca flags on the right.

Avoca Handweavers is situated on the site of the old Glencormac Estate, owned by the Jamesons, the famous distilling family. In 1870 an eleven-acre garden was laid out for James Jameson by William Sheppard, a landscape gardener who worked as assistant to the Victorian garden designer Ninian Niven.

Today the garden is part of the great busy enterprise of Avoca with a huge shop, restaurant and garden centre to distract you. But to enthusiasts, this is known as the home of the Glencormac cypress. Planted in 1794, it was thought to be an ordinary Monterey cypress, a *Cupressus macrocarpa*, but a few years' growth showed that it was something else – a unique weeping mutant, described in a report for Wicklow County Council in 1977 as 'possibly one of the outstanding trees in the British Isles'. The Glencormac cypress, or *Cupressus macrocarpa* 'Pendula' is the only mature specimen in the world.

There are a number of other notable trees in the garden, including huge eucalyptus, giant redwood (*Sequoiadendron giganteum*), blue Atlas cedar (*Cedrus atlantica* 'Glauca'), Scots pine (*Pinus sylvestris*) and a grove of yews of indeterminate age. One of these yews, thought by some to be 2,000 years old, features in the Guinness Book of Records.

Travel up the drive between tree ferns, groves of mahonia and mop-head hydrangeas. Skinny paths slip in off the drive, under the canopy, between more tree ferns onto the open lawns. Take one and wander between cut-leaf beech and liriodendron, cercidiphyllum and acer.

Water is an important feature here. Meandering sunken streams dawdle around the hilly lawns between the various groupings, so keep a close eye on children and watch your footing. The Dripping Pool, an unusual Victorian creation and part of Sheppard's design, is remarkable. According to legend, it has never once dried up since it was built in 1878.

Glencormac is a delightful garden and walk. It must have been even more picturesque when it had an unimpeded view of the Sugar Loaf Mountain. Now, ironically this view is hidden from sight by fine trees.

Avondale House & Forest Park

Rathdrum, Co. Wicklow. Tel: 0404 46111. e-mail: www.coillteoutdoors.ie Contact: Reception. Open: April-Oct. Contact for seasonal hours. Supervised children. Dogs on leads. Special features: House tours. Tearoom. Gift shop. Directions: 2 km south of Rathdrum, on the L2149.

Avondale House, famed as the home of Charles Stewart Parnell, was built in 1779 by Samuel Hayes who was at one time Wicklow's representative in the Irish House of Commons and the person who began the planting seen in Avondale today. In 1788 Hayes presented a bill entitled 'An Act for encouraging the cultivation and better preservation of trees'. In 1904 the estate passed into the care of Coillte, the Forestry Service, and much of the land was laid out in one-acre plots for experimental tree planting. The plots are arranged in the form of a forest garden with three planned walks – the Pine Trail, the Exotic Tree Trail and the River Walk.

A colour-coded map can be obtained at the reception, marking out in detail the array of special plants and trees along each of these. Among the groves of oak, silver fir, pine, larch, maple and beech, there are also scattered specimens of eucalyptus, Serbian spruce, monkey puzzle, red cedar, redwood, Monterey pine, and Spanish chestnut. Underneath these there are ferns, foxgloves and other woodland ground dwellers.

The grove of giant sequoias is singular, an almost primeval-looking area, where the huge trees soar up and the dark, needle-strewn ground is soft underfoot and rippled with exposed roots. This is not a place to be forgotten easily.

At the last visit, upkeep left something to be desired and the place does not look well loved. This is a pity but should not deter visitors.

The Coe Garden

Manor Kilbride, Blessington, Co. Wicklow. Tel 087 2220 238. 087 2470 407. e-mail: rcoephoto@gmail.com Contact: Ann and Richard Coe. Open: Open Day in June. Contact for annual details. Partially wheelchair accessible. Supervised children. Dogs on leads. Special features: Teas and plants. Directions: On application.

I have a memory of an outdoor open covered space, the perspex ceiling of which drips wisteria flowers. Another picture is of a curtain of dangling, tinkling shells and an arch of twisty, gnarled hazel like the entrance to some gothic world and an organic-shaped gazebo with a rustic slate roof. Ann and Richard Coe's garden is full of touches that make it a very individual and personal place. This is not the sort of garden you will come across designed on paper by a landscape company. It is just its attractive self, filled to capacity with plants. Ann says the garden centre is her sweet shop and she obviously has a liking for sweets.

Sitting half way up a hill on the outskirts of Blessington, it is also a windy garden, and should be a cold one too but the microclimate they created four decades ago when they drained a boggy, sedge-ridden field and planted young birch, oak, sycamore and ash, had the desired effect. 40 years later, walking through the informal and flower-filled place feels like walking through a cosseted, well loved country garden.

With the number of tall trees scattered throughout, it feels like a light, airy wood. Under slim larch and birch there are all sorts of flowering shrubs, from magnolias, rhododendrons and camellias to azaras, and all sorts of viburnums. The soil is suitably acid for these.

Ann has little time for plant names. She prefers to work on gardening techniques, like growing plants from seed and playing with topiary, as well as cloud training. She practises her clouds not just in her own garden but in those of her grateful friends – some of which I spotted locally, as I made my way to visit with her. Evergreen shrubs can become browned and hollow inside, and she climbs in among these branches with the secateurs, clears out the dead wood and moulds what is left to produce a desired cloud effect.

Corke Lodge

Woodbrook, Bray, Co. Wicklow. Tel: 087 2447 006. e-mail: alfred@corkelodge.com www.corkelodge.com. Contact: Alfred Cochrane. Open: By appointment to groups as part of the Dublin Gardens Group. Special features: Refreshments can be arranged. House tours. Directions: On application.

Idiosyncratic is the word that comes to mind to describe Corke Lodge. There was an arboretum here when architect Alfred Cochrane, took the garden in hand back in the late 1980s. The villa was built in the 1820s, one of many properties owned by the wealthiest widow in Ireland, Louisa Magan. This was to be her seaside villa, complete with Greek revival façade, 'a sort of theatrical joke,' according to Alfred. The house is surrounded by a romantic Gothic wood garden with cedar of Lebanon, evergreen oak and a cork oak grown because it reminded Louisa of an olive tree. When she died the house and garden passed on to her daughter, Georgina, whose sad life was said to be Dickens' inspiration for Miss Havisham in 'Great Expectations'. It was taken on by the Cochrane family at the beginning of the 1900s and in the '80s Alfred Cochrane redesigned the garden. His architectural background is evident throughout the two acres, and the grounds are strewn with architectural remnants and oddments.

One of his most interesting modifications was to turn a rampant, laurel lawn into a three tiered, stepped feature defined in places with granite benches and mossy paths, under Louisa's by now tall canopy of ash, oak and poplar. The shade is not uniform. In one place the sun spills down on a series of box 'battlements'. Alfred clearly enjoys playing, clipping and hemming all these hedges in.

The cork oak (*Quercus suber*), is famed as the oldest in the country. It is suitably contorted; its trunk is twisted, spongy and cracked. The shape is like something from a willow-pattern plate, and it leans heavily and with some drama, to one side.

A series of elliptical stone arches and gothic follies, ruins, half-arches and mullions stand on an expanse of gravel, interplanted with young eucalyptus, artemisia, fascicularia, bamboo and gardener's garters (*Phalaris arundinacea*). A rose seems to be making its way lightly through one of the arches. This is all seen through an avenue of cordylines that march out from the house, via an opening in the lawn, walled by low box plants. Cordylines make an unusual, well-structured, fairly fast-growing avenue. They endear themselves further to Alfred by taking up a minimal amount of space, casting only light shade and having 'a lovely smell'. To the side of the lawn there are groves of

Portuguese laurel (*Prunus lusitanica*), hydrangea, fuchsia, purple beech, maple, cherry and London Plane or *Platanus orientalis*. A huge stone arch frames the view.

In the woods the gardening is done with a light touch. Between openings and clearings there are combinations of conifers and deciduous trees, such as the unusually pruned *Parrotia persica*. Myrtle or *Luma apiculata* and hoheria, both of which grow like weeds here, need constant culling. There is one particularly superb multi-stemmed myrtle, like so many sprouted cinnamon sticks. Thoughts of cinnamon buns come to mind with the sweet sugar smell given off by the *Cercidiphyllum japonicum*.

Allées lead from the house, between stone sentries to another arch covered in ivy. Box clipped into half circles holds back tree ferns (*Dicksonia antarctica*), grasses, stag's horn sumach, bamboo and eucalyptus.

The garden doesn't depend on flowers apart from a dot of geranium here or some blue hydrangeas there, pulmonaria and cyclamen in autumn and bluebells in spring, occasional roses and delicate, myrtle flowers.

It is a restful, cool, masculine garden in which restraint has been shown in the marrying of an old garden with contemporary ideas.

The Dower House

Rossanagh, Ashford, Co. Wicklow. Tel: 0404 40168. e-mail patriciaannebutler@yahoo.ie
Contact: Mrs P.A. Butler. Open: Mid May-mid July to Groups only (min. 2) by appointment. Special features: Teas by arrangement. Wheelchair accessible. Guide dogs. Member of The Dublin Garden Group. RHSI Partner Garden. Member of the Gardens of Ireland Trust. Directions: Driving south on the M11, take Exit 16. Before Rathnew village turn left onto the R761 and continue for approximately 1km. The entrance is on the left before Hunter's Hotel. Travelling north on M11, take Exit 16 and follow signs for Rathnew. From here, same directions apply for travelling south on M11.

Visiting Patricia Butler's Wicklow garden over the years, it has always felt like one of the brightest jewels in Wicklow's horticultural crown. The house has been here since the 1780s, built as a dower house for the larger, neighbouring Rossanagh House. There are sketches of it dating to that period, made by artist Maria Taylor, alongside a painting she made of the famed preacher John Wesley, giving a sermon close by under a yew tree.

At the end of the 19th century a garden was laid

out around the house and filled with rhododendrons. Today those mature arboreal rhododendrons provide a colourful backdrop for the garden Patricia has been working and developing since the early 1990s. Her garden is sympathetic to both the house, the older garden and the surrounding countryside. The diarist Mrs. Delaney, was able to declare it 'very pretty... and neatly kept' in the late 1790s and that is still the case today. There are links with many historic characters from the Methodist preacher John Wesley to Henry Grattan.

By the house there is an uncluttered, restrained and formal white garden made up of ordered roses, white-trumpet-flowered brugmansia and lilies in pots. The plants in the beds include helichrysum, phlox and white lavender, all overlooking a meadow. In a rather nice spooky touch, having made the white garden from scratch, Patricia went on to discover a picture taken in the 1890s of this area as an almost identical white garden. Behind it the courtyard forms another garden room, with a fig, *Rosa* 'Rambling Rector' running wild and a rampant blue, *Solanum crispum* 'Glasnevin'. With the ripening fruit, the gorgeous scent of creamy roses and the blue of the potato vine, this is one of my favourite garden images. Leading away from the house there are mature runs of rhododendron, eucalyptus and magnolia. The eucalyptus, with its pale camouflage bark, is striking. A small collection of large tree heathers here, commemorates the fact that Patricia's father grew prize winning specimens and won RDS medals for his efforts.

The meadow, spotted earlier is as romantic as a meadow can be in June with sprays of poppies and tulips, ox-eyed daisies and cowslips scattered like jewels in the grass.

A notable specimen of *Camellia japonica* gave Patricia a good deal of pleasure when she found that she could date its age to be nearly 120 years. An elderly neighbour told her that she could recall it from a time when she rode over to visit the house as a young child, and it was already a huge tree.

An avenue of Caucasian limes or *Tilia dasystyla* subsp. *caucasica* leads down to the River Vartry, planted just over two decades ago, it is putting on good growth, giving the Butlers pleasure today and promising to continue doing so into the future.

Festina Lente Garden

Old Connaught Road, Bray, Co. Wicklow. Tel: 01 2720 704. e-mail info@festina-lente.ie www.festina-lente.ie. Open: May-Aug, Tues-Sat, 10.30am-5pm. Supervised children welcome. Dogs on leads. Special features: Assisted riding stables. Partially wheelchair accessible. Allotment courses. Dog training classes. Vegetables for sale. Member of the Gardens of Ireland Trust. Directions: Leave the M11 at the northernmost Bray junction. Go through the roundabout towards the town and approach a set of traffic lights. Turn right. Travel .5 km to a newsagents on the right. Turn right after this and follow the garden signs.

I cannot think of a more welcoming garden entrance than the busy café and shop at Festina Lente where you might pick up a basket of black currants, a plant from the garden and a very good coffee indeed. There are always a few gardeners and stable workers sitting between the giant echiums and drifts of achillea, enjoying lunch or elevenses. They usually include some of the 52 allotment holders who have plots here, swapping notes on growing lavender and potatoes.

Hauling myself away from an ear-wigging session, I set out along along the wall-backed flower border edged with puffs of lavender, and moved onto the allotments. Many of these are regular prize winners in the Delgany and District Horticultural Show. I overtook one small boy busy with a watering can bigger than himself and thought he must be destined to be a future winner.

The principal feature of the garden, originally the

walled garden attached to the Old Conna Demesne, is the reflecting double border. It is set out in the lower part of the garden, in front of the allotments. There are four beds, backed by espaliered apples, measuring 25 metres each, and as the name suggests, reflecting each other. The planting was being rejuvenated on my last visit and the gardeners were replanting phlomis and guaria, cephalaria and asters, melianthus and phlox.

Like many old walled gardens, the place had some old glories of which there are now only reminders. For example, Festina Lente once held the longest run of wisteria in the country, along the long brick and stone

walls. To one side of the garden is what is thought to be an old fernery. The dreadfully overgrown yew hedges were rejuvenated and the twin lily ponds have been saved and replanted. The surrounding beds have been cleared of weeds and replanted beautifully with lavender and the ponds now home a large number of rescue terrapins that can be caught standing on top of each other, sun bathing on a warm day.

Work to restore the garden and open it for the use of people with physical disabilities began in 1996, and every time I visit, there have been big changes. I think it will always be a work in progress. It is a hive of industry and development, affording an insight into how a large walled garden can be better used. All work is carried out using organic methods and the garden is a member of the Irish Organic Trust.

The top garden today homes two long, wall backed wild flower borders with bridle paths between the flowers. These borders are arranged for the disabled riders who trek along the soft mulch paths, between scabious, achillea, hollyhock and verbena, mallow, oregano and centaurea. This is an unusual and handsome double use of the space.

At one end of the second of these walks is the old glasshouse border, which now hosts a great busy dahlia display in late summer. In this reconstruction, the old walled garden has been modified in some clever and inventive ways. The sensory garden incorporates plants noted for scent and texture, with mixes of lemon verbena, lavender, curry plant, chives, rosemary and oregano.

Outside the walls, different types of wild flower borders are being developed – one in the arid dry gravel of the car park, and one under the trees. Both are worth studying.

Glenfield

Thornhill Road, Old Connaught, Bray. Co. Wicklow. Tel: 087 259 2866.
e-mail: noreenkeane22@gmail.com Contact: Noreen Keane. Open: Charity days. See Our Lady's Hospice website for details. Partly wheelchair accessible. No dogs. Children welcome. Special features: Teas and plants. Directions: On application.

The house at Glenfield was built in 1830 on an arm of the Powerscourt Estate. Noreen and Frank Keane came to live here just over a quarter of a century ago and are unsure as to when the garden was laid out, but the layout was already in place when they arrived. Walking around today, feels like taking a tour around an Edwardian country garden, starting with the wavy, nobbled hedge on the boundary.

Noreen knew, 'a moderate amount about gardening' when she arrived. Today, she spends what she says is, 'a ridiculous amount of time working the place.' The drive in past a double white cherry and an apple-scented *Rosa* 'Paul Transon', makes it way between two abundant borders of veratrum and agapanthus, fennel, dahlia, macleaya and cardoon.

A great stretch of *Rosa* 'Buff Beauty' runs the length of the wall behind one of these borders. It is one among many. We had to look at the 'Charlie Robinson' rose, a rose with a story: There were two ladies who lived in a cottage in Monaghan. A mink broke into the house, using the rose as a climbing frame to get in, so in fear of another incursion, they chopped the plant to the ground. A local man, Charlie Robinson took the opportunity to take cuttings. He gave them to friends and one plant ended up here in Wicklow, muddling along with scores of other roses in Noreen's busy flower garden.

Near the house we passed big fruiting figs and sweet chestnuts, grand old magnolias and deep shrub borders of deutzia and *Euphorbia mellifera*.

A little gate leads from here into the 'holding bay' garden with a sunny lawn enclosed in a knobbly lonicera hedge, and beds full of white foxgloves and scutellaria.

Gaps and gateways are a recurring theme, under arches and through hedges, between shrub borders made of daphne, cornus and amelanchier, and on into rose and hellebore gardens. We wandered on, through deep shrub beds of self-seeding myrtles, hydrangea and *Cytisus battandieri*. The view up here beyond the garden is of the Sugar Loaf and Maulin Mountain.

The slate covered house backs onto a raised rockery that is negotiated on route to a secret lane into another garden room, made of concentric stone slabbed paths centred on a sundial and a collection of hybrid tea roses. The route from here is by way of clematis and rose-draped pergolas, eventually reaching the vegetable garden where Noreen grows 'Foremost', the best, first early potato in her opinion. I loved the long tunnel running under a mature *Parrotia persica* and *Rosa moyesii* 'Geranium'. 'It drops its pink petals on the path and I love it!' Noreen said as we walked underneath and came to a huge *Rosa* 'Belvedere' weighing heavily on the summerhouse. For all the gardens considerable informal, flowery charm, my abiding memory is of a tall *Echium pininana* growing out of the mortar on top of the boundary wall.

Glenview Hotel

Glen O'The Downs, Co. Wicklow. Contact: Reception Tel: 01 2873 399.
e-mail: sales@glenviewhotel.com www.glenviewhotel.com Open: All year. Individuals freely. Groups by appointment. Supervised children. Special features: Hotel. Directions: 8 km south of Bray on the M11. The hotel is signposted on the right-hand side of the road.

The gardens at Glenview cover a steep hill in front of one of the noisiest and busiest roads in the country. This difficult site has been transformed into a fine hillside garden, favoured with a great view of the wooded Glen O' the Downs. Sit and take it in from one of the tables up on the hotel ledge, surrounded by anthemis and lavender. There are little stone lined ponds and streams secreted in between leycesteria and buddleia at the top of the hilly garden. Being in the hills, the mist can appear at any time, and even on an August day a light mist playing around the trees and hills can render the place strange and atmospheric.

Leaving this area by a path downhill leads into the garden proper. Paths weave through the beds, travelling down, under and between maturing Japanese acer, copper beech, hoheria and Mexican orange blossom. The paths open onto lawns surrounded by agapanthus, peony and lace cap hydrangea. Blue cedars can be seen, beginning to rise above the neighbouring trees and occasional exotics such as paulownia and acacia peep from out of the scrum. Sometimes the path travels into tunnels of rhododendron. The garden finally, and naturally trails off into blackberries and dog roses as it reaches the bottom of the hill.

Gorse Hill

Cliff Road, Windgates, Bray, Co. Wicklow. Tel: 01 2876 986. e-mail: jd@gorsehill.net www.gorsehill.net Contact: Joan Davis. Open: By appointment. Special features: Somatic Practices. Mindfulness. Events. Art Exhibitions. Directions: See the map on the website for details.

The word 'perched' is often used to describe a location but rarely with such accuracy as here the gardens at Gorse Hill which looks out over the Irish sea from the vantage point of an eagle's nest. I fell for this very eccentric garden the minute I arrived. It sits on top of a windy cliff, looking out over the water, partially protected by a large number of pines, cedars and other conifers, a wild but peaceful place.

The garden is cut into the granite rock face, in rough terraces that pick their way, gingerly downhill on stone and sleeper steps. Rock is rarely far from the surface. Joan confirmed my hunch that there is just about a dusting of soil scattered on the unyielding bedrock. She, and nature insulate those plants that will thrive, into little footholds. Happily a wide range of plants fare well out here in the salt-laden winds. We walked between pampas, and yucca, echium and senecio, abundant clouds of *Cryptomeria japonica* and spiked *Fascicularia bicolor* that grows like a weed here.

The plants weave around Joan's art works. A tree might be studded with marbles. Another small shrub will double as a hanging 'bone garden', another might be draped with stained glass or gleaming white oyster shells. As you make your way down through the garden, there are mounds of rock draped with horse shoes and old electrical appliances, the vertebrae of a large fish or mammal. There is an air of the surreal about Gorse Hill but also one of tranquility. This is a wild creation, a strange and fascinating one, not for the tidy person who likes things ship-shape and in order.

June Blake's Garden

Tinode, Blessington, Co. Wicklow. Tel: 087 2770 399. e-mail: info@juneblake.ie www.juneblake.ie Contact: June Blake. Open: April-Oct. Fri-Sun 11-5.30. Other times by appointment. Partially wheelchair accessible. Supervised children. Dogs on leads. Special features: Plant nursery. Accommodation. Refreshments. Garden bookshop. Guided tours. Member of the Gardens of Ireland Trust. Directions: Leave Blessington travelling towards Dublin on the N81. The garden is approximately 6 km along signposted on the left.

June Blake is without doubt, one of the best plantswomen in Ireland. She has been selling fantastic plants from her nursery outside Blessington for years and her garden has been a favourite among visitors.

When we hear the phrase 'cottage garden', an old-fashioned, traditional flower garden, something along the lines of a Mildred Anne Butler watercolour comes to mind. June has proved that the styles, 'cottage garden' and 'contemporary', usually poles apart, can

be melted together to make something that makes sense. What she has made is modern. It draws in the visitor and wraps them in flowers. It is welcoming, yet stylish, an example of virtuoso design and expert plantsmanship. It also changes constantly, making every visit a new experience.

The garden is laid out in front of a house that similarly marries modern with cottage style. This is a gabled, granite Victorian cottage straight off the top of a chocolate box from one angle, but with a sharp modern extension of glass when viewed from another.

The open flower garden is not far from the main road but it is protected and secluded from the carriageway by a grove of tall trees in front of a field of donkeys. Arriving from under the shade of the trees along the drive, you are confronted with a sea of bright colour ahead and you know that this is something wonderful. Generous beds filled with every conceivable perennial seem to vie with each other for attention. Splashy mixes and combinations of flowers fill the place from early spring to the very end of the year. It is hard to know quite which direction to take first.

June has an enviable eye for putting plants together. In one area the flower mix will make visitors feel like they are walking through a 17th century Dutch flower painting: Dahlias in all sizes and shapes compete with lilies, agastache and persicaria for attention. The colour mixes vary from bold and brazen to subtle and cool. I think of pink sweeps of *Geranium* 'Ann Thompson' and black *Cosmos atrosanguineus*, knotted together. Meanwhile behind and between the flowers, tall grasses like *Carex morrowii*, different stipas and *Miscanthus sinensis* 'Gracillimus', provide swishing back-up.

There are aralias and ricinus, grown for their dramatic foliage, mixed with tall *Lilium lancifolium* var. 'Splendens', *Verbena hastata*, *Dahlia* 'Moonfire', *D*. 'Murdock', slim crocosmias and thalictrum. It is spectacular. June grows most of the plants from seeds and cuttings. The fact that many of them can be bought here just adds to the attraction.

Contemporary sculpture by some of her favourite artists add sparky punctuation. There are also pieces by June, like the warped sleeper staircase that rises up behind the flower beds through a meadow, like an unhinged spiral staircase trying to break free. A changing palette of wild flowers pops up in the meadow grass between the wooden steps adding an extra zap of interest between the wooden steps.

There are other contemporary touches in the hard landscaping scheme: Wide metal edges hold in runs of gravel and some of the borders. I think of its practicality every time I see rotting wooden edging.

Hidden behind tall curtains of flowers and grasses we came upon a formal pond surrounded by stone, a polished cement wall and more metal strips. June uses the local Wicklow granite gravel everywhere. It is glittery and bright, with tiny bits of schist embedded in it. There are all sorts of standing stones and small granite benches placed about too.

Happy accidents are left in place, such as the big cedar, which seems as though it might topple over a path but is always there, hanging in. Another of these opportunistic features is the moss rock, like a green chaise longue. There is so much to drink in here – including a recently uncovered archaeological gem, an ancient pub that once stood on the old road to Dublin.

This is the sort of high-maintenance glamour garden that looks as though it just tumbled out of bed, with tousled hair looking naturally beautiful. You will not be able to do this at home.

Hunter's Hotel

Newrath Bridge, Rathnew, Co. Wicklow. Tel: 0404 40106. e-mail: reception@hunters.ie www.hunters.ie. Contact: The Gelletlie family. Open: Every day. 10am-6pm. Wheelchair accessible. Supervised children. Special features: Hotel. Tours. Directions: From Dublin, take Exit 15 off the M11 for Ashford. In Ashford turn left at the bridge and travel 2 km. From the south, take Exit 16 off the M11. Pass Mount Usher Gardens on the right. Take first right after bridge in Ashford and travel 2 km.

Drive under the carriage entrance into a scene that could still be in the 18th century - a wobbly up-and-down cobbled courtyard and old stables, hay lofts and half-doors. I arrived to a sprinkle of hollyhocks poking out of the cobbles, ferns sprouting over an old water tank, colourful pelargoniums in window boxes and a chef standing by one of the doors with a mug of tea in hand. It looked perfect.

Hunter's is known to many as one of the great afternoon tea spots in the country. The garden is very much part of that old world picture. This is a traditional country garden with a great number of creepers and climbers over the old hotel, swathes of wisteria and tiny flowered clematis knotted with sweet pea, spectacular magnolias and rhododendrons. There are of course box beds, filled with sweet patches of nicotiana and poppies given free rein and even allowed to grow up through the hedges.

Around the lawn a big bed of high summer plants snakes, full of all the border standards, like macleaya or plume poppy, lupins, delphiniums, peonies and the blackest hollyhocks ever. I love the multi-stemmed cordylines. They look like flowers in a giant vase. Hunt out the large, contorted yew umbrellas beside the little thatched gazebo overlooking the River Vartry, in a small touch of the gothic. Sitting out in the middle of the garden, drunk on the scent of flowers and listening to the little river, one could be content even if the tea never arrived.

From here, a gate leads into the vegetable garden, where they grow everything from globe to Jerusalem artichokes and kohlrabi, all sorts of berries and currants. I liked the red cabbage matched with red nasturtiums and the mysterious looking 'bell' of variegated ivy.

Then, as a country garden should, it melts at the edges into native trees, hedgerow plants and meadows. I am foxed, charmed and horrified at the strange feature that is the walk through a field of Japanese knotweed. I could only sympathise with the poor gardener with such a nightmare plant with which to deal. But in the meantime that walk is rather intriguing....

Hunting Brook Gardens

Lamb Hill, Blessington, Co. Wicklow. Tel: 087 2856 601. e-mail: jimi@huntingbrook.com www.huntingbrook.com Contact: Jimi Blake Open: See website for annual dates. Groups welcome. Supervised children welcome. Guide dogs only. Special features: Garden courses. Member of the Gardens of Ireland Trust. Directions: Take the N81 out of Blessington in the direction of Dublin. 6 km along, turn left and travel for 1 km. The garden is on the left.

'Spring is like falling in love for the first time, all over again, every year.'

So said Jimi Blake as we bent down to inspect some of his special epimediums and a little beauty called *Erythronium* 'Harvington Snowgoose'

Jimi has been a dynamic figure in Irish and international gardening for many years. In 2003 he moved back to his homeplace and started a new garden from scratch in a field on the family farm. He built a wooden house in the middle of the site and began to garden. The resulting project has become one of the most highly regarded visits in the country, written up in a range of prestigious gardening journals and gaining fans far and wide. Jimi uses his garden as a classroom and laboratory for the courses he runs and the whole enterprise is a pleasure to visit any time of the year.

The garden is constantly under expansion. These days, the exuberant garden around the house is accompanied by the Wood and Valley Gardens as well as the sunny Ring Field, each of which has afforded Jimi the chance to accommodate his special plants, grown from seed collected around the world. He is a true plantaholic and whenever he speaks, there will be mention of some unusual seedling he has just sourced on the net or found in an obscure catalogue.

Hunting Brook is such an individual's garden, not greatly influenced by anything other than his own deep interest in plants. Jimi loves clashy colours. This is not a place of pale lilacs and pinks. He will mix wine and silver coloured *Persicaria* 'Red Dragon' with rusty *Achillea* 'Terracotta' and *Kniphofia* 'Tawny King' together to produce the sort of look one sees in a haute couture fashion show. Elsewhere he mixes black kale with blood-red amaranthus, purple agastache and orange calendula. There are few plants as dramatic as aralias, particularly *Aralia echinocaulis*. The seed of this strange, fast growing Dr. Seuss-like plant was collected in China. In among the architectural stars like aralia and *Tetrapanax papyrifera* 'Rex', Jimi uses see-through plants like coreopsis, geraniums and alliums.

Between the mass of tall grasses, exotics, herbaceous perennials and bulbs, the paths are almost invisible and the house seems to stand in the middle of a large plantation of ligularia, inula, astrantia, coppiced and pollarded eucalyptus. This could be a cabin in the middle of the jungle. On my last visit, the rain was monsoon-like. We stood on the verandah looking out at what could have been a steaming jungle in south-east Asia.

The polytunnel is filled with the unusual and unexpected bounty from many of his expeditions, but on the way to see that, look at the cactus garden, where he plants out cacti that usually live indoors and they look at home.

A little way off, the wood garden is at its very best in the spring. In here under the magnolia, unusual *Viburnum cylindricum* and large-leafed rhododendron, the ground is littered with the lime-fresh foliage of hesperis, violas and the beginnings of blue Himalayan poppies. The ground teems with arisaemas, trilliums, erythroniums, corydalis, ferns, moss, moss and more moss.

A network of paths edged with the branches of fallen trees give the wood an even more verdant and untamed look, and with mature trees way overhead, the wood floor, dappled with light, is a busy place.

The Outer Wood and Valley Garden, joined in the party a few years ago when he built more hill paths through the valley, planting native and exotic ferns between native wood sorrel. The result is a hanging garden that leads down to the stream. He has built wooden bridges across this little waterway in several places. Look for an unusual foliage plant, *Alangium platanifolium* under the towering beech and pines.

The stone ledges and weirs along the stream are beautiful and the waters edge has been planted up with rheum, rodgersia, ferns and large leafed plants that can be seen from the paths above. We walked between schefflera and *Acer sikkimense* collected as seed in China.

Meanwhile, beyond the wood and valley is the latest project, an equally hilly place, this time a flower meadow with a megalithic stone set between the ox eye daisies and orchids.

I have described the garden as it was on my last visit. That description was different to my previous visit and no doubt it will be different next year. Jimi experiments constantly, changing what others would find perfect, adding in new features and different schemes. I suppose I should not try to describe it but say, just expect to be impressed.

Killruddery House & Gardens

Bray, Co. Wicklow. Contact: Reception. Tel: 01 286 3405. e-mail: info@killruddery.com www.killruddery.com Gardens open: April. Weekends. 1-5pm. May-Sept., daily 1-5pm. Otherwise groups by appointment. Supervised children. Special features: Shop. Café. Play centre. Weekly markets. Occasional plant sales. Tours of gardens and house. Events. Movie tours. Directions: Travelling south on the M11, take the third Bray exit, marked Greystones/Bray. Killruddery is signposted from here.

Killruddery has been the home of the Brabazon family since 1618. The garden is unique – it is the only completely unchanged, 17th-century, classically French-designed garden on the island, partially designed by a student of the great André Le Nôtre, designer of gardens to Louis XIV. Letters written in 1682 state that 'Captain Brabazon has and will make new great improvements there'. A few years later, William Petty, author of the Down Survey and owner of lands in Kerry (See Derreen, Co. Kerry) complained bitterly that his French gardener of 12 years had decamped to Killruddery.

Work started in the 1600s, continued for centuries and as a result today, the gardens' great size, austere,

formal beauty and mature planting make it a singular visit that leaves a lasting impression. It is a garden that looks its best at any time of year as it is not a place that depends heavily on flowers, but on strong lines, mature trees, monumental and large-scale plantations.

Before setting off to look at the garden proper, stand at the house and look up the long sweep of lawn in the direction of the rough granite hill. The contrast between the manicured garden and special trees with the wilderness from which it was wrought is worth noting before seeing the rest of the gardens.

Killruddery's design is based on a number of large-scale features laid out along geometric lines, like an illustrated lecture on garden design for the period. The house stands on a wide terrace of granite, softened with hummocks of rock rose and lavender.

Running south from the house, the twin canals measure 187 metres. They lead to a basin and beyond that to a long ride that runs on for a great distance, imparting an air of grandeur. Le Nôtre pioneered this use of avenues cut into woods, to give the impression, real or otherwise, that the garden owner's land extended as far as the eye could see.

To the side of the canals is the 'wilderness.' This historic term today seems misleading, as the trees are grown in straight, ordered, almost military lines and not at all according to what we would think of as a wilderness.

There is a beech-hedged pond, made up of two tall circles of beech, one inside the other, like bracelets, with a circular walk in between. The inner hedge is cut with windows through which the lily pond in the centre can be glimpsed from the walk. This is a simple but exquisite design. At the time of writing it was undergoing restoration.

A little way off there is another unusual feature, an amphitheatre, or sylvan theatre, with grass-covered stepped seats rising above a stage, backed by more tall beech hedging. Performances and recitals are still held here during the summer. The day I visited a quartet was practising and snatches of the music could be heard, picked up by the wind and audible all around the garden.

The area called 'the Angles' is a series of *allées* between four-and-a-half-metre-high hedges of hornbeam, lime and beech. They meet at two points and radiate out from each other like a maze for beginners. Between the lines of hedging, taller, mature trees add height and some confusion to the otherwise straight-forward maze. There are occasional pieces of sculpture sited about and these days, the area is used to hold temporary sculpture exhibitions.

The rose and lavender garden is a striking sight with charming, uneven box and yew hedges, just the answer for anyone who has ever tied themselves in a knot failing to get the line straight on a hedge. The box surrounds fluffy, grey, scented lavender, roses and the big fried-egg flowers of *Romneya coulteri*.

This garden is overlooked by the house and *orangerie* or statue gallery, built by Richard Turner in the 19th century. It has been completely restored and its statues and tender tibouchina and plumbago can now be viewed as part of a tour of the house. It too is used for small concerts.

From its windows you can seen the ornamental dairy, an octagonal building with stained-glass windows, covered in roses and clematis. This was another feature of the continental late 18th century garden, where fine ladies would play at being milk maids and shepherdesses. Today it is a real tearoom. Running out behind it there is a long colourful mixed border which overlooks a sunken bowling green guarded by little stone putti surrounded by agapanthus and penstemon.

The kitchen garden has been restored, and meticulously smart lines of vegetables around the walls are in strong contrast to the romantic looking hen run in the old orchard.

The latest feature added to the extensive gardens is the Rock Wood, out at the edge of the garden, just beyond a new yellow magnolia walk. In the wood, the ground beneath expanses of existing mature beech and oak has been cleared of lesser scrubby trees and replanted as a woodland flower garden. Paths lined with fallen trunks run through seas of ferns and omphalodes, viola and myosotidium or Chatham Island forget-me-nots. With a canopy that is far overhead, the dappled, light thrown down on semi-shaded flower walks creates a romantic atmosphere. Do not miss a visit to this most recently created new old garden.

Knockanree

Redcross Road, Avoca, Co. Wicklow. Tel: 0402 35628. e-mail: whclarke35628@gmail.com
Contact: Harold Clarke. Open: Mid April-mid July. Mon, Tues, Fri, Sat, 9.30am-1pm. Wheelchair
accessible. Toilets. Pet friendly. Special Features: Coach parking on road. Tours. Member of the Gardens of
Ireland Trust. Directions: 1.5 km along the Redcross Road out of Avoca. Green gates on left after 'Caution
Children' sign.

We stood looking at a hedge of sarcococca, or Christmas box, a plant known for its scented white flowers in the depths of winter. I paced it out. It was 80 metres long, three metres wide and a metre tall. Is it in the Guinness Book of Records? It probably should be. It is only one of many memorable features in Harold Clarke's country garden. Harold has been gardening here since the late 90s, playing with, moulding and adding to a design initially drawn up by designer, Robert Myerscough. Knockanree is in the Vale of Avoca and has its own Meeting of the Waters, one of which is what Harold called 'The Sulphur River', with its ochre tinted stones, glinting through the water.

Knockanree is a tempered wood, with a delicate balance of exotic and native trees, streams and waterfalls, huge Ice Age boulders teased into little Japanese-influenced garden rooms, and everywhere, well placed art, much of which was made by sculptor Niall Deacon. I fell for the legions of shuttlecock ferns *Matteuccia struthiopteris*. Harold told me they are all the progeny of a single plant that came from Strokestown. The ants have carried the spores around, colonising the woods with fine splaying green fountains.

I like the humour of two cannons on a gravel ledge, overlooking the valley, still ready after hundreds of years to keep the O'Tooles and O'Byrnes at bay.

We made our way through the woods on pale gravel paths made of Ballylusk dust, which lightens up the leaf-dappled shade under oak, birch and medlar, magnolia and an occasional scented rhododendron or red-flowering embothrium.

There is another garden here close to the house. There are in fact several other gardens, sharing a wide ledge around the house. In contrast to the woods these are symmetrical and formal with box walls and sharp, clipped pyramids holding in overflows of lime green euphorbia, peonies and roses. Ask to see the concert hall, where Harold hosts charity recitals - The glories a cow byre can attain.

The last memory was of a *Nyssa sylvatica*, whose autumn colour makes it rightly famous. 'Country Life' said that if you can fit one in your garden you should. So he did.

National Botanic Gardens at Kilmacurragh

Kilbride, Co. Wicklow. Tel: 0404 48844. 01 8040 319 / 01 8570 909.
e-mail: botanicgardens@opw.ie Contact: Seamus O'Brien. Open: Nov-Feb. 9am-4.30pm. Feb-Oct. 9am-
6pm. Partially wheelchair accessible. No entrance fee. Supervised children. Dogs on leads. Special features:
Café. Free daily tours. Directions: Travelling south, take Exit 18 from the M11. Take a right and drive
through two roundabouts following the flower symbol signposts. Garden on left after about 3.5 km.

Kilmacurragh is arguably the most exciting large garden on the island. Started in the 1850s, on the foundations of an older garden, Kilmacurragh arboretum is famed for its conifers. Thomas Acton planted it between the years 1850 and 1908 in conjunction with David Moore and his son Sir Frederick, both of whom were curators at the National Botanic Gardens in Dublin. Frederick Moore in particular, recognised that it was possible, in places like Kilmacurragh, to successfully plant exotic trees that had recently arrived in Ireland from plant-hunting expeditions around the world. The slightly milder weather and higher rainfall in Wicklow, meant that many specimens fared better, and had a better chance of survival here than their relations in Glasnevin. Moore worked with Acton, sharing his rare and special plants with the Wicklow garden in the greater interest of Irish horticulture. He worked similarly with Mount Usher and Rowallane.

But the garden fell into decline in the 20th century and for many years it looked like the neglect would never be repaired. Happily, Kilmacurragh is enjoying a renaissance and the chapter of its history that covers the beginning of the 21st century is going to read well. It is under the care of Seamus O'Brien and a programme of repair, restoration and development is galloping along.

Glorious trees have been found throughout the wild garden: The different species of podocarpus, including the largest *Podocarpus nubigenus* on the island, is among them. Marvel at a weeping Kashmir cypress (*Cupressus cashmeriana*) with silvery-fringed needles. We inspected a monster sized pink *Magnolia campbellii*, escaping over the top of the walled garden. This is like a one-tree example of how plant exchange has evolved over the years. It was collected as a seedling in Calcutta in 1830 and brought to Wicklow. Recently one of its seedlings was returned to the Botanic Garden in Calcutta, to repay the favour. So the horticultural world spins. There are so many of the biggest, tallest, widest, first-to-flower-in-the-Northern-hemisphere, rarest and most impressive specimens found throughout Kilmacurragh, including a clove-rock scented *Rhododendron fortunei* and a massive *Laureliopsis philippiana*, a rare tree with citrus scented foliage on a warm damp day – of which there are plenty. There are not just a few *Cardiocrinum giganteum*, but a whole plantation of them. Try to see them flower in July.

The Broad Walk, a rhododendron avenue, was made wide enough to accommodate two ladies walking side by side in huge crinoline dresses. In May it looks like a crimson carpet of fallen petals and has become rightly famous for its spectacular looks.

Recent developments include a series of new gardens, based on plants from South America and in particular Chile. One is the Chilean Ravine to where such rarities as *Jubaea chilensis* were sent by Kew. These baby exotics, will in a century rival the now giant redwoods and Monkey puzzles seen in the distance. There are plants from China and the Himalayas gathered together too, some in the bog garden where rare and special rhododendrons splay over lower storey blue Himalayan poppies. All these gardens incorporate plants brought in from seed hunting expeditions, both modern and historic.

The shaded flower borders, unusual under the light cover of overhead trees and the linked tree fern walks, must be seen. These beds are full of unusual species that have had to prove themselves to be included. The same applies to the Regency border close to the house, designed to be of interest from early spring to the end of the year.

In front of the ruined house they planted a young fossil lawn with ginkgo, Wollemi pine, podocarpus and metasequoia as well as other ancients, like magnolia and drimys. The once closely shorn lawn, is now a large and growing flower meadow planted with species daffodils, fritillaries and crocus, early purple and speckled orchids, cowslips and cardamine. Painstaking restoration has also brought a once-famous sea of blue *Crocus thomasii* that had all but disappeared, back to life. There are now 120 species charted as living in the meadow. The huge, and much loved Japanese cedar or *Cryptomeria japonica* with its foliage that colours up to a deep rust for the winter is as striking as ever.

History is everywhere: The house is an unusual Dutch style building, derelict yet still attractive; protected if not fully restored. The wisteria over one of its side walls dates back to the 1830s.

The remains of an older Dutch style park garden can be seen in some of the vistas looking out from the house, as well as a silver fir planted in the late 1700s. Meanwhile there are memories of the great plant hunters scattered throughout, including William Lobb and his Monkey puzzles and giant redwoods, collected as seeds from Yosemite.

Down among the woods the pond is fed by little trout-filled streams. The yew walk, close by is a great ghostly cathedral-like feature, but it actually started life as yew hedging left to run wild. The small stone building close by, which could have been a tool shed, is nothing of the sort. This was the toll house along the original, cobbled road between Dublin to Wexford, used by Cromwell when he marched on that town. Part of it was planted up as a sessile oak avenue. This is being restored and will measure 1 km long when finished.

The restoration being carried out on the approaches to the garden also involves a kilometre long drive planted with magnolias, as well as the first new Monkey puzzle avenue since 1870, grown from the babies of the tree near the Chilean Ravine. The wholesale clearance of cherry laurel, *Rhododendron ponticum* and weedy growth have been nothing short of amazing.

Kilmacurragh is gardened organically. Mown paths between the trees and a light hand make this garden feel as natural as William Robinson would have wanted. All over the gardens, native hedges are being planted with guelder, crab, holly, spindle, hazel and prunus, propagated from plants grown in the locality and from the best specimens found around the country. Even the shelter belt is of native trees and the collection is a genetic one. Do not hesitate to take a tour given by the knowledgeable guides. This is all free. All free. Taxes spent very wisely.

Arboretum Kilquade, The National Garden Exhibition Centre

Kilquade, Co. Wicklow. Tel: 01 2819 890. info@arboretum.ie. Contact: Manager. Open: All year, Mon–Sat. 9am–6pm, Sun. 11am–6pm. Wheelchair accessible. Special features: Tearoom. Nursery. Garden shop. Directions: From Dublin on the N11 turn left for Kilquade.

For the growing number of people with small gardens, it can be hard to imagine scaled-down versions of Powerscourt and Killruddery. For this dilemma, the National Exhibition Centre is an ideal place to visit, find inspiration and ideas. It is also a convenient place to study the work of a range of garden designers should you wish to employ one. It is a fount of ideas, styles and designs. At any one time there are 19 gardens on display in Kilquade. They represent the work of a whole raft of landscapers, artists, craftsmen and stockists of hard landscaping materials.

The plants and plans are well labelled and explained in each garden, and full details are available on all those involved. The use of water in the garden is a particular strength, from rock pools and naturalistic ponds to mountainside trickles and formal hard-edged water features. The hilly site allows for a variety of different sorts of garden styles while also allowing one take in the gorgeous trees in the surrounding landscape. The general maze-like set up is an enjoyable one, directing you to see different gardens from new angles and vantage points. My best memory is of the fern and stone stepped garden that climbs up into the trees, and makes such good use of multiple Belfast sinks.

Mount Usher Gardens

Ashford, Co. Wicklow. Tel: 0404 40205 / 40116. e-mail: info@mountushergardens.ie www.mountushergardens.ie. Contact: Philomena O'Dowd. Open: All year daily, 10am–6pm. Partially wheelchair accessible. Supervised children. Special features: Tearoom. Craft shop. Guided tours must be arranged in advance. Directions: Situated in Ashford.

Mount Usher is one of a small number of Irish gardens with an international reputation and it has enjoyed this reputation since the late 19th century. It started life as a modest acre under potatoes in front of the holiday home of a Mr. Edward Walpole in 1868. Under the stewardship of his son, E. Horace Walpole, it rose to become one of the places that the famous Irish garden writer William Robinson championed as a perfect example of a fine garden. Walpole improved it using the principles laid out by Robinson, the essence being to combine native and exotic plants in a naturalistic, seemingly artless way. It has rightly been a favourite visit of garden lovers for generations. Today it covers 20 acres along the unusually sheltered banks of the River Dartry, and is home to 5,000 different species of plants.

The shaded and sheltered winding paths make it easy to get lost. Roam freely, perhaps using the tree trail – a list of just 75 of the more special trees here. My own favourite on the last visit was is the huge

Quercus castaneifolia or chestnut-leaf oak, along the river walk. The river runs through the place like an artery, with weirs, bridges and waterfalls spread along its length; it is the soul of the place and the views along it in each direction have been carefully constructed to maximise its beauty. Work has recently been put into clearing and repairing the different features to keep it perfect. Look at the walls of rounded 'boulders' that make up some of the banks – They are in fact small sacks of cement.

Every path seems to lead back to the water at some point, weaving between layered plantings of shrubs and rising up to huge *Magnolia veitchii* and champion *Cunninghamia lanceolata* and *Dacrydium cupressinum*. Two-metre-tall Himalayan giant lilies (*Cardiocrinum giganteum*) set in under the trees shine like visions from out of the shade. Spring meadows sprinkled with thousands of crocuses and miniature daffodils run up against groves of scented *Rhododendron lutea* among scores of other early-flowering shrubs.

Layered, best describes the planting. Graduated canopies made up of multi-coloured acer and magnolia, rhododendron and eucryphia are breathtaking, particularly in autumn. Impressive trees and shrubs spread out from every point, complementing each other in ways that look natural.

The collection includes stunning specimens such as a *Nothofagus moorei* (Sir Frederick Moore, the curator of the National Botanic Gardens in Dublin assisted Mr. Walpole in the early days of the garden). Look also for the *Osmanthus burkwoodii*, and one of the largest New Zealand red beeches (*Nothofagus fusca*) in Ireland. *Eucryphia* x. *nymansensis* 'Mount Usher'

is only one of many plants named for the garden here. Mount Usher holds National Collections of both eucryphia and nothofagus. The eucryphias, covered in white flowers at the end of the summer and into September, are worth a special visit.

The groves of eucalyptus originated back to 1911 when the Walpole's were given a gift of seedlings from Tasmania. The collection has been growing since. Their tall, regular peeling trunks are like giant skinny soldiers in army fatigues. The only impediment to Mount Usher holding the national collection of these, is lack of space. They take up a lot of it and the garden is relatively short on that commodity. Sean Heffernan, head gardener explained, as we walked under some of the towering giants that; 'they have the ability to drop a branch at no notice whatsoever, quick as a blink.' We picked up the pace and made our way back to the open. The path always seems to lead back to the water and the noise of the river can be heard everywhere. Even in the pond garden, where the water is still, among the displays of primula and other wet loving plants, the roar of a nearby fall can be heard. Meanwhile, back on dry land, the double herbaceous borders are all colour and scent, full of favourites like solidago or goldenrod, rudbeckia, eupatorium, phlox and euphorbia.

For the workers who cared for this great garden down through its existence, hunt out the plaques commemorating the gardeners who worked here. Many of them gave almost half a century of service each:

> George Burns 50 years of dedicated service 1921–1971,
> Charles Fox 45 years as head gardener,
> Michael Giffney 44 years as gardener,
> Miles 'Miley' Manning 40 years.

Today Sean holds the mantle. He is working on new wildflower meadows, replacing tired old trees with new young specimens. His is the all-important task of bringing the garden well into its second century. He is extending the colourful maple walk, repairing waterways, maintaining the weirs and walls, and adding new features. Like many of the great open gardens of today, Mount Usher is being worked without chemicals. This might make the work hard, but it is all the more impressive.

Patthana Garden

Kiltegan Village. Co. Wicklow. Tel: 086 1944 547. e-mail: tjmaher100@gmail.com
Contact: TJ Maher and Simon Kirby. Open: By appointment to groups (5+) June-Sept. See Facebook for
Open Days. Not wheelchair accessible. Special features: Teas available. Antique tableware for sale. Directions:
On application.

'There's not one plant here that I don't like' said the artist TJ Maher of his garden. I agree. Patthana is one of the best small, secret gardens in the country, made up of good design and excellent plants. I wish it were mine.

TJ arrived in the mid 90s, taking over an old granite house, ruined outhouses and tattered garden, on what he termed 'a whim'. There were lots of birds here. They swung the deal. Without any previous experience, he bought the place and took to gardening.

The result is a delight: Close to the house, the space is dominated by a variety of paved, flagged and cobbled areas punctured with exotic shrubs, perennials, clipped box and flowers. Unlike more solid paved areas, this area feels very much part of the garden rather than an extension of the house looking out at a garden. Wooden pergolas covered in *Rosa* 'Madame Isaac Pereire' and a stylish summerhouse that TJ built, deliver the backdrop and support for climbing jasmine, clematis and the rather exotic looking flowers of *Akebia quinata*. At the base of sunny walls tender *Beschorneria yuccoides* and olives, bask in the warmth. A small lily pond sunk into the stone runs riot with frogs and newts.

He grows species pelargoniums, including *P. echinatum* in the summer house. 'I think species plants are better for nectar and pollen' he said. He primarily grows plants to feed birds, bees and butterflies.

There is more than a hint of the jungle about the abundance of foliage here and even the cobbles float on a green sea of *Soleirolia soleirolii* or mind-your-own-business. I love it. TJ is engaged in a chemical-free war with it. His is a completely organically run garden.

The pond is both bounded by a waterwheel stairway and fed by a waterfall made of the same round stones. I missed this unusual feature among the dense foliage on first inspection.

Above the courtyard, there is a second garden, reached using those stone steps, up between, draping rosemary, clipped box, an *Acer griseum* positioned to catch the evening sun and a *Betula lenta* that smells of TCP. The top garden is made of island beds full of airy, light plants like stipas and *Verbena hastata* and *Persicaria amplexicaulis* 'Rosea'. *Molina* 'Red Pole' was being pulled over by the weight of tiny birds eating its seeds. Among the light grasses, hydrangeas of different types create the necessary solid presence while kalopanax and its relative, aralia contribute a note of the exotic.

The top garden is surrounded by native holly, hawthorn, and euonymus hedge, spiked with *Arbutus unedo*, the strawberry trees, *Buddleja* 'Blue Horizon', purple hazel and *Rosa* 'Kiftsgate'. TJ cut windows in the hedge to frame a view of an old church spire in the distance. A secret path runs like a corridor between this outer hedge and one of the island beds, offering alternative views across the garden.

A tapestry lawn underfoot is further proof that working with, rather than against nature can be the best and easiest route to take. In this, relaxed country garden this multi-species lawn is as beautiful as any perfect weeded-and-fed lawn.

Powerscourt Gardens

Powerscourt Estate, Enniskerry, Co. Wicklow. Tel: 01 2046 000. e-mail: info@powerscourt.net www.powerscourt.ie Open: 9.30am-5.30pm daily (dusk in winter). Closed 25, 26 Dec. Partially wheelchair accessible. Special features: Play area. Garden centre. Shop. Restaurant. Audio guides. Exhibitions. Directions: Leave the M11 at the exit signposted for Enniskerry. The gates to Powerscourt are a few hundred metres outside the village on the road to Roundwood.

Powerscourt, set in the foothills of the Wicklow Mountains almost needs no introduction. It has long been regarded as one of the great gardens of Europe, as well as one of the best-known, loved and most visited gardens in the country.

The lands here were given to the Wingfield family in 1609 in an effort to have them secure the area against the Irish lords surrounding and encroaching on the Pale. Houses were built and rebuilt on this site until, in the 18th-century, a grand mansion and formal grounds were commissioned by Sir Richard Wingfield, the 3rd Viscount Powerscourt. Unfortunately, much of the house, and indeed all the principle receptions rooms were lost in a fire in 1974 and only a wing remains.

The grounds include 45 acres of formal gardens, sweeping and stepped lawns like the best playground slides ever, flower gardens with lengthy, formal herbaceous borders, perfect clipped hedges, shrubs and woodland walks. Added to these, there are follies, Japanese gardens, rambling trails, a monkey puzzle

avenue, ornamental lakes and a great variety of plants.

The pet cemetery, overlooking a hilly rhododendron display, is the largest in Europe, resting place to a large number of memorialised dogs, cats and horses as well as a Jersey cow that bore 17 calves and gave 100,000 gallons of milk. The arboretum includes so many fine specimens it is hard to choose one. I particularly love the massive *Drimys winteri* near the walled garden and the line of huge baby *Sequoiadendron giganteum* along the path over the terraced lawn.

For all its splendours, there is one feature that no one who has visited Powerscourt ever forgets, and that is the Italian garden, designed by Daniel Robertson in the middle of the 19th century. What we see today took 100 men twelve years to build. It was planned as a series of flamboyant terraces modelled on the Villa Butera near Palermo. These would be filled with bronze and stone statues, among them Apollo and Diana, assorted cherubs and strange creatures, spread out like a gigantic stage set. The spectacle would look down over Triton's Lake, itself complete with a fountain based on the waterworks in the Piazza Barberini in Rome.

But the work was cut short at a point when only the first terrace in Robertson's original design and the lake, were complete. The 6th Viscount died on a Grand Tour and artefact-collecting trip in Italy. The work was continued by his son, in a modified way, yet the result is still one of the most lavish garden features. It is a great confection of wide sweeps of steps, pebble-mosaics in elaborate patterns, statuary, wrought iron work, topiary and stunning views. Beyond the lake, there are mature woods, rough, gorse covered hills and the dramatic Sugar Loaf Mountain. The lake is just the most notable of the water features but everywhere throughout the formal gardens, there are spouting, spraying, dripping and spluttering watery attractions.

For me the Japanese garden never fails, particularly as it glistens on a rainy day. It is a hilly garden, accessed from above, run through by streams and waterfalls. The water gathers in ponds and spills into more little streams between plantations of vividly coloured Japanese acer and cherry, fern and bamboo. The moss-dripping, fern-sprouting stone grotto is magical. It appears wild and untamed, while being nothing of the sort. Much as one might want to visit gardens in good weather, rain should always be laid on when visitors arrive in this corner. Be the person who comes prepared with rain gear and umbrella and you will have the place to yourself in a downpour.

Russborough House & Garden

Blessington, Co. Wicklow. Contact: Reception. Tel: 045 865239. e-mail: info@russborough.ie
Open: Grounds: Mar-Dec. 23, 9am-6pm. See website for house opening times. Special features: House tours. Restaurant. Events. Shops. Maze. Play area. National Bird of Prey Centre. Sheep dog trials. Plant sales. Directions: Signed from Blessington.

In no small part, due its colourful recent history including four art robberies carried out by both the IRA and Martin Cahill, the infamous 'General', the Palladian house at Russborough, reputedly to be the longest house in Ireland, is a place known to most Irish people. The house is a popular venue for visitors keen to see the art collection, including some of the recovered old master paintings. The grounds which overlook the Blessington lakes, its woods and maze have also been pleasant places to walk through.

The walled garden, which was built in 1740 and once supplied the Dublin vegetable markets with produce, had, by 2011 become quite derelict. In an admirable move, it was given over to the Royal Horticultural Society of Ireland, to run and is now well into a programme of restoration. With a volunteer workforce, the four acre garden is being hauled back. It is open, productive, interesting and can be visited on a limited, but expanding basis. The old paths have been reinstated. Aged fruit trees are being retrained and young plants added. There is a very good selection of soft fruit on display.

Ornamental and productive beds have been replanted and in high summer the place is a glory of colour and scent. The old bothy has been restored and the glass houses feature an interesting pelargonium collection. Plants raised in the garden are sold to help the restoration effort.

The walled garden is set within the woods on a trail that lead to Ladies Island, an intriguing feature. This is an 'island' that is not quite an island. Cross a red wooden bridge to gain access to it, and a small collection specimen trees, Scots pine, cedar, cercidiphyllum and rhododendron. As with many garden venues around the country, fairies have seen fit to invade this island, as well as the greater woods. From here, different park walks lead out around the grounds, taking in some impressive trees as they go.

There are views back to the house and over to the lake as well the ha-ha, an ice house and a lime kiln that can be visited only on guided tours. The rhododendron garden, planted by Sir Alfred and Lady Beit in the 1950s, has undergone a renovation and is now one of the prettiest features of the garden, best seen from April to July.

Sculpture In Woodland

Devil's Glen, Ashford, Co. Wicklow. e-mail: sculpinfo@coillte.ie. www.sculptureinwood.ie
Open: Every day. See website for seasonal changes. Partially wheelchair accessible. Directions. Approx 2 km out of Ashford on the R763.

The first sight is of a steep hill of mossy knobbled ground under the tallest, stick-straight beech trees.

That is enough. Looped walks lead between dramatic rock formations, along gullies and between stands of trees so beautiful, it is hard to know what more one might wish for in this world. Some of the rocks look sculpted. The terrain seems as much archaeological, as natural in places. The sculptures are interesting and varied, made by some fine talents from home and abroad, but they have a hard act to keep up in the Devil's Glen, which is surely one of the finest stretches of woods in the country.

Shekina Sculpture Garden

Kirikree, Glenmalure, Co. Wicklow. Tel: 0404 46128. 01 2838 711.
e-mail: cmccann@gofree.indigo.ie. www.shekinasculpturegarden.com Contact: Catherine McCann.
Open: Groups of fifteen and under by appointment. Wheelchair accessible. Supervised children. Special
features: Teas may be booked. Picnics encouraged. Directions: Travelling from Laragh, turn left at Glenmalure
at the hotel and bar. Continue on for 4 km. The garden is on the right, situated on a dangerous bend and
marked by a green wall.

Owned and worked by Catherine McCann, Shekina is unique among gardens in Ireland. Set in the middle of the Glenmalure valley, it was created as a place of inspiration and reflection. The word Shekina is Hebrew for 'the presence of God in a place', and there is an atmosphere of peace and simple beauty in Catherine's sculpture garden.

It may cover only one acre but it feels almost boundless, looking out over the trees of the Ballinacor Estate and the Wicklow hills beyond, it blends seamlessly into both. The garden itself is made up of impressively maintained greenery – impeccable lawn that bounces underfoot, surrounded by evergreen and deciduous trees and shrubs in every shade of green, from moss, olive and lime to grey, purple and gold. Steps edged with little bands of cotoneaster connect different levels, patios and platforms.

Accompanied by Catherine's elegant Saluki dog, we walked around stopping to peer into the lily pond, edged with shiny vinca and ferns. This sits under a bank of purple acer, hypericum and wine-leaved berberis. There are two ponds and a fern and ivy-trimmed stream running through the garden and out into the River Avonbeg. Between these, the whole place is filled with the sound and glint of water.

The plants are only part of Shekina. The central feature of the garden is the collection of sculptures. Catherine began to collect in the mid-1980s. Each piece reflects her interest in God and creation. The collection includes work by the late Alexandra Wejchert. Her Eternal Flame, made from gleaming stainless steel, reflects the leaves of rhododendron and ferns in a slim metallic wave. Other works include Fred Conlon's solid granite loops and circles, and a powerful piece cast in bronze by Imogen Stuart. Paul Page's wrought-iron screen, depicting the sun, moon, stars, clouds, rain, earth, fire and water is reason enough to pay a visit.

Each of the works is given its own complete space, so it is possible to feel quiet and secluded even when there are a number of visitors in the garden. There are benches and seats set everywhere around, including a rose-clad summerhouse. Catherine said that there are 40 places to sit.

She has written a book entitled 'Time Out in Shekina', in which the symbolism attached to the sculptures is explored. The book is available to buy from the garden or by post.

Tinakilly House Hotel

Rathnew, Co. Wicklow. Tel: 0404 69274. e-mail: reservations@tinakilly.ie Open: Every day, by appointment only. Special features: Wheelchair accessible. Supervised children. Special features: Pet friendly. Restaurant. Accommodation. Tours. Coach parking. Directions: Take the N11 south to Rathnew. Tinakilly House is 500m outside the village on the road towards Wicklow town (R750).

Tinakilly House is an imposing, double-fronted Victorian country house that stands on a height, overlooking the Irish Sea. The location is idyllic. The house was built in the mid-1800s of local Wicklow granite and stands on seven acres of terraced lawns, mature trees, stuffed mixed beds and walks. The graduated lawns are joined together by runs of weathered granite steps and urns spouting fountains of phormium. Washy-pink roses, *Crinodendron hookerianum*, the lantern tree and slim, *Cordyline australis* soften the straight lines.

A run of lawn and box enclosed flower beds at the foot of these stone steps is surrounded and bounded by curtains of shrubs and trees, including specimens of white-flowered strawberry trees or *Arbutus unedo*, a young *Sequoiadendron Giganteum* and some tall - very tall eucalyptus. One path leads into the quaintly named Badger's Walk – a sheltered woody, ferny place, shaded by Spanish chestnut (*Castanea sativa*) and a towering silver birch that casts only the lightest of shade.

Following the Badger's Walk leads back to the drive, past a big cedar of Lebanon (*Cedrus libani*) and the Beech Cathedral, a woodland garden with a great circle of tall beech trees, reminiscent of the pillars of a grand church.

Continuing on to the other side of the house there are a series of rabbit-pestered rose and herbaceous beds. This whole area is surrounded by a lawn and partially enclosed by beech hedging and tall trees, including Douglas fir or *Pseudotsuga menziesii*. There is a view of the sea from here and another secluded walk called the Fox's Path. It looks across the garden at the Badger's Walk. Beatrix Potter would have loved it.

Trudder Grange Garden

Newtownmountkennedy, Co. Wicklow. Tel: 01 2819 422. e-mail: vahayes1@gmail.com Contact: Vanessa Hayes. Open: June-Sept. By appointment. Special features: Occasional plants for sale. Teas can be arranged. Directions: On application.

There are few pleasures as easy to fall for as a country garden. Trudder Grange had me at hello. From the enthusiastic dogs that bounced out to do the meet-and-greet, through the sights and scents of the colourful flower borders and vegetable garden, a meadow, shrub borders and a little arboretum, I was smitten.

For a start I could have just stayed in the courtyard with the roses and figs, the wisteria over wooden trellis and clipped box; with the sun, as if to order, beating down on the gravelled expanse. I left reluctantly, through a gate in the stone wall to discover another place in which I could have camped: The flower garden, all long deep borders of scented old French roses and herbaceous fancies.

Next door, the vegetable garden had just the right old-school look, with tidy lines, sturdy fruit cages and a queue of forcing pots, ready to work, and strong trellises to support big crops of beans and sweet peas.

French roses are a bit of an obsession with Vanessa Hayes, who has lived and gardened here for over three decades. We stopped to take in the scent of *Rosa* 'Caprice de Meilland' a fat pink bloom with a fruity perfume. The red apples, growing in the wall-backed beds were just as pretty. This one-acre walled garden, opens out to a wildflower meadow spiked with species narcissi. Vanessa has been experimenting with this for a few years and it is progressing well. Grass paths circle her growing collection of specimen trees including a metasequoia and *Parrotia persica* 'Vanessa', various magnolias, cornus, acers and a *Nyssa sylvatica*.

We tracked back to the house by way of the flower

and shrub borders, where a 30-year-old *Ginkgo biloba* has become a favourite, despite, or rather because of the fact that a dog ate the top off it several years, forcing it to split in a fortunately attractive way. The borders feature more roses, dahlias and plenty of salvias, all of which keep it singing up to late autumn. *Salvia guaranitica* and *S. involucrata* 'Bethellii,' in particular stood out.

We left, and trailed along the shrub borders cut into the lawns, passing combinations of acer and and cotinus, camellia, a pink eucryphia and *Halesia* *carolina*. There were hydrangeas here too tucked under the taller shrubs. In fact they are deployed cleverly at various points under the surrounding trees and boundary shrub borders, brightening up the shade with their big vivid flowers.

The greenhouse with a bounty of tomatoes is almost hidden behind banks of tall dahlias, cosmos and echiums.

I left with a memory of a variegated pittosporum grown as a hedge. Inspiring.

The Shillelagh Cork Oak

Church of Ireland Church, Shillelagh, Co. Wicklow. Open: All year. Directions, in the village at the top of the hill.

One day I could envy Jane Hopkins. She died in 1813 and is buried under a blanket of primroses and bluebells and one of the most remarkable trees in the country, a rare cork oak or *Quercus suber*. It is one of only a few such trees in Ireland. Its spongy, rivulated bark and its fine shape make it worth taking a detour to visit. While there, drive out of the village on the Tinahealy Road, past a line of cottages whose long rectangular gardens are also worth casting an eye over for a whole array of good ideas on how to work a cottage garden.

Warble Bank

Newtownmountkennedy, Co. Wicklow. Tel: 089 4213 064. 01 2819 298. e-mail: warblebank@yahoo.ie Contact: Anne Condell. Open: By appointment only. Not wheelchair accessible. Not suitable for children. No dogs. Special features: Occasional plants for sale. Directions. Leaving Newtownmountkennedy travelling south, pass a filling station on the left and the Newcastle Hospital on the right. The garden is through a gate in a painted wall under a large sycamore tree.

The last time I visited Warble Bank, Anne Condell had just completed renovating one of the borders. The time before that had also followed a renovation. Anne's style of gardening is not for the faint-hearted. A good romantic country garden does not work itself. As we walked up the grassy path between beds of competing beauties, the rolling show had me enthralled. Think black and raspberry tulips, paired with blue camassias, pink peonies and silver blue catmint, all pushing and shoving each other for attention in the long sun-trap borders. Anne swears by planting tulips in a paisley pattern, where the clump tails off naturally. She also thinks the variety 'Black Knight' is a good bulb to come back stronger each year.

Behind these, big strong, rustic poles and fences support a selection of old roses including *Rosa mulliganii and R.* 'Francois Juranville' which smells of apples. On the subject of apples, two of the prettiest old Bramleys stand half way up the border, forming an arch under which Ann placed a bench from which to enjoy the spectacle.

Lines of irises mark the edges of the vegetable beds, rendering the lines of sweet corn and chard as decorous as they are useful.

With fruit bushes and trees overhead, and fair maids of France or *Ranunculus acris* 'Flore pleno' between them, the radishes could only look well.

The stone wall that runs the length of the garden provides support for peaches and *Rosa* 'Sander's White Rambler'. I love the large flowers of *Iberis* 'Betty Swainson,' down at ground level under the skirts of *Phlox divaricata*.

Back in the centre of the garden a cross path, also lined by rustic poles covered in roses, leads out to another series of beds running the length of the site, including a rose border starring the scented *Rosa* 'Ispahan' and Anne's favourite, 'Bengal Crimson'.

The yellow border at the side of the house leads under an arch in a wall, out to the front garden, where an even steeper hill has been carved into for shrub beds, lawns and some fantastically old beech, oak and specimen trees.

On the other side of the garden, instead of a wall, there is a ditch. This is the warble bank in the gardens' name. It is, as Anne calls it is a gorgeous bit of slightly tamed countryside, a grassy bank spiked

with primroses, ferns and foxgloves that rounds off the otherwise impeccably maintained garden in a soft, slightly disheveled finish. Think Dürer's 'Piece of turf'.

Photo: Herma Boyle.

Wooden Bridge Memorial Garden

Woodenbridge, Co. Wicklow. Open: Constantly. Directions: In the village of Woodenbridge, opposite the hotel.

Taking the little sloped walk downhill between periwinkle and shrub roses, under slim birches and past a small wild flower meadow, looking over at the expanse of water in the River Aughrim, you could, for a short while enjoy the simple design and good maintenance of this little volunteer-run garden. Then

the granite columns, come into view, and on them, the list upon list of men who died in World War I from Newtownmountkennedy and Bray, Newcastle, Kilteegan and Rathdangan, Arklow and Aughrim. This is a sad but beautiful garden.

Wren's Wood

Kiltimon, Ashford, Co.Wicklow; Contact: Alexander or Lydia Mattei.
Tel: 01 2810 274. 087 1935 384. e-mail: wrenswoodgardens@gmail.com Open: May-Aug. Daily.
9.30am-1.30pm. Other times by appointment. Partially wheelchair accessible. Child friendly. Dogs on leads. Special features: Tours. Coach parking. Refreshments may be booked. Directions: Take Exit 14 off the M11 to Coynes Cross. Turn left at Coynes Cross under the motorway bridges, (travelling west) and go up a steep hill to T junction. Turn right and Wren's Wood is 150 metres along on the right.

The Mattei's have been working on Wren's Wood since 1990, clearing stone, building walls, clearing stone, making paths, clearing stone, banking up streams with stone, creating standing stone gardens - and clearing stone.

This is an unusual garden, the work of a man with his own slant on design. Alexander Mattei has extreme sympathy with his wild surroundings and the raw materials at hand. These are, in order, stone, trees and this hilly site. Working with his mother, Lydia, he has made a handsome, very personal creation.

The stone is everywhere, so he uses it accordingly. He encloses trees in walls of it. He makes raised, circular beds filled with stone. They look like huge, surreal fruitcakes. He bridges the streams that criss-cross the woody garden, and builds dry-stone boundary walls with quirky stiles. He has a way with stone.

He planted large numbers of oak, beech, birch, hornbeam, holly and yew throughout the 14 acres of wood and wilds, using nothing more than a wheelbarrow. That handmade quality is evident everywhere.

Close to the house there is a more colourful, domestic-scale garden with herbs, vegetables and herbaceous perennials, arranged in simple, strong patterns. Yew and lonicera hedges, some with interesting slopes or batters enclose and back these. These hedged rooms give the feel of a maze, as well as providing the dahlias and zinnias with a backdrop. Curving green walls are such a strong feature, They catch the light and give definition to the place. We stood up on a sun-trap stone platform where he grows figs and olives over cyclamen. What Alexander thinks might be one of the tallest *Azara microphylla* in Ireland can be seen here too.

As the paths lead from the house, the flowers and smaller shrubs disappear and the trees and stones take over. We landed at a platform that overlooks a circle of standing stones above a drop into a valley between the trees. It is, to say the least, impressive. The valley fills with foxgloves in early summer.

We moved from here to the long stone staircase - The 39 Steps - Up through a sea of ferns and tree ferns. The Spring Rock Garden is something special. He incorporated an existing stream and pond into an intricate stone design. The motto 'let cares be far away' carved out here, feels exactly right between the water, the flowering sweet chestnut and a *Magnolia soulangeana.*

I love the handmade, circular, wooden, thatched summerhouse, set halfway up the hill, near a recently discovered rath with a circle of tall wild cherries.

Look out for the line of young sweet chestnuts grown from a bag of Lidl walnuts and the tunnel made from a double line of otherwise unloved sitka spruce.

In 1553, Cardinal Giacomo Mattei, a patron of the painter Caravaggio and 'Protector of Ireland', bought land in Rome that was 'covered in brambles and other wild plants and moreover incapable of yielding anything.' From this he created the Mattei Gardens, which became one of the glories of Rome. It is appropriate that his ancestor should do the same in Wicklow almost 500 years later.

Clare

Bunratty Castle & Folk Park

Bunratty, Co. Clare. Tel: 061 360788. e-mail: reservations@shannonheritage.com
www.shannonheritage.com Open: Daily except Good Friday and Dec. 24-26. See website for seasonal hours.
Partially wheelchair accessible. Children welcome. Special features: Gift shops and restaurants. Medieval
castle tours. Directions: Signed from the N18 travelling west from Limerick City.

Bunratty is something of a guilty pleasure. It is a place of bells-and-whistles exuberance. And while I can live without medieval banquets, the gardens are not so easy to resist. The icing to the cake is provided by the animals, old-fashioned farm and gardening implements and recreated historic dwelling houses with people in costume making butter and bread as well as working vegetable plots. It really should be visited, though, like me as a child, you might be as scandalised by a pub called Durty Nellie's. Before heading to the gardens, lovers of antique furniture will enjoy visiting the castle to see the unique collection of Irish furniture.

The reconstructed village, where the gardens are located, begins in the shadow of the 15th century keep. There is a main street lined with cottages, a school house, a doctor's house and some miserable hovels, recreated farmhouses, from various regions around the country and even a Georgian manor. Each of these, with their settle beds and kitchens, fascinating and sometimes squalid living quarters, are accompanied by period gardens. The prosperous landlords' walled flower garden is the chief attraction but the little vegetable plots, fenced in with rusting bedsteads, are instructive in the mend-and-make-do ways of the time.

The houses and gardens have been faithfully reconstructed and together they illustrate the different social layers of 19th century Ireland. The doctor's house is draped with a handsome sweep of *Rosa* 'Souvenir de Claudius de Donegal'. Each of its big red blooms would fill a bowl. This particular garden is almost too pretty, enclosed with a white picket fence with Jacob's ladder, Welsh poppies and wallflowers peeping through the white painted uprights. Meanwhile at the other end of the scale, the smoke from a damp turf fire clings to your clothes as you walk past the potato and cabbage patch of the one-roomed cottage.

The country house walled garden takes up a sunny slope from the top of which the whole garden can be seen, along with views of the distant hills beyond.

This is opulent, with mixed borders, rose displays and wall climbers. The semi-circular iron cages over which the roses drape are smart. Imagine large upturned hanging baskets supporting the weight of hundreds of sweet-smelling *Rosa de rescht* blooms with blue forget-me-nots underneath.

The long double borders below these are full of vibrant yellow inula, lysimachia and lupin. Black, pink and white hollyhocks soak up all the sun along the south-facing side walls between spreads of jasmine, *Clematis tangutica* and figs. The wall opposite is in the shade and faces north. The cool damp soil suits hostas, ferns, Portuguese laurel and a fruiting Morello cherry.

On the other side of that wall the shrubbery is like a sort of maze with multiple paths that lead eventually out towards the stone-fenced paddock. This belongs to the west Clare farmhouse. These huge slabs of stone were the all-purpose tool of the region around the Cliffs of Moher. They were used for every job, from flooring a cottage and hemming in animals, to marking boundaries around fields and acting as paving and work benches.

The manor house is flanked by an impressive weeping ash, weeping beech and cedar, bounded by a ha-ha or sunken boundary, protecting it from incursions by sheep, goats and deer in the fields nearby. Wildflower meadows, haggards with hay drying on top of stone mushrooms and layered hedges, all combine to make an extensive set of horticultural displays.

Finally the examples of stone walls from around the country point up the almost lost skills and flair of the stone mason. A revival in regional styles of wall building is unlikely but it will remain possible as long as we still have good examples of the different styles, as seen here.

The Burren Perfumery

*Carron, Co. Clare. Tel: 065 7089 102. e-mail: info@burrenperfumery.com. www.burrenperfumery.com
Contact: Susan Seager. Open: To groups of under 15 strictly by appointment. Mini buses and coaches cannot
be accommodated due to lack of turning or parking space. See website for seasonal hours. Special features:
Shop. Tearooms. Perfumery tours. Directions. On application.*

Burrowed right in the middle of the Burren, is the most surprising garden. It is part of the Burren Perfumery, where they make soaps, creams and lotions as well as welcoming visitors to see the processes attached to all of this scented sorcery. From the minute you arrive, having driven in on a bouncy bog road, and travelled through the moonscape and karst limestone flats, it feels like something special.

The layout is a loose courtyard of stone outhouses and cottagey buildings. The garden, several little herb gardens in fact, is surrounded by walls and hedges of native trees, fruiting hazel, hawthorn, and ash. These shelter the place from the gales. Outside that shelter, the landscape is largely one of wind-shorn fairy bushes and rock.

This place has a gentle charm to it. I was sorry to have arrived late in the day. If Ralph Lauren was to conjure up a fictional garden to attach to one of his perfumes, this would be the idyll he would bring us, a perfumery set in the countryside, surrounded by the wild and cultivated plants the perfumers require to operate, grown in informal little garden plots. That would be the marketer's dream. This is real.

The Burren stone is everywhere, turned into up-and-down wobbly paths, walls that curve and swirl, little rocky features, gateways leading nowhere with native flowers and herbs sprouting from every possible corner. Rough, cobble paths and willow hurdles break up splashes and mounds, sprawls and spreads of rosemary and thyme, hyssop and betony, water avens and comfrey. Even the paths are under assault from invading ferns and self-seeding Lady's mantle or *Alchemilla mollis*. Someone with a good eye has scattered the place with little stone decorations, wrought iron flourishes and found objects.

I will come back, knowing that I need a lot more than an hour to enjoy it properly. Once again, not a garden for the fastidious. This is nature letting it all hang out.

Caher Bridge Garden

*Formoyle West, Fanore, Co. Clare. Tel: 065 7076 225. 086 0802 748.
e-mail: caherbridgegarden@gmail.com. Contact: Carl Wright. Open: March-mid Oct. By appointment.
Ring or e-mail for times. Special features: Wildlife talks. Directions: Drive south on the coast road from
Fanore. Turn off the road at Fanor Bridge over the Caher River. Pass the church on the right. The garden
is 1.5 km along on the right, just before the stone bridge.*

With a background in ecology, Carl Wright arrived to live in the Burren three decades ago and took on a hazel and blackthorn-filled field around a derelict farm cottage. With these ingredients, in a landscape generally thought to be inhospitable to cultivation, he conjured up a plantsman's garden that sits remarkably well into its tuck of the hill.

By keeping some native trees, but lifting and moving them to strategic places along the boundary, Carl lent instant structure to the new garden while keeping its wild feel intact.

He quickly discovered that there was no soil worth talking about. So he used the unearthed stones and boulders to make raised beds and imported soil from the locality to fill them. Apart from these beds, Carl uses pots and troughs to grow any plants that would find the going too hard here. Hostas in particular, do better in pots with a deep layer of gravel mulch to deter slugs. He marries big containers of hostas with little ones full of rhodohypoxis, sisyrinchium and saxifraga, arranged in groups at the bases of walls and in sheltered spots. A depth of only two centimetres of soil meant that his 200 different types of snowdrop and crocus, each had to be planted into individually excavated holes between the rocks. The man is dedicated.

The dominant feature to the side and front of the house is the pond, which is unlined and fed from a stream. The native water plants that colonise it include rare *Potamogeton lanceolatum*, meadowsweet, bulrush, yellow flag iris, comfrey and purple loosestrife.

The walls throughout call for special admiration. They are all young but were constructed with such craft that they look as though they might have been here forever. Largely double, dry-stone walls with a core of filler, they sprout polypodium ferns, moss, saxifraga and foxgloves from every crack.

Carl is something of a collector and the garden stars 150 daylilies or hemerocallis and 100 each of hostas, primulas and daffodils. All these are plants associated with soil, which, if not good, should at least be plentiful. Carl found it necessary to import every bit of soil in, sieving it *by hand* and adding home-made compost, to provide a good living for his colonies of drumstick and candelabra primulas as well as the daylilies and hostas.

When he was building the garden, as he exposed stone, he studied the discoveries, and then harnessed them into the most appropriate features. So paths were put where the ground suggested itself amenable and steps were fashioned from existing formations that looked like steps.

Early in the year, his collection of daffodils brighten up one area to the back of the house into which he imported tons of clay to raise the levels.

In doing this he covered nearly 70 cm of the bottom of an ash tree trunk. This was unorthodox but it worked and the ash is now the centrepiece in a little lawn planted up with 2,000 snowdrops and lots of narcissi. There is also a new collection of corylus or hazel, in a sunny field he carved out of the wood at the top of the hill.

There are not many hydrangeas as the ground is not moist enough for them, but *Hydrangea villosa* performs well in this corner. What was to be a temporarily placed *Sambucus nigra* 'Guincho Purple', has also fared quite nicely against a sunny fence. It is one of many Irish plants grown here, from *Galanthus* 'Drummond's Giant' to *Prunus laurocerasus* 'Castlewellan' with white speckled leaves, from the famous County Down arboretum.

There is one pocket of acid soil here. It is in a corner where the cottage turf pile sat for decades. Carl harnessed it to home a collection of ruscus. Behind them a circular moon window visually links this area to the garden beyond the wall. That is a damper, darker, stream-dominated area, full of rodgersia, epimedium, fern and arisaema.

The ash tree in the centre of the garden should not to be missed. Carl discovered it, bolt upright, growing between the old hazel trees, trying to get at the sun and almost incredibly, growing over bare rock; its big roots snaking over and clamped onto the boulders. The dreams of Japanese gardeners are made of such things.

Jim Cronin's Organic Kitchen Garden

Bridgetown, Co. Clare. Contact: Jim Cronin. Tel: 061 372685. e-mail: jimcroninp@gmail.com
Open: For an open day on the August bank holiday. Special features: Teas and plants for sale on open day.
Box vegetable system. Courses. Apprenticeships organised. Directions: See signs in Bridgetown on open days.

Driving through O'Brienbridge looking for Jim Cronin's garden, I met the friendliest customers in Bonnar's Bar and Grocery Shop. I explained that I was looking for a garden. One of the men was looking for a wife – He gave me directions despite the fact that I could give him none.

When I found Jim Cronin's east Clare organic kitchen garden, the first thing was to meet his pair of draught horses. This duo of gorgeous mares carry out all the ploughing, tilling and pulling of manure carts, along the hilly land near Bridgetown.

Jim is famed among organic growers and rightly so. He has been working the land here for 42 years, since he was 16 years old. His parents were market gardeners and he began his education as a small boy, later adding formal training to the knowledge learned at home. Today Jim runs courses in organic productive and market gardening and his classes attract people from all over.

He grows between 40 and 50 vegetable and fruit crops in polytunnels and outdoors in utilitarian rows, as well as in attractive mixed, informal borders on the sloped site, where they soak up the sun.

Planting vivid orange nasturtiums and blue cornflowers between the lines of black kale and leeks makes for a beautiful look as well as keeping the soil covered. Californian poppies and phacelia are both colourful, bee-friendly and ultimately available to be dug into the ground as additional compost matter. In the few places you can see bare earth, it is so well worked that it bears a strong resemblance to crumbly Christmas pudding mix.

Jim told me about growing crops into bales of silage that were beyond their sell-by date. One bale, rolled out, covers about 50 square metres of weedy grass. This is then covered with plastic. Plants raised in pots are inserted through holes into the plastic. Planting bunches of about six leeks together and pairing them with sweet pea increases the chance of survival of the crop against slug attack and the results are a good mix of food and flowers. Meanwhile, the ground beneath the plastic becomes alive with worms, soft and friable and ready to be planted into again the following year. The sweet pea are planted six to a pot also, which means that they require no support. They clamber over each other. This whole project will cover the average new suburban garden.

We walked through the orchard, where he grows and recommends 'Merton Russet' as a good double-use apple, being both a late eater and a cooker. Beyond this is an experimental field of sunflowers being grown as green manure that will be chopped and incorporated into the soil.

The old red and green muck spreader standing beside a great stand of cosmos was my abiding memory. I will make sure and hunt Jim out in the ploughing field at future National Ploughing Championships, where he is a regular medal winner.

Doolin Garden

Ballyvoe, Doolin, Co. Clare; Tel: 087 9147 725. e-mail: doolingarden@gmail.com www.doolingarden.com. Contact: Matthew O'Connell. Open: All year 10am-6pm. Closed Mon. and Thurs. Ring before visiting. Supervised children. Dogs on leads. Special features: Plant nursery. Garden sculpture for sale. Events. No entrance fee although donations to the Doolin Coast Guard are welcome. Directions: Outside Doolin village, beside the cemetery on the road to Lisdoonvarna.

This garden and nursery has been growing since 1987. According to Matthew O'Connell: 'It happened rather than being the product of conscious design. It was based on common sense. If you have a problem you work around it. Use the mound rather than try to remove it.'

The garden is set on what could charitably be called a windy site, so he knew he had to create something that could thrive in that challenging arena, or give up. On one hilarious winter visit, I can remember having to hold onto a pergola with both hands to stay upright in a battering gale. Yet despite the winds, Matthew said his first aim was always to be able to see the patchwork of fields, stone walls and hills beyond the garden. These borrowed views, the stolen landscape of the Burren, makes his garden special and the size appear indeterminate while the actual garden covers about half an acre.

On the minus side however, they rule out the usual shelter belt of big trees. Suffice to say that the plants here are tough. Like the song says, 'if they can make it here, they'll make it anywhere'.

Matthew is a plant magpie and has collected a great many specimens over the years. He has a particular love of Irish plants, like *Agapanthus* 'Lady Moore', named for Phyllis Moore, the talented gardener married to Sir Frederick, the famed curator of the Dublin Botanic Gardens at the beginning of the 20th century. He also grows the tatting fern, or Mrs. Frizell's fern (*Athyrium filix-femina* 'Frizelliae'). This plant was found growing by a riverbank by Mrs. Frizell in Wicklow in the 19th century. She gave it to the Botanic Gardens in Dublin.

Matthew grows his plants in long wide bisecting and parallel borders, under fruit trees and around extensive, sheltering pergolas and arches. There are so many good plants here, but I love the way he uses pale blue *Veronica gentianoides*. It crops up all over, a beautiful unifying plant.

The little outdoor garden room is the perfect link between house and garden. Sandy, grey walls shelter it from the wind and accommodate slightly tender plants like *Melianthus major* and ginger lilies or cautleya, under espaliered fruit trees. The use of benches, containers and gates painted in a rich blue brings out the absolute best in blue and pink flowers both here and elsewhere. Everything in this corner seems to grow in beds of pebbles and gravel.

Outside, the angled sleeper and stone paths create interesting, optical illusions between the borders as well as directing the eye to where he wants you to look.

The garden and nursery bleed seamlessly into each other and it is good for customers to see how plants perform in the ground before buying. Some of the borders are colour-themed. In one bed he marries yellow *Buddleja globosa* and yellow roses, tree peonies, kniphofia and fennel with yellow seed heads. The fern-like tamarisk, has pale yellow flowers, grows well by the sea and is a plant he would definitely recommend for a blustery situation.

The whole garden is full of works of art. Many of these are intriguing sculptures by artist Jerry Cahir. They add considerably to the atmosphere and are in turn well served in their fine surrounding.

Doolin Pier Garden

Doolin Pier, Doolin, Co. Clare. Open public area. Directions: On the roadside beside the pier.

I was sent to see this little garden by Matthew O'Connell. It sits on a wedge of waste land beside the pier, made by the people of Doolin. This is both a simple and perfect use for an otherwise unused corner and it is impressive to see what use can be made of little more than local stone, pebbles and gravel, sea-rounded boulders and rocks, rusting buoys and weathered flotsam and jetsam.

Benches and seats range around the small 'beaches' and 'foreshores'. I like that it is impossible to tell which of the sprinkling of wild and native flowers, like sea thrift and dune grass were purposely planted or self-seeded. In a fit of charming silliness someone has knitted cosies to keep some of the little stones warm.

Doreen Drennan Garden & Art Studio

Coast Road, Ardeamush, Lisdoonvarna, Co. Clare. Tel: 087 9303 755.
e-mail: doreendrennanart@gmail.com. www.doreendrennan.com. Open: By appointment. Special features: Art gallery. Art classes. Member of the Gardens of Ireland Trust. Directions: Leave Lisdoonvarna by the N67. Turn right onto the R477 to Fanore and take the first turn left onto the L5064. The garden is on the right 500 m along.

One would have thought that the first rule of making a garden by the Atlantic coast would be to find a good, big shelterbelt behind which to hide. Laying a garden out on an open hill seems like an exercise in making life unnecessarily hard. Since about 2010 Doreen Drennan has been proving, that it can be done on an exposed site, looking down to Lisdoonvarna and the distant Cliffs of Moher beyond.

Using the 'capabilities' of the site, as a famous landscaper once termed it, Doreen had made use of the fringe of hazel wood and river that runs below the bottom of the site. She turned these into a woodland and water garden, complete with its own waterfall. She grubbed out the brambles and gorse, and replaced them with stone steps, digitalis, hostas and ferns, arums and rodgersia. She then carved out a sheltered, winding path along the length of the river leading from the old stone bridge on the boundary. This native garden is joined to the upper, more cultivated gardens around the house, by a yet another set of steps.

Doreen began gardening here a few years ago, by building a sheltered courtyard in beside the house. She also created a sunken garden to make an even more sheltered place for her rose garden. The courtyard is a fine small space and the cream house walls are complimented by an expanse of golden gravel and a well composed selection of *Hydrangea* 'Annabelle', *Clematis jackmanii*, *Rosa* 'Rambling Rector' and *R.*'Albertine'. Modern Country might describe the style. Doreen is an artist and her trained eye is evident in the way she selects and combines plants, mixing them with hard landscaping ingredients. Her spot use of a similar shade of blue on pots, gates, and wooden features further unifies the place.

She obviously loves agapanthus and the garden features plenty of these overgrown blue and white bobble flowers. There are arches and pergolas used at various points around the gravel and flower borders to shade and shelter, as well as provide the opportunity to grow more honeysuckle, clematis and roses over clumps of agapanthus.

The hill down from the garden has been planted as a three line defence against the wind with *Rosa rugosa*, elaeagnus and fuchsia to give the garden dependable shelter into the future. I am sure it will be great but it is already looking good.

An Féar Gorta

Ballyvaughan, Co. Clare; Tel: 065 7077 023. Contact: Katherine O'Donoghue. Open: June-mid-Sept. Mon-Sat. 11.30am-5.30pm. No entrance fee. Special features: Tea and garden room. Directions: Situated opposite the harbour in Ballyvaughan village.

Set in from the harbour at Ballyvaughan, this garden is a fine example of using local materials appropriate to the landscape. The O'Donoghue's work four small gardens to the front and back of their two seafront cottages, one of which is a classic thatched house. They arrived in Clare in the 1980s to take up a life of gardening and running a tearoom. Cultivated gardens were then thin on the ground in the Burren, and the locals looked on their work with some scepticism. Several decades later, they have won over the sceptics.

Each of the four plots has its own individual style, but they are unified by one thing – an abundant use of local stone. There are dry stone walls, standing stones, rockeries, ledges, arches, patios, and stone-edged ponds.

The front of the first house is a confection of little stone blocks, that step up and down, with simple combinations of seaside plants like thrift or armeria and sedum, pulsatilla, creeping things and alpines, cotoneaster and campanula. Every crack in the flags has been colonised by resilient plants.

The next-door garden is the thatched house and it is more cottagey. Moving from an area of low, ground-hugging plants, this is filled with taller, looser things, crinum lilies, mounds of geraniums, penstemon, melianthus and nepeta with which I spotted a little

cat busily entertaining itself and getting drunk. There are also plenty of flowering shrubs. It being the thatched house, there are of course, roses, jasmine and honeysuckle around the door, stone troughs full of annuals and the scent of clove-scented dianthus to send you wafting along.

Behind the house the area is divided into more small garden rooms, joined and divided by walls and openings, paths and arches covered in spongy *Clematis tangutica* and more roses. One area is sunken, probably for shelter, a mix of stone and gravel with agapanthus and fennel, alliums and blue borage. This is where you can sit out for tea. The O'Donoghues serve a whole raft of delicious cakes and teas throughout the summer so this is a good stopping-off point to fill up before heading out to the herb and vegetable garden. In here peas, scallions and cabbages are planted alongside flowers and herbs in a collection of only vaguely formal enclosures. Yet more boulders and rounded stones have been hauled into edge the beds.

Beautifully constructed dry, stone walls act as windbreaks on the gust-blown west coast. They are placed at all sorts of angles to break, redirect and downplay the wind. They also afford opportunities for climbers to grow and provide a transition between the garden and the wild west into which it gradually melts.

If the geography of the Burren is central to the garden so too is its lore. There is one big stone in the middle of the garden called the 'back stone' on which to rub a bad back in order to receive a cure. There are also heaps of piled-up stones. In the past, people would not pass one of these piles, without adding a stone. The stacks can still be seen scattered by the roadside.

Local superstition is also reflected in the name of the garden: An Féar Gorta means 'the hungry grass' and refers to a patch of bewitched ground. According to legend, when you stepped on the hungry grass you were immediately consumed by gnawing hunger pains. To avoid this, you would carry a crust of bread in case of encountering the dreaded féar. Here, you could just tackle some of those delicious cakes.

Gregan's Castle Hotel Garden

Ballyvaughan, Co. Clare. Tel: 065 7077 005. Contact: The Hayden family. Open: Contact in advance for an appointment to view garden. Small groups and individuals only. Supervised children welcome. Special features: Accommodation. Restaurant. Teas can be booked. Directions: Located on the N67 between Lisdoonvarna and Ballyvaughan.

The countryside of County Clare needs no improvement. Wild, sparsely cultivated, colourful and beautiful, it doesn't cry out for additions, which can make it harder in many ways to create a good garden here than in more tamed parts. It is too easy to plant an incongruous-looking, obviously imported garden into these wild surroundings. A more sensitive hand is required.

This garden depends as much on 'borrowed landscape' as on the work carried out within the boundaries. For example, at the front of the house, the low fuchsia hedge is backed not by the usual beech, bay, yew or hornbeam hedging, but by the hills and huge skies of the Burren. In front of it, lying almost flat, is a border of hebe, Cape daisy, peony and catmint. They melt together and seem to wash in toward the lawn like a tide. Colour is used subtly rather than in overly bold sheets. Soft reds and the purple of fuchsia are the dominant colours.

Look for the secret garden close to one side of the house, through a discreet entrance cut into the overhanging shrubs. In here poor man's box or *Lonicera nitida*, camellia and rampant buddleia, which is found everywhere in the garden, attract large numbers of butterflies. Crocosmia, with its exotic, flame-coloured flowers and strappy leaves, has been teamed with matt-green and frothy lemon Lady's mantle, to fringe and soften the house walls.

Along the river they planted sorbus and betula, leading away from the house and towards a circular rock bed with an interesting and unusual pattern of stonework. Mown paths wind through a newly planted wood of native trees, which, as it matures, will become like a wooded maze. That wood opens onto a great big lily pond, edged with more willow and fuchsia and an island.

Irish Seed Savers Association (ISSA)

Capparoe, Scariff, Co. Clare: Tel: 061 921866: e-mail: tansey@irishseedsavers.ie seedsavers@esatclear.ie Special features: Tours for groups. Courses. Mail order trees and seeds. Seasonal café and shop. Open: Directions: Signed from Scarriff.

The Irish Seed Savers Association was set up in 1990 by Tommy and Anita Hayes. Its aim was to save seeds from endangered native Irish fruit and vegetables varieties, to locate, grow and distribute these plants among gardeners who continue to grow them, therefore increasing the stock of plants all over the country, giving the endangered gene pool a chance to survive and increase.

These days many of us know and grow Irish Seed Saver apples in our gardens. A huge number of the open gardens in this book have orchards full of such varieties, rescued and raised by the Seed Savers. An early autumn trip to their garden in Scarriff should include a walk around Peader's Orchard, where scores of these can be tasted and tested with a view to buying the perfect Irish apple for your own garden.

The Seed Saver's propagate, as widely as possible, plants that would otherwise disappear forever. Fears for the future of these plants are not idle. Since the beginning of the 20th century a catastrophic percentage of the genetic diversity of agricultural crops has been lost. Large seed merchants have reduced the variety of seed available for sale and cultivation. As a result, good old garden varieties of peas and carrots, sometimes, but not always, prone to certain diseases and pests must be saved from extinction. These plants need to be saved because they are diverse, taste different, look different and add to the variety of life.

The gardens in Scarriff, where so many of these endangered crops are grown, are rough and lovely. This is no manicured place. The nettles compete with brambles and docks. The lines are not straight. They are not even apparent in some places. But the setup is admirable. The endeavour is to be applauded and after a visit it is happily possible to bring home some quirky old varieties of broad bean and pea, salsify and carrot, onion and radish.

Knappogue Castle Walled Garden

Knappogue, Quin, Co. Clare: Tel 061 360788. e-mail: reservations@shannonheritage.com www.shannonheritage.com Open: On request. Special features: Medieval banquets may be booked in the summer months. Directions: Driving on the N18 from Limerick to Ennis, take the Quin exit. In the village turn left and follow the signs to Knappogue Castle (3 km).

Having driven along the most idyllic hilly, humpy country roads in Clare, it is not really a surprise to arrive at the fairytale castle of Knappogue just outside Quin village. Knappogue is no intimidating Norman keep or battle building. It feels like a castle into which one could almost move. But apart from its tapestry-draped white washed walls, the castle also still boasts a series of gardens. Attached to the building, is a small terraced, ornamental formal garden made up of seating areas under neat clipped trees between box walls and shaped yews, around rose and perennial beds. Like an extension of one of the reception rooms, this is a restrained, pretty garden room.

The powerful sense of being back in time only hits as you make your way to the walled garden. Walk along a path around the outer castle wall, beneath the keep and up a hill through a meadow. As you do you, pass an ash tree that once grew from a stone wall. The wall is long gone. Only the bulging ancient tree, studded with some of its stones, still stands. Then take the carriage gate into the walled garden, where an ongoing restoration of the once lost garden can be visited for free.

I walked it with gardener Elaine Hiney-Wall, who was in the middle of working and renewing the long central double borders, as well as the surrounding wall borders and herb beds.

There is a small collection of old roses here, including scented *Rosa* 'Paul Transon' growing on a pergola, as well as old sweet peas and peonies, and all the usual herbaceous favourites. As stated, it was being worked on as I visited last time. I look forward to seeing it again.

On the way to see Knappogue stop in Quin. There is a little rose garden by the humped stone bridge in the village. Buy an ice cream in the shop and sit for a while to admire the garden, the fine old bridge and the view over to the ruined abbey.

Vandeleur Walled Garden

Killimer Road, Kilrush, Co. Clare. Tel: 065 9051 760. e-mail: info@vandeleurwalledgarden.ie www.vandeleurwalledgarden.ie Open: All year. See website for seasonal changes. Wheelchair accessible. Children welcome. Special features: Restaurant. Plants for sale. Gallery. Conference facilities. Member of The Gardens of Ireland Trust. Directions: Take the Killimer Road out of Kilrush. Travel 1.5 km and the garden is on the left.

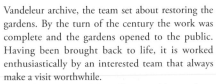

'After we got the approval to buy the walled garden and stables, I walked through the garden and thought 'blast, they'll kill us'. This was Jerry Sweeney's reaction to seeing the ruin of a place, just after he, as part of a committee of local people, had agreed to buy the walled garden and stable block of the Vandeleur estate outside Kilrush in 1997.

The committee's aim was to take a walled field of self-seeded trees, neglected for decades and turn it back into the decorative and productive walled garden it had been a century before, and in doing so, provide local employment and deliver the town a welcome tourist attraction.

The committee carried out research into the history of the Vandeleur family that built Kilrush town as well as Kilrush House. They studied the Lawrence Collection photos to help with the restoration. William Lawrence was a photographer who travelled the length and breadth of Ireland, recording every aspect of life between 1880 and 1910. Using these images with other information unearthed from the Vandeleur archive, the team set about restoring the gardens. By the turn of the century the work was complete and the gardens opened to the public. Having been brought back to life, it is worked enthusiastically by an interested team that always make a visit worthwhile.

Today, in place of the self-sown wild trees, large shrub borders encircle the walls. In the middle, there are spreads of lawn, herbaceous borders, a small tree collection, fruit and vegetable gardens, a maze and a fruit walk, recently rebuilt glass houses, rockeries and gazebos. The people of Kilrush have been busy.

On the south-facing wall there are three-metre tall exotic echiums, towering and flowering. Next to these the informal display includes a fine big fig, airy *Acacia baileyana* 'Purpurea' over rampant hemerocallis, or daylilies and *Melianthus major*. The micro-climate here is benign. The sunny wall is curved to maximise the length of warm wall space and so accommodate a greater number of sun-loving plants. A *Streptocarpus vandeleurii* is one exotic plant doing well in the conditions. It was introduced to Ireland by the Crofton family during the Boer War between 1899 and 1902, having been found on the rocky crevices of the Transvaal. Today it basks in the sun that shines on this alpine bed in west Clare.

The beech maze in the middle of the garden has spent the last decade fattening out nicely and the apple and pear tunnels are also maturing. They must be a sight at blossom time.

Outside the walls, the courtyard has been harnessed into a playground with a living willow for children to climb through. The collection of puzzling farm machines here, should have the most agriculturally knowledgeable person scratching their head.

Beyond the walls there are about 50 acres of wood with several paths and walks. For anyone who feels that lost gardens are not worth reviving, the way the community has taken up this old ghost and resurrected it is a model to gladden the heart.

Cork

Agharinagh Inspirational Gardens

Griffin's Garden Centre, Dripsey, Co. Cork. Tel: 021 733 4286. e-mail: info@griffinsgardencentre.ie
Contact: Reception. Open: Every day. Special features: Garden centre. Restaurant. Directions: In the village
of Dripsey.

Griffin's is a Cork institution, a family run garden centre in Dripsey with a ridiculously friendly staff and good plants. It is also home to a series of 13 little gardens, made to inspire customers with ideas that they can use in their own gardens. Each individual space is based on the sort of small patch attached to the modern home, so the scale is perfect.

They highlight different aspects, from sheltered to exposed, sunny to shaded and dry to damp. The Japanese inspired treehouse garden might be a bit ambitious but I love it. Molly's view cottage garden is covetable and the various water gardens are suitably lush. The trickle and drip, drip of water is always irresistible. The gardens are linked and walking between them gives you the chance to study the compositions from different angles. The panoramic view from a height over the River Dripsey should not be missed either.

Aultaghreagh Cottage Garden

Aultaghreagh, Dunmanway, Co. Cork. Tel: 085 1696474. e-mail: houserocker@live.com
www.aultaghreaghcottagegarden.com. Contact: Christine and Les Wilson. Open: May-Sept. 11am-5pm
by appointment. Special features: Not wheelchair accessible. Directions: On appointment.

To get to Aultaghreagh I drove through Dunmanway and past a sign marked 'site of the ambush.' Most Irish people will know that 'the ambush' was at Beal na Blath, where Michael Collins died, but the sign must leave those unfamiliar with Irish history a little bewildered. Driving on for a few kilometres brings you to Aultaghreagh and the garden that Christine and Les Wilson, a pair of passionate plants people, have been growing and developing in the north west Cork countryside for years.

The magnolia and rhododendron bed by the cottage might suggest that the soil here is acid but this acid bed was made and it is maintained by regularly mulching with pine needles. Making our way through grass and perennial borders under the shelter of oak and black Italian alder, it was hard to see this jungle garden as an unadorned flat field, which is what it was in 1997. Today the slimmest of paths nudge between sizeable tree peonies and blue *Hydrangea aspera* 'Villosa', self-seeding myrtles and white abutilon. The old field is consigned to dim memory. We stopped to feed a huge population of fish in a pond tucked between the massed flowers.

So many of the plants here were grown from seed. Christine is an avid propagator and so the veronicas, unusual lobelias, lupins, delphiniums, sweet Williams, sweet peas and heleniums I admired, are all her own work. The expansive possibilities of what can be grown from seed have always impressed her.

We walked through serene drifts of white foxglove and variegated hosta, lilies and anemones, all pale chalks and creams. From there we made our way into another colour-themed flower garden with a different mood. Clematis is used widely in the upper storeys, over pergolas, up trees and over fences - all made by Les. His pergola works hard, supporting the considerable weight of a *Rosa banksiae* 'Alba', about 20 different varieties of clematis, schisandra, two solanums or potato vines, and an evergreen *Lonicera japonica*.

One among many stealable ideas is the All Seasons Shrub Border, where they grow a series of shrubs arranged to deliver good looks for 12 months of the year.

While the garden is plant rich, there are stylish, hard landscaping touches too. I liked the dug-up stone used to make mowing verges between borders and lawns.

Annes Grove

Castletownroche, Mallow, Co. Cork. e-mail: doneraile park@opw.ie www.heritageireland.ie Contact: The Manager. Open: In the process of a phased re-opening scheme. Check website for changing information. Supervised children welcome. Guide dogs only. Partially wheelchair accessible. Directions: Located 1.6 km from Castletownroche on the Fermoy–Mallow–Killarney road (N72). Signposted from the village.

Annes Grove has long been one of Ireland's favourite gardens. It was largely the creation of the late Richard Grove Annesley during the first half of the 20th century, designed in a style championed by the 19th century Irish garden writer, William Robinson. At the time this 'Robinsonian' style was revolutionary, combining native and exotic plants in a naturalised fashion. Annes Grove, Mount Usher, Derreen, and Rowallane, are outstanding expressions of this mode of gardening. Annes Grove also incorporates an older walled flower garden.

The gardens have sadly slipped into decline over the last few decades and with each visit, the decline seemed to accelerate. In December 2015 however, the Annesley family handed the grounds to the State and they are now in the expert care of the Office of Public Works. Restoration has started and is visible from the front gate, where fallen trees have been cleared and replaced with young oak and beech. Reconfiguration of the drive, back to its Victorian design has been completed, as walls and stone outhouses are being rebuilt and old shrubberies have been smartened up. The work continues.

Blessed with pockets of both acid and alkaline soil, Annes Grove can accommodate an unusually wide range of plants. Richard Grove Annesley was a co-sponsor of Frank Kingdon Ward's plant-hunting expeditions to Burma, Tibet and Yunan. He took full advantage of that bounty and filled his Cork garden with the results of these and other expeditions. Its collection of rhododendrons, including *R. wardii* and *R. macabeanum* are well known.

The walled garden can still be visited, while access is, of necessity restricted as this book goes to press. This is thought to have originally been an 18th century orchard, but the current design is largely Edwardian. Here too restoration has been carried out, including on the well known curved box hedges, called ribbon beds, due to their twisted ribbon-like shape. The path between these is so knobbly and uneven it could more rightly be called a 'rocky road'.

A little distance away there are two long borders where the dominant colours are blue and pink. Their job is to look like lava-flows of flower and foliage, hell-bent on meeting each other in the middle of the flagged path. These are also under restoration but the backing beech walls have already been smartened up.

Pergolas knotted with wisteria, honeysuckle and roses stretch out from the double borders leading in one direction through a shaded, woody walk under cherry and eucryphia, to a lily pond. Beyond the water, the path ducks into the lovely dark gloom of a Victorian fernery, an arrangement of natural-looking stone ledges and mounds built to hold a collection of ferns. This too is being restored.

The last time I saw the gothic summerhouse it looked too late to save from dereliction. The good news is that it is being brought back to life. I look forward to seeing it in all its glory, perched on its little tuffet at the centre of the garden.

Outside these walls, the wood and wild garden spreads in all directions. This once fabulous place is largely out of bounds at the moment simply because it cannot be accessed due to weed growth and fallen trees, but one walk remains open, under and between catalpa and davidia, parrotia and rhododendron.

The huge task of cleaning up and identifying the collection is in its infancy. The simple job of clearing weeds, preventing them from choking out small shrubs is the current concern. The dull but necessary slog is all that will be carried out for the time being. So for now, the bulk of this incredible garden must be remembered rather than enjoyed. I used to love getting lost between the groves of myrtle and bamboo, under clouds of rhododendron, between scented cercidiphyllum, getting bogged down on the walk along the river at the bottom of the valley, looking up at the stunning colours of hydrangea rock. Hopefully soon we will be able to fully enjoy all those gardens again.

Ballycommane House & Garden

Durrus. Co. Cork. Contact: Andy Stieglitz & Ingolf Jungmann. Tel: 027 62799. e-mail: info@ballycommane.com Open: Mar-Oct., daily 9.30am-7pm. Special features: B&B and self-catering accommodation. Self guiding trail. Plants for sale. Children welcome. No dogs. Groups welcome. German spoken. Directions: On the R591 out of Durrus, signposted.

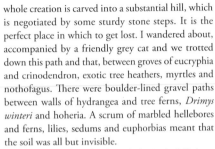

A white picket gate set into a tall mixed hedge gives a sneaky peak into Ballycommane House. This is a pretty sight but somewhat misleading. Nosing over the gate, you would see a gravel path between young oaks and griselinia, hart's tongue fern, ivy, foxgloves and other natives. This is however, only one corner of the larger picture.

Variety is the glory of Ballycommane. It is a welcoming, bamboozling maze of individual garden rooms, all wrapped around the house and its various stone out-buildings, including a little turf house. The

whole creation is carved into a substantial hill, which is negotiated by some sturdy stone steps. It is the perfect place in which to get lost. I wandered about, accompanied by a friendly grey cat and we trotted down this path and that, between groves of eucryphia and crinodendron, exotic tree heathers, myrtles and nothofagus. There were boulder-lined gravel paths between walls of hydrangea and tree ferns, *Drimys winteri* and hoheria. A scrum of marbled hellebores and ferns, lilies, sedums and euphorbias meant that the soil was all but invisible.

The Irish apple orchard on a ledge in the hill above the house, leads up to some towering Scots pines and, remarkably a Bronze Age burial site with standing stones. This is no ordinary garden.

Andy and Ingolf's interest in travel is evident from the many southern hemisphere plants, including *Cyathea cooperi* and *Leptospermum scoparium*, different bananas, palms and a host of exotics. In all directions, there are, and lesser-seen items, living comfortably here thanks to the Gulf Stream. Plants of the Azores are displayed in one flower border, including *Euphorbia stygiana*, a plant now endangered in the wild.

The house sits hidden between a series of patio and terrace gardens, all taking advantage of the sun at different times of day. There are many troughs and containers here, full of succulents and bulbs, alpines and sub-shrubs.

I loved the surprise of the little pond and the whole series of stepped up and down crazy paved paths that eventually lead to a sheltered wood garden, and on out to the greenhouse with its collection of scented ginger lilies. It would be no hardship to find yourself lost in this garden.

Ballymacrown Homestead

Ballymacrown, Baltimore, Co. Cork. Contact Joan de Lacey. Tel: 028 20527.
e-mail: info@ballyhoocottages.com www.ballyhoocottages.com Open: As part of the Baltimore Secret Garden
Trail. See website for annual details. Special features: Accommodation. Wheelchair access to front garden
only. Children welcome. Dogs on leads. Directions: Leave Baltimore on the road to Trafaska. Take the next
left and travel along until you see a group of attached multi-coloured cottages.

Driving on a back road out of Baltimore, I came across a little collection of cottages painted in different colours, banded together, surrounded by an old fashioned country cottage garden. They sat on the brow of a hill, under a big sky. I had to stop.

This is Joan de Lacey's creation, an attractive, informal flower and kitchen garden, built on a sloped, south-facing site and overlooking the mountains and the sea. It is a place full of pretty individual features that mesh together with ease. The sunny rose beds and herb gardens, surrounded by hazel fences, are all scent and colour. The orchard with its mixed fruit trees and bushes is a practical - and equally good looking mix of apples, pears, plums and different varieties of currants. I loved the *Rosa rugosa* hedge that leads you into the middle of it all, flowering all summer and providing the birds with heaps to feast on over the winter. More shrub rose and fuchsia hedges bound little paddocks and there are wild flower meadows, damp peaty spots and all the old-fashioned country flowers, from lupins and roses, to geraniums and stachys.

It would have been good to sit swaddled on a bench in among bee-busy fuchsias if there were time but there were things to see. The cottages are covered in roses with fringes of big bushy white hydrangea. Opportunistic foxglove and *Alchemilla mollis* sprout up wherever they find a spot. The area around the house is topped off with that most romantic of things, a picket fence that does not just look good but also shelters a row of low trained apple trees.

The whole garden and all this busy bounty is grown and cared for organically. Given that, the temptation is to just lie down under a raspberry bush or beside a line of strawberries and pick off a few juicy ones…

Ballymaloe Cookery School Garden & Organic Farm

Shanagarry, Midleton, Co. Cork. Contact: Reception Tel: 021 4646785. e-mail: info@cookingisfun.ie
www.cookingisfun.ie Open: Six days a week. Supervised children welcome. Special features: Garden shop.
Cookery School. Pre-booked guided tours. Courses. Events. Groups can book meals in advance. Directions:
Signed from Castlemartyr on the Cork-Waterford road (N25).

There have been gardens here since the early 1800s when the house belonged to the Strangmans. The Allen family arrived in 1970 and have spent those years improving what they found and creating new features that are now mature, varied and beautiful. If there is one emphasis it must be that, attached to a cookery school, there is a strong emphasis on growing produce, in both practical and ornamental ways.

I can never quite get the shape of the place in my mind despite a good looking map. I love the fact that there are courtyards and little groups of houses and buildings dotted about, adding to a comfortable confusion. Visiting feels like something of a treasure hunt. I would start at the stream garden, beside the restaurant where a gang of wirework ducks and geese, along with a few live versions, congregate by the water. The planting scheme here is one of sedges, vinca or periwinkle, ivy and variegated *Sisyrinchium striatum*.

The fruit garden is not large and its relatively compact dimensions means it is well worth a visit by anyone with a modest-sized plot, dreaming of an ornamental, productive garden. The arrangement is one of gravel paths between fruit trees grown in beds edged by collars of strawberries, rhubarb and pansies. Plums, pears, greengages, peaches and apricots share the space with almonds and olive trees and Irish apple varieties trained over iron arched walks make great use of the paths.

From here, walk through a young beech wood to the *potager* – a French-style decorative vegetable garden. This is a confection of herringbone-patterned paths and *uber*-smart symmetrical beds. You will find no messy gaps here. Tidy parsnips, leeks and Florence fennel stand to attention in measured lines, but marigolds and splashes of orange nasturtium soften the business-like look of the straight-laced vegetables. The willow scarecrows are so good looking that their efficacy must be doubted. I think when a cookery school student comes out to pull some lettuce, they must be under orders to pull that head out uniformly and leave the line looking presentable as they go.

Out on the edge of the potager, a bench surrounded by an arch of golden hop makes a pleasant place to sit and admire tomatoes interlaced with Devil-in-the-bush or nigella. Mop-head bay trees like green lollipops stand over the vegetables.

Lydia's Garden was named for Lydia Strangman whose watercolours of the herbaceous borders as they were in her time, provided a reference for the Allens when they began restoring this corner of the garden. This space is also hedged in by beech and overlooked by a tree house. Tucked underneath the wooden house is a delicate-looking mosaic, created in 1912 with a sign begging visitors not to walk on it. Do as you are told.

The pond garden can also be seen from the tree house. This is a field of rose-clad cherry trees and specimens leading to a Grecian folly and pond. There is an air of cool restraint here, with a simple palette of reflecting water, wildflower meadow and maturing trees.

Next door, the punch that the big double border packs, is a knock-out. These two beds, each 80 metres in length and separated by a wide grass path, are memorable. They carry all the usual herbaceous perennials, from phlox, tall red sunflowers and rudbeckia, to yellow dahlias, cornflowers and bells of Ireland. In early summer there are coral-coloured lupins and bronze fennel. The colour combinations are always bold and strong. This is no softly-softly mushy pastel affair.

The borders culminate in a hexagonal shell house, with walls and ceiling encrusted with a mix of shells, arranged in fantastical geometric patterns. The crowning glory is an elegant coral candelabra.

Beside the shell house the Celtic design-inspired maze of hornbeam, beech and yew is maturing and beyond this, there are some great wildflower meadows. Do not miss the impressive outdoor vegetable beds being worked organically at the edge of the ornamental gardens. These are highly instructive. The huge expanse of greenhouse in which the indoor food crops are grown all year round is equally fascinating. Tours of these remarkable, industrial sized organic productive gardens can be organised and are recommended.

Ballyvolane House Gardens

Castlelyons, Co. Cork. Tel: 025 36349. e-mail: info@ballyvolanehouse.ie www.ballyvolanehouse.ie.
Contact: Justin and Jenny Green. Open: Garden visitors by appointment only. Supervised children welcome.
Dogs on leads. Special features: Refreshments can be booked. Hotel. Events. Directions: Travelling on the M8
from Cork city, take the exit for Rathcormac (R639). Turn right onto the R626 for Midleton and Tallow.
Take the next left to Tallow onto the R628. Take the second turn right towards Midleton at the crossroads.
Take the next left at Britway. Ballyvolane is along this road, signed.

This is a large, mature country garden with a rhododendron and bluebell wood, a walled garden, lakes and parkland. The house was built in 1728 and remodelled in 1847 and the layout is based on the Victorian design. The Greens have been working on the garden since the 1990s when Justin's parents Jeremy and his wife, Merrie, took it over. They began restoring the neglected grounds and planted rhododendrons and other choice plants around the lawn edges as well as tucking them under the mature park trees.

The house is clad in wisteria, splaying cotoneaster, pink roses and actinidia. It stands above a sloped meadow and park that leads down to three interlinked lakes set under old groves of beech and oak. When the Greens arrived, there were two lakes. They added a third. These spill into each other in a surprisingly natural-looking way, providing a scene that can be appreciated from the house. But, if you want to take a bit of exercise, the walk down to the lakes is a pleasant stroll.

Standing at the back of the house, you are lured into an arch of magnolia and up a set of stone steps flanked by pots of nepeta, onto a croquet lawn that might house a rather exotic looking tent which could grace the finest Berber encampment. Huge copper beech, splashes of hydrangea and other flowering shrubs enclose the lawn.

The kitchen garden is tucked behind the trees, to one side of the back lawn. Half of its walled area is being worked at present. Walled kitchen gardens are for many owners something of a millstone: too big to tackle without a sizeable gardening staff. In this case, only part of the area is given to herbs and vegetables for the house. There are also borders and cutting beds of francoa and galtonia, under magnolia and ginkgo. The vegetable garden next to the flowerbeds, is a hive of industry as well as being decorative. Different lettuce, artichokes, Swiss chard, beets, broad beans and red gooseberries, must fight for space with geraniums and roses.

The final feature in the walled garden is a beech hedge *allée* that frames the grazing cows in a paddock beyond. This leads out to another flower border with some flowering shrubs. Myrtle, *Cornus kousa* and buddleia deliver an ever present backdrop to the flowerbeds, providing structure when the herbaceous plants have gone to ground.

The Bamboo Park

Glengarriff, Co. Cork. Tel 027 63007. 086 0628518. e-mail: bambooparkltd@eircom.net
www.bamboo-park.com Contact: Claudine de Thibault. Open: As part of the West Cork Garden Trail.
Spring to Autumn, 9am-7pm. See website for annual details. Partially wheelchair accessible. Dogs on leads.
Special features: Accompanied children free. Tea room. Directions: Just before the Eccles Hotel in the village.

Set on a south-facing slope and surrounded by myrtle, rhododendron and rock, the 13-acre Bamboo Park in Glengarriff is a relatively young garden, but since I first visited 17 years ago, it has matured impressively. Back then the juvenile line of *Dicksonia antarctica* was handsome. Today, walking under those great splayed fronds on top of dark brown trunks is a memorable experience. Time has also marched on in the young plantations of *Phyllostachys nigra* f. *henonis*, which have since become great arching, olive green culms. The spooky rustle of vegetation that only bamboo can deliver makes the lone walker want to step lively along the ghostly paths. When the route eventually leads out to the open, it might be to a squishy bog garden of bulrush and lily ponds, or an extravagant run of *Hydrangea macrophylla* and a stone-edged stream. Inevitably however, the tracks slip back under those bamboos, and eventually out towards the bay and a walk along the waterside.

From here, various paths bring you back through the woods and into open grassed areas, run through by sunken streams and surrounded by towering, slim eucalyptus and acacia, tunnels of white and blood-red camellia, walls of eucalyptus facing walls of bamboo and the suitably situated, *Griselinia littoralis* 'Bantry Bay'.

The path weaves between stands of rhododendron, escallonia and long runs of box clipped in strange formations. Sometimes the route is along crunchy paths made from decades of fallen beech nuts, dappled with light shade cast by the beech trees overhead. This is an experimental garden and the development of plants like *Trachycarpus wagnerianus* and *T. takil,* an endangered native of northern India, will be interesting to follow. More usual specimens, like Chusan palms or *Trachycarpus fortunei* and *Phoenix canariensis* thrive in the warmth and damp. A tree familiar to us through Hollywood films, the LA sky-duster or *Washingtonia robusta,* will be studied to see how high it stretches. Finally, the honey palm or *Jubaea chilensis,* with its coconut-flavoured seed, is not expected to fruit in Cork for a couple of centuries, as it is one of the slowest maturing palms in the world.

Out by the bay, take a seat for a while and admire the view of Ilnacullin and the sun-bathing seals on the rocks.

Bantry House & Gardens

Bantry, Co. Cork. Tel: 027 50047. e-mail: info@bantryhouse.com www.bantryhouse.com
Contact: Sophie Shelswell White. Open: Easter-Oct. April, May, Sept. and Oct: Tues-Sun. 10am-5pm.
June-Aug: Mon-Sun. 10am-5pm. Partially wheelchair accessible. Dogs on leads in garden. Guide dogs only in house. Children welcome. Special features: Accommodation. Afternoon teas in library. Tearoom. House tours. Groups can book tours and meals in advance. Gift shop. West Cork Music Festival venue. Directions: Located on the N71 to Cork, 1km outside Bantry town, on the left.

Bantry House has been in the White family since the mid-1700s when Richard White bought it from the Earl of Anglesey. In the 1940s it opened its gates to the curious and interested, becoming the first stately home in Ireland to do so. As a result, the Shelswell-Whites, as the family is now known, are well accustomed to welcoming visitors. Among garden lovers, Bantry is considered one of the finest, in one of the most extraordinary settings in the world. It is impossible not to be smitten by the place.

For most visitors the glory of the garden is the Stairway to the Sky, an imposing stairs that climbs up the imposing hill above the Italian garden to the side of the house. It reminds me of the stairway to heaven in the David Niven film, 'A Matter of Life and Death'. The formality of this massive feature is somewhat undermined by the constant encroachment of creeping green *Soleirolia soleirolii*, alpine strawberries and quaking grass. This is not as it should be but it is impossible not to be charmed. As well as looking grand from beneath, it delivers a view over the house, garden, Bantry Bay and the headland beyond. This is a view not to be matched. To sit and take in the panoramic sights from the top of the steps on a clear day is a privilege.

Yet for all its beauty, when on ground level, the garden is so full of distraction that one tends to forget how beautiful the surroundings are. The Italian garden is made up of formal box hedging in swirling patterns around a central circle of wisteria. Its knotty century-old trunks are every bit as good-looking as the dangling flowers and leaves they bear. This living trellis surrounds an eccentric-looking, fossil stone-encrusted water feature and pond, used as a *pêcherie*, in which fish were once kept and lived decorously until their presence was required at the dinner table. Today they would presumably spend that time in the freezer.

The sunken flower garden to the side of the house is a busy mix of plants grown in circular beds. In one of these, bobbles of blue and white agapanthus grow under a multi-stemmed cordyline, itself like a series of bobbles on sticks. Around the circles, there are wide bands of *Alchemilla mollis* studded with *Stipa gigantea*, towering blue echiums and big runs of scented phlox. Golden glass balls bob about impaled on bamboo poles, adding a bit of glitter and sparkle.

The yew-and-box garden next door provides a contrast to this frothy, flowery garden: The two hedging plants are being trained, some cloud-shaped, some in more regular boxy lines. From these two garden rooms it is possible to look down over the sloped wildflower meadow, cut through with a mown path.

On the North terrace, at the front of the house there are 14 circular beds in a line, all looking out over Bantry Bay. Phoenix date palm and yucca alternate with two varieties of box, one golden and one plain. Additional weaving bands of coloured aggregates give the feature a final tweak of formality.

Continuing around to the other side of the house, the path leads to the rose garden, edged with cordylines, stone urns and Diana's bed. This is a circular riot of flowers and grasses around a little statue of Diana, goddess of the hunt. With Bantry however, the view is always the thing. Irresistible.

Beechwood

Templeisque, Glanmire, Co. Cork. Tel: 021 4884 489. 086 3157 096.
e-mail: lizkirby101@hotmail.com. www.beechwoodgarden.com Contact: Liz and Ned Kirby.
Open: May-Sept. By appointment to groups only. Not wheelchair accessible. Children welcome. No dogs.
Special features: Refreshments can be booked. Garden design. Directions: See website.

The sight from the road, through a painted iron gate, of a house with flying buttresses of climbing shrubs, topiary and puffs of flower, can make a garden visitor squeal with excitement.

Great gardens are sometimes serene and calm. They are sometimes arch and grand. The Kirbys' is another breed of great garden - A double espresso shot that leaves you feeling energised and sends you home wanting to dig up everything and start all over again

Ned and Liz are part of the enthusiastic band of fine Cork gardeners that leave the rest of us wondering if maybe there is fertiliser in the water down there.

It is firstly a plant-stuffed treat. A walk around should start on the garden side of that enclosing hedge. It shelters a sun-soaked bank of camellias, peeling barked *Acer griseum*, *Acer palmatum* 'Katsura' and winged spindles, planted over and between runs of *Dahlia merckii* and unusual creeping, white-flowered *Cornus canadensis*.

Hidden in behind all this is a secluded, stone-edged path leading to an old fashioned well with a slate roof, built by Ned's father. Ferns sprout from the walls and the ground is thick with hellebores.

Giving good-looking plants the leeway to sprawl and spread is the way they work. The framed views back and forward between the gardens show another

aspect of the design eye working here. Well placed pieces of sculpture add a certain style to each little garden. I love the simplicity of a stone pinnacle from an old convent, topped with an astrolabe.

The house is insulated under blankets of ivy, cotoneaster, climbing lobster claw or clianthus and golden fremontodendron.

Walking past a beech hedge cut into with a small gate, you catch a glimpse of a neighbouring field full of cows - An example of borrowing both landscape and supporting cast. A low, banked bed along the other side of the gravel path spills over with mounds of creeping hardy geraniums and celmisia. Banquettes of clipped cotoneaster and golden privet cones add points of solidity to the loose gravel plantings. Ned used the drop in level between the front and back of the house to create a meandering stone-lined watercourse and pond. Meanwhile, a gateway in between two 'rescue restios' and a tall hedge across the garden beckons. Go through this to the wild garden; a walk through a dizzying maze of shrubs, exotic perennials and tall grasses in irregularly shaped beds dug into the baize-like lawn. Quantities of local brown sandstone have been used to make paths that rise and fall and duck under stands of bamboo, plumes of cortaderia and *Chionochloa rubra* like mad mops of hair. Ned grew the tall birches here from seed. They weave through and tower above the lower planting schemes.

There is so much going on here: We come upon another pond garden hiding behind yet another chest-high beech hedge. This is a sloped, boulder and water, spring garden.

I always leave this garden marvelling at how it manages, at the same time, to be both virtuoso performance and yet an enjoyable and relaxed place to visit.

Blarney Castle Gardens

Blarney, Co. Cork. Tel: 021 4385 252. e-mail: info@blarneycastle.ie www.blarneycastle.ie Contact: Reception, or Head Gardener, Adam Whitbourn. Open: Every day of the year (except Christmas and St. Stephen's Day). See website for seasonal changes. Special features: Blarney Castle and the Blarney Stone. Shop. Restaurant. Wheelchair accessible. Guided tours can be booked. Directions: Situated in the village of Blarney.

Well directed ambition is always a pleasure to see. The work carried out at Blarney Castle over the past few years is cause for a good deal of pleasure. The grounds around the 14th century castle were always worth a visit but today they merit a serious detour. A visit to Blarney gardens and grounds could take all day. It boasts so much more than a slightly scary kissing stone.

Among the interesting experiments being carried out in the grounds is an attempt to put together the biggest collection of Irish cultivars outside of the National Botanic Gardens. These bulbs, perennials, shrubs and trees, can be identified by their green plant labels.

If you can possibly arrive in late April or early May to see the wide spreading umbrella of *Prunus* 'Shirotae' by the entrance gate, do so. At nearly 50 years old, its days are numbered. Until recently it lived with its roots under concrete. Today, enclosed and protected by a low wall, its soil has been fed and mulched and it looks great.

From here, a newly directed curved walk bordered by mixed grasses and perennials, lined with a young avenue of cherries, leads toward the iconic castle, high on its promontory. The route runs parallel to the River Martin and the remains of an old mill race. At one point the river actually runs *over* another little river in an unusual engineering feat.

It also travels through an expanse of semi-wild flower meadow and the Lower Arboretum, which was started by Sir Charles St. John Colthurst in the 1970s. He planted his new specimen trees between older limes, the remnants of historic approaches to the castle. Seed-collecting trips to Vietnam and China form the nucleus of the young collection.

The slope under the castle was recently planted with a mix of ground hugging yew or *Taxus repandum,* spiked with upright Irish yews. Close by, some of the grandest old yews in the park are to be found and on the ground beneath, there are colonies of *Narcissus* 'Blarney' being nursed along.

The trail continues toward Rock Close, one of the glories of Blarney. In the 1750s the owners took the vast reservoir of existing rock formations here - including a dolmen - and added to them to create a romantic garden. This was complete with the weird little Witch's Kitchen, which I would bet good money must have once boasted a hermit. The combination of rocks with trees seeming to grow directly from them, is irresistible. Below this series of spooky entertainments, is the bog garden featuring a zigzagging boardwalk over the river. This leads between big stands of gunnera and ferns and past an impressive tumbling waterfall, on through long willow tunnels and past more venerable, hard-to-age yew. Welcome work has been carried out to protect these special trees. Head gardener, Adam Whitbourn explained how they have forked and loosened the earth around the old yews, mulching the ground to counteract decades of compaction. In some cases they have fenced off the trees to protect them from clambering and climbing.

One of the yews stands supported by a piece of iron engineering under which they have planted a lush hosta garden. (There are over 200 varieties of hosta in Blarney.) As we stood, looking at the hostas, a red squirrel allowed us walk very close to it as it stood, gnawing on a nut.

We next came to a sunny opening and the Seven Sisters, an intriguing looking stone circle garden, before leaving and climbing into the Upper Rockery through the Wishing Steps, a carved out tunnel in the stone, dripping with water and ferns. Adam introduced me to some of the local volunteers, busily weeding the rockery. Over the last few years they have cleared it of sycamore and ash, replacing these with 200 different conifers. The results of their work may be young but they are already exciting. In here there are podocarpus, planted in unusually large numbers as well as sequoias, a champion *Pinus radiata* and a *Thuja plicata* like a mad octopus. 50 years of leaf mould makes for excellent growing conditions.

There are collections of Irish primulas on the route to the Upper Arboretum and the Victorian baronial manor. We admired Spanish chestnuts, magnolia walks and tall eucalyptus. In the other direction, two long double borders and a rose pergola almost as long, run beneath the sunny side of the castle. A good number of the Irish cultivars reside in these borders.

The Belgian Beds are a series of low growing rhododendrons that lead down toward and between big clouds of *Rhododendron arboreum*. See these first from overhead - they are glorious. They have been joined by a selection of plants grown from seed collected in China.

We next landed into the Fern Garden, another of the Blarney treasures. This is a recent feature, a hilly explosion of tree ferns, with trees above and rocks that jag between the growth. You come upon it first from above, from where the tree ferns look like huge green daisies. Climbing down the stone steps carved into the sheer stone, lands you at the bottom of a ravine to stand under cliffs and waterfalls between the lush growth and the green of moss, ferns and, in spring, bluebells.

Among the Irish cultivars, there are 40 apple trees, grown in the walled garden, which is also worth visiting for the Bee Observation Project and the greenhouse range where much of the seed growing and propagation being carried out in Blarney is done. The Poison garden is a bit of fun with its notorious, fenced in cannabis plants, American poison ivy, laburnum arches, ricinus and many many not-so-obvious poison plants including tulips.

Bluebell House & Garden

Gurteenulla, Ballydehob, West Cork. Tel: 087 6886032. e.mail: dohertyw@eircom.net www.bluebellhouseandgardens.com Contact: Liam and Ann Marie Doherty. Open: By appointment. Not wheelchair accessible. No dogs. Special features: Teas can be arranged. Directions: Take N71 from Ballydehob towards Bantry. 1.5 km along turn right, signposted Boleagh. The garden is 1.5 km along on the left.

This is a recently created garden that is settling into its home in the hills outside Ballydehob. In the next few years it will be interesting to see how it matures. From the entrance, the intention to create a spectacle is obvious, from the newly made substantial stone-edged pond surrounded by clusters of young betula and purple hydrangea. Banks of fuchsia and rough grass spiked with wild flowers climb up above these and bound the tended lawn that runs from here to the house. The wilder ground beyond the garden is always there, always visible, leaning in, making itself felt.

The new house appears to have been dropped into the middle of several huge stone outcrops, some covered in moss and lichen, while some are draped in roses. Behind the house there is a sheltered colourful garden, surrounded by fuchsia and mixed shrub borders with sorbus and elder, over hellebores, hydrangea and acanthus. The rocks and boulders, always in the mix, lend the picture drama and solidity.

Substantial beech hedges shelter the house, but more interestingly, there are paths cut between and behind these hedges. They lead into secluded rockeries and hidden garden rooms. It must have been fun making this maze of shrub-bound sunken paths

that surprise and play with the unsuspecting visitor. At various points they open onto pond and stream gardens. I loved the mystery of making my way along, past the scent of daphne and under big umbrellas of Japanese acer. This is a whole little world of water and fern studded waterfalls, surrounded by more acers, grasses and drifts of white watsonia. Eventually, the path steps up, between a grove of hazel and magnolia and arrives eventually, back at the big pond at the drive. Seen at close quarters this turns out to be a swimming pond. The young weeping willow planted beside it in the damp soil will eventually drape over the water.

A forking path leads uphill from the main garden, along a row of more, massive boulders. The old ash trees that were here already have been maintained and underplanted with hydrangea, myrtle and phormium and at the top of the slope there is a young orchard surrounded by mature sycamores. I wondered if I was looking at a sort of fairy fort of sycamores and followed the path around it to arrive at another stone wall and a line of gnarled old crataegus and rain-drenched ferns - and the sound of water too, coming from a stream on the other side of the wall. Magic.

Carraig Abhainn Gardens

Durrus, Bantry, Co. Cork. Tel: 027 61070. e-mail info@carraigabhainngardens.com. www.carraigabhainngardens.com Contact: Eugene, Hazel and Colin Wiseman Open: As part of the West Cork Garden Trail. Contact for annual details. No dogs. Not wheelchair accessible. Directions: In Durrus village on the R591 coastal road to Mizen Head.

My most recent visit to Carraig Abhainn took place the day after a flood had almost washed the place away. 'It's a bit on the wild side today,' was how Eugene Wiseman calmly put it. Any other gardener would have had the barricades up against visitors. Not the welcoming Eugene. We squelched our way around wet lawns between cream flowered *Hydrangea quercifolia*, with the scent of a barley sugar tree or cercidiphyllum

somewhere about. I was amazed at the resilience of the waterside garden. Everywhere there are trees and shrubs with the power to stop you in your tracks. While I paused to envy a perfect umbrella of *Acer palmatum* 'Sango-kaku', the tall liriodendron or tulip tree close by was what interested Eugene. He loves this tree, hard as it is to see its greeny white flowers which are so high in the canopy. He may need a drone to enjoy them.

Carraig Abhainn runs past a stretch of river called Four Mile Water. The place is further divided by streams which they forded and bridged at several points. The sound of water is everywhere. Eugene had to shout to be heard over the roar of the fast moving torrent beneath us as we crossed one stream near the water rams at the bottom of the garden.

Informal grass paths trail between stands of dramatically coloured shrubs and trees, shoe-horned in together. Exuberance is the word. Is it over-stuffed? Yes and gorgeous too. I spotted a guelder rose or *Viburnum opulus* the likes of which I have never seen before size or sheer berrying power. Standing between this remarkable specimen, a variegated sweet chestnut,

a flame red embothrium and a tall trachycarpus, it seemed appropriate to remind myself that we were in Ireland. We passed a replica of one of the Trafalgar Square lions. (There is another out at the front gate.) Remember: Still in Ireland…

Eugene places shrubs and trees to create vistas to lure walkers this way and that. The view across one stretch of lawn might be toward an inviting *allée,* a stand-out tree, a huge outcrop of stone, or the hills in the distance.

The energy of it all, the positive ions, the noise, the colour, this three-acre garden is a different and exciting prospect every visit. In that stretch of river, it also homes what I think is is the best water feature of any garden in the country.

Coosheen

15, Johnstown Park, Glaunthaune, County Cork. Contact: Hester and Patrick Forde. Tel: 021 435 3855 / 086 8654972. e-mail: hesterforde@gmail.com www.hesterfordegarden.com Open: By appointment to groups. Special features: Plants for sale. Snowdrop event in spring. Directions: In Glounthaune, with the church on the left, travel towards the train station. Turn left after the station. Turn right across the slip road and the garden is second last on the left. Park on the slip road near the trees. If travelling by coach ring ahead for parking details.

Coosheen is nothing short of a *tour de force*. Hester and Patrick came to their third-of-an-acre site many years ago when it was given over to gooseberries and apples. They began to experiment and discovered that the soil was rock-hard and that it had once been the site of a quarry. Crowbars rather than shovels were the tools of choice. Thoughts of quarries do not spring to mind today, walking around this jewellery box of a garden, a mixture of precision design and lush display.

An obvious love of woodland plants can be seen everywhere and there are scores of plants that do well in light shade growing under the numerous tree ferns, shrubs and small trees. Japanese acers feature strongly. Actually the number of different trees in this compact garden, is a testament to their skills as designers. It never feels overcrowded or too shaded. Most people with small gardens run a mile from the thought of trees, either from concerns about fear of lack of space, or of too much shade. Anyone who thinks that trees should form an orderly line around the boundary would do well to visit Coosheen.

Apart from small trees, if there is one unifying

item here it must be agapanthus. Their big and not-so-big royal blue, white, peacock and violet flowers seem to be everywhere, even self-seeding into the sides of paths. Such fecundity makes lesser gardeners feel envious.

There are so many other must-have plants too, from *Bessera elegans* which has strange square,

hollow stems, to delicate little species *Gladiolus dalenii*. Contrasting dahlias splash colour about the place from summer to autumn and there are always some roses showing off. On the matter of showing off, I adored the mix of blue and black *Salvia patens* combined with orange dahlias, and purple *Salvia guaranitica*.

The house is on a ledge and overlooks the sloped front garden which is surrounded by a dense boundary of shrubs. This area is in the path of whipping winds that need to be battled. Yet, in farming terms, there are no 'plainer cattle' here. It seems that the sheer number of special shrubs packed together, transforms fine specimens of *Cornus controversa*, young blue cedars and *Acer palmatum* 'Shiro' into shelter belt plants, where they protect both each other and the inner garden. Is that the Cork effect? Squeezed in between the cedars and maples, there are tall grasses, camellias, magnolias and clematis. Actually there are clematis everywhere, from *Clematis* 'Vyvyan Pennell' to the green flowering *C. florida* 'Alba Plena'. Look for them climbing shrubs, trees, poles, obelisks and walls.

The stepped area in front of the house is where the miniatures live: You will want to get down on hands and knees to get a proper look at these fun-sized salvias, eucomis and geraniums, hostas and leptospermums in their scree containers surrounded by miniscule rocks. These could be the plants that might live around a doll's house.

She could rightly be called a plant fashionista with a love for the new and interesting. Be assured that she will be able to show you some impossible-to-find treat. The most recent treasures spotted included a weird, if appropriately named *Colchicum* 'Old Bones'.

Hester never fails to surprise. The most recent change has been the almost miraculous landing of a stylish greenhouse in the midst of the already full garden. How she managed this feat is beyond me. Inside, it is like a sweet shop full of treasures such as spindly little *Pelargonium sidoides* and *Pelargonium* 'Arctic Star'. Hester told me that, despite the high walls and gates, rabbits have found their way into her garden and are driving her mad, eating her lovely dianthus. Even paradise suffers trouble...

Drishane House

Castletownshend, Skibbereen, Co. Cork. Tel: 028 36126. e-mail: jane.somerville@hotmail.co.uk www.drishane.com Contact: Tom and Jane Somerville. Open: For selected days May-Oct. As part of the West Cork Garden Trail. Contact for annual dates. Not wheelchair accessible. No dogs. Special features: Tours of garden and the historic home of writer Edith Somerville. Museum. Accommodation. Events. Directions: At the top of the hill in Castletownshend.

Drishane House was the historic home of Edith Somerville, artist and one half of the famous Somerville and Ross writing team.

The slate-fronted Georgian house comes into view at the top of a drive lined by magnolias, camellias, blue hydrangeas and ferns. The gothic giant of a *Cupressus macrocarpa* or Monterey cypress, only 160 years old, will send a satisfying shiver down the spine of the arriving garden visitor. There have been gardens at Drishane for as long as there has been a house. Care has varied but in different ways each of the nine generations have left their mark. Tom and Jane Somerville are the current owners and gardeners. Tom explained that his parents did a lot here but it was still overgrown when he took it on. 'They didn't have the machines. Too much garden and too little manpower,' is how he put it, as we admired *Magnolia* 'Leonard Messel' *M. stellata*, a flowering cornus, a big copper beech and columnar gingko - all of which were planted by his parents. We walked out from the house between scented yellow rhododendrons and a tall liriodendron or tulip tree. We thanked the senior Somervilles for these too.

Only two pillars and some steps remain of the old kitchen garden. The walls were taken down so it could be turned into a croquet lawn and replaced by a line of white flowering eucryphia and some old daffodils.

The gardens cover about four acres, while another dozen or so are given over to woods, which until recently had become hopelessly choked with laurel.

Tom and Jane, wielding machines, have now carved their way through, clearing laurel and revealing a bluebell, primrose and foxglove wood.

Tom told me that we would visit the Amphitheatre, the home to a 5,000 year-old stone, carved with intriguing looking holes. The amphitheatre is a little opening in the woods overlooking the sea. We sat on a curved stone bench, spiked with hart's tongue fern in under an umbrella of witchy-looking crataegus. If there were ever plays put on here, they were small productions. This is an intimate space. As for the stone steps set into the hill, later we would see them again in a painting by Edith, up at the house. We continued on the newly cleared and restored paths through the wood, to the orchard.

The sheltered orchard is itself overlooked by a stone cottage in which Edith did her writing. It too was hidden until recently, beneath bramble, bracken and rough. The view from here takes in Galley Head and a bay where Spanish ships fought and sank. I pointed to a ruin over on Horse Island and was told that it was built by an ancestor known as Tom the Merchant, to light and guide his ships home.

As we sat and Tom showed and told me about a strange fairy shoe found in 1832 in the Caha Mountains. The shoe eventually ended up in the care of the Somervilles. Tom has a letter dated to 1901 attesting to the shoe's authentic provenance. Edith was obviously not the only teller of tales in the Somerville family…

Dromboy

Carrignavar, Co. Cork. Tel: 021 4884555. 087 0553245. e-mail g.odonoghue27@gmail.com
Contact: Maurice and Gertie O'Donoghue. Open: To groups by appointment and occasional annual open days. Contact for details. Special features: Children under supervision. Dogs on leads. Teas by arrangement. Directions: At Rathduff on the main Cork-Mallow road (N20) take the Carrignavar exit. Continue to T-junction and turn right. At a three road junction take the middle road. Take the next left. The garden is the second entrance on the right.

The garden at Carrignavar comes upon visitors as a surprise. Set on an elevated spot about 200 metres above sea level in north Cork, Gertie and Maurice O'Donoghue's garden is as hard to find as treasure. Even arriving at the gates and travelling up the straight drive, there is little to declare this as the home of something special. Lined with well-clipped conifers, and clean white betulas, the drive is tidy and ordered but not especially indicative of the garden waiting to be seen. However, arriving at the top of the drive the magic becomes apparent in a spread of perfect, rolled, striped lawn, edged in a way that defies nature. They could probably write a textbook on keeping an old-school lawn. Meanwhile, the house, straight ahead, can barely be seen under blankets of climbers, creepers and general growth, giving the impression that the O'Donoghues live inside a garden.

I could certainly live in the hosta groves on either side of the drive: On one side, study the numerous species and varieties, planted in drifts around a little stone-lined pond, under a carved-out *Myrtus communis* or common myrtle. The other hosta garden is built around a stumpery and wooded area. The large mirror set between the trees doubles its size. Wild foxgloves and sprays of native ferns set the hostas off, while cleverly placed boulders finish off this naturalistic look. The contrast between this calm, dark corner and some of the bright flower borders, is almost a shock. In the silver garden, the artemisias, erigeron, astelias, white geraniums, dahlias and euphorbias, illustrate this perfectly. The pink border, next door is just as impressive, a clever confection of every shade of pink geranium, campanula, lupin and poppy. The unusual weeping elm grown like a set of parted curtains, is a fine sight.

Gertie is the plantswoman. Maurice has a talent with hard landscaping and he makes the soulful sculptures that are so much a part of the place. Together they have created a marvel covering about two acres, divided into a number of rooms, each with a different, definite style. If there is a common theme to be found here it is that of impeccable upkeep. The standards set would put most of us to shame. If there is a stretch of gravel it will be free of weeds, loose leaves and debris. If something is clipped, it will be clipped perfectly. I loved the 'lollipop' garden, a collection of clipped box, euonymus and privet, all pruned into different height lollipops. It sounds silly and looks great.

Many of the best vignettes include Maurice's sculptures. In one corner there might be an arch of privet around a little statue in an ivy cloak. Elsewhere it could be a fieldstone pyramid, like a posh insect hotel. The gallery of prehistoric looking stone heads stopped me in my tracks. Maurice unearths boulders in the course of digging. The shape of a stone suggests an idea and he modifies it to further bring out that sense. In so doing, he produces works that add an intriguing extra dimension to the garden.

The surprises are around every corner, from secret pond gardens, sunny dry river bed and scree gardens with silvered celmisia grown in weed-like proportions, to shaded mossy corners, formal flower beds and big bulging shrub borders. At each turn, there seems to be another diverting sight from a collection of pots gathered together behind the house, to topiary works tucked into a corner. Such an amalgamation of features and plant combinations so meticulously minded, calls for the sort of study one visit alone will not satisfy…

The Ewe Experience

Kenmare Road, Glengarriff, Co. Cork. Tel: 027 63840. e-mail info@theewe.com www.theewe.com Contact: Sheena Wood and Kurt Lyndorff. Open: Every day. June-Aug. Check website for annual details or ring in advance. Special features: Interpretative, interactive sculpture garden. Poetry trail. Gallery. Guide dogs welcome. Directions: Travel on the N71 out of Glengarriff toward Kenmare. Well signed.

Gardens are not generally things that relocate, but the Ewe Experience is not a general sort of garden. 22 years ago it was created out on the Beara Peninsula in Goleen. Then in 2004 it gave people a reason to do a double take when it suddenly cropped up in Glengarriff, carved into the side of a seriously hilly and tiered bit of mountain, a few kilometres out of the village. Hearing it described as an 'interactive sculpture garden,' one might expect a sort of museum/ visitor centre with touch screen thingys. That would be a bad description. This is a quirky, inspired, silly, wild, beautiful place. It is a garden for gardeners, and everyone else too.

My most recent visit was on the wettest of days after one of the wettest of weeks in the summer. There were floods throughout Cork and Kerry. The rain, however, served only to improve a walk through the Ewe. From under the canopy of holly, oak, ash and birch, it rained in sheets yet I was able to walk dry, under the trees. For much of the garden the roar of water that can be heard is tremendous. Beside the entrance expect the sight and sound of a waterfall that rips down the hill with nothing short of fury, landing in a turbulent stream below the entrance bridge. First prize for the most exhilarating welcome to a garden in the country? Yes.

From here the route winds through six acres of trees, up and down hills between Sheena Woods' witty sculptures, picking out a route between intricate rustic fences, along alleys lined with boulders, wood sorrel and moss. You might stop to play solitaire on a slate and pebble table. In some places willow walls and wooden pegs hold back the mountain. Overhead there are copper beeches and below, alpine strawberries, ferns and grasses. Good walking boots are recommended because many of the paths feature snaking roots and emerging rocks. At the summit of the hilly wood garden, the path reaches an unexpected sunny opening. A Neolithic copper mine was found in these hills and the information about it is laid out.

While the place feels barely tamed, it is in fact like an intricate web of plants, art and games, horticultural jokes and strange features, ecological statements and general wizardry.

Fernhill Hotel

Clonakilty, Co. Cork. Tel: 023 8833 258. e-mail:info@fernhillhousehotel.com
www.fernhillhousehotel.com Contact: Reception. Open: All year. Partially wheelchair accessible. Children
welcome. Guide dogs. Special features: Hotel open year round. Groups may book a tour. Restaurant.
Refreshments can be booked. Directions: Signed from the town centre.

Four generations of the O'Neills have lived and worked the hotel and gardens at Fernhill. There were well known Victorian and Edwardian gardens here, but as was so often the case, they declined during the middle years of the last century. As they are seen today, the gardens are mostly the work of more recent and current generations. As a hotel garden, Fernhill is somewhat unusual: Part of the wide sloped, site overlooking the town is arranged in the sort of decorous flower gardens one might expect. There are big wisteria-clad pergolas, falling stream and boulder gardens with wooden walkways and boardwalks that cut between the plants and run over the water. There are bamboo walks, flower borders, sheltered arbours and rose gardens. I sat into a swinging bench, tucked under a huge puff of *Cryptomeria japonica* that split in a recent storm, but marches on regardless, looking good.

There is even a summerhouse, home to a little Child of Prague, a character seemingly vital to the business of keeping rain away from wedding parties. The summerhouse is covered in golden hops and fringed with ferns. All the paths are wheelchair accessible, which is a welcome and fairly unusual feature. So much for the first garden. The style then begins to change – at first in subtle ways, then more

dramatically. In recent years designer Mary Reynolds was invited in to advise and with her help, the O'Neills began to create a wild garden that would be sustainable and ecologically sound. Mown grass gives way to longer meadow. The smart trimmed shrubs slide gently into looser more informal shapes. The natural pond, surrounded by raised banks of wild flowers is particularly pretty, spotted with mallow, poppies, ragged robin, iris, and phacelia. Young fig and apple trees have been spot planted here too.

A full native apple orchard, the trees of which were planted by couples that married here, merges into a new wood where they planted 1,400 oak, ash and hazel on terraces. Alder, known as the Rock 'n Roll tree, due to its live fast and die young tendencies, is also included in the mix, making the area look more mature than it otherwise might. These trees will eventually provide a crop of timber, which will be sustainably cut as the wood fills out. The aim is that this will be a wild, productive valley garden.

All water in the garden is recycled. The pond is gravity fed and they are experimenting with every aspect of good husbandry. This is a juvenile garden, being admirably worked. It will be an intriguing one to follow and learn from as it matures.

Fota House Arboretum & Gardens

Fota Island, Carrigtwohill, Co. Cork. Tel: 021 4812 728. 087 79072 99. www.heritageireland.ie www.fotahouse.com. For gardens: Contact: David O'Regan (OPW). Open: All year. See website for seasonal changes. Car charge. Supervised children welcome. Dogs on leads. Special features: Seasonal café. Shop. Wildlife Park. For Frameyard: Contact: Vincent Bartley, (Irish Historic Trust). Tel: 021 4815 737 e-mail: fotahouse@irishheritagetrust.ie www.fotahouse.com Open: Mon-Fri. 10.30am-3pm. Sunday, 11.30am-3pm (See website for seasonal changes). Separate charge to gardens. Special features: Plants for sale. Events. Seasonal café. Directions: Take the Cobh exit off the N25 marked R624. The entrance is approximately 3km along on right.

Fota was formerly known as 'Foatey' which means 'warm turf'. This is an appropriate name for a garden that basks in the mild Cork climate and is blessed with fertile brown earth conducive to rapid plant growth. The Victorian garden designer, William Robinson said that the bamboos grew as well here as they did in their native China.

The garden covers 27 acres and is attached to the grand house built by the Smith-Barry family in the early 19th century. Working well into the 20th century, they planted the finest trees and plants from all over the world. The result was an arboretum of remarkable proportions, a range of pleasure gardens, a fernery, an Italian garden, a lake and a walled garden.

Fota's pleasure garden is well named. Leave the front of the house and cross the expanse of lawn that fills up with picnicking families and kissing couples in the summer. Make for the trees, stopping for a look into the restored *orangerie* with its containerised citrus trees. Two huge Canary Island date palms or *Phoenix canariensis* advertise the location of the arboretum. One of these measured eight metres in 1984. From here there are special trees in all directions, from the Camphor tree or *Cinnamomum camphora* native of Japan to a Mexican *Cupressus lusitanica*. The evergreen oak (*Quercus ilex*) has an awe-inspiring canopy and the Wellingtonia or *Sequoiadendron giganteum* from California measured 31x4.8m in '84. Its spongy-barked trunk continues to rise skyward. Walking between and under the Monterey pines (*Pinus radiata*) is an experience. Making your way along this trail is like taking a trip around the world. It would be hard not to fall in love with trees in Fota. Each visit throws up another favourite. On my last visit it was a monster cork oak or *Quercus suber*.

The fernery is a natural-looking maze-like rock formation smothered in deep, velvety moss, sprouting all sorts of ferns in the shade of sweet chestnut and umbrella-like *Dicksonia antarctica* tree ferns. Visit ferneries in the rain. The leaves are at their best dripping water. Sadly on my last visit, part of the fernery had been fenced off because of vandalising children, climbing on and killing the plants. Behind the wire it will hopefully regenerate soon.

Close by, the lake is a naturalistic expanse of water, with a scattering of lilies over its surface and wild flowers, gunnera, bamboo and grasses around the edge. One tree near the pond, a *Cryptomeria japonica* 'Spiralis' or 'Granny's Ringlets' is like a renegade from a willow pattern plate. Do not miss it.

Within the walled garden, the Italian garden earned its name because of the presence of a decorative 15th century well-head in the centre. I wondered where the scent of thyme came from, and gardener David O'Regan pointed to the fringes of self-seeded thyme along the tops of the walls, the echo of an old, lost herb garden.

Lined along the walls of the larger walled garden, there are beds full of banana plants, verbena, hardy plumbago and a most impressive length of wisteria. In the centre of one long bed are a classical folly and a massive *Magnolia grandiflora,* planted in 1847, that was originally espaliered against the wall. All this overlooks stands of multi-trunked cordylines and yew hedging in the middle of restoration work.

The walled garden also carries a collection of 160 varieties of Irish-bred daffodils. There is a bed of monocots – plants that start life with only one seed leaf and later on, bear often strappy leaves with parallel veins, running the length of one of the walls. Arrangements of libertia, grasses, phormium, tradescantia, iris, crocosmia and hemerocallis make up much of the display. Plants from central and South America and shade-loving plants fill another of the borders. There are generous displays of primula, pulmonaria, hellebore, hosta and astilbe. The old roses above these include showy pink *Rosa* 'Comte de Chambord', *Rosa de rescht* and well named *R.* 'Old Pink Moss',which was bred in 1700.

The latest attraction at Fota is the frame yard, set within another walled garden. This area, with its extensive series of buildings and glasshouses, was once the hub of industry on the estate and home to the gardeners. It had been closed for decades and was derelict. Like the contents of an old attic, all the bits were still in place – if not intact and so a few years ago

a great restoration programme by the Irish Heritage Trust was set up. The result is a real treat for gardening anoraks. Visit the bothys and the little sitting room the gardeners used, the fruit stores and sleeping areas, the rain harvesting systems and the pit house used for growing tropical fruit. The houses are back in business, like new, complete with all the intricate fittings and the fine Valentia-slate staging. Next door in the last walled area, there is a new Irish heritage apple orchard, being worked organically.

Make a point of timing a visit for a day and time during which all parts of the gardens can be visited.

Future Forests

Kealkill, Bantry, Co. Cork. Tel: 027 66176. e-mail: info@futureforests.ie. www.futureforests.ie Contact: Reception. Open: Every day. Times change seasonally. See website for changes. Special features: Nursery. Mail order service. Directions: On the R584, travelling from Bantry to Cork, just under 4 km from Kealkill village.

Future Forests, is appropriately set in the middle of the woods north east of Bantry. This is no ordinary nursery. It spreads out around what looks like a giant, storybook, fairy-tale wooden house, all wobbly lines and bulging gables, with an undulating living roof, made of sedums, houseleeks and grasses.

Once you have stopped marvelling at its weird and wonderful lines, the nursery is also worth looking at. This welcoming place was set up back in the 1980s by Mike and and Cathy Collard. Maria and Mattie Collard Keane, are the next generation, busily

dispatching their ethically grown plants all over the country and abroad.

Backed by the shelter of a big wood, the plants are ranged nicely around the nursery and there are all sorts of interesting specimens to pore over. The whole operation is run on organic and sustainable principles. After 25 years, the Future Forest people have quite a deal of know-how at their fingertips and are happy to impart it. It is rightly popular among gardeners, and well worth a detour.

Garra Fado Garden

Inches, Eyeries, Beara, Co. Cork. Tel: 027 74844. 086 8397149. e-mail garrafado@gmail.com www.garrafadogardens.com. Special features: Nursery. Teas can be arranged. Contact: Connie Torpie. Open: All year 11am-6pm. Dogs on leads welcome. Special features: Nursery. Directions: On the R571. 7 km from Castletownbere and 41 km from Kenmare.

Connie Torpie's nursery garden is a place that should be of interest to anyone considering a seaside garden. She specialises in plants that bear up to the onslaught of salt winds and the nursery is located in a particularly open and exposed spot outside Castletownbere, looking over at the Slieve Mish and Caha Mountains. Connie grows her hardy, tough plants outside, where

they fend for themselves in the prevailing conditions. She reminded me that the garden also sits in a frost pocket. So plants that fare well here will fare well anywhere.

She mixes hydrangeas, tall fennel, teasels and cosmos with rudbeckia and echinops. I like the stone deck around the pond set right into the middle of the borders. This pond is unlined and a testament to how moisture-retentive the ground is. Add to the list of hurdles cleared, the fact that her plants can also deal with soggy ground.

The vegetable garden is reached by way of an arch covered by a huge kiwi or *Actinidia arguta*. It is a functional home to stands of black kale and red lettuce, carrots and beets, all growing well on Connie's seaweed diet. The atmosphere in the nursery is relaxed and the plants are happy. I was escorted around by a busy little dog called Chopper. As I left he joined a new arrival for a tour of the flowers.

Glebe Gardens

The Glebe, Baltimore, Co. Cork. Tel: 028 20579. e-mail info@glebegardens.com www.glebegardens.com Contact: Jean and Peter Perry. Open: April-Sept. Wed-Sun and Bank holidays, 10am-6pm. Groups by appointment. Supervised children. Dogs on leads. Special features: Restaurant. Produce for sale. Directions: Approaching Baltimore on the N71, the garden is on the right-hand side opposite the 'Baltimore' signpost.

Negotiating the tightrope between productive and ornamental is tough, particularly when trying to provide a restaurant with vegetables and fruit. It is even tougher doing it from a garden in the rocky roughs around Baltimore in West Cork. The Perry family have been doing that for many years. Theirs is a market garden that is also aesthetically pleasing, growing a range of vegetables, fruit, flowers and herbs, in a hard-worked plot attached to the family restaurant.

In the summer the little courtyard garden beside the restaurant is tangy with the smell of lemon verbena, purple-flowered hyssop and rue. Golden hops and towering echiums alive with industrious bees fight for space and black kale, dahlias and *Hydrangea* 'Annabelle' soften the corners. The stone arch in the wall has a big cloak of clematis over it and underneath there are pots of scented lilies. There are scores of other pots too, from pelargoniums and cosmos to ginger lilies. On the larger scale there is also a lemon scented magnolia, tree peonies and roses on pergolas. At the centre of the courtyard the big olive tree has been here for years 'and it deals with everything – wind, rain, cold, everything! It even fruits in some years,' Jean said.

To reach the rest of the garden, take a set of steps, bounded by fuchsia and lace-cap white hydrangeas, between borders on top of pencil slim stone ledges, and swoon in the perfume of a *Cercis siliquastrum*. Continue through a gap in the hedge, to reach the Mediterranean garden which actually feels Mediterranean. On my most recent visit, it was a rare dry day and the scent of salvia, golden oregano and thyme battled for dominance in the air as alpine strawberries sprouted from every little crack in whatever bits of low stone walls that were not covered in trailing rosemary.

This garden was hard won. 'We literally dug the herb garden out with a crowbar,' said Jean. 'Even then some of the stone was too tough to move. But herbs like the stony ground.' I cannot imagine how much work went into preparing the ground for the double borders, but looking at the results, it was worth it. All those hot red and rust dahlias, magenta lychnis, red salvias, roses, amaranthus and sweet peas, under puffs of purple cotinus and paulownia are a knock-out.

Beyond all this colour and action, the wider garden is a more sedate place. It is here that Jean is creating an edible wood garden, planting fruit bushes under the existing alder, elder, oak and sycamore. The path through it eventually leads to a pond, green with duckweed, and peaceful. I crossed the water on a rustic wooden bridge, emerging out from under the trees, to a sunny meadow and an amphitheatre where they hold concerts in the summer. Walking along the mown path between runs of meadow grass, I was observed by a pair of stately goats guarding the bee hives.

Glenview Gardens

Desert, Enniskeane, Co. Cork. Tel: 023 8847 230. 087 2535 971.
e-mail: glenviewgardens@hotmail.com. www.facebook.com/glenviewgardens. Contact: David and Mary
Tanner. Open: April-Sept. Daily 10am-5pm. Wheelchair accessible. Special features: Hobbit house. Fairy
trail. Pet corner. Teas. Events. Wedding photos. School tours. Directions: From Clonakilty: Take the N71
to Bandon and take the 2nd left 1 km after Ballinascarthy. Follow signs for 7 km to the 3rd cross roads.
Turn left and the garden is 4th on the left.

Occasionally, a picture imprints itself on the brain and stays there. I had pleasant memories of Glenview, David and Mary Tanner's garden near Bandon, but the most recent trip left me with an image that will stay with me for a long time - A wisteria pergola, 70 metres long, the length of an indoor sprint track. The Tanners like the idea of impact. They started out three decades ago with an acre, becoming more and more entranced with all things horticultural as the years went on. Today, they work about four acres of intensive garden, divided into what feel like dozens of different rooms with different accents and moods. That wisteria pergola is only one small corner. Think of wheels within wheels. A long outer walk bounded by a tall beech hedge, is itself the boundary of another walk hemmed in by silvery, fringed *Olearia virgata*. Using this network of sometimes, almost hidden walks, leads into the different garden rooms and sometimes gets you lost. Mary told me that they regularly need the phone to locate both each other, and mislaid visitors.

I made my own way between formal lawns enclosed within laser-sharp, clipped circular beech hedging, ducking onto a path that forks and forks again, travelling under the arched bamboo, into a hydrangea walk. There are white gardens that morph into madly colourful flower borders, on past water gardens and ponds, woods, Japanese and bog gardens. One route will bring you to a summer house and formal *allée*, a wild flower meadow, a walled vegetable garden or maybe an exotic shrub and tree display.

It is, simply a mad party of a garden and in the middle, do not be surprised to find a display of exotic birds and a viewing platform from where to inspect the large neighbouring field of maize. Finally, follow a plume of smoke that leads to the hobbit house where there will be a wee fire in a tiny hobbit hearth.

Heron Gallery Gardens

Ahakista, Durrus, Bantry, Co. Cork. Contact: Annabel Langrish. Tel: 027 67278. e-mail:annabellangrish@
gmail.com www.herongallery.ie Open: Easter-Aug. Not wheelchair accessible. Supervised children welcome
due to pond. Dogs on leads welcome. Special features: Gallery. Café. Animals. Directions: Take the Sheepshead
road from Durrus. After Arundel's Bar at Ahakista turn right. The garden is 300m uphill on the left.
Signed.

The first time I saw this garden I spent so much time reprimanding myself for not having come to see it sooner I almost ruined the visit. Annabel Langrish is an artist. Looking at her garden just outside Durrus, that is obvious. Her cleverly put-together sculptures are scattered everywhere through her entirely individual garden. From the car park across the road with the lobster pots and buoys artfully hanging on the wall of a stone shed, to the fences made of beach-combed, salt-bleached branches, and the uprighted railway sleeper festooned with broken and worn garden tools, this is a place that oozes style.

I love it all. I particularly love that in such a wild, untamed spot, the garden is worked in a completely organic and sustainable way, planting its small footprint on its surroundings. Even better is the fact that it seems to work to entertain adults and children equally without taking away from either. The Sensory Walk, an uphill route, over a series of surfaces from grass and chamomile to gravel, wooden cobbles, shingles and a host of other surfaces, is clever.

The centrepiece of the garden however must be the large natural pond that takes up a good proportion of the site, surrounded by irises, rushes, grasses and shingle. It teems with wildlife.

Close to the gallery, there are informally arranged, herb, vegetable and flower beds between rocky pebbled paths. The found object sculptures, crop up all over and add hugely to the look.

The site is rugged to say the least and the garden Annabel has created is equally so, at home and at ease in its wild surroundings. She never tries to impose something too alien on the natural beauty of the land, insinuating a clump of zantedeschia or some heirloom primulas, white bluebells and cosmos between boulders and seaside pebbles. It is also a great hilly workout as you make your way through this lightly tamed place.

Ilnacullin

Garinish Island, Glengarriff, Co. Cork. Tel: 027 63040. e-mail: garnishisland@opw.ie www.heritageireland.ie Contact: Donal O'Sullivan. Open: Mar-Oct. See website for seasonal hours. Supervised children. Dogs on leads. Partially wheelchair accessible. Special features: Island garden. Tea rooms. House tours. Directions: Situated 1.5 km off the coast from Glengarriff.

Ilnacullin sits in the harbour of Glengarriff in Bantry Bay, an island with views out to sea and back to the mainland. The Harbour Queen boat was pulling out as I arrived but they came back to pick up this late sailor. We set off, out over the water, past basking seals draped over rocks. The boat made its easy way over the water and the journey was as always, a pleasure. It could not however, prepare me for the pleasure that this latest visit to Ilnacullin would bring. The garden and house have undergone a long needed restoration and the place is looking really well.

The 37-acre windswept, gorse-covered, island was bought by Annan Bryce in 1910. He employed the famous English landscaper and architect Harold Peto to build a seven storey house and garden. This plan was scuppered when the family fortune was lost as a result of the Russian Revolution. Heaven knows what a building of such height would have looked like, but the garden and a smaller house are what we have today.

Bear in mind that everything here is just over a century old. A photograph of the island in 1913 shows bare rock. Yet botanists say it has undergone the equivalent of two centuries of growth since Peto's plans were put into effect. While the Gulf Stream and huge annual rainfall make it possible to grow exotic plants from Australia, New Zealand and the tropics with success, Ilnacullin was not without its difficulties. That rock had no more than a miserable sprinkle of rain-leached soil, low in organic material and fertility. The island was no paradise. It required enormous quantities of imagination for Mr Bryce to create a garden here. The struggle to cart equally huge amounts of good soil over the water and fight salt-laden winds in the early years can only be imagined. In 1928 the Scottish gardener Murdo Mackenzie arrived and applied himself to erecting a shelter belt within which the more tender plants could begin to grow.

Today a visit starts at the restored house, which adds hugely to the *turas*. It has been faithfully restored to what it looked like in the early decades of the 20th century, containing Bryce's collection of Greek and Roman antiquities, alongside Peto's plans. The little garden in front of the rose-covered house, lies in a man-made valley. Its half-door, flanked by pots of brugmansia, looks out on five huge, perfectly centred pines. From here the path leads to the Italian Garden, past stands of mature myrtles over drifts of pink crinum lilies.

The Italian Garden is the most famous feature here, with its casita or tea house and pergola, built from golden Bath stone and incorporating variously coloured marbles, from prestigious Carrara to local Connemara, all used to tile the rectangular central pool. The plants used include venerable bonsai, flowering leptospermum, myrtle, camellia and rhododendron, wisteria and sprawling clematis. On different visits, different plants stand out. This time *Abutilon* 'Cloth of Gold' and *A.* 'Ashford Red' were the stars. The surrounding yew hedges were in the middle of being restored by hard cutting back. To the southwest, the Sugarloaf Mountain is an exceptionally dramatic backdrop to all of this.

Leaving here, the trail leads in several directions. One wide rough, stone path leads uphill to a Grecian Temple to a point where the formality of the lower garden is cast off in favour of slightly tempered wild growth. Big stands of blue agapanthus and a fine Chilean fire bush or *Embothrium coccineum* welcome you into the temple to enjoy a view out over the sea. The straddle stones on either side of the path were once used to drape corn, keeping it out of the reach of rats as it dried. From here, the trail swoops downhill and into Happy Valley, a walk past an impressive *Dacrydium franklinii* from Tasmania and lower layers of flowering shrubs. The ravages of the 2014 storms are still visible among the older trees and replanting is underway to replace the losses. The rock is never far from the surface, peeping out and reminding visitors that this garden was gouged, using dynamite.

There are so many special trees, like the *Phyllocladus trichomanoides,* or celery pine from New Zealand that is one of the biggest specimens growing outdoors on these islands. Close by the extent of sweet scented *Drimys winteri* had us entranced. As did a ten metre tall *Cinnamomum camphora* planted in 1991. The path leads between ferns and recumbent pines hugging and mimicking the rock as it climbs back uphill, toward the Martello tower. This was built at a commanding point on the island at the time of the Napoleonic wars. In summer alpine strawberries grow in the shaley earth below, basking in the sun and begging to be eaten. Donal O'Sullivan told me how the tower was designed so that only a left-handed soldier climbing the interior stairs would have an advantage over the defenders overhead, and the number of left-handed people was lower than it is today. Standing on top of the tower lost in the beauty of it all, it was hard to imagine this place as something designed for hand to hand combat.

The track continues back down towards the garden by way of a rocky gorse-and-heather-strewn outcrop called the Viewing Point. It eventually leads into the walled garden and back into all things preened and tended. Two double borders dominate the space, filled with echinops, watsonia and phlox, asters, cimicifuga and *Cardiocrinum giganteum*, campanula and verbascum. These are all planted tightly, cheek-by-jowl, all holding each other up.

A side path leads from this explosion of flowers over to a Roman sarcophagus from 600 AD. Having left the flash borders to see this we were now in a little wildflower area with roses on wires and espaliered fruit trees. I loved the *Pileostegia viburnoides* that climbs the tower at the outer wall. The boat was due so we left reluctantly past an impressively large *Magnolia grandiflora*.

Inish Beg Gardens

Inish Beg Estate, Baltimore, Co. Cork. Tel: 028 21745. e-mail: info@inishbeg.com www.inishbeg.com. Contact: Paul and Georgiana Keane. Open: All year 10am-5pm but ring in advance to check, as gardens close on wedding days. No dogs. Partially wheelchair accessible. Special features: Accommodation. Children's Pirate and Fairy Trails. Café in summer. Catering for groups can be booked. Events. Directions: Situated on the R595 approx 6 km south of Skibbereen. Turn right just after the sign for 'Canon Goodman's Grave' and travel over the bridge to the island.

On my first visit, I couldn't find this garden. An exasperated phone call was answered with directions to 'turn off the road and drive over the bridge to the island.' Those words, 'the island' have a fizz of extra excitement about them. From the outset, Inish Beg has that fizz. It feels like the sort of place Agatha Christie could have had a wonderful time killing off people in a country house whodunnit. From the stone bridge over the water, the drive leads under some dramatic Lebanese cedars, onto a sunken avenue that then climbs a hill lined with beech and oak. A second stretch of avenue includes a lower storey of cherries under the oak and beech. Add masses of bluebells, ferns, hostas, cyclamen, tulips and daffodils naturalising on the ground under these. Now that is what I call an entrance.

The house looks out over lawns bounded by unusual, beach-stone walls, groves of flowering myrtles, magnolias and some old white cherries.

The main body of the garden however, is taken up with walks through 40 acres of woods planted back in 1895, between groves of ferns and tree ferns, and along sunken, stone-lined streams. One of these leads out to the River Ilen as it makes it its way to the Atlantic. One could be convinced that this is simply a case of nature untamed, wild and perfect. It is in fact, a carefully tweaked, worked woodland garden. The older, mainly native woods have been enhanced with specimen trees and shrubs. Japanese acers have been planted under the tall canopy of ash and beech with camellia and bamboo in the shelter of those skyscrapers. The place is a maze of 'barely there' paths

that become even more barely there as the summer goes on. Apart from the large area covered by woods, there are also newly planted orchards and walks out by the sea. Look out for the ponds named for deceased family bulldogs, Boadicea and Pumpkin.

The jewel of Inish Beg, is the walled garden built from found fieldstone on the estate. Its walls come to just about to eye level, a height that means this decorous garden can be seen and enjoyed from outside as well as in. Within the walls, the ground, once cleared of weeds with a team of helpful pigs, was divided by wide paths into big square beds to hold the vegetables and flowers. A notable feature is the use of sturdy metal obelisks and ornamental wigwams for beans and other clambering crops like clematis and roses. The bone structure is good: The low stone walls planted with box hedging enclose large beds of rudbeckia, 'Daniel O'Connell' peas, cosmos and black kale. In other beds, sedum, asters and Florence fennel as well as divine little *Dianthus carthusianorum* are all tidily hemmed in between the box walls. Where box has failed, *Myrtus communis* subsp. *tarentina* has been deployed. Head gardener Tony O'Mahony finds it a useful alternative. The large beds contradict the idea that small beds are easier to work. By secreting mulch paths between lines of heleniums and verbena within the bigger areas, these invisible paths and kneeling spaces render the beds as easy to work as narrower

borders.

The whole walled garden contains only one original plant. This is a big old contorted apple tree that lords it over the young garden giving an air of maturity to proceedings. As a reminder that this is mild west Cork, there are healthy olive trees growing outside. The shelter is provided by a great buffering encirclement of mature trees around the walled garden. Ask to see the auricula theatre. Either full of pots of fancy auriculas in late spring, or empty for the rest of the year, it is a little beauty.

Kilravock Garden

Durrus, Co. Cork. Tel: 085 2015507. e-mail: garden.kilravock@gmail.com www.kilravock.garden Contact: Ronnie Halligan Open: By appointment only. No dogs. Special features: German also spoken. Groups welcome. Directions: 1.6 km from Durrus on the Kilcrohane Road. The garden is on the right and signposted (small blue oval sign).

When Ronnie Halligan retired having lived, worked and gardened in Munich for many years, he set out to walk the length of Ireland, from Malin to Mizen. When he arrived in Durrus, he saw that the garden created by the well known gardeners, Phemie and Malcolm Rose, was for sale. He was smitten and bought it, describing it as 'a thing of beauty and a job forever'.

Kilravock is now approaching its 30th birthday. It is a lush, mature yet hard won garden, created from a stony, boulder-laden site. Rock is never far from the surface and always in the way of where one might want to get a spade or fork into the ground. It was with hardship that it was wrested from the tough Atlantic coastal landscape. Getting things to establish on the edge of the ocean is in itself indication of a large mountain conquered. Once establishment is achieved however, not too much care is required. The plants more or less take care of themselves.

The garden gets a great deal of rain. The free-draining nature of the ground and the warm climate permit a population of unusual, rare, and seldom-seen plants from all over the world. There are scores of different restios, a collection of over 70 species and varieties of sorbus, including a square fruited *Sorbus hostii*. The birds adore its fancy fruits.

The garden is not just made of the rare and exotic however. Out in the open section, collections of acacias and acers grow beside the more humble pheasant berry or *Leycesteria formosa*. If a plant is good-looking it is good-looking.

The house stands on a south-facing ledge, wrapped in blankets of climbing plants from the delectably scented *Trachelospermum jasminoides* and *Jasminum officinale* 'Aureovariegatum', to the bluebell creeper *Billardiera heterophylla* and *Cissus striata*, the evergreen ivy of Uruguay. Underneath, pink flowering, fuzzy, *Echium tuberculatum* grows like a weed, as does strobilanthes, which elbows its way in between mounds of hardy geraniums. Bees adore the pink echium flowers.

The oriental area beside the house has been a long-time favourite of visitors. It features raked gravel, a stream, Japanese anemone and a spreading umbrella of *Acer palmatum* 'Dissectum' which, like many of the other acers here, is draped over a rock. The big *Rhododendron sinogrande* by the water is also gorgeous. Above this area, the spring garden is made up of more rhododendrons and huge acacia overhead. Meanwhile lobelia, salvia, hosta, primulas and ferns fight for space in the damp streamside.

Ronnie has a simple approach to adding to the garden. He takes a fancy to a plant, reads up on it and then tries it out, usually with good results. Sea hollies, or eryngiums, are a current enthusiasm. We also stopped to admire the fascinating geometric arrangement of berries on a young *Pseudopanax laetus*.

The two-acre garden is ice cream-cone shaped, with the narrow end reached through a tunnel of white wisteria, golden hop and clematis. Finally, there is the Mediterranean tower. Yes, a Mediterranean tower, in Cork.

Specialist, complicated gardens such as this rarely survive from one owner to another. Kilravock is a happy exception.

Lag Bridge Garden

Rath, Baltimore, Co. Cork. Tel: 028 20148. e-mail: beacondesigns@eircom.net www.beacondesignsknit.com Contact: Bebhinn Marten. Open for the Secret Gardens of Baltimore Weekend and at other times by appointment. Wheelchair accessible but paths are grass. No children under 12. No dogs. Special feature: Designer woollen boutique. Directions: Driving from Skibbereen to Baltimore, the garden is on the right hand side, signposted.

Bebhinn Marten told me that what she does in her garden is simply add to what is around her. 'I don't try to improve it'. Given the extraordinary location, this is both sensitive and sensible. The garden is laid out along the edge of the water on the outskirts of Baltimore. Massive outcropping boulders rise like icebergs and the garden actually appears to wash like the sea up against them. 'It would be difficult to make a bad garden here,' she said.

That stated, weather and salt are two very real conditions that need to be tackled. Every few years, floods soak the ground in salt water and salt winds play havoc with any plants not equipped for seaside life. So Bebhinn grows almost all her plants from seed. She thinks that home grown plants are sturdier and stronger, able to manage better in the salty environment. 'You end up with a silver and blue garden,' she says. This is no bad thing. The garden is made of 13 big beds distributed around the rock strewn site. Most of the beds are colour matched, with deep blue agapanthus and white veronica in one place. Next door, pink and purple rule in a mass of dahlias, liriopsis, thalictrum, *Viburnum bonariensis*, *Papaver* 'Patty's plum' and perennial wallflowers. Red hot pokers and dahlias are among the most used plants here. It is clear that Bebhinn also likes bearded irises. They are even allotted their own specific bed.

Given that they are surrounded by rock, nature and chaos, Bebhinn keeps the beds looking immaculate and well-hemmed on the garden side with neat brick mowing verges. The lawns too are maintained perfectly. All this order makes the rock look even more untamed and dramatic. I love the mix of wild flowers and occasional self-sown garden plants that sprout from the huge boulders. As the garden melts off out to the surroundings, plants that hug the ground proliferate: Cotoneaster creeps over the outcrops and creates a handsome, changing blanket of colour, flower and berries. The actual boundary is a mix of heather and gorse, clipped tight with a hedge cutter, to mirror the shape of the rock it stands on.

Lassanroe

Skibbereen, Co. Cork. Tel: 028 22563. e-mail: rjstonard@eircom.net Contact: Janet and Robin Stonard. Open: Daily by appointment. Groups welcome. Children supervised. Partially wheelchair accessible. No dogs. Special features: Plants for sale occasionally. Directions: On application.

Lassanroe is everything one might think of when a Japanese garden comes to mind. You enter through a hand-made wooden gate with a bamboo latch. It is its own little world, ruled over by the charming and talented Janet and Robin Stonard. Robin has always been interested in things Japanese. He joined the Japanese Society at an early age. He grows Japanese plants. He even built a small teahouse. (We couldn't go in however because a family of swallows had taken up residence.) Being a potter, Robin makes his own lanterns. They sit, waiting to be lit at night, under draping acers and behind stands of rhododendron and camellia, beside gleaming white lilies and free-flowering fuchsias.

The plants make this garden memorable, from the New Zealand celery pine *Phyllocladus trichomanoides* to elegantly pruned-up, dissected acers and bamboos of every description, grown over mounds of mossy rock and surrounded by lakes of mind-your-own-business or *Soleirolia soleirolii*. Among the finer bamboos, and there are a number of these, *Semiarundinaria Fastuosa* or the 'Temple Bamboo' a tender and rare plant, is Robin's favourite. In an other area we looked at a dramatic looking Chilean *Chusquea cunninghamii*, which is strange and spiked, as well as nasty to fall on, according to Robin. It might be a good choice for an anti-burglar plant. Bamboo dominates the garden and not just as the most widely grown plant. It also provides the material to make windows, gates, plant supports and fences. As Robin takes care of all this, Janet is the greenhouse woman. She grows all the usual things like chillies, as well as a supply of ornamental gourds for a friend who uses them to make banjos.

Not surprising, this special garden, and I assume its two bold King Charles cavalier dogs, has featured on US TV programmes.

I left, emerged back out into County Cork where I was chased down the road by a sheep dog. The west Cork roads seem ruled by these herding dogs...

Lissard Estate Gardens

Castletownsend Rd, Russagh, Skibbereen, Co. Cork Tel: 028 40000. e-mail: events@lissard.com Contact: Reception. Open: Gardens: For the summer from late May, Wed. and Thurs. 9am-5pm or by appointment at other times. Sky Garden: By appointment only. Contact for details. Partially wheelchair accessible. Accompanied children welcome. Special features: Light lunches and teas in house. Accommodation. Events. Directions: On the R596 out of Skibbereen.

The grounds and gardens at Lissard have been a point of fascination for many years. To start with they are extensive, made up of wild and semi-tamed landscapes, wild ponds, wetlands, mature woods and coppiced ash and hazel woods, wildflower meadows and cultivated walled, flower gardens. I was intrigued, in particular by the Cork university Bee Project being carried out here.

Walk downhill between stands of blackberry and under oak trees, into a meadow, and from there back under the trees. The smell of wet vegetation is invigorating, between banks of foxgloves in spring and later in the year, ferns. Tiny trickling streams run parallel to the paths and steps. At various points, these enter ponds, big and small.

Other log-lined paths head back to the woods, past stands of trees and knots of new planting. In different places the trees are mature and towering. The fairy garden in one dark corner of the woods, is suitably Potteresque – in both the Beatrix and Harry senses

of the word. This wood is as good a use of rampant laurel as I have ever seen. Hide and seek here would be nicely scary.

The waterside walks are alive with the sight and sound of birds and other wildlife. Eventually all paths lead back to the woods however. Pick your way downhill to the bottom of one wood. Take the step stone bridge over a stream. Climb a stile into the waterfall garden and march over the bridge past the noisy fall. A final set of steps lead down to a strange cobble and tree fern garden, both native and exotic at the same time.

For all this beauty, Lissard has one other extraordinary feature - The Irish Sky Garden. It is set in the middle of the woods and from the outside it is not quite clear what the tall, grassy mound is. A long, stone-lined tunnel that makes me think of the pyramids, leads in under and through the mound, and at the end of this tunnel, a set of steep steps leads up towards a clean rectangle of sky in the roof. This leads out to the middle of a large crater. Sitting at the bottom is a strange-looking altar or bench. Lie on this, head below feet, and look up at the sky. The fish-eye effect of the circular sky edged by the cut-grass crater edge brings with it a profound experience: both moving and disorienting. The Irish Sky Garden makes Lissard worth going out of one's way to visit. It is important to know that it must be booked in advance.

Lisselan Estate Gardens

Clonakilty, Co. Cork. Tel: 023 8833249. e-mail: info@lisselan.com www.lisselan.com
Contact: Mark Coombes. Open: Daily, 8am-dusk. Groups must book. Supervised children. Dogs on leads.
Partially wheelchair accessible. Special features: Guided tours. Teas can be booked. Golf course. Fly-fishing
Directions: Located 3 km from Clonakilty on the N71 travelling towards Cork city.

I have spent years mispronouncing Lisselan. It is, it seems 'Lis-el-awn' as in 'lawn' and not 'Liss elen' as in 'Sue Ellen'. Either way, this most memorable garden takes up 20 acres of sheltered valley along the River Argideen just outside Clonakilty. It was laid out by the Bence-Jones family in the last century following the principles of William Robinson, the Irish garden writer and designer. It must be among the most romantic, peaceful and handsome gardens on the island, a perfect combination of water, flowers, wildlife, trees, tranquillity and taste.

In Cork they believe you can never have too many flowering hydrangeas. In late summer, the blue lace-caps on the drive into Lisselan will get the visitor a bit excited. Add in some immense specimens of *Abies grandis, Cryptomeria japonica* and the Irish Girth Champion, *Pinus radiata* as well as a *Podocarpus salignus* to die for, and the excitement goes off the scale.

Having arrived up that gorgeous drive, the next view is of the house and its rock garden. The building is reminiscent of a French chateau, all turrets, flourishes and gables, draped in Virginia creeper. It stands on a cartoon-like precipice which is laid out as a rock garden, falling away from the base of the building down to the river valley floor. For visitors with the footing of mountain goats it is possible to climb the rockery. However, be careful not to step on the thousands of seedlings in the paths – walking on these feels like committing plant infanticide. There are innumerable cyclamen, primulas and ferns, lysimachia and dianthus – the tiny progeny of parents growing in the beds.

Drag yourself from here to the west of the house and into what is more or less a jungle of fine shrubs with mature pines overhead and acacia, myrtle, robinia and vivid-coloured rhododendrons in the middle storey. The Ladies' Mile leads through this, along by the river and through the rhododendron woods. Take the rough-paved steps under arched trees, edged with dahlias and other flowers down to this river walk.

At one point, the water is spanned by a white, wisteria-covered bridge that leads over to an island with a lily-stuffed pool, and then out past weirs, sluice gates and more branches of wandering waterway.

Flowering camellia and bamboo take up one side of the river path, and primula, ferns and irises take the other. Hidden in the middle of the rampant growth, look for the bamboo summerhouse surrounded by libertia.

Today the old walled garden is the home of the Fuchsia Garden. This iconic flower is almost the official plant of West Cork. Most species of these often tender plants would not survive outdoors on the rest of the island, but there are over 30 species in this collection, living outside in good health.

My last visit was in September the day after a freak flood. The lower garden was under water and its statues were up to their waists in water. The gardeners were philosophical. I was told it would be grand. It always is.

Mardyke Gardens

Fitzgerald's Park, Mardyke, Cork City. Open: All year round. See website for seasonal hours. Special features: Gallery, restaurant, Events. Directions: Take the Mardyke walk off the N22 heading west out of the city centre.

The Mardyke Gardens were closed, restored and reopened with a fanfare a few years ago to the usual mix of claps and sneers. As the dust has now settled, it can be seen for what it is, a perfectly good city garden with some flourishes. I love the bandstand, an extravagant sweep of curved white, set out in front of a grand rectangle of lawn, invariably draped with sun-loving bodies the minute there is anything approaching decent weather. There are smart wooden benches set about on equally sharp expanses of formal paved area, all buzzy with people walking and playing about.

The centrepiece of the garden is the pod made by Diarmuid Gavin for the 2012 Chelsea Flower Show. This is the Sky Garden, a pink Egyptian Eye of steel with a living houseleek roof, perched on the banks of the Lee, inside which lovers can sit and smooch or smoke. Gavin's signature spheres, executed in clipped box and polished steel form the main body of the garden around the pod. They are as much playground as garden and there is no shortage of kids to slide off the side of the curved metal balls, so the planting is of necessity made of hard wearing grasses, pachysandra and box under a light canopy of betula. Having passed the quaint fairytale gatelodge by the entrance, the modern zap of all this is both strange and welcome.

There has not been too much tinkering with the old Fitzgerald Park which is still a confection of mature specimens of magnolia and chestnut, acer and yew, set into big sweeps of lawn along a handsome river walk under an avenue of maples. Spot the tree with the cordyline sprouting from high up in its trunk.

This all leads toward the restored Victorian duck pond with its display of old and new sculptures. Walking along the riverside, the views of the elegant old Mardyke suspension bridge is only partially successful in drawing the nosy walker away from inspecting the back gardens of some of the posh denizens of Cork across the River Lee.

Mill Cove Garden & Gallery

Beara Peninsula, Castletownbere, West Cork. Tel: 027 70393. e-mail: millcovegallery@gmail.com www.millcovegallery.com. Contact: John Goode. Open: As part of the West Cork Garden Trail. May-Sept. See website for seasonal times. Other times by appointment to groups and individuals. Wheelchair accessible. Dogs on leads. Special features: Gallery. Exhibitions. Directions: Travelling east from Castletownbere on the R572 just outside the town on the right. Signposted.

Pulling on off the road, through a wall of trees and down a little incline, Mill Cove holds out the prospect of a woodland garden. It quickly becomes clear that the gallery is every bit as important as the garden, which serves both.

The first sight is of strange gingko-inspired sculpture in a sunlit opening between curtains of tall maple and pine. Standing stones peep out from beneath trees and even the low walls made of pencil slim stone have a sculptural air about them.

There are sculpted plants too, with pruned-up acer and crinodendron revealing gorgeous tactile barks. But there are more than enough wild looking specimens to make the place feel like a green jungle – constantly springing surprises on the first-time visitor in the shape of huge eyeballs and other strange and good looking pieces of art peeping from out of the trees. Much of the garden is wood, that regularly opens up onto bright areas, where puffs of hydrangea and agapanthus add zappy spots of colour to the many greens.

The whole garden is a running lesson on placing art in a garden. There are traditional and contemporary bronzes and stone pieces, mixed media and steel works scattered about. The exhibits change regularly so

there is always something fresh to see and I think few sculptors could resist having their work surrounded by this gorgeous rock and moss background.

The ruin of the old mill, after which the garden takes its name is nestled between the trees, giving something of a hint of the long, convoluted local history. A gentle stairway leads down between more art works toward the sound of water, opening out to a view of the cove and a stone bench cut into the hill from which to enjoy it. The path back uphill, runs under bamboo tunnels and out again to a dappled area and a canopy high above of *Magnolia grandiflora* and not quite as tall, myrtles and olearias. Be sure to see the huge catalpa behind the gallery before leaving. And be sure to inspect the gallery too…

Bruno Nicolai's Exotic Garden

Blackrock, Cork, Co. Cork. e-mail bnicolai@eircom.net Contact: Bruno Nicolai. Open: By appointment in Aug -Sept. to groups and for occasional open days. Contact for annual details. Not wheelchair accessible. Children accompanied by an adult at all times. No dogs. Special Features: Refreshments can be arranged at time of booking. Directions: On application.

Bruno Nicolai's Cork garden has been a source of great interest to Irish gardeners for some time. This young enthusiast has been working his pocket-sized tropical jungle close to Cork harbour for a few years, testing the boundaries of what we think we can grow in Ireland. Prepare to pick your way between *Schefflera macrophylla* and *Cyathea medullaris*, brushing past runs of sweet smelling gingers, persicarias and cannas and to instantly forget that you are in a suburban garden surrounded by houses. Bruno's lair has more of the air of a tropical glass house than the garden of a semi-detached home.

This is a plantsman's laboratory as much as a garden. Skinny paths shimmy between and under a sizable and intriguing collection of rare, unusual and tender plants, from herbaceous perennials to shrubs and small trees, bamboos and tall grasses.

This expertly tended tangle includes the well named *Salix magnificum* with 10 cm long catkins and *Fatsia polycarpa* which has giant 50 cm leaves. While tucked in under their exotic skirts, you can seek out a fascinating collection of swanky begonias, persicarias and ferns. The canopy of exotics runs from *Paraserianthes lophantha* or Cape wattle, to a loquat with a madly flowering bomarea climbing its trunk and onto spiny, scary-looking aralias.

This impressive cram of foliage and flower is largely grown without much soil addition or fertiliser. Even the use of a hoe is foregone and Bruno believes that the mossy carpet that covers his moist, heavy soil makes good ground cover as well as being a natural weed barrier.

Neither should a rigid routine of protection be assumed. The number one rule appears to be that what goes in the ground stays in the ground with no winter wrapping or protection ever used. 'I only seem to suffer losses when I fuss too much, he said rather infuriatingly.

For all the variety, the garden is more than just a gathering of plants. It is a thing of beauty. Bruno's eye for design is as obvious as his talent in rearing and tending, often temperamental plants. All this exotica is framed by and within wooden arches and pergolas, edgings and bookend wooden structures, all made from found wood. These materials prove as stylish in the hands of an artist as any pricy custom-made features. Bruno's garden is an example of how talent and style trumps a big cheque book any day.

Mary O'Connell's Garden

Passage West, Co. Cork. Contact: Mary O'Connell. Tel: 087 2254909. e-mail: connellm@eircom.net Open: For occasional charity days. Otherwise to groups by appointment. Children over 12 welcome. Dogs on leads. Special features: Refreshments can be arranged. Directions: On application.

There is a grand specimen of *Acer griseum* in the centre of Mary O'Connell's hilly Cork garden that catches the evening and morning sun in its fluttering, copper, peeling bark. 'I'd die if anything happened to it,' she told me. It cost Mary the considerable sum of £40 in 1983.'My mother nearly had a stroke when I told her.' Gardening matters to Mary. A lot. It is in her blood. This garden was started by her uncle, who also built the house on a hard-to-negotiate, three-levelled site in hilly Cork. As we squeezed our way through the densely planted, jungle of good and unusual plants, that really should not fare so well outdoors in Ireland, but do here, I could only marvel and be jealous.

There were grand spans of lawn when Mary took on the garden in the 1980s. No more. She needed the space for plants, for *Acca sellowiana* and *Dodonaea viscosa*, for *Hedychium* 'Helen Dillon' and tree dahlias that she manages to get to flower. She has filled this place with plants and to walk between them is to take a horticultural trip around the world, under pillars of blue *Echium pininana*, and explosions of red embothrium, on gravel and sleeper paths, between trachycarpus and fine acers with *Rosa*

banksiae climbing their trunks, into shaded gardens and out to open flower beds full of verbena scented like sherbet and flame-like *Kniphofia* 'Christmas Cheer'.

Mary is besotted with plants and collects from all over, from gardening friends throughout Ireland and from obscure nurseries here and abroad. She is a fund of tips about caring for difficult plants, and a generous woman with both information and cuttings.

I love this garden because it manages to be both horticulturally first rate and still a place that is welcoming and enjoyable to just wander through, brushing off the soft plumes of restio, and under the light-filtering leaves of acer, between flowering shrubs and perennials, into little pond gardens where Goldie, a venerable fish born in 1983, lives alongside his giant younger relatives.

I love the way the house seems to have been squashed down into the middle of a large flower bed, rising above fringes of eupatorium, aconites and spring bulbs. Mary opens it for a charity day each year but I am not sure how the visitors fit, given the abundance of plants – I assume it is a case of 'single file please.'

The Old Deanery Gardens

Kilboy, Cloyne, Co. Cork. Tel: 021 4652 204. 087 2716 249. e-mail: edwaelec@eircom.net Contact: Martin and Janet Edwardes. Open: May-Sept. By appointment to groups only. Directions: On application.

'We bought a walled garden by mistake', Janet Edwardes told me. What they bought was an old deanery outside the historic, ecclesiastic village of Cloyne. One day, their daughter squeezed through a rickety gate in a wall and found herself in the middle of a secret garden, a walled garden that appeared to have been thrown in with the house for good measure. This was the stuff of novels. They employed two goats to eat their way through the overgrowth and finally, Janet and Martin got to work, transforming it into a proper walled garden.

They led me past lines of autumn raspberries and irises, under arches covered in golden hops, between rows of potatoes and roses, from 'Albertine' to an impressive *Rosa mutabilis* on the south-facing wall, which flowers for ten months of the year.

I wondered about the amount of work involved and was told that they are the only gardeners. Impressive. Not being millionaires, the whole operation, as Janet told me, 'works from seed.' Even more impressive.

Outside the walled garden they discovered a stream

that dries in summer and roars with water in winter. So they turned it into a stream garden, under the shelter and shade of a canopy of existing tall trees. They planted lines of camellias, ferns and more roses, turning it into a dreamy, atmospheric corner that eventually leads out to the open.

Out in that greater garden, I discovered that

there are 27 different types of magnolia, including the beautiful *Magnolia hypoleuca* and *Magnolia tripetala*, the umbrella tree. As we met one after another, it was necessary to suppress a smile as Janet insisted that she is not a collector. Some of the magnolias are found in the area around the lake, a body of water fed by rainfall, filled with frogs and newts and wonderfully natural. The path from it leads to the 'sort of oriental garden' as Janet calls it. This is a light-dappled wood with stone-lined paths where they grow unusual ferns like tender *Blechnum chilense,* and the Chinese chain fern, *Woodwardia unigemmata* under a handsome Japanese snowbell tree, *Styrax Japonicus* and *Decaisnea fargesii* the blue bean plant.

Leaving the water, we walked out past a skyward-bound *Cedrus deodara* on the lawn and a growing collection of specimen trees including a number of different oaks.

The courtyard garden is reached through an arch of *Rosa* 'Wedding Day' and clematis. The cobbles here had to be unearthed and restored along with rebuilding the old wall. There seems to be no part of the garden that did not require major work. Looking at this beautiful garden today, still in its teens, the levels of work and dedication that Janet and Martin have poured into the place are to be applauded. Before you leave, ask to see the miniature railway.

Pine Tree Lodge Garden

Cloonkirgeen, Dunmanway Co. Cork. Contact: Erika Treutler and Harry Sexton through Facebook Page. Open: To groups by appointment through Facebook and for occasional open days. Supervised children welcome. Dogs on leads. Directions: Coming from the R586 Dunmanway to Bandon Road, turn onto the R637 and follow Signs to Pinetree Lodge. From the R599 Clonakilty to Dunmanway Road turn onto L4635 and follow signs.

Set in the hills above Dunmanway, this garden is well hunkered into what is an exposed, windy site. Erika and Harry have earned their gardening spurs creating a garden so admirably adapted to its handsome but challenging surroundings.

From the gateway, looking in at the 200-year-old farmhouse and a covetable *Luma apiculata* set into a sweep of gravel, the urge is to investigate. And visiting in the company of Erika and Harry when you find

out how they achieved it, makes the garden even more interesting.

The situation might be open and windy, but it is also south-facing and frost-free, so the mature *Trachycarpus fortunei* they planted many years ago made it through the nasty 2010 winter. Shelter belt trees, grown and later thinned out to allow light in, are the reason Erika and Harry have shelter enough for camellias and magnolias.

This site started out strewn with blue-grey limestone, which is an unusual rock in west Cork. They took advantage of it to build steps as well as stone walls, some free-standing and some butting against the house, creating a number of sun traps for their flower borders and special shrubs. They also restored the outer stone walls. These walls, combined with the natural rocky outcrops, which they also incorporated into the design, tie the garden firmly to the land. With the place suitably anchored, they then mixed native and exotic plants together, arranging them between newt and frog ponds, alongside meandering walks, and beside boulders and benches. The result is a charm.

Before leaving, we climbed into the tree house overlooking the garden, including the wilder, outer reaches where we could see beehives, before the garden melts off into the surrounding fields.

Pip's View

Gorteanish, Ahakista, Durrus, Co. Cork. Tel: 027 67263. 086 1780007.
e-mail: pippabiagi@gmail.com www.biagi-art.com Contact: Pip Biagi. Open: As part of the West Cork
Garden Trail. Contact for annual details. No dogs. Directions: Leave Ahakista on the Kilcrohane road.
The Ahakista bar (tin pub) is on the right. Park here and walk up to garden (signposted).

It is hard to see what Pip Biagi envisioned when, in 1996 she first came upon the site of her future garden. This was the roughest, untamed few acres of scrub imaginable. Pip is an artist however, whose taste is equalled by her appetite for work. Today the rough plot is a charming garden sensitively tucked into its exceptional surroundings.

Pip describes it as a flower and boulder garden with an unusual number of trees and small woods spread out over the up-and-down rugged site. Pip grew all of these, pocket-planting them into the rough in the early days and letting them get on with the business of surviving the harsh winds, or being uprooted by the wind and blown away, which happened too. I asked why the trees do not appear wind-sheared as trees so often do out on the coast. 'It's because the wind comes from all directions!' She laughed. Pip mixes natives with imported plants and, because as she explained 'the soil is so shallow, if something is willing to put itself in here I will not go against it.'

We had just looked at a tender little unnamed fuchsia, a gift from renowned Cork gardener Mary Walsh. 'I'm gardening on the edge with that one,' she said. I also spotted an olive tree over a splash of blue flowering lithodora and the exotic climber *Rhodochiton atrosanguineum* inching up an arch. These are also managing nicely 'on the edge.' Pip need not concern herself with the hardiness of the busy, bright red crab apple, or the *Cornus alternifolia* 'Argentea' she brought from Yorkshire. Trial and error is the phrase and 'if at first it doesn't succeed, give up!'

We walked around the garden, uphill and down, trying not to step on ferns and violas that had seeded in the paths. Under the dappled shade of birch trees, strung with dangling works of art made from beach combed objects, Pip has planted stands of bright, striped phormium and special shrubs, like her favourite, *Halesia monticola*, which has white dangling blooms. 'I love them so much,' she said.

Beneath the trees, expanses of rock emerge from under blankets of moss and fern. It is this stone that Pip used to make the extensive network of paths, walls and ledges seen everywhere. Stone is such an integral part in this barely tamed garden. Some boulders simply emerge from the ground. Pip works with, and plants around them. Some have been purposely placed. She turns some into enigmatic sculptures. She has moved heaven and earth to make the garden.

Poulnacurra

Castle Jane Road, Glanmire, Cork. Tel: 086 6025791. Contact: Mairead Harty. Open: For charity days. See local press for annual dates. Otherwise by appointment. Directions: Driving from Cork city to Glanmire, turn left at the traffic lights. The road forks just after that. Take the right fork onto Castle Jane Road.

It is stating the obvious but the most enjoyable gardens are those where the enthusiasm of the gardener is visible. I love when it is clear that the gardener has fun with their 'baby.' Mairead Harty's Poulnacarra sings of her enthusiasm. Every corner is busy, worked and loved. This three-and-half-acre garden, set around the Queen Anne house is however, despite its historic setting, quite recent. Just 20 years years ago it was the site of a great number of trees and Mairead was busy doing other things. Then, as she says, the late and highly regarded garden designer, Brian Cross happened along. Things would never be the same again. The result of the collaboration between the two is a veritable spree. All Mairead wanted was an easy-to-mind, no-fuss garden. Brian had other ideas. Those ideas would sweep her up, and fire her with an enthusiasm for plants and designs she didn't know she had. These days she happily spends her time lavishing her high-maintenance super model-garden with the care it demands.

The stars here are the mirroring borders, cutting up through the centre of the garden on either side of a path made of rough hewn slabs suitable for only the most sensible walking shoes.

Working out from the path, in order, the borders are made of expanses of catmint or nepeta, coupled with shell-pink and fuchsia-coloured roses. These are

backed by impeccably clipped variegated euonymus. Behind these, there are taller acers, lined up like sentries. Just standing at the bottom of the hill looking up at it is a pleasure.

At the top of the garden, running at a right angle to the double borders, is the mill wheel walk, a path made from about a dozen big mill wheels. These were unearthed, from underneath decades of fallen leaves and garden detritus, when the garden was being restored. They make for a dramatic feature, running down the centre of an avenue of hydrangeas, under the shade of more acers. At one end of this walk, a gate in the stone wall leads into a new meadow and garden leading to a wood walk that Mairead is currently working on. At the other end, one path forks off onto another mill wheel walk.

There is more. In through a gate at one end of the mill wheel walk there are great explosions of flowers, roses and herbaceous perennials. This much looser arrangement is quite different to the restrained double border palette in the lower garden.

To one side of this flower fest, a strange-looking tall ash tree, seems to rise out of a mound of big round river stones. The big stones gradually morph and shrink into an expanse of gravel spiked with *Verbena bonariensis* and clumps of hakonechloa grass and celmisia.

The individual garden rooms are punctuated by large, well-maintained lawns and divided by groves of acers, camellias and roses, all placed in combinations that either block off or open up views of different areas of the garden.

In stark contrast to this smart main garden, there is another, hidden across the drive, a wild wood and meadow, made up of dog roses and weeping juniper, variegated azara and embothrium, arranged in a more haphazard, natural-looking way. This is where Mairead takes the opportunity to play with a selection of plants in ways not possible in the formal areas. The little cottage garden beside the small lodge at the front of the garden is another ongoing project. The work continues.

Ringfield House

Ballindenisk, Watergrasshill, Co. Cork Tel: 021 4889175. 087 6492342
e-mail: anne@thegardendesigncentre.ie Contact: Anne and Liam Griffin. Open: May-Sept. By appointment
to groups. Directions: On application.

I left Ringfield House stretching for the the right word to sum up Anne and Liam Griffin's north Cork garden. As I made my way along the country road, the word dawned on me – 'nailed'. They have the style they endeavour to achieve nailed. Their teenage garden, over its two acres, and multiplicity of little rooms, is exactly what it aims to be. The acers and magnolias, rhododendrons and other trees, mound and mix, blend and fuse in ways one would want them to, swirling around well tended lawn and along paths in the most pleasing fashion. The little water features bubble and gurgle as they should. The secret gardens within clipped beech and yew walls are as secluded as they should be - until you find them. The topiarised, cloud-trained and pollarded box, bay, cypress and daphne are coiffed to perfection

and the lines are strong, strict, architectural and sculptural. Not surprisingly, the Griffins put vast hours into its care and development. 'There *is* a lot of work,' Anne nodded as I marvelled. She is the Maintenance Department while Liam is the gardener with expansionist tendencies. Since I last visited, he has colonised another area, a little wood at the edge of the garden, redesigning it with mossy boulders and tree ferns, log-lined paths and dry stone walls, native and exotic trees and woodland plants.

I had remembered the long double herbaceous borders from previous visits, the rills and ponds, and the greenhouse big enough to move into, with its collection of cacti, the damp bog garden and dry river bed, all minded beautifully. I have no doubt there will new surprises to be seen on the next visit.

Rolf's

Baltimore, Co. Cork. Tel: 028 20289. e-mail: info@rolfscountryhouse.com www.rolfscountryhouse.com
Open: All year. Special features: Accommodation. Restaurant. Wine Bar. Partially wheelchair accessible.
Directions: In Baltimore village, before descending the hill toward the harbour, turn left and left again
and follow the signs.

The Haffner family arrived in Baltimore to run a business nearly 40 years ago but the garden is a more recent venture. Friederike Haffner told me that her mother began it all, that she is the gardener. The rest of the family have not been slow to get involved either. This is a place of great character, starting with a rather surprising tropical courtyard surrounded by terracotta coloured buildings that could easily be in some hot steamy corner of the world. Massive gunnera leaves and swishing bamboo, sharp phormium swords and exotic-looking aralia add to the lush atmosphere, making it feel more like a jungle than mild, damp Ireland.

The ground storey beneath these shrubs is dense with hostas. They love their hostas, 'but we despair of the slugs', Friederike says shaking her head. I noted that the slimy ones do not go after the spiky agave.

The site is hilly so one side of this garden appears sunken. We took a set of stone steps up under towering *Echium pininana,* alive with bees, landing up on a rockery that Friederike is developing on the height above the courtyard. The yuccas and aeoniums love it. I was charmed by the huge eucalyptus, lying along the ground like a sort of serpent plant. It fell in a gale and just continued growing.

The natural rock happens to be shaped like conveniently aligned steps and Friederike is exposing these as she develops her rockery. The stone walls come courtesy of her father and brother. This is a family affair.

At the top of the hill the desire to grow shrubs is let loose around an expanse of lawn, so there are roses and dahlias, and the darkest *Hydrangea macrophylla* 'Merveille

Sanguine' alongside eucomis and *Luma apiculata*. The lawn runs out to the rocky surrounds where the natives take over, with digitalis and ferns, a field of donkeys and a gaggle of Indian runner ducks.

Rosewood House

Lough Hyne, Baltimore, Co. Cork. Tel: 028 20149. e-mail: oreganmichael62@yahoo.ie Contact: Sheryl and Michael O'Regan. Open: As part of the West Cork Garden Trail. Contact for annual details. Groups by appointment. No dogs. Not wheelchair accessible. Special features: Accommodation. Stone wall building courses. Teas. Directions: Driving uphill from Lough Hyne in the direction of Baltimore, travel through several hairpin bends. At the top of the hill follow the Baltimore sign. The house is second on right with Rosewood written on the wall. Park at the next junction.

An entrance through a little apple orchard must be the perfect way into a country garden. Happily the garden around Sheryl and Michael's house turned out to be pretty perfect too. The building is, on one side disguised as a wall of ivy, and a bed of white hydrangeas and Japanese anemones with windows. On the other side, it seems to rise out of a deep dark pond with an impressive waterfall that looks pretty realistic given the extreme hilly nature of the land around it. Only a boardwalk stands between house and water. This is unusual. Michael created it in place of a lawn. Wildlife has more use for water and the garden is, as Sheryl told me 'all for the wildlife'. Frogs, rather than fish inhabit the pond.

The hill that rises above the house does so under a canopy of crab apple, field maple and guelder rose, ash, willow and even a few old, and plenty of young elms, one of which is allowed to lean down over the hill and house. There are pignuts or *Conopodium majus* on the ground underneath, along with moss, ferns and other natives.

These four acres were plain fields when Sheryl's grandfather gave her the land. Since then she has turned them into an enviable country garden, planted 2,000 trees, created wood and water gardens, fruit beds and greenhouses, shrub borders and hedgerows. It has become a haven for wildlife and native plants, used beautifully and only occasionally augmented by imports and exotics.

There are stone withholding walls and ledges erected to break up and define different areas. Michael created all of these. They are like works of art. We took a path made of sleepers set between huge boulders, powder blue ceanothus and shiny box. It led to the woods, passing fallen and decaying trees, being slowly returned back to the earth.

What really struck me however was that they created a new boreen on the land, lining it with fuchsia and *Rosa rugosa* hedges, with exits leading over stone stiles and through little gates into paddocks with donkeys, goats and chicken runs, surrounded by digitalis-spiked walls.

Stepaside Garden

Cross Road House, Ahaliskey, Ballinascarthy, Clonakilty, Co. Cork. Contact: 023 8839224. 086 8625132. e-mail: sineadmurphycork@gmail.com Contact: Bernadette and Larry O'Leary. Open: As part of the West Cork Garden Trail. Contact for annual open dates. Directions: On the N71 travelling from Clonakilty turn right in Ballinascarthy and travel for 2.4 km. The garden and house are on a corner.

Bernadette and Larry had me at *Begonia* 'Bonfire'. I do not like annual, bedding begonias, or at least I did not, until I saw their display of single variety hanging baskets stuffed with these mad exotics. The O'Learys have lived in and worked their welcoming roadside garden outside Clonakilty for decades, creating their own particular sort of garden magic. They combine good plants with enviable upkeep and the result adds up to a charming garden that also takes in views of the patchwork fields in the surrounding hills.

The gales that whips uphill through the garden can be considerable. Bernadette countered them by carving out secluded walks under the canopy of trees and between tall stands of flowering shrubs.

From the crossroads at which the old cottage stands, the hint of a garden is there, in well-reined privet hedge and a multi-stemmed *Cordyline australis*. Creeping *Parthenocissus tricuspidata* and several varieties of fuchsia also peep over the sharp green hedge walls and whet the appetite. Then, from the gateway, the sound of water can be heard. It turns out to come from a hidden water feature, almost invisible under a big mop of deep red *Acer palmatum* 'Dissectum'. The outhouse beside this is all but invisible under a mix of *Parthenocissus quinquefolia* and rampant roses that must be full of birds nests.

All around the house, there are narrow slab stone paths that make their way under rose arches and between puffs of *Cryptomeria japonica*, Portuguese laurel and myrtles. Out in the larger garden, there are more multi-stemmed cordylines over beds of variegated hosta, and a circling shrub border. Around the sloped lawn tree ferns, tall echiums and other delicate plants shelter under and inside the tall natives hedgerow shrubs and trees. This is a loved garden.

St. Mary's Collegiate Gardens

Emmet Place, Youghal, Co. Cork. Tel: 087 7140473. 024 91014. Open: Daily 9am-5pm, as part of the Ring of Cork Open Gardens Trail. Special features: Entry free. Historic ruins. Guided tours can be arranged. Events. Directions: In the centre of the town.

In the middle of the historic Walter Raleigh quarter of Youghal there is a gate in a stone wall that leads into St. Mary's Collegiate gardens. I stepped through it, without any knowledge of what to expect and was struck by a sense of something special. It is not surprising. These gardens go back to the 1500s and can be seen on the Pacata Hibernia Map of Youghal drawn up in the 1600s.

Today the hilly garden is given over to lawns and shrub borders, with some herbaceous planting between the more solid plants, some specimen trees and bits of archaeology in the remains of old walls and buildings, a few intriguing looking old specimens and a gnarled hawthorn growing from the top of an old wall which must have a story to it. There are benches and seats everywhere. A children's play group was doing relay races and elderly couples sat in the sun. In reference to the defences set up to protect Youghal in the 1641 rebellion, a cannon stands at the top of the hill.

At one end of the garden, an arched gate in the wall leads into the remains of an old orchard and above that, a graveyard. In 1616 over 100 apple trees were brought in from Bristol to create a college orchard. There has been an orchard here ever since, although these days it is a modest affair. From the top of the garden the view out over the bay and some buildings that go back to Raleigh's time, is tremendous. The feel of civic pride in this historic park, is a strong one.

Templebreedy Grounds

The Old Rectory, Templebreedy, Crosshaven, Co. Cork. Tel: 021 4831480. 086 2888776. e-mail: b@templebreedy.com www.templebreedy.com Contact: Bee FitzGerald. Open: May-Aug. By appointment to groups. Directions: On application.

Although the rectory at Templebreedy has been standing on its scenic site overlooking Crosshaven since 1815, it is home to a relatively recent garden. Bee FitzGerald and her husband Michael moved here looking for a garden to work in the 1990s and encountered a blank canvas around a fine old house and courtyard. Bee has been playing with it ever since.

The little woodland garden to the side of the house

acts as an informal welcome. There is a mature beech wood just beyond it and the borrowed view of the towering old trees makes Bee's young wood garden feel both more extensive and a good deal older than its teenage self.

An almost invisible trail winds between stands of camellia and rhododendron, acer and hydrangea, over ferns, erythroniums and epimediums. This too eventually leads out to the wood and the Priest's Walk that runs around it. The more cultivated garden around the house beckons first.

The early owners may not have gardened but they played tennis and the old court is still here, set out on a platform overlooking the harbour. Being a ballboy was no easy job.

On the garden side, the tennis court is bounded by a wall of pleached limes over a lower wall of beech. So the view is something like a wide cinemascope picture framed by the two elongated bars of foliage. In front of the house more clipped beech encloses a topiary garden with box beds, yew cubes and cones. This enclosed corner is best enjoyed from inside the house. Coming around the side of the building, there are much looser shrub beds made up of spreading *Cornus controversa* 'Argenta' and *Fatsia japonica*.

The house is just below the gravelled drive and its basement windows look up at the ledge on which Bee has placed a line of iron obelisks to support exotic annuals like ipomoea or morning glory.

The courtyard is the sort of little room that would make any gardener's heart leap. Every spare bit of the red sandstone wall is covered in honeysuckle, *Hydrangea petiolaris*, and clematis. *Rosa* 'Mermaid' and *Exochorda* 'The Bride' share and do well together on the north-facing wall. Stone troughs of tulips and alpines line the walls and a great splay of ginger lilies fills an old brick trough in a shady corner. The sound of water comes from a spouting stone feature between all the asters, peonies and thalictrum. Bee calls it her mad flower room.

The side of the house is where the mixed borders live. These start looking good in spring with hellebores and camassias, followed by alliums, eremurus, martagon lilies and delphiniums.

When not in among the flowers, Bee will be found playing with the berry garden, experimenting with josta berries and blueberries.

Looking up from the vegetable plot, the view is of the old and unusual looking ruin of Templebreedy church. It was built in 1769 yet beyond use after only 80 years. Do not leave without admiring the fine gate made a Pat Ronan of Bandon.

Blarney Rose walk

Kerry

Ard na Sidhe Country House

Carragh Lake, Killorglin, Co. Kerry. Tel: 066 976 9105. e-mail: reservations@ardnasidhe.com
Contact: Reception. Open: Ap-Sept. By appointment. Not wheelchair accessible. Supervised children. No
dogs. Special features: Hotel. Tours and refreshments can be booked. Directions: Traveling west on N70
in Kilorglin, turn onto Annadale Road and continue onto Langford Street. From here turn right onto
Farrantoreen Road and drive for 4 km. Continue onto Glannagilliagh and follow signs to Ard na Sidhe.

This unusual arts and crafts style house, built in 1913 comes as something of a surprise on the edge of

Carragh Lake, but the soft coloured sandstone and low rise elevation couch it comfortably into the landscape. The first sight is of beech trees like the arches of a cathedral, but the gardens proper are to the front of the house, leading down to the lake.

The building overlooks a series of terraces, that step up and down, linked to each other, each individually enclosed by low stone walls. The heights are kept low so that the lake can always be seen. The ledges are variously divided into stone patios and squares of lawn, surrounded by hydrangea and hardy geranium, blue-tinged *Melianthus major, Arbutus unedo* and lavender.

Moving downhill from here, the style softens and shakes itself out in a series of more informal areas, sunken stream and fern gardens, under the shelter of fat, fluffy *Cryptomeria japonica* and contrasting, shiny camellias. Make your way through a gate in the wall and into a hilly, slightly wilder garden with rhododendron, young apple trees and clumps of bamboo, like islands in a green lake. Another gate leads to the rockery. This is an undulating, boulder strewn, mossy place with paths between stone lanterns and under the well named Chinese lantern tree, *Crinodendron hookerianum*. This informal and welcoming garden is attached to a hotel. As I left, I wished I was staying…

The Austen Garden

Sneem, Co. Kerry. Tel: 087 9112 876. 064 6689 251. Contact: Stephen and Louise Austen.
Open: By appointment to groups (Only mini buses possible.) Contact for an appointment. Directions: On
application.

The Austens have, what is known as 'form' when it comes to good gardens. For many years they worked a well known private garden in Wicklow. At the turn of the century they bought a derelict cottage on a windswept and beautiful bog near Sneem. A little

over a decade has passed. What they term, some 'extraordinary growth' has taken place and that boggy land is now an expanding garden, made up of growing and developing arrangements of magnolias and camellias, rhododendrons, acers and pines. Beneath and between these, there are great lower layers of herbaceous plants and bulbs.

They dug a whole network of steps into the hill, parallel to each other, up and down the slope, threading between the burgeoning rose and shrub beds, groves of white betulas, tree ferns and restios. The stairs all give onto grassed walks with different views of the fast developing borders. The acer and hellebore garden, running alongside one of the stairways, is already handsome but as the trees stretch up into their characteristic umbrella shapes it will become quite a sight. This is a garden very much in development.

Out on the edge, the new wild garden is where Louise spends much of her time. She took a hill with some tall spindly self-sown native trees, laid down mulch and trunk-lined paths and planted hostas and lilies, baby rhododendrons and ferns among the already existing wood sorrel and violas. This is a quiet, subtle spot in an otherwise busy garden.

Since my last visit Louise has added a tree fern ravine to the boundary and work was well underway on a grand new pond at the very bottom of the garden.

I loved being introduced to plants that came to the garden, as cuttings grown from cuttings, that grew from cuttings, stretching back a half-century to both of their childhood gardens in England. Everywhere you look there are plants with stories.

At its outer edges, the garden melts into the bog and into plantations of native oak, willow, betula and holly. I liked the touch of the surreal, red painted wooden walkway that seems to float out over the grassy expanse, just above the boggy waterways.

Finally, there are not many gardens graced with a three-chambered souterrain and a megalithic standing stone. Looking at these is a reminder that this garden is simply one extra layer on a landscape which stretches back to prehistory.

Dawros Gallery & Garden

Dawros, Kenmare, Co. Kerry. Tel: 087 6875461. e-mail: charlotteverbeek@me.com. Contact: Charlotte Verbeek. Open: Strictly by appointment to groups and individuals. Not suitable for children. No dogs. Special features: Art and jewellery gallery featuring work by artist/owner. Refreshments can be arranged for groups. Directions: On application.

This is an exciting garden, built around a cool modern new house set comfortably into the mountainous land on Beara. Charlotte and her husband built their sharp, new home from the old stone on the site of a ruined cottage. They continued this trend when it came to making the garden, which is moulded lightly into the land.

That stated, the area attached to the house stands apart from the rest of the grounds. It is stark and contemporary, with an unadorned cement patio leading to an overflowing pool with step stones. To counteract this hard-edged look, explosions of waving *Verbena bonariensis*, cortaderia, eupatorium and other tall, constantly moving and swishing grasses soften the look of the concrete, minimalist wooden benches and sunken fire pit. Charlotte told me that she shears all growth to the ground in spring and the resulting bed spends the rest of the year putting on an ever-changing show.

Beyond this 'fashioned' area, the wild garden begins, sweeping down and away from the house and patio, into a wet, sedge and grass garden that then rises back up to a birch wood full of intriguing looking pieces of sculpture and a wooden thatched summerhouse. Before investigating these, make your way downhill from the house, on a path bounded by a cleft oak fence around a native Irish apple orchard over sweeps of blue camassias. Charlotte swears by the 'Russets', as versatile apples as well as 'Kerry pippin' which nevertheless needs to be eaten immediately. The wall at the bottom of the hill wanders along, side-stepping and navigating its way around the oak trees that end up appearing to grow from the stone in some places.

In one hollow, Charlotte made a little wood garden where she incorporated camellias, acers and magnolias under the existing canopy of natives. A pond and a huge boulder complete the arrangement. I was struck by the iron ring emerging from a stone wall, yet another interesting piece of sculpture.

The mummified, equally sculptural *Cardiocrinum giganteum* seed heads are also gorgeous. She also re-deployed a dead tree fern trunk as a plinth for another sculpture. This is like a little woodland gallery. At the front of the house, a line of light, white betulas over a ribbon of miniature rhododendrons and *Gaura lindheimeri* again show Charlotte's eye for design.

From here, the way leads into the vegetable garden, which she decorated by adding cross paths that glitter with colourful pieces of glass and ceramic set into the gravel. It is like walking on jewels. While she works here, Charlotte can look out over the wild garden. This expanse of grass and sedge is simply weeded for

brambles. Apart from that it is left to its own devices. The birch wood on the other side, stands beyond a reconstructed stone wall and moon window. The view back across the sedgy valley to the house and more tended garden is an arresting one.

Over here, more ponds and pieces of sculpture vie for attention. Willow sculptures and boardwalks span the wet areas. The water gathers into ponds between stands of molina, miscanthus and young pines – which Charlotte, disclosed, the invading deer love to eat. She is however, philosophical about these marauders. Not many of us would be so understanding and accommodating.

Derreen

Lauragh, Killarney, Co. Kerry. Tel: 064 6683588. e-mail derreengarden@gmail.com www.derreengarden.com Contact: Reception. Open: 10am-6pm all year. Supervised children welcome. Dogs on leads. Special features: Tearoom. April-Oct. Large groups please ring ahead. Guided tours can be arranged. Directions: Derreen is 24 km from Kenmare on the R571 travelling toward Castletownbere. Signposted.

Derreen is a singular garden, a place of such charm and beauty, it lodges in the memory in a way that much showier gardens rarely manage. Completely man-made, it nevertheless has an air of nature untamed about it. When lists of quintessentially Irish gardens are made, it is the always at the top.

In the 1600s the lands at Derreen were among the massive tracts owned by the Cromwellian, William Petty, author of the Down Survey, which was the first great land survey of the south and west of Ireland, drawn up to facilitate the redistribution of lands confiscated from Irish landowners. Petty was paid for his work with 270,000 acres in Kerry of which he wrote, that 'for a great man that would retire, this place would be the most absolute, and the most interessant place in the world, both for improvement and pleasure and healthfulness.' The lands moved through Petty's family and a series of tenants until the 1850s when the Lansdowne family, the then owners began to take an interest in the property.

Today, Derreen is a large woodland garden, created through the improvements carried out by the 5th Marquess of Lansdowne in the 1870s on the rock and scrub around his house on the Beara Peninsula. Back then the first job carried out was to plant

a windbreak of trees, including recently introduced North American western red cedar, *Thuja plicata* and Western hemlock or *Tsuga heterophylla* on the rocky land that was to become the proposed garden. From these beginnings a lush, green jungle grew and matured into a place that is simply perfect. Today it is rightly known as one of the most beautiful on the island. Despite the shelter, there were large losses in the Valentine's Day storm of 2014 and throughout the garden it is heartening to see new young trees being planted to replace fallen giants.

The garden visit begins close to the house by the Big Rock, a massive, flat, smooth outcrop, known since ancient times as a meeting place. Today it rises out of a sea of lawn, and gives the visitor some idea of the original quality of the land.

Within the woods, some of the individual gardens have brilliantly descriptive names, like the King's Oozy and the Little Oozy. On wet days, of which there are no shortage, the term oozy seems particularly apt as boots slurp through mud. The annual rainfall here can be as high as 200 cms.

One of the best areas in the garden is the Knockatee Seat, perched to take in a view over the woods to Knockatee Hill. A knobbly path picks its way up between rocks, over snaking roots, towards the seat. The wild feel is enhanced as you make your way over a bridge built to straddle and save the exposed roots of a huge eucalyptus tree. Remarkable trees abound here, including the largest *Cryptomeria japonica* 'Elegans' in the world. Even growing on its side, it still reaches over 18 metres. Under the sheltering taller trees, there are wonderful mature tree ferns, mostly *Dicksonia antarctica*. Derreen has become famous for them. They grow in such numbers that it is almost possible to become *blasé* about them as they naturalise and self-seed like refined weeds.

The magic here lies in its wildness. Huge barriers of bamboo cross the path, making the visitor feel that a pith helmet and machete might have been a good idea. But this wildness is contrived. We have to remind ourselves that if it was really wild it would disappear under native weeds. The areas devastated by the already mentioned storm is a reminder that nature is a battlefield.

Walking through the woods, at one point, brings you out toward the water, past a private island reached by a bridge, mysterious and out of bounds. Even on a dull, rainy day and late in the evening it is a surprise to emerge into sunlight and to be able to look across the sea to the Caha Mountains on the other side of Kilmackilloge harbour. Take the path back in under the trees to walk between moss carpets studded with little fountains of fern. A romantic soul might be moved to lie down on the moss and commune with nature.

Driving up and away from the garden as the land once again gets rougher and wilder, look back down to the fertile fields and the sheltered bay in which Derreen snugs. At the top of the pass gather your breath with a HB Ice cream in Don's Mountain Cabin before the hair-raising, hairpin ride back down the valley between steep drops into the rock and sheep-busy rough. There was a huge tour bus heading up the hill as I drove away. 'The Italian Job' came to mind...

Derrynane National Historic Park

Caherdaniel, Co. Kerry. Tel: 066 9475387. e-mail: derrynanehouse@opw.ie Contact: James O'Shea. Open: All year, daylight hours. Free admission to gardens. Partially wheelchair accessible. Supervised children welcome. Dogs on leads. Special features: Café. House tours. Directions: 3.5 km from Caherdaniel, off the N70. Signposted.

Memory of trips to Derrynane involved picnics on the grass in front of the slate-sided house and guided tours of Daniel O'Connell's' home. Today Derrynane conjures up pictures of Wellington-clad expeditions through a fascinating and growing plant collection.

A number of years ago the garden was linked with the Edinburgh Botanic Gardens and chosen to trial an array of seeds and plants collected in far flung places. Today Derrynane is home to the resulting experimental garden. What makes this horticultural laboratory most remarkable is the way head gardener, James O'Shea and his team, grow these plants. Once again, the magic fairy dust of the western Irish garden is in evidence: The entrance to the garden is through a stone arch under the driveway. Curtains of clerodendron and mulberry hang over the arch and walking under it and into the garden, instead of finding laboratory-conditions and a neat Botanical garden look, the plants are arranged as they might

be found in the wild. Rhodochiton snakes along a fallen tree trunk. Fascicularia emerges from a stump in among a mass of native ferns. *Salvia corrugata,* black *S. discolor* and *S. confertiflora* all grow through in loose splays among the long grass. To see the Chilean bellflower, bomarea, growing like a wild plant is a privilege. Watsonia sprouting from a crack in a boulder is also quite a sight.

James is an enthusiastic plantsman who talks engagingly about the little and not-so-little orphans in his care. Listening to him pour forth added immeasurably to the visit: He spoke about how *Fascicularia bicolor,* is hybridising, growing in different places, under the skirts of white-barked myrtle, exotic Chilean *Weinmannia trichosperma* and *Fuchsia boliviana.*

Heavy rainfall, lush growth, sheltering neighbours and soft climate bestow the conditions that allow plants such as the rare Chinese elm, *Ulmus chenmoui* grow so well. The seemingly loose hand with which the garden is minded actually cossets the plants. So everywhere there are specimens from Chile, Argentina, Brazil, Australia and New Zealand, all growing outside, cheek by jowl. Tender tree ferns like *Dicksonia squarrosa* and *Lophosoria quadripinnata*, thrive like natives here. An old stone ruin has been pulled into service to shelter some of the collections, again adding to the natural look. It was rare to see *Xanthoria australis* doing well outdoors, along with tender Norfolk Island pines or *Araucaria heterophylla* and *Taiwania cryptomerioides*.

Much of the garden is taken up with expanses of sheltered lawn around these loose island beds and protruding rocks. The tall oaks overhead tower so far up that they cast only the lightest shadow on the proceedings below. Shaded spots like the fern and rock garden, link the open areas to the iconic Tree Fern Field. Finally, do not miss the folly in the woods.

Dhu Varren

Knockreigh, Miltown, Co. Kerry. Tel: 087 7596 414. 066 976 7770. e-mail: dhuvarrengarden@yahoo.com www.dhuvarrengarden@yahoo.com Contact: Mark and Laura Collins. Open: By appointment to individuals and groups. Not wheelchair accessible. Children welcome. Dogs on leads. Special features: Tours and presentations may be arranged for groups. Plants for sale. Directions: Take the N72 Killorglin, Ring of Kerry Road. Turn right at the Golden Nugget Pub (R563) and continue for approx 10 km. The garden in on the left.

Laura and Mark Collins have been building up their remarkable garden since 2000. Each visit sees it marching on and become more impressive. The last trip felt as though it should have been undertaken dressed in safari khakis. To steal a phrase from Dorothy in '*The Wizard of Oz*', we were 'not in Kansas anymore'. From the front gate to the very back of what was once a field, this is an extravaganza of trees, shrubs and grasses, a large number of which are tender and rare. There are twin Koi ponds with mirroring waterfalls, a Japanese tea house, with a raised bamboo walkway, a jungle house high above the trees, separate tropical and succulent houses and a rockery that took two truck fulls of rock to build. Each area and each garden room has been stuffed to capacity with collections of plants from far flung parts of the planet. The influence of the Gulf Stream and the subsequent mild, damp Kerry climate is further enhanced by the shelter that the mature trees and shrubs here afford each other. Yet it is still marvelous that such things as aeoniums and South African proteas grow outside all year. I was introduced to *Pitavia punctata*, a rare evergreen Chilean tree with white flowers, supposedly not hardy, yet defying the odds here.

Jubaea chilensis also looks as though it should be in the greenhouse but this baby, at 23 years old, lives successfully outside. In any case there would be no room for it in either greenhouse: Mark is busily decapitating towering cacti to stop them hitting the double height glass roof.

The hot conditions in the tropical house suit Burmese and Indian natives as well as papayas from Mexico. *Billardiera heterophylla* with pink flowers like bells is one of scores of plants stretching up greet a selection of bromeliads dangling down from the roof.

All sorts of echiums were met as we walked around, from plain and variegated *Echium canadensis* to *E. pininana* and hybridising babies of these, alongside the orange flowered foxglove relative, *Isoplexis sceptrum* from the Canaries. We made our way under skyward-bound 16-year-old *Sequoiadendron giganteum*, between rare white flowering *Magnolia cylindrica* and tree dahlias, weeping *Taxodium distichum* and *Cinnamomum camphora* the camphor tree.

In the middle of the damp jungle garden, Mark pointed to *Hydrangea aspera* 'Bellevue', a plant for wet ground and also the hydrangea with the biggest leaves. Here in this area, the route is by way of a raised wooden walkway over the water-logged borders. Enchanting for the visitor, it must be even more so for the frogs and newts, safe in the shelter of the canopy. We stood up high in the raised jungle room looking out over the garden, taking in plants from all over, from India and America to Vietnam and New Zealand - before returning to Kerry outside the gate.

Dunloe Castle Gardens

Beaufort, Killarney, Co. Kerry. Tel: 064 6644111. e-mail: reservations@thedunloe.com www.thedunloe.com. Open: May-Oct, by appointment only. Contact: Reception. Supervised children welcome. Dogs on leads. Directions: 10 km from Killarney on the Killarney-Beaufort road (R562). Note: Hotel and Garden closed until 2018 for restoration.

The number of superlatives needed to adequately describe the settings of some of the gardens in the southwest is a bit embarrassing: Bantry House sits on the edge of Bantry Bay. Ilnacullin basks in Glengarriff Harbour and Valentia Island shelters Glanleam. The Dunloe Castle Gardens, looking straight at the Gap of Dunloe, is another magnificently placed retreat.

The castle at Dunloe has a disputed origin. It may have been built in 1213 by the MacThomas clan, but it is also reputed to have been built by O'Sullivan Mór. Yet another source claims it as a Norman keep built by Meyler de Bermingham. Whatever the facts, the garden is built on what is clearly a favourable site, overlooking and commanding passages across two rivers, the Laune and the Loe. Presumably because of that enviable position, the castle has seen multiple onslaughts and plenty of fighting, including an attack by Cromwell's forces, who left it in ruins. Rebuilt after his departure, it continued to be inhabited until the 19th century, when it was left to decline.

Dunloe had to wait until the 20th century to be rescued. It was bought by Howard Hamilton a keen plant-lover from America, who created the garden. He bought the property and set to work at a furious pace and, with his considerable means, within only 16 years (1920–1936) he had produced a huge collection of trees and shrubs, many of them rare and unusual specimens.

The exposed site, meant that he had to begin with a windbreak of Monterey pines (*Pinus radiata*), sycamore and beech. The choicer plants were then bedded within this belt. These include a number of specimens which have since been catalogued by the renowned British plantsman Roy Lancaster. Lancaster began advising on planting at Dunloe in the 1980s, taking over from another giant of English horticulture, Sir Harold Hillier.

The shape of the garden is a bit amorphous and, to be honest, not that relevant. This is not a place of framed views, apart from that of the Gap. This garden is about the plants.

The tower house castle overlooks those plants. A little stone path travels from here through newly planted camellia and hydrangea beds, downhill to a lower walk, bounded by low walls on one side and a three-metre drop down to a beech wood on the other side.

The arboretum is filled with specimen trees and flowering shrubs. There are varieties of camellia, athrotaxis and magnolia, including the most fabulous *Magnolia delavayi* and a *Cornus mas* that looks as though it could collapse under the weight of flowers and then fruit. Two podocarpus worth looking for are, *Podocarpus totara* and *P. salignus*. The Japanese banana (*Musa basjoo*) is as exotic as its looks suggest and there are dawn redwoods or *Metasequoia glyptostroboides*, rediscovered in the 1940s in China, have previously thought to be extinct. The southwest's most famous tree, the strawberry tree or *Arbutus unedo* grows here in great numbers. Myrtle or *Luma apiculata* comes from Chile, but it might as well be a native, self-seeding freely, clumping into multi-stemmed specimens and decorating the garden year-round with dark green leaves and tiny white, fragrant flowers in August. Another multi-stemmed tree to love is the big *Pinus wallichiana,* while *Illicium anisatum*, the Japanese star anise tree and a huge *Osmanthus yunnanensis* tower above the lower layers of magnolia and camellia, tree ferns and hedychium or ginger lilies.

There is far too much in this garden to take in on a single visit and for many, the handy 'Around the World in Thirty Minutes' leaflet, which marks out thirty of the most remarkable trees, will be a welcome introduction.

The Gardens of Europe

Listowel, Co. Kerry. Open: All year, dawn–dusk. Directions: Coming into Listowel from the Limerick to Tarbert road (N69), turn left towards Listowel Golf Club and look for the signposts. The Gardens are next to the golf course.

Between the 1940s and early 1990s the land now occupied by this garden was the Listowel town dump. The Gardens of Europe provide a perfect lesson on the better use of public space. The site, which was given to the town by Lord Listowel, covers about three acres. It was ringed by mature oak trees and this handsome surrounding provided a stately and mature backdrop for the planned garden. Cleaning up the site, putting a drainage system in place and importing huge amounts of topsoil preceded the more interesting part of the creation. (Building a garden on top of three metres of rubbish is no straightforward task).

A statue of Oskar Schiller, the man who wrote the words to the European anthem 'Ode to Joy', was placed at one end of the garden, representative of the highest ideals of the European project. To balance this it seemed fitting to commemorate the holocaust and the mass slaughter of World War II by placing a sculpture by Irish artist Gerry Brouder at the opposite side of the garden. This is a monumental, enigmatic and brooding work, suggesting imprisonment and freedom.

The garden between the two works was divided into 12 bays or individual gardens – representative of the 12 countries that made up the European Union at the time of the garden's creation. The planting in each bay varies – different bays are devoted to camellias, roses, heathers, herbaceous perennials and sculptural plants.

In the years since the garden was put in place, there has also been the addition of a riverside walk and a circular looping wooded walk around the town. A great number of trees have been planted throughout. Well done Listowel.

Glanleam House & Garden

Valentia Island, Co. Kerry. Tel: 066 9476 176. e-mail: mail@glanleam.com www.glanleam.com Contact: Meta and Jessica Kreissig. Open: Easter-Oct, daily, 11am-7pm. By appointment. Supervised children. Dogs on leads. Special features: Musical events. Accommodation and meals. Events. Directions: Leave Knightstown and turn left after the Church of Ireland, which is itself on the left. Drive on and Glanleam is on the right, signposted.

On my most recent visit to Glanleam, the faint sound of chamber music drifted out the front door, sending me off to see the gardens on a wave of music. Like Derreen and Derrynane, Glanleam is another of the great 'wild' gardens of Kerry. It was the creation of Peter Fitzgerald, the 19th Knight of Kerry. In 1830 he took the bare rock of Valentia Island and began to mould it into a garden. He used his many connections to fill it with rare and unusual plants, many of which are still here. Today the gardens are worked by the Meta and Jessica Kreissig, who open the house to visitors.

The ornamental garden is long and narrow, made up of walks through sheltering and lightly shading trees, with occasional openings and clearings. Close to the house there are lawns and a semicircular walled kitchen garden where they grow vegetables organically. There are also acres of woods to explore. This is a large and ongoing project.

The list of exotic and special plants is long: The lily-of-the valley tree, or *Clethra arborea* reaches up 23 metres here. This is extraordinary, as they generally reach only about seven metres in their native Madeira. Embothriums, also attain heights in Glanleam that they never manage in Chile, where they come from.

In the Knight's Garden there are special ferns growing wild, including the black tree fern, *Cyathea medullaris*, the European chain fern (*Woodwardia radicans*) and the rare little Killarney fern (*Trichomanes speciosum*). Because of a craze among Victorians for collecting ferns, this little plant was almost collected to extinction. Collecting hordes would descend on woodlands like corseted and tweed-clad locusts, digging up everything ferny, with a particular enthusiasm for anything rare or weird-looking. They would then bring these home where most promptly died. It is therefore heartening to see the native ferns doing well here. Regarding tree ferns, a group of New Zealand scientists recently did tests on one of the huge specimens here and discovered that it was over 450-years-old. The aged trunks were brought in ships as ballast in the 19th century and planted into the ground where they started to grow.

The Upper Walk is the home of the camellia collection, which starts flowering at the end of November, and like a tag team, continues in succession right through to summer.

The perfect blue water in the bay is reminiscent of the setting for a Bond movie and the mild climate adds further to that impression. Fuchsias thrive in the wet warmth but almost wilt under the weight of flowers. Make sure to see the Dell, deep in the garden where the tree ferns grow in remarkable numbers and sizes. Another of the great sights is that of massed myrtles (*Luma apiculata*) with glossy dark leaves, bark like rust and sweet white blossoms. 'Such clean trees', Meta calls them.

The famed variegated *Luma apiculata* 'Glanleam Gold' with green leaves, edged in gold, originated in this garden.

The Spring Rice Garden is a small corner set out in memory of one Elizabeth Spring Rice who died exiled in France as a consequence of smuggling IRA arms in 1916. Agave and ginger lilies or hedychium

are grown alongside a circular water feature made of finely wrought stonework. Lengths of Victorian decorative pebble drains are in the middle of being unearthed and restored here, as they are throughout the garden. The Kreissigs are constantly finding and repairing stone walls and sets of steps in the garden, as they clear rampant growth. Meta says a lot of time also goes into rooting out the too-prolific hoherias.

We made our way along a fern and dierama walk, overhung with fringed acacias. In the spring, all bare ground fills up with bluebells, followed by libertia. To the front of the house, walk along the gunnera walk past more naturalised tree ferns and a thundering stream. There are waterways everywhere here. Some were hidden until recently under great groves of *Rhododendron ponticum*. As they clear this pest and uncover the streams, they are slowly restoring the stone work along these pretty channels.

The results, good and bad, of storms and subsequent tree losses are remarkable: Losses invariably reveal previously hidden features like the 30-metre-high monkey puzzle tree, or *Araucaria araucana*. Meanwhile, a *Podocarpus andinus* from the Andes, fell over in a storm yet continues to grow on its side. Close by the remains of a huge fallen cordyline gave rise to hundreds of seedlings and these have since been planted out as a young *allée*.

More than 22,000 oak were planted in the early 1990s, along with 15,000 ash. These huge plantations have been greatly improved by being cut through with dark, tunnelled paths and trails. Within the woods a holy well was uncovered and an intriguing healing garden has grown up around it.

Green Shutters

Sneem. Co. Kerry. Tel: 086 836 9997. Contact: Rose Cross. Open: To small groups by appointment. Directions: On appointment.

'This is Brian's garden,' said Rose Cross, widow of the renowned gardener and designer. We were standing, looking over the seaside garden before setting out to walk around. 'I'm just minding it,' she continued.

Brian began gardening here in 2003 before even beginning to build a house on the site. It was designed as a getaway, an easy garden to care for, requiring a

minimum of effort, away from the high maintenance Lakemount, his well known garden in Cork city. It was to be, as he put it a 'chop and drop' garden, meaning that whatever was chopped or pruned, could be left to mulch down naturally, a method of operating that suits the wilder sort of garden. That is precisely what Green Shutters is, a wild garden, informal and interesting, a mix of the native and the exotic in warm, subtropical South Kerry.

Situated in the crook of a sheltered bay on the south of the Iveragh peninsula, the garden enjoys a deal of protection from the worst of the Atlantic ocean. This coupled with the influence of the Gulf Stream, it can accommodate all sorts of precious things, from schefflera and eucryphia to *Cyathea cooperi*, the New Zealand tree fern and a number of different restios.

It is a higgledy piggeldy place, stretching in an organic flow from the house, out to the wild surroundings. The building stands on a wide gravel apron, set with slate and stone slabs, that step through it as through water. The gravel is softened considerably by multiple seedlings of self-sown *Verbena bonariensis* and different grasses, clumps of vivid pink *Nerine bowdenii* and agapanthus. All these these wave about, noisily swishing within sheltering fuchsia and hydrangea walls and the occasional tall cordyline. Add in pieces of well placed sculpture and strange looking hulks of bleached bog oak. I love it.

This shelter makes it possible to sit, immune to the wind on the blusteriest day, under a tall *Trachycarpus fortunei*. A pina colada might not be out of order.

From here wide, lightly defined gravel paths, also set with stepping stones, head off into the hilly garden on one side, and out to the rushes and water on the other. They wind back and forth over twice bridged streams and ponds, under fast growing Japanese acers and stands of bamboo, sometimes pruned up as in the case of a *Phyllostachys aurea*, sometimes not. 'Brian regretted planting bamboo,' Rose said. I wished that more people knew that before the embarked on a foray into growing these sometimes troublesome plants.

The garden climbs up a hill by way of grass paths, bounded by old fern-sprouting stone walls, to a viewing area above the canopy of acer and rhododendron, hydrangea and magnolia. The view over the canopy below and the garden near the house is charming but it is set to change. Soon even this viewing point will be below the canopy and this will increasingly become a flower wood.

Kells Bay House & Gardens

Kells, Caherciveen, Ring of Kerry, Co. Kerry. Tel: 066 9477 975. 087 7776 666. e-mail: billy@kellsgardens.ie www.kellsgardens.ie Contact: Billy Alexander. Open: All year. See website for seasonal changes. Partially wheelchair accessible. Children welcome. Dogs on leads. Special features: Accommodation. Groups tour may be booked. Restaurant. Special plant nursery. Directions: Travel from Glenbeigh on the N70 towards Caherciveen. Turn right at the sign for Kells. After 1.6 km turn right towards the beach. The entrance is 800 m along on the right.

A wet summer has its advantages. Arriving at the gate into Kells Bay Garden one of those advantages was seen tumbling over a cliff in the shape of a great gushing waterfall, crashing into a pool in the woods.

A little while later, I was standing in the restaurant looking out at the front garden, through sheets of rain. The view was a wedge of choppy Atlantic waters framed by the rocks. Closer in, a green sea of lawn washed around its own big boulder islands.

The front of the house is taken up by the tropical garden and its young trachycarpus over scree beds full of succulents. The pots of agave and aeonium, brugmansia, abutilon and yucca, between little statues of Buddha, are diverting.

Look behind however, to the garden that extends to the rear of the old house, to the wooded canopy.

Then start walking. Follow the noise of the water into what feels like a maw of bamboo, hedychium, tree ferns and rhododendrons. The noise turns into a roar. Within metres it is necessary to remember that this is Ireland, and not the jungle.

I took a walk with Billy Alexander, whose baby this is. Only metres into the garden we had already passed Ireland's tallest *Phoenix canariensis*.

'As long as it stays standing,' he laughed. The wood gardens are divided into two looped walks. We started on the Red Walk in the Ladies Walled Garden. This is a dark, moody and beautiful place, with some special plants including *Blechnum magellanicum*, arisaemas and *Musa basjoo*.

The path cuts between the light waving fronds of *Cyathea cooperi* and mad looking pseudopanax.

In every direction in this intimate area there are good things to see; the tree fern that has grown into, and almost become a part of an ancient stone wall, is unforgettable. This is a suitable introduction to what Billy told me is the biggest collection of tree ferns in the northern hemisphere. The collection is mostly made up of *Dicksonia antarctica*, some *D. squarrosa* and *D. fibrosa* from New Zealand. We stood surrounded by these dinosaur plants drinking in the splendour of it. Trees leaning over and continuing to grow along benches, give it a whacky sort of look too. *Blechnum nudum* is plant to look for too, naturally teaming up with *D. antarctica*. The tufts of *Microsorum pustulatum*, a fern that grows in abundance on the trunks of oak trees, are wonderful and I was taken by the handsome *Todea barbara* on the ground below.

We made our way into bamboo walks, drenched by their long culms, lying over temporarily after a heavy shower.

Billy spent a long time clearing these woods of *Rhododendron ponticum* before bringing in his Southern hemisphere plants. We passed a Jurassic-looking gunnera pool that feeds a big waterfall. The gunnera had the biggest leaves imaginable. On we went, past artist Peter Konig's tremendous dinosaur and the point where Billy was getting ready to built a rope bridge across the roaring torrent, ten metres below us. We continued uphill between native oak and ferns, moving into plantations of rhododendron, unusual Taiwanese *Fatsia polycarpa,* hostas and moss and low growing *Sasa veitchii.* The sasa needs constant chopping back. I needed to be reminded that there is only one full time gardener working here!

We ended up on top of what seemed like a cliff. I

loved the unpredictability of the terrain. We marched on past natural and man-made ledges thick with self-seeding tree ferns, eventually ending up down at the bottom of a ledge, in the bog garden, making our way along on wooden boardwalks, over streams. This is not a place for the un-booted. Kell's Bay is rightly becoming one of the best loved gardens on the island.

I left, driving through the International Dark Sky Preserve on the way to Kilorglin.

Killarney House & Knockreer House

Killarney, Co. Kerry. Tel: 064 6670164. e-mail: pat.dawson@ahg.gov.ie Contact: Reception. Open: All year Round. Wheelchair accessible. Children welcome. Dogs on leads. Special Features: Killarney National Park visitor centre. Courses. Tea room. Shop. Events. Directions: In the centre of the town.

Killarney House, built by the Browne family, Earls of Kenmare, in the reign of Queen Victoria, and visited by her in 1861, no longer stands. All that remains is a rather impressive stable block, which was turned into a comfortable home by a subsequent owner, John McShain, an American who subsequently handed both

it and the lands attached to the Irish state in the 1970s.

Today that stable block is home to the headquarters of the Killarney National Park, around which a new garden has been created and opened to the public. These gardens run from the stables down to the iconic lakes of Killarney. Using archaeological surveys and historical records, part of the old garden has been recreated. They began by building a boardwalk, on the site of two long herbaceous borders that were here in the 19th century. This is made up of a wide path in Kilkenny limestone and Killarney pink stone, which runs for about 100 metres alongside an equally long border of grasses, bulbs and perennials. A cherry walk featuring *Prunus* 'Kanzan' and fat, white-bloomed *P.* 'Shirotae' next door, was planted to replace an original, lost cherry walk.

Meanwhile, out in the centre of the large lawn, they traced and reinstated the network of old and lost garden paths. The new walks now run between formal bedding borders. They retrained and shaped the clipped yews and planted up a formal beech and lime *Patte d'oie* 'maze' and an oak, beech and Spanish chestnut 'wilderness'. The Irish oak for the wilderness was sourced from Tullynally in Westmeath. The intricate parterre was designed using *Ilex crenata* rather than box as a measure against box blight.

The garden takes in a host of styles, from the 18th, 19th and 20th centuries. The centrepiece is a fine sculpture set in the middle of the parterre dating to the 1700s. It has a long history in these gardens.

Adjacent, but not open to the public at this time, is what was once described as the finest example of a stable block in the country, with a beautiful two-storey dovecote and slaughterhouse, a carriage and horse bath and an unusual inner surrounding of pollarded limes. Outside the walls, a new walnut avenue has been planted up between mature magnolias.

These young gardens will take a few years to bed in but they are undoubtedly an addition to the amenity of the town.

A long trail leads from Killarney House through a wood, uphill for a few kilometres, past the historically interesting remains of several lime avenues. It passes Dervock Cottage, a quaint little building with the most improbably tall, dominant chimney. (Today its is used as a seasonal tearoom). The route eventually leads to the unrestored gardens of Knockreer House, another Kenmare property, also gone, which was, in its lifetime known to the people of Killarney as 'The Mansion'. It was built in 1870 and lost to a fire in 1913. The unrestored gardens here are haunting, slowly disappearing under wild growth. Wander through, and wonder about the old terraced Italian gardens, looking out over the rounded mounds of rhododendrons in the lower reaches of the grounds, and beyond these to ancient Ross Castle in the distance. It is a handsome ghost garden. Some day it may be restored, adding even more to Killarney's network of historic pleasure grounds and gardens.

Muckross Gardens

Muckross House, Killarney, Co. Kerry. Tel: 064 6670 164. e-mail: killarneynationalpark@opw.ie Open: All year. 9am-6pm. Closed Christmas. No entrance fee to garden. Greenhouses by appointment to groups. Partially wheelchair accessible. Supervised children. Dogs on leads. Special features: House tours. Craft shop. Restaurant. Self-guiding trails, including a trail for the visually impaired. Traditional farm. Directions: Situated 6 km from Killarney on the N71 to Kenmare.

Set among the woods and lakes of Killarney, Muckross is a garden I always look forward to visiting, if possible, arriving in a jaunting car. Slowly driving toward the gardens with your jarvey, ducking under the branches of roadside trees and seeing the woods at close quarters is the perfect way to begin a visit.

The house was built in 1843 for Henry Arthur Herbert. It transferred to the Guinness family and on to the family of Senator Vincent Arthur who presented it to the State in 1932. It stands deep into the park, surrounded by lawns that run smoothly down toward the famous lakes. Clipped hedges and topiary cones add a dash of formality and tidiness to these front and side lawns. Old shrub roses butt up against the building, along with an ancient wisteria, whose almost architectural trunk runs up along and blends in with the grey limestone window arches. From the terrace there are views over the lakes to the mountains beyond, the beginnings of the arboretum and a stand of sculptural Scots pine to the foreground.

The house looks out on a sunken garden with beds full of roses, clematis, annuals and herbaceous perennials. Following a set of steps from here into the rockery, is one of the great pleasures in Muckross. Scramble up, down and around the rocks, which sprout cotoneaster, cornus, small Japanese acers and a vicious-looking *Rosa sericea* subsp. *omeiensis* f. *pteracantha* with an improbably long name, winged, blood-red thorns and butter-coloured, single flowers.

This rock garden has a sort of tempered wildness about it. It is full of knotted heathers, native strawberry trees or *Arbutus unedo* and *Rubus thibetanus*. There are unusual, lesser-seen and interesting shrubs, creeping plants and trees growing on the sprawling rock face, and the full extent or size of the rockery is difficult to see from most points within it. Through shrubs and stone outcrops, one catches glimpses of the manicured parkland in one direction and the arboretum and extensive plantations of rhododendrons beyond.

Before heading off to the far reaches of the wood and tree collections, visit the walled garden. This is a smart and ordered place with lollipop viburnums, box-enclosed beds full of wallflowers, tulips, antirrhinums and forget-me-nots. The rustic fences backing the borders work well. The gravel paths between are perfectly swept and the tidy lawns are ruler-straight and manicured. I discovered the hard way however, that the greenhouses, stuffed full with orchids and tender exotics can only be visited *by groups and by appointment*. You might have to settle for a nose pressed against the window.

Take a walk through the nearby water garden, which strongly contrasts with the manicured walled and flower gardens. The paths trail alongside stone-edged streams, with sprays of ferns and tufty moss, big clumps of crinum lilies and hostas. The little stone walls and slab-stone bridges over the water are charming. The mature trees overhead leave in enough light for hydrangeas and other shrubs beneath. On my last visit, I discovered a promontory bounding the water garden and arboretum. This huge outcrop can, like the rockery, be climbed for better views of the rest of the garden. The arboretum, which underwent shocking losses in the Valentine's Day storm of 2014 was still under restoration on my last visit. A huge toppled pine having crashed, causing huge destruction in its path, just missed a little *Podocarpus salignus* by inches. How will the little one fare in its now light-filled position?

Sneem Community Garden

Pier Road, Sneem, Co. Kerry. Open: All year. 8.30am-12.30pm. As this is a productive garden there is little to see between November and April. No entrance fee. Special features: Vegetables and flowers on sale. Directions: In Sneem turn off the square for Pier Road. The garden is a down the road on the left.

The Pier Road Garden is a little community-run vegetable, herb and flower garden set on the edge of the village of Sneem, carrying all the usual crops and some unusual food crops also. It is not over-prettified but rather is a simple working garden that anyone with a plan to start a vegetable plot should visit and note.

It also includes a privet maze, some rose walks, raised mixed beds and a stream garden that wanders through the long plot, decorated with little stone bridges. It makes sense that the gorgeous village would have a pretty community garden.

The Water Margin

Cappanacush East, Templenoe, Co. Kerry. Tel: 064 6682 998. e-mail: thewatermargin@eircom.net Contact: Aly Peh and Neal Cahill. Open: By appointment. Directions: On application.

Not many new houses can call themselves 'moated.' Aly and Neal's almost can. The Water Margin is a well named garden. Laid out on a wooded hill, it is almost completely encircled by a small river. The gardening duo have become accustomed to being surrounded by water. My overwhelming memory is of the roar of water, as we walked along Corrib slate paths, between beds of flowers and grasses, along the drive that circles the house. I could not see the water but even when invisible, it made its presence felt.

Aly laid the garden out along Feng Shui lines: The house has its back to the hill and faces Kenmare Bay.

Felled trunk and rustic fence-lined paths pick their way through the wood garden, between ferns, tree ferns and rhododendrons. The site is wet. The river overflows at various points, washing soil away as it does and as a result there is only a very thin layer of soil sprinkled over the rock. They explained that establishing plants is not always easy, but working with what they have, they plant moisture-loving plants such as astilbe and rodgersia.

A small, natural lily and frog pond fed from the stream, adds another element of the natural to the garden. Nature is supreme and the lines of beautiful fungi growing in linear patterns on the tree trunks along the path are remarkable.

Aly and Neal also incorporated the old stone walls that were here before they arrived. The stone makes for a handsome backdrop to their hydrangeas, including Aly's favourite, *Hydrangea paniculata* 'Vanilla Fraise', which has a flower that moves from white to pink as it ages.

They grow hundreds of hostas, all in pots and containers, as both a slug fighting measure and because these scores of different varieties, from the gigantic *Hosta* 'Empress Woo' to brilliantly white variegated *H.* 'Minuteman', are well suited to life in pots.

The garden, with its strong oriental feel, not surprisingly carries a good number of acers and bamboos, planted around statues of Buddha and stone lanterns. One of these lanterns is an elegant terracotta example, made by Aly.

The main route is a circling one, with the river always on the outer boundary. Not many gardens can boast anything like the spectacular waterfall, thundering over the stepped-down boulder ledges in this little river. In other places it rolls along as a gurgling stream, quietly gliding over rocks. The path along it at one point, turns onto a Japanese-style, zigzag stepping stone bridge. In another it leads over a little wooden bridge. It becomes a raised wooden walkway in places and finally ends up on a tall wooden platform that towers over the lower garden. This platform is a fun piece of design, part outdoor dining room surrounded by wisteria and part viewing platform, with a bird's-eye view out over the double white *Prunus* 'Oku Miyako' and a lace-cap *Hydrangea villosa* 'Anthony Bullivant.' Make sure to seek out the 'erratic stone'.

Limerick

Adare Town Garden

Main Street, Adare. Open: Every day.

The village of Adare could be described as a garden. It is a planned village, unusual for Ireland, built around Adare Manor and featuring a number of quaint thatched cottages, some of which are further enhanced with typical cottage gardens, full of climbing roses and all the old-fashioned favourites.

It is worth stopping the car to take a walk along the main street, as you will probably be stuck in traffic anyway. It is a notorious place for traffic jams. Take the time to stroll through the village and enjoy the show. The town park is worth investigating. This is a well presented park with groves of trees, island beds full of grasses and perennials, an avenue of hornbeam and wisteria arches. Make a point of seeing the village washing area by the front gate, where the women once came to do the washing in the cold water.

Ballynacourty

Ballysteen, Co. Limerick. Tel: 061 393 626. e-mail: stacpoole@iol.ie. Contact: George and Michelina Stacpoole. Open: May-Sept. By appointment to groups only. Not wheelchair accessible. Supervised children welcome. No dogs. Member of Gardens of Ireland Trust. Directions: Driving from Limerick to Foynes on the N69, turn right onto the L6006. Drive onto the T-junction and turn left. The garden is 2 km from the turn on the right. Tall hedges and stone pillars mark the entrance.

All-green gardens are quite rare. This stylish type of garden is not as widely seen as it should be. There are a great number of effects that can be achieved confining the palette to lawns, hedging, trees and shrubs. It might not be particularly low-maintenance but neither is it in the highest-maintenance bracket.

Half a century ago Ballynacourty was 'a plain, unadorned, old farmhouse'. Today the handsome garden has the appearance of a place that never knew a plain or unadorned day in its life. The years since

moving to Ballynacourty have been well spent by the Stacpooles. They have turned the grounds into a sophisticated, handsome garden with references to historic landscaping. The lines are architectural. They are the lines that hedging delivers. Everywhere there are long and tall beech hedges, with the line of one substantial run standing out and above the contrasting line and colour of a second hedge, travelling in another direction and at another angle. The garden has the feel of a maze with little architectural surprises found at the bottom of each.

Start with a house draped voluptuously in a mantle of wisteria. Just visible under its trailing branches is a loggia-cum-conservatory. It feels as much Lombardy as Limerick.

A walk through the garden proper begins through an arch cut into a big hornbeam, hedge that runs out from the house, into the first of the garden rooms where a substantial double curve of privet, tall and expertly cut, dominates. Privet is their favourite hedging plant. It is easy to shape and makes a good dense screen but it does need several cuts a year, making it the choice for those who do not mind work.

From this point, at the end of the hedge, the garden meanders in several directions: 'One Christmas George thought we'd go this way,' explained Michelina

Stacpoole, as she led the way into one particular garden room in the six-acre plot. This route takes in a lavender walk that leads towards a wildflower area with grass paths cut through the buttercups, cowslips and meadowsweet. We arrived up on a bank overlooking a grassed area, a sea of daffodils and the River Shannon beyond. The cherry walk is for George, 'paradise' in the late spring, while the long runs of blue and pink hydrangea, specimen camellia and aralia, magnolia and spindle, provide him with equally edifying sights at different times of year. He says he feels lucky in having pockets of both acid and lime soil here.

Ballynacourty is an easy garden in which to get lost. Only when the path leads up a hill that overlooks the garden, can the shape and plan of the place, with its feature gates, pillars, statues and hedge walls be seen in context.

Apart from the hedges, the other feature vital to the look of Ballynacourty is the statuary, and the place is filled with eclectic works that trick and surprise, from chimney pots salvaged from Dublin Castle to witty 'classical' sculptural works made from items bought in TK Maxx. The jokes and references are scattered through the garden.

The Stacpooles derive as much use from the natural features the land throws up as those brought in and built: Old wells and stone outcrops peeping out of the well-kept lawns are used like stepping stones across a green lake. In addition to looking good, these boulders give some idea of the sort of rocky ground out of which the garden was hewn. Finally there are some fine specimen trees. I loved the mature walnuts and huge sweet chestnuts, as did the two mad springer spaniels that joined us on the walk, racing each other, running tight circles of the trees.

The Boyce Garden

Mountrenchard, Foynes, Co. Limerick. Tel: 069 65302. e-mail: phylboyce@icloud.com www.boycesgardens.com. Contact: Phyl Boyce. Open: May-Oct. Daily, 10am-6pm. Other times by appointment. Partially wheelchair accessible. Groups welcome. Not suitable for children. Special features: Member of Gardens of Ireland Trust Directions: The garden is 1 km from Loughill, travelling towards Glin, off the N69. Signposted.

Phyl and her late husband Dick Boyce began working this well known one-acre garden in 1983, and it has clearly known decades of love and dedication. The house and garden are built on the site of six labourers' cottages. That history is visible in the six varieties of hedging that run along the roadside in front of the present-day garden, each being a reference to one of the old dwellings.

From the moment you enter from the road, through a door in the wall, past a *Magnolia wilsonii*, it is clear that this is far from the garden belonging to a humble cottage. Instead, it is a maze of complicated rooms in different styles. Arched tunnels under blankets of clematis and honeysuckle lead from one compartment to another. The look changes constantly, morphing from a painted Japanese gate garden featuring young cut leaf acer and little bonsai chestnuts to a perfect small alpine garden facing south and baking in the sun, and from there on into a pair of long double borders that 'may yet be done away with'

according to Phil Boyce. These days she is moving in the direction of using more shrubs with only spot use of perennials. There is no shortage of flowers here in any event. I love the recently made wisteria arch that greets the visitor who comes into the garden by the second, gated entrance. This route leads into a series of secret walks between a host of specimen trees, tree ferns and shrubs, including variegated clerodendron and a small tree that is special to Phil. The well aged *Corylus avellana* is a sight, winter and summer. As is the elegant myrtle or *Luma apiculata*, intertwined with *Rosa* 'Nevada'. The double use of soil and space is something small-plot gardeners must learn to master to get more bang for their buck. The flowers of the host tree and the roses come into bloom one after another and are in turn followed by the berries on the neighbouring elder. A pruned up shrub of *Griselinia littoralis* 'Bantry Bay' graces the lily pond.

Griselinia is a slightly tender plant, as many people have discovered over recent hard winters. It does well here in the shelter however. Growing shrubs as standards is a favourite trick in this garden. Pruning up the lower branches and making a 'tree' shape, or lollipop, out of what would normally be a multi-stemmed, ground-sweeping shrub is also another route to expanding the number of plants that can be fitted into a small garden. Pruning out the bottom branches allows the insertion of shade-loving plants into the soil below, plants like spring bulbs, winter cyclamen, ferns and hellebores. Topiary is another feature in the Mountrenchard garden, and a golden myrtle trained as a perfect two-metre cone must be the star among the trained plants here.

Phil is a keen produce-grower and her raised bed vegetable garden is an example of what can be achieved in a compact space. She is a great lover of home-made compost and has been extolling its virtues for many years. Her vegetables are a testament to that compost: The brick wall behind the vegetable shelters a little peach tree. It catches the sun and holds the heat to help the peaches ripen above the lines of cut-and-come salad crops.

You do not see the the greenhouse until nearly bumping into it, so abundant are the distractions around it. It is a small treasure trove, full of grapes, succulents, an Australian *Todea barbara*, *Fuchsia* 'Annabel' with flowers like white ballet dresses, plum-coloured *Rhodochiton atrosanguineus* and a jam of other exotics. Outside in a little shaded area is where she grows her ferns in marked contrast to the wild colour party inside.

At the lower end of the garden there is a boggy area with, among other things, a Japanese pagoda tree or sophora with zigzagging branches and minuscule, sweet flowers. The garden is full of good plants and Phil is equally full of knowledge and good advice which she kindly shares with her visitors.

Cahernorry Church & Gardens

Cahernorry Church, Ballyneety, Co. Limerick. Tel: 086 260 9068.
e-mail: desneyland1@gmail.com. Contact: Kathleen and Des Kingston. Open: May-Sept. By appointment to groups only. Not wheelchair accessible. Children welcome. No dogs. Special features: Teas provided by appointment. Directions: Drive on the R512, old Cork Road from Limerick for 9.5 km to Ballyneety Village. Turn right at the Garda Station to Cahernorry Church 500 m along on the left.

Cahernorry is a small, former Church of Ireland place of worship, built in 1809, dismantled in 1862 and re-built on this site. Today it is a private home with an unusual garden attached. This is the work of Kathleen and Des Kingston, a couple with the rare ability to bring wit and fun into a garden.

The space around the house is clearly divided into several garden rooms, each distinct and complete within itself. The Kingstons restored the old graves that were here when they arrived, placing them in a dignified, peaceful, hedge-enclosed area at the side of the garden. Outside that reverential corner, the garden simply takes flight in a spree of 'shrines' and obelisks, found object art, topiary, trees, water and flowers. There are what might be described as cabinets of curiosities with bits and pieces of architectural salvage from 1950s' cars, old industrial signs and eclectic sculptures ranged about on ledges and shelves, in the corners of borders and under the trees. The outdoor living room needs to be seen and do not miss the covered bridge over the pond. I thought the shed made from aged planks and sleepers was beautiful. Des is a man addicted to making and creating. There is even a round tower.

The planting, courtesy of Kathleen, is a pleasure. It features lots of well worked topiary, maturing shrubs and tall native trees, busy and pretty herbaceous borders and plenty of natives. This is a charming, very personal garden, owing less to outside influences than to the individuals who made it. I suspect they have a lot of fun with it. As we left, I spotted the nose cone from a passenger jet. Apparently Des has a plan for it.

Coolwater Garden

Fedamore, Co. Limerick. Tel: 087 2584 716. e-mail:kevinjamesbegley@gmail.com
www.coolwatergarden.com. Contact: Kevin Begley. Open: By appointment all year as part of the Secret
Gardens of Limerick. Member of Gardens of Ireland Trust. Directions: Traveling 11 km on the R512 from
Limerick towards Kilmallock, turn right at Kirby's Hunting Lodge and drive to a T-junction. Take a left.
The garden is 100m along on the left.

Coolwater is primarily the garden of an individual with his own particular take on the sport of gardening. Sitting out one day several years ago, Kevin Begley decided that he had had enough of cutting grass and invited a friend with a JCB to see to the problem. The result is a half-acre garden, almost 50 percent of which is a pond, a great expanse of lily-covered and rush-surrounded water that is many times more vital, dynamic and entertaining to sit and study, than grass. Kevin then built an octagonal summerhouse and dining room with a commanding view of the water. It makes for a perfect hide from which to study the constantly changing wildlife show.

The garden initially presents itself as a rock and wood garden, an upward sloping expanse of gravel and sandstone boulders, stepping-stones, sleepers, pillars and unusual shading parasols. These run between and under *Acacia baileyana* 'Purpurea' and a *Cedrus glauca* 'Glauca' and lines of Japanese acer. The ground beneath is also busy, with native ferns presented to him by friends from Skrule Hill, which can be seen from the garden.

There are stone circles partially smothered under mounds of creeping *Thymus citriodorus* 'Aureus', like golden lava. Recumbent cotoneaster, pachysandra and dead nettle, similarly spread out like different shades of spilled, liquid greenery. Bright variegated *Euphorbia* 'White Swan' and bergenia sprout upwards from these spreading blankets. In spring the place is awash with crocuses, while spreading cyclamen decorate the ground in autumn.

I was busy enjoying the rockery until I spotted the containers, lots of them. The only thing to do was get down on hunkers and investigate, container after container, full of intricate miniature landscapes, little plantations grown around rocks, slates, and mounds of scree. They are like small mountain ranges with tiny forests of miniature shrubs, perennials, alpines, bulbs and grasses.

Nail-scissors and tweezer-preened, these scaled-down worlds are like little marvels. In one of the metre-wide, shallow, circular containers we looked at a tiny conifer, *Picea pungens* 'St. Mary's Broom' with a shrublet of *Polygala chamaebuxus* around some artfully arranged rocks. This was just one of many such creations, each a little vision of perfect little mountain range-gardening using inch-high rhododendron and lewisia and every sort of saxifraga and sedum, thyme and erodium. The stone in each container came from friends who know Kevin to be a man who can put a stone to good use. He uses Killaloe slate and tufa, limestone and granite as well as sandstone from the local Ballyhoura hills.

He constructed a shelter to give some of the containers an arid, desert habitat which suits and all sorts of cacti as well as a *Beschorneria yuccoides* that recently flowered on a spike 5 metres long.

We eventually made our way to the pond, home to newts, sticklebacks, fish and birds, surrounded by weeping sedges, purple loosestrife, bog-bean, bulrush and meadowsweet. We had left the rarefied world of the containers for the native pond. The only exotics here are the waterlilies. The surrounding trees are not so local however: There are loquats and *Magnolia* 'Gold Star' and more Japanese acers. The more I saw the more time I needed – especially for those containers…

Glin Castle

Glin, Co. Limerick. Contact: Tel: 068 34173. e-mail: catofglin@gmail.com www.glincastle.com
Open: By appointment to groups only. Directions: Enter the village of Glin from the Foynes–Listowel Road
(N69). Go to the top of the village and turn right at O'Shaughnessy's Pub. The castle is at the end of this
short avenue.

Glin Castle has been the home of the knights of Glin since the late 1700s. The Georgian manor, built in 1780, was transformed into a 'castle' in the 19th century, complete with turrets, crenellations and Gothic features. It stands on the Shannon Estuary, more handsome than imposing.

The castle is covered lightly in wisteria and is fronted by bay and yew cones. Close by the building there is a formal garden with classical busts perched in niches cut into the hedges and avenue of clipped yew pyramids and a little green garden room lead out from here. Very little colour or flowers are allowed to invade the restraint in this area apart from occasional roses and hydrangeas.

There are sundials on little stone islands and pieces of statuary scattered about, standing free and set into hedges and under trees. A witty swagged wall covered in lichen finishes off this garden and marks the border between the formal areas and the wood and wilder place beyond.

Over the past few years, the lawns leading from the house have seen the addition of young acer and magnolia, camellia and eucryphia, trachycarpus and underneath, mounds of hydrangea. More mature

specimens of *Cornus capitata*, *Magnolia campbellii* and *Pinus radiata* look venerable beside the babies.

Walk uphill through a meadow, past benches on viewing points and intriguing sculptures, into the shade of the wood, where the fast-running stream makes quite a racket. The place is full of native ferns to which they added tree ferns under the oak canopy.

Hunt out the early 19th century grotto, snug in the wood: 'The grotto was completely covered in rubbish when they found it a few years ago. We didn't even know it was here,' Madam FitzGerald told me when I last visited. Once found, its history came to light too: It appears that it was an unofficial bower for courting couples and it enjoyed excellent business over the last two centuries among estate workers.

The modern standing stone folly is much younger. Set in a clearing, it is surrounded by huge, stately and aged trees, which have the effect of making it look ancient too. Images of druids spring to mind. A great number of rhododendrons have been planted in the wood, adding to the fine and a most impressive snowdrop tree or *Halesia carolina*.

Leaving the woods, you go through a great, heavy wooden gate into the walled garden. This is a proper working garden, covering two acres and brim-full of vegetables and flowers: Cosmos, walls of sweet pea, seas of cornflowers, nigella and other annuals decorate the beds of asparagus, Swiss chard and lettuce. Everything is grown in substantial blocks.

The temple with a headless statue of Andromeda is surrounded by white roses. Long deep beds of acanthus and geranium, phlox and agapanthus shoulder in on each other while out in the centre, there are hot borders of crocosmia and helenium, kniphofia and sedum all jumbled in with ornamental grasses. Making your way between heavily fruiting trained fruit trees, walk on further between the smart clipped yews. At the bottom of the slope a little, rounded, wrought-iron seat will invite you to sit and look up the garden to views of sweet pea, yew and a big fuchsia hedge grown as an arch among the flowers.

Knockpatrick Gardens

Knockpatrick, Foynes, Co. Limerick. Tel: 069 65256. 087 9485 651. e-mail: hob@eircom.net Contact: Tim and Helen O'Brien. Open: May-Oct. By appointment. Charity day in May. Contact for annual dates. Not wheelchair accessible. Supervised children welcome. No dogs. Special features: Plants for sale. Member of Gardens of Ireland Trust. Directions: Take the N69 from Limerick for 34.5 km. About 1.5 km before Foynes village follow the sign for Knockpatrick. The garden is 1.5 km from the cross and marked by an arched entrance.

The garden at Knockpatrick was started by the O'Brien family nearly 80 years ago. Since then three generations of Tim's family have worked and developed the three-acre plot, which enjoys an enviable view over the Shannon.

From the gateway, the drive leads enticingly under an arch of dripping gold laburnum, and along a route being slowly encroached upon by magnolia, liriodendron and peeling barked Japanese acer. Tim's father planted all these. Tim is not too pleased with the bulging, colonising habits of these great trees as they push out onto his drive, but if one has to be bullied by plants, let it be by a smarter sort. On the other side of the drive is a steep rock garden with a waterfall, on top of which the house appears to stand. It is unusual, a sort of plant-stuffed mini-mountain.

When Tim and his wife Helen began gardening here, Knockpatrick was a calmer place, centred on a collection of rhododendrons and camellias, both of which love the acid soil which predominates. The husband and wife team maintained these treasures, including the big 80-year-old *Parrotia persica* or Persian ironwood tree. But they also set about adding to and varying the planting. They brought in everything from bamboos and tree ferns to trees like cercis, drimys and embothrium, blue Himalayan poppies, candelabra primulas, hellebores, and unusual shade lovers like *Diphylleia cymosa*, the umbrella leaf plant.

'We have the time to work the place and really we're at it all the time,' said Helen of their almost all-consuming project. Under their care this has become a more varied garden, divided into different levels by pools, streams and stone features, including a moon-gate, or circular gateway that joins and separates two garden rooms. Their latest project is a newly developing arboretum. It is filling up fast with interesting specimens, particularly of magnolia.

The whitewashed yard is a bright sun-trap and they take full advantage of the warmth by growing *Echium candicans*, actinidia, and a range of different abutilons against the gleaming white walls, in nothing more than the soil that a single sleeper holds against the wall. This area gives a whole new meaning to the phrase patio gardening. Backed by the lime-washed stone, this range of exotics look great. I felt I could have been somewhere on a Greek Island.

My favourite area must be the long stream, a ribbon of primulas and ferns, rhododendron and hydrangea, leading along a rough path to a gate in the distance.

For all the new plants, the busiest and best time of the year in O'Brien's garden is late May when most of the rhododendrons bloom and they hold a charity day. Plants are potted up and teas and cakes are prepared for the crowds that arrive to enjoy the fleeting flowers and party atmosphere. Helen laughed at the thought of the amount of work that goes into it: 'Every year we say this is the year and every year we do it all over again!'

Terra Nova Garden

Dromin, Kilmallock, Co. Limerick. Tel: 063 90744. 086 0658 807.
e-mail: www.terranovagarden.com. www.terranovagarden.com Contact: Deborah and Martin Begley.
Open: Mar-Oct. As part of Secret Gardens of Limerick. By appointment. Families and groups welcome.
Special features: Complimentary refreshments in self-service teahouse. Fairy shop. Directions: Travel through
Bruff and towards Kilmallock (R512), for 2 km. Turn right at the crossroads and follow the signs for Terra
Nova Gardens.

The last time I wrote about Terra Nova, I stated that no matter how often I visited it, it always felt that it had just been given a complete overhaul. This has happened again - the fairies have arrived or at least evidence of them in the shape of doors in tree trunks, little houses and bits of paraphernalia. Visitors with small girls in tow will find themselves well served.

It is a small garden, covering half an acre, but incorporating the sort of clever use of space that the Japanese would envy. It is almost impossible to describe how many plants in such good combinations that Deborah and Martin Begley manage to shoe-horn into a finite area. The Begley's are fanatical gardeners and a walk through Terra Nova almost brings on a bout of sensory overload. Meanwhile, the changes and developments are so marked between each visit that my notes could refer to different places altogether.

Begley's garden is, for want of a better name, a laboratory. They subscribed to seed-collecting expeditions to locate unusual plants like African hemp or *Sparmannia africana*, with exquisite white flowers and big showy leaves. Deborah is fond of using exotics like *Ricinus communis* the castor oil plant and *Amicia zygomeris* as annuals. The frost will get them and they will die, but treating them in the same way the rest of us deal with petunias means that this does not matter. She loves arisaemas, strange-looking plants like hobgoblin arums. Among the huge number of plants there are other grotesques too, like the memorable voodoo lily or *Dracunculus vulgaris*, which smells like a baby's bad nappy: 'The flies love it,' Deborah told me.

Considerable thought has been given to the design. Look for the betula-and-verbena circle, the unusually placed oak gate in the woods and the fun-sized fern garden at the shaded front of the house. This little corner boasts such oddities as the upside-down fern *Arachniodes standishii*, and huge *Polypodium vulgare* 'Whitley Giant'. Glimpses of stained glass seen in various places around the garden comes courtesy of Martin and his glassworks.

A great love of trees and only a half-acre to play with means that small trees are the order of the day, from small calycanthus and heptacodium to a locally-bred betula, known as *Betula* 'White Light'. It has a particularly stark, white peeling bark and good autumn colour. I loved the combination of *Acer dissectum* that were planted together as seedlings. They are all slightly different to each other in the way that seedlings often are.

Martin is head of hard landscaping, maker of features like the little bridged frog pond, edged with canna lilies, golden gardener's garters and bulrushes. His Thai house is surrounded by big tree ferns, including a *Dicksonia squarrosa* and the beautiful tassel flowers of *Amaranthus caudatus*. When I first saw the Thai house, there were three women also seeing it for the first time. They were speechless. The path away from it leads along through a snaking pergola walk, built to hold a number of roses including the yellow *Rosa* 'Teasing Georgia' and an unusual green *Rosa chinensis* 'Virdiflora'. In every corner there is a little bench, wooden structure, bunch of ceramic balloons or something diverting.

This is an inspiring garden, especially for those who work in a restricted space. It is a testament to what flair, passion and back-breaking work can achieve.

Tipperary

Ashfield Garden

*Lisnagaul, Bansha, Co. Tipperary. Tel: 062 54882. 087 2899 800.
e-mail: breadfhayes@gmail.com. Contact: Breda and James Hayes. Open: For the Tipperary Garden
Festival. See annual details. Other times by appointment. Directions: Leave Bansha on the R663. The
garden is approximately 5 km from the village on the right. A two storey farmhouse and stone gateway with
a green barn.*

When we were small and the teacher asked us to draw a house, we drew it with a door in the middle, four regularly placed windows on either side and a path running in a straight line from gate to door and on either side there were flowers, flowers and more flowers. No grass, Just flowers. We never came across this in real life. But it was what we drew.

Near the little village of Bansha in the Glen of Aherlow, with a view of the Galtee Mountains I finally came across the house I constantly drew as a child.

It is Ashfield and it belongs to the extraordinary flower gardener, Breda Hayes.

In real life it is further enhanced by a racing green coloured barn covered in jasmine, a subtle green that foils the exuberance of the dahlias, rudbeckias and asters, cosmos, aconites and roses.

Calling it a simple flower garden would be to lie. The wide straight borders, divided by a gravel path, also include flowering trees and shrubs. Standing over the persicaria and lavender there are small trees and big shrubs, spreading acers and *Cornus kousa* 'Rainbow', roses of all descriptions, mahonia and plum-coloured calycanthus. To some extent, lines of berrying cotoneaster and laurel hedge hold in and frame the beds of variegated azara, hardy geranium and nepeta. Breda has a talent for growing flowers in simple and attractive ways. The mixes she puts together give the garden such personality. Even the seasons seem to bend to Breda's will. I looked at bearded irises and lupins still flowering with gusto in mid October.

The place is a bit like a different impressionist painting from wherever you view it and discovering the secret paths, hidden behind a border and between the flowers, adds a few more pictures to the gallery. Meanwhile, the cattle in the field next door, looked over with more than a little envy. Those flowers probably looked as tasty as they were pretty.

Ballyboy House

*Ballyboy, Clogheen, Cahir, Co. Tipperary. Contact: John and Breda Moran. Tel: 052 7465297. 087 6360
296. e-mail: ballyboyhouse@eircom.net. www.ballyboy-house.com. Open: As part of the Tipperary Garden
Trail. See website for annual details. Otherwise all year by appointment. Special features: Accommodation.
Plants for sale. Teas can be arranged. Partially wheelchair accessible. Directions. Situated on the R665.*

A garden is more than plants. This garden was created around Ballyboy, a handsome Georgian house in the Tipperary countryside and it is very much the garden that belongs to its house. The stone outhouses, grain stores with steps leading up to lofts, half-doors, arched carriage gates and slabbed courtyards, shape and determine the sort of garden that works best here.

This is not Big House gardening, harnessed and smart and carried out by a staff. It is approachable, easy, country gardening. Think Jamie Oliver rather than Patrick Guilbaud. One could nearly believe that the roses and clematis just appeared on the back walls of the house, that the phlox and sisyrinchium in the stone lined beds and sprouting from cracks in the slabbed areas, simply put themselves there. Well they did. But garden visitors know that more than these welcome plants self-seed.

The house garden is informality itself, a series of stone paved areas, patios and a courtyard, old walls covered in climbers with beds of Japanese anemones fringed below. There are sprays of flower and foliage tucked in between the slabs and it is busy with bees. As the garden travels out from the buildings, it is into, unusually, a flower wood. there are paths in several directions, one leading towards a moss-covered, dripping fountain. The trees way overhead filter light through to sheets of aquilegia, hellebore and lupin below. From here, bamboo and shrub lined walks lead past vegetable gardens lined with ancient digging tools.

We followed a gate out through a stone wall and past an unusual ruin, to another wood. The River Tay marks runs along the bottom of the hill and we made our way down to it on a path carved out by John and Breda's daily walks. In spring this is all bluebells.

Back at the house, another arch leads to the front and a rock garden with a mix of lavender and hydrangea, cistus and geum. The view here is of a wide span of lawn with more shrub and flower borders, specimen trees including *Liriodendron variegata*, dawn redwood and Indian chestnut.

There is an ash wood too, appropriate for an ex-Tipperary hurler such as John. Paths lined by *Rosa rugosa* lead into it, and eventually to a lake, about a half acre in size, with an old boat house and a rough trail around it. Wild it feels and wild it is. The sound of birds was almost deafening.

Ballyhist House

Ardfinnan, Clonmel, Co. Tipperary. Contact: Joe and Mary Johannes. Tel: 052 7466 788. 087 7996 169. e-mail: johannesmaryjoe@yahoo.co.uk Open: As part of the Tipperary Garden Trail. Contact for annual details. Other times by appointment. Directions: Take the Clogheen road from Ardfinnan for 2.6 km to Ardfinnan church. Turn right to a pink bungalow on the left.

The winds whip through Joe and Mary Johannes's garden with a ferocity that can lift a wooden bench and throw it across the garden. That could be off-putting for some gardeners. Not Joe and Mary. I think they could be described as gardening triumphantly against the elements.

Just 15 years ago, they brought in 120 tons of topsoil to improve the hard 'yellow soil' that greeted them at their new home in Tipperary. The late designer Brian Cross gave them a plan for a garden and they have been playing with it ever since, planting against and with the wind to make an attractive distinctive garden.

The drive runs in past a 'river' of creeping cotoneaster, to a house that looks like part of a border. The building sits anchored in a flower border between lilies, pink *Paeonia* 'Bowl of Beauty', daphnes, arums and pink *Rosa* 'Bonica'. There are pots too, of amsonia and huge *Hosta* 'Sum 'n Substance'. This busy start continues as the garden spreads out from the building in a series of different areas all linked by widespread use of gravel. Joe told me that they find that half-inch gravel is best to walk on. As well as being practical, alliums and irises, grasses, geraniums, and boulders stand out well over an expanse of gravel.

To counteract the wind, they plant things very small, giving the plants the chance to adapt. I admired the bed of well adapted *Hydrangea* 'Annabelle' and was told they take a chainsaw to these once a year. There is no molly-coddling here.

Joe is responsible for the stone work. His sunken wall in particular stands out, dug into the gravel. Boulders emerge like icebergs through the sea of stones and overhead, mop-head and lace-cap hydrangeas and variegated azara form a floral necklace. The wall, draped in an impressive white wisteria functions to protect a precious *Grevillea rosmarinifolia* and callistemon from the skelping wind. Tamarisk might look exotic but it needs no protection.

Planting pines provided the shelter allowing them to grow *Acer shirasawanum* 'Aureum', which has such spectacular red fringed leaves.

There are covetable little features everywhere, from a set of steps draped with a carpet of *Cerastium tomentosa* or snow-in-summer to a line of four clipped golden euonymus balls in the gravel. We inspected the ex-lily pond, now a damp bed where they grow

primulas, astilbes, and hostas, surrounded by a recumbent juniper. Here and elsewhere in the garden, they use taxodium needles under the hostas as part of the war on slugs.

The pergola is most useful, holding up and supporting *Clematis* 'Lady Diana', *C.* 'Dr Ruppel', roses, jasmine and a wisteria. The view of this puff of flowers from the house is one of Mary's favourites. And, seen through beds of phlox, gladioli, blue and white campanula, day lilies and Japanese anemones, it looks even better. The anemones arrived courtesy of the birds', Joe told me.

Do not miss the courtyard garden, around which the house is built. In this one completely wind-free, tranquil hideaway, they can sit, surrounded by the scents of *Rosa* 'Gertrude Jekyll', lilies that stretch to the roof, *Fatsia japonica* 'Spider's web' and more hostas.

Curraquill

Ballycommon, Co. Tipperary. Tel: 087 7696 527. Contact Lulu Bergin. Open: One annual charity day. See Facebook Page for details. Wheelchair accessible. Supervised children. No dogs (free range fowl). Special features: Self-catering accommodation. Directions: Signposted from Newtown and Nenagh on open day.

The surprise of finding that Lulu Bergin's garden, in the north Tipperary countryside, only covers one acre was, to say the least, big. I had been walking around for a long time, through what felt like a garden at least twice that size, up one grass path and down another, under pergolas and through bamboo circles, under specimen trees and shrubs, past deeply planted up ponds, between long borders of day lilies and scented 'Bonica' and 'Chapeau de Napoleon' roses, inspecting *Magnolia soulangeana* and skyward-bound liquidambars. I got lost. Lulu's garden is an informal, happy concoction that trails off in all directions, on all sorts of little missions. When I admired a low hedge of *Sedum spectabilis* she told me that she ran out of money for box. I suspect the large number of bees busying themselves on its flowers are happy that she did.

Fancy fowl, including little silkies and some swanky geese scattered, discommoded, as we turned up to look at their various favourite sitting spots. They vacated stands of phlox and lupin and took cover in among a run of solidago, some secreting themselves under a stand of ferns.

As we walked, Lulu told me that the soil is pure lime, yet she manages to keep magnolias looking happy and healthy. She wanted to try them out, being curious and the experiment paid off. Lulu works the place completely organically and told me that her Call ducks are the ultimate slug deterrent, as we investigated a sweep of hostas doing nicely in the care of these slug terminators.

At any one time she may be experimenting with different growing systems, to reduce water requirements and the necessity for digging. We took a look at one of these; a base of timber covered with layers of grass, herbaceous cuttings and compost and then planted into with vegetables and annual flower seeds. The timber becomes a reservoir of water as it rots, reducing the need to water the bed. The results are proving interesting.

An air of busy work pervades the place although, as a wild garden, do not expect that business to include massive energy spent on weeding. Wild is wild, and in this case it is also handsome.

Dundrum Nurseries

Ward Park, Dundrum, Co. Tipperary. Tel: 062 71303. Open: Seven days, half day Sunday. Special features: Garden centre. Directions: In the village of Dundrum.

The nursery at Dundrum is famous for the number of different plants it stocks. It is also well known for stocking mature specimens. The garden, too has been of interest to visitors for many years. The emphasis is on shrubs and trees, waterside plants grown in an informal style. At the time of writing, it is undergoing a renovation due in large part to enthusiastic growth and subsequent overcrowding. It will be good to see how it fares in the next few years.

Fairy Hill

Clonmel, Co. Tipperary. Tel: 089 2509910. Contact: Mary Donovan. Open: By appointment to groups. Not wheelchair accessible. Not suitable for children. No dogs. Directions: On application.

There is a huge *Sequoiadendron giganteum* planted about 30 metres from the house at Fairy Hill which does not dominate the view from the house, or from any point in this wonderful garden. I think that this succinctly sums up Mary Donovan's creation. The growth and the scale of the plants in her country garden are remarkable. Even more remarkable however, is the fact that this country garden is in the town of Clonmel. If ever a garden deserved the description secret, this is it. I had spent a lifetime driving past without even knowing that it existed. But once inside the gates, this secret, hiding in plain sight is as bewitching as its name suggests.

Mary has been working and developing the three-and-a-half acres, mostly by herself, since 1978. There was a garden on the site when she arrived. The house dates to the early 1800s it is properly a combination of old and new, of mature and growing trees and special shrubs and flowers.

The long cone-shaped site runs along the banks of the River Suir, in shaded trails and walks underneath rhododendron and hoheria, mahonia and towering oak. It even has a family of otters living on its watery boundary.

The trees are tall and dominant, from beech and oak, to lime and sycamore with holly and pittosporum stretching up too in places. Great explosions of climbing roses and clematis clamber up their trunks and long rustic pergolas stretch between and underneath them, like caves. Wisteria branches hang, like Tarzan ropes from the canopy. It is another world.

Walk on paths busy with the snakes of barely submerged roots, and up and down on rough stone steps, between rustic gates and long walks through loosely cut box hedging. The lines are organic. The feel is informal and the scale is large.

Little areas of bright sun-spilled lawn interrupt the gorgeous gloom. Open sunny, sheltered spots are home to wildlife ponds and sun-trap, seating areas. The spring is Mary's favourite time, with all the bulbs and new ferns and emerging hostas all opening, fresh in the light shade. I lost both Mary and my way several times as I wandered around. This is good. You are meant to get lost in woods.

Fancroft Mill & Garden

Roscrea, Co. Tipperary. Tel 0505 31484. e-mail: millgardens@gmail.com www.fancroft.ie
Open: By appointment. Partially wheelchair accessible. Supervised children (water). Dogs on leads. Special features: Working mill tours. Music events. Tea room. National archive of Mills and Millers of Ireland Association. Directions: See website for details.

It is 12 years since Irene and Marcus Sweeney took the brave move, and bought the house, mill and garden at Fancroft, taking over its stewardship from the formidable gardening force that is Angela Jupe. Angela had created a beautiful and interesting garden around the old house and huge deserted mill, building a new walled garden in the process. Moving on to a new project in nearby Shinrone, Angela found worthy successors to mind Fancroft in the Sweeneys.

In the time since they have taken over, they have cared for and developed the garden, as well as taking on the gigantic task of restoring the five storey mill, complete with mill wheel and all the wherewithal to grind corn.

As we looked around the wheelhouse, swallows flew in and out of the wheel opening and scooted over our heads, not in the least discommoded by the restoration.

Outside, Irene has been gardening. Before walking around we looked at photos depicting the place Angela created, as well as the developments since the takeover, including the return of the pond to being an area of wetland. Angela gave birth to the garden, Irene is is its second mother, caring for and bringing it into the 21st century.

The Offaly and Tipperary border runs through the garden and as we walked around the side of the house along a beech hedge and a little stream, to the kitchen garden, I was told that we had crossed that county border. The stream runs along the back of the house, sunken and stone-lined. It is known as a spill stream, built to prevent the house from flooding. Standing at the back of the wisteria covered house wall, beside a dripping laburnum and a fine magnolia, we looked over a little bridge across the stream and along its length to an intriguing circular window in a stone wall. There was also sight of a rose-and-trellis-clad

summerhouse, and wide spreading cherries. Romantic was the word to sum it up. We took the catmint-lined path to the greenhouse. The beds beyond those ribbons of hazy blue are mixed, with maturing *parrotia persicaria* and *Cotinus coggygria* over stipa, arum and obelisks twined in clematis.

I have always loved this greenhouse, built from the salvaged windows of the old conservatory in the long gone Jervis Street hospital in Dublin. Today, in Tipperary, it homes a *Clematis armandii* and a big *Cytisus battandieri* as well as pots of pelargoniums and found birds nests.

The way into the walled garden is up a little lane of shrub roses, past a round tower with a turret, and in through one of the stone walls. This is an unusual walled garden, first in that it is new, and secondly in that it is oval in shape, divided by curved and rounded walls of box. Within the solid structure of walls, cobbled paths, stone circles and sunken stone ponds, the planting is loose and soft, made up of of young magnolias *Drimys winteri* and roses, clematis and climbing dicentra. These provide height in the centre and around the walls, while the mainstay plants on the ground are perennials like blue omphalodes and hardy geraniums, hellebores, phlox and pulsatilla.

The spring fed stream is clear and clean and busy with frogs.

The moon window, previously seen from the house, gives a view out along the stream, with a frame of *Rosa* 'Perle d'or' and white *Hydrangea paniculata*.

One path out of the flower garden is through the developing wood, where young oak and beech grow over more seas of snowdrops and hellebores.

'Angela's Fancroft babies' as Irene calls them.

The wood is about a decade old now, cut through by log-lined paths. It is a good spot for studying mushrooms. The way through it eventually leads down to the boathouse, the old pond and the river cabin, where they sometimes hold music events.

A rustic bridge over the boulder-lined stream leads off to another wood, of alder and ash, and a walk back through Tipperary to the house, via a slowly developing laurel lawn, and a collection of developing trees, some interesting birches, euonymus, zelkovas, and oaks.

This is an expanding, fascinating visit for garden visitors, historians and music lovers.

Garryhochaill

Bansha, Co. Tipperary. e-mail: glencush1@gmail.com Contact: Margaret and Bill Kingston.
Open: An open charity day in early June. Contact for annual date. Directions: On application.

Sitting half way up a hill looking across at both Galtee Mór and Galtee Beag, Garryhochaill enjoys a setting not unlike the famous hills in 'The Sound of Music'. When Margaret Kingston arrived here 30 years ago, she saw its potential as a garden and started to play with her hilly Tipperary field. She began planting immediately so the house now boasts mature specimens of *Luma apiculata* 'Variegata' and a skyward-bound *Cedrus deodara.*

The shelter belt of trees she initially planted to protect the new garden from the skelping south westerlies is today the raw material she is working on to make a wood garden in its own right. As I arrived Margaret was busy laying felled trunks along the paths between the trees. She had already added ferns and native bluebells, lamium and cyclamen, foxgloves and epimediums to the existing ground cover. She generally looked to be making merry with the place. Juvenile it might have been but it was already looking good.

Margaret's new garden joins the ribbon-shaped flower and shrub garden that decorates the stream which runs the length of the site. The garden is riddled by springs, which she and her gardening husband Bill have cleverly steered into the main waterway.

The mix of shrubs and perennials is an easy, informal one. There are tree peonies, acers and *Melianthus major*, callistemon, drumstick primulas, *Daphne bholua* and *Dahlia australis,* all growing together as comfortably as natives.

Gardening is a funny business. We studied a collection of *Rhododendron macabeanum* planted 20 years ago in a grove. One is about three metres tall and wide. One is a little smaller and one is no more than a third the size of the biggest plant. Micro-climates giveth and taketh away. The winds have a powerful curbing effect on growth here. Raiding deer are another problem to contend with, but the garden marches on despite their input - or rather out-take.

We walked between stretching *Abies koreana* and cut-leaf beech, liriodendron and davidia, tree-sized griselinia and *Parrotia persicaria*, under which and between, Margaret is busy planting more rhododendrons and native ferns. Gunnera leaves that could be turned into beach umbrellas reminded us that this is a wet site.

The garden is shot through with meandering paths. This is no place for straight lines. One leads off the lawn, past the raised vegetable squares near the house, and into a little rose garden, tucked away behind a circular, arched beech hedge. Sit in here, surrounded by pink carpet roses and lavender, winter jasmine, under a sort of cave of *Cryptomeria japonica*, a sheltered spot in the middle of what is becoming a little arboretum.

Hough's Garden

Ballinderry, Nenagh, Co. Tipperary. Tel: 067 22175. 086 8466 461.
e-mail: mwilkinson12345@outlook.com Contact: Michael Wilkinson. Open: May-Sept. By appointment to groups. See Facebook page. Partially wheelchair accessible. Supervised children. Special features: Meals can be arranged. Directions: On application.

This was a garden conceived and started before the house it surrounds was built. That is Michael Wilkinson's way of doing things. As he planned the house, he knew where the garden paths were going and the sort of garden those paths would run between. He had picked a handsome little field to start with, beside a wood, on rich, loamy lime, at the top of a mile-long drive. I would find out later that Michael works the wood too. Having cleared it of scrubby undergrowth, he planted an all white under-storey of snowdrops, aconites and *Cyclamen hederifolium* 'Album'.

The drive emerges out of the smartened up

wood onto an opening in front of the house and the overwhelming sense is of flowers, flowers and more flowers. We set off, diving straight in, along the shadowy border, where naturally, everything is dark. The palette takes in plummy cercis and cotinus, dark red *Dahlia* 'Arabian Night' which has foliage as dusky as its flowers. Lighter shades set off the night time colours in the shape of pink *Paeonia* 'Bowl of Beauty,' monarda and blue *Delphinium* 'Clifford Sky.' These were bought from Finlay Colley, whose plants Michael likes. His shrubs include black *Sambucus niger* and physocarpus, mixed with pale, variegated philadelphus. These mixed borders work from early summer to the end of autumn.

The path along the border leads down to a sunny sitting spot at the bottom of the field, with an old iron bench surrounded by scented nepeta and red achillea. It is almost necessary to battle through the nepeta to get to the bench.

The ground is damp down here, so Michael built a pond and is planning a bog garden beside it, with rheums and rodgersia, both of which like wet feet.

The sight, back uphill, is of the house and the colourful borders we had studied as we walked. Only now did I notice the sloped meadow. Michael explained that it is too fertile for wild flowers.

As we walked back up he spoke about deer,

the bane of his life. 'Nothing keeps them out.' Not an electric fence, and certainly not the pretty cleft chestnut fences that he uses around his various borders. Deer like the finer things in life, including his paulownias. He has taken to hunting for plants they do not like. Buddleia seems to work.

Back at the house, I was smitten by the hosta display, collected together in pots on the shaded side of the building. There are also box and herb gardens, and ribbons of nerines lined along the path. As a keen cook, Michael grows a range of fruit and vegetables in the productive plot at the sunny side of the house.

Before leaving we looked at the double border with its white dahlias and delphiniums, michaelmas daisies, veronicastrum and dramatic-looking purple *Verbena rigida*. Michael told me that this was supposed to be an all-white border but colour has a habit of making its way into the mix. 'So I left it.' Golden marjoram lines the path in one place, with nepeta behind it and lines of fuchsia at the back, mixed with variegated holly and peonies. I thought that the *Magnolia* 'Leonard Messel' looked well growing on this pure lime soil. In fact all his magnolias do well – if he can keep them from the deer.

Out at the edge of the flower borders, a boundary of *Rosa* 'Blanc de double de Coubert' might look good but the deer like it too...

Killurney

Ballypatrick, Clonmel, Co. Tipperary. Tel: 052 6133 155. 087 9444 662. e-mail: rowswork@eircom.net Contact: Mildred Stokes. Open: Open days June. Contact for annual dates. By appointment at other times. Partially wheelchair accessible. Special features. Teas can be arranged. Directions: Driving from Kilkenny on the N76 turn right at the Ormonde Stores. Take the third right signed for Killurney. Take the first turn left after the school and the house is first on the left.

Driving through the gates at Killurney, past a little stone ruin with a fern, hosta and hellebore garden, looking up the drive, through peepholes under the trees, it is clear that this is a place worked by an assured talent. Everything spells expertise, and flair. The woman responsible is Mildred Stokes and this has been her domain for over a quarter of a century.

When Mildred first arrived she was greeted by a congested one-acre site around a Georgian house. That acre was dark and shaded, hidden under and behind heavy conifers. As she describes it, one can feel the

oppression and gloom, although, most likely, the trees must have been planted to perform as miniatures.

Once these were dispensed with and the place was opened up to light, Mildred began to design and build her own garden. She did it all herself, from digging out beds and building paths, to directing streams and creating ponds, with all the hard work those jobs entail. Mildred is a hands-on gardener. The garden was designed so that, standing at the front door, two generous flanks of shrubs, trees and flowers act like huge theatre curtains, framing a view of the Comeragh

Mountains.

While the view is important, Killurney is principally the garden of a plant lover with all the abundance and plant action that this involves. Mildred is a devotee of the layered garden, so there are multiple and constantly changing layers of herbaceous plants, shrubs and trees in fluid, easy groupings. Between the plants, and within the beds, stone paths lead into, out of, and around the different compositions. These routes can be hard to find until you are actually walking along them in summer, because so many well-fed plants seem hell bent on going out meet their pals across the road. Mildred knows how to keep order however.

The idea of harnessing a natural sunken stream that ran along the boundary of the garden was inspired. Water was brought into the centre of the plot so that it could be directed to run between the vegetation. The path meanders back and forth over the little waterway on stone bridges. The stream, at one point opens to a pond, planted with waterside drumstick primulas, astilbes and lilies. The sound of water, even when it is not always visible, is attractive and its trickle can be heard everywhere.

The feeling of privacy and intimacy is achieved by the strategic placement of taller plants, which then have to be skirted around in order to see more of the garden. The effect of this is to entice the visitor on to further investigation. The maze of paths delivers the walker in between runs of *Rosa* 'Bonica', past tall stands of dahlias and under a peeling *Acer griseum*, towards groves of ferns in the deep shade out at the boundary. In parts the borders are shaded by small trees like *Aralia elata*, *Acer palmatum* 'Senkaki' and *Cercis canadensis* 'Forest Pansy'. In part they are open and sunny.

The real wow is the gravel garden to the side of the house. The sunken stream makes it way into this area too, side-planted by waving dierama. Big boulders create natural-looking leaning posts and shelter for mounds and tufts of miniature alpines.

The latest garden room is a sun-trap built around a much loved *Cornus kousa* 'Satomi' planted over splashes of honesty, a grand stone wall and a bench from which to enjoy the show.

Kilmacomma Garden

Kilmacomma, Clonmel. Co. Tipperary. Tel: 052 6122 525. 087 7632 231.
e-mail: patheg@eircom.net Contact: Pauline Hegarty. Open: To groups by appointment. Special facilities: Partially wheelchair accessible. Plants for sale. Supervised children. Dogs on leads. Directions: Drive on the R671 from Clonmel to Dungarvan. The garden is attached to the first two storey house on the right after Ball Alley Cross.

Pauline Hegarty has been working her garden in the picturesque Nire Valley for 46 years and every single day of that four-and-a-half-decade's-worth-of-work can be seen. From the cleverly pruned up shrubs, to the lawn like green baize, the tended flower borders and well considered combinations of plants, it is a bit of a *tour de force*. Paulines' is an all-go, full-on, busy flower garden.

Throughout the place there are examples of the better sort of flowering shrub and small tree. She loves acers and she has chosen some of the best, from an exquisite red-leafed *Acer* 'Shiraz' to the improbably red *Acer* 'Beni Komachi' and *Acer griseum*, so loved for its peeling, colourful bark.

Fine maturing specimens of 20 and 30-year-old *Cornus kousa*, *Carpenteria californica* and pruned-up *Cercis canadensis* are arranged around the lawns, over beds of lilies and roses, hydrangeas and aconites.

From every angle in the open garden the plants have been placed to frame and create good views, over and back across the lawn, taking in an old stone wall supporting clematis and roses in one place, or a little seating area in another, or a grove of *Cornus kousa* 'Miss Satomi' with a multi-stemmed white betula, pittosporum and mad coloured *Cornus florida* 'Rainbow'.

'I'm happier outside than in.' Pauline said. That is easy to believe. The levels of care and attention lavished on this garden are first rate. Textbook is the word that springs to mind and yet the air of one of welcome. This is a garden with a charm that stayed long in the memory between two very well spaced out visits.

Petrovska Garden

Old Spa Road, Clonmel, Co. Tipperary. Tel: 052 6182 969. 087 9576 129. e-mail: eamonnoriordan@eircom.net Contact: Michael and Snezana O'Riordan Petrovska: Open: May-Oct. By appointment. Supervised children welcome due to water features. Directions: On application.

Wild is a term worth considering properly when describing gardens. Genuinely wild means brambles, nettles and scrubby trees. Michael O'Riordan and Snezana Petrovska began gardening in 2000 on a hill outside Clonmel, with selection of all of the above and a swamp. 'Our ambition was just to strim a path down through it. It was all we thought we could do' Michael explained to me. Strimmed paths through the rough are a distant memory today. The pair may have started to garden modestly, but the bug took hold in a bad way and today the seven acres add up to a whole series of gardens, as varied as they are attractive.

We walked between tended jungles of large leafed perennials, hostas and lilies, under exotic looking trees. The water features and ponds are everywhere, tucked into every corner, from cool, hard-edged contemporary to rough, wildlife ponds - and that swamp. There are flowering shrub and perennial borders, lawns, container gardens, raised beds and surprise features, such as the outdoor shower and a grown-up treehouse.

The swamp of old, instead of being drained, was embraced and transformed into the anchor of a new wood and water garden. They created a whole spider's web of paths, made of bark chippings, boardwalk, grass and gravel. These divide the whole affair into bite-sized individual features.

The star of the garden is the young wood. Michael planted 500 willows before decisively flooding the swamp at the bottom of the hilly site. The water is so deep in parts that it was necessary to sink telegraph poles to support the boardwalks. Walking through it is like being in the tropics.

Next door is the other wood garden. Until a few years ago, this area was all impenetrable brambles and closely planted, un-thinned Christmas trees. Snezana climbed in, hacking her way through it, discovering a new stream as she went. She cut her way, little by little down through the Christmas trees and spent years clearing the brush and rough from under those trees. Then she pruned them up and stacked piles of logs around the woods. The result is a remarkably beautiful deep dark wood garden. 'As you get to know the land it speaks to you,' she said. It speaks to her, loud and clear. In one opening beside the conifer wood, there were three tall, stray conifers. They added a telegraph pole to these and built a treehouse platform, a place to enjoy tea high up in the canopy of ash, oak and holly. From up here we spied more mystery paths we would investigate when we climbed down.

Out on the boundary they planted a number of young oaks, the self-seeded children of a line of century-old trees we could see in the distance that were planted by two Quaker ladies who lived here once.

Michael and Snezana live in the garden. They get up at first light and walk it. They eat, shower and work out here. They use it all day long and share it with dratted deer and welcome ducks, water hens, herons, otters, birds and frogs.'But we go for a walk with a secateurs in our hand!' Snezana told me.

Roscrea Heritage Garden

*Damer House, Roscrea, Co. Tipperary. Contact: Reception. Tel: 0505 21850.
e-mail: roscreaheritage@opw.ie. Open: All year. Contact for seasonal changes. Special features: House and
castle tours. Admission to the garden free. Directions: In the centre of Roscrea.*

To start with, the OPW, which cares for the Roscrea Heritage garden should be proud of the women who work as guides at Damer House. They are enthusiastic, friendly, engaged with the place and keen to share it with the public. I discovered this when I visited early on a wet Sunday morning. They mind the wonderful Damer House, a Queen Anne building, along with an older tower house and the various outhouses, courtyards and gardens that make up what is a unique historic monument in the middle of the Tipperary market town.

The garden is the Roscrea Heritage Garden, a walled town garden, restored in the 1990s by the OPW. The guides showed me photographs of it before it was rescued and then lent me an umbrella and sent me out to see it in its restored glory. It is a series of flower and shrub borders and wide gravel paths, radiating out from and converging on a remarkable looking fountain and pond dating back to the 1740s. The fountain was designed by Samuel Chearnley an architect and designer known for his work on both Birr Castle and the town of Birr in the 1740s. The fountain alone is worth the visit.

The garden is pretty too however: The box surrounded flower beds with roses and scented jasmine, antirrhinums, hemerocallis and agapanthus, eucomis and geraniums, are healthy and colourful and the benches ranged about about make for a perfect sit down in the middle of the town. Looking out over the walls at the old buildings of Roscrea gives one a good idea of just how historic this often overlooked town is.

Swiss Cottage

*Kilcommon, Cahir, Co. Tipperary. Tel: 052 41144. Contact: Head Guide. Open: All year. Contact for
seasonal changes. Children supervised. Special features: Guided tours. Riverside walk to Cahir. Directions:
Leave Cahir by the road to Ardfinnan (R670) and travel for 1.5 km. Well signposted.*

The Swiss Cottage is one of the loveliest small buildings on the island. Designed by architect John Nash, architect of Regent's Street in London, it was built in 1817 for Richard Butler, the Earl of Glengall. In common with so many historical sites, the Swiss Cottage suffered for many years from neglect and it fell into a state of disrepair so dreadful that the house was reduced to the status of a stable in the 1980s. However it was restored in the 1990s by the OPW.

At the end of the 18th and beginning of the 19th centuries, a fashion grew up among the gentry for little houses built into naturalistic, romantic, landscaped gardens – a fashion sparked by Marie Antoinette and her peasant village, the Hameau de la Reine at Versailles. World-weary aristocrats played at being peasants and enjoyed 'simple country living' in these idealised rustic cottages, while the real peasants quietly organised the comforts of life in the background. In the case of Swiss Cottage, this was in a below-ground kitchen.

Swiss Cottage is set in the middle of a garden, on a pleasant slope down to the River Suir, which meanders along below the house. The building was designed so that no door or window resembled any other. No wall is straight, nor is it the same length as any other.

The surrounding garden is filled with classic cottage garden plants, similar to those that would have been planted in the original garden. Thyme, hyssop, oregano, lavender, chamomile and sage are grown up against the house, and the little building fills with the romantic scent of herbs through the windows and open French doors on sunny days. Meanwhile, achillea, *Campanula glomerata*, perennial sage (*Salvia superba*), periwinkle (*Vinca minor*), and *Geum coccineum* flower merrily around the trellises and clutter the porches.

Wisteria, old-fashioned French climbers and Bourbon roses like 'Albertine', 'Mme Alfred Carrière', 'Louise Odier', 'Cécile Brunner' and 'Mme. Isaac Pereire' decorate the porches with voluptuous shades of pink. A wide belt of sheltering beech, oak and other park trees, including Florence Court yews and monkey puzzle trees, surrounds the little garden. None of these compare to the ancient yew growing beside and over the house, said to be around 1,000 years old, but yew is notoriously hard to age.

The wrought-iron fence, mimicking thorny rose stems, divides the garden from the woods. I love it.

Turtulla

Thurles, Co. Tipperary. Tel: 0504 21839. e-mail: tandksheedy@icloud.com Contact: Tom and Kathleen Sheedy. Open: By appointment, Mar-Sept. Wheelchair accessible. Supervised children. Dogs on leads. Special features: Groups may book refreshments. Directions: Leave the M8 at Junction 6 for Thurles. Drive as far as the garage on the left. A few meters beyond this, there is a bend and the garden is the second house after this, on the bend (marked by crash barriers).

Tom and Kathleen Sheedy have been working their garden since 1971.

'We're in the garden all the time,' said Kathleen. It is their plaything. It is what they do and they do it with enjoyment as well as enthusiasm: There are over 300 roses here. At one time there were over 400. It might be good fun but it is serious good fun. Turtulla is very much a his and hers garden. Kathleen is a flower arranger and in charge of the perennials and bulbs, containers and all things floral. Tom grows trees 'probably too many', he confessed. The result is an engaging garden that will probably, in centuries to come, bequeath a fine little arboretum to the plains outside Thurles.

The air of cheerful bustle is everywhere, from decorative iron church gutter tops, which came from Templemore, redeployed as flower pots, pinned to the white-washed shed, to the ever-present roses. This is an enjoyable place of horticultural endeavour.

It is also a garden from which to learn. Thurles, gets very cold in winter. This was one of parts of the country where all the phormiums, cordylines and pittosporums were lost in recent cold winters.

Yet *Rosa banksiae*, a supposedly fairly fussy rose, is still thriving alongside more rampant roses such as Félicité et Perpétue' 'Keep it safe from the north wind' was the advice.

We made our way through the 'Her' area, in the fine company of *Clematis* 'The President', 'Nelly Moser' and 'Mrs Ruppel'. On the ground underneath the show is all go with flowering strobilanthes and alstroemeria, lilies and geraniums, peonies and achillea. Even the pond and its waterfall were hauled in to host a rambling *Rosa* 'Albéric Barbier'.

The gravelled area, reached through yet another rose arch near the house is set about with an array of blue painted chairs and tables.

Out in the 'field', Tom's area of influence, the ever-growing collection of trees will need to slow down at some point but for the moment he continues to plant: cedar and davidia, acer and cornus, viburnum and golden elm, liquidambar and sorbus, red oak and cut-leaf beech. There seems to be room for everything here including a few magnolia and eucryphia. Many of these are acid lovers and this is a lime garden yet they look healthy. An experiment is always worth trying.

Waterford

Abbey Road Garden

Abbey Road, Ferrybank, Waterford, Co. Waterford. Tel: 051 851111. 087 2209026.
e-mail: abbeyroadgardens@hotmail.com Contact: Margaret Power. Open: As part of the Waterford Garden
Trail, by appointment. Contact for annual details. Special features: Wedding photos. Partially wheelchair
accessible. Teas can be booked. Plants for sale. Directions: From Waterford railway station turn onto the
R711 towards Belview Port. Stay in the centre lane. Go through the traffic lights and turn right onto Abbey
Road. The garden is on the left.

It had been a few years since I last visited Margaret Power's garden and it has changed. Margaret has worked here for many years and she has no fear of remodelling. The entrance, once dark and tree-tunnelled has been swept away, replaced by a new and open south-facing space with a lively flower border. Her love of plants is evident here, as it is throughout the garden. She thinks of her plants in terms of the people who gave her cuttings and seeds. So we admired *Salvia confertiflora*, given to her by Neil Porteus of Mount Stewart, a little geranium gifted from Cappoquin House and zantedeschia and *Dahlia australis*, which all turned out to be souvenir plants with stories attached. 'Grow good plants and you'll have good plants to share' is Margaret's philosophy.

On the other side of the drive, she felled a huge *Cupressus macrocarpa*. It needed to be taken down, but the still useful stump stands at the centre of another sunlit bed with sprays of different grasses

including the much-loved *Calamagrostis* 'Karl Foerster', tree peonies, acanthus and phlox over clmps of snowdrops in spring. The expansive *Rosa* 'Rambling Rector' climbing an iron arch, refuses to stay on the arch yet she loves this bold, free-ranging white rose too much to be cross. Margaret likes roses and there are roses around every corner, from David Austin varieties to older types like *Rosa* 'Cécile Brünner' and 'Souvenir de St. Anne's'. Corners are in no shortage either, as the garden is divided again and again by hedges and stone walls, making it undiscoverable in one sweep.

Self-seeders such as *Verbena bonariensis* and different grasses have been encouraged in the open gravelled areas around the house and outbuildings, and all walls have been harnessed too, to accommodate more roses and wisteria, climbing hydrangea and honeysuckle. One of the house walls is particularly sheltered so this is where many of the tender plants can be found, from *Rosa banksiae* and *Jovellana punctata*, *Polygala* x. *dalmaisiana* to a beautiful *Fuchsia arborescens*, which is tender yet can flower here until November. Elsewhere, scattered around the courtyard, the roses, include *Rosa* 'Bengal Beauty' and *R. mutabilis* but *R.* 'François Juranville' is her favourite. This is a plant that flowers throughout the year and hides the whole roof of a big stone outhouse.

The little pond, with its glinting water is tucked away under maturing liquidambar, betula and acer. Cardiocrinums underneath the trees light up the shade too, alongside fairly hardy white *Abutilon* x. *suntense*. The ground in the spring wood garden is busy with bulbs and hellebores, under *Rhododendron augustinii*, *R. sinogrande*, *Daphne bholua* 'Jacqueline Postill' and *Davidia involucrata*. I was more than impressed with a five-metre tall fruiting loquat in one favoured corner.

All together this collection of secret garden covers three-quarters-of-an-acre and like its enthusiastic owner, is a pleasure to visit.

Ballylin Gardens

Lismore, Co. Waterford. Tel: 058 54608. 087 7939101. 087 6348404. e-mail peterlraven@aol.com sarahjraven@gmail.com www.ballyingardens.com Contact: Peter and Sarah Raven. Open: April-June and National Heritage Week. See website for exact annual dates. Groups at other times by appointment. Not wheelchair accessible. Supervised children. No dogs. Special features: Accommodation. Directions: On the left 500m from Lismore Bridge on the Ballyduff Road. (R666).

Ballylin is a house with a history stretching back to the 1700s. It has variously been hunting lodge, land agent's house and home to the Dean of Lismore Cathedral. The gardens have a correspondingly long history, linked with Lismore Castle and the Duke of Devonshire. Over the centuries they benefitted from the importation of choice plants from abroad, in particular rhododendrons. The history is obvious and evident in the sight of a great Monterey cypress or *Cupressus macrocarpa,* a tree with a girth of nearly nine metres, and holder of the Waterford girth record.

In 1906 King Edward VII saw fit to take a turn about the Ballylin gardens when staying in Lismore and a great deal of planting went into preparing the garden for that visit. The place went into decline however, after the Second World War. When Peter Raven arrived in 1983 he began to restore and he has been at it ever since, more recently joined by his wife Sarah. The garden is once fortunate to have two dedicated gardeners caring for and developing the riverside site. It is naturally a spring and early summer garden, made up of flowering rhododendrons, camellias and magnolias, so Peter and Sarah are now trying to extend the flowering season with roses, abutilon and herbaceous perennials. Sarah's particular love of salvias is useful for a later summer and autumn show.

The Monk's Garden is a serene little spot tucked in behind the house, combining old stone walls, white clematis, silver artemisia, and wisteria with box and some of Sarah's blue salvias. I like the use of cut-flower beds between the vegetables. Dahlias, daylilies and aquilegias rub shoulders well with kale and onion.

The secret courtyard garden features a little bell tower. This both faces and corners the sun and is as a result warm and sheltered, and through the summer, full of the scent of wisteria, rose and white fuchsia. Out in front of the house, I was taken by the unusual raised stone ledge bed where Sarah's salvias, penstemon and roses share the space with native ferns and moss-clad stones.

From here, we moved on to the greater garden, by way of a curved set of fancy cobbled steps that disappears downhill under the trees. Emerging from beneath this green tunnel into the light, the view back up the hill is one of impressively big clouds of rhododendron, arranged into varieties and species that between them, deliver a rising and rolling display of flowers from late winter to early summer. High in the hill, a thatched summerhouse appears, squeezed in between the trees. On the other side, the springy, wide grass path is bounded, for a decent stretch, by the river. Eventually the path leaves the waterside to climb back up, under those rhododendrons. We finally arrived at a long mixed border, featuring shrub roses and myrtles, that leads back to the house. The rounded capping on the wall behind the border is beautifully made.

Along with all its west Waterford neighbours, this is a garden worth noting.

Cappoquin House

Cappoquin, Co. Waterford. Tel: 058 54290. 087 670 4180. e-mail: charleskeane@cappoquinestate.com www.cappoquinhouseandgardens.com Contact: Charles Keane. Open: All year round except Sundays. Guided tours of garden and groups by appointment only. House open in April, May and for Heritage Week. Not suitable for wheelchairs. Children under strict supervision. No dogs. Directions: Entering Cappoquin from the N72, turn right at the T-junction in the centre of the town. The garden is 200m along on the left, with a stone gateway.

Cappoquin House is a fine Georgian house built on the site of, and incorporating the walls of one of several FitzGerald castle's on the River Blackwater in west Waterford. Like Dromana upstream and Tourin, Salterbridge, Ballylin and Lismore downstream, Cappoquin was built close to the river because the waterway was, in essence, the motorway of its day. It was easier to travel by boat than over land and the river cut its way through the countryside, efficiently, carrying goods and people for centuries, from the port at Youghal, inland.

The house has been the home of the Keane family for nearly 300 years and the garden has the air of a place that has been tended and minded for all of that time. It is chiefly the result of the 19th century inhabitants however, with additions made by Lady Keane between the 1950s and 2002. There are also vestiges of older gardens and garden buildings. Meanwhile, work and development continue to this day under the stewardship of Sir Charles Keane and his head gardener Mark Windross.

The drive leads through an arched carriage entrance into a welcoming courtyard, all white-washed walls, wisteria and climbing roses, including Mark's highly recommended *Rosa* 'Emily Grey'. You leave this heat trap by way of two big colourful mixed borders on each side of another arched gateway to the croquet lawn garden and a huge *Eucalyptus coccifera*.

The greater garden seems to be of indeterminate size, wandering off in all directions from the centrally placed house which looks out over the town, down to the river and Lismore Castle in the distance. The garden proper however, covers about five acres into which a great deal care has been poured. Stylish colour mixes, particularly with the many rhododendrons scattered throughout, avoid the headache-inducing effect too often seen in rhododendron gardens, where glaring oranges scream at their fuchsia pink and bright yellow neighbours.

A maze of grass paths lead through meadows, alongside ponds, between groves of notable trees and shrubs, including a rarely seen *Griselinia litoralis* grown as a specimen tree, and a huge Turkey oak or *Quercus cerris* with a girth of three-and-a-half-metres. They meander between damp beds of meconopsis, euphorbia, the odd clipped lonicera and puffs of hydrangea. One route leads past a little rose garden, snug in the shelter of an ancient ha-ha. This is an easy tangle of geraniums and Gallica, Damask and modern roses, including *Rosa banksiae, R.* 'Dentelle de Malines', *R.* 'William Lobb' and *R.* 'Wild Edric'. Between them they provide flowers from April to November. At one end of the wall, a little stream emerges from underground, creating the conditions needed for a damp garden busy with ligularia and gunnera. In spring a collection of snowdrops brightens up this corner. Close by, surrounded by a number of other shrubs, a healthy olive tree, proves just how sheltered some of the planting pockets here can be.

The specimen trees at Cappoquin include a cropping walnut tree (*Juglans nigra*), a weeping beech or *Fagus sylvatica* 'Pendula', a 400-year-old cedar, groves of myrtle, or *Luma apiculata* and what must be one of the largest specimens of *Cordyline australis* on the island. Make sure to see the eight-trunked sixty-year-old acer planted in 1946. We know that it cost 10/6 and came from the Slieve Donard nursery because Lady Keane kept records. Record-keeping in historic Irish gardens is as rare as it is welcome.

To the front of the house is the wing garden, a mix of lawns, raised beds full of lamb's ears or *Stachys byzantina*, perennial wallflowers, or erysimum, wild strawberries and pink osteospermum, twining through black grass, all under more mature magnolias and acers. This is an intimate, domestic spot, overlooked by an elegant conservatory, the home of velvety-purple tibouchina, oleander and succulents lined up on staged shelves, sharing the space with a scented

Rosa 'Ophelia.'

The only formal area is here at the front of the house. This is a sunken sundial garden, with stone paths, bleached white with lichen, mirroring beds full of clove-scented dianthus, penstemon, lupin and iris, lavender and white hydrangea. Beyond its balustrades you can see the wilder bog garden, under the shade of a big holm oak.

The side of the house looks out at the croquet lawn and two borders full of acers, azara and the already mentioned huge eucalyptus. In spring, daphne, winter sweet or *Chimonanthus praecox* and witch hazel perfume the air.

The garden continues to evolve and one of the latest additions is a new rhododendron garden. Mark also spends time designing new routes through the various plantations. He studies the way visitors make their way around the garden and subsequently 'directs the traffic' by creating interesting plant compositions, staging points, rest spots and trails to best display its treasures. The views and vistas back and forward between ruins covered in roses, aged stone gateways leading seemingly nowhere, labyrinths cut into the grass and folly-like buildings between groves of trees, are the glory of this fine garden.

Curraghmore

Portlaw, Co. Waterford. Tel: 051 387134. 086 8211 917. e-mail: info@curraghmorehouse.ie
Contact: Alan Walsh. Open: House, Gardens and Shell House: Easter-Sept., Wed-Sun. and bank holidays, 10.30am-4.30 pm. Guided tours 11am and 2pm daily. Oct.-Easter: By appointment only. Special features: Tearoom during visiting season. House tours. Theatre events. Bluebell Day. Events. Directions: The turning for Portlaw is off the main Waterford–Cork road (N25) at Kilmeaden. In Portlaw, the gate to Curraghmore is 0.5 km northwest of the village.

There has been a castle at Curraghmore since 1176 when the le Poers, later Powers, settled on the site close to the Comeragh Mountains, west of Waterford city. They have been here ever since. The Norman heritage is loudly signalled above the house by an extraordinary family crest: a huge stag with the Cross of St. Hubert set between its antlers. The house itself is a remarkable sight, partly 12th century, partly 17th century, with strong French influences.

As with most great houses, the gardens have been remodelled many times over the centuries. Records exist of a garden in the mid-1700s made up of great canals with cascades, formal terraces adorned with statuary and a 'wilderness' – every inch the fashionable demesne of its time. The canals and terraces were swept away in the later years of that century when a romantic, less formal landscape was put in place. The wilderness is still in evidence however. These days it is set beside an even later garden close to the house: a Victorian formal terrace with a man-made lake and wide gravel walks flanked by clipped yews and rhododendrons. Dramatic-looking and intriguing 19th century French statuary marks the edge of the woodland and wilder garden. At the outer reaches

there is a park and a wood boasting possibly the tallest Sitka spruce or *Picea sitchensis* on the island. In early summer, the woods at Curraghmore have become well known for bluebell displays. Do not miss the Shell House in the spring garden. Inside is a statue of a woman with a scroll that reads:

'In 261 days these shells were put up by the proper hands of the Rt. Honourable Cathne Countess of Tyrone 1754'.

Presumably, this means that Cathne, the lady represented by the statue, created the shell-covered walls herself. It is a stunningly good job. Many of

the shells came from tropical seas, and are arranged in swirling, organic, three-dimensional patterns, spread over every inch of the ceiling and walls of the quatrefoil-shaped building. Apart from the massive job of piecing the work together, the acquisition of these shells, some from as far off as Madagascar and the Maldives, was a feat. The colours are still vivid and the whole work is well preserved.

Another feature of Curraghmore and also found in the woods, is King John's bridge which spans the River Clodagh. It is reputed to have been built for the king when he came to Ireland in the 12th century. The restoration of the waterfalls below it are welcome and work continues both to the river and in

the woods, along the mile-long drive into the house, and the Japanese garden. Several old paths have been re-opened through the woods and gardens. Bring good walking shoes.

Curraghmore has another claim to fame: It was the training ground of the famous gardener and designer William Robinson, whose work had a huge influence on gardening on these islands in the late 19th and into the 20th century. Robinson served part of his apprenticeship as a garden boy at Curraghmore.

Before leaving, look out for two noble looking goats, regularly seen sunning themselves on the porch of the lodge at one of the side gates onto the estate.

Dromana

Cappoquin, Co. Waterford. Tel: 024 96144. 086 8186305. e-mail: bgrubb@eircom.net www.dromanahouse.com Contact: Barbara Grubb. Open: As part of the Waterford Garden Trail. April-June. See website for annual times. Other times by appointment. Special features: Accommodation. House tours. Exhibition. Refreshments can be booked. Directions: Leave Cappoquin on the N72 towards Dungarvan. On the outskirts of Cappoquin on the first sharp bend, leave the main road, direction Clashmore/Villierstown, with a brown sign for 'Dromana House and Gardens'. Then follow the signs for 'Dromana House and Garden', 'Dromana Drive and Villierstown'.

Before reaching Dromana House you will come across the Dromana Gate, an incongruous, Indian-style gothic gate lodge built in 1849 by Henry, Lord Stuart de Decies. The FitzGerald de Decies have lived here on the banks of the River Blackwater for eight centuries. As a lure there are few more effective than this strange feature.

In the 1400s the first tower house was erected here and since then, there have been grounds and gardens at Dromana. Today they are undergoing restoration thanks to Barbara Grubb, the 23rd generation of her family. Barbara and her husband Nicholas, with small additional help, have saved this old garden from falling off the cliff. The image of cliffs is an appropriate one as they feature strongly at Dromana. The house stands on a precipice looking over the River Blackwater in a manner that would make one hope there are not too many members of the family suffering from vertigo.

We began the visit and left the house on its precipice, passing flower beds and lawns, by way of a young and developing plantation of cornus including *Cornus* 'Norman Hadden' and *C.*

capitata. Barbara's little favourite here is a young rhododendron that will be named 'Dromana Eight Hundred' in honour of the garden.

Out in the grounds, we came across more drops to the river, some sheer some gentle. These are overlooked by walks through the wood gardens that Barbara and Nicholas have been clearing of of *Rhododendron ponticum* for nearly a decade. Barbara used information gleaned from a map drawn up in 1751 to guide her and today, where there was wild rough growth, there is now a cleared, planted up, refreshed wood establishing itself under a light canopy of mature, taller trees. They have planted 2000 trees since my last visit.

It felt special to walk along paths that had not been trodden on since ladies in long dresses made their way along these tracks. We passed 50 different varieties of camellia, as well as newly planted mahonia and eucryphia. Along the route we came to steep stairs cut into the hill, leading from one level to another.

The soil is fertile and perfect for Barbara's young *Rhododendron falconeri* and *Rhododendron arboreum* var. *cinnamomum*. A six-year-old *Paulownia tomentosa*, at six-metres tall, is testament to the good going and mild climate here. I liked the little *Dichroa febrifuga*, a rarely-seen member of the hydrangea family. Barbara showed me a specimen of *Emmenopterys henryi* which she says has been called the finest tree in the Himalayas. Roy Lancaster broke it to them that it will however, 'never flower in Ireland'. In summer the wood steams with heat. I noted countless self-seeded embothrium, 'although the dogs eat them,' according to Barbara.

As we walked on newly opened paths, we came to the stone picnic house overlooking the river with its smart 18th century graffiti, and continued on to Grand Junction, where all the paths in the woods converge. Finally we got to the Bastion, a formal terraced platform over an old boathouse built in 1750, and as we did around 100 whooper swans arrived along the river, having come from Iceland. The noise was remarkable.

Dromana is all about the woods and the history, the vistas and walks. It is a place that will probably look as Barbara wants it to look in another two generations, but working on a site that has been in the family for eight centuries years, what is another 50 years?

I left, having been given a few good tall tales as any to keep me entertained: The first was the story that Sir Walter Raleigh planted the first flowering cherry here. Later, Barbara's ancestor Catherine, Countess of Desmond fell from that tree and was killed at the age of 140. A walking stick made from one of its branches can be seen in the house museum, apparently proving the story

Fairbrook House Gardens

Kilmeaden, Co. Waterford. Contact: Clary Mastenbroek-Muller. Tel: 051 384 657. 085 8131448. www.fairbrook-house.com Open: As part of the Waterford Garden Trail. May-15th Sept., Wed-Sun. See website for changes. Not suitable for wheelchairs. No children under 12. No dogs. Special features: Group tours must be booked. Museum of contemporary and figurative art. Teas. Plants for sale. Concerts in August. Directions: From Waterford on the N25, take the Carrick-on-Suir roundabout in the direction of Cork (N25). After just over 1 km take the first turn to the right with a sign for a low bridge. The garden is on the right.

For those who like their horticulture with a good dose of art, archaeology and history, Fairbrook House is just the place. The garden itself was built over the past two decades on an historical industrial site, by Dutch artists Clary Mastenbroek-Muller and Wout Muller.

I suppose it could be called a water garden, because water plays a vital part in the design. There are streams, rills and ponds at every turn, some of these being part of the waterworks that were once part of an 18th century woollen mill on the little River Dawn. The mill closed in 1927. At different times of the year the river either roars and swells to great levels, or trickles sedately along.

The creative stonework is everywhere, from walls to cobbled paths and there are all sorts of little follies and jokes. The stone features are divided into those that were here for centuries, and those made by Clary. Most recently she created a new bridge to span the river, bringing it even more centrally into the garden design.

For all the water works however, there is one feature that comes to mind when I think of Fairbrook - two lengths of alternating, clipped box. On one side the box plants are pointed, like green soft peak meringues, or pixie hats. On the other side, the box has been shaped into cushioned, roundy mounds of greenery. Caught in the morning sun with cobwebs draped over them, they are indescribably lovely. They also need to be trimmed every three days throughout the summer. No wonder this is not the sort of feature that is widely seen.

Snapping on its heels for attention is the little room made of blue hazy lavender and white *Rosa* 'Winchester Cathedral' under-planted with chives and black 'Queen of the Night' tulips. Fairbrook is, in essence, a collection of different rooms that lead one to another. A weeping mulberry arch provides an unusual entrance to the Dye House garden, the ruined old dye house which Clary used as a base for her reed bed and lily pond. The reed bed doubles as a water purifier. Wander around beech and hornbeam mazes, into fern gardens and an all-green garden made of lime green hellebores and ribes, kniphofias, nasturtiums and euphorbias with green bracts. Then take a rosemary-lined path into the cruciform wisteria pergola. Clary obviously likes pergolas. There is another nearby, supporting trained crabapples. The knot garden, which features black *Pittosporum* 'Tom Thumb', lavender and box, again shows her very personal style and the bonsai garden is a series of miniature delights. Can I pick a favourite? No.

The use of sculpture is widespread. See it in niches, secreted around corners, in secluded spots and out in the open. The buildings and planting schemes provide each piece with the perfect exhibition space. Fairbrook is an object lesson in placing art in a garden.

For all the cultivated plants here, there are also a good number of natives. At the edges of the garden, in particular, the planting blends out into the surrounding countryside: Clary matches smart specimens of magnolia, acer and eucryphia with horse chestnut and wild hawthorn, hazel, ash and holly with success.

Lafcadio Hearn Japanese Gardens

Pond Road, Tramore, Co. Waterford. Tel: 087 0960 013. e-mail: info@lafcadiohearngardens.com www.lafcadiohearngardens.com Contact: Janet Carey. Open: Tues-Sun. See website for seasonal times. Children free. Partially wheelchair accessible. No dogs. Special features: Teas and coffees in summer. Tours may be booked. Directions: In the centre of the town, well signposted.

Patrick Lafcadio Hearn is a 19th century Irish writer, almost unknown in this country yet hugely famous in his adopted country of Japan. In 2012 one of his descendants sat in a small public space in Tramore, overlooking the sea. He had come to see the house and garden in which Hearn had spent much of his youth. As they sat, his guide, Agnes Allen, a Tramore woman with a knowledge of Hearn, hatched a plan to create a commemorative garden on that spot.

With thanks to the Tramore Development Trust and all sorts of other local bodies and individuals, by 2015 the idea had been turned into a garden that is now among Waterford's treasures. It is situated on a steep hill right beside the main shopping street, with a

view of the famous strand. They could not have found a more perfect use for what was an awkward site. It has been transformed into an impressive Japanese garden that tells the story of Lafcadio Hearn's life and work. The whole is divided into ten separate gardens recounting the story, from his birth in Greece, upbringing in Ireland and careers in America and ultimately Japan, where he died. The gardens are beautifully made, full of imagery from Japanese folklore and culture. They incorporate stone, water, wood and plants arranged in the Japanese style. Well composed plantations of *Euonymus alatus*, *Fatsia japonica*, camellias and juvenile pines sit between faithfully constructed waterfalls and streams. Tree peonies and tall grasses, ferns and creepers stand over restrained, raked gravel. The difficult terrain was harnessed to create naturalistic rock formations, cliffs and precipices over formal and natural ponds. There are even stone lanterns, carved by a visiting Japanese artist and a grassed amphitheatre laced with fragrant herbs.

The young garden is already handsome and will only improve as it matures. Created under the canopy of some fairly mature tall sycamores, oak and beech, it already seems older than its single digit age. I would say that the wooden bridge with its beautiful curved banister as well as the little spring and waterfall in the Stream Garden are worth the visit alone.

As if all this was not enough, there is also a faithfully reproduced Victorian walled garden set beside the 19th century house, commemorating Hearn's childhood which was spent here with his aunt Sarah Brenane.

Lismore Castle Garden

Lismore, Co. Waterford. Tel: 058 54061. e-mail gardens@lismorecastle.com
www.lismorecastlegardens.com Open: As part of the Waterford Garden Trail. Mid-March to mid-Oct.,
7 days, 10.30 am-5.30pm. Art gallery accessible to wheelchairs. Group tours by appointment during
opening times. Supervised children welcome. Dogs on leads. Special features: Contemporary sculpture in
grounds. Directions: Situated in the village of Lismore.

Lismore is one of the most beautiful towns in Ireland, overseen by one of the most romantic looking castles. There has been a castle on this spectacular elevated site since the 12th century with a colourful collection of past inhabitants, including Sir Walter Raleigh, Robert Boyle, the father of chemistry and Estelle Astaire, sister of Fred. The castle seen today is largely a 19th century creation remodelled for the Sixth Duke of Devonshire, into whose family it passed in the 1750s.

The gardens are divided into two areas: The upper and lower gardens. The upper garden, built on a slope, is reached by way of a rickety stairs up through a stone riding house. This is an unusual, crooked little building, built in 1620, that spans the drive into the castle. The garden is one of the oldest, continuously cultivated walled gardens on the island, first laid out in the 1600s. Recently, the wall that held the upper garden up, collapsed and a major restoration had to be carried out.

The orchard and wildflower garden is cut through with informal, mown grass paths. This romantic orchard is the first part of the garden seen from the riding house entrance. Beyond it, a beech hedge marks one side of the double mirroring borders that climb up the central axis. Eucalyptus and white hydrangea, abutilon and callistemon or bottlebrush shrubs reflect each other back and forth across the path. This bed leads up to the first set of steps. From here, a rose and lavender double border continues up to more steps, covered in santolina, snow-in-summer and thyme. The borders continue up the hill, and morph into a more contemporary style, using sharp black phormium, ophiopogon and trachycarpus.

At the top of this there is a cross path which runs north-to-south, bordered on one side by colour themed beds. The contrast between loose, massed pink lupins and formal, nail-scissors-smart yew hedges with topiarised pyramids and acorns is very satisfying.

Long runs of venerable yew, beech and box hedging divide the garden into smaller compartments and sheltered rooms, like the white garden, a confection of sculpture, stone benches, white flowers and lush green ferns under a canopy of white cherries.

The art gallery is surrounded by a dramatic new exotics border, set about with chairs in which to sit in summer. Echiums and trachycarpus, teasels and ricinus, bake in the heat and look over to a manicured bowling green with intriguing little drainage 'arches' made of stone and slate.

The accordion-shaped greenhouses designed by Sir William Paxton are unique in Ireland. They contrast well with the modern, bleached wood and stone arbour lower down the slope.

As I made my way between lines of artichokes, sprouts, leeks and cut-flowers, the sound of a soprano practicing outside the wall, for a concert in the

grounds later in the day, made it feel as though I had stumbled into the set of a period drama.

The way to the lower garden is back through the riding house. Emerge from the little building out onto a cobble-edged gravel path that makes its way past lines of magnolia, rhododendron and other special plants. This part of the garden is also built on a slope and this top walk allows one to see the flowers on some of the blooming eucryphia and rhododendron, from above. The wall on the other side of the path is lined with a variety of climbing roses, clematis, cottage garden herbaceous flowers and varieties of euphorbia.

It is in the lower garden that the famous yew walk, laid out in the early 1700s can be found. Tree ferns and woodland bulbs, anemones and bluebells carpet the ground under the tree canopy to the side of the walk. The garden boasts a number of important contemporary sculptures, and it is here that one piece by British artist Antony Gormley has been placed. This is a ghostly, powerful work placed in just the right atmospheric spot. Close by, in the middle of some rhododendron, Cork-born artist Eilís O'Connell's blue, patinated, swirling flourish of metal sits supreme. The English artist David Nash also has a work in the garden. The use of contemporary art at Lismore adds an additional layer of variety to the garden and shows a place with a future as well as a past.

The latest tree fern and wood garden at the bottom of the slope, leading to the river, was designed with children in mind. Would that all children's gardens were so cool.

Mount Congreve

Kilmeaden, Co. Waterford. Contact: Reception. Tel: 051 384115.
e-mail: admin@mountcongreve.com. www.mountcongreve.com. Open: Mid March-Sept. 11am-5.30pm.
Last entry 4.30pm. Thurs-Sun. and Bank Holidays. Special features: Tea room. Garden shop. Occasional
market. Partially wheelchair accessible. Guide dogs only. Directions: Leave Waterford on the N25 heading
towards Cork. Turn at the second crossroads after the Holy Cross Pub, following brown signs. Continue on
and turn left at the second crossroads. The garden is on the right.

Mount Congreve is an astounding place, built on a scale completely different to that of any other garden in Ireland. Created over the last century, it is more akin to one of the great estates of the 19th rather than the 21st century.

Containing one of the biggest collections of rhododendrons in the world and certainly the biggest in Europe, Mount Congreve is a place of superlatives. Think of 3,500 cultivars of rhododendron, 650 named camellias and 350 named cultivars of Japanese maple, lilac and tree peony. This is the world's largest plant collection, assembled in the last half of the 20th century. It was started by the late Ambrose Congreve, a man of considerable wealth who decided, at the age of 11, to begin planting and never stopped. Under curator, Michael White, the development of new plants with Mount Congreve provenance continues, in particular rhododendron, magnolia and mahonia.

The main body of the garden is woodland and its attractions are the flowering magnolia and camellia, rhododendron and cherry, acer, azara, eucryphia, pittosporum and prunus. The scents can be heady, even at times of the year when very little is in flower. At the height of the late spring blossom, the word overpowering might better describe it. All of these flowering shrubs and trees are overlooked by 18th and 19th century plantations of oak and beech, many of them with stretches of clematis and rambling roses shimmying up their huge trunks.

There are over 16 miles or 27 km of paths wandering in and around the plants. It is genuinely too easy to get lost. There are also surprises: Every so often the paths open onto a secret garden, a rolling lawn planted through with spring bulbs, a secluded dell, a private garden room or a temple garden. The Chinese dell is a glory, a sunken garden at the bottom of a 12-metre drop into the quarry from which the stone to build the house was mined. You look down to see a circular pond with a little pagoda standing on an island. Moving on from here, the path leads through a forest of *Magnolia campbellii* towards an 18th century ice house, via a grove of tree ferns.

There are massed bulbs everywhere. During late spring the carpet of bluebells is so dense that much of the place looks like it's planted through water. The bluebells are joined by countless snowdrops, daffodils and fritillaries. The overall feel of abundance comes from the grouping of plants, not in the usual threes and fives, but in 25s, 50s and 100s. One doesn't come across a single witch hazel but groves of them, not a single Japanese acer but an avenue of them, as for the numbers of rhododendrons and camellias – get out the calculator. The varieties are invariably rare and unusual.

A huge natural outcrop of stone provided the opportunity for a cascade of water, which tumbles down toward the path but finishes in two stone ponds. The damp atmosphere the spray creates, make it ideal for wet-loving meconopsis and primula. Another bank of rock provided the base for a football pitch-sized rock garden and a maze of little paths.

The eight, layered beech trees are unforgettable. Ask to be shown this unusual sight. It is too easy to miss one among countless features here.

There are also four sloped acres of walled garden, arranged into May, June, July and August borders. These are like a feast of usual and unusual herbaceous perennials and include special iris beds and long runs of hydrangea in north-facing beds, as well as double borders of peony, nepeta and roses. These three, planted together really are irresistible.

Every sort of vegetable that can be grown in Ireland is grown here, interspersed with beds of asters and chrysanthemums. Fruit trees fill the middle beds while the surrounding walls home long runs of wisteria and the biggest *Clematis armandii* in these islands. The last marvel in the walled garden is the Chilean bellflower, or *Lapageria rosea*, sheltering from the salt winds that sometimes bluster over the wall.

Wander through the extensive greenhouses past walls of nectarines, a mind-bending display of orchids and bromeliads, rare fuchsias and almost extinct varieties of cyclamen and clivia. Numerous pots of streptocarpus, regal pelargoniums, hibiscus and gerbera grown from seed vie with masses of tall carnations. A visitor could buckle under the sheer extravagance of it all.

Salterbridge House & Garden

Cappoquin, Co. Waterford. P51H985. Tel: 058 54952. 087 2030763.
e-mail: pjwingfield@gmail.com www.salterbridge-houseandgarden.com Contact: Philip and Susie Wingfield.
Open: By appointment. Groups welcome. Partially wheelchair accessible. Supervised children. No dogs.
Special features: Teas can be arranged. Tours of the historic house. Directions: Leave Cappoquin by the road
to Lismore. About 1.5 km along the gate lodge is the first house on the right.

Salterbridge is a country garden of charm, and one of a cluster of interesting gardens in and around Cappoquin and Lismore, along the River Blackwater. Having negotiated its long drive under a canopy of trees, past big plantations of pittosporum grown as a florists crop, the drive opens out to reveal a fine old house on a ledge overlooking the wooded valley below it. The cork oak to the side of the building was, until recently thought to be the biggest on the island. (It has since been overtaken by one in Clonmel.) Meanwhile the four Irish yews close by must be among the first planted after the discovery of the Irish yew at Florence Court in Fermanagh. Philip Wingfield gave a slightly despairing laugh at the aged larch, close by which seems to drop a branch yearly.

Still standing by the house, we looked across the lawn to a distant huge cloud of rhododendron. The centre of one massive plant in the plantation was blown out in a storm about five years ago. 'Come back in 50 years and you will see it looking right again,' Philip said. This speak volumes of Salterbridge. Like its neighbours at Tourin, Cappoquin House, Ballylin and Dromana, this is a place to see plants grown on a large scale, planted with centuries rather than decades in mind. Flowers, when there are any, tend to come courtesy of flowering shrubs and trees rather than flower borders. On the subject of flowers, we passed a huge camellia with a *Clematis montana* and bindweed climbing through its solid glossy bulk. Philip told me that his annoyance at the presence of bindweed was somewhat lessened when a visitor told him that Gertrude Jekyll once recommended it as a good climber.

The lawns are studded with magnolia and camellia, flowering, scented daphne and rhododendron, euonymus and eucryphia. Attacks from rabbits and deer invariably take their toll on young plants but do not deter Philip from planting interesting new specimens, particularly large leafed rhododendron.

Down below the house the loss of a huge yew beside a bridge set into a fold in the landscape, offered the opportunity to make a sheltered new 'sunken' garden which is now full of hydrangea, gunnera and Japanese acer, whose canopies look great from overhead. I love the flowering *Cornus kousa,* reaching for the sky at only a decade old. This picturesque spot was a bramble-knotted mess before Philip got to work on it a few years ago.

The hilly lawns run between developing liquidambars, Korean pines, *Halesia monticola* and Indian chestnuts. In particular, a Cox's juniper, *Juniperus recurva* var. *coxii* with long fringed leaves, cries out to be admired. Beneath, the lower storey plants are no less interesting, from edgeworthia to massed hydrangeas. The 'dry' pond surrounded by a circling wall of white marble and ferns, irises, primulas, and hostas, is at its prettiest when the fountain is running.

On a height above the house and the stable block, there is a sheltered walk that tracks between hamamelis and more Japanese acer, bounded by the stone buildings and a raised stone ledge, alive with ferns and echiums, busy colonising the cracks. The fine *Rhododendron macabeanum,* with soft yellow flowers and softer, furry leaves is a favourite here. Before I left, Philip pointed to one more favourite, an unusual white-flowering *Zenobia pulverulenta* - 'ravishingly beautiful', a bit like the gardens themselves.

Shady Plants

Coolbooa, Clashmore, Co. Waterford. Tel: 086 660860. e-mail: molly@shadyplants.ie www.loveferns.com Contact: Molly Dukes. Open: By appointment. Special features: Fern nursery. Groups welcome by appointment. No children due to deep pond. No dogs. Directions: From the N25, turn on to the R671 between Youghal and Dungarvan towards Clashmore. When coming out of the village turn right at the wide junction, signposted for Dungarvan. Look for a wooden house and polytunnels 500m along on the left.

For a number of years, the Shady Plants nursery in West Waterford has been known to fern enthusiasts all over the country, as a source for all sorts of special and desirable plants. Mike Keep and Molly Dukes have mainly sold their wares at plant fairs and by mail order. Finally, now it is possible to visit the gardens attached to this excellent nursery.

This is exciting because those gardens are akin to the laboratory for the plants they sell. They grow and trial plants here and therefore have a better sense of what various species and varieties require. It comes as no surprise to be told that they work without chemicals. The sense of unsullied nature is overwhelming walking around this beautiful place.

The garden covers several acres but it is hard to get a sense of the overall size because its is so well divided into different spaces. This is a series of informal, very natural, gently tempered gardens in the hills above

Ardmore in Waterford. Naturalistic is the word that describes the woods and waterways, ponds and streams. The use of water in the garden is exceptional. The little stream that runs through it has been gently played with, added to by the tweaking of and altering existing small waterfalls. They have bridged and then side-planted the water with both native and exotic ferns in such a way that it could pass as completely natural.

Native trees, birch and ash, oak and holly, have been added to by a selection of exotics, beautifully coloured cut leaf acers and magnolias, under which winding paths squiggle between plantations of hosta and ferns, hellebores and spring bulbs.

Closer to the house, where it should be, is a little vegetable garden, sharing its space with dahlias, which Molly has fallen in love with and with which she is busy experimenting. Apart from the shelter of the woods, there are open areas too: Sunny lawns surrounded by prairie borders of perennials and tall grasses that seem to engulf the wooden house, which is tucked in between the plants, and weathered to a state of gentle camouflage. Filled with the sounds of birds and swishing wind rustle, this is a seductive, garden that will repay visits at different times of year.

Tourin House & Gardens

Cappoquin, Co. Waterford. Tel: 05854405. 086 8113 841. E- mail: tourin@eircom.net www.tourinhouseandgardens.com Contact: Kristin Jameson. Open: As part of the Waterford Garden Trail. April-Sept. Tues-Sat. 1-5pm, otherwise by appointment. Supervised children welcome. Dogs on leads. Groups by appointment all year. Not wheelchair accessible. Special Features: Guided house and garden tours. Refreshments can be arranged. Art classes. Events. Directions: 5 km south of Cappoquin on the road to Youghal. Signposted from both Cappoquin and Lismore.

Tourin is one of a string of historic gardens dotted along the river Blackwater in and around the town of Cappoquin sharing similar climates and soils. They have shared and swapped plants over the centuries, yet there are differences that make each garden worth seeing.

Among the group, Tourin and Salterbridge are closest in relation to one another, having been built for brothers who lived on either side of the river.

Tourin boasts an interesting mix of old and new. The garden as it is today was created around the 19th century house and an even older castle dating back to 1560. It was developed further by Kristen Jameson's parents. Today, Kristen and her sisters Andrea and Tara hold the baton.

Having taken in the very modern, reflecting pool placed perfectly in line with the old house, and some beautiful specimen trees, including a huge multi-stemmed rhododendron, the main garden is reached by way of a wide straight path, bounded by old, clipped yews.

From this point on, formality is dispensed with. The path moves into the woodland gardens and starts curving and bending. In here, the combination is of new and special trees tucked in under the older park trees and specimens planted in the 1950s, when their mother arrived and began her work on the gardens. Kristen told me how the late Mrs. Jameson climbed in among tangles of overgrown trees, unearthed a lost rockery and replanted it with low growing woodland plants as well as camellias and rhododendrons. Today, more work is being carried out and the result is a woodland that meanders along, taking in *Magnolia*

grandiflora, Magnolia x. *soulangeana* 'Speciosa' and *Rehderodendron macrocarpum,* an unusual Chinese tree. One among so many fine plants here is an old unidentified bright red rose that thrives in the shade. The great mounding rockery has been planted up with disporum and mini rhododendron, fritillaries, special snowdrops and cardiocrinum under strongly coloured acer and an unusual *Cornus* 'Dwarf Pink'.

Spring gardens made of cherries and camellias criss-cross between the network of low dry stone walls that Kristen's mother also made. They add to the structure and eccentricity of what is a very attractive feature. In winter, the air is scented by *Camellia sasanqua*. Hostas and primulas, lily-of-the valley and foxgloves take over the show later in the year.

The Japanese acers are used to good effect in the sort of layered plantations that suit the style here much. Layered arrangements are desirable but complicated when the layers include much loved evergreen oaks under which it is hard for other special things like *Rhododendron arboreum,* to survive. Judicious pruning is an ongoing task. 'Gardens develop and you have to deal with that development,' is what Kristen says.

An arboretum is about to be planted on the outer edge of the garden, close to a huge London plane or *Platanus* x. *hispanica* that could possibly have the biggest girth in the country, although the specimen at Salterbridge, could be bigger – another reason for visiting these gardens together.

The walled garden is divided into borders, fruit gardens, vegetable plots and greenhouses full of tomatoes. In the middle of all this action, there is a row of cherry trees, growing fruit for sale to the local shops. They carry the best cherries I have ever tasted. Tara is fond of irises and she grows over 100 varieties of them in here, lined up along the paths. Some of the walls are given over to fruit but there are also acacias and climbers, including *Solanum crispum* 'Glasnevin', while on the ground, pale blue *Agapanthus* 'Dublin' is a favourite. I liked the experimental bird seed bed, filled with sunflowers, flax, and other annuals, designed to provide the birds with food.

The courtyard is the home to a small collection of roses they collected as cuttings from derelict cottages around Ireland. Meanwhile, in the outbuildings, artist Andrea has her studio. There is a venue for garden talks and even cinema shows and the long refectory-style tables were all made from trees that had to be felled in the garden. Appropriately, a cherry walk leads from here out to the river, through a plantation of 65 acres of hardwood trees. It leads to Tourin Quay and passes original 16th century tower house that the Victorian house replaced.

Woodhouse

Stradbally, Co. Waterford. Tel: 051 293 105. e-mail: 1woodhouseestate@gmail.com Contact: Cathy Maitland. Open: For occasional charity days. Contact at beginning of year for annual dates. Other times, to groups by appointment. Special features: Museum. Refreshments can be arranged. Children welcome. Dogs on leads. Directions: On the coast road to Dungarvan out of Stradbally.

Driving out of Stradbally a few years ago I noticed something. There was a grand old house at the bottom of a hill that had always caught my eye but now something seemed to be stirring. There were men repairing, with great skill, previously crumbling stone boundary walls, including the old stiles. Inside the wall, the evidence of laurel and *Rhododendron ponticum* clearances could be seen. New trees were being planted and there seemed to be a whole programme of work in train. So when I heard in 2016 that the place was opening for a charity garden fete, the nose got the better of me.

It turned out that Woodhouse, built by a branch of the Desmond Fitzgerald's back in the 1700s, and having been through a large number of owners in the past 30 years, had been bought by a man with a local background, and was being brought back to its former glory. Jim Thompson, whose family left Ireland in the 1850s, moving to Yonkers in New York, bought the house in 2012. He has been restoring both house and garden ever since.

The steeply sloped walled garden, ever so slightly visible from the high road above the estate, is something of an awakening charm. The amount of rebuilding carried out on the walls alone, is itself a marvel. The greater space divides into two separate walled gardens, one, being a recently re-planted orchard of free-standing apples and wall-trained plums and pears. The other is the ornamental garden. This has been newly planted up with beds of purple and white, hydrangea and phlox, lupins and roses, including a rose named for Jim's mother, Sadie. This new garden is being coaxed along within the soft, pink, brick walls. A piece of sculpture by David Harbour, which seems to emerge from a brimming central pond, stands in interesting contrast to the traditional setting. At the top of the garden there are a line of restored garden buildings that overlook the borders. Beyond the lower walls, the river garden and walk runs the restored stone-lined River Tay. Above the walled garden is where the new greenhouse stands.

Throughout the greater grounds, new bridges have been built over the river and old ones restored, including an ancient three-spanned stone bridge. One of the new bridges leads across to a tennis court and pavilion with a small fern garden, and a walk along new avenues of young trees. Old, almost lost walks through the woods have also being reopened and restored.

The house looks out on a witty box and rose garden, to a restored lawn and a grand old oak for which the description venerable could have been coined.

Finally, up behind the house, the stone stable block is in the middle of being restored to provide the home for a museum to Woodhouse and its history.

Antrim

Antrim Castle Gardens

Clotworthy Arts Centre, Randalstown Road, Antrim, Co. Antrim. BT41 4LH. Tel: (0044 28) (048) 9448 1338. e-mail: culture@antrim.gov.uk Open: All year. No entrance fee, apart from organised guided tours. Wheelchair accessible. Supervised children welcome. Dogs on leads. Special features: Guided tours. Art gallery. Café. Events. Directions: Off the Randalstown Road (A6), about 150m from the Ballymena Road (A26).

The gardens at Antrim Castle are unique in Northern Ireland. Along with Killruddery in County Wicklow, they are the only remaining example on the island of a style of gardening almost completely superseded by later tastes and fashions. In the 17th century this style, which began and developed in France and Holland, started to infiltrate Britain and Ireland. It spoke of order and symmetry, grandeur, power and confidence and involved the creation of large and elaborate water features and expansive vistas. This impact was produced by cutting long *allées* or paths through extensive woods that enabled the garden to spill out into the countryside beyond and thus appear more all-encompassing than it really was. Symmetrically arranged walks and avenues made of pleached trees, often lime (*Tilia* x. *europaea*), trained like hedges on stilts, led between features. The French landscape architect André Le Nôtre is the most renowned gardener who favoured this style and his designs for King Louis XIV at Versailles and Les Tuileries in Paris are the most well known.

In the 17th century, Sir Hugh Clotworthy, and later his son Sir John (the first Viscount Massereene), created an Anglo-French garden on their lands in Antrim, attached to the new manor house on the site of an older fortified castle.

The garden was made up of ornamental canals, a parterre, a round pond and an ancient motte. This gargantuan creation was executed at a time when the country around it was in a state of civil chaos, making their achievement even more remarkable, if slightly crazy. Sir Hugh built the castle in 1613 and between that date and 1662, during which period Cromwellian troops dispossessed the Irish, he violently resisted plantations and civil war, and with Sir John, managed to complete the gardens. Today the castle is gone, burnt in a fire that swept through the buildings, not in the midst of conflict, but during a ball in 1922. An arts centre is located in the old stable block which was converted to living accommodation after the fire and was occupied by the Clotworthy family until 1956.

The gardens cover 26 acres. It was intended that the visitor be awed by the size, style, manpower and wealth employed in creating the spectacle. This visitor was certainly awed. The main feature of the garden is the parterre, an immaculately laid-out vision of ruler-straight, box-edged beds and yew topiary, divided by generous paths in pale pea gravel, while *Lychnis coronaria*, eryngium, dianthus, lysimachia and various herbs escape like floral explosions over the box walls. A line of pleached limes mark one end of the parterre, surrounded by tall hornbeam and yew hedges, and the deepest purple beech. These are all well maintained and look like a series of green curtains and walls butting into one another. A recently erected stage overlooks the picture. In contrast to the order here, the arts centre is surrounded by frilly, colourful flower gardens.

The restored long canals and cascades are impressive, planted with lilies and surrounded by more walls of clipped lime and hornbeam. Hunt out the pet cemetery, flanked by a suitably sombre grove of yews. One Victorian dog interred here, having died in Dublin, was brought in procession to Antrim and all dogs on the funeral route were expected to wear black headscarves!

The last time I was here, I had the gardens to myself and the place seemed rather forlorn; in particular, the motte seemed a sad, fenced-off scruffy affair. A motte is a man-made hill, on top of which they built wooden fortifications. The motte at Antrim Castle had been incorporated into the garden design as a viewing mount. Since that visit, the motte has been opened to the public. You follow a spiral path around and up the little hill, to enjoy a grand view. All around it, is a series of newly restored and created gardens, from a modern sculpture garden to some substantial flower borders that mark the edge of the old walled garden.

The Belfast Cat Garden

Belfast Castle, Antrim Road, Cave Hill, Belfast. BT15 5GR. Co. Antrim.
e-mail: bcr@belfastcastle.co.uk Tel: (0044 28) (048) 9077 6925. Open: All year. See website for seasonal
details. Special features: Restaurant. Museum. Walking trails. No entrance fee to garden. Directions:
Travelling north on the Antrim Road from the Crumlin Road, turn left onto Innisfayle Park and drive on
to the Castle gates.

The prospect of a cat garden will instil one with either horror or delight. For those who like the thought, the legend is that good fortune will attend visitors to Belfast Castle as long as a white cat lives in the grounds. With this in mind, a cat garden was created a few years ago around the romantic-looking castle on its perch above the city.

The garden is littered with sculptural cats – appropriately, nine of them, although I came across only seven, none of them the real white cat.

The castle, with all its turrets and flourishes in warm brown sandstone, is graced by the well-tended cat garden, laid out on ledges and surrounded by mature woods. There are well composed herbaceous borders with block plantings of blue nepeta or catmint and hosta, iris, sedum and berberis. I loved the sloped, shaded fern and gunnera beds tucked in beside the building. Long walls of clipped box hold these in and divide them off from the bowling-green lawns and gravel paths. One white stone cat sits, licking its paw in the middle of a limy fluff of *Alchemilla*

mollis. Another, clipped from box, hunches down in the middle of a lavender circle, threatening to pounce. There are mosaic cats best seen from overhead, and small cast iron cats on posts.

Expect good plants, well-placed and well-minded, enhanced with witty pieces of sculpture. This is an attractive garden with delightful views out over the city and harbour.

Benvarden Garden

Dervock, Ballymoney, Co. Antrim BT53 6NN. Tel: (0044 28) (048) 2074 1331.
Contact: Mr. and Mrs. Hugh Montgomery. Open: May, by appointment. June-Aug., Tues-Sun., and
bank holidays, 11am-5pm. Not wheelchair accessible. Groups should book. Children supervised. No dogs.
Special features: Farm implement museum. Plants for sale. Seasonal tea room. Directions: From the main
Belfast-Coleraine road, take the B62 ring road to Portrush. At Ballybogey, turn right onto the B67. Drive
2.5 km. Just before the bridge over the River Bush, turn right. The garden is marked by iron gates.

There is an uplifting air of endeavour at Benvarden, from the girl who takes care of both the gate and vegetable sales, to Mr. Montgomery, deadheading roses as he walks about the place, chatting about plants his mother brought to the garden and checklisting his jobs.

The estate on the banks of the River Bush had a colourful start. In the 1760s it belonged to a notorious

man, John MacNaughton, known in local history as Half-Hanged MacNaughton. A student at Trinity College, Dublin, he eloped with a 15-year-old heiress, Mary Ann Knox, whom he then killed, according to the stories, by mistake. In a botched execution, he was twice hanged for his crime. Benvarden was subsequently sold to the Montgomery family and they have been there ever since.

The walled garden is one of the oldest continuously cultivated gardens on the island: The two-and-a-quarter-acre feature appears on a 1788 map drawn by James Williamson of Dublin. Over 230 years later, it is still being worked and is a model of its type. Enter by way of the vegetable garden, which is, unusually, surrounded by a fairly low wall topped with railings which make it feel open and airy. A greenhouse full of tender plants doubles up as ticket shop and all around it there are neat crops and plants raised in the garden, which are for sale.

Next door is the ornamental walled garden. Here, the first sights that stand out are the unusual double

rows of box hedging around the herb borders and flowerbeds. The outer hedges, which are clipped higher, enclose inner, lower, stepped-down hedges, to strong sculptural effect. All around the brick walls are deep herbaceous borders crammed with delphiniums, spiky irises and clouds of blue and pink campanula. The radiating rose garden is a charm, like a bicycle wheel, where the beds form the triangles between the knobbled stone paths which make up the spokes. They all converge on a central fish pond and small fountain. Mr. Montgomery showed me his favourite *Rosa* 'Else Poulsen', a soft pink floribunda that has been going strong here since the 1950s.

Scented rose arches are present at all the cross paths, leading between shrub borders stuffed with hydrangea, abutilon and fuchsia. *Rosa* 'Paul's Scarlet Climber' fairly smothers one such cross path arch, while the pergola, laden down with wisteria, leads away to the peach and grape house.

The tennis court is surrounded by a fence being colonised by a long stretch of *Rosa* 'Albertine'. Mr. Montgomery told me that the court, built by his father in 1920, had cost an outrageous £300. Close by, investigate the restored garden bothy or hut where the garden boy who stoked the hothouse boilers, slept.

Separated from the leisured world of tennis parties, the vegetable garden is made up of industrial-sized beds. Regiments of strawberries line out along the outside of tidy lettuce beds; to pick something from these sumptuous rows would feel like a crime. The fat tomatoes, guarded by straight rows of marigolds in the greenhouse, are as perfectly arrayed. There are apples on the walls and a lichen-covered sundial which has been telling the time on sunny days since 1705.

Leaving the walled garden by a little gate in the wall, under an arch of Japanese acer, leads one to the pleasure grounds. These include a grassy path through a green, damp fernery, and a yew walk, past towering copper beech, pine, rhododendron and willow. The path trails along a woodland pond with a quaint little humped stone bridge between festoons of ferns, primulas and other damp-loving plants. Wear wellingtons here. It is a quiet place made up of glittery water, dappled light and teeming wildlife. The mown grass continues along to the River Bush and the elegant iron bridge with a 30 metre span, built in 1878, a testament to splendid Victorian engineering and design.

The Botanic Gardens

Botanic Avenue, Belfast, BT7 1LP, Co. Antrim. Tel/Fax: (0044 28) (048) 9031 4762. Contact: Reception. Open: Throughout the year, during daylight hours. Wheelchair accessible. No entrance fee. Supervised children welcome. Dogs on leads. Special features: Guided tours can be arranged. Events. Directions: The gates to the park are on Botanic Avenue.

The Belfast Botanic Gardens are well situated in the centre of the city, close to Queen's University. As a result, the gardens are regularly frequented by visitors and natives alike, for leisurely walks, a quick shortcut and summer sunbathing, as well as the more obvious pastime of plant studying.

The gardens were founded in 1828 following an upsurge of interest in botany and horticulture, fuelled by the thousands of new species being brought to Europe from the Americas and the Far East by plant hunters and explorers.

The first large task undertaken in the new Botanic Gardens was the creation of a pinetum, or a plantation of pines and conifers, as well as a collection of deciduous trees, mainly varieties of oak. These were laid out between 1838 and the 1850s and included trees like the newly discovered swamp cypress (*Taxodium distichum*) and a sky-scraping Douglas fir (*Pseudotsuga menziesii*), brought to England only a few years before by one of the bravest plant collectors in history, David Douglas. The remains of these collections still stand today in front of the Ulster Museum, which is situated within the grounds.

In 1839, a palm house was built to a design by the architect Sir Charles Lanyon (see Ballywalter Park, County Down). This was one of the first curvilinear glasshouses ever built and the work was carried out by Richard Turner, who modified the original design to make it more practical. ('Curvilinear' refers to the placement of the glass panes, arranged at angles to maximise the absorption of the sun's rays.) The Belfast palm house preceded the curvilinear ranges in both Kew Gardens and the Botanic Gardens in Dublin. Some of the original plants placed there in the mid 19th century still thrive today, including a heady *Rhododendron fragrantissimum*. The palm house was in the middle of vital restoration work when I last visited.

In relation to glasshouses, Belfast's greatest claim to fame is the tropical ravine, built in the 1880s by the then curator Charles McKimm; it was built to resemble a sunken glen. Visitors enter and walk through the warm damp-house on a raised mezzanine that overlooks the huge plants growing in the ravine below, like a jungle, steamy and hot. It too, still includes plants from the original Victorian layout. The dombeya is one of its famed plants, flowering in February and emitting the smell of caramel, alongside orchids, tree ferns, bromeliads, sugar cane, papyrus and cinnamon. It too was closed for restoration on my last visit. I look forward to seeing it again when finished.

The best walks through the park lead deep into the middle of the garden and take in the double borders of herbaceous perennials on one side and multiple swishing grasses on the other. Parallel to these is another double bed, even deeper, mixed on one side and largely herbaceous on the other. There is also a substantial rose garden. My most recent favourite route leads into the shaded stream garden, between log-lined plantations of ferns under conifers and rhododendrons, different species of crataegus and mahonia. Light-reflecting gravel paths brighten the shade, making the whole effect gorgeous.

The Botanic Gardens in Belfast are unlike those in Dublin, where education is a crucial aspect of the work being carried out. The Belfast gardens are more pleasure grounds. This is quite simply a good-looking, friendly, busy and well-used city park.

Brocklamont House

2 Old Galgorm Road, Ballymena, Co. Antrim. BT42 1AL. Tel: (0044 28) (048) 2564 1459. e-mail: glynn.margaret@gmail.com Contact: Mrs. Margaret Glynn. Open: May-Sept., by appointment. Groups welcome. Supervised children. Dogs on leads. Directions: Leaving Ballymena on the A42 to Portglenone, the garden is 0.75 km outside the town on the right, marked by black iron gates, opposite the Ballymena Academy.

The house on Old Galgorm Road is a classic Victorian villa overlooking a two-and-a-half-acre garden, created largely by its current owner, Margaret Glynn. Mrs. Glynn's strong feel for both plants and design is evident from the first step inside the gate where a convertible multi-stemmed *Acer Griseum* stands over a small gravel garden, carpeted with *Viola labradorica*, Corsican mint and cushions of hepatica. Off and away from here, one's attention is drawn towards alluring stands of trees and sloped lawns punctuated by shrub borders and flowers.

Mrs. Glynn's favourite plants are, in order: Irises, hellebores and geraniums. She grows scores of each. She also cultivates 300 types of galanthus. Ferns are favourites too and, as well as fitting them into corners throughout the garden, she built a fernery at the bottom of one of the slopes. This is a damp area under an umbrella canopy of Japanese acer and magnolia with an array of ferns that look like so many green shuttlecocks.

Overhead, sky-dusting pines lead the eye back up. As they grew, Mrs. Glynn regularly pruned them, to create more scope for under-storey planting. Pruning-up also permits the creation of a network of views and vistas through tunnels of trees, back and forth across the garden. Through one opening, the view might be of a bridged pool and a wedding cake tree or *Cornus controversa* 'Variegata', teamed with white hydrangea. In another, there will be a view of open lawn. In yet another direction, the picture will be of a little wood, run riot with primulas, trilliums and aquilegias.

There is a giddy abundance of troughs by the house. Done well, these are always a pleasure. Here the rows of miniature gardens, filled with fun-sized alpines are the best. Mrs. Glynn is a keen member of the Alpine Plants Society.

The old walled garden has been converted and part of it is now a sunny patio and terrace garden. Two borders, one herbaceous and one annual, stand on either side of the path. Someone called this the Botticelli garden and the two flower-filled expanses are certainly voluptuous enough to deserve the name, with mixed poppies, cosmos, periwinkles and osteospermum elbowing each other for attention.

Remember to ask to see the compost system. Enviable is the only word.

Joey Dunlop Memorial Garden

Castle Street, Ballymoney, BT53 6JR, Co. Antrim. Open: Year round. Admission free.
Directions: In the centre of Ballymoney, signposted.

I found myself following signs that read 'Joey Dunlop Garden' in Ballymoney and they led me to a touching memorial garden honouring two of Ulster's motorcycle heroes. It comes as something of a surprise with its life-size statues and monument walls surrounded by a tidy flower and shrub garden; well-minded with colourful bedding and perennials spread out under a series of white betulas and Japanese acers, planted by relatives of Joey and his brother Robert Dunlop. The laurel arch is particularly apt.

The Cairncastle Sweet Chestnut

St Patrick's Church Graveyard, Ballymullock Road, Cairncastle, Co. Antrim. Open: At all times.
Directions: Turn off the A2 coastal road and drive to Cairncastle village. Take the Ballymullock road out of the village to the church.

Several people recommended that I visit this tree so I followed their directions and arrived at the picturesque cemetery that looks out at the sea. Standing over, indeed growing out of, a grave in St Patrick's church graveyard is a rather tatty, gnarled, sweet chestnut. The tree leans precariously to one side and has as many dead branches as living. It could star in an old-fashioned horror film.

The story is that a sailor, washed up from the Spanish Armada is buried here and the tree grew from a seed in his pocket. According to stories, seamen carried these and chewed them to prevent scurvy. The story sounds like a romantic one yet dendrochronological tests have shown that the tree does date to the 16th century.

Carnfunnock Country Park

Coast Road, Ballygally, Larne, Co. Antrim BT40 2QG. Tel: (0044 28) (048) 2826 2471.
e-mail: carnfunnock@midandeastantrim.gov.uk. Contact: Park Manager. Open: Daily. Wheelchair accessible. Groups welcome. No entrance fee. Parking charge. Supervised children. Dogs on leads. Special features: Café. Miniature train. Maze. Play area. Golf course. Directions: Travel north on the A2 from Larne for 5 km. Garden signed.

The two-acre walled garden of the Carnfunnock Country Park Estate is another Big House garden without a house. As seen today, the garden, which looks out over the Antrim coast, is planted in a contemporary, modern style. It is laid out in a pattern that is heavy on shrubs and good hedging, with a network of walks and a big circle of hornbeams. A Time Garden, with a varied collection of sundials can be found within the walls, ranged about the separate hedged rooms, providing a visual chart of the progress of timekeeping instruments over the centuries. One is made of marble slabs set into the grass; several others are wall-mounted and a good number are the more usual free-standing sculptural types.

Clouds of mature rhododendron overlook the show and pergolas covered in actinidea and wisteria span the paths, further dividing the garden rooms.

One of these garden rooms is a small enclosure of box beds filled with pink, white and raspberry cosmos, each with a central tall cordyline, all enclosed between fat hornbeam hedges. There are some vibrant colours, witness red begonia bedding in front of blue lobelia.

The maintenance is as exceptional as I remember it many years ago when I first visited.

Children will enjoy the hornbeam maze, complete with a helpful viewing stand to aid escape. There is also a wildlife garden and walk. Lose the children in the maze. Place the Thomas the Tank Engine fans on the tiny train. Send teenagers to the golf range. Escape to the garden and everyone can meet for a walk by the sea when they are finished. Carnfunnock is a great place for a family day out.

The Cottage Garden Plant Centre

154 Ballyrobert Road, Ballyclare, BT39 9RT. Co. Antrim. Tel: (0044 48) (028) 9332 2952. e-mail: information@ballyrobertgardens.com Contact: Joy and Maurice Parkinson. Open: Mar-Sept. daily. Other times by appointment. Groups welcome. Supervised children. Dogs on leads. Special features: Plant nursery. Teas by arrangement. Directions: Just under 1 km from the centre of Ballyrobert, on the Ballyclare Road, opposite golf club sign.

Planting a garden of cultivated flowers within a surrounding of wild countryside is not easy. If treated without due care, it can jar badly with its surroundings. Ideally, it should blend in, almost unnoticed. The Parkinsons could give lessons on how to blend in.

Maurice and Joy have been working here since the early 1990s. The venture started out as a cottage garden, attached, appropriately enough, to an early 19th century farm cottage. Close to the buildings and yard, the style is still one of a classic cottage garden, a sea of old-fashioned flowers, an abundance of bloom and colour, scent and foliage, busy with butterflies and bees, the very picture of a chocolate box garden. But as it travels out from the house, the garden becomes more native and loose, finally meeting with, and melding into, the rough Ballyclare landscape in a series of sedge gardens shaped as spirals and St. Bridget's crosses.

The area in front of the house is called the field garden. It comprises two large mixed beds, divided by grass paths that resemble nothing so much as a green shag pile carpet. The beds are chock-full of lupins, asters, irises, hollyhocks and violas and divided into colour blocks. The most striking is the 'hot' bed, a wild party of reds and wines, plum-coloured hemerocallis or daylilies, scarlet crocosmia and chocolate cosmos or *Cosmos atrosanguineus*, with the scent of a big bar of Bourneville.

Tucked behind the house, is a box garden with more favourite flowers, a dovecote, a restored stone barn and original cobbled paving. Apart from the house and barn, the garden features old iron farm gates with distinctive pillars peculiar to this area of County Antrim.

At the outer edge of each of the gardens, the cultivated plants butt up against wilder natives to dramatic effect. There is a marked contrast between bowling-green lawns and loose meadows of buttercups and wild grass. In the formal garden, the fronts of the beds are edged in clipped box while the backs are bounded by undulating fieldstone walls, behind which a native wood trails off into a meadow and on out to the rough fields.

The borders are backed by a mixture of exotic and native small trees. The gradual balance between import and native shifts from the cultivated to the wild: Japanese acers and magnolias blend with, and then are replaced by native hawthorn, blackthorn, ash and birch.

The orchard is the sort of unusual feature in which a lazy gardener will delight. Maurice planted apple trees into raised mounds of compost, simply laid down on the soil in a field at the edge of the garden. Keeping the mounds weed-free is all that needs to be done, while the young trees romp along, growing strong in the rich soil, gaining strength and stature before their roots hit the surrounding field.

Out by the lake garden, the plants are much more native and the views over little stiles, beyond the boundary, are of the carved and sculpted rush and sedge gardens and a young wood.

17 Drumnamallaght Road

Ballymoney, BT53 7QX. Co. Antrim. Tel: (0044 28) (048) 2766 2923. www.ulstergardensscheme.org.uk Contact: Mrs. Dorothy Brown. Open: All year by appointment to groups. Not suitable for children. No dogs. Special features: Alpine plants for sale. Directions: On appointment.

Mrs. Brown has been tending her suburban garden, growing and minding her hard-to-mind plants since the late 1990s. Like a diamond, it is small but gleams. Despite its size, I think I could discover something new here no matter how many times I visit.

We stood in the front garden looking at an arrangement of troughs overflowing with alpines and miniature plants, ancient-looking, twisted, squat shrubs and rockery arrangements which could cheerfully turn me to crime. Mrs. Brown introduced it by explaining that the initial idea had been to create a scree garden, planting everything directly into the ground. The soil proved too wet for that. The garden is on the boundary of the Leslie Hill estate and enjoys the shelter of its mature trees, but it also lies at the bottom of the hill in question and as a result, is soggy and damp. Resolution lay in raising the alpines, which crave free-draining soil, into troughs and raised beds, pots and other containers.

Mrs. Brown propagates most of her plants and, given that many of them are hard to come by, that talent with seed is most useful. Among some of the more beautiful small plants are the gorgeous green pillows of *Azorella trifurcata*. They grow like solid little jade hillocks in the gravel.

Any plant that sets seed is welcome and allowed to do so freely. Those plants that seed in unsuitable spots are simply removed. The effect of this is that everything *looks* natural, even in troughs. Mrs. Brown recommends the benefits of membership of both the Alpine Plant Society and the local horticultural society.

The main garden to the back of the house includes a small lawn like a green rug, surrounded by shrubs, modest-sized trees, such as the eye-catching *Robinia pseudoacacia* 'Lady Lace', and an overstuffed lily-and-iris pond. Good as these are, they are only the backdrop to the cabinet of curiosities that is the collection of pots, troughs and planters, including a pot of fabulous orange *Isoplexis canariensis*, the Canary Island foxglove. Mrs. Brown has a particular talent for arranging containers – an underestimated skill. I was particularly taken by a collection of little acers in pots gathered on the steps.

The conservatory, a calm place to sit in summer, cannot be accessed in the winter for the sake of migrating plants. This is because a good proportion of the plants here are tender and need indoor sanctuary over winter. We sat in the glass room looking out at the plants that a few months later would be sitting in our place.

At the same time, many of the plants here little toughies that just look tender and exotic-looking. She grows some of these in the crevice garden, between slates, laid on end and inter-filled with gritty compost to create the desired crevices. Tiny alpines and other half-pint plants have been insinuated into these miniature landscapes. The wide, shallow pans look like self-contained worlds. I admired an exquisite *Fuchsia* 'Lottie Hobby', a shrub the size of a teacup. Venerable-looking willows, hug the ground and spread out only 30 cm. Elsewhere, an arrangement of succulents on a series of ledges looks like a sweet shop display.

On my most recent visit, Mrs. Brown asked if I would like to see her new garden. I wondered where on earth it might be as I was led towards the back boundary, to discover that the burgeoning *Rhododendron sinogrande* was not quite the boundary. Underneath its spreading branches, there is a sunken stream that she recently planted with ferns and hostas, arisaemas, fabulous *Athyrium felix femina* 'Dre's dagger' and tall white ranunculus. We climbed down, almost into the water, to inspect it. Any further expansion will need to be made onto the roof of the house.

Glenarm Castle

Glenarm, Co. Antrim, BT44 0BQ. Tel: (0044 28) (048) 2884 1203. e-mail info@glenarmcastle.com
Open: May-Sept. Mon-Sat., 10am-5pm. Groups welcome. Supervised children. Guide dogs only. Special
features: Tearoom. Gift shop. Castle tours and trails by arrangement. Plants for sale. Events. Disabled
parking. Directions: Glenarm is on the A2, north of Larne. The castle is in the village.

Glenarm Castle is set at the foot of one of the Glens of Antrim in one of the most scenic settings on the island. The drive around the coast along the A2 is a rare pleasure, devoid of ribbon development and scatterings of new houses. This peaceful tour would be reason enough to make a visit to Glenarm, even if the gardens were of no worth. Thankfully, that is not the case. The first time I visited, I approached from the wrong direction, and drove into the village, arriving at a bridge over what looked like a moat. It is in fact a river. On the other side is an elaborate, castellated gate lodge. This not-so-little gate lodge was built in the 1820s in a gothic style complete with arrow slits, battlements and a portcullis. It was clearly created with more than the needs of a gatekeeper in mind, but designed as a place in which to entertain. Make a detour in the village to see it before visiting the gardens.

In a Top of the Pops countdown of the gardens on the island of Ireland, Glenarm would certainly be in the toss up for the Number One slot. Dating back to the mid 18th century and covering four acres, the walled garden is a *tour de force*. Enter it via the former mushroom house, today a tearoom. This whitewashed building, along with the gardener's cottage and a line of potting sheds, overlooks the first small walled garden, an area devoted to decorative vegetable beds.

Sitting with a cup of tea and cake, before setting off to oversee lines of Swiss chard, artichokes, strawberries, fat carrots and lettuce, is a good plan. The wall-trained roses married with same colour sweet pea, can be inspected from this vantage-point too; deep, quartered, plum-coloured flowers, so pretty they could be artificial. At the top of the garden a huge fig marks the place of a long dismantled greenhouse. A modest lip of glass on top of the wall protects it from the weather and, possibly as a result, the tree carries a good crop.

In the greater garden over the wall, there is still a long run of intact greenhouse, almost 100 metres long. Within the greenhouse there are trained vines, bounteous apricots, peaches and iridescent blue plumbago. Outside the glass, a long ribbon of blue nepeta or catmint runs the length of the building. This is cut back in July to encourage a second flush of flowers. On the other side of the path bordering this, pleached limes stand to attention, like a hedge on stilts.

From here the rest of the walled garden spreads out, like a series of festivities, beginning with mixed beds of pink love-lies-bleeding or amaranthus, pink everlasting sweet pea, ruby cosmos, red pheasant berry or leycesteria and aubergine-coloured cotinus. Flowering buddleia and tree peonies are used in repeat patterns over the length of the wide beds, to create continuity. Next on the inspection list are the purple beds, with *Papaver orientale* 'Patty's Plum', purple pansies, blood-red roses, purple salvia, toned down a little by more hazy-blue nepeta and pink geraniums.

The surprises are everywhere: mirroring double border of silvers, blues, yellows and variegated foliage shrubs line one path leading to a central sundial, which is surrounded by a tall yew circle, reputed to be the oldest in Ireland. The sundial seems to float over plumes of fennel and borage. The trick to making this work is that the inner planting scheme cannot be seen from outside the yew circle and so it comes upon the visitor as a surprise.

The centre of each curved yew section opens out to another garden room. One of these is a serpentine beech *allée* which leads to a beech circle with a raised pond and fountain. This gives onto another short beech avenue. Every time visitors think they have seen the full extent of this garden, another flourish appears from around a corner. I love the yew 'battlements' and the perfectly presented *Luma apiculata* on the centre of one of the lawns.

Since last visited, there has been no let up in Glenarm's expansion. One addition is the formal stream that flows downhill between lines of gleaming white and jet black cobbles from the beach outside the castle walls.

The next new attraction is a feature usually found in 18th century landscape gardens: A viewing mound, negotiated by means of a spiral path up to a sometimes windy point from where you can take in the entire tremendous garden. From here, lines of newly planted box and beech rooms can be seen clearly. Each room contains a fruit garden from an individual crab apple garden, where the trees grow over squares of wildflowers, to quince gardens and mulberry gardens. The most outstanding is the pear garden with a circular rail on which two varieties, 'Conference' and 'Chanticleer', are being trained. The most unusual of the fruit enclosures is the medlar garden where the trees have been trained as supported two-metre standards. The new cornus garden around the base of the mound will be interesting as it develops.

Nearby is another unusual feature: box enclosed squares of kniphofia, stipa and alliums, with one flower type per square. These are formal and modern.

In another direction, the mood loosens out with a wildflower meadow dissected by mown paths centred on a wooden obelisk. Along with native flowers, they grow vivid blue camassias in the grass. The mown paths can be seen best from the top of the viewing mound, as can the parkland beyond and a view out to sea.

The meadow is cut to about 5 cm in August; the grass is left to lie, dry and drop its seed, before being raked. Yellow rattle helps inhibit it from growing too vigorously, rendering the meadow a better environment for wildflowers. They also plant 8,500 tulip bulbs each autumn for a tulip festival in May.

Glenarm is a singular garden: Ambitious, clever and attractive. Yet it is maintained by just two men. These are the remarkable Whally brothers, Billy and James.

Greenmount Walled Garden

45 Tigracy Road, Antrim, Co. Antrim, BT41 4PS. Manager. Tel: (0044 28) (048) 9442 6669. e-mail: enquiries@cafre.ac.uk Contact: Alan McIlveen. Open: Selected open weekends. Contact for annual details. At other times by appointment to groups. Wheelchair accessible. Directions: From Antrim town follow the signs for Belfast Airport on the A6. At the mini roundabout, take the second exit and after 2 km turn left into Tirgracy Road. After 1 km Greenmount is situated on the left.

The garden attached to a horticultural college is a garden worth investigating. I walked around chatting to the extraordinarily friendly workers at Greenmount, marvelling at the place. Picture a Celtic knot garden like the most delicate green lace. Add in long, busy herbaceous borders, pleached lime *allées*, roses grown along swags, and wall borders full of well-matched shrubs and herbaceous perennials. There are arbours, a maze and excellent topiary. The curvilinear glasshouse had undergone some work and was closed when I visited, but it looked perfect, even though it could be seen only from the outside.

The apples are trained, not one but four ways – as step-overs, vertical cordons, angled cordons and classic candelabra espaliers. Wildflower borders sit well inside perfect box walls. The pergola and gazebo, are made from classic wooden trellis and covered in healthy tangles of wisteria and golden hop, underneath which, there are dark fern and hosta beds. We left this area by way of a gateway at the back of the gazebo and entered a sort of secret garden. It is a Japanese-inspired pond garden woven through by a series of paths between and under acers, aralias, magnolias, nothofagus, conifers and bamboos, over shade-loving foliage plants and waterside iris and rodgersia.

Those familiar with the BBC Ulster garden

programmes will recognise the Greenmount television garden, which is here too.

My favourite area is the corner of lavender combined with a huge *Echium pininana* that looks as though it were pretending to be lavender, coupled with *Rosa* 'Bengal Crimson' and golden hop grown on ropes.

The larger pleasure gardens are studded with mature trees, in groves and as single specimens set into the lawns. There are perfect shrub borders and fashionable vertical garden walls, as well as bedding displays, which will turn the head of the most 'bedding averse' among us. If you like blade-sharp edges and grass like a billiard table, hedges clipped with a nail scissors and perfect spacing between bedding, this is the garden for you. It is a well-presented and beautiful place run by staff that CAFRE should bottle. Ten out of ten.

Kilcoan Gardens

240 Middle Road, Islandmagee, Larne, Co. Antrim, BT40 3TG. Tel: (00 44) 7703 519 564. e-mail: cherry@kilcoangardens.com. Contact: Cherry Townsend and Jane Robinson. Open: April-Sept. Wed-Sun. 12-5pm. Special features: Garden tours. Courses. Cut flower sales. Self-service tea barn. Directions: Take the A2 south from Larne as far as Whitehead then take the B150 north, forking onto Middle Road. The garden is up a laneway to the left.

Walking around Kilcoan, it is necessary to remind yourself repeatedly that it is a productive garden, a market garden. Cherry Townsend sells cut flowers from her impossibly romantic garden and has been doing so for several years.

The site, on top of a windswept hill on the Islandmagee peninsula, might seem strange. After one has negotiated a series of lanes between wind-scalped fields, the sheer abundance and luxury of the growth here comes as a surprise. Cherry explained that all she thought of in the early days was shelter. She put shelter belts everywhere until by the early years of the century, the shelter she craved was largely

Photo: Cherry Townsend.

in place and she was finally able to lay out her cut-flower borders. Today, scented beds full of peonies and nigella, hesperis and sweet William, rose and iris, bask in the climate Cherry created for them.

First, drive downhill to the house, with its spade-shaped door knocker, set in a yard of pots bursting with perennials and old tin watering cans.

The first of the garden rooms is an old-fashioned cottage border filled with big clumps of delphinium and lupin, rose and campanula. From here, the maze begins. Go in one direction under a rose arch cut into a native crataegus, honeysuckle, holly and wild rose hedge, to reach yet more flower gardens, cut through with grass paths. Another route leads through gates in farther hedges, out past cut-flower borders and on into pond gardens and wildflower meadows, herb gardens, orchards and vegetable plots.

There are young plantations of special trees, as well as nearly 20 acres of natives.

Cherry mixes wild roses with cultivated varieties, wild flowers with more exotic species and varieties of native hedging and trees in combinations that look good, but which also benefit wildlife. The garden was a past winner of Britain's Bee Friendliest Garden. Remember as you walk, that this garden is worked organically.

Picking your way between meadows spiked with species gladioli, bear in mind that this Flake-advert-made-real did not just happen. The team responsible is made up of Cherry, her mother Jane Robinson, and her aunt, Jo Adams. Together they are the terrific trio that work the garden and, if they chose to do so, could probably run a country. Let it not be forgotten that Cherry's brother William, keeps the all-important grass under control.

The Mill House

140 Ballynashee Road, Glenwherry, Ballymena, Co. Antrim. BT42 3EW. Tel: (0044 28) (048) 2583 1223. e-mail: jimandhilary@btinternet.com. Contact: Hilary and Jim Rafferty. Open: By appointment to groups and individuals between May and Aug. See website for additional details. Directions: On application.

Occasionally you will come upon a sight with the power to stop you in your tracks. The garden that Jim and Hilary Rafferty have been making since the early 1990s in the Antrim countryside is such a sight. Back then, the Raffertys bought a farmhouse with some stone outhouses, surrounded by an unpromising few fields, and began to work, using what might have been wands and spells, rather than spades and barrows. Today, groves of young birches stand over seas of spring flowers; hostas and ferns grow where there were once flat fields. Small oak and beech woods and rhododendron walks were laid out, with tracks trailing through.

The site was wet, so it was natural that water should be brought to bear on the garden. As a result, the small river that runs through the five-acre site was incorporated into the design, with the excavation of a sizeable pond. This substantial body of water is now surrounded by ribbons of primulas and arums, irises and rushes, shrubs and flowers. It could well have occurred naturally. A mesmerising feature here is the little whirlpool, like that created by the emptying of a bath down a drain. The pond is only part of a series of linked watercourses. One of the outhouses is a 300-year-old mill that has become Jim's pet project, along with the 1950s' tractor with which he works the garden.

So far he has repaired the engines that run the mill race. This restoration project has rendered the garden interesting on a wider level than the simple horticultural one. I love the noise of the mill. The wildlife its waters has attracted is also impressive. Kingfishers and otters, moorhens and ducks are only some of the animals sharing this haven.

Close to the house is the busiest of the gardens, a series of flower borders grown up on ledges that house alpines, trailing plants and low-growing perennials where the visitor can get right in to investigate the treasures nose-to-nose.

Jim and Hilary have created a virtuoso garden that also manages to ooze charm. It felt like a real find.

Photo: Hilary Rafferty.

Sir Thomas & Lady Dixon Park

Upper Malone Road, Belfast, Co. Antrim, BT17 9LA. Tel: (0044 28) (048) 9091 8768. www.belfastcity.gov.uk/parks. Open: All year during daylight. No entrance fee. Supervised children. Dogs on leads. Special features: Annual Rose Festival. Directions: Located south of the city on the Upper Malone Road, signposted.

On a recent visit, on a sunny 12th of July, I was met by the sight of a gang of people gathered in the car park, wearing running gear and skis and carrying ski poles. I could see how a spot of cross-country skiing might be the order of the day in snowy December, but as a meeting point for skiers wanting to practice in sunny July, it seemed that this city park is nothing if not versatile.

The grounds and gardens that make up the Sir Thomas and Lady Dixon Park were given to the city of Belfast by Lady Dixon in 1959. They were part of a demesne founded in the 18th century, attached to a house that is now gone. The main body of the park is made up of mature woods and rolling parkland, along the banks of the River Lagan.

The park is best known for its rose gardens and as the home to the International Rose Trials, set up in 1964. For many people, rose gardens are not the easiest of gardens to love. Roses are beautiful and the scent and variety of the flowers cannot be denied, but beds full of hybrid tea roses with bare, stumpy or gangly legs are not to many people's tastes. The words 'beautiful' and 'rose bush' do not always sit happily together. Old shrub roses can have a more attractive shape but, in general, we grow roses for the flowers rather than for the shape of the plant.

That stated, the large beds of roses look good, streaming off into the distance like coloured ribbons draped over the hills, in all directions in this huge park. The sheer scale of planting in the displays is the key. The 130-acre park is an attractive place, with dramatic sweeps of lawn rising and falling in hills and hollows between groves of park trees. The rose beds, containing over 25,000 plants, run in long swathes of single colours. The climbers, shrub, patio, floribunda, heritage and Irish heritage roses are all grown, like with like, in spirals, over festive-looking tent-supports and along pergolas. There is a rose here for every situation and occasion. The long arched walks, between scented climbers and ramblers, are a dream at the height of summer. Among the displays, the Dickson and McGredy beds take pride of place and celebrate the achievements of two famed, fifth generation, Irish rose-breeding families. Both have been in the business since the 1870s.

The park has more to offer than roses however. There are also 100 varieties of camellia grown in trial beds. When I was looking for these, I hit upon some rhododendron and magnolia walks, wrapped around a children's playground. From here, I made my way down a yew avenue and into a hilly meadow dotted with orchids. Paths mown through the grass ran in all directions. Taking what was obviously the wrong path, I became lost and ended up in a plantation of oak and dawn redwood. I stayed lost for a long time, in the woods and then outside, coming across more expanses of rhododendron, trails through exotic trees and a smaller series of gardens around Malone House at the edge of the park.

Do not miss the Japanese Garden, which is also hard to find if you are as directionally challenged as I am. This was added to the park in the 1990s, a green valley dotted with mature specimens of acer, cornus, cryptomeria and picea, planted between boulders and a bridged lily pond.

Kilcoan Gardens, Co. Antrim

Small Pots £3·50
Medium £4·00
Large £5·00
X Large £6·50

All plants grown organically

Bee friendly!

The Ledsham Garden

*11 Sallagh Road, Cairncastle, Ballygally, Larne, Co. Antrim, BT40 2NE.
Tel: (0044 28) (048) 2858 3003. e-mail: ledshamd@aol.com. Contact: David and Janet Ledsham. Open:
Mid-April to mid-Oct. by appointment. Small groups preferred. Special features: Unusual plants for sale.
Directions: From the A8, turn left onto the B148 signposted for Cairncastle. After 6 km, leave the road
at the 'Old Dairy Cottage' and fork left onto Sallagh Road. The house is just under 1 km along, below the
road, on the right.*

The Ledshams came to this spot in Larne, with its view over the sea to Scotland, in the mid-1990s. They bought an exposed two-acre sheep field surrounded by other exposed sheep fields. I studied the almost impossible-to-believe photograph of that original site. Standing in the middle of David and Janet's wild alpine garden, full of containers filled with cacti, proteas and small shrubs, at the base of a wall of trees and shrubs rising dramatically above us, I could only wonder where the exposed field might have existed. Above us, towered massed ranks of flowering cherries, Japanese acers, *Rosa* 'Alister Stella Grey', evergreen oaks and a rare, curry-scented escallonia. Perched on their height, they seem like an impenetrable wall of flower and foliage. However, it is through these that the entrance to the garden proper can be found.

The climb up under a canopy of hoheria, between phlomis and cistus lures in the visitor. There are plants in every direction, overhead, underfoot, in front and behind. A delicious smell of cloves floats on the air, coming from an unusual, spidery *Dianthus superbus*. David pointed to a line of willows in the middle of the knot of plants. These were originally stakes, hammered into the ground to mark an old boundary. Nearby an apple tree grown from a pip, reaches skywards, alongside rather more refined *Acer griseum* and nothofagus. This is a garden with room for all-comers. Making it more remarkable is the fact that everything has been grown from seed and cutting.

I commented on the natural rocky outcrop we were scrambling around as we made our way between plants and boulders. I had not seen it in the photograph. David explained that it was no more than the remains of some lost field wall dusted with a thin layer of soil. This impressive illusion is only one of many. The ground here is wet. Because of this, much of the planting has been achieved by making camouflaged raised beds under the trees. The fact that it was also once a windswept hill can be seen deep in the undergrowth where David left the remains of the old shelter barrier, to remind himself that this was not always a sheltered wood.

One could learn a great deal here about how to make an exceptional garden from an unpromising site with, as David reminded me, bad soil. It now houses collections of special plants like hepatica and trillium, snowdrop and gentian in impressive numbers. Overhead, pruned-up acers and pittosporums deliver the dappled light the ground-dwellers love.

Halfway up the hill, the sound of water can be heard, coming from a stream that, over the course of its way through the garden, is banked into ponds three times. One of several bridges leads to what David calls the 'Donegal garden' where all the plants come from that county. These include an aspen which arrived as a sucker taken from an ancient multi-trunked tree in Carnlough. The ferns, of which there are many, are all native, yet they sit perfectly beside exotics and rarities like *Anemonopsis macrophylla* and *Glaucidium palmatum*.

We emerged, blinking, into the sun and another,

different garden made up of Japanese *Hydrangea serrata* and lilac-flowered strobilanthes. It took me aback to see clump of *Saxifraga stolonifera* growing outside. This is normally a houseplant, known to many as mother-of-thousands. Another greenhouse plant that lives outside all year round here is *Tibouchina urvilleana*.

Out in the sun, the path runs between wild-looking hilly flower borders full of irises, echiums, more proteas and campanulas, planted on free-draining scree, as they would grow in the wild. Farther along, the dry riverbed garden might be something of a horticultural joke, although it was no joke to make, according to David. This bleached, stony garden like everything here, appears as though it naturally occurred.

Staggering out, under sensory overload, I learned that this is David's first garden! When he was fifty years old, this trained artist who knew 'a bit about botany' bought the place and began to work it with Janet, who had always gardened. David found that he had a talent and together they have produced this remarkable experimental garden. Since I last visited, he has fallen for snowdrops and now grows over 200 different species and varieties. 'I catch the bug in December every year and lose it in late spring,' David said. Just so.

Musgrave Park & Therapy Gardens

Musgrave Park, Stockman's Lane, Belfast, Co. Antrim, BT9 7JB. Tel: (0044 28) (048) 9038 1581. Contact: Reception. Open: All year. Seasonal hours. See website for details. Directions: Off Stockman's Road.

Musgrave Park is a large city garden with pleasant walks between trees and shrub borders, some classic, well-maintained, colourful bedding borders, sunken gardens and specimen trees, set between playing fields and running paths. The interesting features here are the therapy and allotment gardens. These are obviously well-used community gardens. Some were created by local schools, others by social groups. There are all sorts of projects from experimental greenhouses made from plastic bottles to sensory gardens, wildflower and wildlife gardens. Raised beds on hard surfaces for disabled groups sit cheek-by-jowl with vegetable beds and sitting areas. You will meet people working their plots and picking vegetables for dinner.

59 Richmond Park

Stranmillis, Belfast, Co. Antrim, BT9 5EF. Tel: (0044 28) (048) 9020 8623. Contact: Adrian Walsh. Open: Only by appointment to groups, between June-Oct. Directions: On application.

Adrian Walsh moved into a 1920s' town house 12 years ago and proceeded to surround it with a garden worthy of the dwelling's character. From the front, the work of a design-minded plantsman is evident. The shrubs that encircle the space and decorate the red-brick house include a *Crinodendron hookeriana*, which came from the famous Slieve Donard nursery in the 1960s, a fine *Betula albosinensis*, with a warm, rust-coloured bark, and a distractingly pretty twisted hazel, *Corylus Avellana* 'Contorta'. Underneath, Adrian grows knots of *Geranium psilostemon, G. palmatum, G. pratense,* hellebores and spring bulbs, small rhododendrons and acers. He pays great attention to pruning-up the shrubs to better accommodate the under-storey plants. The effect is of well presented layered planting. 'I aim for a planned, unplanned look' is how he puts it. I doubt that bare earth is ever allowed to show its face here. In spring, bulbs, hellebores and epimedium kick off proceedings. These are followed by aquilegias and astrantia. Adrian loves astrantias: We saw them many times as we walked about. He is fond of Kennedy primulas too and *Euphorbia polychroma,* through which *Geranium* 'Ann Folkard' entwines itself in a zinging, lime-and-magenta show. The euphorbia insinuates itself into various spots around the garden being a good mixer plant if ever there was one. The considerable shade is dealt with by growing *Podophyllum* 'Spotty Dotty' and *Galium odoratum* or sweet woodruff. Adrian is a plantsman who knows his stuff, and as we walked and talked, I felt I was being introduced to friends. He minds his friends well.

At the back of the house, a lot more sun makes itself felt, particularly in the stone-slabbed breakfast area where the stones appear to be grouted with erigeron, a pretty if rampant plant. This spot provides a cool foil and a place of rest at the edge of the main garden, which is a veritable sea of plants.

When Adrian arrived to live here, he was greeted with 'one lawn and one path', an old-fashioned, no-maintenance garden. He began by building a network of paths which now break up what is in essence one huge mixed border. All roads lead to a central point, a funky pond that must be the best use I have seen for a pig feeder apart from providing pigs with their dinner. Using it with clever box topiary, this little feature begs to be seen. Overhead, towering, parasol-topped aralias flutter over *Salvia* 'Amistad' and dahlias of every colour and size. Everything appears to compete with everything else for attention in a most decorous way. It

is particularly impressive when you know that all these plants were grown from seed. We made our way under towering *Echium pininana* and past orange *Helenium* 'Sahin's Early Flowerer', known as sneezeweed, and more astrantias, grasses, clematis and other climbing glories.

For a city garden, there is a lot of sky visible. The neighbouring houses do not loom over the garden, which feels open. Indeed, Adrian counts himself lucky to have his neighbours' trees as borrowed landscape. Meanwhile he increases the available light by lifting the skirts of fuchsias, revealing peeling bark trunks, and even washing the white trunks of his betulas. If there is a special plant here, it could be the see-through *Cercidiphyllum japonica* wafting around the scent of barley sugar. There are roses, climbing aconites and *Akebia quinata*. But even here, in a paradise garden, Adrian does not have it all his own way. We looked at a line of gorgeous purple asters of unknown nomenclature. He loves them but told me that 'they'd take over if I let them.' As I left I noted that Adrian grows hostas in pots on a table, up and away from the slugs, a tip for the tiny garden gardener.

The Ledsham Garden Co. Antrim

Armagh

Ardress House

*64 Ardress Road, Portadown, Co. Armagh. BT62 1SQ. Tel: (0044 28) (048) 8778 4753.
Contact: the Administrator Open: Grounds all year. Apart from Christmas and New Year. Partially
wheelchair accessible. Supervised children. Dogs on leads. Special features: Tours of house. Events. Directions:
Ardress House is 13 km from Portadown on the Moy Road (B28).*

Ardress House was built as a farmhouse in the 17th century. In the 18th century it was improved and enlarged by its owner, the architect George Ensor, who created a neo-classical-style manor house. The house and grounds are filled with fine furniture and paintings, old farm implements and rare-breed livestock.

The drive to the house cuts through a working apple orchard, made up of the iconic Armagh Bramley. This is the focus of an annual apple festival, where picking and juicing events are all open to the public.

From the orchard, a short drive leads up to the house, which stands on a slightly raised plateau overlooking a sloped lawn. The side wall of the house bows inwards and around in a niched curve that holds various classical busts. On my last visit the wall was being whitewashed and the statues sat rather comically wrapped in plastic rain scarves. Clipped bay trees in pots and large containers of blue agapanthus and pelargoniums stood out against the bright walls basking in the sun trap.

The gardens are understated and elegant, in keeping with the restraint of the pale-pink Georgian house. The planting proper and a bit of exuberance begins as the wall trails away from the house into a mass of creepers. The border beneath is about 75 metres long, filled with herbaceous perennials and flowering shrubs, including lacecap hydrangeas, red-leaved *Cotinus coggygria*, berberis, and laburnum, over phlox and Japanese anemone. Behind these, climbing roses, vines and clematis run rampant up the wall.

When you reach the end of this border the little rose garden comes into view. It sits at the bottom of a small stone stairway edged with more shrubs. The roses are accompanied by dark-green leafed choisya, silver, feather-like artemisia, greyish-purple sage and more wine-coloured cotinus. The soft colours and textures mesh together. A sundial in the centre rises over a collar of blue iris and small-leaved bergenia. The border in front of the stone wall is scented and pretty, all grey-blue nepeta foliage, creeping rosemary or *Rosmarinus officinalis* 'Prostratus' and roses, which look particularly good in front of the stone which is encrusted with lichen. A low yew hedge encloses the garden on the other three sides. The surrounding parkland sweeps off and away to the hills in the distance and by taking the Ladies Mile walk, the best of the woods can be enjoyed.

The Argory

*144 Derrycaw Road, Moy, Dungannon, Co. Armagh BT71 6NA. Tel: (0044 28) (048) 8778 4753.
e-mail: argory@nationaltrust.org.uk Contact: The Administrator. Open: Grounds open all year apart
from Christmas and New Year. Groups welcome. Parking fee. Supervised children welcome. Dogs on leads.
Special features: House tours. Events. Shop. Directions: Travelling toward Dungannon, leave the M1 at
Exit 13 and follow the signs.*

The Argory is a fine Victorian house surrounded by beautiful woodlands, oak plantations, lawns and two formal gardens. Built in 1824 by the Bond family, the house, laundry, stable yards, coach houses and an acetylene gas plant have all been maintained beautifully by the National Trust. It has the appearance of a household preserved in aspic, waiting for the Victorian inhabitants to return. There was even a sign welcoming visitors to become a stable hand for a day.

The Pleasure Garden begins with a sweep of lawn that rolls downhill from the house and stable yards. This is wrapped around by an impressive mixed border, the strength of which derives not from flowers but foliage. Shiny bergenia forms a low collar along the edge of the bed. Above this there are waves of big, dark-veined rodgersia leaves, strappy agapanthus and spiny acanthus. There are touches of subtle purple in the shape of buddleia, occasional clumps of geranium and blue agapanthus balls to set off all this foliage. I love the two huge yew arbours out on the lawn. They look so like two giant Darth Vader helmets, into which you can sit. The lawn finishes off in a ha-ha, or sunken walled boundary that overlooks a path to the woods. On either side two quaint stone summerhouses with Chinese-style windows, frame the picture. One stands under a peculiar looking but handsome cedar. I love the liriodendron on the lawn with its equally strange looking 'elephant foot' trunk. The whole garden overlooks a stretch of the River Blackwater, where a huge heron stalked about looking for fish. The lime tree walk, shading the riverbank is handsome.

The second of the formal areas is a small rose and sundial garden. This is a perfect domestic-scale space, held in by double, stepped box and yew hedges. The roses are all pale pinks and whites, standards and patio varieties. Delicate is the word that describes this, and the scent from the roses and lavender lining the walls is intoxicating.

The woods are being restored as many of the trees at the Argory were felled during the World War II and *Rhododendron ponticum* marched into the clearings. This has had to be grubbed out in order to allow new young trees to develop. On previous visits the new planting looked raw, and while still juvenile, the growth has been impressive. Today the woods make a fine walk.

Derrymore House

Bessbrook, Newry, Co. Armagh Tel: (0044 28) (048) 8778 4753. Contact: The Administrator: Grounds open all the time. Treaty Room in house for occasional days in summer. See website for annual details. Groups welcome, by appointment. Supervised children welcome. Special features: Unusual thatched manor house Directions: Off the main Newry–Camlough Road (A25). Bessbrook is 3 km from Newry.

Derrymore House is the largest thatched manor house in Ireland. Isaac Corry, Newry's representative in the Irish Parliament for 30 years, built the house in 1776. It is an unusual building; a symmetrical single-storey house topped off with a thatched roof. There were several of these buildings in Ireland as early as the mid-18th century. Later in that century the numbers would increase and more elaborate cottages, such as Swiss Cottage in County Tipperary and Lord Bantry's Lodge in Glengarriff, County Cork, were built. However, Derrymore remains an impressive model of this architectural period. It was at Bessbrook that the Act of Union between Britain and Ireland was drafted.

The landscaping around the house was carried out by John Sutherland, one of the most celebrated disciples of Lancelot 'Capability' Brown, the renowned English 18th century landscaper. Today some young planting of rowan, sycamore and silver fir, alongside the older mature parkland trees, surround the house. A small, cottage garden stands to the side of the building. This soft planting lightly anchors the house into the land. Sweeps of daffodils cover the lawns in spring.

The McKelvey Garden

7 Mount Charles, North Bessbrook, Co. Armagh. Contact: Mr and Mrs William and Hilary McKelvey. Tel: (0044 28) (048) 3083 8006. M: (0044 79) 3436 6560. e-mail: hemckelvey@gmail.com See Facebook: The Model Garden. Open: By appointment to groups. May-Aug. Not wheelchair accessible. Supervised children welcome. No dogs. Directions: On application.

Carving a niche out of the rock to build a house in North Bessbrook must have been quite some headache

if Hilary and William McKelvey's front garden is anything to go by. When they arrived to live in their house, that north-facing space was under grass. Hilary thought she might dig a border and in the process found the natural rockery that lines out along the front of the house. Life provided her with rocks and she made a rockery. She planted it up with arum lilies and astilbes, codonopsis and species tulips in the early summer, followed by alpines and flowering shrubs later in the year. Expect colour and flower and variety, from scented gold and rust rhododendron and unusual treats like the miniature Scottish willow, *Salix boydii*. Hilary found herself short on deep wells of soil, so she grew hostas in troughs. They look wonderful. This little front garden is however only the hors d'oeuvre.

A long slim sweet shop of a garden stretches out behind the house, full of notable plants, smartly arranged. There is something desirable to see and inspect in every direction, shoe-horned into tiny spaces and teased into ways that make the whole show a boggling delight. *Clematis chiisanensis* 'Love Child' is a hard plant to pass without reaching out to stroke the little mop-head seed heads. The lime flowers are fairly show-stopping too. Helen is a plant collector and she has amassed over 140 different types of clematis in the garden.

In another corner we looked at the unusual *Rosa* 'Narrow Water Castle' from Warrenpoint, planted over more troughs, this time full of tiny orchids and epimediums, rhodohypoxis and miniature alliums.

Arches link one garden room to another, allowing for clever changes of mood and tone. Deep flower borders and grassed areas take over from a room of planters, crevice gardens and raised beds. In the border, deep ruby *Rosa* 'Nuit de Young' accommodates both pink hardy geranium and raspberry-coloured phlox.

Things fare well in Hilary's care and as a result, this garden is one in which the visitor most certainly should carry a notebook. There are so many things worth studying and she is wonderfully free with her information.

At the back of the garden, the mood changes again, to a gravelled circle where a colony of self-sown red watsonia show how giving a plant the right conditions is all you need. The rocky soil is perfect for alpines. I particularly fell in love with white *Dactylorhiza* 'Eskimo Nell' under the skirts of *Paeonia mlokosewitschii*.

For all the high powered plants, this is a family garden and Hilary still manages a swing and play area for her grandchildren, decorated of course with with *Rosa* 'Félicité et perpétue' and *Clematis integrifolia*. On the ground there are more baby hostas. Helen has a serious addiction to miniature hostas. There are more dactylorhizas under the skirts of the taller shrubs, like the special local *Pieris japonica* 'Daisy Hill'. Helen began with three little orchids 15 years ago. Today she has several hundred.

Cavan

Pergola Nursery

Ballyjamesduff Road, Virginia, Co. Cavan. Tel: (049) 854 7559. e-mail: info@pergolanurseries.ie
Contact: Donal McEvoy. Open: All year. Special features: Nursery. Directions: Leave Virginia on the road
to Ballyjamesduff. Nursery on the left, just before Virginia Park Lodge.

'We're not a lifestyle shop!' Donal McEvoy warned me as I entered into the jungle of plants that make up the greenhouse at the front of his plant nursery. I had almost crashed the car at the sight of the place - A big glass house, almost out the road, stuffed to capacity with plants. It had to be investigated.

There is no fear of being accosted by floral wheelie bin covers and scented candles in here. Instead, prepare to pick your way along narrow alleys between plants growing in explosive proportions. Kiwis and vines drip from the roof and, along with an impressive nectarine, they are the undoubted stars of this choc-full greenhouse/front shop.

Behind the greenhouse is a long garden, just as busy as the glass house, stuffed with perennials, trees and shrubs through which you have to negotiate a route without getting lost.

Donal McEvoy is a man on a mission. He grows his own stock and employs a host of different ecologically friendly armies to keep the garden pest-free, from nematodes and gnat-eating beetles to parasitic wasps. Listen out for for him on the Garden Show on Northern Sound Radio.

Virginia Park Lodge

Virginia, Co. Cavan. Tel: 049 854 6100. e-mail: info@virginiaparklodge.com
www.virginiaparklodge.com Contact: Reception. Open: By appointment to groups. Special Features: Dining.
Venue hire. Events. See website for details. Directions: On the road out of Virginia to Ballyjamesduff.

Until the early years of the the 20th century, at the height of its glory, the garden of a great house would supply that house and estate, as well as a town house, with food enough to render the household almost self-sufficient.

The fascinating thing about the 21st century garden at Virginia Lodge Park is that its aim is to render both this Cavan estate house, as well as Richard Corrigan's London restaurant as close to self-sufficiency as possible, in vegetables and fruit. The project is in its early stages. Plans to raise poultry and pigs, cattle and deer (from the deer park) are some way off, but in the pipeline. In the meantime, the gardens and poly tunnels are busy producing vegetables, herbs and soft fruit for both town house in England and country house in Cavan. Apple orchards have also been planted and even the wild bounty of the 100-acre estate is being harvested for use in both kitchens.

For anyone interested in productive gardening in an aesthetically pleasing way, this is a place to investigate.

From the lavender garden with its oyster shell mulch, created on the site of the old tennis court, to the cut-flower beds, vegetable fields and the old woods and pleasure grounds, this is a fascinating and evolving garden.

I visited in the company of Donaill Murtagh the head gardener and we walked through the various projects, from the laurel lawn being hauled back into shape, to the smartened up lime avenue that leads into the house. We made our way up and down hills. This is drumlin country after all; under the canopy of trees, between ferns and splashes of hesperis, passing fairy forts and specimens of rhododendron and magnolia, lines of fine old yews and lawns that lead out to Lough Ramore.

The house stands on a ledge overlooking all this and surrounded by formal box and rose beds as well as big puffs of nemesia in urns and hydrangeas against the house walls. The courtyard, with its decorously stacked firewood, is sheltered and sunny and the stone walls are covered in more roses, hydrangea and fuchsia. I made a note to come back and eat.

Derry

Buchanan Garden

*28 Killyfaddy Road, Magherafelt, Co. Derry. BT45 6EX. Contact: Mrs Ann Buchanan.
Tel: (0044 28) (048) 79632180. Open: March-Sept. Wed-Sat. Not wheelchair accessible. Groups welcome.
Supervised children. Special features: Refreshments can be booked. Directions: Leaving Magherafelt on the
Moneymore Road, turn left opposite the petrol station and travel 1.6 km. The garden is 200 metres from
the new bypass, signposted.*

'The mowing space is getting smaller.' Ann Buchanan felt it necessary to tell me on my most recent visit to her busy garden outside Magherafelt. On a previous trip, it had appeared that they would continue to expand into the surrounding fields. The prediction turned out to be accurate. This garden just keeps growing.

The Buchanan's moved here in 1971 and immediately got to work. By the mid-1980s, expansion to a plot across the road was necessary. 'We never intended to grow on that spot,' Ann explains with the puzzlement of the truly addicted. That stated, the rate at which they work the garden meant that incursions were inevitable. The garden across the road is mostly made up of herbaceous plants. Its overall style is dictated by the plants. Yet the garden is no untidy jumble. It is a bustling series of borders full of well-tended, well-matched flowering plants. In a place with so much herbaceous planting, the dreaded task of staking could be a big job and a bigger headache. Not so at Killyfaddy Road. Ann says that she has done away with the need to stake by planting everything cheek-by-jowl: 'Everything holds everything else up.' For lesser mortals, it could be a case of everything knocking everything else over. But here, monarda, larkspur, agapanthus and foxgloves, still flowering like mad at the end of August, looked wonderful, planted *en masse* in one stuffed bed, where they did indeed, all hold one another up and looked good doing it.

There are paths everywhere, but most cannot be used in the summer because the plants just spread out, take over and hide them. Where there are grass paths, they invariably sprout wild orchids that need to be side-stepped and mown around.

If something looks good, the Buchanans leave it as it is. 'A variegated tropaeolum appeared a few years ago and it self-seeds around like anything' said Ann. She continued: 'It's a bit of a weed, but we like it.' Close by there was a shoving match taking place between a *Hoheria sexstylosa* and a *Pittosporum tenuifolium*, in a fight for space. They were grown from seed and the principle of survival of the fittest will decide the outcome of this Posh Plant Fight Club bout.

The plant cram is impressive, even in the woody area where the apple trees emerge from seas of hellebores, hostas, cautleyas and primulas. These are further decorated by sizeable puffs of mistletoe growing on their trunks. The pond, or 'puddle' as Ann calls it, is almost hidden among all this. Its clear water teems with water snails and sticklebacks, and the edges are deep with irises and *Potentilla palustris*.

Simple things are often the most memorable: In the main garden, on the other side of the road, the spread of *Pratia pedunculata* in the grass, is like a sea of pale blue stars. This side of the garden has more shade, but it also has its own 'sunset strip', a border with a view of the west-facing fields beyond. Take the path that leads up along it, to the Sunset Seat at the top. It is likely to be blocked at several points however, by spreading herbaceous plants, making the walk a bit more challenging. Some of these spreading culprits happen to be pyramidal orchids, marsh orchids and *Fritillaria meleagris*. The Shetland ponies in the field looking in on this may admire, but the flowers are teasingly just out of their reach through the fence. Meanwhile, I was teased by the barley sugar tree or *Cercidiphyllum japonicum*, which wafted its characteristic smell of barley sugar about.

Harking back to the expansion, the neighbour's field next door was annexed a few years ago when Ann jumped the ditch and planted up the boundary of his paddock with a variety of woodland plants. Now they both have something good to look at and the expansion continues...

Downhill Castle & Mussenden Temple

Mussenden Road, Castlerock, Co. Derry. Tel: (0044 28) (048) 70848728.
www.nationaltrust.org.uk/downhill-demesne-and-hezlett-house Open: Times vary. See website for seasonal
details. Not wheelchair accessible. Supervised children (Cliffs). Dogs on leads. Special features: Events. Shop.
Directions: 8 km west of Coleraine, on the coast road (A2).

If you decide to visit the gardens at Downhill Castle, arrive from the west on the A2 rather than from the east. From this approach the scenery is awe-inspiring. I would also recommend lingering until dusk to see the sun sink over Mussenden Temple, which lies at the very edge of the North Sea on one of the most beautiful deserted beaches on the island. There are also some spectacular coastal and woodland walks and trails through the grounds, with more being developed all the time.

Frederick Hervey, the Earl of Bristol and Bishop of Derry, created the demesne at Downhill between 1777 and 1788. He was an enthusiastic builder and in its heyday Downhill was an imposing limestone house, surrounded by an elaborate collection of replicas of classical buildings, a walled garden, the famous temple, ha-has and several gardens. Today the house is in ruins. The walled garden had vanished, apart from the ice house and dovecote. The walled garden is happily under restoration as I write and an orchard with a range of native Irish apples has been planted up, including the disgustingly named 'Greasy Pippin.'

Out on the boundary, only one of the stone cats on the Lion's Gate survives. (The name is misleading, as these were in fact leopards from the Bishop's coat of arms.)

The rotund Mussenden Temple, perched out on the cliff, is both precarious and magnificent. I took a walk around it with ranger, Paddy Gorman and two National Trust volunteers, who were preparing the place for a wedding ceremony the next day. Mark, one of the volunteers, translated the Latin inscription around the dome for me. The temple, built on a line with the central axis of the house, is just one example of the Bishop's mania for the circular form. He named it indiscreetly after his cousin, Mrs. Mussenden. The views out to sea from its windows are breathtaking, but so too is the wind that sweeps around it. Stories are told of how the servants had to crawl from the house up to the temple on hands and knees in the howling winds to save themselves being blown over the cliff. The Bishop is reputed to have had a particularly rotten sense of humour, so this was possibly part of his enjoyment of the building.

These days walking, and hopefully not crawling, up to the temple in the summer brings you through a spectacular hay meadow full of wild orchids. Until a few years ago, the sward was grazed by sheep, yet, as soon as they were sent packing, the orchids shot up and flowered again, after decades of grazing.

Today the horticultural glory of Downhill is the developing garden by the Bishop's Gate entrance to the estate. This was created by Lady Bruce in 1910. It fell into ruin and was restored by Jan Eccles, a warden who came to look after the place in the 1960s and stayed until the 1990s. Jan Eccles' garden is hilly, floral and informal, a singular place that looks natural and melts into the surrounding mature sycamore and beech wood. A great deal of restoration and development continues today with welcome help and advice coming from the experts at Mount Stewart. The bog area in the middle of the mixed garden is a treat, stuffed to capacity with flowering primulas, cowslips, flag irises and wild orchids. It is all splashes of pink, gold, yellow and purple.

Several paths take off from here in the direction of the ruined house. One runs beneath the hill and under spreading native and imported cherry. The path begins to rise uphill and the trees get taller. These include mature acers and liriodendrons. The gardening team have cleared the woods, made the paths easier to negotiate and placed benches everywhere. They have also deployed ruined statuary and bits of architectural salvage from the old house, showing that the chipped top of an old Doric column set into a lawn can be as beautiful as a perfect monument. A new secret garden has been developed beside the little gate lodge with a range of ferns and tree ferns. The planting around it is colourful and pretty and I look forward to seeing it mature.

John Gault's Garden

84 Broad Road, Limavady, BT49 0QH. Co. Derry. Contact: Mr. John Gault. Tel: M (00 44 77) 1493 3394. Texts preferred. e- mail: jlandmaureen@aol.ie Open: April-June 20th and otherwise by appointment. Directions: Leave Limavady on the Coleraine Road. The garden is about 1 km along on the left, signed.

John Gault began gardening when he was three years old. He started growing and breeding rhododendrons when he was 16 and his nursery and breeding gardens are over 60 years old. This is quite an operation but John explained that it is just his hobby. Like his father before him, he is first and foremost a farmer.

The land is hard around Limavady. As he told me, if you dug a clod out of the ground and put it in the oven, you could use it to build a house. As a result he plants his rhododendrons on enriched, raised mounds of good compost. Rhododendrons are shallow rooting plants so working like this delivers good results.

We made our way between lines of young plants, so many of which looked promising, but they were not promising enough for John. The vast majority had already been condemned by him to the compost heap as not quite perfect enough, while only a few choice successes will be grown on and studied further.

The rhododendrons might be the main business in this garden but they are not the only show in town. Apart from a fine oak, planted in 1726 on the lawn in front of the house, there are a series of long, handsome and mature shrub and tree borders featuring a grand mix of conifers, magnolias, acers and of course rhododendrons. These substantial beds rise and fall with sometime rounded and sometimes sky reaching canopies, in contrasting colours and textures. A fascinating garden worked by a charming and informative gent.

Hampstead Hall

40 Culmore Road, Derry, Co. Derry. BT48 7RS Contact: Liam Greene. Tel: (0044 28) (048) 7135 4807. e-mail noramariegreene@gmail.com www.ulstergardensscheme.org.uk Open: May-Sept. by appointment to groups and for occasional open days. Contact for annual dates. Not wheelchair accessible. No children (Water). No dogs. Special features: Refreshment by appointment. Directions. Travelling out of the city in the direction of Culmore and Greencastle, turn left at the sign for Baron's Court. The garden is on the right marked by a stone wall and new gateposts.

Over the past 30 years Liam Greene has been creating a garden of full of horticultural surprises around his home on the outskirts of Derry city, which it also overlooks. On arrival, it appears to be a decent garden, made up of raised mixed borders, on top of dry-stone walls, small formal lawns with sentries of clipped yew and Portuguese laurel in straight lines, leading to the front door of the old house. There are some strong shrub and tree combinations with mixes of arbutus, embothrium and trachycarpus together. It is all ordered and smart and it complements the Georgian house.

Yet there is more: Swing around the side of the house to discover Liam's Japanese garden. Much of the space here is taken up with a pond, side-planted with miniature trees and creeping greenery. A wisteria-wrapped bridge and stepping stones, span the pond and the view across is of a wooden summerhouse and a big parasol canopy of cut-leaf acer. The plants that really get the tone right are two podocarpus - *Podocarpus salignus* which has shiny, waxy foliage that begs to be stroked, and *Podocarpus nivalis*, a rarely seen and handsome shrub with a splayed habit. Liam teamed it with a weathered stone lantern and some close cropped junipers beside the water. On the ground, under these perfect shrubs there is a carpet of moss and spreads of *Soleirolia soleirolii*. It is a compact, perfect little garden room.

This is not the whole show either. Around the corner is yet another completely different garden.

This is a courtyard behind the house, where soft brown sandstone outhouses and the unusual bow-backed house, between them, enclose a sunny sheltered area. There are big camellias, a tall *Magnolia grandiflora* 'Exmouth', *M. campbellii* and *Clematis armandii* against the sunniest of the walls, all knotted through with jasmine and roses. A rather grand looking one-eyed white dove pottered between terracotta pots planted up with clipped bay and frothy pelargoniums. Lucky bird, this is where he lives.

There is yet more: Through a gateway in the wall lies another garden room. This one is reminiscent of the sort of enclosed garden spotted through an open gate down a side street in the old quarter of a southern European city. It is a formal space, made up of a square of box. At each corner there is a five-metre tall Italian cypress, *Cupressus sempervirens*. Set into the

back wall, a spouting lion's head provides the sound and glint of water and on the side walls there are well maintained box balls, white magnolias and a fruiting fig. Everything is preened and perfect.

This in turn leads down a set of steps to yet another formal topiary garden, with more clipped box around a square pond, *Fatsia japonica*, *Agave americana*, and *Cupressus* 'Castlewellan Gold'. This little room looks good from above but its main job is to be admired from the basement windows of the house and it works best from that angle, importing the garden successfully into the building.

For no one reason I can put my finger on, for all its formality this feels like a garden with which Liam has real fun. It has a warm and relaxed atmosphere and an enormous amount of style - two things not often found together.

Springhill

20 Springhill Road, Moneymore, Magherafelt, Co. Derry, BT457NQ. Tel: (0044 28) (048) 8674 8210. e-mail:springhill@nationaltrust.org.uk www.nationaltrust.org.uk/springhill Contact: The Administrator. Open: Grounds, every day except Christmas and New Year's Day. House, seasonal changes. See website for details. Partially wheelchair accessible. Groups welcome. Supervised children. Dogs on leads. Special features: Costume museum. Café and shop. House tours. Plant sales. Events. Directions: 1.6 km from Moneymore village, on the B18.

'Good' Will Conyngham, a soldier who made a name for himself as one of the defenders of the walls during the Siege of Derry, built the house at Springhill when he married Anne Upton in 1680. The marriage settlement required that he build 'a convenient house of lime and stone, two storeys high with the necessary office houses'. He fulfilled the brief and subsequent generations of Conynghams and Lenox-Conynghams lived in and enlarged the original house. In 1957 the house and all its contents were left to the National Trust

The house Will Conyngham built is a somewhat unusual for an Irish house, a handsome whitewashed building, with deep slate roofs, curved gable ends and clean, simple lines. At the front is a forecourt and planted on one side of this is a really handsome myrtle or *Luma apiculata*, the cinnamon coloured bark of which stands out against the white wall. Four big, fat bay cones, joined by low box walls, march out from the house, past the sort of well-raked gravel that would

do a Japanese garden proud. The effect is formal and minimalist. The lawns, studded with daffodils, lead out to the original gateway from here. This restraint is loosened around the outbuildings, where climbing roses and spreading rosemary or *Rosmarinus officinalis* 'Prostratus', soften the walls and anchor the house.

To the side of the building and just off the courtyard car park, there is a long, sloped, narrow, walled garden with a path on one side. Recent changes have seen this planted up with a number of different clematis. Along the path, there is long bed of lime-coloured carex and daylilies in front of wall-trained *Hydrangea petiolaris* and yellow roses.

The path leads down to the inexplicably named Dutch Garden. This is a romantic little spot, planted with roses in four colour themed beds, with pink, plum, white and yellow. The beds are further boosted using perennials like hosta and thalictrum, *Crambe maritima, Hesperis matronalis* and hardy geraniums. The romantic garden is perfectly accented with a decorated shell house at the top of the slope, providing a sitting place for fatigued visitors.

Further down the hill there is a little herb garden with slab paths and herb beds on raised stone ledges and white currants trained on the stone walls.

Over the walls, towering beech and oak invite the walker out of the garden to the park, but not quite yet. First of all the route leads into another, much bigger walled garden with a slate sundial, on an ancient-looking stone plinth, surrounded by hostas and more daylilies. The whole area is a feast of flowers, full of white phlox, purple clematis, pink Japanese anemone and yellow potentilla.

An entrance from the front of the house passes the garden and leads out through a small, gothic arched doorway, to a set of steps covered in roses with rosemary and agapanthus at their feet. From here a gunnera-lined pond on the edge of the woods can be seen. There are also mature and not so mature specimens of magnolia, Spanish chestnut and cut-leaf beech. Take another route, along the young, but maturing beech avenue that strays off towards a folly on a hill above the house. Following this path reveals several other paths into and through the woods which are deep and dark and peaceful.

Hampstead Hall, Co. Derry

Donegal

Backleas

Stranorlar, Co. Donegal. Tel: 074 913 1107, 087 2516 806. e-mail: gallinagh@eircom.net www.donegalgardentrail.com Contact: Tony Gallinagh. Open: As part of the Donegal Garden Trail. See annual dates. Otherwise April-Sept. by appointment. Special features: Tree nursery next door. Directions: In Stranorlar, take N13 to Letterkenny. After 500m turn left at the Presbyterian church. Travel 1.5 km. Garden on an open elevated site on right.

As I walked around Backleas garden in the company of its owner, Tony Gallinagh, I was reminded of the local women who once walked through this fascinating piece of living agricultural history. As I passed by the cold, spring fed stream where they churned butter, I thought of the tough lives these women led. We ventured further along a relief water system, built in famine times by labourers working for a penny a day, which transported water to Ballybofey and stopped to look at an old fort and a collection of mill wheels scattered through the garden.

Tony's family have worked the land here for generations, and in 2000, when he decided to create a garden and a new home, he chose a hill on the farm, with a fringe of wood to one side, and an enviable view of the Barnsmore Gap on the other with its magnificent patchwork fieldscape that spills down to the horizon.

So far so good but the soil was not fertile and initial attempts to grow roses failed. Undeterred, Tony noted that the pH was acidic so he began to grow rhododendrons, camellias and heathers.

The wood bounding the site is an important feature which, while handsome, had a strictly practical start. Tony explained: 'It was a bit of useless land and we were tortured with cattle breaking in'. The trees put an end to that carry-on and today the wood is a glory of oak, ash and beech that in spring, fills with bluebells. He laid out a series of paths through the trees and walking along one, we came to a little 'cave' made by the hole a mature beech left when it fell. It continued to grow on its side. Tony does not strim the paths. Instead, he walks them every day. This provides his exercise and prevents the grass from growing too long. There are no lawns here. Tony has no time for lawns. Expect to find shrubberies, terraced borders and raised heather beds, broken up by contorted pieces of bog oak and bog pine. Today troubles come in the shape of self-seeding ash and hazel which regularly make their appearance between Tony's precious photinias, mahonias, rhododendrons and weigelas. He lifts and donates them to friends in need.

Beltany View

Braehead, Raphoe, Co. Donegal. Tel: 074 9144 974. e-mail: marbeltony@hotmail.com. www.donegalgardentrail.com Contact: Marjan and Ton Bangert. Open: By appointment only. Directions: On application.

Marjan and Ton bought a field on a hill outside Raphoe 15 years ago. They had gardened before, on flat, sandy, free-draining, rock-free Dutch soil, not an ideal preparation for the stony wet ground outside Raphoe. 'We started by planting a hedge out on the west side of the field because that's where the wind comes from,' Marjan said. The existing hedge, with its ditch and stream, on the east side 'merely needed to be cleaned of brambles.' Ton got to work on that, clearing a metre a day. It is a long hedge and the bramble thicket was dense, to put it mildly. I was in awe of the amount of energy he must have expended on this work.

Extracting stones and boulders from the ground became the next, metre-a-day operation. When they got a digger in to create a pond, the learning process continued as the hollow filled with water and did not drain. They discovered that it would not need liner. Today it is surrounded with dug-out boulders, native ferns, white *Libertia formosa*, native orchids and irises, and looks as though it were always there, although scores of golden orph, whipping around like poorly camouflaged torpedoes, add a touch of the tropical.

Once the hard slog was finished out on the boundaries, Ton created a border on the east side. He simply added to the native mixed hedge, filling the foreground with combinations of fuchsia, *Alchemilla mollis* or lady's mantle, silver *Santolina chamaecyparissus* and *Iris* 'Black Prince'.

He used the same light touch working the boundary at the top of the hill. This is a deep gorse hedge grown over a fieldstone wall. It looks well and keeps out the cattle. Still, it needs constant paring back because gorse likes to march. Where they are lucky to have shelter on the east they planted rhododendrons and Japanese acers over more purple irises and thalictrum and they are all thriving.

Below the house on the sunny rockeries they planted clumps of nepeta and dierama, *Schizostylis coccinea*, tiny blue-flowered *Sisyrinchium angustifolium* and miniature irises in a vibrant, colourful splash. This is a garden that proves what can be achieved on a windy, wet, rocky field, with endless energy and a good dollop of talent.

Bruckless House

Bruckless, Co. Donegal. Contact: Joan Evans. Tel: 074 9737 071. e-mail: info@bruckless.com www.donegalgardentrail.com Open: By appointment between May and July, as part of the Donegal Garden Trail. See website for annual details. Directions: Travel 18 km west from Donegal town on the N56 to Bruckless. The house is indicated beside signpost for Bruckless village.

If I think of a perfect country house garden Joan Evan's handiwork comes to mind, from the first glimpse of the plant-frilled Georgian house as the car rounds the drive, to the atmospheric little wood at the bottom of the garden, at the edge of the sea. This is a finely balanced combination of smart and informal.

Like the best country gardens, it feels as though it was always here and as though it simply came about. There is no bolshy design manifesto beating its chest, telling you how great it is, just an organic flow of good flowering shrubs and trees, subtly deployed perennials and imposing woods.

We walked between mixed borders full of purple cotinus and foxgloves, purple hardy geraniums and white lupins, and along the the edge of hydrangea-fringed woods, on raked gravel paths and beside well maintained lawns. The views across the grass take in rose pergolas and stone-slabbed seating areas strewn with flowers. I was caught between enjoying the relaxed atmosphere and being impressed at the amount of work that went into making it look that relaxed. Between puffs of geraniums and phlox, tightly, minutely clipped pieces of topiary stand out as a nudging reminder that this is a place of work. The tools are never far around the corner.

She loves her roses and there are explosions of them everywhere, clambering over trees and arches and up the house walls where the voluptuous *Rosa* 'Madame Isaac Pereire' makes its way through white *Clematis* 'Marie Boisselot' like a mass of French fancies. Pale lemon *Rosa banksiae* 'Lutea' is here too, doing well in the shelter. *Koelreuteria paniculata,* known as the golden rain tree is something Joan is particularly fond of and it too does nicely even in this windy spot. In the shelter of the wood, she grows *Rhododendron macabeanum* and *R. loderi* 'King George'.

The game here is one of patience, playing with and adding to what was in the garden when Joan began

working it in the 1990s. She pointed to the 20-year-old *Magnolia campbellii* by one of the stone outhouses. 'And it only took 19 years to flower', she laughed.

We made our way along, shooing chickens out of the path, walking through the woods, which Joan has gradually cleared of brush and bramble, underplanting the old sycamores and oaks with hellebores and hesperis. As she worked on these clearances, she unearthed the original stone-lined paths that had been lost under decades of leaf mould.

I left Bruckless with a vision of the many-shaded blue hydrangeas in the woods - all grown from cuttings.

Cannon's Garden

Doonan, Donegal, Co. Donegal. Tel: 086 1082 029. e- mail: maureencannon@eircom.net www.donegalgardentrail.com. Contact: Maureen Cannon. Open: In July by appointment. Directions: From the Mill Park Hotel roundabout on the outskirts of Donegal take exit signed 'Letterbarrow'. The house is ninth on the right after the hotel entrance.

Driving down the laneway to Maureen Cannon's garden it is obvious to which house the open garden belongs. A dormer bungalow engulfed in flowers would best describe it. Maureen likes flowers. There is little doubt of that. I passed at least six different shades of purple and lilac tradescantia in the first border alone. There is a lot to be seen and the low picket fence that fronts the show, generously allows passers-by to enjoy it as they come along the lane. The fence also supports various plants, including climbers winding their way between the uprights along its length.

My most recent visit took place on a summer's day that resembled a monsoon. The rain came down in buckets, yet did nothing to stop it looking first rate. Between several developing liquidambars and *Tamarix ramosissima,* which Maureen loves, there are good Japanese acers too. The best of these, a multi-trunked specimen, came about when it appeared to die in the bad winter of 2010, but came back to life as this new improved specimen. Nearby, I got seed, breed and generation of a big shrub of *Viburnum mariesii* grown from a slip, that itself was grown from a slip of a plant that Maureen shared and lost in the same bad winter. Clearly it pays to propagate and share.

The clamber of plants is extraordinary and it took a while to spot *Rosa* 'Teasing Georgia' knotted through a mass of other climbers on the summerhouse that Charlie, Maureen's husband, built. Meanwhile, the main house is hidden behind heavy sheets of parthenocissus, clematis and more roses. Its windows appear to peep out through curtains of *Rosa* 'Aloha', *Clematis* 'Multi Blue' and *C.* 'Rouge Cardinal.' Maureen loves 'Aloha' best because of its habit of changing colour. For me, red *Rosa* 'Bantry Bay' twined through a white and green *Euonymus* 'Silver Queen' is the inspired combination. On the ground underneath, the primulas come thick in early summer. Maureen's talent is for combining colours and textures.

The garden is not large. It covers about half an acre but it is so jam-packed and stuffed with plants of all description, that the extent of the plot is rarely apparent. What is important is that with space at a premium, only interesting plants can be countenanced and the barrier over which they must vault is high. Plants need to boast a combination of attractive berries, foliage and flowers. Several seasons of interest are even more desirable.

There are roses grown over obelisks as well as every other solid item, from sheds and fences, dead trees and badly performing shrubs. Even the covered work space at the back of the house, also built by Charlie, hosts a big grape vine. Under this shelter, the huge, sawn-down trunk of an ash that needed to be felled, works as an eccentric potting bench. I look forward to seeing the place on a sunny day but I doubt that it could look any better.

Carrablagh House

Portsalon, Co. Donegal. Contact: Jan Bradley Tel: 074 9159 113. e-mail: jonmul@eircom.net or Brendan Little (Gardener) 085 1092 956. blittle@eircom.net www.donegalgardentrail.com Open: As part of the Donegal Garden Trail. See website for annual dates. Directions: In Portsalon pass caravan park and golf club and Pier Road on right. Continue uphill following long stone wall to the 2nd drive on right, signposted.

When a garden takes up a perch on the scenic Fanad Peninsula, with a view out to Lough Swilly and Inishowen, it would want at least, to justify itself in the good looks department. Carrablagh more than earns its unique situation. It is a place of extraordinary natural beauty, further improved by the clever planting carried out by Mr and Mrs Henry Hart who lived and gardened here in the 1850s. A debt is due also to its current owners Jan Bradley and John Mulcahy who continue to care for this important historic garden and its plant collection.

The bulk of the 35 acres is given over to woods shot through by a network of tunnelled walks under mature trees and shrubs. They climb up and down the hills and occasionally open onto views of the sea. There is a healthy smattering of rare plants, including rhododendrons placed strategically along these routes. There is also a walled garden and a sunny, sheltered kitchen garden. The range of different gardens within the grounds is itself an entertainment.

My most recent visit was in the company of Brendan Little, who has worked Carrablagh for many years with such obvious affection for the place.

We began admiring the huge *Halesia carolina* by the drive, the first of many special trees here that date back to the Harts' time. The site should be blasted by gales but the walled garden enjoys a favourable wind-free corner and the impressive *Davidia involucrata* inside the gate is proof of that shelter. A ground-sweeping *Magnolia soulangeana* at the top of the slope, is however, the glory. Sitting on the bench underneath its spreading canopy it is impossible not to give thanks for the generosity that allows visitors inside these graced walls.

Walking under what feels like a cave of *Parrotia persica,* where you can get right in to see its knobbled trunk, is another pleasure. Leaving it, walk on, under a *Drimys winteri* with great leathery leaves and waxy white flowers. The routes through the walled garden trail along step-stone paths and little slab bridges over frog ponds, past views of sunny, lily-strewn borders,

underneath tall scratchy looking *Trachycarpus fortunei.*

We eventually left the walled garden and took one of the stony paths into the gorgeous gloom under a canopy of *Rhododendron sinogrande, R. grandis* and *Metrosideros lucida,* over sheets of moss, spiked with hart's tongue ferns or *Asplenium scolopendrium.* The paths branch and branch again and one could get lost among *Rhododendron lindleyi,* a plant that, according to Brendan 'won't win any beauty contests but has a great scent.' *R. augustinii, R. racemosum* and *R. ciliatum,* are just as special and a lot prettier. *Rhododendron barbatum* is rightly one of his favourites. It has a dirty pink bark and deep red flowers.

We made our way under a massive self-seeded *Clethra arborea,* also known as the lily-of-the-valley tree, and looked up at its dangling flowers before looking down to where the mossy floor was like the best Navan carpet.

Light spilled through the canopy and we emerged, blinking out to the sun trap that is the kitchen garden. This is a charming spot, relaxed and informal but well tended, with lines of flowers and vegetables, fruit cages, a grand orchard and a busy greenhouse. I could visit this garden every day of the year and never tire.

Celtic Prayer Garden IOSAS

Derryvane, Muff, Co Donegal. Tel: 074 938 4866. Open. Seasonal times. See website. Open: Contact for seasonal times. Special features: Accommodation. Retreat. Organic box vegetable scheme. Events. Directions: From Letterkenny drive to Bridgend and take the first exit off the roundabout signposted 'White Oaks Rehab Centre /IOSAS Centre.' Take next right. Turn right at next T-junction and follow signs.

'We need a place such as this so that Christianity can recover its nerve.' – John Moriarty. So reads a plaque at the entrance to the prayer garden. This wild place, only barely tended in some parts, is a strange sort of garden set in a remote corner of Donegal. Paths and raised walkways have been laid out and built between various planted up areas that between them, make up the shape of Ireland. There are ponds and small buildings, stone towers, and standing stones, beehive huts and thatched prayer rooms. I half expected to come across a hermit in a stand of bog cotton, heather and sedge. Native birches that do so well in this surrounding, make up the bulk of the trees. It is a serene, peaceful place but it could well do with a few of the faithful coming in to help on the upkeep.

Cille

Kill, Co. Donegal. Tel: 074 9738 107. 087 6712 341.
e-mail: martincille@eircom.net www.donegalgardentrail.com Contact: Carmel and Martin McLaughlin. Open: For selected open days as part of the Donegal Garden Trail and other times by appointment. See website for annual details. Directions: Leave Killybegs on the R263 toward Slieve League. Drive for 6.4 km. The garden is on the right before the Blue Haven Hotel, marked by an old stone wall.

Think of a hairpin bend, then think of tightening it, making it even hairpinnier and bendier. You may now think of Martin McLaughlin's Cille, outside Killybegs. Coming to see this garden for a second time, I wondered if it would be as impressive as the first time I saw it. It was better. It is an unusual creation in several ways. For a start, it is sited on the side of the road while remaining completely obscured from the road. Carmel is chief weed-puller and under-gardener, and she told me that even some of their neighbours are unaware that there is a garden on this almost unworkable, steep site.

The house, stands at the very top of the garden, looking out over the Atlantic and with only a hint of a view of the first of the ledged gardens beneath. Taking a series of paths, zigzagging down, back and forth on the previously mentioned hairpin bends, a trail leads the visitor down the difficult slope by way of several rooms linked with steps and stairs. Each room has its own style, different in character to those above and below. Some are open and sunny, with strips of lawn and mixed flower beds. Some are shaded and green, dark, lush and almost forest-like. One is wet and drippy, filled with ferns and glistening stony overhangs. The garden paraphernalia and sculpture arranged at strategic points catches the eye as the route moves from one level to another.

Martin has been working on the site for 34 years, playing with what has become a most individual, good-looking, plant-stuffed, hanging garden. His modesty struck me when I met him first. He had taken no gardening classes, and with no particular interest in garden books or manuals, he told me that he 'just buys plants and tries to grow them.' The famed Kerry footballer Mick O'Connell came to mind as my gushing praise was fobbed of and made little of. Carmel told me that Martin spends all his spare time tending his creation. Mostly it works with ridiculous-looking ease. I left quite jealous. Later in the day I bumped into Martin, in Cluain na d'Tor nursery and garden, stocking up on supplies. The plants were going to a good home – although I am not sure when he planned fitting them in. I am sure I saw not a square centimetre of bare soil anywhere.

Cluain Na D'Tor

Ballyconnell, Falcarragh, Co. Donegal. Tel: 087 6267599. e-mail: cluainnadtor@eircom.net www.seasideplants.net www.donegalgardentrail.com Contact: Seamus O'Donnell. Open: As part of the Donegal Garden Trail. See website for annual details. Special features: Plant nursery. Design service. Events. Directions: From Falcarragh crossroads turn down by the Bank of Ireland. Take the first left. The nursery and garden are on left 400m from the crossroads.

Falcarragh, on the north Donegal coast, is not where one expects to come across an exotic garden and that was not what Seamus O'Donnell found when he took over the field and house that his grandfather built in 1920 when he arrived home having made his fortune in Alaska.

Seamus is an experimental gardener. He began planting a shelter belt, 50 metres wide, using whips of sitka spruce, alder, ash, oak, wych elm and hazel. This permitted him to make a garden that two decades later would attract a documentary crew making a film about the Gulf Stream. They wanted to see the Gulf Stream garden he has grown around his nursery. What they found here was a substantial garden, subdivided into several individual areas.

The dry, seaside garden is the first of these, all gravel, pebbles, boulders, flotsam and jetsam, scattered between swishing molina and miscanthus grasses. Big agapanthus bobbles, silver-leafed potentilla and delicate-looking *Diplarrena morea* flowers flash like sparks in the grass and pieces of found-item sculpture peep out from under trees like *Elaeagnus* 'Quick Silver'.

The garden leading to the house is Seamus's rather individual take on a cottage garden, with pink campion and *Alchemilla mollis* under skyrocketing echiums and cordylines. His talent for placing sea-bleached branches and tree roots, pieces of blue and green glass and found objects here is worth studying. His style is as informal as style comes: 'I am all the time collecting plants. I have no overall plan,' is how he puts it. There are however some strong themes. The exotic garden really is ridiculously exotic, filled with cannas and restios and *Ferula communis*, the well named giant fennel, alongside tree ferns, red flowered *Metrosideros lucida*, trachycarpus and cautleya. All this shelters between the trees, like a splash of the tropics, combined with scores of natives, divided between willy nilly paths. The exuberance is giddying.

There are wet and dry meadows, a developing wood, a maze, raised vegetable beds and a notable number of unusual and special plants. Out in the wet garden, bring your wellies for the squelching grass path that circles the pond, picking between clumps of vivid blue irises, *Echium fastuosum* and wildflowers, from orchids and ragged Robin to eye-bright and all sorts of clovers.

When I was leaving the garden I met Martin McLaughlin, the gardener who owns the impressive Cille, outside Killybegs. Mr McLaughlin, who knows a thing or two about plants was stocking up at the nursery here. Praise indeed.

Lower Cranny

Inver, Co. Donegal. Tel: 087 9895 099. e-mail: j2donleavy@eircom.net
www.donegalgardentrail.com Contact: Joan Donleavy. Open: As part of the Donegal Garden Trail. See
website for annual details. Telephone before visiting. Special features: Directions: Take N56 from Donegal
town towards Killybegs. After 8 km turn left to Cranny Lower L1665, before crossing Inver bridge over
Eany Water River. Straight on for 500m. Turn right at crossroads for Trá and see the stone walls marking
the 4th house on left.

Joan told me, she simply cut grass here until 1999. In such a natural setting, surrounded by woods, water and wildlife, that makes sense. At a certain point however, she decided to take the garden on in a more concerted way, but the design she came up with needed to be worked out with ease of mowing in mind. It was also designed with the gardens' enviable wild location firmly to the fore. The result is a spree of woods, meadows, streams, lakes, waterfalls, and flowers. Joan gardens it organically with her husband Paddy. He builds benches and bridges to span the waterways. She plants herbaceous perennials within the borders around the house, and together they clear the woods of brambles and scrub, encouraging bluebells, snowdrops and other natives.

They dug out a lake on the site of an ancient, dried up lake and to their surprise, the lilies that spread out over this new expanse of water, arrived spontaneously - along with an otter and some water hens. Water is important here. They took the river that runs through the woods and turned it into the focus of one of the walks, restorating old sluice gates to release water into the river from the new lake. We walked along the edge of the water, on log-lined paths between sheets of bluebells, under birch, alder, ash and rowan. The views out of the woods give onto open sloped and sunny meadows.

The meadow was too fertile when Joan decided to play with it, so she added yellow rattle or *Rhinanthus minor,* to weaken the grass and since then meadowsweet, ragged Robin, twayblade and dactylorhiza orchids have all appeared on the slopes overlooking the pond and house. A mown path gives it a slightly tamed look, but only slightly. It is cut once a year in August.

Even when she decided to create a formal hedged circle as a special feature in the garden, Joan carried it through in a style that kept with the easy and native feel of the greater plan, using a soft mix of beech, guelder rose, blackthorn and fuchsia.

While keeping the larger area of garden wild and mostly native, Joan understandably loves to use more cultivated plants too. So hardy geraniums, thalictrum, lupins and peonies, can be found in the borders around the house. But even here, they share the space with populations of native foxglove.

This is a garden of understated style, worked by a woman who has well earned her place in this heavenly corner of Donegal.

Dunmore House

Dunmore, Carrigans, Co. Donegal. Contact: Amelia McFarland. Tel: 083 8028625.
e-mail: info@dunmoregardens.ie www.donegalgardentrail.com. www.dunmoregardens.ie Open: As part
of the Donegal Garden Trail. See website for annual dates, otherwise by appointment. Directions. Travel
through Carrigans village on road to Derry. Dunmore is on the left just outside the village marked by large
stones outside gate.

On my most recent visit to Dunmore, Andy, who has gardened here since he was a child in the late 1940s, was eyeing up a reverting branch on a cut-leaf beech. It was planted in the early years of his own father's career here. Today, it is big enough to bear a swing. This tree is one of a number of fine specimens in the atmospheric country garden but the glory of the garden is on the other side of the wall. It is a sloped walled garden with an indefinable air of charm. From the gate, the long beds, come spilling out onto the paths and the place is all busting and bustling and stuffed with flowers. They grow vegetables too but they are disguised between roses, peonies and flowering shrubs. Most of these roses are old and of unknown nomenclature and they were here before Andy arrived. He says 'they're still going good and there's no need to spray either.' As we emerged from under one rose and clematis arch, he stopped and instructed me to climb in under the bird-proof net to try what could be the tastiest strawberry ever, a variety called 'Marshmallow'.

From here we paced out the length of a *Rosa* 'Rambling Rector' on the south-facing wall. It measured 26 metres and while it might only get one flush, Andy under-plants it with climbing nasturtiums which make their way up its branches and carry the flowering season through the summer.

Dotted through the loose, informal garden there are examples of topiary that are impossible not to notice. Andy has a passion for clipping greenery and has decorated the place with a selection of his projects. He favours box and we came upon a line of rabbits, llamas, (possibly) and bears, alongside corkscrews, lollipop and even the spades, diamonds, clubs and hearts from a pack of cards.

Generations of gardening predecessors have left their mark on this garden. We walked up a set of stone steps built in 1956 by one such man. He told Andy that these steps would be his memorial. Having admired them before, I liked them even more now.

Andy's own family goes back a long way back in this garden. He remembers as a tiny boy when his uncle started here. He got the job and travelled to Derry to buy a hat one Saturday, in order to begin on Monday. His father too worked here from the age of 11.

I was not surprised to hear that Agatha Christie is reliably said to have visited Dunmore. It is easy to imagine her wandering along the little arts-and-crafts, crazy paving path between the strange shaped, linking ponds and the surrounding damp beds full of drumstick primulas, ferns and hostas. There is over half a mile of paving threaded through the walled garden, winding in and out of the multiple, deep, flower borders, wire-trained roses and runs of scented *Rhododendron luteum*.

Andy told me the story about a big stand of arums, or *Zantedeschia aethiopica*, in one of the wall borders. Back in the dark days of the Troubles a bomb exploded on Bishop Street in Derry, blasting the arums out of their greenhouse. A clump was found by a passing woman and she brought it home, grew it in her cottage garden and then shared a bit with the McFarlands.

Finally, arranged around the garden there is a fascinating collection of sundials, some straightforward, some frankly impossible to figure or fathom, all of them intriguing and many made by Col. Robert McClintock, the last of his family to live at Dunmore. He left in 1940 a few years after a terrible tragedy that thankfully, has left no trace on the warm atmosphere of this beautiful garden.

Foxrock

John's Brae, Shroove, Greencastle, Co. Donegal. Tel: 074 9325 969.
e-mail: margotcaldwell@btinternet.com www.donegalgardentrail.com Contact: Margot Caldwell. Open:
By appointment in summer months as part of the Donegal Garden Trail. Musical Open Day in August.
See website for annual dates. Partially wheelchair accessible. Supervised children welcome. Dogs on leads.
Special features: Directions: Travel from Moville on the R241 with the Foyle on the right to Inishowen
Lighthouse north of Greencastle. The gateway is in a beech hedge along the brae.

Some gardeners are blessed. Margot Caldwell is one such person. I arrived to find a pair of her obliging friends taking orders with regard to a weeding session they were about to start. They would later make soup for us after our hard mornings' walkabout. I wanted to kidnap them but first they were going to help Margot ready the garden for a charity open day she was planning. She is further blessed with the most remarkable situation, looking out across to a view of the Inishowen lighthouse and beyond it, the Mussenden Temple and the Antrim coast. There is no such thing as perfection however: 'The soil was all rock and rubbishy dust,' Margot said of the prospect that greeted her 30 years ago. The garden is built on a steep glacial dump of rock, with crevices and gaps, hardly ideal for making a garden, but she set to work with a pick axe, tucking plants in wherever she could on the rock-strewn hill.

After three decades, the result is a successful garden that trails down the hill, interrupted by ledges and rockeries and zigzag paths, down from the house, towards the pond and a lawn at the bottom of the garden. It is a rewarding, if keep-your-wits-about-you trip down the slope. Then from the bottom of the hill, the view back up is of a completely different garden. In a welcome touch it provides passers-by with a full show.

We tip-toed downhill between spreads of recumbent juniper and heather and I was smitten by the combination of *Microbiota decussata,* which is like an upturned mop, teamed with cushions of *Hebe* 'Broughton dome' and *Azorella trifurcata,* which sort of oozes like a liquid, yet solid, green alien over neighbouring rocks as it grows. There are long runs of herbaceous and flowering plants too, full of blue delphinium and lupin, nepeta and foxglove.

A healthy sprinkling of trees from blue cedars to Japanese acers add height and variety to the planting, framing views and enclosing particular corners. Many of the plants came as gifts from friends and bring with them, all sorts of dear memories. *Osteospermum* 'Lady Leitrim' has been here for nearly as many years as the garden. It too came as a gift. The garden is like a living list of gardening pals. A strong design, well planted on a challenging goat-track site.

Glebe House & Gallery St. Columb's

Churchill, Co. Donegal. Tel: 074 9137071. e-mail: adrian.kelly@opw.ie www.donegalgardentrail.com
Contact: Head Gardener or reception. Open: Garden, all year every day, dawn to dusk. Gallery. See
website for seasonal changes. Special Features: Garden and gallery free. Historic house tours available. Café.
Directions: On the shores of Lough Gartan below Churchill village, signed on the R251.

If you have travelled as far as Glenveagh, it would be a great pity not to finish your visit with a trip to Glebe House and Gallery. There must be something in the air in this part of Donegal that imparts a sense of philanthropy on its inhabitants. Glebe House was the home of artist and collector Derek Hill, who left his home and art collection including works by Picasso and Oskar Kokoschka to the Irish nation.

The gardens can be spotted from the road as it rounds the lake. Giant gunnera and rodgersia leaves stand out against the grassy hill, enticing the traveller. The bank is also spotted with groves of tree ferns or *Dicksonia antarctica,* thriving in the shelter of taller trees and shrubs. Huge boulders glower on the grass reminding you that this is a tamed garden - in a harsh landscape.

The garden around the house has undergone an impressive improvement in the past few years. There seem to be roses everywhere, all around the building, in drifts of scent and bloom. It is like a busy celebration of fat pink roses, further enhanced with clematis, honeysuckle and jasmine. There are peonies too. The house actually seems to grow from out of a great mixed border. On one side, it floats above a hill of bergenia and tree peonies. The paths and steps around the building have been laid out with so many pots that walking along the paths is an impossibility. Given that this is a public garden this is a very un-institutional scrum. The open verandah at the side of the house is unusual, featuring ornate wrought ironwork around a jasmine-surrounded window at the top of a set of steps. Gravel paths take you down a level into a courtyard full of clematis, hydrangea, hostas, single red dahlias, and more large shrubs, all grown against the walls. Take an arch out of here out to the lawn and a route into a more intimate cottage garden with beds of herbaceous plants and more roses.

The little garden of herbs and soft fruit, known as Grace McDermot's garden, is filled with strawberries, red, black and white currants.

To walk around the park is to meet with some great trees, including a number of Japanese acers and betulas with toffee coloured trunks, *Acer* 'Crimson King' and laburnums. A quite surreal feature is the beech tree with a brick wall built into a hole in its trunk. A bualadh bos to the OPW for minding this garden as it deserves to be minded.

Glenalla House

Ray, Milford, Co. Donegal. Tel: 086 6064 409 e-mail: patrickburkitt@yahoo.ie www.donegalgardentrail.com Contact: Patrick Burkitt. Open: As part of the Donegal Garden Trail. See website for annual dates. Special features: Donation to charity. Directions: From Ramelton take Rathmullan road for 5 km to Ray bridge. Turn left after bridge and drive 1 km to grotto. Take right fork and continue for 2 km past gate house. Take next right over cattle grid.

The estate of Glenalla dates back to the 18th century, and in the 19th century it was home to Henry Chichester Hart, owner of Carrablagh House in Portsalon. (see elsewhere in this chapter) He was a renowned naturalist and botanist. The seven acres of garden surrounded by 270 acres of wood, both wild and planted, as seen today however, are largely down to the Franklin family. Netta Franklin, a political, educational and religious reformer from England came to live in Ray in 1913 and took an interest in the gardens.

While the stone courtyards and outhouses behind the house have an air of aged venerability about them, the garden feels younger, very much the Edwardian, classic country garden. From the house, a sloped lawn, quickly morphs into wildflower meadow and leads down to the surrounding woods. Close to the building there are small box gardens with crazy paving paths between sprawls of bergenia. Arbours and pergolas and old tennis court fences have been used to support rambling roses. These are the general elements we expect in a pre-war garden.

Out in the meadows, two huge limes stand alongside specimens of weeping beech and rhododendron, some bred in the famous, lost Donegal nurseries at Mulroy. The fallen copper beech that still grows on its side is a bit of star too. The mown paths run between loose, wind-blown grass and buttercups, before heading for the woods and the surprise of a labyrinth. This is a maze with only one route through. In the centre is an enigmatic standing stone marked on Ordnance Survey maps. It feels ancient but whatever age, these grounds makes for a pleasant tramp about.

The route along the bottom of the meadow looks back up to the house and the sloped wild garden, before heading off to a series of water gardens that include an old flax pond and the original sluice gate. One route makes its way eventually past these and up a hill into another wood from which an impressive clearance of over enthusiastic *Rhododendron ponticum* and laurel has been carried out. The trail hauls up past a noisy, impressive waterfall and continues up on mossy paths and stone steps, under the trees and further into the deeper woods that would not be out of place in a Grimm tale. From here, the specimen trees, rhododendron and eucryphia growing out in the open can be seen from above.

Glenveagh Castle Gardens

Glenveagh National Park, Churchill, Letterkenny, Co. Donegal. Tel: 076 1002 692. e-mail: sean.ogaoithin@ahg.gov.ie www.glenveaghnationalpark.ie www.donegalgardentrail.com Contact: Reception. Open: All year 10am-6pm. Last admission at 5pm. Guided tours available. Groups welcome. Supervised children welcome. Special features: Admission to grounds free. Interpretive centre. National park. Restaurant. Castle. Directions: Take the N56 north out of Letterkenny. Turn left on Termon onto the R251 and follow the signs for Glenveagh National Park.

A great garden is a living thing, not to be placed in aspic, but grown and developed. Head gardener, Seán O'Gaóithín and his small team of gardeners, understand this. As a result, every visit to Glenveagh shows an ever-changing, ever-developing project. Today Glenveagh is run on organic principles. Given that the 19th century castle sits in the middle of a 36,000 acre demesne of mountains, lakes and woods, this is good news. It makes Glenveagh the biggest single protected area of land in Ireland.

The gardens were laid out in the 1850s and since then a succession of design and gardening talents have combined to make it a contender for the position of Best Garden On The Island.

Although it is not associated with north Donegal in the way that it is with Kerry and west Cork, the Gulf Stream is responsible for the favourable microclimate in Glenveagh. The deep shelter belt of Scots pine (*Pinus sylvestris*) around the castle and lake, further improves the climate. The northerly aspect helps too by leading to sturdy, hardy growth. As a result, plants from China and the Himalayas thrive here. It is not all good news however: Glenveagh faces northwest and in winter many parts of the garden receive no direct sun at all during the day. It is hard to believe, but one of those dark spots is in the walled *jardin potager*. This *potager*, which covers an acre, is an important laboratory dedicated to Irish plants and good horticultural practice. 'In here we grow everything from seed. We are growing more and more perennials and digging less and less.' Seán explained as we made our way under an arch of fast growing peas spanning the path. They also favour Irish cultivars, rare and unusual plants and vegetables

that are losing ground in the wider world, including Irish apples. Seán's favourite is 'Irish Pitcher' a self-rooting cooker. He spent years collecting old Donegal roses from cottages and ruins around the county that this collection is here too. The *jardin potager* is at its best between July and August when the flowers and vegetables are in full swing. Seán pointed out the exceptional performance of *Geranium psilostemon* and a dainty-looking red *Dahlia* 'Matt Armour' – an apt memorial to the great gardener who worked here for half a century.

Among the welcome developments in the potager is that the gardener's cottage has been turned into a garden archive, with information on everything from its history to the price paid in 1947 for a *Rhododendron sinogrande* (£12.6.0). The little garden outside the cottage is itself a confection of box walls enclosing lilies, alliums, chives and origanum, as well as some rare native perennials in need of close supervision. As I left the walled garden I looked down to see the paths edged with ribbons of primula and alpine strawberry and thought that this is just one of many examples where the gardening team at Glenveagh seem to deliver just that bit more.

A lead urn-capped gate leads from here, into a camellia and rhododendron 'corridor' that has the feel of a cool hallway leading out of an impressive reception room in a grand house. Seán pointed out that because the urns are made of lead, they subside over the years under their own weight and need to be repaired.

Out in the pleasure grounds, the atmosphere is tropical. In quick succession we pass tree ferns, including self-sown specimens, eucryphia, hoheria and the fragrant, magnolia-like flowers of *Michelia doltsopa*, a Chinese native.

Glenveagh receives a substantial annual rainfall, and this gives the place its steamy, damp, glistening look, as well as promoting growth. Everywhere there are impressive plants like *Nothofagus dombeyi* and *Davidia involucrata*.

In 1996 a seed-collecting expedition was made to China's Yunan province resulting in a whole range of new plants coming to Ireland. Glenveaghs' share of the seed collected was planted in 1999 in a new Chinese garden beside the lake. One day this will be one of the great features of the garden.The list of special rhododendrons here is a long one and includes a variegated specimen called *Rhododendron* 'Mulroy's Variety', unique to the garden.

One of the great designers who worked here was Lanning Roper, whose penchant for silver and purple plant combinations is being echoed today. We looked at a composition of black elder, wine-coloured *Cotinus coggygria* and a silver hebe. The layered planting style that delivers several storeys of trees and shrubs in one spot is one that has been brought to perfection here. It delivers a three-for-one deal: Under a big Scots pine, spot *Prunus sargentii* and under it, a bottom storey of *Rhododendron sinogrande*. Long swathes of *Hosta fortunei* have been planted like striped ruffles along the edge of those layered-up borders. They do not use slug pellets, yet the hostas look very healthy. Look for the gazebo, built without nails, using huge larch planks and silvering beautifully as it ages.

An impressive set of 67 steps leads up through the woods to a belvedere, or viewing garden, set out with Italian terracotta pots. This was laid out in front of the upper glen and Lough Veagh with a view out over the castle, gardens and lake. At the moment the steps are out of bounds as they are waiting to be restored.

The other features within easy walk of the castle, are the rose garden and the Swiss Walk, so named because of its apparent resemblance to the mountains of Switzerland. The Belgian Walk, was created by recuperating Belgian soldiers during World War I. The Italian garden is full of 18th century Italian statuary, paved with Donegal slate and planted around with rhododendron and pieris.

For those who do not wish to take the shuttle bus, there is now a long and scenic cycle and walking path, from the outer gate to the castle and garden. Keep the whole day free.

Greenfort

Kerrykeel, Co. Donegal. Tel: 087 7574 823. e-mail: perrypat70@yahoo.co.uk
www.donegalgardentrail.com Contact: Paddy Perry. Open: As part of the Donegal Garden Trail. See website for annual dates. At other times by appointment. Directions: Driving from Kerrykeel to Portsalon on the R246 turn right onto R268, signed Rathmullan/Ramelton. After 300m fork left down a lane with 'no through' sign.

The house at Greenfort has a history that began back in 1711. There was a splash of good fortune in the boom of 1815 when the Napoleonic Wars led to a surge in prices, and the house was subsequently enlarged. When the Perry family arrived in the 1960s however, they bought a building in a poor state, but with a view worthy of a Bond film. Standing at the front of the house, looking out, the vista is of the sea framed by two plantations of trees and arboreal rhododendrons.

A ridge of land to to the south, protects the garden from the prevailing south westerly gales. Much of the planting here is about 50 years old and nicely maturing. Paddy Perry told me that his job is mainly 'maintenance, conservation and the odd addition'. One of his additions is the little wildflower meadow, visible from the house, where, in the summer there is a grand population of wild orchids, self-heal, speedwell and daisies, like a collection of small jewels in the grass.

The large walled garden is on a stepped-up ledge from here, a relaxed and informal place where the love of roses is obvious - every opportunity to include a rose seems to have been pounced on. We looked at them strung along wires, over arbours and pergolas, on strong metal supports and up old apple trees, on walls and standing free. I admired *Rosa* 'Narrow Water Castle, from County Down, a pale pink, rarely spotted, yet vigorous rose. The old apples were espaliered at one point and so they are nicely knotty and contorted into attractive shapes. They are also all cookers and one is appropriately called 'Mrs Perry's cooker'.

It might not be the obvious thing to expect but the Buddhist temple at the top of the garden, is charming. This was built by Paddy's uncle, using the portico pillars from Ards House, near Portsalon, which he bought at an auction in 1965 'for ten bob'.

Apart from the roses, there are some good specimen trees, weeping hoheria, fine myrtle, abutilon, embothrium and a scented *Rhododendron nobleanum* of which Paddy is very fond. There are also camellias, magnolias and a rhododendron, that having blown over in the wind, was righted and is now held up at all four corners by ropes. In the spring, the place is awash with bulbs, particularly snowdrops.

The *Rhododendron ponticum* at the front of the garden needs to be cut back hard annually but Paddy feels it is worth the bother as it shelters some precious plants. Under its skirts big mounds of mop-head hydrangea look like replacement jewels when the rhododendron is not flowering. We took a walk down between these, finishing off in the recently planted wood, where 13,000 ash, oak, alder and rowan have been planted between grassy paths and some 'beautiful but doomed elms' as Paddy called these handsome young trees that will no doubt succumb to Dutch Elm disease soon. We left having looked at the hollow beech tree into which Gus Barton, the then owner of Greenfort, carved his name in 1906.

Mrs Jessie Mahaffy's Garden
....

Blackrock, Lifford, Co. Donegal. Tel: 074 9141216. Or text 086 1759162. e-mail: mahaffybelinda@hotmail.com www.donegalgardentrail.com Contact: Belinda Mahaffy. Open: As part of the Donegal Garden Trail. Contact for annual dates. Special features: Directions: Leave the N14 and travel on the R265 to St. Johnston for 1 km. Pass yellow cottages on the left. Blackrock House is the 5th house above the road after this, marked by white washed walls and beech trees.

As Belinda Mahaffy talks about her garden, it feels as though you are meeting the cast of her family, going back to 1911 and the time of her great uncle and aunt who planted the line of beech trees at the front gate as a hedge, to keep sheep and cattle away from the old farmhouse. Then there was her mother and the roses she planted here. This is a garden full of plants with stories about people, from the old lady in Castlefinn from whom her mother also bought the predecessors of the double primulas we admired in the rock garden. (Every year the lady grew 13 lines of primulas and sold them along with eggs, to make ends meet.) We then met the ghost of a lady from Rathgar, from whose wedding bouquet Belinda grew a pretty apricot rose. Best of all was the potentilla from William Robinson's garden 'Gravetye' in England. Robinson, one of the most famous gardeners in history, was related to the family and this is very much a Robinsonian garden.

The rockery is without doubt *the* feature here. Forget ordinary rockeries and imagine instead an old quarry and the sort of steep walls found in such a place: Such is the rockery here, with dramatic stone ledges jagging out from the verticals. It is an impressive, if daunting planting medium. How the generations of Mahaffys managed to turn it into a garden would be beyond most of us. Yet this is what they have done, mulching and enriching it with ash and leaves. As a result, its dripping wet walls and stone steps are studded with *Asplenium scolopendrium* and different dryopteris, hostas and aconites, daylilies and *Vinca major* 'Variegata'. The ferns were real favourites of Belinda's late mother.

The outhouse garden is also a dream. Every stone wall has been smothered in roses. There are spreads of *Rosa* 'Louise Odier' and the ever-rampaging *Rosa* 'Rambling Rector' doing battle with a *Paulownia tomentosa*. I love the tree peonies under the beech trees and the sprinkling of soapwort or *Saponaria officinalis* which Belinda grew from roadside seed she found in Kerry. The place is full of charming, rampant plants. The gravel in front of the stone outhouses is all but invisible under a blanket of Virginia creeper. When I admired a red chestnut, it turned out to have been grown from a nut her mother was given.

Belinda's stories about the old gardeners could have held me all day. However, the most recent credits must be given to her. A few years ago she began clearing scrub from, and planting up the existing wood with ferns and woodland flowers, making a whole new wild place that Robinson would, I am sure, have loved. I left with a tip for planting *Geranium phaeum* to smother out ground elder.

Oakfield Park Demesne

Raphoe, Co Donegal. Tel: 074 9173 068. e-mail: gardens@oakfieldpark.com www.oakfieldpark.com www.donegalgardentrail.com Contact: Brian McElhinney. Open: April-Oct. Check website for seasonal details. Large groups by appointment. Special features: Garden tours by appointment. 4 km narrow gauge railway, open weekends in summer. Tea rooms. Picnic facilities. Toilets. Partially wheelchair accessible. Directions: Take the Letterkenny to Lifford road (N14). Pass the exit for Raphoe and continue for 1.5 km. Take the next right (L2374) by the burnt out Cross Pub. Travel 1.5 km to the car park on the left. The garden is on the right.

Arriving to Oakfield Park for a first visit can be overwhelming. Take 100 acres, insert several new man-made lakes, huge walled gardens, follies, acres of woods, a collection of oaks, several huge flower meadows, parterres and large scale formal gardens, complete with glasshouses, sunken gardens, Japanese gardens, kitchen gardens, a flax field, tennis courts and ponds. This is exactly what Sir Gerry Robinson and his wife Heather did – not in the 18th or 19th centuries, but in the last two decades. This is a remarkable achievement and further improved by their having thrown open the gates to the public.

It all started when they bought a derelict Georgian deanery in Raphoe and 55 acres. Once the house was restored they took up gardening – with what seem like bottomless reserves of energy and money.

The soil here is blue marl, a difficult, heavy soil type that holds onto water. This may account for the numerous pond building projects here, on the 'if you have lemons, make lemonade' policy. The ponds naturally hold their water. But this heavy soil means that the husbandry of the rest of the garden needs to be thorough. The impressive growth seen throughout is a testament to the work and care invested in both feeding and lightening the soil.

In the walled garden lines of yew pyramids flank one path and look like they have been here for decades. The pergola over a little pool is laden down under the weight of roses and clematis and the swagged brick wall behind it, lovely as it is, can barely be seen behind the cotoneasters, tall betulas and acers. The distractions

are everywhere. In one corner we came across a secret 'room' planted up with aralias, white-barked betulas and paulownias over bright white anemones. The dizzying route leads between pagoda gardens and into an oval Koi-pool with unusual borders of white alliums and dicentra. The stream and rill garden is a different picture of perfection. The acer collection, planted on an ivy bank and backed by a beech hedge is developing impressively. The kitchen garden is substantial and filled with well-tended vegetables and trained fruit trees. The latest floral feature is the cut-flower meadow behind a picket fence, keeping visitors away from the beehives within.

This is a high-maintenance place and as no endeavour is without its problems, neither is this. The box parterre is impressive but it is suffering from box blight which they are working to eradicate organically.

Flax was once grown widely in the area to produce linen, and its luminous blue flowers were a common sight. A man from Raphoe, one of the few people left in the country with a knowledge of flax, now grows it here in as sweet a little stone-enclosed field as ever existed. Come in June for the flowers.

In another field, running down a hill they planted the September wildflower meadow, with corn marigolds, wild rape and poppies. A four-acre expanse of these waving in the breeze was enough to make me want to move in.

A huge area of the ground is given over to woods and in keeping with its name and history, the Robinsons are building a young collection of oaks, which currently stands at around 100 species.

Creating views and vistas is an ongoing preoccupation. The most ambitious example of this is the view from the house, downhill, over and beyond the pond and its classical summerhouse, and on through an *allée* between trees, to a distant mound planted up with 15,000 box plants. The opportunities to create such large-scale features are rare.

In one of the woods, the most recent item of interest is the 1800s water ram which pumps water from the stream to the upper garden. These days, the entrance is via the train station – Yes there is a train station, complete with tea room. It homes two narrow gauge trains that chug through the woods, past an another lake, through acres of reed beds and alongside a sham castle/viewing tower. All bells and whistles? Absolutely. Finally I should add a thank you to the friendliest, most informative coffee van girl in the country. She makes a mean carrot cake too.

Rathumullan House

Rathmullan, Co. Donegal. Tel: 074 9158188. e-mail: info@rathmullanhouse.com. www.donegalgardentrail.com Contact: Mary Wheeler. Open: All year. Special features: Hotel. Supervised children welcome. Special features: Hotel. No admission charge. Directions: In Rathmullan turn left off the R247 at Patton's Butcher. Gates on right.

On my most recent visit to Rathmullan House, it poured rain but it did not matter. The metre-and-a-half tall arums (*Zantedeschia aethiopica*) in the flower garden were like creamy, upturned trumpets and the pink lupins looked as happy as the outrageously cheeky rabbits that I had to shoo out of my way on the lawns.

Elaine, at reception laughed at my surprise at the rabbits: 'They think they own the place!'

I set out with Bob Wheeler to revisit the gardens. The flower garden to the side of the house, with its arums and lupins, is an exuberant place, wrapped up in wooden trellis, coloured a soft green shade of eau de Nil. It is like an explosion of flower, centred on a piece of hard-edged contemporary sculpture that is in good contrast to the soft, fuzzy lavender and *Rosa* 'Galway Bay', solanum and crinodendron. This area was once the site of an ammunition shed. (There were two gun emplacements mounted at Rathmullan during World War II)

'Chef and gardener' are the themes in the main body of the garden. We made our way into the productive kitchen garden, by way of a sign that read 'Hens Out. Keep Closed.' Inside the walled garden, Bob, announced, as he tended a pipe, that we were now in 'the workhouse'. The Wheelers supply as much of the produce for the hotel as they can and in an informal, attractive way. We passed climbing beans winding their way up a rusting old garden gate, clipped bay trees and long runs of flowers.

Bob's big interest is fruit, and he aims to grow as much of it as possible, principally for jam. We inspected his rhubarb, raspberries and strawberries, loganberries and gooseberries, blackcurrants and jostaberries. Around these are an array of well trained 30-year-old apple trees. Everything is shot through with bloom and flower, from angelica and lupins to a rambling rose up a past-its-prime apple tree. In the tunnel, they grow tomatoes, lemon verbena and grapes. The large fig manages outside nicely on the south-facing wall over a splash of wine coloured *Knautia macedonica*. In the middle of the garden, the remains and base of an old lost green house, were transformed into a cosy sitting room and herb garden, with hip-high walls, sprouting golden oregano and thyme, sage and mint. This is an organic garden and inside the walls, the ongoing battle is predictably, with the old garden villain, bindweed. As we left we looked at the ledge above the walled garden and the new heritage apple garden that will begin to produce in a few years.

To the side, and out in front of the house, there are some specimen trees; magnolia, crinodendron, eucryphia and among them, an old weeping elm and an impressive evergreen oak with branches that steel over the grass. A trail down the lawn leads to the woods and 'Batt's Walk', which makes its way eventually to the village by way of the lough.

Riverside Park

Dungloe, Co. Donegal. Open: At all times. No admission. Directions: In the middle of the village.

On December 3, 1910, a woman called Ellice Pilkington travelled to Dungloe, armed with a map, a thermos flask, and a passport in Irish, given to her by the President of the Gaelic League, Douglas Hyde. Her task was to establish a bilingual, co-operative society calling on the skills that the women and girls of the area were known for. She harnessed the possibilities of knitting, cottage gardening, dairying, and jam-making and helped them set up one of the first ICA branches in the country.

It is fitting in the centenary year of the branch, that the ICA women of Dungloe should be memorialised in this waterside cottage garden of roses, geraniums and catmint, with flowering trees, a little wildflower meadow and a pond. It is a testament to the enterprising women of the ICA.

Ros Bán Garden

Near Mongorry, Common, Raphoe, Co. Donegal. Tel: 074 9145336. 086 0805214. e-mail: rosbangarden@gmail.com www.donegalgardentrail.com Contact: Ann and Bob Kavanagh. Open: Easter to Autumn. Contact for seasonal details. Directions: Take the Mongorry road from Raphoe. Take the first right after .5 km and the garden is the 5th house on the right.

I met Ann and Bob Kavanagh one day and they gave me a little leaflet, that read: 'A modest garden which contains, for those who know how to look and to wait, more instruction than a library.' This was a prospect to be looked into. Ros Bán covers one acre, but it feels bigger, divided as it is into a series of walks and occasional openings, between substantial plantations of native shrubs, trees, grasses and perennials. It is a busy place.

From the car park the nature fest begins: The gravelled area was covered in alpine strawberries as well as rampant fox and cubs or *Pilosella aurantiaca* with orange daisy-like flowers. From here the way into the garden is under a series of arches heavy with philadelphus and bright golden hop or *Humulus lupulus* 'Aureus', scented *Jasminum officinale* and lilac abutilon. You then pass a bustin' out all over greenhouse filled with vines and figs and arrive onto a tightly mown lawn centred on a sorbus with a wooden bench like a necklace around it. White *Clematis montana* combines well with sorbus. Underneath, orchids seem to grow in weed-like proportions. The Kavanaghs simply mow around the little clumps.

This is an educational garden and there are information plaques dotted about. I like the one that quotes Oliver Goldsmith:

'Beside yon straggling fence that skirts the way.
With blossom'd furze unprofitably gay.'

The sound of a stream is audible everywhere. Sometimes the water can be glimpsed and at the bottom of the garden, where it is properly on show,

stand and look out of the shaded, snug, wood garden over a buttercup meadow and a centuries-old fieldscape beyond. Overhead Indian chestnut and rhododendron join ash and oak. It is an utterly quiet, peaceful place that has the effect of slowing the visitor down to dawdle and inspect the varieties of lichen on a branch, or try to understand the marks on an ogham stone, or consider what a stand of cow parsley and native fern might look like in their own garden. Another sign: 'A weed is a plant whose virtue has not yet been discovered.'

Nail-clipper gardeners, keep away.

Nora's Rose Garden

85 Blue Cedars, Cappry, Ballybofey, Co. Donegal. Tel: 087 7900 490. e-mail: singh_nora@yahoo.ie www. donegalgardentrail.com. Contact: Nora and Jeet Singh. Open: As part of the Donegal Garden Trail. Contact for annual details. Directions: Travelling on the R252 from Ballybofey, pass Jackson's Hotel on the right. Blue Cedars is on the left after 2 km. Take the 3rd left. No 85 is on the left.

Imagine how many roses can be fitted into a small front garden. Then double that number. Now squeeze in a few more. I give you Nora Singh's rose garden, a feast of flower on a lucky suburban road in Ballybofey.

Brought up in the Philippines, where roses were prohibitively expensive, Nora would walk past the house of a rose-growing neighbour every day as she went to school, stopping to smell the flowers. 'She used to roar at me!' Nora laughs. 'She was grumpy. But I never missed a chance to walk past.' When she arrived in Ireland Nora was delighted to find that rose gardening can be an accessible interest and five years ago she began her own rose garden.

'I joined the Finn Valley Garden Society and

the exchange of ideas was so good. Now people ask *me* about roses!' She seems amused at that thought.

Nora starts the morning throughout the summer at about 6.45am when she gets up, says hello to the roses and begins the pruning, deadheading or whatever job might be in need of doing on the day. She grows them in pots and containers, in the ground, up obelisks and arches. This is high maintenance stuff. Between the roses there are splashes of nepeta, lupin and other perennials. An occasional Japanese acer and apple tree trained on a wall add permanence and variety – but mostly it is roses.

In the back garden, she also grows cauliflowers in pots and herbs in tyres. Does that sound a bit mend-and-make-do? Nothing could be further from the truth. This is a smart, tidy, eat-your-dinner-off-the-floor garden. Nora's beetroots grown in wooden boxes are stage-set perfect. I could not imagine digging them up. Still the emphasis is always on the roses. With regard to growing roses in containers, Nora's advice is to 'just change the top layer of compost in spring and feed the bushes every two weeks with tomato feed through the growing season. Give them a good soaking. Then let them almost dry out.' Simple. How many roses does she grow? 'Maybe a hundred?' She hazards too busy to count.

Cille, Co. Donegal.

Salthill

Mountcharles, Co. Donegal. Tel: 074 9735387. e-mail: etemple@eircom.net
www.donegalgardentrail.com Contact: Elizabeth Temple. Open: As part of the Donegal Garden Trail. See
website for annual details. Other times by appointment. Special Features: Garden talks. Groups welcome.
Directions: Take the N56 from Donegal town towards Killybegs for 3.5 km to the Mountcharles Pier sign
on the left. Follow signs to the pier and continue straight on until the road bends right. Continue for 200m.
The garden is the second gate on the right.

Salthill is a classic story of a country garden brought back from the brink of extinction. It covers about 1.2 acres enclosed within tall walls behind a Georgian house on the edge of Donegal Bay. When Elizabeth Temple arrived here, she saw drawings of the garden on old maps. It seemed to date to about 1820 but it was wildly overgrown and it was hard to see what shape it should have. So Elizabeth began to redraw a new garden within the walls.

The entrance is through a courtyard surrounded by old farm buildings including a byre. This is like the starter in a substantial meal. The courtyard garden could in all honesty have been lifted by spaceship from somewhere hot and dry, and beamed into Donegal. Visiting it on a sunny day certainly added to the sensation. Giant eucomis or pineapple lilies, looked so healthy and bustling, they could have been natives. Tall pink echiums, waves of phormiums, miscanthus with white agapanthus flowers dotted through them, look right at home, although it is far from a Donegal yard that these plants came.

The fun of this garden is that having accustomed ourselves to the idea of a Mediterranean garden in chilly Ireland, like Alice, we wander through a gateway to a completely different world. This is the main walled garden, a place that had been used as a dump in the years before Elizabeth arrived. That once lamentable fact turned out to be a blessing in disguise. Life as a dump rendered the garden perfectly fertile. Add a sheltered aspect and a talented gardener to the fertile soil and the result is a great bustle of a place, full of good and unusual plants. The design revolves around the plants. Curtailing them to fit in with a hemmed-in plan would not meet with Elizabeth's approval. We wandered past heavily flowering *Cornus*

mas, competing with a *Buddleja alternifolia* for attention, only to be side-tracked by *Euonymus cornutus,* a rare flowering shrub with seed heads like extravagant crowns. An arch of *Hydrangea aspera* leads past a greenhouse, stuffed with heirloom tomatoes.

The seaside location means that there is always a plentiful supply of seaweed. The roses thrive on this. *Rosa* 'Ferdinand Pichard', *R.* 'Californica plena' and the thornless *R.* 'Zephirine Drouhin' all bore heavy flower, cargoes and wrapped us in perfume as we went.

At the top of the garden, Elizabeth grows her vegetables in high, ridged beds. I admired an abutilon on the wall behind the rows of leeks and spinach and was told that it came as a seed from Central Park in New York. Beside it, we looked at a shrubby *Clematis heracleifolia* with purple bells, and a creamy, greeny- white *Clematis rehderiana.* The herbaceous borders run perpendicular to these massed shrubs. Grass paths allow the visitor to get right in between the drifts of day lilies, phlox and white sanguisorba and the flowers stretch in all directions, including upwards, into the trees, in the shape of a climbing aconitum twining through the branches of a variegated azara. The fascinating stripey snake bark on an *Acer forrestii* acts as a reminder that no garden should be without one of these exquisite acers. Ginger lilies or hedychium grown outside, and fat stands of crinum lilies again make me think I am somewhere exotic. The week before my walk around, Charles, Prince of Wales had visited. He must have wondered if he was in Donegal or Madeira…

Sea View

Salthill, Mountcharles, Co. Donegal. Tel: 074 9735 350. 087 9131 393.
e-mail: dorothyjervis@gmail.com. Contact: Dorothy Jervis. Open as part of the Donegal Garden Trail. See
website for annual details. Directions: Drive on N56 from Donegal toward Killybegs. After 3.8 km turn
left to Mountcharles Pier. 200m along, turn left into a cul de sac and drive uphill for 500 m to the garden.

Dorothy is the fourth generation of her family to live and garden at Sea View. She could actually be the fifth generation but the records are thin. Standing at the front door the view is simply one of the sea, interrupted by a long, century-old flower border known as 'Granny's Bed.' This was named for Dorothy's grandmother, the first gardener in the family and it is suitably old-fashioned and cottagey, full of peonies and roses, salmon-coloured oriental poppies and sprinkles of white *Hesperis matronalis*. Dorothy wonders where her grandmother got her plants from at a time when plants were not easily come by. One item in point being *Rosa* 'Old Blush China' also known as the Monthly Rose.

'I often have that on the table for Christmas Day,' she told me. The phlox in this bed also goes back to the first garden, as do the aconites. 'I can remember there was always a stand of aconites in the orchard.'

Off in the distance, two curtains of tall ash and pine frame the view of the water, and across the bay, Merva Beach, Garrison in Fermanagh and, when the conditions are really good, Ben Bulben. Those trees

afford the garden much of its precious shelter. Back inside that garden, the stone wall that runs down the middle of Granny's bed provides a line of support and shelter. Originally this was the dividing wall between the yard and the haggard. Walking around the bed, leads downhill and into a second distinct area, a sunken flower garden that looks over a paddock to the sea beyond.

Here in the sunken garden, Dorothy can work away on the windiest day, being below the whip of whatever gales zip past. It is a welcoming spot, circular in shape, surrounded by flowering shrubs and perennials, and benches from which to enjoy them. In the enclosing beds the theme is a white one – with an occasional splash of purple. We admired white iris, astilbe and lupin, arum and the stand out star - *Gladiolus colvillei* 'The Bride'. A white *Cornus kousa* 'Teutonia' creates height and flower and a number of hydrangeas contribute both white and purple. I like the use of purple *Salvia forsskaolii* here.

The soil is slightly acid heavy clay which suits her magnolias. A younger bed, started by Dorothy out by the gate, homes the David Austen roses and more magnolias. Take the secret path from here into the bottom garden. It weaves between lines of bergenia and *Primula bulleyana* as well as more iris and astilbe.

'The ground here is not just damp. It's wet!' Dorothy told me as we made our way between lush 'rivers' of francoa in front of shrubs like *Azara microphylla*, *Magnolia stellata* and more hydrangeas. As well as purple flowers, she uses purple foliage throughout the garden to good effect. She pointed to cotinus, berberis and black elder. Before I left I had to see the pittosporum hedge made of *P.* 'Irene Paterson' matched with a fat pink *Rosa* 'Harlow Carr'. This is charming garden worked by an equally charming woman with a good eye, a sure sense of what works and a sea of knowledge.

Summy

Portnoo, Co. Donegal. Tel: 074 9545 242. 087 4366187. www.donegalgardentrail.com
Contact: Michael Classon. Open: As part of the Donegal Garden Trail. Contact for annual details.
Directions: Leave Ardara on the road to Portnoo. Turn left onto the L7713 to Rosbeg. The garden is attached
to a two storey house in the trees on the left.

As the directions say, Michael Classon's house can be found 'in the trees'. Add to that, that it is in the wilds. Summy is that perfect blend of wild and cultivated, found more often dotted along the western seaboard than anywhere else. Hunkered down in the middle of the almost untamed hills west of Glenties, this is a place of real beauty. If it were a supermodel it would be Kate Moss, a bit unkempt, with tousled hair, roots showing a bit, and still fabulous. Forget straight lines and edges. There are none here. There are great plants though, tucked in between the bracken and sycamores, ivy, brambles and hazel. Then there are what Michael calls his 'rescue roses.' Many of them were found growing around derelict Donegal cottages. A lot are different varieties of pink, cabbagey, scented, flowers, resistant to disease, and very desirable. They climb the house, climb trees, and drape themselves over shrubs looking at home and relaxed in his garden.

Summy is in a valley and so the hills and hollows are the defining features. At the bottom of one such hollow is a grand sized natural pond that, once Michael dug it, filled itself and continues to be filled from a number of natural springs that make their way down the hill, colonised by ferns. Michael added some lilies to the pond, as well as a little chubby Putto missing an arm. He sits on an island surrounded by bulrushes and wild irises. They just arrived and thrived.

The hilly walks that lead down to, up from and around the pond, are dotted with special shrubs, many from old Irish gardens, such as the purple hazel *Corylus maxima* 'Purpurea', a gift from the late Corona North in Altamont (See Co. Carlow) It sits snug between massed ranks of *Buddleja globosa*, white flowering abutilon, camellia, magnolia, a range of rhododendrons and a handsome run of *Rosa* 'Grootendorst', which has frilled pink flowers.

A sheltering encirclement of sycamores gives this wild valley plot the shelter that allows Michael grow some surprising things this far north. The *Paulownia tomentosa* that he was told 'would never do in Donegal,' gives him the greatest pleasure. As does the performing *Magnolia wilsonii* and a juvenile *Ginkgo biloba*. There are lots of native Irish apples too. He recommends the tip-bearing 'Irish Peach' as well as the old English 'Gladstone', an early eater. He has fruiting almonds too which are not often seen in Irish gardens.

From the open colourful garden, to the front and side of the house, take the hill up through the wood, on trunk lined paths under sycamores and hazels, ferns and in spring bluebells. Bring a walking stick.

The White House Garden

CPI Complex, Castlefinn, County Donegal. Contact: Michael Carlin. Tel: 074 9143976. 087 2655525.
Email: info@ clipped.net www.donegalgardentrail.com Open: As part of the Donegal Garden Trail. Check
for annual dates. Other times by appointment.

Hillsborough Castle Garden, Co Down.

Down

Ballyalloly House

19 Ballyalloly Road, Comber, Co. Down. BT23 5SPN. Contact: Augusta Nicholson.
e-mail: aamcmurray@hotmail.co.uk or augustanicholson@aol.ie Open: By e-mail appointment only. May-
Sept. Not wheelchair accessible. Children welcome. No dogs. Groups of 10 maximum. Refreshments can be
arranged. Directions: On appointment.

I have had the vision of this garden in my head for a long time. I first saw it about ten years ago and the picture of an heroic sweep of shrub-studded lawn down to a lake and a backdrop of fine trees stayed with me. Seeing it for a second time felt like coming home. Few places live so successfully up to fuzzy, rose tinted memory. The 1930s house stands high on a stone ledge. It is from this vantage point that my vision took place. Standing on the height, all attention is pulled and drawn down the slope, towards great clouds of rhododendron and sky-rocketing blue cedars and massive copper beech and huge oak. The hill simply begs you to roll down it – I imagine that regardless of age you might wish you had the place to yourself. The fallen cherry half way down the slope, likes this place so well it continued to grow on its side having toppled. Who would blame it?

Areas of long loose meadow grass makes the shorter cut sward look like expensive green carpet and the white iron benches in among the meadow grass and under flowering rhododendrons look as though they were placed by God himself.

This is the forty shades of green garden. It is also one for the wellies, even in summer, because at the bottom of the hill, the ground is squelchy. Expect to slop happily along the waterside, past frills of primula and martagon lilies, rodgersia, rush and iris. The air always seems to be warm and the feeling is slightly exotic. It becomes even more so when the grass gives way to mulched paths under the trees. This walk through the lovely murk stretches out for about a quarter mile by the water, leading eventually to Bluebell Hill. As you walk, the gleam of *Magnolia wilsonii* flowers will lure you over to an opening, to see them at close quarters.

Years of clearing laurel has freed up a number of species rhododendrons so *Rhododendron sinogrande* with its cinnamon trunks can be seen again. Augusta Nicholson, who works the garden with such enthusiasm, is constantly adding new plants for future generations, as well as clearing and smartening up the secret garden that is the walled garden.

As we walked she sang the praises of Shoo Shoo Stephens who predated Augusta and her daughter Emma as the guardian of this lovely place. Shoo Shoo was a friend of Mrs. Vera Mackie, the famed gardener of Guincho and Ringdufferin. (See elsewhere in the chapter). Mrs. Mackie's influence can be seen in this garden.

Ballyglighorn Garden

19 Ballyglighorn Road, Comber, Co. Down. BT23 5SX. e-mail: aamcmurray@hotmail.co.uk
Contact: Adam McMurray. Open: By e-mail appointment only. May-Sept. Groups of 10 maximum.
Children welcome. No dogs. Special features: Refreshments can be arranged. Plants for sale. Directions:
On appointment.

Adam McMurray has been working his country garden since 2013. It feels more mature than that because there were a great number of big native trees dotted around the site to start with, particularly ash, of which Adam is hugely fond. The garden is also surrounded by some impressive native hedges that make the place feel protected, sheltered and mature. The ash trees line both the boundary fields and tower over parts of the garden.

His garden is organic, flower-filled and informal, even slightly wild in parts. There are bees living and working here in great numbers and it is the sort of place that townies like me dream of. I love the mix of flowers and vegetables, jumbled together in the small stone-enclosed vegetable garden.

Prepare to swoon at the scents of the mint garden, a scrum of pineapple, ginger, apple and spearmint as well as banana mint which *does* taste of bananas.

Apart from the mints, I left with a note to try both 'Red Bore' black kale and tree spinach.

A good range of ornamentals ensures that this area is as pretty as it is productive. I was smitten by the red lantern flowers of *Abutilon megapotamicum* against the stone wall of an old shed. We followed through a gate from here into the front garden, again dominated by a grand old ash. This area is a jungle of stipa and hellebore, echium and *Rhododendron macabeanum*.

The field garden is Adam's next project, He was busy layering *Rhododendron falconeri* in preparation for life here. Among the most interesting plants is a Japanese *Magnolia obovata* with a white bark and beautiful waxy flowers.

The house is barely visible under blankets of passion flower and clematis, as well as *Rosa moyesii*, eucryphia, leycesteria and variegated ceanothus.

Adam's talent also runs to building with stone, including little circular walls and unusual arches, like

pieces of sculpture between the plants. We looked at stands of hellebores and lilies under arbutus and *Olearia ilicifolia* beside the stream, which he diverted. We took wooden walkways through plantations of hebe, dierama and *Rosa glauca* becoming more and more lost in this lovely garden.

5 Ballymoran Road

5 Ballymoran Road, Killinchy, Co Down. BT23 6UE. Tel: (0044 28) (048) 9754 1012.
Contact: Knox and Shirley Gass. Open: By appointment. Directions: On application.

Knox Gass has been a well known man in the world of Ulster gardens for many years. The garden at Ballymoran Road is his most recent creation, a new baby in the hands of an expert. Mr. Gass began working the site in 2009.

'It's beginning to bulk up now,' he mused as we stood looking down on proceedings before walking around. The garden covers one acre, yet seems a lot bigger, as that bulking up has transformed it into a nicely subdivided space. The house is being slowly colonised by exotic looking *Berberidopsis corallina*, pseudopanax and *Parthenocissus henryana*, which turns a rich shade of plum as the year winds down. Underneath, mounds of pale francoa are used to good effect. Francoa is an easy good looker that is not used as widely as it should be.

A tender *Lonicera × tellmanniana* hints that this garden is favoured with good shelter and the orange

in its flowers is set off well by yellow *Rosa* 'Gloire de Dijon' and *Hibbertia scandens,* a delicate plant from Queensland, which Mr. Gass said is 'still here after the two bad winters.' He chose the site well.

The garden leads away from the house, running downhill in repeating arcs of dry stone walling. These are made of dark whinstone which stands out effectively against the golden gravel paths. Hard landscaping plays second fiddle to the plants however.

We started down a path between hydrangea and agapanthus, turning a corner into a deep mixed border. In all directions there are special plants, from a sideways-growing Chilean tree fern, *Lophosoria quadripinnata,* whose dark feathery foliage looks so good against pale variegated pittosporum. Elsewhere I had to admire *Pterostyrax hispida*, the epaulette tree with white flowers, exactly like, well, epaulettes.

Mr. Gass does the rounds with what looks like

The Great Book of the Garden. This is a sizeable tome, filled with the names of what look like several thousand plants. Every time I saw something I did not know, which was often, he had the details in the great volume at his fingertips. We made our way on cross border paths, passing silver and lilac *Olearia* 'Henry Travers' and an even more ghostly, silver shrub called *Gomphostigma virgatum*, all the time moving downhill towards the river and the wet garden, where the scents and colours come from masses of primulas, from *Primula helodoxa*, a yellow fragrant bloom to *Primula burmanica*, in contrasting purple. The splashes of *Trollius chinensis* 'Golden Queen' with its exaggerated orange stamens, alongside dark-stemmed

Iris 'Gerald Darby' went on to my must-have list. Low growing jungles of epimediums and ferns cover the ground under Japanese acers and young eucalyptus. One of the dark stone walls has been used to direct a *Rosa* 'Rambling Rector' sideways, allowing it to be handled and tamed with more ease than when left gallop up a tree to cause chaos.

For sheer informal floral beauty, this is a garden that is hard to beat. Add the desire to get to know some lesser spotted herbaceous plants and shrubs, and it is of the first order. Add to that, that with all its exotic inhabitants, it still manages to feel like an old-fashioned cottage garden.

64 Ballystockart Road

64 Ballystockart Road, Comber, Co. Down. BT23 5QY. Tel: (0044 28) (048) 9187 0133. Contact: Robert Russell. Open: By appointment only. May-Sept. Not wheelchair accessible. Supervised children. Dogs on leads. Directions: On application.

From the sunny courtyard, with its stone sheds and the back of the house, smothered in fat pink roses, honeysuckle and winter jasmine, to the softly shaped hedges and mad explosions of *Echium canadensis*, and mounds of pink *Geranium palmatum*, this garden opens its welcoming arms from the start. The mood is relaxed, floral and pretty. It is exactly what you expect from a country garden around an old farmhouse.

Down the straight garden path from the front door, massed ranks of lupins, hardy geraniums and more roses, line up in a welcoming guard of honour. The plants come out of the bed to greet you rather than doing the eyes-front, formal thing. Laburnum

and twisted hazel, peeling barked eucalyptus and sweet chestnut, a good *Magnolia soulangeana* and *Buddleja globosa* crowd around the lawn, and a *Rosa* 'Paul's Himalayan Musk' clambers up an old apple tree. It is gorgeous.

We made our way through an old gate and into the outer garden.

Here the place is heady with the scent of *Rosa rugosa*. Walking around between clipped crataegus hedges, on mown paths with a cram of shrubs and trees, like acer and *Cornus kousa*, ducking under rose arches leading into a little sitting down area, everything about the garden says welcome. This is a mill of good plants, from more roses to *Styrax japonica* and liriodendron. It will change dramatically as the juvenile *Metasequoia glyptostroboides* and neighbouring eucalyptus begin to reach for the sky in years to come.

Another gate, old and painted white, led into the kitchen garden with its lavender-trimmed greenhouse and little fernery. From here, we left and went out to the meadow that runs down a hill to a wood with hazel and apples. This flowery, meadow is straight out of the textbook of Wildflower Meadows We All Want. When we arrived the top of the hill, the way back into the garden was under another arched wooden gate covered in roses.

Ballywalter Park

Ballywalter, Newtownards, BT22 2PP. Co. Down. Tel: (0044 28) (048) 4275 8264.
e-mail: enq@ballywalterpark.com Contact: Mrs. Sharon Graham. Open: By appointment to groups. Special
features: Teas by arrangement. Events. Wedding photographs. Directions: Turn off the A20 at Grey Abbey.
Take the B5 and turn right at the T-junction. Continue to the gate lodge on the right.

Out on the windy Ards Peninsula, Ballywalter Park was built in the 1850s by the English architect Charles Lanyon for the Mulhollands, Lords Dunleath. The drive runs past stretches of wild flower meadow and stands of impressive trees, through which there are excellent views both across the park and up to the house. These light-splashed openings are all recent and owe their existence to much needed clearances by Lord Dunleath in recent years. As he and his team worked, all sort of surprises were thrown up, including a pond and several groves of magnolias that had been completely lost and forgotten under decades of rampant *Rhododendron ponticum* growth.

The greater gardens are chiefly comprised of a landscape park. In addition to the house, Lanyon also laid out a plan for the grounds and a great gardening programme was undertaken with 93,500 trees and shrubs planted in the winter of 1846. There are walks and rides past a lake through impressive stands of *Rhododendron falconeri* and *R. sinogrande*, which has huge leaves and creamy-yellow flowers. A series of streams meander through the park. Bridged waterways were also designed as part of a naturalistic, picturesque landscape. Informal plantings of ferns, rodgersia and primula edge the water. The views over the well positioned bridge, up toward the house or down to the woods, are like pictures of nature perfected. Among the small groves of trees there are two fine Monterey pines, both in the Irish Tree Register.

The house stands unhampered and handsome, on a terrace overlooking the park, with its European flag fluttering overhead. The restored conservatory was also designed by Lanyon. Along with the house, it had degenerated over the years until a major restoration of both began back in the 1960s. The work had been first recommended by the poet Sir John Betjeman when he visited for tea in 1961. In any case, after decades of work, the whole place sparkles today. Lord Dunleath is particularly proud of the work on the conservatory, and describes with pleasure the painstaking operation involved in getting the details right. I arrived on a

bright sunny day to see a gleaming edifice, full of citrus fruits and bananas in pots; showy displays of alpine pelargoniums on staging along the walls and an inviting table in the middle, set up with cake and tea. Unusually, instead of lilies in the little pond there were shoals of skittish tropical fish.

Behind the house, there are long wall-backed mixed borders full of scented fennel, hebe, euphorbia, tree peonies and mulberries. Leaning up against the wall, a dramatic red-flowering embothrium stands out, as it is not a tree often seen outside the shelter of a wood garden. Long draping lengths of wisteria cover the rest of the wall. The walk from here leads to the walled garden where four statues guard the entrance, goddesses depicting the four seasons, minus the wheat sheaf that Miss Summer should be carrying.

Inside the walls, take the rose walk under a red brick pergola, under-planted with cornflowers and sweet William. It leads to a whole range of glasshouses, the first of which is fronted by a line of tall cardoons. There are seven houses here. They are all still standing and some have been restored and now home succulents, nectarines, apricots and peaches. It is unusual to see so many houses still intact. I love the sunken house and the restored sheds. The work on these continues.

The fruit garden can be found behind a wall of

yew trees. The fruit trees themselves are divided into 12 sections. There are circles of espaliered trees and free-standing specimens.

The water garden out beyond the lawn has been worked on in recent years also. The stream, with the dripping stone waterfalls spotted earlier at the front of the house, is sided by little islanded rockeries, damp bog gardens full of primula and pink bog rush or *Butomus umbellatus*. A magnolia on top of a hillock in here charmed me and overhead, there are stands of rhododendron and parrotia, limes and cedars. The stumpery and a sweet chestnut straight out of Harry Potter rounded off yet another great visit.

Bangor Castle Gardens

Valentine Road, Castle Park, Bangor, Co Down. BT20 4BT. Tel: (0044 28) (048) 9127 1200. www.ardsandnorthdown.gov.uk Open: March-Oct. See website for seasonal changes. Wheelchair accessible. Children welcome. Dogs on leads. Special Features: Museum. Café. Arboretum, Walks. Guided tours can be arranged. Directions: In the centre of the town.

Looking at the last comment I made on the walled garden at Bangor Castle it read: 'Well done Bangor County Council.' On checking the official literature, I discovered that this should read 'Well done Ards and North Down Council'. In any case well done.

Start at the car park of the North Down Museum with its various exhibits including a fascinating history of local cinema. A walk around the gardens starts in the arboretum, between some suitably impressive trees. In particular, I passed a fine weeping lime, a *Pinus strobus* or Weymouth pine, *Ulmus carpinifolia*, the smooth leafed elm and a handsome *Metasequoia glyptostroboides*.

Having already enjoyed this, the entrance to the walled garden comes as something of a bonus. The restored garden covers 1.5 acres and has been open since 2009. Using the plans from the garden that the Ward family built here in the 1840s, the new design is divided into four quadrants, and sub-divided by long arched rose walks starring particularly fine scented roses. There are well presented vegetable plots and several double borders. My favourites were the dark borders with heavily scented *Rosa* 'Nuit de Young' and 'Falstaff', teamed with black cimicifuga and dark purple cotinus, carpets of *Sedum* 'Black Jack' and the darkest delphiniums imaginable. There were children enjoying a playful sort of maze made of grass paths between beds of wildflowers in all colours, with different cornflowers, poppies and soapwort. A well labelled young orchard takes up one of the quadrants and on the walls, some very versatile ways of training apples are worth studying.

The shaded wall holds a hosta collection and the huge rockery into which you take a sort of spiral path, between massive boulders, is well made. The ground here is damp and the seas of orange, yellow, apricot and pink primulas all smooching into each other, bear witness to that damp ground. The scent of *Primula japonica* 'Apple blossom' is delicious.

Beechgrove

Castlewellan Forest Park, Castlewellan, Co. Down. Tel:(0044 28) (048) 4377 8275. Contact: Mr. Sam Harrison. Open: By appointment all year. Groups welcome. Entrance fee donated to charity. Supervised children. Directions: Set within the forest park in the village of Castlewellan. The house is the first turn left inside the gates.

Sam Harrison was head forester at Castlewellan Arboretum for many years. Separately, he began working his own garden within the grounds of the arboretum in the 1970s and that garden became, unsurprisingly the plaything of a tree-besotted man. In recent years, his wife Esther arrived bearing more flowers and herbaceous perennials.

You would understandably expect plenty of special plants here, from a superior form of *Crinodendron hookerianum* 'Ada Hoffman' to a *Metasequoia glyptostroboides* 'Gold Rush'. You might not necessarily expect great design however. You would be mistaken. There is wit in this garden and it is as much a pleasure for the design inspired gardener as the plants man or woman. While you might marvel at a maturing Roblé beech (*Nothofagus obliqua*), its placement beside a little wooden hammock house that Sam built, does the tree further justice. A huge number of insects live on its trunk, making it an attractive tree for the birds, so the view show on from the hammock is a fascinating one. Walking under cathedral-height trees, a hooped metal moon gate with a bright thread of golden hop or *Humulus lupulus* 'Aureus' calls attention to itself. Elsewhere, a tree draped with blue glass bottles is also designed to stop you in your tracks.

The garden is arranged in peninsulas of layered grasses, perennials, shrubs and trees that jut into runs of perfect lawn, making a walk around the one-acre garden a zigzagging affair. We moved between lines of hostas and bamboos and trees like '*Eucryphia* 'Pink Cloud' which is 'a must' according to Sam. The good compositions were everywhere from maturing tetrapanax and fine podocarpus over iris, carex and bergenia, or well placed, maturing Japanese acers like rounded domes over hydrangea and ferns. He does obvious things that come as revelation to most of us, for instance, placing scented plants with the prevailing winds so the perfume wafts along the most used paths.

The rounded frog pond overflows into damp ground, making it ideal for hostas, primulas and ferns. Close by is a bronze work by Betty Newman Maguire, the sculptor known to Dubliners for her Viking longship on the Liffey quays. The garden is full of good and well placed sculptures.

One of his many pride and joy plants is the *Juniperus recurva* 'Castlewellan'. 'It had three upheavals before it came here, but it will not have to move again,' he promised.

A little trickle of water runs the length, of the rockery at the front of the house, fringed by tatting ferns, a dwarf lilac, fountains of royal fern and dierama. A spread of bearberry cotoneaster or *Cotoneaster dammeri*, closely contours the ground by a little humped bridge midway along. It is really handsome.

A whole array of plants conspire to hide the house under vegetation. Several sunny sitting areas by these green walls make meals an outdoor affair for much of the year which is fine because this is an all-year garden.

3 Brooklands Park

Manse Road, Newtownards, Co. Down, BT23 4XY. Tel: (0044 75) 6148 8367.
Contact: Miss Gillian Downing. Open: As part of the National Trust Open Garden Scheme. Contact for annual details or see the NT leaflet. Directions: On application.

Gillian Downing is a member of the Rose Society. She grows 123 different roses in her compact town garden, the majority of these in pots. This is a garden that even rain bucketing down could not wash out. Every conceivable inch is taken up with plants. They creep right out to the very edge of the footpath that runs past her garden. I envy the neighbours. This is a lesson in layered planting. Overhead, contorted hazel and hoheria, creamy yellow rhododendron bloom and grow, with evergreen *Clematis* 'Avalanche' and thornless *Rosa* 'Zephirine Drouhin' both clambering up the canopy. Rising up to meet the overhead canopy of acer and crab apple, there are also drifts of *Lychnis coronaria*, veronicastrum and lupins. Climb in between camellias, ribes and *Prunus serrula* on secreted paths that must become quite a squeeze as the season goes on.

Meanwhile the house walls are lost behind more climbers, include a sweetly scented soft yellow *Jasminum officinale* 'Clotted Cream' and *Luma apiculata* 'Variegata'. I left this jam-packed treat of a garden with the secret to the happy growing of roses in pots: You need rose fertiliser, grit and a feeding regime that starts in spring and continues until July, every six weeks. Stop at that point. Plant in big containers and change the top few cms of soil each year. Finally, stick to disease resistant varieties.

Castle Ward

Strangford, Downpatrick, Co. Down, BT30 7LS. Tel: (0044 28) (048) 44881204. Contact: Mike Gaston, Property Manager, or Andy Dainty, Head Gardener. Open: Grounds open all year, dawn–dusk. House, see seasonal changes on website. Partially wheelchair accessible. Groups welcome. Supervised children. Dogs on leads. Special features: Cottages to rent. Shops. Café. Farm museum. Rare-breed animals. Children's playground. Theatre facilities. Caravan site. Events. Directions: Travel on the A25 for 11km from Downpatrick or for 3 km from Strangford. The garden is well signposted from either approach.

Castle Ward is not as well known at it should be given its many attractions. To start with the house is an extraordinary place, seemingly the result of a disagreement between Bernard, Viscount Bangor, and his wife, Anne, who could not agree on an architectural style for their home. Their accommodating, anonymous architect created a compromise whereby the back of the house was designed in the Gothic, 'Strawberry Hill' style, according to Anne's tastes, while the front of the house reflected her husband's more sober, neoclassical preferences. To this day, the guides attest that women seem to take to the Gothic façade while men prefer the classical style. The house, which was built in the 1760s, overlooks Strangford Lough and is set in parkland filled with architectural features, including a temple set high on a hill over a massive man-made lake, replete with swans and several artificial islands. The 700-acre demesne also includes woods, farmyards and landscaped gardens.

The main garden lies at the bottom of a hill below the house, which stands on a ledge overlooking the pleasure grounds. A sunken lawn garden centres on a circular pond with a little statue of Neptune, whose modesty is guarded by a porpoise. Above this the walled walk is planted with cordyline, trachycarpus,

embothrium, pittosporum and clianthus, under which are healthy *Bergenia stracheyi*, *Sisyrinchium striatum*, melianthus and roses.

The garden today has changed from the original 18th century design. Today the style is mainly Victorian. Proof of this is found in an 1850s painting by Mary Ward, found hanging in the house. The painting depicts the garden as it can still be seen. The Irish yews that dominate one side of the sunken lawn can be seen in the painting, as can the banks and cordylines that now take up so much space. The garden went on to become a rose garden. The roses were taken out about 20 years ago and replaced by shrubs and a selection of perennials from veronicastrum and agapanthus to nemesia and mallow. One interesting development in this garden is a new 'yew' hedge, actually an experimental hedge of podocarpus.

The pleasure grounds include a Victorian rock garden and a pet cemetery where the names of the interred animals are spelled out in snowdrops. The rock garden is a fine specimen, full of red armeria, saxifraga, echium, ginger lilies and watsonias.

Among the groves of specimen trees, one of the more important is possibly the biggest griselinia in these islands, with a girth of almost three metres, which stands almost unnoticed beside two gangly, adolescent, 150-year-old Wellingtonia (*Sequoiadendron giganteum*).

Seven acres of lawn have been planted with drifts of daffodils. One walking route out through the park (not explored by nearly enough visitors), is that leading toward the original Audley's Castle and past a temple, ice house and lake. This path also passes a large grove of yew. Once upon a time a walk through these was likened to walking through a cathedral. However, in desperate need of rejuvenation, these have been pruned back very hard and it will be a number of years before they return to their former grandeur. A new avenue of limes leads to where a previous Ward home once stood, with views of Strangford Lough and Scrabo Tower.

The walled garden is now empty, but its semicircular wall is impressive. One elderly man who worked here as a young boy was able to provide the gardeners with the information to draw up a plan of the walled garden as it was in the early 20th century. Should the chance to restore the garden present itself, they will have an authentic base from which to work.

Castle Ward is the most complete estate in the care of the National Trust in Northern Ireland, surrounded by seven miles of walls, with a laundry, farm, corn mills, pleasure grounds and meadows. The farmyard is popular for school groups and it contains watermills, animal pens, now used for rare-breed animals and walks along 'cattle creeps', built to keep the livestock out of view as they were moved around the estate. The walks continue out to the lough. When I visited, there was a Viking longboat parked at a boathouse, making ready for a re-enactment of a raid on the estate.

A fine garden, interesting historic estate walks, an impressive working yard, a collection of rare farm animals and the Vikings: If the family cannot fill a day here, there can be no hope for it.

Castlewellan Forest Park

Castlewellan, Newcastle, Co. Down. Tel: (0044 28) (048) 4377 8664. e-mail: customer.forestservice@dardni.gov.uk Contact: Reception. Supervised children. Dogs on leads. Open: All year. 10am-dusk. Groups welcome. Special features: Maze. Tearoom. Adventure centre. Tours and forest walks can be booked. Conference centre in castle. Caravan parking. Directions: Situated in the village of Castlewellan.

The Annesley family moved to Castlewellan, north of the Mourne Mountains, in the mid -1700s, and between that time and the 1960s they built, gardened and created a demesne of outstanding beauty in the hilly landscape of south County Down. In 1967 the grounds were acquired by the Northern Ireland Forest Service and opened as a national arboretum.

The house dates only to 1856, but the walled garden was created in 1740 when the family first arrived. In 1874 the 5th Lord Annesley began to develop the arboretum, initially confining his work to the 12 acre walled area but over the years moving out to the greater parkland. He realised that Castlewellan's favourable microclimate, created by the shelter provided by Slieve Donard, would allow him to plant exotics in his garden. It was he who planted many of the more unusual trees and shrubs that grace the estate today. Planting continued through the years, and under the care of the forestry service the arboretum has grown to over 100 acres. It is acknowledged to be one of the most outstanding tree and shrub collections in Europe, and a regular attraction for enthusiasts from all over the world.

The Annesley walled garden is the focal point of Castlewellan. It dates back to 1740 when it was built as a kitchen garden, alongside the pleasure grounds. It was built on a slope and contains yet more fine trees – at one point the visitor stands, like an ant, under a huge pair of Wellingtonias or *Sequoiadendron giganteum* or a multi-trunked *Chamaecyparis pisifera* 'Squarrosa'.

A few steps past these, stop and overlook the garden and the canopy of rare conifers, rhododendron and Japanese acers. A number of plants carry the garden name, including the much-loved *Juniperus recurva* 'Castlewellan' and the rather less loved *Cupressocyparis leylandii* 'Castlewellan Gold'. There are so many beautiful trees. In May, the fire bush or *Embothrium coccineum* from Chile, dazzles with bright red flowers. Later in the year a eucryphia walk produces a mass of creamy-white flowers as beautiful as cherry blossom. Podocarpus and southern beech are also planted in numbers.

The large walled garden is divided into two gardens and separated by a gate guarded by two huge, wobbly Irish yews. In the top garden, a double border of *Paeonia lutea*, geranium, yellow iris, echium, poppies and daylilies rises up to a fountain and pond surrounded by mixed ferns and the gaudiest azaleas in a range of dazzling shades. The mixed border continues uphill, backed by yew hedges. Colourful runs of London pride, rodgersia and acanthus share the bed with two huge eucalyptus trees.

Castlewellan is a space in which the visitor is constantly distracted and side-stepped by one great tree after another. Attempting to admire the famous Castlewellan juniper, one is pulled away by a gorgeous weeping *Cedrus deodara* 'Pendula', with one-metre-long branches, and a big Algerian fir or *Abies numidica*. Great topples of yew line the paths and the huge west Himalayan spruce (*Picea smithiana*) is only one of 50 varieties of picea in the garden.

Outside the walls, spring gardens of heathers and dwarf conifer, autumn tree walks, ponds and cherry groves are only some of the many attractions. There is a good day's work to be spent trying to see the full extent of Castlewellan. Happily, a period of neglect has come to an end and there has been welcome rejuvenation in the garden. So far this has included scrub clearance, replanting and impressive repairs on the greenhouse which was being readied for replanting when I last visited. Standing up on its ledge, the view over the newly cleared pink trunks of arboreal rhododendrons sent me home happy.

Coille

15 Finnebrogue Road, Downpatrick, BT309AA. Co. Down. Tel: (0044 28) (048) 4461 1266
Contact: Agnes and John Peacock. Open: As part of the National Trust Open Gardens Scheme. See leaflet
for annual details. Directions: On application.

John Peacock told me that when he and Agnes arrived here to set up home 19 years ago, the last occupants had been some chickens. The buildings they took on included a set of ancient kennels, a dairy and and a cow byre once inhabited by a herd of fancy short horn cattle.

The Peacocks are not people to be put off and two decades later their little bit of heaven in the hills of County Down is just that, floriferous, informal, quite wild and full of good things. The house walls host *Clematis armandii*, honeysuckle and sweetly scented *Rhododendron luteum*. The various outhouses and remains have been turned into quirky garden compartments, used to make ledge gardens and raised beds where they keep containers of alpines. (They are members of the Alpine Garden Society.) Unusual slate drinking troughs were reincarnated as water features and harts tongue ferns sprout from the old walls.

One little wall-enclosed area now lives on as a sunny sitting room, decorated with pots of agapanthus and alpines, all satisfyingly near eye level for close inspection. A fruiting fig peeps over one half-wall and a pink *Rosa* 'Dortmund' over another. Leaving this series of intimate garden areas around the house, we walked out along a line of golden upright yews over runs of variegated *Euonymus fortunei* and equally golden *Rosa* 'Graham Stuart Thomas'.

We walked past mixed borders, full of Japanese acers, camellias and *Rosa glauca,* as well as black *Sambucus niger,*' over splashes of *Salvia involucrata*. There are unusual shrubs, like the gorgeous *Stachyurus praecox*, a shrub with great dangling spring flowers, in all directions. Sunny beds of *Cephalaria gigantea*, delphiniums and day lilies stand in front of taller cotinus and golden cornus.

The pond started life as a hole dug to accommodate a tree, which says a lot about the levels of water in the ground here. Today, it is surrounded by a run of hairy *Bergenia ciliata* with hosta, erythronium and primula.

Darker corners, under the shade of tall surrounding trees, abound. Figuring out what would do well in this shade took the Peacocks a long time but the experiment has been a success. They teamed up kirengeshoma and monkshood under a golden elm that according to Agnes 'lights up like a light bulb'. We walked under eucryphia and beech, past more camellias and under an arch of *Exochorda korolkowii*. They think this is a better performer than the more usually seen *E.* 'The Bride'.

They love their irises, particularly *Iris sibirica* so there are lots scattered through the place, even in the shade, including the delectable black *Iris chrysographes,* Japanese water iris or *Iris ensata,* and *Iris louisiana,* a hard-to-mind species that likes both water and heat. Looking up, we admired a pair of buzzards, giving their fledgling a flying lesson.

Glenkeen

12 Dunlevy Road, Portaferry, Co. Down. Tel: (0044 28) (048) 4277 2418. e-mail: mikem4498@gmail.com Contact: Mr. and Mrs. Mike and Ann Miall. Open: May-Sept. By appointment only. Partially wheelchair accessible. Children over 10. No dogs. Special features: Teas can be arranged in aid of Poraferry Lifeboat. Directions: On application.

An atmosphere of industry and endeavour runs through this attractive garden on the windy Ards Peninsula. It is clear that Mike and Ann enjoy working the fertile soil, after years of trying to work the hard clay of Lincoln in England.

'We're like children in a sweet shop,' Ann said as we stood at the front gate looking at the young apple orchard, the two giants, *Rosa* 'Paul's Himalayan Musk' and 'Rambling Rector' putting a big ash tree to the test, over puffs of hydrangea and little avenues of hellebore beneath.

From here it is all go. We investigated a young stumpery being created out on the boundary and walked under a rose pergola from which we could see Scrabo Tower in the distance. Ann told me that the golden hop came with her from England to join the camellias, rhododendrons and cornus. In the flower beds, two metre tall peacock blue, *Salvia concolor* proved that the going is indeed good here, as did healthy stands of lilies and beefy agapanthus. Beyond the slate, stone and fern water feature, we made our way into the vegetable garden where the real action begins.

Built around smart wooden trellises, they grow and train thornless blackberries and tayberries over beds of sage and chives, parsley, strawberries and lines of irises. All woven together, the flowers, herbs, fruit and vegetables are as pretty to look at as they are useful in the kitchen. Mike particularly recommended the Irish apple, 'Ecklinville' a good looker and tasty cooker raised here in County Down, near the village of Portaferry. Do ask to see the wood turning shed before leaving. These are talented people.

The Grange

The Grange, 35 Ballyrogan Park, Newtownards, Co. Down. Tel: (00 44 28) (048) 91 821451 Contact: Gary Dunlop. Open: Weekends and evenings in the summer, by appointment only. Telephone for an appointment either at about 8am or after dark. Groups welcome. Entrance fee donated to charity. Not a garden for a family outing. Special features: National collections of euphorbia, celmisia and crocosmia.

Mr. Dunlop's garden covers about three acres and is situated on an exposed site at the northern end of the Ards Peninsula. A lush, mature garden filled with great plants, it comes as something of a surprise at the top of a windswept hill. The garden is well planted, perhaps one might even say stuffed, a plantaholic heaven. At every turn there are colourful specimens to study and with which to fall in love. Woodland plants and bulbs are grown in the terraced and raised beds. Shrubs and trees range along the paths in colourful waves of *Acer griseum* and *Garrya elliptica,* pruned up podocarpus and spiky *Trachycarpus fortunei* over lower storey planting of hellebore, camassia and geranium. At the highest point in the garden is a natural rock garden that houses Mr. Dunlop's national collection of celmisia. Great rock formations, sometimes with waterfalls of cotoneaster tumbling down, both natural and manmade, create a backdrop for the plantings of both the ordered collections and the informal mixed beds. The views from the celmisia rock encompass the whole of County Down, the Mournes, the Isle of Man and Scotland.

A separate garden, covering half an acre, faces south. This contains a collection of South African plants, like crocosmia, agapanthus, roscoea, angel's fishing rods or dierama, schizostylis and watsonia, phormium, phlox and euphorbia. Throughout the garden statuary has been used to frame views and redirect the visitor. Thriving plants encroach on little paths and the walker must pick their way gingerly through beds of agapanthus and red hot pokers or kniphofia, allium and penstemon. Notebook at the ready....

Forth Cottage

67 Lisnacroppin Road, Rathfriland, Co. Down. BT34 5NZ. Tel: Tel: (0044 28) (048) 4065 1649. Contact: Helen Harper. Open: By appointment to groups of ten and under. Directions: On application.

I would have stopped at this attractive cottage garden for a quick look even if I did not know it was the open garden for which I was hunting. Helen Harper's cottage stands on the side of the country lane, behind an informal and pretty flower garden set into the roadside gravel. Orchids, irises, *Verbena bonariensis*, lavender and celmisia are not your usual side-of-the-road flowers. In the spring there are crocuses too. 'But no snowdrops. It is too dry for them.' Helen explained.

This was her granny's and her mother's garden. It is her modern, cool style however that sets this cottage garden apart. Having been charmed by the front, and what Helen can do in a restricted situation, I should not have been surprised to find something special behind the house in the main attraction.

If there is one word that would sum up the whole creation it would be *detail*. Everywhere in this very flower filled place, the detailing is what sets it apart. From the repeat use of *Viola cornuta* as a binding and unifying plant to the use of smartly presented troughs, from paths edged with tufts of silver raoulia spiked with little dactylorhiza, to well-maintained borders and raked pea gravel paths, the details of this garden are all spot on. Add to these an eye for colour and it is a winner. Pink *Nepeta racemosa* 'Amelia' drapes alongside blue nepeta out over the path. Intense blue *Allium sikkimense* is used to great effect as well.

'I pack everything in,' Helen told me. On the walls around the garden, there are 'Arthur Bell' roses and clematis, while on the ground there are different shades of purple heuchera, penstemon and violas. Helen grows her violas from seed, removing the poor performers at an early stage.

The garden is divided into rooms. We took a gate into another area, through a wall draped in wisteria, akebia and *Clematis viticella*. This led to the field bank garden, where she grows different thymes on a sunny dry stone wall bed, mixed with blue campanula. These are glorious when the thyme is in flower. *Euphorbia*

'white swan' and golden oregano add their bit to the show too, surrounded by an arc of ferns and white digitalis,

The rude health of a swamp cypress or *Taxodium distichum* seems to run counter to the dry free-draining, sandy conditions here. Under the cypress, an arrangement of boulders being colonised by mint and white *Viola cornuta*, is gorgeous and scented. A smart beech hedge encloses this garden room. From here the garden changes again, morphing into something looser, with native hedges and tall grass spiked with wild orchids, ox-eyed daisies and yellow rattle.

I love the mastery and control that still allows for exuberance.

Glenmount

34 Dunlady Road, Dundonald, Belfast, BT16 1TT. Co. Down. Tel: (0044 28) (048) 9041 9717. Mob (0044 78) 0821 6446. Contact: Nick Burrowes. Open: Nursery and garden: Telephone for an appointment. Not wheelchair accessible. Groups welcome. Supervised children welcome. Dogs on leads. Special features: Nursery selling plants and herbs from the garden. Directions: Travelling from Belfast to Dundonald, pass the Ulster Hospital and turn left at the second main set of traffic lights after that. The garden is 1.6 km along the Dunlady Road on the left, at the top of the hill.

Nick Burrowes' garden is an informal, relaxed place on a sunny hill that looks across at Scrabo Hill and Tower. The plot rises up from the back of his house in a riot of shrubs, trees and herbaceous perennials, vegetables and herbs. Since I last visited, much has happened. It went through a period of time when Nick was unable to work it and this led to some serious growth that he is now in the process of bringing under control.

Cloud pruning many of the large shrubs has been his favoured way of bringing light and space back into the mature garden as he rejuvenates it. Nick created the garden in the mid-1990s and propagated most of the plants himself, building up a collection of mints, which are now dispersed among the beds. We walked on grass paths between beds of these, including sweet little *Prostanthera rotundifolia* with bell-shaped, purple flowers. The garden design is simple, almost like one large hillside bed with wide paths cut through it. The plant combinations are good: In one bed blue lobelia, variegated golden euonymus, white creeping nettle and a rich, dark, glossy-leaved pittosporum sport

together easily. We passed the summerhouse, fringed with *Bergenia ciliata*, the hairy bergenia, teamed with erigeron and a fine lavender hedge. These beefy plants were raised from seed. The unusual pond made from a series of Belfast sinks is a witty touch, as is the oak circle Nick was restoring as I visited.

Swathes of what he calls 'savage hostas' make for a lush, cool look in one corner while tall *Echium pininana* towers above the grass path further along. Masses of colour, texture and the smells of thyme, rosemary, apple, spearmint, onions and roses, leave the senses boggled and satisfied in equal measure. A small working nursery beside the garden allows visitors to bring home a few pots of herbs as a souvenir of a visit.

Walking around with Nick is an entertaining and informative experience, particularly in relation to the herbs. One of the things I learned was that wormwood or artemisia, when dry-fried and then lit, will rid a house of flies.

Grey Abbey House

Grey Abbey, Newtownards Co. Down. BT22 2QA Tel: (0044 28) (048) 4278 8666. Contact: The Hon. Mrs. Montgomery. e-mail: daphnemontgomery@greyabbeyestates.com. www.greyabbeyhouse.com Open: To groups by appointment. Not wheelchair accessible. Special features: House and garden tours. Refreshments can be arranged. Directions: In the village of Grey Abbey.

Grey Abbey House stands on a hill overlooking the Cistercian Abbey after which it was named on the Ards Peninsula, as well as Strangford Lough.

The Montgomery family have lived here since 1604, building, improving and laying out grounds. They continue developing the gardens to this day.

There are some fine old and existing shrub, wood and flower gardens, walled kitchen gardens and parkland. Certain plants stick in the mind, such as an old cork oak with character to spare. Standing on a lawn leading out from the house, it sprouts ferns from its fork.

The house looks down over a sweep of parkland bounded by mature trees, but the first of the gardens is accessed in by the side of the house where a little path

disappears into a shrub border graced by a dramatic red *Rosa chinensis* 'Bengal Crimson' mixed with the purple candlesticks of *Echium canadensis*.

This lands you on a croquet lawn, leading into to another, slightly more secret lawn. The view off across the park, between trees, is of the ruined abbey.

The mixed borders backed by barns and outhouses are busy and attractive with a mix of black *Sambucus niger* and *Rosa glauca*, black persicaria and phormium with white hydrangea and foxgloves. Tall blue salvias and delphiniums, phlox and lupin vie for attention before the path leads off toward the walled garden, and a walk through the woods.

The most recent feature is the Southern hemisphere garden at the bottom of the hill, surrounded by sheltering woods, hidden behind the strealing skirts of great old oaks.

Grass paths run between the tall semi-shaded shrub and tree groves of embothrium, azara and abutilon over woodwardia ferns. High overhead, tall Scots pines cast dappled shade on the big mounds of gunnera in the seas of grass below. Arboreal rhododendron and young nothofagus, crinodendron and restio do well in the partial light and moist soil here too. With baby dawn redwoods, this is a young jungle in development decorated by strange sculptural works like great totem poles, a good opportunistic use of some deceased Scots pines.

At the bottom, I discovered a swan lake complete with swans.

Grey Abbey Physic Garden

Grey Abbey, Co. Down. Tel: (0044 28) (048) 4278 8585.
Open: April-Sept., Tues-Sat, 10am-7pm. Sun, 2pm–6pm. Groups by appointment. Wheelchair accessible. Supervised children. Dogs on leads Special features: Monastic ruins. Directions: Situated in the middle of Grey Abbey village.

In the Middle Ages, abbeys, monasteries and religious houses created many of the most important early gardens in Europe. The monks ran orchards, kitchen gardens and medicinal or physic gardens to feed and care both for themselves and for their visitors. At the Cistercian abbey of Grey Abbey, the monks would have been as self-sufficient as their brethren throughout Christendom.

The physic garden at Grey Abbey is a small garden laid out in the grounds of the 12h century abbey. Historical records and archaeological information on the makeup of physic gardens were called on to help in the design. The results of these investigations is a plot created along the lines of a medicinal herb garden from the Middle Ages, but it is of necessity an interpretation of what such a garden might have been like. No actual gardens of the sort remain intact anywhere.

Each bed was designed for practicality, holding a single herb and fenced in by woven wicker hurdles. They make a simple but pretty overall picture of usual and unusual herbs. A small information centre is attached to the garden where the medicinal uses for each of the various herbs are explained. I noted that mugwort wards off evil, and rue can be used against witches and the plague. But betony must take a bow as it can cure 47 different diseases.

Guincho

69 Craigdarragh Road, Helen's Bay, Co. Down. Tel: (0044 78) 0821 6446. Contact: Nick Burrowes, Head Gardener. Open: April–Sept., by appointment to groups of 15 or more and for charity days (see local press or National Trust Garden Scheme for details). Not wheelchair accessible. Supervised children. Dogs on leads. Directions: From the Belfast to Bangor road (A2), take the Craigdarragh Road. The garden is 0.5 km along on the left-hand side.

The gardens at Guincho are known as one of the best private gardens on the island. They were created by Mrs. Vera Mackie in 1948 on a sloped, 12-acre wooded site near the County Down coast.

Guincho suggests to the visitor however that it has been here for a lot longer than just over 70 years, particularly in the case of the four acres of woodland. The garden is substantial, full of variety and beautifully maintained. In 1982 it was added to the Northern Ireland register of gardens of outstanding historical importance.

This is a place of huge sweeping lawns enclosed in a wide collar of woods, filled with unusual and rare plants, some of which came from the Kingdon Ward plant gathering expeditions as well as from collectors such as Lord Talbot of Malahide. The woods contain and shelter long walks past substantial swathes of bulbs, ferns and hydrangea, beneath sheltering oak, pine, eucryphia, cordyline and rhododendron. Winding, mossy paths open every so often onto expanses of lawn, letting in daylight and views across the garden, to well-designed combinations like the massive silver fir beside a large plantation of gunnera or a sea of blue hydrangea.

The path leads alongside a huge *Cryptomeria japonica* that looks like a monster climbing-frame or a single-tree adventure playground. Continuing along, the stream garden takes up another clearing that feels tropical, full of wet tree ferns and trachycarpus. The mood changes again as it reaches an oak, ash, chestnut and beech wood. The paths rise and fall down to the stream, leading eventually to a grove of large-leaved rhododendron.

Emerge from the wood to a cultivated area of lawns edged with myrtle and willow, with splashes of geranium, *Fascicularia pitcairnifolia* and cotoneaster draping over a stone wall. Among the special plants found at Guincho is a handsome *Rehderodendron macrocarpum,* a rare plant with creamy flowers and shiny, tapered leaves.

In the area close to the house there are smaller, more domestic-sized garden rooms with select and unusual small trees and flowering shrubs knotted through with climbers. The round garden contains the champion *Pseudopanax crassifolius* as well as the original *Sambucus nigra* 'Guincho Purple', a famous shrub, with blackish-purple leaves and pale-pink flowers. It was found growing in a hedge by Mrs. Mackie in the Scottish highlands in the 1960s. She took cuttings and grew them on. She gave some of these to Sir Harold Hillier whose nursery brought it into cultivation. The original still grows here.

The terraces and balconies around the house are decorated with old varieties of apples and pears trained as balcony fences. Standing on the terrace, looking down from a height, over these and to flowering magnolias and cherries in the garden below is an experience, especially when the full scent of coconut wafts towards you from the double gorse. One last touch is the slim arch of cotoneaster wound tightly around and over the front door.

Hillsborough Castle Garden

Main Street, Hillsborough, Co. Down. Tel: (0044 28) (048) 9268 1300.
e-mail: hillsboroughcastle@hrp.org.uk www.hrp.org.uk/hillsborough-castle Open: Grounds open daily.
Wheelchair accessible. Supervised children. See website for changing seasonal times. Special features: Royal
Palace. House tours. Exhibitions. Events. Directions: In the centre of the town.

I arrived at the soft, coloured sand stone gate way of Hillsborough Castle with no notion of what treat awaited me beyond the gatehouse and the mannerly gents who guard it in their livery and top hats. This is a tremendous garden and apparently, one due to become even more tremendous. I visited, having been told that it was 'still a work in progress.' Would that all

half finished landscape projects looked so wonderful.

From the informal planting directly into the York stone terrace in front of the castle, I was smitten. The wide expanse of stone slabs has been gently interrupted by irregular little tufts and compositions of iris and lavender, thyme, fennel and *Verbena bonariensis*. On a warm day, perfume adds another element to the pleasure of this place. The style is soft and un-stuffy. There are puffs of pink *Lychnis coronaria* and hardy geraniums too. As Dolly Parton nearly said: 'It takes a lot of effort to look this effortless.' Enjoy it from within, then enjoy it from without, from a seat in the little temple that also looks down the sloped walks to the pond and fountain.

The white garden with its tall wands of foxglove and monarda, brunnera and campanula is another and different sort of charming garden room. Stands of *Cornus kousa* and box walls deliver more permanent structure to the airy, seasonal flowers. Throughout the grounds the raked gravel paths feels as though they were raked only moments before you walked on them.

Follow an opening through a hedge like Alice down the rabbit hole and land in the rose garden, all formal beds full of good roses, cut into perfect grass, overseen by big mixed herbaceous perennial beds. The white roses trained on wires over a bed of lime *Alchemilla mollis* is an infinitely stealable idea. Taking another gate out, the paths divide, travelling in different directions, toward the castle and deeper into the grounds, where an inspection of the commemorative trees could fill a few hours. A new lime tree avenue has been planted to mirror a mature one nearby, and restored yew walks lead down to the lake and Temple.

The riverside walks are a glory, shaded and green, between moss covered rocks and abundant ferns. The river trips down in little falls and is bridged in a few places too. Stone overhangs, green with self-seeders, seem to have been built to mesmerise. The views down along the valley are equally handsome, drawing the eye towards compositions of trees and shrubs in the distance. Seeing baby acers planted beside mature specimens, well into their second century is a rare sight.

Clouds of rhododendrons and well ordered shrubberies and plantations of trees, draw you on and on and out through the park. The land is hilly. It dips and ducks under a sweet chestnut here and a weeping willow there. There are iconic cedars of Lebanon and spreading oaks, each one distracting from its neighbour. Continue along and the way leads into a pinetum, suitably shaded and atmospheric under tall chamaecyparis and thuja, cedrus and abies. Did I mention the perfectly raked gravel?

11 Longlands Road

Island Hill, Comber, Co. Down. Tel: (0044 28) (048) 9187 2441. Mobile: (0044 77) 59424997. Contact: David McMurren. www.ulstergardensscheme.org.uk Open: For one weekend each year. Contact in spring for details. Partially wheelchair accessible. Directions: On application.

As we picked our way along what is really an insinuation of a gravel path between an explosion of fennel and delphinium, orange lilies and astrantia, potentilla and spotted aucuba, I thought to myself that David McMurren does like to do things his own way. I had spent the last summer being reminded of the importance of a good wide path – The wider the better in many cases, wide enough to fit two people side by side comfortably. Not here. David likes a path just wide enough for one to squeeze along. 'More room for plants' was his explanation.

David has been developing this garden since 1989 and in that time he has learned much about maximising space. As an example of this at the front gate we looked at a *Philadelphus* 'Belle Etoile' hosting *Rosa* 'Zephirine Drouhin', doubling the floral possibilities of both plants without taking up any extra space.

The plants wash right up to the edges of the building and the garden seems as though it might invade the house: A bulging hosta pond placed right beside one of the windows gives the indoor onlooker more to look at than any television. The *Acer palmatum* 'Osakazuki' beside this is under-lit, so it can be seen and enjoyed from indoors at night, as well during the day. He uses lights widely through the garden in this way.

At the front of the house the are two long serpentine herbaceous borders, with perfect striped lawns and well maintained box walls that I remember seeing on my last visit. There have been fairly dramatic changes. Shrubs have replaced much of the grass, and very successfully. Acer and berberis, miscanthus and rose, eucryphia and choisya are more fun than grass.

Hedges are a vital part of this garden. Their straight, smart, green lines frame and enclose, divide and wrap around swathes of herbaceous plants and create little garden rooms, for sitting and dining. This is a virtuoso small garden, in which David manages to pack a huge number of plants and features into a site of only half an acre.

From each little space there are a number of views across hedges or through arches into other rooms and areas. Add real skill in choosing plant combinations and a perfectionist's attention to detail and the result is a polished gem of a garden.

There are sharp ideas at play everywhere, like the 'secret' gravel walk down the centre of a wide herbaceous border already mentioned, designed to do more than than space save.

From head-on, this appears to be one solid border. But a little path through it turns it into two, and the splashes of Jacobs's ladder, daylilies and aconites can be enjoyed from different angles as one walks between them. Close by, what looks like the outside of a large maze, is in effect an unusually shaped and placed privet hedge, that splits the space.

Working the soil to this extent means that the garden needs to be kept very fertile. Liberal doses of organic matter are required with the sandy free-draining soil if everything is to be maintained at full tilt.

Expansion onto the outer boundaries, seen previously, has continued and today, along the outside of the hedge, there is a long colourful border of lavender, penstemon and Californian poppies.

Moira Demesne

High Street, Moira, Co. Down. Open: Daily all day. Directions: On High Street.

The demesne at Moira was once famed for its collection of trees, many dating back to the 18th century plant hunting expeditions. Today the 40 acres of parkland are still picturesque, with some of the old trees still here to be enjoyed. Previously constant mowing has been replaced with more judicious and less frequent cutting and the reappearance of meadow species is welcome. Some box beds and herbaceous borders can be seen out at the front of the park. On my recent visit, these looked at though they needed attention however. The village of Moira is a charming one, and worth visiting too.

Montalto

Ballynahinch, Co. Down. BT24 8AY. Tel: (0044 28) (048) 9756 6100. e-mail:info@montaltoestate.com Contact: Keith. Open: To groups by appointment. Partially wheelchair accessible. Special features: Venue hire. Events. Tea room. Occasional open days. Catering can be arranged. See website for details. Directions: In the town of Ballynahinch.

In the late 1700s Lord Rawdon, the Earl of Moira, set the tone of the estate at Montalto for centuries to come by planting thousands of exotic trees from the first of the plant hunting expeditions to the New World. The glorious and mature trees ranged around this large estate are partially thanks to that auspicious start. Although Montalto would become known less for its trees than as being the site of the Battle of Ballynahinch for much of its history.

The house and grounds have gone through several owners in their time. There have been house fires and neglect, periods of wealth and hard times. Since 1994 however, Montalto's latest owners have been restoring and renewing both house and gardens in a massive project that will see it take its place among the best gardens on the island.

I have seldom seen a feature quite as beautiful as the perfect, formal garden by the house with its statue of Mercury on a soft sandstone circle, surrounded by box, lavender and clipped bay. The amalgamation of vivid lavender, smart green foliage and soft sandy colours, is divine.

The house looks out over a park and lake, which seems to be fish shaped. There are plantations of trees, including champion liquidambars and sycamores. A summerhouse, the remains of which were found on a slope overlooking the water and park, was restored and rebuilt.

This lake, far from being simply decorative, was put to good use and almost emptied in the 1970s when it was needed to put out a huge fire in the house.

A rockery, made from natural rock formations has been augmented by more imported stone and restored. In the meadows and along various avenues of trees, great drifts of spring daffodils have been planted. Soft mulch paths were laid out to open the extensive woods, leading in places, to wood gardens. The woods have undergone great clearances of scrub and *Rhododendron ponticum* and the cleaned spaces have been planted with ferns and native bluebells. Today rather than the accursed ponticum, enjoy runs of *Rhododendron arboreum* and *R.* 'Altaclarensis', *R. macabeanum* and scores of other species and varieties.

The hilly land so characteristic of Ballynahinch has been employed to accommodate rising and falling paths between copses of trees and shrubs, including magnolias, stewartias and cornus. Spot-planting of blue hydrangeas look wonderful in the distance under tall and ancient oak.

The carriage rooms were restored and are surrounded by rather cool but colourful modern flower gardens and replanted orchards. Then there is a restored walled garden with lawns enclosed by box and yew walls, rose arches and wall trained fruit trees, as well as a greenhouse. The long borders are once again full of nepeta and lupin, hosta, campanula and lavender.

Leading away from here, a grassed-through orchard, planted up with Irish heritage apples, leads to the river and a waterfall. We finished our visit in a new cutting garden. This is a real colour treat in an outlying field, pretty in itself, but also supplying the house with flowers. Something about the simplicity of the straight lines and big busy blooms charmed me as much as all the grandeur.

Mount Stewart

Newtownards, Portaferry Road, Newtownards, Co. Down. BT22 2AD. Tel: (0044 28)(048) 4278 8387 / 4278 8487. e-mail: mountstewart@nationaltrust.org.uk www. ulstergardenscheme.org.uk. Contact: Neil Porteus. Open: Mar., daily, 10am-4pm. April, daily, 10.am-6pm. May-Sept., 10am-8pm. Oct., daily, 10am-6pm. Partially wheelchair accessible. Supervised children. Dogs on leads. Special features: Tearoom. Shop. House and garden tours. Events. Directions: Situated on the A20 between Newtownards and Portaferry.

Everything about Mount Stewart is aimed to impress: The fact that it already covered 90 acres, but has recently been added to by an additional 900, sets the tone. Visitors adore the enormous variety within its many gardens, the care employed in its upkeep and the wit of the design. It is a horticultural place of excellence.

The house is an impressive pile in honey-coloured stone, unusually not standing in splendid isolation on a lawn or on a wide spread of gravel but in the middle of a jungle of the finest plants, doing battle with vegetation for attention, clambered over by *Rosa gigantea* and a collection of other climbers and 'leaners'. Even the paving around it sprouts lavender, crinum lilies and *Desmodium elegans*. Tall, peeling eucalyptus, elegant conifers and seas of variegated phlox, waving anemones, great Florence Court yews, cordylines, clipped bays, irises and a thousand other plants, do everything they can to distract from the house.

The garden was designed by Edith, Lady Londonderry, in the 1920s. When she arrived to live in Mount Stewart, she declared it a 'damp and depressing' place, situated as it was between the Irish Sea and Strangford Lough on the Ards Peninsula. Employing first 20, then another 20 and yet another 20 gardeners and ex-servicemen, she set to turning her ideas of a garden into reality. By the time she had finished, Mount Stewart was home to an extraordinary series of gardens. The damp climate, once thought to be its drawback, allowed her to grow a great number of tender plants. As a result, the place has more than a touch of the tropics about it. Tree ferns, *Podachaenium eminens* or the Mexican giant daisy tree, acacias and olive trees all grow happily in the temperate climate.

This was designed as a pioneering garden, and not one to be frozen in aspic. Thankfully, it continues to be a pioneering place. It has come into the new century firing on all cylinders, using Edith's garden notebooks as a loose reference. Neil Porteus, head gardener, is fascinated by this suffragist and magpie garden designer and builder, who regularly cornered unsuspecting visitors with a wheelbarrow and an order to, 'go and weed Bluebell Wood', after a quickly scoffed down lunch.

The rethinking of the garden is an ongoing process and so it continues to fascinate and engage visitors. Experiments are evident everywhere, from the borders around the house to the recently cleared woods where

substantial new rhododendron and tree fern gardens are being planted up using seed from recent seed hunting expeditions. Back in Lady Edith's day, 300 rhododendrons came to Mount Stewart from the Frank Kingdon Ward expedition.

Work on an eight acre outer walled garden with an ornamental dairy, is beginning. Hunt out the famous yew hedges on top of which romp devils, hunters, the whole Londonderry family in a boat, riders on horseback and stags. These topiary figures were created from grafted Irish common yew, and now increasingly, Chilean yew. Only a few of the characters are left of the original 30 but work to restore the lost, as well as redefine the existing figures is well in hand, and can be studied as it goes on. Mount Stewart's most famous feature has also been smartened up: the Shamrock garden with its huge Red Hand of Ulster picked out in red bedding, begonias and double daisies set into gravel. The hand is set off against a green topiary harp, which towers four and a half metres over it.

The most evocative of all the gardens is the Mairi garden, created for Edith's daughter, Lady Mairi. This was where the little girl would be brought for her daily turn in the pram. A little bronze fountain incorporates a statue of baby Mairi spraying water at unsuspecting visitors. The original layout of this garden was drawn up by the English gardener Graham Stuart Thomas, who planned it as a rose garden. The roses never quite took however, and the planting has been changed several times in the pursuit of getting it to work perfectly.

There are wonderful statues of gryphons, turtles, crocodiles and dodos scattered throughout the Ark Garden, references to historical, cheeky, political and family in-jokes. The great bay umbrellas and drums, flanking the house were bought for £99 8s 9d as a job lot in the 1920s. They still look divine. Look under their skirts to see the frames.

The formal gardens are broken into large 'rooms.' Between the Spanish and Italian gardens, the huge, iconic leylandii cypress or *Cupressocyparis leylandii* hedge is cut with nail scissors' perfection into a series of arches that resemble a huge green viaduct. Saline incursion into the Lough is causing concern and could cause long term problems for the plants that grow here, including this famous hedge and it is being monitored.

Mount Stewart is a full day's visit and it might

even be two, if you really want to study the individual gardens and then take in the lake, the lily wood, and the other woodland walks as well as the famed Temple of the Winds overlooking the Lough, reckoned by some to be the finest garden building in Ireland. It was built in 1782 to designs of James 'Athenian' Stuart, and based the 1st century BC building of the same name in Athens.

The lake walk is becoming more and more beautiful, a site of wonderful, ever changing trees. As has Tir na nOg, a hill garden leading up to the family burial ground, full of delightful plants from acers and magnolias, beauties like *Kalmia latifolia* and oddities like *Doryanthes palmeri*, the giant spear lily.

Once evenly mown lawns are, today, left to grow longer and the number of natives that have reappeared as a result is wonderful. Populations of orchids that had been mown down for decades are now thriving. While it is a fine idea to take a guided walk, the specimens are clearly marked and identified, so an unescorted browse can be just as enjoyable and instructive.

The Nixon Garden

48 Ballydoran Road, Killinchy, BT23 6QB. Tel: (0044 28) (048) 9754 3336.
e-mail: katherinenixon48@sky.com Contact: Katherine Nixon, for art exhibition details or an appointment.
Open: On occasion by appointment to small groups.

Gardens built around, and for the display of contemporary art, are rare. Katherine Nixon gardens what she terms 'the little habitats' of her garden with the accommodation of her art, and that of her artist colleagues in mind. So when she makes a garden room or space, its ability to take on a piece of art is as crucial to her as the siting of the plants. As I arrived, the place was being readied for an impending group exhibition.

This garden is expansive and hard to pin down, set out at the edge of Strangford Lough with the cry of birds and the tang of the sea everywhere. There is history too. The 6th century monastic site, Nendrum, can be seen across the Lough.

It is an organic and sustainable garden, with its own hives of Irish black bees, busy working the flowers, both native and exotic.

The variety and range of different gardens that slide and melt into each other is what makes it most attractive. You might begin in a sunny slabbed courtyard with vanilla scented *Luma apiculata* and variegated pittosporum, and move on to a colourful shrub and lawn garden, land out by the water in an informal littoral setting, and from there, head to a carefully husbanded yet wild, hilly meadow and wood garden. The trick is that all these different areas hang together within this very privileged location.

It is divided into a series of small worlds: from the hide-and-seek garden created for grandchildren, to run between fat fuchsia, tall echiums, anemone and foxglove. One of Katherine's sculptures sits in the centre of this snug corner, a work cast in the sand of Errigal mountain. This is also where the golden bay is, a plant that has lived in every garden Katherine has lived in since her birth.

Down by the sea, the mood is wildest and most relaxed. As we stood at the old boat house, surrounded by figs, artichokes and teasels, the view was of the waters edge and a colony of samphire. This is probably the most lightly tended of the spaces.

In the fruit garden I discovered the good sense in growing fruit like yellow raspberries and white currants - The birds don't go for these oddities. The wall trained trees are intricately pruned and include a selection including 'Egremont russet' 'Irish peach' and 'Cobra'. We walked up through the meadow to see the turlough Katherine had been playing with, placing step stones across this occasionally wet, occasionally dry pond, through clumps of *Primula bulleyana* and variegated flag irises and arums. Intense splashes of purple in the form of native orchids are what please her most in the meadow, as do the birches which are growing apace in the wet, exposed ground. Some Scots pines, a walk of evergreen oaks, damsons, medlars and hazels are the other trees that will more and more shape this garden as the years march on.

Old Balloo House & Barn

15-17 Comber Road, Balloo, Killinchy, Co. Down. Contact: Moira Concannon and Lesley Simpson. Tel: Lesley Simpson (0044 28) (048) 9754 1485. e-mail: m.simpson197@btinternet.com. Moira Concannon. Tel: (0044 74) 8464 9767. e-mail: moira.concannon@gmail.com Open: By appointment, May-June. Not suitable for the infirm. Supervised children. No dogs. Directions: On application.

'It's not for the faint hearted,' Moira and Lesley told me, when I arrived to visit their joint gardens in the village of Balloo. 'There's a certain amount of wilderness,' they added, looking reassured to see me in my stout boots. There certainly is an amount of wilderness, although it is tempered, minded wilderness; planned, arranged, and I should add handsome. These are gardens for the sure-footed mountain-goat garden visitor, although nothing could be less apparent from the front of the two adjacent houses, originally one house and its barn, built in 1809.

The gardens have been worked by long standing neighbours, Lesley Simpson and Moira Concannon for three decades. The initial gardens seen are full of flowers, with gravel and cobbled areas, neat trees and shrubs, roses and stands of francoa. Lovely as they are, they do nothing to prepare the visitor for the rollercoaster collection of gardens that lie behind the houses.

These range from exuberant jungle gardens made up of violet coloured rambling *Rosa* 'Veilchenblau' tangled with purple sweet pea over hostas and ferns. There are vegetable gardens here with as many roses and flowers as peas and beets. Meanwhile, next door there is an actual rose garden so fragrant and pretty it could send a poor visitor into a swoon between

the battling perfume of *Rosa mundi* and *R.* 'Pleine de grace'.

Moira is an avid propagator, which is just as well because the overall gardens take up a large, if hard to measure area. The more plants you have from seed and cutting, the fewer you need to buy.

Having made our way through a new raised bed garden with seas of epimedium, pulmonaria, white *Viola cornuta* and penstemon, 'walls' of ivy being trained on posts and wires, under old apple trees smothered in clematis, we made our way onto the 'Field Garden'. Do not miss the clever water feature, made from a trough, found objects and slate. These women have such style.

The Field Garden is the glory of the place, a ridiculously steep wood garden that Moira and Lesley have been planting up for many years. It cannot have been easy, working the slope, but the result, seen from above, below and from across the garden, is a horticultural pleasure. The plants that grow here must be able to fend for themselves, which allows for widespread planting of species roses such as *Rosa complicata* and the tough *Rosa* 'Belvedere'. Look up to liriodendron and purple beech, rhododendron and white cherry, and look beneath these to seas of white daffodils, francoa, crocosmia and *Lunaria rediviva*, or perennial honesty.

At the bottom of the steep hill there is the River Blackwater, and an expansive area of wet ground being colonised by *Primula bulleyana* and *Primula* 'Miller's Crimson'. As well as planting the slope, they have built wooden viewing points that allow the visitor view the garden from different angles.

The last of the garden rooms holds a mixed shrub, tree and perennial border, with a serpentine path woven through it leading back to the house. This border is bounded by the main road, and pruned down at various points so that the neighbours can see in and enjoy the garden. A delightful set of gardens gardened by a delightful, knowledgable and generous pair of gardeners.

Old Barrack House

7 Main Street, Hillsborough, Co. Down. Tel: (0044 28) (048) 9268 2329.
e-mail: dawn.dmitchell@btinternet.com Contact: Dawn McEntee. Open: By appointment to groups and
occasional open days. Special features: Cream teas in the byre. Art exhibitions. Directions: On application.

After more than ten years of opening it to visitors, and having featured on Dermot Gavin and Helen Dillon's champion garden television programme, Dawn McEntee's favourite garden achievement was having it 'droned' for the same programme. The sight of your garden from above for the first time must be exciting but this garden is a treat from any angle. From the entrance through a carriage gate of this Georgian townhouse on the main street, you arrive into the peace of a secluded courtyard surrounded by house, carriage house, and stone sheds including a byre. There is also an old petrol pump from the days in the 1920s when the house was an RIC station. This is the start of Dawn's welcoming, excellent garden.

When she arrived 30 years ago it was a weed sanctuary, particularly favouring equisetum or horsetail. It took three years of ploughing, setting grass and mowing to see to that. The garden started life with nothing more than three interesting old apple trees and a crinodendron.

We picked our way through some of the densest planting, starting right at the byre, smothered as it is in honeysuckle. Dawn says her motto is 'to stick something in the ground and hope for the best.' Her hopes seem to be generally answered because the growth is phenomenal. The range of plants is equally impressive. I was amused by the occasional stand of rhubarb among the *Achillea grandiflora*. Space is tight here so vegetables need to squash in between ornamentals. During the war however, the whole garden was given over to grow vegetables for the village.

Today, layered ornamentals are the order of the day. Rampant *Akebia quinata* and jasmine clothe the walls, with puffs of white hydrangea at their skirts.

The place is divided by rose, honeysuckle and clematis pergolas and hedges, into a series of secreted garden rooms, each with its own style. One of these, the dining room, is filled with purple foliage plants, sambucus and cotinus, cimicifuga, acer and cherry, planted around a sunny open gravelled area and a piece of sculpture. We left this stylish dining room by way

of an arch covered in golden hop, contrasting with the different shades of purple. The next room again features Japanese acers and contorted hazel. On the ground there are geraniums galore and overhead the light shade of a tall tall betula.

In another snug, *Cornus kousa* is underplanted with white and purple *Viola cornuta* in a simple, effective mix. We looked along a pergola of *Laburnum* 'Vossii' to a little statue beyond and of course were drawn down to see it. Dawn's husband Ken made the copper, arched pergola here, as he did the unusual copper gate that leads into the garden.

The trails lead under eucryphia and young gingko, down to a mossy pond that her bold rescue puppy springer spaniels are a bit too interested in. The thought of them leaping in was too much to take. This is a really jungle-like part of the garden, wild with ferns and gunnera. The water soldiers or *Stratiotes aloides* dotted on the surface of the water are native but look exotic and the bulrushes are dramatic too.

I left watching Dawn trying to rein in the two boisterous springers. She is a saint…

Orchard Garth

Orchard Garth, Old Kilmore Road, Moira, Co. Down, BT67 0LZ
Tel: (0044 28) (048) 9261 9449 / 9261 9584. e-mail:johnklund@btinternet.com Contact: Mr. John
and Mrs. Erica Lund. Open: By appointment in summer months. Directions: ON application.

It feels like there are several gardens at Orchard Garth. The front garden is quite traditional, what one might expect, down the straight garden path of a 1910 farm house with lawn, some shrubs and perennials, fluffy ladies mantle, good old-fashioned hydrangeas and thalictrum marching up either side of the path. This then trails off to an orchard and a little productive raised bed vegetable garden. (Growing strawberries up on a height is a clever way to keep them away from slugs and rain splash.)

Meanwhile, just a few short steps around the house and around the corner there lives a wild flower party that speaks of a different mindset altogether. In the sunny sitting room with floor to ceiling windows, the flower borders seem set to march in and take over your seat. All there is for it, is to be spirited away by the mad exuberance of it all. Erika Lund likes flowers and she lets them do their thing.

This garden is informality itself, a mix of what she and her husband John like; jumbled together in a good looking way. Long mixed borders run out to what they call the Field Garden, mixing aconites and veronicastrum with broad beans and potatoes, roses and clematis, acers and cabbage. It works. You walk up one grass *allée* and down another around these substantial, truly mixed borders. Out at the boundary, the feeling is more woodland than open garden with hostas under the trees, adding a lush feel to the shaded areas.

Add in a long pond, running alongside the house set into the longer gravel border full of nemesia and evening primrose, dianthus and erysimum. The pond was built using the stones of an old stone railway bridge nearby that was knocked. The Lunds even bought the Victorian graffiti on the old bridge and this is still to be seen in a memorial to the workers who built it.

It all looks over at an old stone byre covered in clematis, roses and wisteria, a building that is as much vegetation as stone, and quite lovely. Erika told me that the plants here 'do their own thing.' With more than a little help I imagine.

Ringdufferin

Ringdufferin Road, Toye, Killyleagh, Co. Down. Tel: (0044 28) (048) 4482 8276.
Mobile (0044 77) 6802 7286. e-mail:ringdufferin@btconnect.com Contact: Tracy Hamilton. Open: By
appointment to groups. Directions: On application.

Ringdufferin House and garden are set on the shores of Strangford Lough. Indeed the view of the Lough from a gateway in the walled garden must rate as one of the best sights in County Down.

The house was built in 1780 and the grounds carry features dating from all periods since. From the middle of the 20th century, however Tracy Hamilton's grandparents and parents, embarked on a substantial programme of planting trees. Tracy continues that work today and as a result the gardens will march on into the 21st century looking as good as they should. We met some of her favourite trees as we meandered around the grounds. Among these is a *Cupressus macrocarpa* or Monterey cypress, with the widest girth of any on the island. We also looked at a lovely *Davidia involucrata*, fine Turkey oaks or *Quercus laevis* and two silver firs or *Abies alba* that have improbable, quirky looking 'elbows'.

The gardens are home to some grand rhododendrons, including cinnamon-leafed *Rhododendron falconeri* with big white flowers, and magnolias, most of which were planted in the 1950s and 1960s. The huge *Magnolia campbellii* looks older than that. I admired the knobbled, snaky bark of a *Metasequoia glyptostroboides* and discovered that it too was planted in 1952.

The walks through the park take in banks of camellia and groves of tree ferns, a big *Drimys winteri*, oaks and cut-leaf beech. Occasional wild flowers can be spotted through the lawns in summer, and in damp areas of which there are few according to Tracy, there are runs of candelabra primulas too.

The walled garden, which once would have been almost completely productive, is today largely given over to ornamentals, with sweeping, wall-backed mixed borders. It is a bit of a flower fest, a melange of tree peonies and deutzias, *Fremontodendron* 'Hidcote' and explosions of *Philadelphus coronarius*, tall acanthus and agapanthus. The view from the top of the hill is really good. A long wisteria covers much of the wall as it runs down the slope and there are sweeps of airy-looking white willow-herb and daylilies. Ducking into the deep shadow of the yew circle, I half expected to see a white lady, headless horseman or some other sort of ghost. The circle is thought to have been planted

in 1820. It is wonderfully spooky.

We passed apple trees spiked with mistletoe and one with the more onerous task of supporting huge *Rosa* 'Paul's Himalayan musk'. The sheltered nature of this walled garden can be seen in the health and vigour of a tender *Myrtus lechleriana,* known for its delicious smelling flowers. Under the ferns, pachyphragma gleams out like white fireworks while overhead there is more white in the shape of a spreading white cherry.

Utilitarian vegetable rows long gave way to flower and decor, like the big yew 'helmets' shot through with red *Tropaeolum speciosum* and a *Rosa roxburghii* planted in 1954 which takes pride of place.

The farm around the garden is worked with bees in mind. I had already passed a tree creeper climbing a trunk, and stopped the car on the drive to watch two baby foxes wrestling with each for about five minutes. A heavenly place.

Rowallane Garden

Saintfield, Ballynahinch, Co. Down, BT24 7LH. Tel: (0044 28) (048) 9751 0131. e-mail: rowallane@nationaltrust.org.uk Open: Changes seasonally. See website for details. Partially wheelchair accessible. Children welcome. Dogs on leads. Special features: Walks for the visually impaired can be arranged. Home of the National Collection of penstemon. Tearoom. Gift shop. Second-hand garden book shop. Ceramic pot shop. Directions: 1.5 km south of Saintfield, off the A7.

In 1903, Hugh Armytage Moore, a man deeply interested in plants, inherited this 1861 house and garden just outside Saintfield from his uncle the Rev. John Moore. He started growing some of his special plants in the yards and fields around the farm and went on to create the garden we know as Rowallane today, a 50-acre spree of landscaped gardens, wildflower meadows, rhododendron plantations, woods, rock and walled gardens.

Arriving at the gate you come upon an intriguing line of huge stone cairns or pyramids made of boulders alerting you to the possibility that Rowallane will be a garden out of the ordinary.

The larger garden is a wild, Robinsonian-style garden that ranges over the hilly, rocky drumlins of south Down. It is renowned for its spring displays of daffodils and rhododendrons but in truth it looks wonderful all year. Mr. Moore subscribed to all the great plant-hunting expeditions and he planted

seeds from these in throughout Rowallane. The rhododendrons reach their flowering peak in May.

The Rowallane rock garden is famous and was created by relieving a huge outcrop of the local stone called whinstone, of its soil. Pockets were then backfilled with acid soil and planted up with meconopsis, including the locally bred *Meconopsis* x *sheldonii* 'Slieve Donard,' as well as gentians, primulas, erythroniums, celmisias, heathers and leptospermum.

To the side of the house, I stopped to admire the huge yew cones. The man cutting them told me that they take two weeks each summer to clip.

It is in the walled gardens that many of the treasures are to be found. Hunt in the outer walled garden to see *Chaenomeles* x *superba* 'Rowallane'. Large wisteria and a *Hoheria sexstylosa* by the entrance and the greenhouse bed need to admired too. This area covers two acres and varies between strictly clipped, box-enclosed, ten-metre runs of agapanthus, even longer runs light, yellow *Cephalaria gigantea*, penstemon and looser beds of tumbling peony and bergenia, inula and camellia. The large, rare *Magnolia* x. *watsonii* is a sight.

The dates 1828–1883 are carved on one of the gateways. In fact, throughout the garden there are dates scattered around, pointing mysteriously to landmarks in the garden's history. There are all sorts

of small stone buildings dotted through the grounds too, housing second hand gardening book shops, tea rooms and shelters from the rain, complete with signs welcoming you to rest. The wider pleasure grounds are also marked at various points by old stone walls, some of these are farm walls and boundaries, but some seem to have been built for the fun of it. They are pretty and serve to render the directionally challenged visitor even more lost than they might otherwise be.

At one point, a hilly grass path between colonies of orchids, leads between groves of spectacular trees, towards the most beautiful *Cornus kousa* 'Chinensis' I have ever seen. When in flower, it is like a magnet in the centre of the garden, attracting mesmerised visitors from all corners like a beacon.

If it is raining, retreat to the little shed where the stock of old garden magazines is kept, and dry off while poring over the thoughtfully provided publications. Having met some of the garden staff, an incredibly welcoming and enthusiastic crew, I was not surprised at the inclusion of such a generous facility.

One final point. Forget about the map. It makes no sense and anyway getting lost here is part of the pleasure.

The Sanctuary

230 Ballywalter Road Millisle. Co. Down. Tel: (0044 28) (048) 9186 1278.
e-mail: heatherfarmer1@btinternet.com Contact: Heather Farmer. Open: By appointment April-Sept.
Special features: Refreshments can be arranged. Directions: On application.

It is impossible to miss this cheerful seaside garden. For a start, it is surrounded by a bright red picket fence which has the almost impossible job of holding in a busting-out explosion of pink and white campion, *Lychnis coronaria* and Michaelmas daisies, all growing from an expanse of beach gravel. It is a most welcoming place. The red front door is surrounded by a big tangle of *Clematis montana* with pink flowers and dark purple leaves. Heather's great garden continues around the house, with old stone baths full of *Geranium palmatum* and blue *Meconopsis betonicifolia* – This could be a good way to grow the fussy perennial if you do not have the correct soil. 'I just stuffed those in there. It goes to show doesn't it?' Heather said of the meconopsis.

The pergola is not just covered in clematis but

hanging baskets too. Actually there are hanging bicycles in this garden. The sight of nasturtiums piling out of buckets and churns sums up the easy charming mood of the place.

The main garden runs in a long straight hill up behind the house. It is made up of an avenue of cordylines on either side of a wide grass path, with two beds of grasses and shrubs, mulched with pea gravel. The style is still very seasidey, with large driftwood sculptures between the plants, and plenty of space and air between drifts of peony and geraniums. She grows black kale and shiny lettuce in between the ornamentals. I like the style. It is very individual, very Heather, with roses and phormiums between broad beans, lobster pots, upturned boats and rusting metal spirals on the gravel. This is the garden of a woman who knows her own style.

Sit at the top of the hill on a bench with an arch of *Rosa* 'Wedding Day' overhead to look down on the proceedings. It is simply pretty. The outer hedge surrounding all this is one of native crataegus. I left having taken a picture of the most wonderful old washing mangle ever, a work of art…

Seaforde Gardens

Seaforde, Downpatrick, BT30 8PG. Co. Down. Tel: (0044 28) (048) 4481 1225. e-mail: info@seafordegardens.com www.seafordegardens.com. Contact: Charles Forde. Open: Easter-Sept., Mon-Sat., 10am-5pm. Sun., 1pm-6pm. Partially wheelchair accessible. Groups welcome. Supervised children. Special features: Guided tours can be booked. Butterfly house. Tearoom. Plant sales. Home to the National Collection of eucryphia. Directions: On the Belfast to Newcastle road. Look out for the signposts in the village of Seaforde.

The drive up to Seaforde is like a mossy valley under tunnels of mature trees, between walls like hanging ferneries. It is magical. At the top of the drive you are greeted or at least regarded by a large number preening peacocks sauntering around the car park like fine courtiers.

The garden dates back to the 1750s, and was probably the work of the great landscape gardener, John Sutherland. Its involved extensive woodlands, shelterbelts and screens. There was also a network of winding drives. It was in the 19th century that many of the trees seen here today were planted however. These include the Wellingtonias and huge Monterey pines, riddled with holes made by little tree creepers. Seaforde is made up of woods and a walled garden encompassing five acres, full of rare and interesting shrubs. Many of these specimens are the fruits of the well known plantsman, Patrick Forde's numerous seed-collecting expeditions abroad, particularly to Vietnam in the decades up to the 1990s.

The main body of the walled garden was at one time formal, laid out in the type of smart beds still seen in many walled gardens today. This format had descended into a wilderness of bramble and laurel until the mid-1970s when Mr. Forde took it in hand and began to bring the garden back to a presentable state.

He planted a maze of hornbeam in 1975. This is now a large puzzle complete with an arbour and statue of Diana. It could keep the directionally challenged visitor away from the rest of the garden for too long.

Today Patrick's son Charles, gardens Seaforde, continuing to develop and care for the maturing garden. He has formalised the area around the maze, adding wide, straight gravel paths.

Next to it is a new hobbit-esque gateway into the garden proper, home to the maturing well laid-out groves of rhododendron, including over 100 different *Rhododendron falconeri* as well as large shrubs, like the incredibly tall mahonia, home to a romping rose. Huge acacia and eucryphia are grand by themselves but even more distracting with melianthus and hostas planted in numbers underneath. The peafowl population makes itself useful by eating slugs and saving the hostas from attack. The ground is moist and damp too, which the hostas also appreciate.

It is not hard to get lost. Duck into a rhododendron tunnel and re-emerge into the sun and a eucryphia walk, laden down with white and pink flowers, in the case of *Eucryphia lucida* 'Pink Cloud' and *E. milliganii* 'Pink Whisper' both of which have shell-pink blooms. These are part of the National Collection of 23 species and hybrids.

Scattered alongside the rising and falling path under the trees, are surprise clumps of sweet-scented white *Lilium* 'Casa Blanca' and sprays of native ferns in between the more exotic tree ferns. Eventually it leads into a clearing where the damp ground around the pond could be described as having been conquered by primulas.

The place is full of rarities including an unnamed rose that Charles collected in Bhutan, on the border between China and India. It has unusual orange, hairy hips.

One of the great pleasures of this garden is standing back and enjoying the sight of maturing groves of trees, the cloud-like canopies of rhododendron and acer and great explosions of *Cryptomeria japonica* across a sunny, grass valley.

Charles has the required enthusiasm both for the garden and its special plants. He continues to collect seed in the wild and his interests lie in Japan. His advice is to collect seed on the north side of a mountain if the plants are to stand a chance in our long damp winters. Also, high up in the canopy he pointed out some epiphytic *Rhododendron maddenii* recently planted in the upper branches as part of an ongoing experiment here.

Apart from bringing new plants to the garden he spends a great deal of time relocating paths to accommodate the considerable growth and spread of the maturing trees and shrubs in the ever changing garden.

There is a butterfly house to occupy non-gardeners. This is set in a huge greenhouse planted like a jungle. It is home to hundreds of colourful butterflies that fly freely about, settling on branches and leaves, camouflaging themselves only to surprise visitors by suddenly taking flight in front of them.

Timpany Nursery & Garden

77 Magheratimpany Road, Ballynahinch, Co. Down. BT24 8PA. Tel: (0044 28) (048) 9756 2812. e-mail: s.tindall@btconnect.com. www.timpanynurseries.com. Contact: Susan Tindall. Open: Seasonal and varied. See website for details. Groups welcome. Special features: Alpine nursery. Mail order catalogue. Refreshments can be arranged. Tours. Directions: Take the Newcastle Road from Ballynahinch, then take the Ballymaglave Road to the right after the Millbrook Hotel. Take the first left onto the Magheratimpany Road. The garden is on the left.

This handsome large garden has been in development for many years. The area around the house and alpine nursery includes a cottage garden, which in summer is filled with iris, peony and astilbe, astrantia, hemerocallis and rudbeckia. Tumbles of the best flowers jostle with each other for attention. I liked having to pick my way between so many Japanese acers grown in containers. Troughs of tiny rhododendron, miniature Himalayan poppies and scores of little alpines are lined up for inspection too. The rockery and alpine bed is raised to one side of the flower garden so that its treasures can be inspected, close up. There are little mounds of mat-forming alpines tucked into every crevice and crack, politely competing with

each other for attention.

Next door is a wood, almost primeval in nature, strewn with ferns under the dark, mature canopy. The greater garden covers about 25 acres and is like a cabinet of arboreal delights, with a range of special magnolias and rhododendrons, cherries and oak, betulas and eucalyptus, liriodendron and camellia. Mown paths between the trees lead eventually to a lily pond with an island.

There is a satisfying layered look to the trees, shrubs and herbaceous plants. This is a garden with such a range of plants that there is something to look at throughout the year.

The Walled Garden At Helen's Bay

Craigdarragh Road, Bangor, Co Down. BT19 1UB. Tel: (0044 74) 2943 4918.
e-mail: thewalledgardenhelensbay@gmail.com. Contact: David Love Cameron. Open: By appointment to
groups. Special Features: Vegetables sold at Bangor monthly market. GIY Courses. Box system vegetables
sold. Directions: Coming from Belfast on the A2 turn left onto Craigdarragh Road and continue for about
800m before taking turning left into a private lane with a school bus stop. Continue all the way to the
garden.

This organic productive garden is run by talented organic gardener, David Love Cameron, who grows vegetables for sale to restaurants in Belfast. Set in the large old walled garden belonging to Craigdarragh House, it is very much a workplace. There are some good old apple trees to decorate it and the hills of the Craigdarragh pleasure grounds are visible over the walls.

David and his team of volunteers aim to grow as many heritage varieties as they can so I looked at lines of Gortahork cabbages from Donegal (a large headed cabbage that overwinters well). Among the many heritage vegetables here David recommended a County Down bred pea called Carruthers' Purple Podded Pea, a very tall variety with pretty purple and pink flowers and a fruit that has been likened to a cross between a broad bean and a pea. The apple trees include rare varieties, 'Widow's Friend' and 'Munster Tulip'.

This is a horticultural venture to which I could only wish the best.

Glenkeen, Co. Down

Ballywalter Park. Co. Down

Fermanagh

Tully Castle

Churchill, Co. Fermanagh Tel: (0044 28) (048) 9082 3207. Open: Sunday. 12pm-4pm. Groups welcome. Supervised children. Dogs on leads. Special features: Entrance free. Castle ruins. Directions: Signed off the Enniskillen–Beleek road (A46).

Tully is a 17th-century tower house castle with a restored garden, that is the only plot of its type on the island in both style and period. The castle belonged to Sir John Hume, the largest landowner in Fermanagh in the 1600s. In 1641 Rory Maguire set out to recapture the land where Hume's castle stood. This had once been the Maguire's land and castle. Everyone was killed in the ensuing battle and the castle went to ruin.

The garden, which ebbs away from the front of the castle shell, has now been restored to that period. Low box hedges encircle beds of bluish-grey rue, tall umbels of angelica, violets, geranium, marigolds, deep-blue cornflowers and some shrub roses. Wattled hazel fences enclose beds, effectively holding in the plants. It is a surprising, poignant garden.

Monaghan

Hilton Park

Clones, Co. Monaghan. Tel: 047 56007. e-mail: mail@hiltonpark.ie. Contact: Joanna Madden.
Open: May-Sept. By appointment to groups only. Supervised children. Special features: Refreshments by
prior arrangement. Accommodation on site. Directions: Leave Clones on the Scothouse Road, taking the
right fork at the Lennard Arms Hotel. Hilton Park is 5 km on, on the right.

Travelling up that most desirable feature, a mile-long drive, provides glimpses of the house, which is fronted by 200 metres of yew hedge battlements. Planted in 1911, this is the longest hedge of its kind in the country. It guards a croquet lawn and a stately Georgian house.

Hilton Park has been home to the Madden family since the 1730s. It is known primarily for its oak woods, which hold exceptionally tall trees for plants grown so far north. As with many big houses, there have been several gardens on this site since the 1690s, for which the current owners, Lucy and John Madden, unearthed documentation when they began work here several years ago. The Maddens have discovered all sorts of mysteries about the older gardens, including work by the well-known family member 'Premium' Madden, one of the founder members of the Royal Dublin Society (RDS) and one of the great 'improving' landowners of his time. Another of the Maddens who added to the garden was the Victorian, John Madden, who brought many North American trees to Hilton Park. These are still growing in the estate. The current family are no less interesting: Lucy Madden is known in her own right as an author and expert on the potato and its history.

Visiting Hilton today, the first feature you see is a Victorian garden. To the side of the house, the lawns drop down dramatically to a perfect Maltese cross design made of yew and box. This parterre and the Pleasure Grounds, were laid out by Ninian Niven, the renowned designer who worked on the Iveagh Gardens, The National Botanic Gardens and the Phoenix Park. The pattern in box and yew is seen to best advantage from the house above it.

Set in behind the building, the herbaceous borders are deep and full of tall plants – four-metre-high grasses, buddleia and rust-red sunflowers. A huge stone wall covered roses and clematis backs the bed with its strong lines and bold colours. The walk leads into the herb garden. This is a compact garden, inspiring for small-scale gardeners. Anchored on a stone ledge, you negotiate it by way of little paths that are almost impossible to get through at the height of summer due to the overflow of billowing catmint, chives, parsley, dill and borage. This whole area is backed by low hornbeam hedges and bounded on the outside by shade-loving hostas, primulas and hellebores.

The woods leading to and from the lake are filled with fine big native trees as well as rhododendrons, specimens of Douglas fir (*Pseudotsuga menziesii*), and coast redwood (*Sequoia sempervirens*). There are two lakes, a summerhouse clothed in roses, an island and a lovers' walk. The older, romantic, 18th-century parkland is beautiful – A treat not just for lovers.

Rossmore Park

Monaghan, Co. Monaghan Open: All year. No admission. Directions: situated 3.5km from Monaghan
town, on the Newbliss Road (R189).

The attractions at Rossmore are the lake and its walks, the walled garden and an old yew walk. Travelling up an avenue of big beech trees that tower over a carpet of naturalised white wood anemone or 'wooden enemies' and an iris-filled stream, the entrance to the park at Rossmore is perfect. By the stream *Rhododendron ponticum*, the bane of many a great garden and woodland in this country, looks far too lovely to be a pest.

Like many old estates around the country, Rossmore is long past its sell-by date as one of the great gardens. All that is left are the ghostly remains of some of its features, and even more ghostly remains of the house; a raised platform above the lawns with a few bits of stone marking the spot. Majestic steps leading up a blank grass plateau where the house once stood, look slightly absurd.

Wandering along the half-forgotten paths, rustic stone bridges peep shyly out from the overgrowth. This being Monaghan, the terrain is hilly and it makes for very enjoyable rising and falling walks through the woods. You find yourself ensconced at the bottom of a canyon of trees, then a few steps on and you are above the level of the trees, looking out over the countryside for miles. Hidden within the woods is the Rossmore mausoleum which was described by the 4th Baron Rossmore as 'so beautifully situated that it may well be said to make one fall in love with death.'

Blessingbourne Estate, Co. Tyrone.

Tyrone

Blessingbourne Estate

Murley Road, Fivemiletown, Co. Tyrone, BT75 OQS Tel: (0044 48) (028) 8952 1188.
e-mail: info@blessingbourne.com www.blessingbourne.com Contact: Colleen and Nicholas Lowry.
Open: By appointment to groups. Special features: Refreshments in the coach house. House tours.
Costume museum. Carriage museum. Self catering accommodation. Directions: On application.

The house was built in the 19th century in the Jacobean style using soft yellow sandstone. Large but not imposing, it looks out over a series of stepped down, sunken gardens that lead to a lake and a surrounding of woods.

The central small garden, close to the house, is a little rectangular flower garden, surrounded by low balustrades. Inside there are box squares and pyramids, set with informal flower borders and divided by slab stone paths. This was created by Nicholas Lowry's mother. Outside the railings, large but pruned up rhododendrons drip flowers from early in the year. The lawn sweeps out from here, to larger plantations of cloud shaped rhododendrons.

A sunken formal lawn divided by a wide gravel path, leads toward the lake. In the middle of this otherwise formal sweep, I wondered about the presence of an incongruous, probably opportunistic but attractive hawthorn or 'fairy tree', as Colleen called it. The small tree fell over in a storm many years ago but instead of taking it out and restoring the formality, Nicholas's father and a few lads managed to right it and set it off growing again. Best to be safe.

The woods wrap right around the 20-acre lake, a good mix of lime, beech oak, sycamore and rhododendron. There are 14km of paths and trails through the trees for walking and biking. We walked in the woods marvelling at Colleen's much loved multi-stemmed *Thuja plicata,* wondering which of it's many trunks might be the original. There are some fine old yews here too.

In 1874, William Robinson was employed by the then owner, Mrs. Montgomery to design a rockery down in these woods. Colleen and Nicholas are in the middle of plans to restore that rockery so watch this space. I left looking at the oak that was planted to commemorate the US forces that were stationed here in the house in advance of the D-Day landings in Normandy.

Old Methodist Manse

52 Moyle Road, Newtownstewart, BT78 4JT. Co. Tyrone. Tel: (0044 78) 6485 5315.
Contact: Mr Uel Henderson. Open: April-June. By appointment to groups. Not wheelchair accessible. Not
suitable for children. No dogs. Directions: On application.

Mr Uel Henderson's Victorian house had nothing more than a line of ten large Scots pines and one elm when he arrived to live here 40 years ago. The jungle garden that today fills the long riverside site on the edge of Newtownstewart is, as the saying goes, all his own work.

This is a garden to wander through and at which to marvel. There are a great number of good plants to be seen, particularly trees and shrubs. Mr. Henderson loves trees so it seems only right that this is the home to a rare, mature, surviving common elm or *Ulmus minor.* This grand tree is 140 years old and a treasure. He collects its seed for the Woodland Trust who are making investigations to see if it might be immune to Dutch Elm Disease. In the meantime he wonders if the collar of ivy around the trunk, could possibly be protecting it. We walked along a path strewn with millions of its silvery seeds, past golden philadelphus and magnolia of all sorts, including *Magnolia* 'Star Wars', *M.* 'J.C. Williams and 'Heaven Scent.' Other paths run under clouds of rhododendron. There are over 80 varieties and specimens in the garden, including a rare scented and inordinately pretty *Rhododendron yuefengense.*

Among the many roses, we stopped to look at was *Rosa* 'Pat Austen'. Mr. Henderson says that if you want a really good rose, pick one the breeder named for his wife as he will always name the best roses for her.

The garden covers about four acres, including a riverside garden which he has bridged twice. He has also built a 47-stepped staircase down to the River Mourne which runs through the garden, before it eventually flows into the Foyle. Hanging over the water, in places, we passed a well named *Rhododendron* 'Old Port' with ruby coloured flowers and an equally plummy *Acer palmatum* 'Bloodgut' growing out over a ravine. Nearby, *Acer* 'Butterfly' is actually growing in the water. Acers can be versatile trees. Across the river the big leaves of *Kalopanax pictus* are only one of the many show-off plants, competing with *Magnolia cylindrica* and *Salix magnifica*.

As well as admiring unusual specimens like the rare *Ilex yunnanensis, Betula raddeana* and *B. tatewakiana* we trailed between some well placed stone features, summer room temples created from architectural salvage and intriguingly placed gates between different garden rooms.

The image of a *Eucryphia nymansensis* planted right beside the building and now stretching above it it, will remain with me, as will the advice that the 'Perla' variety of broad bean is well worth trying.

Tattykeel House & Gallery

115 Doogary Road, Omagh, Co. Tyrone. BT79 0BN. Tel: (0044 28) (048) 8224 9801.
e-mail: tattykeelhouse@hotmail.com www.tattyleeldesignstudio.com Contact: Hugh and Kathleen Ward.
Open: By appointment to groups. Partially wheelchair accessible. Supervised children (Busy road).
No dogs. Special features: Gallery and studio. B+B accommodation. Refreshments can be arranged.
Directions: Approximately 4 km from Omagh town centre on the main A5 Dublin to Belfast road.

'I always tell visiting groups, don't be in a rush to get started on a garden' Kathleen Ward told me. When she and her husband Hugh arrived here 30 years ago, like many novices, they did not realise that plants do not grow successfully on builder's rubble. The impressive garden seen today was a hard won thing: Three decades of Hugh taking care of the hard landscaping and Kathleen, the artist on the team, tending the plants, have turned their country garden into a perfect model of the type, run by two perfectionists.

Kathleen continued to explain that they started their garden at a time when shrubberies were popular, and so there are good numbers of mature shrubs and trees here, arranged in boundary and island beds, divided by impeccable lawns. Hugh built the little summerhouses and pergolas that peep from between the trees and over borders, as well as erecting obelisks for Kathleen's many roses and clematis. As they worked and learned, a garden worthy of the name took shape. It is a picture of perfection.

Under the mature canopies of *Cedrus deodar* and acer, many of them pruned up, there are whole other worlds of perennials and foliage plants from hosta and big cardiocrinum, to allium and crinum, phlox, delphinium and every conceivable sort of perennial.

Kathleen trained as a textile artist and she has an eye for contrasting textures. This is obvious throughout the garden. She also creates pictures and vistas, cuts openings and tunnels into the borders and shrubberies, to open up views across the garden, highlighting different pictures.

Just as I thought I had seen a perfectly satisfying garden, she led the way under the trees - into *Hugh's* garden, a hidden green, rock, fern, water and wood garden. This is another world altogether, made by a man who really knows how to create a stream. Perfection? Yes, welcoming, hospitable perfection.

Index